DELIUS: A LIFE IN LETTERS

1909–1934

DELIUS

A Life in Letters

II

1909–1934

Lionel Carley

SCOLAR PRESS
in association with
THE DELIUS TRUST

First published in Great Britain 1988 by
SCOLAR PRESS
Gower Publishing Company Limited
Gower House, Croft Road
Aldershot GU11 3HR

Gower Publishing Company
Old Post Road
Brookfield
Vermont 05036
USA

Published in association with
The Delius Trust
(Trustees: Musicians' Benevolent Fund and Norman K. Millar)
16 Ogle Street
London W1P 7LG

BRITISH LIBRARY CATALOGUING IN PUBLICATION DATA
Delius, Frederick, 1862–1934
  Delius: a life in letters.
  2: 1909–1934
  1. English music. Delius, Frederick,
  1862–1934. Biographies
  I. Title
  780'.92'4

ISBN 0–85967–717–6

Printed in Great Britain
at the University Press, Cambridge

Front endpaper: Grez-sur-Loing, the garden
Rear endpaper: Grez-sur-Loing, the river

Contents

List of Letters

Epilogue

List of Illustrations

The illustrations in this book are largely drawn from the collection of the author or from the archive of The Delius Trust. Other sources are given in the captions. Where known, the name of the artist or photographer is recorded in the captions.

Introduction and Acknowledgements

'I have no hesitation in declaring the life and work of Delius to be the greatest and most far-reaching incident in music during the last fifty years.' Thus Sir Thomas Beecham in 1929. Just twenty years earlier – when this book opens – the subject of his remarks is at the height of his musical powers. Among works completed during the two previous years are *Songs of Sunset*, *Brigg Fair* and *A Dance Rhapsody*; and *In a Summer Garden* has been revised to become perhaps the composer's finest purely orchestral creation. Delius's works are now frequently performed throughout Europe and are shortly to gain a foothold in America. However, it is in England that he now takes the centre of the stage. Many conductors programme his music, but Beecham is the one who for over half a century will prove to be its greatest admirer and its principal exponent.

In general terms the composer's life continues to be well reflected in this legacy of letters; but those of his wife now begin to assume a much greater importance in telling the tale. Delius's correspondence with publishers is for example in large measure conducted by Jelka, and it is at times difficult to guess whether he himself has dictated and signed a letter to Harmonie, Tischer or Universal – to take the three foremost publishers of his middle years – or whether it is his wife who has composed it and imitated his signature. Sometimes the letter ends with her own signature, so closely involved does she become, from these middle years, with the preparation and publication of – and indeed propaganda for – her husband's printed scores. She is often involved, too, in the translation of his English texts into German. This is not to say that Delius himself does not write to his publishers: he does so on many occasions. But much of the onus is removed from him through the dedication – and determination – of his wife. This is particularly obvious when the letters need to be written in German.

As time goes by Delius's health begins to deteriorate, and Jelka's role in his correspondence becomes crucial. By the early 1920s she has become the composer's pen, not only as a writer of letters but also in her efforts to take down his music by dictation and to make fair copies of his scores. It is anyway at least as easy for Jelka to write to their friends as for Delius to dictate to her, so closely does the thinking of husband and wife coincide. Delius's dictated letters rarely attain the flow of some of his earlier writings; and it has to be admitted that even in those earlier, active days he could not exactly have been described as ever the most fluent of correspondents. The cogency of his musical thought was not usually reflected in the written word. Perhaps wisely, in the circumstances, he wrote little for publication; and he was never to embark upon an autobiography.

In reflecting a life worthy of biography, letters have many competitors. The events that make up the life of any composer will of course have little significance to the reader who has neither heard a note of his music nor, perhaps, studied his scores. The music that he creates is, after all, the composer's universal legacy, not his correspondence. The process of sound recording and radio can in modern times add to the overall dimension by allowing us to hear a subject speaking and reflecting on his life and works. A still wider dimension may be offered by film and television, with the man recorded for later generations as he walks and talks. By the year of Delius's death the arts of recording, whether for the gramophone or the cinema, had become sophisticated, and their exploitation was commonplace and indeed worldwide. But no recording of Delius's voice has been found, nor is any such recording documented. Similarly, no film of the man, either in middle or old age, is known to have been made. And the objects that he possessed in his lifetime have been scattered far and wide, for the most part irretrievably. Music apart, the record of this particular life, then, rests in the word and in the still, silent image that a photograph or painting is given leave to represent.

In one respect at least the letters in these two volumes can only imperfectly illuminate or describe the people who wrote them. The registering of *visual* impressions by friends and colleagues – even by chance acquaintances – is almost always effected at one remove from the subject and his immediate correspondence, and not by the subject and his friends writing to each other. Beecham would not have written to the composer himself in the terms of his later reminiscence of that first encounter with 'a stranger of arresting appearance . . . with fine and ascetic features that might have been taken for those of a distinguished ecclesiastic had it not been for the curiously eager and restless expression both in the eyes and mouth.[1]' And Basil Dean could still later remember how in 1920 'Delius was unlike the popular idea of a composer. His thin aesthetic face and precise diction suggested a professor, perhaps of philosophy, rather than a musician, while his faint North Country accent and brisk manner hinted at business training.[2] The power and attraction of these and other observations (see also Letter 397, note 2) derive from the fact that they are

---

1   *A Mingled Chime*, p. 63.

2   *Seven Ages*, pp. 145–6.

not made in letters *to* the subject, but they are made *of* the subject by people who knew him well.

The most intimate and intense picture of all is probably that drawn by Fenby in his book published just two years after the death of the composer. Delius, at the end of his life, is more surely alive in these closely observed pages than in any other book, and we are irresistibly drawn into the almost macabre atmosphere that descended on the house and enwrapped its inhabitants during these very last years. Cecil Gray, never above malice, went so far as to refer to an 'indescribably sinister' quality of which he was conscious in the household, but Fenby, too, remembers how from Delius there 'emanated a presence that was absolutely sapping . . . you could even feel him when you were in the garden.' The urbane Hubert Thieves, the most sophisticated and likeable of Delius's male nurses, was to confer in 1933 the title of 'the Plot House' on this closely-contained autocracy, with its tensions and its displays of temperament, exemplified above all by frequent – and often fearsome – rows between Jelka and her touchy housekeeper, Marthe Grespier. In between, there were the hours of silence, Delius being utterly averse to small-talk and forbidding social intercourse between the members of his household and the villagers of Grez. The letters of the Deliuses during the last year or so of the composer's life, with Jelka dedicated to preserving 'face' to the outside world, and with what their friend Alden Brooks was to describe as Delius's 'colossal egoism' at this stage dominating all else, simply cannot convey the picture of a household virtually in ruins – a picture that can only fully be drawn by the more objective views that we have from immediately outside the circle.

So it is that in a life documented alone by the letters written to or from its subject, something of the objective as well as the 'pictorial' view will inevitably be lacking. Neither subject nor correspondent will be found dwelling on the subject's appearance or manners. Delius's last twenty years, however, give a twist to the tale in that his painter wife Jelka gradually takes over the role of principal correspondent – perhaps more so than the proportion of her letters in this book indicates. She reports on how her husband looks and feels and on what he is saying and doing, and colour and movement are present in many of her letters – qualities that are found much less frequently in those of her husband.

Mention of colour and movement brings us to another reminiscence of Delius – this time of the young man in Paris. Astonishingly vivid, it is addressed direct to its subject by the composer's painter friend, Charles Boutet de Monvel, and its almost surreal, daydream-like quality is somehow heightened by the passing of time and the feeling of distance:

I walk along the avenue d'Orléans, Lion de Belfort – take the Rue Ducouëdic – go up the four steps [to Delius's apartment] – knock and nobody there. Off I go again, shutting the yellow door – past the post office, back down the Rue Brézin – It's strange, travelling in one's mind like this, and it's so precise. I cross the place de la Mairie, leave the square on my right and take myself down the Rue du Château – there, I go and knock at Floquet's and I hear the barking of all his dogs and the bizarre calls of his parrot. Then the gruff voice of the master of the house sounding annoyed at being disturbed – but soon showing that he's pleased to see you. Then along I go down the rue Vandamme – the gate at the level-crossing is closed and I hear the noise of the steam – psssshhhh . . . the concierges at their doorsteps, sweeping – the women coming back from their shopping. And the big carriages jolting along the cobbles and cluttering up the street till they can move off again.

– In my part of the town, in the park, an enormous sprawl of greenery taking over everything, quite superb, and perfect disorder inside it – then, back home, I hear rapid steps in the courtyard and the noise of a walking-stick on the cobblestones – the little door opens, there's a knock and it's you with your big, light-coloured cloak – you want to go to the hautes Bruyères because it's sunny. I propose that we go and see Molard, – and we're off. Now we're in Rue du Moulin de beurre, by those terra-cotta lions, so funny those lions. We leave the studios to our right and turn into the Rue Vercingétorix – the big entrance-door – the big courtyard – the marble-cutters – the scowling concierge – the well-polished staircase, clean and gleaming. We knock, the key's in the door. Warm welcome, Ida's off right away to make some coffee – we make ourselves comfortable in the big rocking-chair and the smoking chair, but there's the feeling that Leclerc must be somewhere round the corner ready to pounce on us. Vague feeling of unease – You talk music with William – Ida's grinding the coffee while Judith shows me some new and rare plants she's growing in a pot. – You see the state of mind I'm in and these leaps that one makes back into the past – where one undertakes the same journeys in times that are no more with companions who are no more . . .

This particular picture of Delius and his Parisian circle, drawn several years later, is of the composer in the early 1890s. Properly, the letter from which it is taken belongs to the first of these two volumes. The fact that it does not appear therein helps to make another point in defining the principles and at the same time the limitations of this overall selection. It simply was not available when Volume I went to press, but was found when some fifty letters that had been separated from the Delius Trust's Archive for many years finally came to light. At the same time a quantity of musical manuscripts was passed to the Trust – one result being that some revision of the chronology of established works became necessary, and another, that some minor works were added to the known Delius canon. This new musical material is fully documented in Robert Threlfall's *Frederick Delius: A Supplementary Catalogue*, and its accession to the Archive accounts for a considerable proportion of the list of additions and corrections to Volume I at the end of this book.

Without that further letter of Boutet's to Delius, we should obviously be the poorer. There are, however, other important omissions in the record. Those affecting the reporting of Delius's early life are recorded in Volume I, pp. xxv–vi, where, among others, the loss of the letters from Fenby to Delius is noted. The letters from Philip Heseltine to Delius have not, unfortunately, been accessible to me, and this has meant that Heseltine himself can only sparsely be represented in the present volume, his own words having to be plundered from some of the usefully extensive quotations in Cecil Gray's *Peter Warlock*.

In fact there are considerable and often inexplicable gaps in both the incoming and outgoing extant correspondence of Delius. C. W. Orr's letters to him, for example, have not survived; nor have those of Sydney Schiff (the novelist Stephen Hudson). The last letter from one of Delius's closest and best-loved friends, Norman O'Neill, dates from December 1909, only two years after the correspondence was initiated. The Deliuses' side of this correspondence, however, *begins* in October 1909 and continues for many years, even if twenty-five letters are all that remain. Then Beecham's letters to Delius fall almost entirely between December 1907 and June 1915. All that remain otherwise are isolated letters in 1916, 1919 and 1933. At least we are more fortunate here than in the reverse correspondence: the earliest letter from Delius to Beecham that has so far been found dates from 1933. As with Beecham, so with Balfour Gardiner: twenty-four letters written to Delius between 1907 and 1910. After that, just three more items found of what must in fact have been a voluminous correspondence. From Delius to Gardiner, almost incredibly, even less has been found than to Beecham – just one postcard, so far, from 1914. Then again all the letters from the intimate American friends, Henry and Marie Clews, have gone. One note from Henry to Delius, presumably never sent, was found among the large collection of letters from the Deliuses to the Clews that, thankfully, had been carefully preserved by their recipients.

Again, almost nothing, unfortunately, remains of the letters of Ida Gerhardi to the Deliuses. And of Jelka's correspondence with members of her own family, virtually all that has been found are the letters written to her by her brother and sister-in-law in the 1930s. If most of the letters from the Deliuses to Grainger seem likely to have survived (although clearly there are gaps), there is an odd hiatus between 1922 and 1932 in the reverse flow. Just as in the cases already cited, it is quite clear that the correspondence nonetheless continued during those years.

There are further gaps, on the one side or the other, in Delius's correspondence with various publishers. Here it should be stated that a representative sample of some of the more interesting of the communications between Delius and his publishers is what is offered in this edition. It should be borne in mind that a voluminous business correspondence, of which these examples will give, I hope, a fair flavour, underpins the musical achievement and shows Delius and his wife at best to be perfectionists in their efforts to see clear and fault-free scores through the press, and at worst a publisher's nightmare in an endless (and at times, it must be said, clearly justifiable) quibbling over detail, particularly in relation to financial matters. Whether or not Delius was, in his lifetime, unlucky with his publishers, or whether the reverse may have been the case, is very much a matter for future consideration and judgment, and is certainly beyond the scope of the present work.

One may therefore be tempted to wonder just how fully the last twenty-five years of Delius's life can, then, be documented by the composer's correspondence alone, when such swathes of it conducted with central figures like Beecham, Gardiner, O'Neill, Clews and Fenby are gone. The answer of course is that, as with the first of these two volumes, a great deal of the other side can continue to be inferred from the side that is preserved, and that, furthermore, letters to and from other, perhaps even peripheral, figures can also be ransacked for such pertinent information – as well as for interesting sidelights – as they may contain.

Yet another unhelpful element in the story is the tantalizing matter of letters which we know, from other sources, were preserved after Jelka's death, but which soon disappeared. Among a list made by Dr Berta Geissmar for Sir Thomas Beecham in 1940 were 'several letters' from Bartók and 'several letters in a special bundle' from Elgar. These are, thankfully, at least preserved in transcript, but the whereabouts of the originals is unknown. Another typed synopsis tells us of 'numerous letters and telegrams dated and undated but circa 1913' from Lady Cunard, and of a number of letters from Beatrice and May Harrison dated 1916, 1917 and 1920. None of these has been found. Also evidently missing is a letter (or letters) from the Munich critic William Ritter. An earlier schedule, made only shortly after Jelka's death, details letters 'apparently of importance found at the house at Grez', and among the names of correspondents figuring in it are Bjørnson, Berg, Ibsen, Le Gallienne, Messager and Oscar Wilde. Wilde is certainly out of court, the reference undoubtedly being to a third party's letter responding in 1903 to Delius's enquiry concerning the rights to *Salome*. It seems quite possible, on the other hand, that letters from one or other of the Bjørnsons (cf. Vol. I, pp. 59–60) could have survived, as from Richard Le Gallienne (I, pp. 61 and 71), André Messager (I, pp. 208–9) and Henrik Ibsen (I, p. 54). It seems however rather more likely that Berg is a misreading of (Herman) Bang – although Alban Berg should perhaps not be entirely discounted in view of the assertion, in 1971, by the conductor Jascha Horenstein during the course of a BBC interview that Berg was very impressed by Delius and particularly by the *Mass of Life*.

Among the Trust's documents it is also recorded that the German painter Julie Wolfthorn, in Berlin, on learning of Jelka's death asked for the return of her own letters to Jelka. Not just letters such as these, but many other of the Deliuses' more preciously personal possessions were to be dispersed after Jelka's death, seemingly beyond recall. On 28 February 1936 almost all of the household furnishings at Grez came under the hammer at the Hôtel des Ventes in Paris. Among the more interesting items were one bronze and one plaster bust of Delius, artist unspecified; some 'wooden figures' – almost certainly comprising the Gauguin carvings that Delius was known to possess; '11 engravings by Munck'; no less than 56 'paintings', simply described as such; three lots of 'canvasses', numbering 38 in all; '21 framed engravings'; '18 unframed pictures'; '25 unframed sketches'; '12 sketches'; and a 'Case of sketches'. Apart from the Edvard Munch pictures, which fetched 2,700 francs, the rest went for a song. Most of the paintings and sketches would have been by Jelka. The whereabouts of only a few of these is now known; of much the larger portion there is no trace. Finally, a number of fine books, several of them from the sixteenth century, Jelka bequeathed to her brother, while many minor and relatively modern titles were passed to the British Hospital in Paris.

In spite of all that is missing, it can be reasserted that Delius's extant correspondence continues to reflect largely – and accurately – the pattern of his life and work. With his fame now established at home and on the continent of Europe, the correspondence from 1909 onward shows the composer consolidating the pre-eminent situation so recently earned by his music. So it is that one-third of this selection from his letters takes us up to the First World War, when the high plateau that Delius has reached, with settled periods of composing at Grez punctuated by occasional weeks of social and musical acclaim – idolatry even – in London and indeed in other European cities, is left for ever. The next third reflects unsettlement and the struggle to compose despite adverse external circumstances, compounded by a gradual breakdown in health. And the final third of the book takes us through the Deliuses' last decade at Grez-sur-Loing, the restless wanderings that have otherwise so strongly characterized the composer's life now at an end.

From today's perspective, however, it could well be said that the musical divides in Delius's creative life fall elsewhere. The works completed during the Great War should surely no longer be considered as representing a significant diminution in the composer's creative powers. The Requiem, *Eventyr*, the second *Dance Rhapsody*, the Double Concerto, the Violin Concerto, the String Quartet: all these works – and others – written in an unsettled period during which the composer was at times troubled by both physical and nervous disorders, can now legitimately be seen as a continuation – a development and extension even – of the cooler note that was becoming apparent in his music during the immediately pre-war years with *Fennimore and Gerda*, *An Arabesque*, *The Song of the High Hills* and *North Country Sketches*. Curiously enough, it was to be during the final stages of the war that there came the signs of a breaking-away from the comparative astringency of these larger-scale works of the preceding years. *A Song before Sunrise* and *Poem of Life and Love*, written in Biarritz during the hopeful summer of 1918, may be seen as preludes to a late and luxuriant flowering that was to be represented, by the Cello Concerto, *Songs of Farewell*, first drafted in 1920, and *Hassan*, all but completed in 1921. But the personal battle with ill-health was inexorably to take over and become the dominant factor in the composer's life, so that what course, in other conditions, Delius's work might subsequently have taken – with that re-found element of warmth and affirmation and hope – must remain a question ultimately without answer.

From the mid-twenties on, with the battle against chronic invalidism lost, we had no right to expect more music from Delius, by then a physical wreck even if – extraordinarily – quite undiminished in mental power. But once again the pattern is distorted. With Eric Fenby's arrival in Grez comes the last, unhoped-for period of creativity. By the beginning of 1929 a joint *modus operandi* has been established and the pencil jottings of many years earlier are taken up one by one and fully composed by dictation, a process that is to continue, with interruptions, until the end of 1932 – only a year and a half before Delius's death.

This triumphant musical valediction within the framework of wretched physical breakdown is well documented, both in the Deliuses' correspondence and in the memoirs of Eric Fenby and others. Its astonishing affirmation of mind over matter may perhaps poignantly be contrasted with Elgar's desolated withdrawal from creative endeavour following the death of his wife in 1920. 'I felt that I was no longer "in" the world,' he wrote, 'or rather, that the old artistic "striving" world exists for me no more; so my one short attempt at life was a failure.' Delius on the other hand, years later still composing and still almost exasperatingly Nietzschean in outlook, was to tell Fenby: 'I have seen the best of the earth and have done everything that is worth doing; I am content. I have had a wonderful life.'

There is little variation from the previous volume in treatment of the subject-matter. As before, my general practice has been not to correct errors in the spelling or punctuation of the original letters; and to preserve the original layout, as far as has been possible, both of the body of the letter and (if more approximately) of the address headings. Where elements of the date were pre-printed in a letterhead, they are here given in italic numerals, and written numerals that were added are given in Roman fount. Some standardization has been accepted in respect of the layout of letter endings and signatures; and the use of double quotation marks has been adopted throughout. Where envelopes have survived, I have tended this time to record details of postmarks and addresses with rather more consistency, in acknowledgement of the fact that for the student of other personalities who play a part in Delius's life such information may well be of use. Where I have referred to the writings of Eric Fenby, a bibliographical reference is generally given. On the other hand, 'Fenby remembers' indicates oral reference, recorded as a result of conversation with Dr Fenby or from remarks made by him in the course of lectures on Delius given in more recent years. During the final decade in Grez there were to be many visitors, Delius himself being unable to travel. I have tried at least to mention the more interesting visits, but there must have been more, often undocumented.

As before, 'RT' numbers, referring to Robert Threlfall's 1977 *Catalogue* and to its 1986 updating, are assigned to Delius's compositions where the latter are listed at the end of the introductory notes to each year.

It should perhaps be reiterated that the originals of the letters in these volumes come from a variety of sources and not simply from the Delius Trust's files. If the search has, finally, been less than thoroughgoing, the blame must lie with the writer. There will surely be more letters from Delius lying quietly in private collections, and as they are brought forward, fresh light will inevitably be cast on the composer. The Trustees of the Delius estate will obviously be grateful to learn of the whereabouts of such letters.

As before, translations into English from letters originally written in other languages are in large measure my own. In a number of cases, already-existing translations from the German have been revised, and here Evelin Gerhardi has again offered invaluable advice. The language of the original is stated in the notes following each letter only if that original is not in English. This is in contradistinction to the practice in Volume I, where a far larger proportion of the letters printed were originally in languages other than English.

The reader may on occasion need to refer to both volumes for bibliographical information, since the bibliographies are complementary. Works mentioned in Volume I are not given repeat listings in Volume II, whose bibliographical section comprises books and articles on the second half of Delius's creative life, as well as some of the more important recent writings generally on the composer. I hope, too, that I have rectified a number of omissions from my Volume I listing, in particular some of the excellent essays published over the years in *The Delius Society Journal*. Under its present editor the *Journal* sets ever-higher standards in the presentation of British-music scholarship and has become an important original source of information on Delius and various of his musical contemporaries. As before, my bibliography is not intended to cover essays of purely musical analysis or commentary, which are in Delius's case legion and of which some of the best examples (Fenby and Palmer among others) are anyway to be found in concert programmes or in the literature associated with recordings. The aim has rather been to list works that on the whole deal with the life *and* the music, since both are, after all, the subject of these two volumes.

That the life should here be seen as a primary concern will be no surprise to those students of Delius who may by now have become aware of the minefields of factual error scattered among the critical writings of three-quarters of a century and more on Delius. Some of these errors have become enshrined almost in consequence, it would seem, of their own antiquity, others because of the august reputations of those who first perpetrated them. *A Village Romeo and Juliet* provides suitable examples in both areas. Study of the letters in the Delius Trust's Archive and in the Gerhardi/Steinweg collection in Lüdenscheid reveals that Keller's tale had first attracted Delius some years before the composer was to write his own English libretto in the summer/autumn of 1899. Later in that autumn of 1899 he was hard at work on the music, 'composing the whole time'. However, many years later and presumably with Delius's approval, Universal Edition were to give out a vocal score with the opera's precise dates of composition shown as 1900–01, and all subsequent editions of the work have borne these dates. Much more serious in its consequences has been the legend that Delius composed the opera to a German libretto, a libretto sometimes presumed to have been written by his wife and at other times said to have been written by Delius himself. It has furthermore been said that Jelka translated it into English. Any study of the letters soon reveals that Delius's German, if quite fluent, is not perfect, and the hypothesis that he wrote his libretto in German may be discarded, the conclusive evidence finally being supplied by Letter 533. And the translations that Jelka made for him are all into her own native language, German, and certainly not into her acquired English.

It can only have been in this mistaken belief that a 'new translation' of the opera was commissioned for the Delius Centenary production, in 1962, in London and Bradford. Inevitably it is inferior to the original, being a hotchpotch of Delius's own text (with Beecham's emendations) and, one can only presume, of the original German translation back-translated into English. One need only listen to the final love-duet as sung in both English versions to realize what savagery has been perpetrated. Elsewhere even the 'Juliet' has been relieved of the mellifluous name by which both Keller and Delius address her, and Vreli becomes – in an English setting – Vrenchen, calling for vocal contortion all but absent in the original. Myths like these still clinging to *A Village Romeo and Juliet* and its libretto are hard to dispel: it was only recently that the truth of this old legend was once more averred to me, with the greatest confidence, by a distinguished conductor.

Then, for example, some of Delius's English and German publishers have consistently misprinted the names of a number of those foreign poets whose texts he set, something that has occasionally led English commentators down the same path. To be fair, it is often Delius himself, careless in spelling, who has initiated the process. But even in recent years references to Bjørnsen (or Björnsen) in the Delius musical literature must be mildly irritating, at the very least, to Norwegians for whom Bjørnstjerne Bjørnson was their country's great nineteenth-century patriot poet. A similar reaction might be felt by Swedes for whom Ernst Josephson – rather than just 'Josefson' – was a distinguished late Romantic poet and painter; and by Danes who must certainly find it galling to see Delius's song 'Let Springtime come' still published to 'words from the *Swedish* [my italics] of J. P. Jacobsen'. Rather more forgivable is the English habit of ignoring the fact that *aa* is the final letter of the Norwegian alphabet: strictly speaking it is, therefore, wrong to describe 'The Homeward Way' as a 'poem by A. O. Vinje'. The poet's name was Aasmund, etymologically and phonologically the English Osmund, and in Norwegian it can only be abbreviated to Aa. O. Vinje. One hopes that the recording of even such relatively minor points within these covers, as elsewhere, may ensure that we get it right from now on.

I suppose one of the better examples of musical history going slightly awry lies in Beecham's misreading of Bartók's address (Budapest, Teréz-körut 17.IV.23) as also comprising the date. No matter that the first of the sequence of six communications from Bartók is clearly dated 7 June 1910. In his biography of Delius Beecham squarely places the correspondence, and consequently the friendship, in 1922–23, hauling in not just Kodály but also a (1911) Viennese performance of *A Mass of Life* on the coat-tails of this chronological clanger. In isolation it is just one of a number of factual errors in what is, at heart, a wise and sympathetic book. But there are those who succumb completely to the magisterial authority of Beecham, with the result that the late-dating of the Bartók/Delius friendship has gained undeserved currency, Beecham's book remaining uncorrected in subsequent editions.

These almost random samples of by now institutionalized errors in the Delius literature are to be found multiplied a hundredfold when serious study is given to that literature. Once accepted as a fact of life, this condition may be seen as largely remediable by returning to first sources – represented in diminishing ratio by those alive today who actually knew and even worked with the composer, and in conversely increasing ratio by the correspondence of the protagonists, as more of it steadily comes to light. So it is that some of the lessons pointed by the following pages will inevitably have to be modified (but, one hopes, only rarely unlearned) as further material touching on the composer and his music is uncovered. Only on the world's last day can 'definitive' biography after all be written, and then to no earthly purpose. Indeed, it seems to me that this particular epithet, more regularly applied to the genre than any other, is the one that should logically never accompany it.

Max Chop in 1907 had little to go on except his own very recent exposure to Delius's music and his consequent conversation and correspondence with the composer. His monograph may therefore confidently claim to be based on primary sources, as may the later books of Philip Heseltine and Eric Fenby. Each work when it was published provided major new insights into Delius and his world, as Beecham's biography was to do much later still.

Commentators on the music alone have on the other hand tended, usually of necessity, to draw factual background from the volumes most readily available to them, and into the net of musical sources have been drawn a number of other books ranging from the broadly sympathetic to the simply unacceptable. Alan Jefferson's biography in the *Master Musicians* series remains a useful work of reference by a writer who knows his Delius. It is only let down by the fact that closer study generally of Delius's life was only just getting under way when it was published, with the result that some factual matter has been amended by more recent studies. Hutchings's biography was a holding operation necessary in its time but impossibly handicapped by Beecham's iron grip on the contents of the Delius Trust Archive, a grip that was not to be relaxed until Beecham himself finally found time to write and publish his own biography of the composer, fulfilling after the passage of a quarter of a century a promise he had originally made to Jelka. The more important part of Arthur Hutchings's book dwells on the music, and this is always worth reading, for the author has a profound empathy with Delius's work, and he is never dull.

The first full biographical venture after the composer's death was, however, undertaken by Delius's sister, Clare, who was (like Hutchings in due course) rigorously denied access to her brother's papers. Her memories of his childhood are valuable, her notions of the rest of his life impossibly vague and romantic. Many years later, a gifted American historian and travel writer, Gloria Jahoda, also denied access to the Delius papers, took unfortunate refuge in the wispy imaginings of Clare's daughter, Peggy, and produced an uncharacteristic piece of romantic fiction, apparently aimed at a younger audience but nonetheless laying claim to authentic biography. Like the Clare Delius it is at times more than faintly ridiculous.

Another work aimed at a younger readership is Fenby's second Delius book, written for *The Great Composers* series. As might be expected, however, this is a model of its kind and represents a valuable addition to the Delius literature. Christopher Redwood's admirable compilation *A Delius Companion* is, too, an indispensable book for Delians, although again with many of the pieces being by Delius's contemporaries a modicum of care is well worth the taking if it is to be trawled for factual matter on the composer's life. And we are indebted to this husband-and-wife partnership for Dawn Redwood's book on Delius as seen at the time of *Hassan*, where fresh fields have been thoroughly researched. A still greater debt is owed to John Boulton Smith, whose last major publication was his long-awaited study of Delius and Munch. This is the work of a fine scholar, deeply informed by the eye of the art historian as by the ear of the musical connoisseur. Finally there is the lone outpost represented by Christopher Palmer's *Delius: Portrait of a Cosmopolitan*, a curious but successful amalgam of biography and musicological enquiry, tempered with wide and perceptive comment on a number of Delius's contemporaries and disciples. Here is unquestionably a highly original approach to the study of Delius and his music, full of sensitive observation and judgment – qualities based solidly on a profound insight into the man and the workings of his mind. Palmer's book, much less a biography than a major first attempt to analyse both the influences at work on Delius and the hitherto much underrated influence he has had on others, stands aloof but not inaccessible. It comes as close as any to defining the Delius mystique.

This brief conspectus of Delius biographies, while not exclusive, may provide a pointer to what the literature has lacked and to what this edition must set out, in some measure, to supply: a full and reliable chronology which may safely be used to underpin the study of earlier texts at the same time as offering as wide a perspective as possible on the composer and his times.

Finally, a note should perhaps be added on the subject of concert reviews, to which, for reasons of space, only sparse reference can be accorded in this book. The pattern shows a distinct change, with the hostility evident in a range of reviews in 1909 and the period immediately following being replaced by comparative euphoria in the post-war years. Delius was himself strongly antipathetic towards music criticism in most of its published manifestations. 'It is only *now* they begin to see there is anything in my music at all,' he wrote to Charles Kennedy Scott in 1928. '. . . I have more faith in the music-lover than in the music critic. Every one of my works has at one time been damned by the London critics – from *Sea-Drift* to the *Mass*.' (See Letter 520.) Delius, of course, had some justification, no doubt remembering what the *Musical Standard* had had to say about the Beecham/Austin performance of *Sea Drift* early in 1909: there was, it ran,

> no excuse for its dullness and labouredness . . . abominably monotonous, barbarous and totally ineffective stuff . . . ugly and meaningless dissonance . . . Let Mr. Delius re-study (say) the Prelude to Tristan and Isolde and endeavour to understood how clumsy, seriously lacking in contrast and often downright bad his music is from an harmonic standpoint. He will also see the value of melody.

Again, in June the composer would have been able to read the views of the critic of the *Daily News* on his *Mass of Life*, on the day following its first performance:

> His writing for the chorus . . . is as ugly as it is trying to the voices . . . When Mr. Delius should be ecstatic he is only noisy, cacophonous and monotonous. Nor has he only failed in the big climaxes. The solos are singularly pointless and unexpressive of anything that approaches emotion.

Not all, however, was condemnation. Even the *Daily News* had had to allow that 'where the composer has been able to place the burden of description on his orchestra he has been very successful indeed.' Younger and more sympathetic critics, like Robin Legge and Ernest Newman, were meanwhile rallying to the defence of Delius's music, and *The Daily Telegraph* of 8 June 1909 carried a lyrical review of that same performance of the *Mass*. But the musical establishment was not easily to abandon the offensive, and Delius was to find strange bedfellows in *The Scotsman* in the context of a review of a

Beecham concert given in Edinburgh on 22 November 1915: 'It was perhaps unfortunate that the attention in the second portion of the concert was devoted to such examples of modernity as Stravinsky, Delius and Borodin' – an extraordinary statement as seen from today's perspective, given that Delius was represented by *The Walk to the Paradise Garden*. However, only seven years later Aldous Huxley was to give expression to the degree of acceptance at last accorded to Delius's music by a generation that was becoming accustomed to even stranger sounds:

> Where shall we look for that long pure line of melody that gives to the best of Mozart's works an outline like the silhouette of a beautiful city of cones and towers? It is difficult to think of any such melodist today with the solitary exception of Delius. He most certainly possesses the gift of pure melody, as the long, beautiful lines of his 'Village Romeo' attest.

We have come a long way, then, from the *Musical Standard*'s strictures, addressed to Delius in 1909, on 'the value of melody'. Huxley was in no doubt at all as to Delius's 'real contribution' to music: '. . . he has extended the boundaries of musical expression and has added a new province to its already opulent empire.'[1]

I must confirm my gratitude to colleagues already acknowledged in my first volume, with a special second thank-you to Eric Fenby, Evelin Gerhardi, Stephen Lloyd and Lewis Foreman for the breadth and generosity of their continued help. To that first list must be added further benefactors, with my gratitude for advice and, where appropriate, for permission to reproduce material. I am particularly indebted to: the Bartók Archive in Budapest, John Bishop, the late Sir Adrian Boult, Mary Cahill, Patricia Cleveland-Peck, Denham Ford, Thomas Gunn, Alan Hancox, Margaret Harrison, Roy Henderson, Katherine Jessel, the late Eric Marshall Johnson, Alice Kadel, Michael Kennedy, Mme Sarolta Kodály, Jonathan Maddox, Jerrold Northrop Moore, Barry Ould, Henry Roche, Bertha Sander, John Kennedy Scott, Sophie Royde Smith, Eva Smirzitz, Rolf Stang, Fred Tomlinson, Jane Wilson and Alan Woolgar.

The extract from *Great Morning* by Osbert Sitwell (Macmillan), quoted on p. 133, is reproduced with permission. The extract from *Overture and Beginners* by Eugene Goossens (Methuen London), also quoted on the same page is reproduced with permission.

My deeply appreciative thanks go to James Price of the Scolar Press; and

1   Cf. Basil Hogarth: 'Aldous Huxley as Music Critic'. *The Musical Times*, December 1935, pp. 1079–82.

I also gratefully acknowledge the help and encouragement of Sean and Cece Magee and of Antony Wood, for their commitment in helping to bring each of these two books to publication. The continued encouragement and support of the Delius Trust and its distinguished members has been invaluable, and is again acknowledged with gratitude.

Lionel Carley, 1988

'One of the most charming, the most original, and the most golden of men'

Ethel Smyth on Delius *(from Beecham and Pharaoh)*

1909

Delius spent the first five months of the year mainly at Grez, at work on what was to be his last essay in operatic form, *Fennimore and Gerda*. Invitations, however pressing, to attend committee meetings of the Musical League in England, and indeed to attend performances of his music in England and elsewhere, were ignored. There were occasional visitors to Grez to be entertained – Beecham and O'Neill, among others – and there were undercurrents to divert him from his preoccupation with *Fennimore*: Balfour Gardiner had his solicitor commission an agent in Atlanta to survey and report on Delius's Florida plantation; Delius himself had instructed a Berlin solicitor to look at his position with regard to Harmonie Verlag as, disillusioned with his dealings with his publisher, the composer was seeking to disengage himself from the company; and there were preparations to travel to London for the first full performance, on 7 June, of *A Mass of Life*. Delius attended Beecham's rehearsals at the beginning of June and was back in Grez by the middle of the month.

Both he and Jelka fell victim to influenza in July, but Delius recovered sufficiently in time to set off on a walking holiday in the Black Forest with Norman O'Neill. This was in mid-July, when for a few days the two men stayed in the Feldberg area: 'I dont care for it here much – it is overrun with tourists & too civilised. However I pretend to like it so as not to spoil O'Neill's pleasure ... All this is nothing to Denmark & Norway.' The countryside around Neustadt, 'quite primitive & not a soul', pleased him much more and a further note to Jelka informed her: 'I walked 20 miles to day – I am better but getting coughing fits', a passing reference to a stubborn bronchial infection induced by his earlier influenza.

Jelka joined him at Hamburg at the end of the month, and the beginning of August saw them both in Denmark, on the way to stay at the country estate of their Danish friends, Einar and Elisabeth Schou. 'Austin's children are also there,' Delius had told Jelka; and it seems that they both stayed for most of the month.

One further trip to England followed. Delius had two important commitments there. The first was to conduct the first performance of *A Dance*

Rhapsody at the Shire Hall, Hereford, during the course of the Three Choirs Festival. 'I wish I had not accepted the thing,' he had written to Jelka in July, aware that he would not have at his disposal an orchestra of the size that the work really demanded; 'fancy to be in England the whole of September!' He was then to attend the Musical League's first festival, in Liverpool. Although unwell in Hereford, he nonetheless conducted his piece, but was subsequently forced to retreat, with Jelka, to London, complaining of 'a very bad bilious attack'. Plans to travel to Liverpool were abandoned completely and as soon as Delius felt well enough to travel, the pair left London for a period of recuperation in Grez. Jelka too was under some strain and had still not fully recovered from the debilitating effects of her summer influenza. Any further work by the composer on *Fennimore and Gerda* this year would have been confined to a few weeks at Grez later in October and in November, when he was restored to fitness.

December saw the Deliuses again on their travels, arriving in Elberfeld a few days before Haym's performance there of *A Mass of Life* on the 11th. They went on to Berlin where they stayed for a week or so and where Delius could at last discuss in detail with his solicitors his problems with Harmonie. The end of the year found them once more at Grez. Apart from the two performances of the *Mass*, 1909 had seen other significant performances: *Sea Drift* in London, *Appalachia* in Prague and Basel, and the Piano Concerto in Munich, Leipzig and Budapest. For the first time, too, a major work had been given in the United States: the Boston Symphony Orchestra had performed *Paris* in Boston in November.

Fennimore and Gerda, opera 'in eleven pictures' (Delius, after J. P. Jacobsen) (RT I/8). Begun.

(301)

Frederick Delius to Granville Bantock

Jan 7th 1909
GREZ SUR LOING,
S. ET M.

Dear friend

Thanks for your letter: for goodness sake do not resign from anything whatever
– There are so many active men in the wrong direction & we might get one of
these on the Committee – Let the others examine the rest of the Scores[1] – Have
you found anything worth playing? I asked D^r McNaught only to send me the
likely ones to look at – Debussy, d'Indy & Schillings will not fill up more than
$\frac{1}{2}$ a programme – Mahler's Symphony will take 1 hour of the Choral Concert
– So we have any amount of room yet – The Festival ought to be a great attraction & a pecuniary success – Mahler, as Conductor, is always a great draw – he
is perfectly wonderful – In the Symphony I proposed that he should conduct
there are beautiful things – It is No. 2 – Enclosed I send you a list of mistakes
in the Score & parts of "Appalachia" get somebody to correct them carefully –
it will save you a lot of trouble – Do not let the Chorus stand up until just
before the funeral march which heralds in the a capella chorus – The la la la
sound much more mysterious thus – Please tell me when it comes off – if I
can I will come[2] – I am now working at my new Dramatic Work, "Niels
Lyhne"[3] – Have you already addressed the University–? Do tell your students
not to continue to write classical music or to imitate what they think is deep or
severe music – England seems never to get over this sort of nonsense & the best
result only seems to rise to a weak imitation – Since Beethoven the Symphony
has gradually become weaker & more meaningless – à travers Mendelsohn,
Schumann, Brahms. *Tschaïkowsky* managed to put a spirited march or tune
Valse Lento into it which gave a slightly new color to it – but very slight, but
somewhat more human –

It has been very cold here & the snow is still lying on the ground – it is still
freezing – Give my love to your wife & write me again when you have a
moment to spare.

Yrs ever
Frederick Delius

Autograph letter, signed and dated, written on headed notepaper.

The original is in the Delius Trust Archive.

1 'I am afraid I shall have to give up all active work on the [Musical] League,' wrote
a hard-pressed Bantock to Delius on 4 January. Recently appointed professor of music
at Birmingham University, while remaining principal of the Birmingham and

Midland Institute School of Music, he was resolved to resign from the League's music-selection sub-committee, 'having already looked at nearly 20 scores'.

2 Bantock was hoping to conduct *Appalachia* in Liverpool, but the project fell through.

3 *Fennimore and Gerda*, after J. P. Jacobsen's novel, *Niels Lyhne* (1880).

(302)
Frederic Cowen to Frederick Delius

THE WINDSOR HOTEL,
GLASGOW
JAN^y 17th '09

Dear Mr. Delius

I am *very* sorry that after all I cannot do "Brigg Fair" here this season – The fact is, I find our time for rehearsal now is more limited than I thought, owing to many Concerts & travelling; we tried the work through the other day, & I find it *very* difficult, not technically, but as regards detail of parts & general effect, & I would not venture to do it without a *great* deal of rehearsal – It would also be unfair to the Composer, & I would wish to do it every possible justice. I am sure you will understand, & would yourself prefer to wait until you can be made to shine in a proper light. I will arrange differently next season & give it, or something else of yours, a proper chance. Thanks for all the trouble you have taken which I regret should have been in vain (at least for the moment)
With best remembrances

Yours sincerely
Frederic H. Cowen

The Score & Parts shall be returned safely to B. & H. –

Autograph letter, signed and dated, written on headed notepaper.

The original is in the Delius Trust Archive. It is the second of two communications from Cowen to Delius in the Archive; a postcard from 54 Hamilton Terrace, London N.W., dated 4 October 1908, was written to suggest a meeting on Sunday 11 October.

Frederic Cowen (1852–1935): English composer and conductor. A child prodigy, he studied music in Leipzig and Berlin from 1865 to 1868. He conducted most of the major British orchestras and was from 1900 to 1910 chief conductor of the Scottish Orchestra. He was knighted in 1911.

(303)
August Schmid-Lindner to Frederick Delius

München, 22 January *1909*.
Königinstr. 73.

Dear Herr Delius,

I thank you most sincerely for your repeated kind cards and can only apologize by saying that it has been because of a great deal of work that I have not yet got round to replying to you. I should only like to tell you now what you perhaps already know, namely that your work created an extremely favourable impression among the experts, and had a considerable success with the public too.[1] As to your plan of altering it again somewhat, I must confess that a little toning-down of the orchestra would naturally be welcome to the soloist.[2] But I believe this could only be a matter of minor retouching because the whole design of the work requires that the orchestra should remain the dominant element and naturally no alteration can be made in this respect, nor is any necessary of course. For the most part, at the places where the piano comes in, the orchestra is quiet and there are only a very few places, e.g. towards the end of the slow movement, where perhaps some of the additional parts in the orchestra might be dispensed with. In my humble opinion any radical alterations are out of the question, the pianist must just accept this work for what it is: a symphonic orchestral work with piano obbligato.

Incidentally, I should like to ask you whether you have read what the press writes and whether you might like me to send you on some newspapers.

You will have received the picture postcard which Ludwig Hess and I sent you recently. We were at the time together on a little concert excursion and took advantage of a beautiful winter afternoon before the start of the concert to find some enjoyment in the beauties of nature.

If you should wish to make any alterations to your concerto, I shall always be very interested to get to know it in its new form.

In the meantime I am with best wishes

Yours most sincerely
Aug. Schmid-Lindner

I apologise for having to type this for lack of time.

Typed letter (with handwritten postscript), signed and dated, written in German on headed notepaper.

The original is in the Delius Trust Archive. It is the fifth of six letters and postcards from Schmid-Lindner to Delius, dated 28 April 1907 – 23 January 1909, that are preserved.

1   Schmid-Lindner, soloist in the first Berlin performance of the Piano Concerto (I, 308–10), had given the work again, in Munich on 8 January under Felix Mottl.

2   A spirited correspondence was continuing between Delius, pianist Theodor Szántó, and publishers Harmonie Verlag; and Mottl and Schmid-Lindner were now also being consulted. A number of relatively minor alterations (mainly dynamic markings) just made by Delius reached Schmid-Lindner too late to be incorporated in his performance. Szántó's radically revised version of the concerto was, as the composer informed Harmonie on 4 January, on no account to be given again. For a discussion on the subject see Threlfall in *A Delius Companion* (ed. Redwood), pp. 239–47.

(304)
August Schmid-Lindner to Frederick Delius

München, 23 January *1909*.
Königinstr. 73.

Dear Herr Delius,

Felix Mottl informed me today that you were seeking advice about alterations to your concerto, and asks me to reply to you on the matter. He said he could not himself possibly see what there was to be altered. I already informed you yesterday that I was more or less of the same opinion. Your work is certainly not a clear-cut piano concerto & any attempt in the future to categorize it as such would, in my opinion, be bound to fail. The amount the piano has to say is already given in the basic design and can hardly be altered later. At the most the volume of the orchestra might be reduced just a little here and there; but that too only in a few insignificant places. I respect the work enormously as a melodious and sensitively beautiful orchestral piece in which an obbligato piano part is integrated. I do not ask for more – nor is it at all necessary to do so. I believe that the work would be bound to lose in naturalness if a more dominant role were forced upon the piano part than had been allotted to it in the basic design.

With most cordial greetings

Yours most sincerely
Aug. Schmid-Lindner

Typed letter, signed and dated, written in German on headed notepaper.

The original is in the Delius Trust Archive.

(305)
Thomas Beecham to Frederick Delius

28/1/09
Highfield,
Boreham Wood,
Herts.

Dear Delius –

I am delighted to hear your Concerto went so well with Mottl –

Last Monday my new orchestra[1] made it's first appearance – they played very well and got a few brilliant notices – (*not* in the Telegraph) – the Times noticeably. I do not however have the full contingent until Feb. 22nd when I fire off my first heavy gun –

I can quite honestly declare that I shall have by then an orchestra which will simply wipe the floor with all the others combined –

The few last men of the "New Symphony" whom I want have joined me and I have sneaked some from the other orchestras –

The wind are splendid –

The 1ST Flute I prefer to Hudson.

   "   1ST oboe is the best in the country

I have two clarinets whom I prefer to Draper

"   "   the best Bassoon in the country

The Trumpets are the same and the Trombones – headed by the 1ST Trombone in London – are very good –

The Tympani is a fine fellow who used to be with Wood and had to retire for a long time through illness –

The Horns are not finally settled –

The Violins will be lead (I think) by Louis Zimmermann

"   Violas *are* lead by Lionel Tertis who is the best Viola I have heard anywhere

"   Celli by Boris Hamburg or Herbert Walenn

"   Basses – Claude Hobday who is far & away the best man here –

The rank & file are excellent and I think almost every-one has been a scholar or gold-medallist – The new crowd are tremendously keen and very well behaved –

The Principals are all on contract – The Syndicate is practically formed –

I was unable to attend the last League C^{TEE} meeting[2] or I should have "sat on" the absurdities perpetrated. English people have passed into the grand-motherly state in dealing with these matters –

I have made enquiries about the Tonic-sol-fa for the Mass;[3] I think that it could have been done cheaper by Novellos. McNaught for instance does the translation himself – But as Breitkopf has the agency for the work, I do not think the other firm would undertake it. Outside of them, Curwens are the only other people in London, and I think as the work is difficult, it would not be advisable to hunt for a cheap man in the Provinces – If I cannot find anyone else in the next few days, you had better put [it] in the hands of Curwen without delay – Time is pressing and the Choir ought to have it soon – I will write you again first thing next week –

Love from us both

Ever yours
Thomas Beecham.

Autograph letter, signed and dated, written on headed notepaper. Envelope addressed: Frederick Delius Esq/Grez-sur-Loing/Seine-et-Marne/France. Postmark: LONDON.W. JAN 29 09.

The original is in the Delius Trust Archive.

1   The Beecham Symphony Orchestra.

2   Present at the committee meeting of the Musical League on 10 January in London were Elgar, Bantock, Wood, McNaught and Allen Gill. Afterwards McNaught wrote to Delius to ask for an assurance that the 'eminent men' from abroad, suggested by Delius as participants in the League's first festival, would be willing to come without fee. The next committee meeting was held on 31 January; Delius was again unable to attend.

3   Beecham was planning to give *A Mass of Life* with the North Staffordshire District Choral Society, and a tonic sol-fa edition of the choral score was required.

(306)

Ethel Smyth to Frederick Delius

One Oak,
Frimley.
Feb 10th [1909]

Dear Mr. Delius,

If you know Messrs. Novello you will not be surprised to know that tho' they have had "On the Cliffs of Cornwall"[1] (the piece I wanted to shew you for the Musical League concert) since Sep last it is only a proof of the Full Score I can send you even now! However, as it may yet be months ere they are ready, quite, I send that –

I have made Mr. Beecham's acquaintance, to my great delight & he is doing it & some other things at his May concert – I am looking forward more than I can say to hearing "Sea Drift" on the 22^{nd2} & later to the "Mass of Life". It is splendid to hear him talk of you – it is above all splendid to meet someone in this country not afraid to use big words about a real person.

Mr. B. is going to let me know in a few days whether his Opera scheme comes off – but I expect it will –^{3}

What glorious fun for you & me!

Hoping you may turn up on the 22nd & that I shall see you

Yours sincerely
E M Smyth

Autograph letter, signed and dated, written on headed notepaper.

The original is in the Delius Trust Archive. It is the first of five letters and postcards from Ethel Smyth to Delius, all dated 1909, that are preserved.

1   A concert arrangement of the Prelude to Act II of the opera *The Wreckers* (1903–4).

2   Beecham and his orchestra were to give *Sea Drift* at Queen's Hall on 22 February, with Frederic Austin as soloist.

3   Beecham was planning an opera season in London and had *The Wreckers* and *A Village Romeo and Juliet* in mind.

(307)
Frederick Delius to Ethel Smyth

GREZ SUR LOING,
February 17, 1909.

Dear Miss Smyth,

Many thanks for your letter and postcard. Novello sent me the proof of *On the Cliffs of Cornwall* which I read with great interest and pleasure. You have "Stimmung", which is a rare thing for English composers and I am looking forward to hearing your work this autumn – I hope at the Musical League Festival. Shall I keep this proof or send it back to Novello's, and will they send me another copy so that I can submit it to my colleagues of the Committee?

I am very glad you met Mr. Beecham. He is quite a remarkable man and musician and really understands and likes modern music. He feels and understands what the moderns are trying to do – the real moderns I mean, for there are also the false moderns. He is wonderfully gifted and destined to play, perhaps, the most important part in the development of modern music in England. My prophecy! Don't forget it!

Music now is exactly in the same stale state as painting was in France at the time of Manet, Turner etc. I say in France, as painting has scarcely begun in England and music hardly. Handel paralysed music in England for generations and they have not yet quite got over him.

As far as I can judge, the English race is lacking in emotion, the essential part of music. Conventionalism and respectability did it, and they live and think and work in cut and dried forms. That is why they love the formalists in music so much, and do not understand the colorists in any art whatever.

Still I believe the coming generation may cast off this spell and express something human, and it was with this hope that I started the Musical League.[1] Up to the present in music they have produced nothing but bad imitations of the German classics. Mendelssohn and Brahms are the two musicians who the English people really like after Handel. Wagner they like because Richter plays him, and they like Richter much more than Wagner or any other composer – and the older he gets the more they will like him. Just like Joachim! – and that is the bane of music in England and that is what we must all try to get rid of ... When I come to England you must show me the whole of *The Wreckers. I am really very much interested.*

I am so sorry I can't come over for *Sea Drift* but I am hard at work on something new[2] and dare not break off. Let me know how the performance went off, and believe me,

Sincerely yours,
Frederick Delius

From Ethel Smyth: *Beecham and Pharaoh*, pp. 25–7.

1   Delius's claim to have started the Musical League was well-founded: in an undated letter he received from Norman O'Neill later in the year, he is referred to as 'the inventor' of the League.

2   *Fennimore and Gerda.*

(308)
Oda Krohg to Frederick Delius

Paris 22–2–09

Dear Delius

Does the hotel Chevillon[1] still exist or is there another hotel at Grez where Per[2] and I could stay for a week or so. Would you be so kind as to send me a postcard to 114 rue Vaugirard?

Kind regards to your wife and au revoir

Yours
Oda Krohg

Autograph letter, signed and dated, written in Norwegian. Envelope addressed: Monsieur/Delius/Grez sur Loing/S et M. Postmark obscured.

The original is in the Delius Trust Archive. It is the only item of correspondence from Oda Krohg to Delius that is preserved.

Oda (Othilia) Krohg, née Lasson (1860–1935): Norwegian artist. She painted landscapes earlier in her life, but among her more mature works are a series of fine portraits, including those of her husband, the painter Christian Krohg, and her lover Gunnar Heiberg. Heiberg's play *Folkeraadet* was dedicated to her.

1   The Hôtel Chevillon had been the resort of a galaxy of Scandinavian (and other) artists and writers, among them Christian Krohg, Carl Larsson and August Strindberg (see L. Carley: 'Carl Larsson and Grez-sur-Loing in the 1880s'). No reply from Delius to Oda Krohg's query has been found.

2   Per Krohg (1889–1965): Norwegian painter. Son of Christian and Oda, he studied under his father and Matisse and had already exhibited at the age of fifteen at the Christiania Art Society. He was perhaps to become best known for his murals in some of Norway's foremost public buildings.

(309)

Thomas Beecham to Frederick Delius

Feb. 27th/09

LANGHAM HOTEL,

LONDON.

Dear Delius

"Sea-Drift" has come and gone – I am sending you some of the Press notices, and you can see what they say about it – Everyone, even the Press, agree about the Band, that it is firstrate. The critic of the "Times" told Ethel Smyth that it was the finest performance he had ever heard – They certainly played splendidly, I have never heard anything like it before, anywhere –

Sea-Drift went stunningly, the Choir were beautifully in tune and quite safe and Austin's tempi were much better. Of course, his voice is very trying, but his share of the work was much better and more elastic – Generally, it was a far and away superior performance to those *you* heard.

The Band were frantically enthusiastic, and if you had been there, you would have had a great ovation –

They are really a wonderful lot, the richness of tone and delicacy of the wind are remarkable –

I am so thankful now that I have got rid of that d—d N.S.O.[1]

We shall have a glorious time when the *"Mass"* comes off[2] – I will see about that affair of the contract right away – It is most necessary to have the Sol-Fa parts soon – *Clark*[3] is very keen on his part, he talks about it everywhere – We shall have a fine "house" for it – people are coming from everywhere to hear it – Do "buck up" Harmonie about the voices –

The critic of the Standard (that mug Trevor)[4] says – apropos Sea-Drift – that you "traverse the whole gamut of *aquatic* emotion"!!! Seems to take you for a sea-serpent or dolphin –

Love to you both

Ever yours
T. B

Autograph letter, initialled and dated, written on headed notepaper. Envelope addressed: Frederick Delius Esq/Grez-sur-Loing/Seine-et-Marne/France. Postmark: LONDON.W. FEB 27 09.

The original is in the Delius Trust Archive.

1   New Symphony Orchestra.

2   Beecham was to give *A Mass of Life* at Queen's Hall on 7 June. His enthusiasm for Delius's works seems to have inhibited any reference to his present dire financial position, and his agent Thomas Quinlan wrote on 1 March to tell Delius that Beecham's 22 February concert had lost between £400 and £450: 'There is no doubt that Beecham is at his wit's end for money ... What we want is a strong subscription list, & until this comes, his Concerts will never pay. The blasted public won't come.'

3   Charles William Clark (1865–?): American baritone. A pupil of Henschel and Randegger in London, he was to sing the 'Zarathustra' role in Beecham's first *Mass of Life*, and again when Beecham gave the work for a second time, at Covent Garden on 10 March 1913. He also sang the *Mass* for Haym at Elberfeld on 11 December 1909.

4   Harry Trevor was musical editor of *The Standard*, London.

(310)
Ethel Smyth to Frederick Delius

One Oak
Frimley
March 5 [1909]

Dear Mr. Delius

What must you think of me? But when I tell you that between the "Sea Drift" concert & now all is settled and that Mr. Beecham & his band & I and Beerbohm Tree[1] produce "The Wreckers" on the 25th June ... you will understand & forgive –

First of all – Would you be so very kind as to send Novello those proofs of "On the Cliffs" – & he will paste them, and send to Mr. Beecham. – I had (at last) got the M. S. Score back from Novello & sent it to him. But he is giving the thing in April not May (– because they are doing a thing of mine in Paris on May 18th –) So he wants to begin rehearsing next week – & who knows whether Novello can paste up another score in time!! so better have yr proofs

Sea Drift went magnificently – as to orchestra & chorus, of course – But I thought F. Austin monotonous & . . . well . . .! monotonous. When one has said that one has said all –

(I am a slow listener & whoever the people may be who grasp very deep & new thoughts, & jump to a new outlook in one minute, I am not one of them. But I felt of course all through the performance pages of such divine exquisite beauty – that I have absolute confidence in the other pages that connect them even tho' their content may be less irresistible on superficial acquaintance – and via Austin's overdone monotony & lack of backbone. The whole thing remains in one's mind as a great vision – I am longing to hear it again ..)

Thank you for the kind things you say about being interested in my work – I wonder much if you will like it – & do hope you can be here on June 25th – Your letter made me laugh – I do so agree with what you say about England tho' I think the place is teeming with creative talent – We shouldn't agree about German music. I am very catholic in my taste – learned when I was over 40 to appreciate Racine, tho' I started by hating him – & had all the Anglo-Saxon twists about him – I have fearful fights with Mr. Beecham, whom Mrs. Woodhouse & I love! . . . He is splendid – & I think about his future as you do – I hope to see you in May –

I hear you know Mme de Greffuhle[2] . . She has been very kind to me – Do you know my friend Mme de Polignac?[3] She is worth knowing – a grand musician.

Yours ever sincerely
E M Smyth

Autograph letter, signed and dated, written on notepaper headed WARWICK HOUSE, ST. JAMES'S, S. W. (crossed out).

The original is in the Delius Trust Archive.

1   Herbert Beerbohm Tree (1853–1917): English actor-manager. Knighted in 1909, he was one of the most celebrated actors of his generation.

2   Hélène de Chimay, a friend of Ethel Smyth and sister-in-law of the Comtesse de Greffulhe, had 'pulled strings', and the Comtesse had tried to arrange a performance of *The Wreckers* at Monte Carlo.

3   Princesse Edmond de Polignac. Delius did indeed know her (I, pp. 149–50). Adela Maddison had earlier written to him from Berlin on 11 February: 'Mme de

Polignac was here for Elektra (passing through) & asked if you ever came up from Paris –? She wanted to do something of yours chez elle.' On 14 April Mrs Maddison wrote to Jelka: 'Mme de Polignac is longing to see you both – write & ask her to come down to you one day, & say you *can't* come up to her.'

(311)

Frederick Delius to Granville Bantock

GREZ SUR LOING,
S. ET M.
[7 March 1909]

My dear Bantock –

Firstly let me apologise for my naivté about the Arabian nights – The English & German versions I have read are as different as night & day from the *Mardrus Version* – The point of the whole – the climax is always missing in the English Version – I am reading Mardrus with great pleasure and entertainment – So you are really giving up Liverpool – I suppose Liverpool wants to imitate Manchester! Things really look rather hopeless in England – What you say about staying away from England may be quite right for others, but not for me[1] – What good would it have done me to be on the spot – I know nobody in Birmingham & certainly dont intend to waste my precious time trying to be performed at Festivals in England – Where one receives an entirely inadequate performance – I should not even have handed in my "Mass of Life" if you had not asked me to do so – Besides I am beginning to appreciate what it means – "The English Ears" – Ears that have listened to vulgar & formal commonplace music for a hundred years without protesting, & which hail, as a work(s) of genius – Music that belongs to the Mendelsohn period with a little bit of Wagner thrown in – We shall now see how the "League" will pan out – If the good will of McNaught has to be attained by engaging his son as assistant Sec (a sinecure) (In Germany the whole business is done by the "Treasurer" – a very busy business man – There are 800 members in the German Society) then the outlook is not promising & the thing will fizzle out anyhow – What you are trying to do in Liverpool, Beecham is trying to do in London at an enormous sacrifice to his pocket – The London Symphony Orchestra did not desert Beecham[2] – How could it? He engaged the whole lot for every Concert – I was there at the time that Beecham gave them an ultimatum about the deputy system & said that if they did not accept it – He would form another orchestra – They refused this ultimatum & Beecham left them & formed his present Orchestra – which is far better – Beecham ought to be encouraged by every modern & progress loving musician in England – He is the most worthy of it – You seem to have something against him[3] – I cannot make out what it is – He is no intriguer   What hast tha gotten agin im, lad? He is more musical, modern & progressive than Ronald, who is an opportunist of the first water & a courtier − & cares as much for music as your gardener − A weak imitation of Nikisch − We want pioneers my boy, & *men of courage & not bourgeois*   As far as I can judge one of the Characteristics of the English race is *want* of moral courage − Beecham has this courage in a high degree & that is why I appreciate him & recognise in the man the qualities which go towards the making of a big man − There are so few in England of this sort, that one ought to try to gather together & unite − I recognised in you, what I recognise in Beecham. That is why I should so much like to see you more united − With best love & wishes for Omar − part III[4] − also to your wife from us both   I remain,

Yrs affectionately
Frederick Delius

Autograph letter, signed and undated, written on headed notepaper. Envelope addressed: Granville Bantock Esq[re]/Broad Meadow/Kings Norton/nr Birmingham/Angleterre. Postmark: GREZ 7 -3 09.

The original is in the Delius Trust Archive.

1   'You ought not to stop too long away from England,' wrote Bantock on 21 February. 'I am sure that if you had been on the spot, a work of yours would have been put in the Birmingham Festival programme. When you leave the country, you are soon forgotten. You have to show yourself continually, & go about a lot, if you want performances.'

2   *Not* the London Symphony Orchestra: 'Do you know,' wrote Bantock in his letter of 21 February, 'that the New Symphony Orchestra deserted him, & have appointed Landon Ronald their conductor.'

3   The fact was that Beecham's unreliability was irritating League committee members, and he had to be 'threatened with serious consequences' for not bothering to send on scores to other members of the reading committee.

4   Bantock was at work on the final part of his cantata *Omar Khayyam*.

(312)
Granville Bantock to Frederick Delius

BROAD MEADOW,
KINGS NORTON.
March 11.09

Dear Lad!

What hast tha gotten agin the ole countree? What's use o' crying aboot th' English Ears, if tha wa'nt do summat to help syringe 'em? What's use o' protesting? Lad, tha must keep on poomping and poomping at em', wi'out givin' o'em rest. The poor ignorant fools know dinna kenna no well better. Of course they'll suck Mendelssohn's soothing syrup, as long as they have hold o' the bottle. What we have to do is to get the bottle awa' from 'em, and ye canna weel do it, by pitching yer tent over the hills and far away, any more than I can by caravaning to Mecca, & visiting the Ka'abah. If ye can't drive the donkey or yer pigs to market the proper way, then you must let 'em think they driving you, and once you get them to follow, why, lad, you can pull their noses all the time.

Once & for all, get it oot o' thy skull that I've anythink agin B. I don't know him as well as you do, but I give him credit for what he is doing for orchestral music, & for his sacrifices in this direction. He ought however to answer his letters, and particularly mine, if I am to maintain any interest in his work. I am not going to wait any man's pleasure, & the man who is straight & frank with me will find me willing to reciprocate. I've no time to solve mysteries however, or to remind other people of their duties. My own keep me sufficiently occupied. At the same time I see no reason for deprecating others at the expense of individual glorification. Of course we need pioneers; above all, comrades, willing & ready to work side by side *for* the best in Art always, & not *against* the worst. It's no good to be Anti-anything; better be Pro-something. Get the B out o' thy bonnet, lad! There's no lack o' moral courage hereaboots. Let's gather together & unite, & follow the teaching of Rabelais. O'Neill seems to be making a good energetic Secretary,[1] and all seems to be going well. Cum' oot o' thy shell, lad!

Yer affeckshunet fayther
Sambo.

Autograph letter, signed 'Sambo' and dated, written on headed notepaper.

The original is in the Delius Trust Archive.

1   O'Neill had written to Delius on 1 February: 'I was yesterday elected Hon Sec to the League!'

(313)
Norman O'Neill to Frederick Delius

The Music Selection committee meets on Tuesday 23. I will then tell them what you say with regard to conductor etc. If the other members of the committee have not seen Miss Smyths work of which you speak so well they had better do so. Perhaps you will send it to Bantock. You are an ex officio member of committee but I am going to suggest that I take over the selected scores to France with me if you want to see them & give [them] to you myself if I am able to get to Grez! – With regard to Chamber music I think we should do some of the good stuff by Bax, Dale,[1] Gardiner, etc, published by the Soc: of British composers. Let me know of anything you want to put before the music committee. Bantock is doing all he can to push *Brian* in & we shall have a fight for it! – I wish you were not so far away! –

Greetings to you both yrs aye
N. O'N.
March 14.09.

Autograph postcard, initialled and dated. Addressed: France/F. Delius Esqre/Grez sur Loing/Seine et Marne. Postmark obscured.

The original is in the Delius Trust Archive.

1 Benjamin James Dale (1885–1943): English composer. He studied at the Royal Academy of Music, where Frederick Corder was a mentor of his – and of which he was later to become Warden. He was to make a piano transcription of Delius's *Eventyr* which was published by Augener in 1921.

(314)
Frederick Delius to Ethel Smyth

GREZ SUR LOING,
15th March, 1909.

Dear Miss Smyth,

Firstly let me tell you how delighted I am that your opera will be brought out in June and that Beecham will bring it out. You will only understand Beecham entirely when he has brought one of your own works out. Then you will realise how deep the man goes into your work and how he personifies himself with it. Of course I shall do my utmost to be present . . .

You must have misunderstood me about German music. I am a great admirer of the great German composers. I protest only against the school which imitates them and would palm its imitations off as the real thing – the so-called classical direction. The Russians and French have tried to break away, and partly the Norwegians – Grieg. The English and Americans, however, go on stolidly creating dead works.

The French, although perhaps not great composers, know that their force lies in charm and grace, and the light touch in the orchestra. The Russians also try to give that strange mixture of the Orient and Occident; the half barbaric – the peculiar mixture of Wagner and the "Danse du Ventre". Grieg has given us charming and poetical music based on the Folk Song, the English nothing. They go on conscientiously working on foreign models and on biblical subjects, and indeed the public is *abruti* to that degree that they will listen with respect and awe to any twaddle having Jesus or the Virgin Mary as a subject. And when it is more than usually dry and long they call it "noble and severe".

Handel is the creator of this public and of the "genre ennuyeux", which is still the bane of music in England, and every conductor in England flatters that public except Beecham. I believe there is lots of talent of England and that it will gradually become more daring and independent, but there is as yet very little to encourage it.

I consider Percy Grainger the most gifted of all the young composers I have met, and he is again Australian. Have you met him? He does quite remarkable things and is most refreshing. I shall be in London for June 7th (*The Mass of Life*) and hope to see something of you...

I am extremely glad to hear you like Beecham and hope you will be able to get him subscribers for his concerts. He deserves the support of all the best London musical people. We ought all to write and push in one direction in order to form a new public and create a new musical centre.

Very sincerely yours,
Frederick Delius

From Ethel Smyth: *Beecham and Pharaoh*, pp. 28–9.

(315)
Frederick Delius to Granville Bantock

Grez sur Loing,
S & M
16 March 1909

My dear old Pal –

Ow can thee axe me what ie's gotten agin the ole country? Asnt tha gotten sacked at Liverpool! & you've been poomping & poomping at em pretty long & really trying to bring a little fresh air into the musical atmosphere – The question is, is it worth "poomping" & spending ones energy and strength on a musically apathetic race – I know there are splendidly musical people in England & also lots of courage & enthusiasm but it is rather thinly spread & suffocated by the others – You see, they really love knocking balls about – either kicking them about or knocking them about in to holes – & that is devilish bad for music – Another example! Why did Beecham give a concert in Manchester? because they had been writing for years about the bad Richter Programmes – that they never got anything new etc, etc. Beecham got hundreds of letters asking him to come & give a concert – He did so & brought that excellent Hanley Choir & there were not 200 people in the Free Trade Hall! His faith in musical Manchester wanting novelties cost him £250 – I believe if we all unite we may create a musical centre & precisely thro' the *League* we will be able to create a special musical public who will always attend our meetings – I am very glad that you have nothing against Beecham I never heard him deprecate others for his own glorification – But when we look things straight in the face he is really almost the only man that we can look to with hope & who is dead in earnest – The others are making money at any price & pushing their own little affair –

What you say about the pioneers my boy is entirely wrong. *Listen*! You cannot work *for* the best in Art & not against the worst – it is entirely impossible – You know that where the place is limited you have to *take away* before you can *add* – The bad & mediocre is always standing in the way of the good & excellent & the Mediocre people are more numerous than the superior people & therefore when a superior one comes along who has the power or the influence – the first thing he will always do is to *knock* or try to eliminate the bad & mediocre & not go patting mediocre people on the back simply to get their support – He loves making enemies of fools & incapables He loves the fight – Opposition – anything but acquiescence in a rotten state of affairs – In art there never was evolution – it was always revolution against an existing accepted art – which everyone had already got accustomed to – The danger of custom is enormous "Habitude" it destroys all keener perception & sensitiveness –

O'Neil is coming here shortly & will bring me the scores for the Festival – I have not seen one yet – Try & arrange to come back with me here in June – Perhaps Newman will also be able to come & we might have a jolly time. I am well on in my new Drama *Niels Lyhne* –

With love to you both
I remain

Your affectionate
Frederick Delius

Autograph letter, signed and dated.

The original is in the Delius Trust Archive.

(316)

Thomas Beecham to Frederick Delius

Highfield,
Boreham Wood,
Herts.
March. 29.09.

Dear Delius;

I am going to try to run over to Paris next week, but it is not certain.

Of course I do not agree with the programmes chosen for the League festival, but these will not be allowed to stand. The last selection committee meeting was carefully called on a date when everyone on it except our friend Bantock had a concert to conduct. – I myself had one on at the Queen's Hall.

We have another meeting on April 6th & you may be sure that the programmes will be quite changed on that date.

At this moment I am kept in the house with Bronchitis & my wife is writing this.

The last concert went off very well, and Austin's "Rhapsody"[1] had a great success – composer recalled many times & all the rest of it –

The work of Vincent D'Indy I gave "Jour d'Eté" came off extraordinarily well – & sounded quite remarkable on the band.

I am sending you some notices but I must ask you to return them when you have done with them – as they have to be used.

There are some quite exciting musical developments here; about which everything when I see you.

The New Symphony Orchestra have started on their own & have taken on Landon Ronald as their permanent conductor – They are now giving a Series of Concerts at which they play for nothing – They are now recognized as a *first rate* orchestra and the Press patriotically palpitate with their virtuous and disinterested policy. They have even gone to the extent of producing a *British* Novelty, a work by William Wallace, conducted by the Composer – which all the critics have acclaimed as a masterpiece.[2]

But I have invented one or two simple and effectual expedients and remedies, which if I can carry into effect (and I hope to be able to do so by next autumn) will alter the whole state of things here – Opera – Concerts – Critics & all within the space of twelve months.

I have more or less recently discovered a tremendous ally – in the shape of Ethel Smythe who is at present the one and only genuine fighting asset in Great Britain.

We have on foot the most exciting things and I find that as a worker she is worth, ten times over, all the male composers here put to-gether, besides having the additional virtue of being able to run straight as a die for a longer period than half an hour at a time.

My little group of soloists for the "Mass of Life" are all suffering from some mysterious brain trouble as the result of much study of their parts. Alexander is the safest of the lot[3] and Clark who is the best Artist is the least reliable – But they will be alright – I find hardly anyone here who cares about taking a serious *financial* interest in music. Nearly all the country is in a hopeless state of dilettantism – especially the composers. I am giving a work of *Bax* at my next concert – I think *he* will do something – he *works* –

Love to you both

Toujours votre
T B

Letter (and envelope) in the hand of Utica Beecham, initialled and dated, written on headed notepaper. Envelope addressed: Frederick Delius Esq/Grez-sur-Loing/Seine-et-Marne, France. Postmark: BOREHAM-WOOD MR 29 09.

The original is in the Delius Trust Archive.

1   Austin's *Symphonic Rhapsody: Spring* was also given by Wood, at a Promenade concert in 1907, and for some years his orchestral works were to enjoy a modicum of success.

2   William Wallace (1860–1940): Scottish composer and writer on music. *Villon* (1909) is the work referred to. The fifth of a series of six symphonic poems, it was the most popular and was played widely in Europe and the United States. Nine letters and postcards he wrote to Delius in 1909, largely concerning his translation into English of the text of *A Mass of Life*, are preserved in the Delius Trust Archive.

3   In the event the tenor soloist was Webster Millar.

(317)
Thomas Quinlan to Frederick Delius

THOMAS QUINLAN,
MUSICAL AGENT AND IMPRESARIO.

318, REGENT STREET,
LONDON, W.
1st. April, 1909.

My dear Delius,

I have induced a very good American Soprano to sing at her Recital on the evening of May 6th. a good selection of modern British Works, including a group of your songs. I suppose you will not be in London about that time? I send you the Prima Donna's Programme of her last Concert.[1]

Matters are moving splendidly, but I wish I could have just ten minutes with you. I am very anxious to alter something in Beecham from a managerial standpoint, which will add greatly to his popularity, and instead of going from my Office across the road to Boosey's, he is – through certain mannerisms, – idiosyncrasies, or call it what you like, going all round Regent Street and Oxford Circus to get there.

To my mind he has the first Orchestra in London, but he is the most unpunctual devil imaginable. In many things if he could only see himself through a mirror, he would be the first to recognise how foolish he sometimes is. I speak to you as to no-one else, and what I really want is, to get you and Beecham in my little Study for a few hours, because I feel you would back me up and drive home my argument. It is only his friends who would tell him of these barriers against rapid recognition and progress. I have induced fifty people to attend his Concerts, and without a single exception he has rubbed everybody up the wrong way. If you do not come, I shall tackle him myself, and if he does not see what I mean, and nip it in the bud, it will take him years to reach the goal that he ought rightly to take *immediately*.

Let me hear from you some time soon. You know I have the cause at heart.

With best wishes,

Believe me,

Ever yours,
Tom Quinlan

Typed letter, signed and dated, written on headed notepaper. Addressed at head of letter: F. Delius Esq., Grez-sur-Loing, Seine-et-Marne, France.

The original is in the Delius Trust Archive. It is the fourth of six letters from Quinlan to Delius dating from 13 February 1909–6 January 1910 that are preserved. A pencilled note scribbled by Delius on the verso of this letter: 'Minds om en sommar-morn paa Hau ku li fjeld' [= Haukelid Fjeld] evidently rehearses a Norwegian inscription for a photograph of himself shortly to be sent to Nina Grieg, and acknowledged by Nina in a letter of 22 May. The portrait, now framed, hangs in the Grieg Museum, Troldhaugen.

Thomas Quinlan was manager of the Beecham Opera Season. He was also engaged in organizing provincial tours for the autumn of 1909 for the Beecham Orchestra, as well as for Caruso, among others.

1 The programme has not been preserved among Delius's papers.

(318)

Hans Haym to Frederick Delius

E[lberfeld]. 2 April 09

Dear friend,

Yesterday evening the concert management decided to perform the *whole* of your *Mass of Life* on the 11th December! I really ought to have sent you a telegram straight away, but it is better still to express one's delight over this sort of thing by letter. I am happy that I may now also bring your principal work to life for the first time in its entirety. We intend to put enormous effort into it too. For the principal baritone role I thought of writing to Dr Felix v. Kraus. I feel he would be the best. Messchaert has not got the strength needed, otherwise he might perhaps be more subtle. But Kraus, if he is interested in it, will also do the thing splendidly. In the meantime I will wait a few days more until I hear your opinion. Alto: Frl. Philippi? Soprano: Mientje Lammen? (who sang the part in Munich) Tenor: —?[1]

Do please return the Prague newspapers to me.[2] We must make propaganda for you here in plenty of time, and for this we need everything that has been written about the "great Delius".

Are you rather pleased?

This will be yet again a real event in this otherwise somewhat problematic existence. Hartmann the bookseller[3] turned the scales with an enthusiastic vote for your work. If you know him, you could send him a special thankyou.

Best wishes

Yours
Haym

Autograph letter, signed and dated, written in German.

The original is in the Delius Trust Archive.

1   Haym's final tally of soloists was Emma Tester, Meta Diestel, Matthäus Römer and Charles Clark. Felix von Kraus was an Austrian baritone who came to prominence at Bayreuth in 1899 and who was now teaching singing at the Royal Academy of Music at Munich. He was not to sing Delius for Haym until 1911 when he was the baritone soloist in both *Sea Drift* and *A Mass of Life* – and when, for the latter work, he was joined by his American-born wife, the contralto Adrienne von Kraus-Osborne.

2   Haym wrote to Delius on 18 March: 'I congratulate you on your new disciple in Prague, Prochazka, who has just written to me full of admiration for Appalachia & sends newspaper cuttings about the performance there.' Haym gave the cuttings to Szántó to take to Delius.

3   The firm of B. Hartmann dealt in books, music and art from their premises at
Neumarkt 26, Elberfeld. One letter to Delius from the company, signed Hans
Hartmann and dated 24 September 1909, is preserved in the Delius Trust Archive and
discusses Harmonie's charges for orchestral and choral material for the Elberfeld
performance of the *Mass*.

   Haym's performance on 11 December is discussed in L. Carley: 'Hans Haym:
Delius's Prophet and Pioneer'.

(319)
Frederick Delius to Granville Bantock

Grez sur Loing
S & M
24 April 09

My dear Bantock –

I received a letter from Dr Sinclair[1] of Hereford asking me for a short
Orchestral work – In reply I proposed my "Dance Rhapsody", just finished
and taking about 10 or 12 minutes to play. I suppose this is your doing again
& I can tell you that I appreciate it most thoroughly – It will also afford me an
opportunity of hearing "Job" by our mutual friend H.P.[2] How a man rolling
in wealth, the lord of many acres & living off the fat of the land can write
anything about Job beats me entirely – unless it is a cantata expressing H.P.^{s}
satire & derision at Mr Job's mode of life – I am really curious! – Will you be
able to come up for the "Mass" on June 7th? I do hope so & try to arrange to
come back with me to Paris – I want to spend a few days with you there &
shall probably have a little appartment at my disposal where we can both stay.

   My wife wants a letter from Mrs B. The garden is simply lovely & my new
Music drama is well advanced.

   What is the new Suite for Hereford?[3] Tell me some news – With love to all.

   Yrs ever
   Frederick Delius

Autograph letter, signed and dated.

The original is in the Delius Trust Archive.

1   George Robertson Sinclair (1863–1917): English organist and conductor. He
became organist at Hereford Cathedral in 1889 and was a guiding spirit of the Three
Choirs Festival, at which he conducted frequently from 1891. From 1899 until his
death he was conductor of the Birmingham Choral Union. He wrote to Delius on 21
April: 'you may like us to produce a short orchestral work of yours under your

conductorship', adding that Bantock, Elgar, Parry and Walford Davies were also to conduct works of their own. Eight other letters from Sinclair to Delius, all dated 1909, are preserved in the Delius Trust Archive.

2   Sir Hubert Parry's oratorio *Job*, composed in 1892 and first performed at the Three Choirs Festival in Gloucester that same year.

3   Bantock conducted the first performance of his *Old English Suite* for small orchestra at the Three Choirs Festival in Hereford on 8 September, at the same concert in which Delius conducted his *Dance Rhapsody*.

(320)
Gustav Mahler to Frederick Delius

[Vienna, Rennweg 5]
[13 May? 1909]

My dear Herr Delius,

I must apologise for not having sent a reply to your very kind letter of December. – To tell the truth – after having delayed in the first instance for some reason or other, I subsequently forgot about the matter. I am now reminded of my offence by a letter from the Musical League, which has been sent on to me from New York. – I now hasten to send you a reply and would also ask you kindly to inform the gentlemen of the Committee of its contents.

I thank you again most sincerely for having thought of me, but to my genuine sorrow am obliged to decline your kind invitation.

I cannot possibly conduct a work of mine without *abundant* rehearsals – in the past I have often been obliged to withdraw on just this account. In point of fact I should be doing neither you nor myself a service were this to happen – The least that I require for a performance of a work of mine – in the case of an orchestra which has not played anything of mine before, is 4–5 full rehearsals. – I quite understand that in your still precarious circumstances this is not possible, and so I beg you to excuse me on this occasion.

With best wishes

Yours very sincerely
Gustav Mahler

Autograph letter, signed and undated, written in German. Envelope addressed: Frankreich/Mr. Frederic Delius/Grez sur Loing/S. et M. On the reverse: Absender: Mahler/Rennweg 5. Postmark: WIEN/13 [. . .] (Postage stamp detached and rest of postmark missing.)

The original is in the Delius Trust Archive. It is the only item of correspondence from Mahler to Delius that is preserved.

The question of Mahler's participation in the League's festival had arisen frequently since Delius first suggested it in November (I, pp. 374–5). 'Do you see your way to extract the asked for promises from Mahler etc?' McNaught enquired on 16 January. Delius sounded a cautionary note to O'Neill on 27 January: 'Mahler has written no work that takes less than 1 hour – the Symphony he will probably conduct takes 1 hour & has good things in it – (Chorus)'. O'Neill responded the following day: 'I think an hour of Mahler (at least 3 hrs rehearsal mind you!) is a bit too much!' On 24 March he returned to the charge: 'I don't see how we can possibly give him enough rehearsal or orchestra!' Delius then evidently replied with further advice for the committee, for O'Neill wrote again on 28 March: 'I will tell them what you say with regard to Mahler.' The chapter finally closed on 20 May, when O'Neill wrote to Delius: 'So Mahler is off! I suppose *you* got the reply to my letter?'

(321)
Clare Delius Black to Frederick Delius

4 Victoria Avenue
Ilkley

June 9th 09

My dearest Fritz

It's too bad, I have to address this to your publisher, as I don't know where you are in Town – & I want to raise my voice in praise & congratulation – If you had let me know I'd have come up to hear the Concert[1], I wanted most awfully to hear one of your things. I am awfully glad it was such a success. I suppose it's no use reminding Jelka that she owes me a letter for a *year*.[2] You remember Elsa – She is coming home from S Africa – with her husband who has been made Secretary to the Prime Minister; so I expect she will give me a jolly time. How is Tante Albertina? Is there no chance of your coming up here – after all your excitement. I haven't heard from Mamma for ages – Have you seen any of them? Since I last wrote you – I have been staying in Dinard & Jersey for seven weeks. I have some very good friends there, who, having heaps of money, sent me a cheque & insisted on my coming, & Missie like a good girl, gave me some dresses – I had a lovely time. If you can tear yourself away from your admirers – for a second – let me know how you are going on – & *do* if you have one, send me a Photo – I have not got one of you at all. Have you ever met a man called Rohan Clensy? He is a great admirer of yours, & a friend of Beecham's? Give my love to Jelka – & with best love to you

Your loving sister
Clare

Autograph letter, signed and dated.

The original is in the Delius Trust Archive. It is the only letter preserved in the Archive from any of Delius's sisters.

Clare Black, *née* Clara Edith Delius (1866–1954): Delius's favourite sister, married in 1889 to J. W. A. Black. She was later to document her relationship with her brother in her *Frederick Delius*, published a year after the composer's death.

1   *A Mass of Life* had just been given, on 7 June, by Beecham at Queen's Hall, using William Wallace's new English translation. While in London the Deliuses stayed at the Kensington home of Norman O'Neill.

2   Jelka duly replied, on 15 June from Grez: 'We thought so much of you in London – but were so frightfully busy that we did not write. Fred was so surrounded – and his work, altho' such a very difficult one was a huge success. It was splendidly performed – Dr Haym, the Concert-Conductor from Elberfeld came over to hear it, as he is going to do it in December there. So I was very much taken up with him – shopping and sightseeing – The time passed like a dream – I only saw my own relations twice and of your family no one but Karl Collmann who came over for the Concert. Your mother has not heard any of Fred's music yet.' Beecham's success was to be echoed by Haym in December, when a near-capacity audience in the Elberfeld Stadthalle gave the composer a rousing ovation.

(322)
Thomas Beecham to Frederick Delius

Aug. 2/09
Highfield,
Boreham Wood,
Herts.

Dear Delius –

I have been so busy lately or would have written you – My father and I have patched up our grievances at last, and we are on the way more rapidly than I expected to being friends again. Amongst other things he has declared his intention of "running" my musical affairs "himself" – What this means exactly I do not know, but I fancy his idea is to run them successfully against all the others here. Well, I hope he does and smashes about a bit for I am getting rather tired of certain conditions here.

I learnt for the first time the other day the secret history of the "New Symphony Orchestra's" indifference to discipline last Winter and their rejection of my proposals. Just previous they had had a Committee meeting to consider a letter from our friend Landon Ronald in which he said he was prepared to "adopt" the orchestra and make the fortune of everyone in it provided they had nothing more to do with me. This charming document was to an organization created and "run" exclusively by myself for nearly two years and which had received from me £4000 in fees and expenses. I do not believe that they ever had one engagement that I did not secure for them.

The result of this has been that since last Christmas, this orchestra has been playing for no fee at all and paying Landon a salary for his conducting!!!

I really think all this is very delightful and a touching commentary on British intelligence –

The "Wreckers" finished (as you probably heard) in a sort of blaze of glory[1] – all very amusing – *and* – useful – at this juncture – as it impressed the old boy, my father. We had a hell of a time with the damned thing, making it go. The woman has some good notions, but she is hopelessly narrow and amateurish. I discovered – "inter alia" – she did not know the difference between $\frac{6}{4}$ and $\frac{3}{2}$ time!

I wonder if you are coming over in September – I have arranged about the *Bass Oboe* for Hereford. I find out however that Sinclair has been writing to another man who plays the "Heckelphone".[2] I am told though that this particular instrument is a filthy affair and will not do – The man who played the Bass Oboe in the "Mass" has overhauled the instrument and got to the bottom of it. He makes it now sound most beautiful and it is quite in tune. I find that it is built to suit either high pitch or low, this being determined by crooks. These latter we did not have for the "Mass" – hence the weird noises –

But now it sounds enchanting, and it is also the only one there is –

If I were you, I should write to Sinclair and tell him this or else you will be saddled with this other instrument which I am sure you will not like.

My wife is getting on very well indeed – also the new boy – he is very dark in complexion – evidently a philosopher – for he lies awake for hours without uttering a sound, looking (with two enormous eyes) into space –

We are giving up this house in a month and moving nearer London –

I have quite decided that to do anything here well, one must play the social game for all it is worth – after all they are the only people who have the money to spend on Music – the "people" – i.e. – the mob – do not care any more about it, and have no cash to throw away, even if they did –

Let me know when you come over here – if we are settled in our new place you must faithfully promise to stay there –

My wife and Adrian send love to you both

Always yours
Thomas Beecham

P.S. Please let me have "Dowson"[3] as soon as possible. Send to Elstree.

Autograph letter, signed and dated, written on headed notepaper. Envelope addressed: Frederick Delius Esq/Grez-sur-Loing/Seine-et-Marne/France. Re-addressed: Palsgarrd/ bei Juelsminde Danemark. Postmark: LONDON. W. AUG 4 09.

The original is in the Delius Trust Archive.

1   Beecham had already written on 23 June about the first performance: 'Yesterday we produced the "Wreckers", a very fine performance and the public liked it. Ethel Smyth is quite delighted.'

2   Wilhelm Heckel's recent invention (prompted by Richard Strauss) was a more sophisticated version of the bass oboe required for *A Dance Rhapsody* at Hereford. Although Delius initially had the heckelphone in mind for this work (as a draft score shows), it is the bass oboe that is nominated in the published score.

3   *Songs of Sunset*.

(323)
Frederick Delius to Ernest Newman

[Grez, 30 September 1909]

Dear Newman – I note your new address. I am so sorry I did not see more of you in Hereford – I had a very bad bilious attack & spent most of the time in my bed – In London I got worse & only managed to get back to Grez after 3 days in bed – I hope our Festival went off alright. of course I could not possibly come. Kindest remembrances to you & your wife from us both

   Frederick Delius

Autograph postcard, signed and undated. Addressed: M Ernest Newman Esqre/ Trythorpe/Wake Green R^d/Moseley/Birmingham/Angleterre. Postmark: GREZ 30 -9 09.

The original is in the Delius Trust Archive.

Most of September was to have been spent in England, where during the course of the Three Choirs Festival Delius conducted the Festival Orchestra in the first performance of *A Dance Rhapsody* – at the Shire Hall, Hereford, on 8 September. In Hereford, Delius stayed at the Queen's Arms, an old pub in Broad Street, spending evenings in the bar talking with the locals – a reaction, perhaps, to George Sinclair's innocent letter of 16 August: 'The Bishop of Hereford will write to invite you and Mrs Delius to stay at the Palace, so there is no occasion for you to engage rooms. Sir Hubert Parry will also be staying at the Palace.' Two local boys took Delius, at his own request, on their favourite walks along the river Wye and to Dinedor Camp; and one of them, many years later, still remembered the composer's 'condemnation of the "smart set" in the hotel opposite, his strong socialist views, his silences bidding the boys listen to the sounds of nature.' (*The Delius Society Journal*, 88 (Winter 1986), p. 23.) After Hereford Delius was then to have been present at the Musical League's festival in Liverpool, but had to miss it completely because of illness.

(324)
Adine O'Neill to Frederick and Jelka Delius

London 3^d October 09.

My dear Friends

I am awfully sorry to hear you have been so seedy and that you were in a nursing home in Paris   I hope you are much better by now and we should like to have some news. I thought it would interest you to hear about the Liverpool Festival by an Eye Witness! – Well, I went without my good man alas![1] but a few of my "tame robbins!" (read admirers of a very platonic type!)

The first concert,[2] chamber music was a rather depressing affair as it was not well attended, there was an orchestral rehearsal the same evening, and Austin, Gardner and Co all rushed to that from the concert, so one could not have a word with them, no gemüthlich talk over pots of beer! dear me no, we went back to the Hotel to find that after 11 o'clock they would not serve us anything! – Now to the programme. Balfour's string quartet, very jolly, sort of British Humour in it, good work, not too long – Songs Cycle "Bhanavar the Beautiful" by Bell, very difficult, it was not enough rehearsed, there are some beautiful things in it but also some rather obscure ones –

Sextett of Holbrooke, quite good, but at times vulgar. Three songs by Agate rather dull.

Three pianoforte solos by Scott and Grainger beautifully played by the later.

Three songs by Nicholls (a Liverpool man) quite pleasing but common place.

And to finish a string quartet by McEwen   it does not reveal anything new but is good Kamer Musik and sounds well.

I hear there was a supper that evening but I was not invited! – The next morning there was the general meeting   very few people turned up. Elgar made a little speech and for a wonder did say the right thing   There was a luncheon at the Town Hall offered by the Maire (who by the by) was present at all the concerts with his wife. There, Elgar made a very good speech. –

The Afternoon Concert[3] was better attended, the Philharmonic Hall is a beautiful concert room and the best in England for accoustic. –

Rhapsody by Frank Bridge (he conducted it very well) good work, full of go, not original but effective. – Your songs were lovely especially "Through long long years" and Edith Evans sang them very well. The symphonic Poëm

"Isabella" by Austin (he did not conducted well) I found dull, I am told it is well orchestrated   I quite believe it, they all do that well now our days! but it was "constipated" music   too much restrain, it did not come off somehow. – Sceana for Tenor & orchestra "The Dying Swan" by Hathaway I did not like; and I thought the swan was rather long dying! –

The Nocturnes by Debussy were well done, too heavily handed but the ensemble good and it was beautifully sang by the Choir. Harry Evans quite a decent sort of conductor. And to finish the concert, "Antar" by Rimsky-Korsakoff. In the evening it was very jolly "coup d'oeil"; good many people and something very cheery about it. The whole of the concert[4] was enjoyable. Fatherland for Tenor, Chorus and Orchestra by A. Bax. Sort of glorification of Ireland   pompeous, sonorous and effective work, but has not got the originality which characterizes most of his other works. –

The two songs of Ethel Smyth were *very good* indeed, full of spirit, amusing   they had Huge success, she conducted herself in a sort of japanese gown, and danced about the desk, so excited she grew – and seemed to me, like a priest throwing Holy water at the orchestra, Austin sang them beautifully. – The two Folk song settings of Grainger "Irish tune" and "Brigg Fair" sounded lovely and they are gems, they were beautifully sang by the choir and had the greatest success. "By the waters of Babylon" of Havergal Brian has some clever things and is spontaneous which is a great deal for an English work but it lacks a refinement for beauty, it is rough and unpolish work. –

"Willow Wood" cantata by Vaughan Williams is just the opposite, very refine poetic, but on the verge of dullness through want of vital power.

Three "Idylls of a Summer's Day" by Ernest Bryson (a business man of Liverpool) I did not like; some musicians there, thought them beautiful so I bow, and say nothing as I dont pretend to know anything about composition   I can only tell the effect they make on me! –

I thought there was something amateurish about these things and he never knew when to stop, they ought to have been short slight sketches. – To finish the Cantata of Bach, Praise Jehova   A good joint of Roast beef! – Then there was a delicious supper at the Adelphi offered by Johnson. On the whole for a first attempt it was artistically speaking a decided success. –

Norman is awfully busy with his theatre and I see little of him. Patrick is quite well and the new nurse successful. –.

My people are coming Wednesday and I play Friday at the "Prom" a Mozart Concerto – The weather is dull, warm damp and we have a good deal of rain. These are all the news. Now do let me know how you are getting on.

With love from us both to you both

Yours affectionate
Adine.

I received the £6 safely from Aaron. – Thank you. – Everybody was sorry at Liverpool about the absence of Mr Delius.

Autograph letter, signed and dated, written in English (but betraying Adine's non-English origins!).

The original is in the Delius Trust Archive.

1   Norman O'Neill wrote on 22 September to tell Delius that he could not attend the Festival, being needed at the Haymarket Theatre, where he was conductor. 'Adine will be there & represent me.' He felt that it was 'a disaster' that Delius could not be present.

2   The first (chamber) concert, given at 8.00 pm on Friday 24 September at the Yamen Rooms, in Bold Street, consisted of: Balfour Gardiner's String Quartet, W. H. Bell's song cycle *Bhanavar the Beautiful*, Holbrooke's Sextet No. 4, three songs by Edward Agate, piano pieces by Scott and Stanford (arr. Grainger), three songs by Frederick Nicholls, and McEwen's String Quartet in E minor.

3   The second (orchestral) concert, given at 3.00 pm on Saturday 25 September at the Philharmonic Hall: Frank Bridge's *Dance Rhapsody*, four songs with orchestral accompaniment by Delius ('Wine Roses', 'In the Garden of the Seraglio', 'Through long, long years' and 'Let Springtime come then'), Frederic Austin's symphonic poem *Isabella*, Joseph C. Hathaway's *Scena: 'The Dying Swan'*, Debussy's *Nocturnes* and Rimsky-Korsakov's *Antar*.

4   The third (choral) concert, given at 8.00 pm on Saturday 25 September at the Philharmonic Hall: Bax's *Fatherland*, two songs by Ethel Smyth, 'Irish Tune' and 'Brigg Fair' for chorus by Grainger, Brian's *By the Waters of Babylon*, Vaughan Williams' *Willow-Wood*, Ernest Bryson's *Idylls of a Summer's Day*, and the Bach cantata *Praise Jehovah*.

(325)
Frederick Delius to Adine O'Neill

GREZ SUR LOING,
S. ET M.
7 Oct 1909

Dear Mrs O'Neill –

Many thanks for your long letter with the account of the Festival. I was so glad to hear that everything went off so well & that it was an artistic success   2 suppers & a lunch surpassed my most sanguine expectations – "I hope now that many new members will join the *League*". I am quite alright again altho' I have not yet started work – The weather has been muggy & wet – but yes-

terday & to day are simply devine Autumn days – sunny & still. My indisposition was a severe bilious attack – prepared in Denmark & brought to a
crisis by a fortnights stay in England – on associating with the better class of
people – the English bourgeois has always this effect on me – but as I stand it,
as a rule, only a day or two, it has no serious results. This time, however, I had
an overdose. No other nation but the English would put up with the state of
affairs you write about – "Nothing to eat after 11 p m" – *I suppose it is considered
bad for you.* Please tell Norman to inform his undersecretary that Grez sur
Loing. (Seine & Marne) France is not in England – Every communication I
receive from the Musical League, I have to pay double – I must have paid
about 5 francs by now – It is not the money, but I am called down every time
to the postman at 8 a m –

I am also very glad that Elgar turned up & made a decent speech – With
love to you both from me & Jelka – I remain

Yours affectionately
Frederick Delius

Autograph letter, signed and dated, written on headed notepaper.

The original is in the Delius Trust Archive. It is the first of twenty-five letters from
the Deliuses to Norman or Adine O'Neill, presented to the Trust in 1986 by Mrs
Katherine Jessel, granddaughter of the O'Neills. Also with this collection is one
further letter, written to Adine's daughter Yvonne (Yvonne Hudson) by Jelka on 8
January 1928.

(326)
Frederick Delius to Theodor Szántó

[20 October 1909]

HOTEL DU QUAI VOLTAIRE
        PARIS

Dear Szantó –

I am afraid Klemperer[1] cannot come this evening & as it is very doubtful about
Ravel[2] as well I should like to put off our little dinner & use the evening for
the theatre
Best wishes

Yours
Frederick Delius

Autograph letter, signed and undated, written in German on headed notepaper. The date '20 Oct, 1909' is added in another hand.

The original is in the Library of Congress.

1   Presumably the German composer and cellist Oscar [Oskar?] Klemperer (1877–?). There are a number of references in the Delius correspondence to this friend of Delius's. His mother, we learn, lived in Rotterdam and Jelka was in touch with her in 1913. He himself settled, for a time at least, in Paris, and composed chamber and orchestral music. Delius admired a quintet of his.

2   Ravel figures only rarely in Delius's correspondence, but this letter shows that they kept in touch, however intermittently. The Library of Congress also has a note from Ravel to Szántó, which appears to refer to this proposed meeting: 'I shall be delighted to see Delius again, whom I have not seen for years. You can count on me tomorrow at 7 o'clock.'

(327)
Norman O'Neill to Frederick Delius

HAYMARKET THEATRE, S.W.

Oct 23. 09

Dear Fred,

I have been meaning to write to you for a long time but I am so awfully busy that I never get a moment. I am writing this between cues! – My wife sent you an account of the successful festival which really seems to have gone off splendidly & made a great artistic success. There is a loss of £300 – for which the guarantors will have to stump up! – There is a meeting in Nov: (I have not been able to get the committee together sooner) to decide (or talk about!) place of next festival & *talk generally* about our affairs! – I am so glad you are better. I hope quite all right by now. I am busy with the Blue Bird music[1] which promises to be a beautiful production. We are doing a very good play now – I have only entracte music to play so I manage to write some letters during the acts! – I stayed with Balfour last week end. He is going for Beecham with the arm of the law! I don't blame Balfour after the way he has been treated. It seems that our Tommy owes a good deal of money so I doubt if he'll pay –[2] This won't prevent him living in state at the Langham! I am taking various steps to boom the League all I can. The *press* was fine. More members are what we want now. So that we may become self supporting. Adine is going to give a concert of English music in Paris in January. What are your winter plans? – No further news of Beecham's opera at present! My "in Springtime"[3] has two performances next week. Ronald is going to do my "Belle Dame"[4] & I have a commission to write music for "Richard III" so you see I am fairly full up! – It seems my fate ("Oh terrible fart"! as the German tenor sang in the Carl Rosa Co!) to write for the stage! With best Love to you both

from yours always
N. O'N.

Tell me how the opera is getting on.
We are meeting (McN & I) Corder[5] & McEwen[6] to discuss the League's joining the Soc of British Composers.

Autograph letter, initialled and dated, written on headed notepaper.

The original is in the Delius Trust Archive.

1   O'Neill's incidental music to Maeterlinck's *The Blue Bird*, op. 37 (1909).

2   'He knows his cheque was dishonoured a fortnight ago, & yet he does not write to me,' Gardiner told Delius on 13 September. 'It is abominable treatment & I have had enough of Beecham to last me the rest of my life.'

3   Overture: *In Springtime*, op.21 (1905–6).

4   *La Belle Dame Sans Merci*, for baritone and orchestra, op. 31 (1908).

5   Frederick Corder (1852–1932): English composer. He studied at Cologne and at the Royal Academy of Music, where he became professor of composition in 1888. He was founder, in 1905, of the Society of British Composers.

6   John Blackwood McEwen (1868–1948): Scottish composer, and a mainstay of the SBC. He studied under Corder at the Royal Academy of Music, where he was now teaching, and where he was later to become principal.

(328)
Thomas Beecham to Frederick Delius

THE TURRET,
WEST HEATH,
HAMPSTEAD, N.W.
Nov. 29/09

Dear Delius

Just a line to ask how you both are, and to tell you that I am producing Romeo & Juliet on *March 1st* next at *Covent Garden*. I am giving the whole season there instead of at "His Majesty's" which is too small for my purpose. I have also signed a contract with Strauss's publisher by which I give both Elektra & Salome.

For these two, I am bringing over "en bloc" the Berlin opera folk, and some from Hamburg (Edith Walker) and Vienna (Mildenburg), so I think there will be some fun. The prospectus will be out in a day or two and you will have one. The English text of *Romeo* will have to be entirely overhauled. I have already mentioned the matter to Wallace – But apparently there is only one Piano copy in existence and that is in my hands, but with no German text.[1] What's to be done? Is it any use asking Breitkopf about it? The last time I was there, they had none – The singers will soon have to be looking at it. I find that Miss Artot de Padilla is now at the *Grand* Opera House Berlin – There may be some difficulty about getting her, as I have already engaged so many Berliners, and every one tells me she is too "small" for Covent Garden. But I have several possible people on the list. The only person I am concerned about is the – Black Fiddler – I have an excellent Tenor – quite splendid voice and fine appearance –

Best love

Yours ever,
Thomas Beecham.

P.S.

Do you think in the Prologue that the parts of Vrenchen & Sali should be sung by two girls, both of very small stature, one a mezzo-soprano & dressed as a boy? I think myself this would be much more natural – They have very little to do – only a few lines –

Autograph letter, signed and dated, written on headed notepaper.

The original is in the Delius Trust Archive.

1   Beecham, like many subsequent commentators, seems to have been unaware that Delius had composed *A Village Romeo* to his own English text.

1910

The year started promisingly, with Scheffler preparing to conduct *Appalachia* in Hamburg on 4 February, Beecham advertising his forthcoming London production of *A Village Romeo and Juliet*, and with *Brigg Fair* listed for performance at the Tonkünstlerfest in Zürich. But Delius was unwell once more by the time of his birthday, a prelude to a more serious breakdown in health that was to mark the year out as exceptional in his middle life. He was in England again early in February, staying as Balfour Gardiner's guest at Ashampstead for a week and then in London, where from the middle of the month he was kept busy attending rehearsals of *A Village Romeo*. He did not stay long after the first night at Covent Garden, on 22 February, and returned to Grez where through the spring months he was largely to remain. His nervous condition was in part exacerbated by an increasingly acrimonious correspondence with Harmonie Verlag, whose staff he regarded as incompetence personified. Delius travelled to Zürich late in May to hear Volkmar Andreae give *Brigg Fair* at the Tonkünstlerfest. Schuricht, Haym and Bartók, among others, were there. The performance was excellent, and as a result more performances of his works were planned for a number of European cities, *Brigg Fair* itself being given several times during the autumn season. While in Zürich he took the opportunity to consult a specialist, who advised a month's stay at a sanatorium in the Swiss resort of Mammern. Delius returned to Grez at the beginning of June, and left for Mammern in the middle of the month. Ida Gerhardi saw him off in Paris and wrote to her sister that Jelka was 'very depressed, as she is so very worried about Delius (& she has good reason)'. The symptoms were in fact ascribed at Mammern to tertiary syphilis. In a letter to Delius shortly after his departure Jelka herself wrote: 'I found it very lonely – and all your things about and not *you*.' Letters between them reflected something of Delius's nervous state. 'Dont overstrain yourself,' he told Jelka on 20 June, '. . . I am sure you want a thorough rest after having undergone my bad-temper for so long . . . The people here are awful & I am always alone.' 'Heaps of wishes and lovingest thoughts' came to him a few days later from 'Yr old Jelka'; she was sorting out a number of songs to offer to Tischer & Jagenberg who now wanted to publish some of his compositions. On the 27th

Delius wrote that he was 'feeling better', and on the 30th: 'I want to work again.' 'Since 8 days it is raining & storming,' he wrote early in July, despatching irritable postcards to Jelka to complain that money and newspapers he had asked for had not arrived. A despairing letter came in response: Jelka was doing her utmost to prepare everything for her husband's return, and she was distracted too by troubles with the new maidservant: 'please write me *nicely* soon so that I am not miserable.' In the meantime the money had arrived and Delius wrote an immediate and contrite reply. On 12 July, during the final stage of the return journey between Paris and Grez, with Ida accompanying him on the train, he became ill again. Pain and general debility were, then, characterizing 1910.

At least there was good news on the musical front. Schuricht had programmed *Sea Drift* for 7 November in Wiesbaden, and in August Beecham wrote that he hoped to give *Koanga* and *A Village Romeo and Juliet* in the coming season. This did not happen, but at all events *Paris* was down for 7 November. In September Delius was well enough to continue composition: 'hear you have nearly completed your "Nils Lyhne"', wrote Bantock on the 27th.

On 4 November Delius's travels resumed, to Frankfurt and Wiesbaden for Schuricht's *Sea Drift*, then on to Elberfeld where Haym gave the same work on 12 November, following which the composer continued to Dresden for a cure at Dr Lahmann's Sanatorium which was to last into the new year.

Fennimore and Gerda, opera (RT I/8). Continued.

(329)
Ida Gerhardi to Frederick Delius

108 B^d du Montparnasse
Paris 28.1.10

Dear Fritz, Now it's your birthday & you have to be ill, I am so terribly sorry & if I had not to stay in bed myself tomorrow & the day after, I would certainly have come along to look after you for a while, – I hope this time the attack is not as bad as last time but nonetheless I would almost beg you to consult a *German* doctor specializing in liver & gall complaints, because it is just in gall & liver matters that *German* doctors are acknowledged to be the best in the world. However much I like Dr. Bas personally, generally speaking I have no great confidence in Fr. doctors; they don't go into things so carefully; for the most part are more interested in the money. I think you ought for a while to live under controlled conditions in a German sanatorium for these things & then perhaps in a short time you would be perfectly fit; and that above all else is what you must be in this new year of your life! – Don't be angry with me for suggesting this to you, it arises only from my great desire to see you well. I am sending you a few roses in honour of tomorrow, I had made them into a chemin de fer parcel, but was sent away again with them from the B^d Raspail as parcels are no longer handled by the line from gare de Lyon, – so I had to cut off all the lovely long stalks &, as prescribed by the regulations, make up a small parcel for the post & the roses are not even as nice as they should have been – they should have been just beautiful white ones mais il n'y a pas d'"arrivage". The terrible floods are of course bringing everything to a standstill, – the religious people say that this fate was bound to befall Paris sooner or later, Rodin's Quartier is completely under water. Yesterday was a bright day & I went to look at this Deluge; the ponts & quais which were not roped off were thick & black with people, an anxious air about them all, whilst across from Notre-Dame the sculptured saints look on in immutable majesty & *just at this very moment* the goatherd is passing by playing his familiar tune, setting the seal on my good wishes for you so that they will be fulfilled! To both yourself and Jelka cordial greetings[1]

    from
    Ida

Autograph letter, signed and dated, written in German.

The original is in the Delius Trust Archive. It is the first of three letters from Ida Gerhardi to Delius dating from 1910; two earlier letters, dated 1899, have also survived.

1   In the tone of this letter and the 'cordial greetings' it conveys we find almost the earliest evidence of the reconciliation of Ida with Delius since the break that apparently occurred between them in the spring of 1902 (see Letter 135 and notes). According to Jelka, in a letter written to Grainger on 5 December 1934, there had been no quarrel between Ida and herself over Delius, the separation having occurred 'when Ida began a great intrigue with Oscar Klemperer, which greatly annoyed Fred.'

(330)
Robert Phifer to Frederick Delius

My dear Mr. Delius

It was a surprise and a very welcome one too a few days ago to receive by mail a copy of your Appalachia[1] which you had sent me thus reminding me of yourself and of your old Danville days.

It is a long cry back to those days but I still recall them – the town has very much changed since your time – Large factories now occupy where we once walked. North Danville has now become a part of Danville having been annexed some years ago. Mrs. Richardson still lives at the old house where you and Hoppe once lived.[2] Her two daughters are married and have children – One of her sons-in-law is dying with consumption. Old man Rückert who moved to Washington a year or so after you left has since died of Cancer of the lip. I saw his son in law Dodson about two years ago here in D. Mrs. James (Annie Wilson) still lives at her home on Main st – they are rich.

As for myself I have not been in good health for some time – I really don't mind if I go one of these days. My children are all grown now and what matters. The Averetts are just the same – Miss Pattie still teaching. Edmonds Averett has died leaving a wife and several children – She returned to her fathers.

You know we have prohibition here now. So Hoppe's business has busted if he were still here. – I congratulate you upon your acchieve in the line of your lifes work. I remember when the Appalachia was first given in Berlin. The music papers spoke of it in favorable terms. In the Schirmer Collection I noticed they spoke a couple of weeks ago in mentioning the European novel-ties of your "Paris – a night piece". I enclose a likeness of you – It came out in the Etude a monthly music paper widely read in America.[3] – We all – my wife and children still speak of the delightful evening you and your friends spent with us on your way South to the orange grove – By the way the severe winter has done much injury to the orange industry this year. – Where is Mr. Leminoff? and your singer – what is her name.[4] We were all much interested in the great floods at Paris etc.

I did not know till I saw this paper that you were married – Please pay my respects to your wife – I hope you will not have to die to have your works receive their just dues.

Believe me yours sincerly –
Rob[t] S. Phifer

Danville Va.
Feb. 16th 1910

"Say Telius does you make much money out of your composing pisness"
Summerfield[5]

Autograph letter, signed and dated.

The original is in the Delius Trust Archive. See also Letter 53.

1   The 1907 Harmonie piano score is inscribed: 'To my old Danville friend/Robert. S. Pfifer/from/Frederick Delius/Grez sur Loing/(Seine & Marne)/France/Jan 25th 1910' (cf. Mary Cahill: *Delius in Danville*, p. 32).

2   Miss Cahill has recently identified Delius's Danville address as 208 Church Street (the site has since been rebuilt). He lodged with the family of Henry P. Richardson (probably the 'Mr Rishton' of Letter 1). His friend and fellow lodger, F. W. Hoppe, was at the time apparently in the employ of one of the local saloons and later became manager of the Anheuser-Busch brewery in Lynchburg, some sixty miles to the north of Danville: hence the reference to prohibition below.

3   Delius was accorded a short note on p. 80 of the February 1909 issue.

4   Halfdan Jebe ('Mr. Lemmanoff', as a Danville newspaper spelled it, but perhaps also known as 'Cyril Grey') and, it is believed, the Princesse de Cystria ('Madame Donodossola'), had travelled under assumed names with Delius in 1897. They had given a recital, which included some music by Delius, at the Danville College for Young Ladies (later Stratford College).

5   A Danville personality already referred to in I, p. 87. Phifer's letter of 16 February is also printed in Mary Cahill's *Delius in Danville* but, contrary to the credit, is not from a transcript made by the present writer.

(331)
Frederick Delius to Granville Bantock

7, PEMBROKE VILLAS,
KENSINGTON, W.
[early February 1910]

My dear Bantock –

I have just arrived in London for the rehearsals of "A Village Romeo & Juliet" Will you be able to come up for the Première on the 22nd? I should so much like to see you & my wife hopes M^{rs} B will come too – I am extremely busy, but everything is going on well
    With kindest greetings to you both –

    Yrs ever
    Frederick Delius

Autograph letter, signed and undated, written on headed notepaper.

The original is in the Delius Trust Archive.

Delius travelled to England around the beginning of February, staying for about a week with Balfour Gardiner at Ashampstead, Berkshire, before taking up residence at Gardiner's London home. Almost the first news to reach him here came from John Julia Scheffler, conductor at Hamburg: *Appalachia* had been well received there on 4 February. In the event, the London production of *A Village Romeo and Juliet* proved something of a disappointment and was not a critical success. The Deliuses returned to

Grez rather sooner than expected. Beecham noted that the composer had been far from well, suffering from chronic nervous indigestion and pains in the back. There was to be some improvement by May, Delius writing from Zürich to Jelka: 'I am very comfortable & feeling quite well'; and Ida Gerhardi consequently reported to her doctor brother: 'he suffers of course from neurasthenia & a little gladness & good fortune give a lift of course to his whole condition – the dreadful winter with its failure in London certainly contributed to his state of depression.'

(332)

Harmonie Verlag to Frederick Delius

BERLIN, 5th March *1910*

Dear Herr Delius,

I am replying personally to your communication of the 3rd inst., for which I thank you. I write as head of the department concerned and even more as the person dealing with your business. I shall not reply to the insults thrown in my face, though I might be justified in doing so, partly so as not to inflame the vicious thoughts you already entertain about your dealings with Harmonie, but even more because I realize that you had every reason, under the circumstances, to be on edge, dissatisfied and unwell. By way of explanation let me tell you that:

No-one is entitled to hold another person responsible for a third person's acts or for unforeseen events, difficulties, etc., which one neither could nor should have foreseen. There could not be a case where this maxim is more relevant. Herr Lindemann[1] had always produced work of the finest artistic quality. We were most conscientiously acting in your and your work's best interests when we gave him the job. How could we anticipate that he would let us down in the most irresponsible way imaginable when it came to delivering the manuscript? Witnesses:

Herr Mädler, proprietor of the Berliner Musikaliendruckerei, G.m.b.H., the said firm's employees,

Herr Kwis, the copyist,

our firm's employees and many others.

All these can vouch for the fact that I did everything in my power to get the work back sooner from Lindemann. There were scenes which beggar description. I did everything I could think of but all to no avail. Again and again Lindemann gave promises which he later failed to keep. I had to make my plans on the basis of his definite promises.

The printing works did all they possibly could, under circumstances which were complicated and which every printer will know were extremely difficult. Unfortunately various difficulties made it absolutely impossible for the print-

ing works to keep their word as regards the final delivery date. These difficulties included the engravers' refusing to work overtime, the threat of a strike,
resulting in lack of goodwill amongst the workmen involved, and the English
proof sheets not being delivered on time, etc.; witness: Herr Mädler, proprietor of the Berliner Musikaliendruckerei, G.m.b.H., and specially in charge of
the printing order for "A Village Romeo and Juliet" by Frederick Delius. He
had also undertaken to have the proof sheets corrected by an English proof-
reader on his staff. He specifically assured us that this man was English, as to
which I again cite Herr Mädler as a witness. Moreover I give you my word of
honour that everything I wrote to you about the lost score sheets was true.
I will let you have any evidence of this which you require. I can let you see
our notification to the police, our investigations and our advertisements. I can
also produce a witness as to this in the person of our permanent copyist, Herr
Kwis, who had the job of dealing with the musician, Herr Haffke, to whom
he made an advance payment of 20 Mk. and delivered the score sheets. We
have been guilty of absolutely no negligence whatever. Herr Haffke had already written the extra parts for us. You will admit that this work was perfectly and most conscientiously performed in every line, which he again marked in
blue. In addition, he had already worked, on a previous occasion, with Herr
Kwis, who had always found him completely satisfactory, as we had ourselves.
You know as well as I do that that sort of work gets sent out. One could only
make certain such things did not occur if one had the time to have everything
done on one's own premises.

I now come to your last point, which is that my account of the despatch of
proof-sheets and printed copies is untrue, meaning that it was a deliberate lie,
and that it amounted, to be quite frank, to fraudulent deception.

I have already told you that the printers did not keep to what they had
promised and why this was. I am ready to let you have the clearest proof that I
at all times genuinely believed that the information I passed on was correct. If
printers clearly and unambiguously promise that goods will be despatched
tomorrow evening, I cannot report anything else to you. I have also held the
printers liable for the fact that the libretto is unusable and was, in any event,
despatched too late. I have also reproved the printers for not sending off the
piano score as promised but two days later. At the same time the printers
cannot alone be held liable, as Lindemann delivered the manuscript in a completely irregular manner and then only bit by bit. The printers were never able
to keep the engravers continuously occupied and had to give them other work
to do part of the time, as not enough of the manuscript was available. Herr
Mädler told me quite categorically that he had never anticipated such difficulties and that, if he had foreseen them, he would never have taken the job
on if he could have avoided it.

Finally let me tell you that it is with great reluctance that I give you references concerning myself. I will merely say that I am known to Herr *Fried*,

Herr *Gustav Brecher*, Dr. Richard *Strauss* and a considerable number of public personalities, composers and authors as an absolutely reliable and, above all, completely truthful man, who is not in the habit of paying insincere compliments. I am very sorry you ran into such difficulties but neither "Harmonie" nor I was in any way whatever responsible for them. I think you are entitled to complain about all the things which went wrong but that you are not entitled to hold us liable for them, as we did all that lay in our power. We ourselves will have to have recourse to the persons who caused us the loss. Let me repeat that I hope your personal relations with "Harmonie" will not be adversely affected. If you like, I will in future have your business dealt with by Herr Jadassohn or another member of our firm, as the whole affair has truly earned me nothing but ingratitude.

Yet despite everything I retain the greatest interest in you as an artist and in your works and hope sooner or later to be able to prove this to you by myself succeeding in getting your opera performed in Germany.

Yours truly
Kurt Fliegel.

Typed letter, signed and dated, written in German on the headed notepaper of "HARMONIE"/Verlagsgesellschaft für Literatur und Kunst, and addressed: Herrn/ Frederick Delius,/c./o. H.B. Gardiner Esq.,/7 Pembroke Villas,/Kensington n./ London.

The original is in the Delius Trust Archive.

The correspondence with Harmonie, begun in 1906 (see Letter 186), draws to a close. Apart from a few extant carbon copies of letters written by Delius to Harmonie (cf. Letter 295), the progressive acrimony in the exchanges between composer and publisher is largely charted by the Harmonie side (Delius's letter of 3 March has not survived). An even more aggrieved letter from Harmonie just a week later refers to 'the obviously improper form' of Delius's letter, refutes an evident accusation by Delius of lying, and coldly informs the composer that 'in future Herr Jadassohn will correspond with you.' (Jadassohn and Fliegel were brothers-in-law.) Harmonie's final extant letter to Delius is dated 13 June 1910.

1 Otto Lindemann made the vocal score of A *Village Romeo and Juliet* that was published by Harmonie.

(333)
Ida Gerhardi to Frederick Delius

108 B^d du Montparnasse
Paris 13.5.10.

Dear Fritz,

I have just received Jelka's lines telling me that you are not well & that you have pains in your back & that you still have to be extremely careful about what you eat. Now would you not prefer to use this summer to go into a sanatorium under medical supervision & get well? instead of going off of your own accord into the cold Norwegian mountains where you are sure to over-exert & strain yourself with long marches, for your nature is such that it knows no moderation, allows itself to get carried away & *doesn't in the least understand* what is good for it! As chance would have it Frau Stoop[1] wrote to me yesterday to say that it would be so excellent for you in Dr. Dengler's Sanatorium in Baden-Baden – even if Frau Stoop thoroughly upset me with her autocratic manner, she is nevertheless an *intelligent* woman & moreover takes an active interest in us all & might be able to arrange matters so that this sanatorium would be payable[2] for you, – for you see, in my opinion something *must* be done to put your health right because life really has no point at all if every-thing has to come to a standstill through illness. And at the same time the baths at Baden-B., which are second only to Kreuznach, would do Jelka an infinite amount of good.

For almost everyone there comes a time in life when sacrifices have to be made for the sake of one's health & if one does not or cannot make them, the penalties will be all the more severe. So take yourself to task & ask yourself whether this is not the very time when you ought to be making this sacrifice.

It seems to me far more important that you should preserve your health, nota bene your creative powers, that infinitely delicate, sensitive flower rather than go walking on the high Norwegian mountains, – there is a time and a place for everything in life. I hope your state of health remains tolerable, no-one wishes that more sincerely than your painter friend

Ida

It was warm today & now it is raining again. Best wishes to Jelka & tell her my nice green dress was ruined by the paint-spots & had to be dyed black –

Autograph letter, signed and dated, written in German. Envelope addressed: M. Frederik Delius/Grez sur Loing/Seine et Marne. Postmark obscured.

The original is in the Delius Trust Archive.

1   There are a number of references to the Stoops in the Delius letters. Bertha Stoop, of Dutch origin, and a friend of the Gerhardi family, was the subject of a particularly fine portrait painted by Ida in London in 1910. British by naturalization, she was the wife of Frank Stoop, the rich art-collector who on his death was to leave to the Tate Gallery paintings by Van Gogh, Cézanne, Rousseau, Matisse and Picasso. Bertha Stoop loved music and frequently held musical soirées in her home at 9 Hans Place. In a letter to Percy Grainger Jelka mentions her death in 1928, and six years later we find her writing to him again and recording the death of Frank Stoop, 'so that that hospitable little house in Hans Place exists no longer.' Clearly the Deliuses must for a time have been frequent visitors to the Stoops' London home; and now in 1910 the Stoops in their turn, together with Ida Gerhardi, are to pay a short visit to Grez at the end of May, staying overnight with Jelka while Delius is in Zürich.

2   *affordable*: in French in the original letter.

(334)
Frederick Delius to Jelka Delius

Zurich[1] Monday [30 May 1910]

Dearest Jelka —

Your letter just arrived: I am glad everything is alright & that you are better again – The performance of "Brigg Fair" was wonderful – the best I have heard – Andreae[2] is a splendid fellow & the work made a tremendous effect – quite a triumph – Wolf[3] in Berlin at once acquired the first performance in Berlin & Hamburg – So Nickish will have to do it in Berlin – The Zuricher quite excelled in Gastfreundlichkeit – even better than Basel[4] – We had a lovely day on the Lake yesterday & on our return at night the whole Lake side was illuminated & fireworks & we were escorted from the steamer to the Tonhalle where we were received by hundreds of Zuricher in Native costume – then a procession in the Tonhalle with dances (national) & Ringkampf etc & quite beautiful costumes from all the Cantons – I am taking great care of myself & feel quite well   I shall leave for Paris on Wednesday morning & hope to find you at Ida's – Will write you the exact time – The Fest is really quite amusing & I am enjoying it very much – In haste

yours ever
Fred –

Autograph letter, signed and dated.

The original is in the Grainger Museum.

1   Delius travelled to Zürich on 26 May in order to be present at the first performance outside England of *Brigg Fair*. It was given, in the context of the 46th Festival
of the Allgemeine Deutsche Musikverein, in the Grosser Tonhallesaal on 28 May.
Delius stayed c/o Frau H. Haeberlin, Stockerstrasse 49.

2   Volkmar Andreae (1879–1962): Swiss conductor and composer. He was director
of the Zürich Symphony Concerts from 1906 to 1949. Two communications from him
are preserved in the Delius Trust Archive: a letter dated 2 April 1910, and a postcard
of 19 May: 'Your "Brigg Fair" is going excellently and is a *splendid* piece.'

3   The concert agency of Hermann Wolff.

4   The 1903 Tonkünstlerfest had been held at Basel, when Delius's *Mitternachtslied
Zarathustras* had been performed.

(335)
Zoltán Kodály to Frederick Delius

[early June 1910]

Dear Herr Delius,

We must tell you of an incredibly funny thing. Our publisher insists that the
name of a foreign musician must be printed on the piano pieces he is now
issuing, as "revisor". If that is missing, (f. example: Revised by F. Delius)
then the things are pirated in America, as Hungary is not yet a member of this
International Convention. (Like Russia)

   Well, if another name has to appear on our music, there is hardly any other
we would sooner see there than yours. So if you do not object, (we must simply
accept the matter as a formality or a joke) then please write to Bartók (Bpest
VI   Terézkörut 17) just saying "yes". (If at the outside you were an American
citizen, it would be of no help to us!)

   As the matter is urgent please reply as soon as possible.

With friendly greetings and kindest regards
Z. Kodály

Autograph letter, signed and undated, written in German.

The original is in the Delius Trust Archive. Apart from the postcard jointly sent by
Bartók and Kodály in February 1911 (*qv*), it is the only item of correspondence that is
preserved from Kodály to Delius.

Zoltán Kodály (1882–1967): Hungarian composer and teacher. Together with Bartók
he attended the Tonkünstlerfest at Zürich, where the two young Hungarians befriended Delius and heard *Brigg Fair*. Bartók was soloist in his own *Rhapsodie*, op. 1,

at the same concert, and Kodály's String Quartet No. 1 was given the following day. Bartók recalled of the occasion, in a letter to Heseltine dated 24 November 1920, that Delius was 'very pleased' with the Kodály quartet (János Breuer: 'Kodály in England, A Documentary Study (I: 1913–28)', *Tempo*, 143, p. 3). No letters from Delius to Kodály have been found, but the younger composer placed on record an irritable complaint by Delius in 1910: German conductors were 'amazingly stupid; they could not imagine the compositions away from the written notes and always wanted me to play it. On the piano(!) an orchestral composition, although I cannot play the piano!' (*The Selected Writings of Zoltán Kodály*, London, Boosey & Hawkes, 1974, p. 195.)

(336)
Béla Bartók to Frederick Delius

Budapest, Teréz-körút 17.
7 June, 1910

Dear Mr. Delius,

I fear that you will already no longer be at home when my Suite[1] and this letter arrive. For my Suite there is time enough of course, and perhaps someone will be able to send my letter on to you. I should so much like to describe to you – and yet find it so hard – what a great joy it was for me – I might almost say an event – to get to know you. That is – music quite apart! To see you simply as a human being! I am afraid that it may not seem natural to you for me to write about these things, which you would have sensed in any case from my conversation, but I cannot restrain myself from mentioning it again. I am so alone here, have no-one to talk to, apart from my only friend Kodály, and have never met anyone anywhere else to whom, right from the start, I have felt so close as to you. And this is what made my time at the Zürich Festival one of the most beautiful periods in my life.

Now you are going to your Norway again or are already there – unfortunately I cannot leave the city this summer – and all I can do from here is to yearn for the wild regions you told me about. Could I have news of you sometimes? I should also very much like to know whether the Suite makes a favourable impression on you?

With best wishes

Yours
Béla Bartók

German typescript, dated, in the Delius Trust Archive. Of the six communications from Bartók to Delius that are recorded, only one – the joint Kodály/Bartók postcard of 18/19 February 1911 – has been found in its original form, the remainder surviving in typed transcripts. All six items, dating from 1910 and 1911, are reproduced in this volume.

Béla Bartók (1881–1945): Hungarian composer and pianist. At this time he was teaching piano at the Royal Academy of Music in Budapest. His Budapest address, given as Teréz-körút 17.IV.23 at the head of three letters, has led earlier commentators to suppose that his friendship with Delius dated from 1923.

1 Suite No. 2 for orchestra, op. 4 (1905/7).

(337)
Frederick Delius to Béla Bartók

Grez sur Loing,
(Seine & Marne)
11 June 1910

My dear Mr Bartok –

Your kind letter gave me the greatest pleasure: I felt exactly as you did & am glad to have found a new friend in you.

I am afraid that I cannot go to my beloved Norway this summer as in a week's time I have to start on a cure in a sanatorium – Wasserheilanstalt[1] Mammern (am Untersee (Boden-See) Schweiz) – I would be awfully pleased to hear from you there – I have received the "Suite" & will read it with much interest & then let you know my opinion – Mr Kodaly wrote to me about the business of your publishers – If it can be of use to you my name is of course at your disposal –

Please give our warmest greetings to Kodaly & also my best regards to your wife –

In cordial sympathy

Yours
Frederick Delius

Autograph letter, signed and dated, written in German. Envelope addressed: Monsieur/Béla Bartók/Terez-Körut 17/ Budapest/Hongrie. Postmark: GREZ 12 –6 10.

The original is in the Bartók Archive, Budapest. It is the first of two letters from Delius to Bartók that are preserved in this Archive. See also Letter 344.

1 Hydropathic establishment.

(338)
Frederick Delius to Jelka Delius

Mammern
17/6/10

Dearest Jelka

I arrived here last night at 10.19. The train left Basle at 6–15 & not
7–5   Suter was at the station & I had a nice chat with him & a cup of tea – He
is doing Brigg Fair & Appalachia again – I am lodged in the Villa 2nd Etage –
but my room looks out on to the chemin de fer & trams go bye altho' not many
& the last at night at 10.19 – I was woken up this morning by someone
practising the (the) Cello!!! Scales & exercises – A man from Zürich – one of *the
Fest Commité*   I shall make a row if it continues every morning – The piano
downstairs in the big Establishment is going all the morning – horrible   The
place is full of old men & women – fat & ugly – and heaps of careworn,
wrinkled middle aged females – most of which seem to play the piano – How
ugly humanity is! what expressions! A lot of men ataxique – stamping about
with a man holding them. I had my consultation – The doctor is nice & I
think clever   He examined me thoroughly with all sorts of instruments   He
noticed at once that one of the pupils of my eyes the left one is smaller than the
other. That seems to be a sure sign of *Nervenkrank*[1] – He said my liver &
stomach were absolutely alright – I am not in the slightest artritique or
Rhumatique – My trouble comes from the Central Nerven System & may have
something to do with my old Syphilis – I dont believe this at all – He gave me
a bath tepid at 4 – which did me good   A man rubs you in the water for about
5 minutes & then you dress & take a walk for half an hour – tomorrow at 11. I
have an electric bath – After dinner & supper I have to take a tablet of *Sajodin* a
preparation of Jod[2] – one of Beyer's schweinereien – Elberfeld – I shall see how
things go before judging the place – It is beautifully situated & the Park is half
flooded – Lots of Russians here – These few words in haste – Thanks for the
block Haglem – Just what I wanted – Hope you are well & will go with Ida to
Paris & not bother yourself about anything until the servant comes –

yr affectionate
Fred –

This is the face of a russian baby boy

Autograph letter, signed and dated.

The original is in the Grainger Museum.

1   German: *Neurosis*; *neurasthenia*.

2   German: *Iodine*.

(339)
Frederick Delius to Tischer & Jagenberg

Wasserheilanstalt
Mammern
Untersee, – Bodensee
Schweiz
[mid-June 1910]

Dear Herr Doctor,

I have just received your letter of the 4th inst – I do not understand why there should be a limit to my share of the royalties – After all, it is only just that I, the composer, as well as my heirs should have a share in the profits – All my contracts have the conditions which I proposed to you – All my large choral & orchestral works published by "Harmonie" as well as those published by F. E. C. Leuckart –

All I sold outright were 3 small choral songs to Harmonie for 600 Mk.

Since I believe in the future of my music, I have always preferred the conditions that I have proposed to you, instead of settling for one large once-for-all payment –

And just now my music is beginning to make headway –

There cannot be many more copies at Breitkopf's in London – You can of course ask for precise information & at the same time inform Breitkopf's that you are now going to publish these songs. You could also withdraw the remainder as soon as the new edition is ready – In one song I have a small alteration to make "Venevil" I would however like to read the *proofs* of all of them – I am staying here for another 8–10 days & then I return to Grez Would you accept Breitkopf & Härtel as agents in London? If you agree please send the 500 *Mk* to Gebr Arons, 34 Mauer Str Berlin, for my account – With kind regards

Yours sincerely
Frederick Delius

Autograph letter, signed and dated, written in German.

The original is in the Delius Trust Archive. It is the first of nearly seventy communications from the Deliuses to the firm of Tischer & Jagenberg between June 1910 and June 1929 that are preserved. An incomplete draft letter of 23 June 1910 (from Delius to Tischer) is in the Grainger Museum.

Gerhard Tischer (1877–1959): German music publisher and editor. From 1906 he was editor of the *Rheinische Musik- und Theater-Zeitung*, and from 1909 head of the publishing firm of Tischer & Jagenberg, Cologne, which he himself founded.

Tischer had recently written to enquire about publishing some of Delius's songs, and Jelka, writing to Delius on 16 June, added her own encouragement: 'I wish you *would* publish a few songs and fill the Reise Kasse. Shall I send you the 2 Verlaine Songs printed or written off? and a few others? I see that this Rheinische Musikz. makes proper propaganda. It is very handy as Tischer himself edits it. Please write a card at once if you are willing, and try not to be unwilling!'

(340)
Frederick Delius to Jelka Delius

Mammern, 23/6 1910

Dearest Jelka –

Enclosed I send you the Korrectur Bogen[1] of Sea Drift, kindly correct & send to Harmonie – I received The Dance Rhapsody & the songs today   Send me the letter to Tischer here & I will copy it off & send it – enclosed is what I want to write – I will offer him the 7 German songs & the 4 new ones for 1500 Mk or the 7 German for 1000 –

The weather today is cold & rainy with sunshine in between – I miss very much sun baths & Air baths which one does not get here – I think Lahmann would suit us better. I spoke [to] a man here who had been there & was delighted with it – walking about naked & bathing of some sort all day – This place is very slow & there is nowhere to sit when the weather is bad – I will stay a month or 3 weeks & come back to Grez for sun baths, we can then go away for the winter somewhere – If you feel you want a cure then come here – There is one man who is interesting a Mr Moser – a great traveller in the East & a great collectioneur of Persian & oriental things – Do you think I ought to offer the songs first to Sander[2] – I dont see why I should – Write me a letter to him asking him if he wants songs of mine & also what I want for them & then we will see who accepts my price – We will try & be clever with these d — d verleger – The Tauchnitz books came from Zürich today nearly a week & cost 25 centimes a volume more than in Paris! A man lent me some books here so I am alright for the present – Send me one of my Photo postcards & I will send it to Clare – They are in the lefthand drawer of my working table – I eat a lot & feel quite well – Nervous pains a bit when the weather is changing – The electric bath does me good I believe – but sun baths I am just longing for –

I am so glad the garden is looking so well & that there are such [a] lot of strawberries – Get Salomon to roll the lawn – Was the grass spoiled? The butcher will have to take it now I suppose anyhow. The park is half flooded & the roads outside very muddy.

I hope all went off well with Daniel & family – How does the Gauguin look?[3] – Are you going to copy it or do something new?

There is only one russian family here & they seem only to speak russian –
With many kind thoughts & love

yrs always
Fred

Autograph letter, signed and dated.

The original is in the Grainger Museum.

1   German: *Proof sheets*. Carl Schuricht had been pressing for the corrected score of *Sea
Drift*, which – as he had informed Delius a week earlier – he was to conduct on 7
November.

2   Martin Sander (1859–1930): Director of the German publishing house of F. E. C.
Leuckart, in succession to his father Constantin Sander (1826–1905).

3   Daniel de Monfreid had borrowed Delius's precious Gauguin canvas, *Nevermore*, in
order to have it restored. On 17 June he wrote to propose that he and his wife call at
Grez; should Delius be at home, he could deliver the picture personally and so see his
old friend again. This was not to be, so the Gauguin was left instead at Ida Gerhardi's
Paris apartment for Jelka to fetch when convenient.

(341)
Jelka Delius to Frederick Delius

Grez 27.6.1910
posted[1] before 7 p.m.

Dearest,

Inclosed came just now; No news from you to-day – I've sent the Korrekt.
Bog. to Harmonie. – I picked 11 Pounds strawberries yesterday – an awful
work and made them into jam to-day – I also began the Gauguin copy[2]
yesterday, and worked at it all the afternoon to-day – It is most interesting. It
is so beautifully drawn, when you come to imitate it, you get so much more
intimately into its beauty. When I think of Ouvré explaining, how the hip
and all was not drawn at all – It is so wonderfully drawn with the slightest in-
flections in the outline – that a hairbreadth wrong makes an abominable difference. I am very uncertain about being able to copy it – I must say I can't
share Ida's optimism there again. What troubles me too is, that I must do it
one little bit lighter than the original, because those mixed colours are bound
to sink a little. The "how much" of that bothers me. No, I am not as naïve as
Ida – But it interests me immensely – and in this delightful servantless quiet,
with the thrush singing in the garden it is a happy occupation. Of course I am

only drawing as yet, and shall try to get a very good drawing before I do paint.

How are you, dear? You never tell me what you drink for meals? Do[3] you sit eating with others or by yourself? I find it so dull eating alone. The weather has been better to-day – we were going towards another flood with these torrential rains. I had a nice letter from Mrs Schou[4] – she will not yet give up hoping for our visit; they had all looked forward to it *so much*. She asked for your address, which I'm sending, as she wants to send you some books. I should like to know whether the letters posted[1] at 12 or those at 7. go to you quickest. Please tell me. I met Hilma[5] and baby, supposed to be very well but looking very thin and with a red rash. Everybody sends their love and wishes to you – Roger, carpenters Soulange, Lea – Hilma –

Thursday and friday morning I shall be in Paris, so please address there, if you write on wednesday. I'm curious how you decide about the songs.

Be loved and kissed from your old

Jelka –

Tono-Bungay[6] is delightful.

Autograph letter, signed and dated.

The original is in the Grainger Museum.

1   The original has 'postet'.

2   While staying briefly in Paris with Ida Gerhardi, Jelka wrote to Delius on 24 June and signalled the return of the freshly restored *Nevermore*: 'Oh the Gauguin is here – and perfectly lovely, glossy and golden-toned – I'll take it with me to-morrow and copy it. It is really immensely improved and so beautifully waxed – but it is not on a rough canvass – it is on the same fine canvass, as it had before. God knows it is a difficult enterprise to copy it – but I must try.' (Cf. I, p. 141.)

3   The original has 'To'.

4   Elisabeth Schou was the wife of a successful industrialist, Einar Schou, pioneer in the manufacture of margarine. He had a large factory which included, among other advanced social amenities for his workers, a concert hall. More recently he had purchased Palsgaard, a large estate near Juelsminde in Jutland, where he built an emulsion factory. He lived for the rest of his life at Palsgaard, where his wife, who had artistic interests, was able to entertain many musicians. The Deliuses stayed at Palsgaard in August 1909 and in October 1915. Three letters, dated 1908 and 1909, from the Schous to Delius are preserved in the Delius Trust Archive.

5   Hilma, daughter of the painter Francis Chadwick and wife of Alden Brooks: friends and neighbours of the Deliuses at Grez. Alden Brooks, an American, was a graduate of Harvard and subsequently taught at the United States Naval Academy.

While he lived at Grez (and in Paris) he was a particular friend of Delius; and Eric Fenby recalls him as a notably kind man. He was a correspondent for the *New York Times* early in the first World War before enlisting in the French Foreign Legion and serving as an officer in the artillery of the French army throughout the war. He was a gifted writer, notably of war stories, and was in 1937 to publish a book on Shakespeare. During Delius's later years at Grez, Brooks was probably the most frequent visitor to the house, delighting Delius with all the latest art gossip from the capital, where he spent most of the week. This particular side of his character is referred to in a letter Jelka wrote to Delius, then in London, on 27 February 1920. Brooks had called on her in Grez: 'He is nice, but, God, how tactless, lets himself go much more with me than with you. He wishes *very much* for you to find out whether Wells has besides Mrs Wells another menage with a person called Rebecca West, by whom he has a child?'

6   Novel by H. G. Wells, first published in 1909.

(342)
Frederick Delius to Ida Gerhardi

[Switzerland, 9 July 1910]

Dear Ida – Your card received – Have just written to Jelka   Let's go to Norway then & shut the house up. The weather in Norway is dry & warm – so I hear – Servants ruin one's life[1] I now intend to settle more into the life of a nomad[2] – I arrive on Monday evening

   Best wishes
   Fr Delius

Autograph postcard, signed and undated, written in German. Addressed: Frl Ida Gerhardi/108 B^d Montparnasse/Paris/France. Postmark: AMBULANT 9.VII.10.

The original is in the Grainger Museum.

1   Ida had helped Jelka procure the services of a young German girl, Bertha Groeschke, for the house at Grez. The girl soon grew homesick and now wanted to leave.

2   Writing to Jelka on 29 June, and pondering spending the winter in the sun, Delius had proposed: 'We might first try Spain & then Cairo.' His good spirits were returning: 'I am getting stouter here –,' he wrote a day later, 'so it seems to agree with me...I want to work again.' A further change of plan then came about with a letter from Milly Bergh telling of fine weather in Norway; but the setback in his health which occurred while he was actually on the way back to Grez on 12 July brought a reluctant acceptance that the rest of the summer must be spent at Grez.

(343)
Frederick Delius to Tischer & Jagenberg

GREZ SUR LOING
S. ET M.
24.7.1910

Dear Herr Doktor,

I have received your letter of the 21st & am very pleased that you are going to bring out the songs so beautifully & tastefully. Blue gold should look very well on parchment.

I will easily be able to do the third Verlaine song, as I already had this lyric in mind myself. The translations into English are seldom good. The Corder ones that I am acquainted with are bad. In any case I must see all translations first. Wallace, I know, is fine.

I meant to sell the three Shelley songs to Novello, as I need the money – However, I am ready, if you really would like to have these Shelley songs too, to let you have these and the new Verlaine song under the same conditions as the others, with an advance of another 300 Mk. –

Otherwise I would advise you to publish the 2 Verlaine songs & the Vinje song separately. I have as usual sent the contract to my legal adviser in Germany to look through. Apart from the "Performing Right", over which as a member of the Genossenschaft I have no control I see nothing that needs altering in it & think you can already begin your work whilst awaiting the return of the contract

With best wishes

Yours
Frederick Delius

Letter in the hand of Jelka Delius, dated, written in German on headed notepaper.

The original is in the Delius Trust Archive.

An earlier letter from Delius, on 13 July, shows that an agreement with Tischer was in sight: 'I have received your contract form and will return it to you in a few days.' The composer was distinctly reluctant to have his German and French songs sung other than in the original language: 'The French songs must on no account be translated into English as well' – partly because it was particularly muddling to have three lines of text cramped together in the printed copies.

(344)
Frederick Delius to Béla Bartók

GREZ SUR LOING
S. ET M.
13 August 1910

Dear Mr Bartók

Forgive me for having left you so long without news – I spent 4 weeks in Switzerland undergoing a cure and had thought that my wife might have brought your Suite for me which was not the case, so I have only just now been able to read it through. The work interested me very much – I like the slow movement best – which I find full of genuine feeling – After that the First movement, then the scherzo and least of all the last movement. Just as in your piano music, which you have played to me, I find in the Suite too that you sometimes employ dissonances, which are not in themselves called for by the music, in a characteristically arbitrary way. I imagine that you feel this as a certain reaction against the banal, which can indeed be perfectly fair: I believe, however, that music should be apart from all such preoccupations – flowing purely from one's own feeling and without too much intellectuality. – So, feeling! I consider Berlioz and Strauss to be purely intellectual composers. In spite of their technical perfection and many other interesting points, both lack what for me is the soul of music – They try to make up for it by purely superficial means – I feel you are cut out for something quite different – The Suite must sound splendid and I should very much like to hear it – Shall I send the score back to you, or shall I keep it here still? I shall not of course be able to do a great deal before the winter while I am here. I could however send it, if you wish, to Dr Haym in Elberfeld, he is a friend of mine and is interested in modern things – I am afraid I was unable to go to Norway this summer as I did not feel strong enough and the weather was so bad – Perhaps you will come and visit me here in Grez, it would give me the greatest pleasure: I shall be here until the end of October. What are you doing? Are you composing anything now?

Do write to me soon, I should be so glad to hear from you.
– Best wishes to you and your wife and also to Mr Kodaly

Yours
Frederick Delius

P.S. I hope your publisher business is settled.

Autograph letter, signed and dated, written in German on headed notepaper. Envelope addressed: Monsieur/Béla Bartóking/Teréz-Körut 17/Budapest/Hongrie. Postmark: GREZ 13 -8 10.

The original is in the Bartók Archive, Budapest.

(345)
Béla Bartók to Frederick Delius

Budapest, Teréz-körút 17.IV.23.
[September 1910]

Dear Mr. Delius,

Since I received your letter we have had nothing but worries. My wife was and still is ill, though now almost recovered. I could not write earlier, before all of our troubles were out of the way, otherwise it would have turned out to be too sad. – Your candid opinion gave me great pleasure – yes, I too really felt the last movement to be the weakest, with less invention in it, and parts of the scherzo, too, sound contrived and not at all right. In many ways, though, I prefer the 1st movement to the third. What in this Suite was intended more as a contradiction of the commonplace recurred in the later little piano pieces however as the result of a peculiar mood I was in at the time and which is hardly ever likely to return. I think the language of this piano music is not so contrived and deliberate as that of the Suite. Since the piano pieces I have become more "harmonious" again, so that I now no longer need the contradictory accumulation of dissonances to express the feeling of a mood. This may possibly be a result of my giving way more and more to the influence of folk-music. The business of the American copyright of our works is indeed a nuisance. An outsider might wonder for God knows what dubious reasons we should be using your name. In fact it looks rather worse in print than I imagined. I am now seriously considering whether it might not be possible somehow to acquire another citizenship, which would ensure the protection of my compositions in America.

It is with great pleasure that I can tell you that your Brigg Fair is to be performed here in February – under a relatively quite good conductor[1] (we have plenty of bad ones, and how bad). I should like to suggest some Grainger to this conductor for the following season – actually only because I should like to hear it. But I do not know how to come by a score etc., whether the composer will agree to a performance at all, what to choose. – Please advise me on this. And please mention me to Grainger when you have an opportunity; I should like to write to him on the subject of folklore, and would not wish to do so as a complete stranger. How I should like to accept your invitation, but we poor music teachers are very tied – the school year lasts from the beginning of Sept. until the middle of June. If only someone would give me a position where I could have the job of collecting folk-songs scientifically, that is something I would do with great enthusiasm. But I can work up absolutely no enthusiasm for giving piano lessons to untalented youngsters who regard music as a means of earning a living. But ours is a poor country which is able to make little contribution to the solution of scientific and artistic problems. (I must point out that my motive for collecting folk-songs was certainly not "scientific curiosity".) We were very sorry about you in your sanatorium – I can imagine life in a sanatorium to be very disagreeable. Let us hope you will soon have no further need of this sort of thing.

Would it perhaps interest you to make the acquaintance of some Rumanian folk-music (on paper)? If you have time for it, I should very much like to send you something from my collection to look at. And in March you will be sure of course to keep your promise and pay us a visit, so that I can introduce you to the peculiarly oriental character of the music of the Rumanian countryside, in its vivid reality. How enjoyable that would be!

With best wishes

Yours
Béla Bartók

N.B. Please do *not* send the ii Suite back; I have several copies of it.

German typescript, undated, in the Delius Trust Archive.

1 *Brigg Fair* was given in Budapest on 15 February 1911, with István Kerner conducting the orchestra of the Hungarian Philharmonic Society. Bartók's view was that the work was full of 'colours of marvellously fine texture, the magic atmosphere of folk-tales: that is the impression gained in listening to it by anyone with an ear for music' (Demény, ed.: *Béla Bartók Letters*, p. 389).

(346)
Frederick Delius to Tischer & Jagenberg

Grez sur Loing
S. et M.
25.9.1910

Dear Herr Doktor,

Yesterday I received two of the Shelley Songs, which I am returning to you by the same post. I greatly regret that you did not send me these texts before engraving them, for I must say that your two translations are not as successful as the others and cannot possibly be published as they stand. Also, just as with the Verlaine Songs, Shelley's beautiful words must appear above, and the translation below.

Perhaps you are not proficient enough in English for you have missed the sense, the delicacy of expression. You have also come to grief with the rhyme, which is better omitted altogether if it is impracticable musically.

Right at the beginning you have: *Kaum entschlafen sah ich dich, aus dem Traum bin ich erwacht* – there is no connection, no coherence – *Den alten* – *bis erwacht* too stilted.

The following lines are too banal & do not convey the sense, with the result that the beautiful landscape does not become visible to us.

Es sinken Düfte etc & the following line is too vague. Rather keep literally to the text.

Ach fühlst Du meinen Schmerz is not at all suitable. Rather no rhyme at all than the familiar "Herz – Schmerz."

"O reich mir Deine Hand" is much too tame and *ich sterbe hier im Gras* is impossible with the big crescendo in the music; in the following line the declamation is not good either & the expression is too direct

"Treu bis in den Tod" is quite out of keeping with the whole passionate Indian song – (even Germans are not true unto death)

I hope you will not misunderstand me, I have quoted everything en détail so that you will see why this translation is not to my liking.

I therefore suggest that for this song you should print my wife's translation[1] which renders the Shelley poem faithfully & fits the music exactly.

The same goes for Love's Philosophy & my wife is about to translate this too & will send it on as soon as possible, probably tomorrow.

I await a further proof of the Verlaine Songs.

With kind regards from myself and my wife

Yours
Frederick Delius

Letter in the hand of Jelka Delius, signed by Frederick Delius, dated, written in German.

The original is in the Delius Trust Archive.

1   Jelka's translation of 'Indian Love Song' was enclosed.

(347)
Frederick Delius to Granville Bantock

Grez sur Loing
S & M
26 Oct 1910

Dear Bantock –

Many thanks for your letter: I, also, shall not have anything to do with this society: The information Mr Bonnaire sends me is much too scanty & every-

PLATE I   Frederick Delius.

PLATE 2   Gustav Mahler, caricature by Hans Boehler.

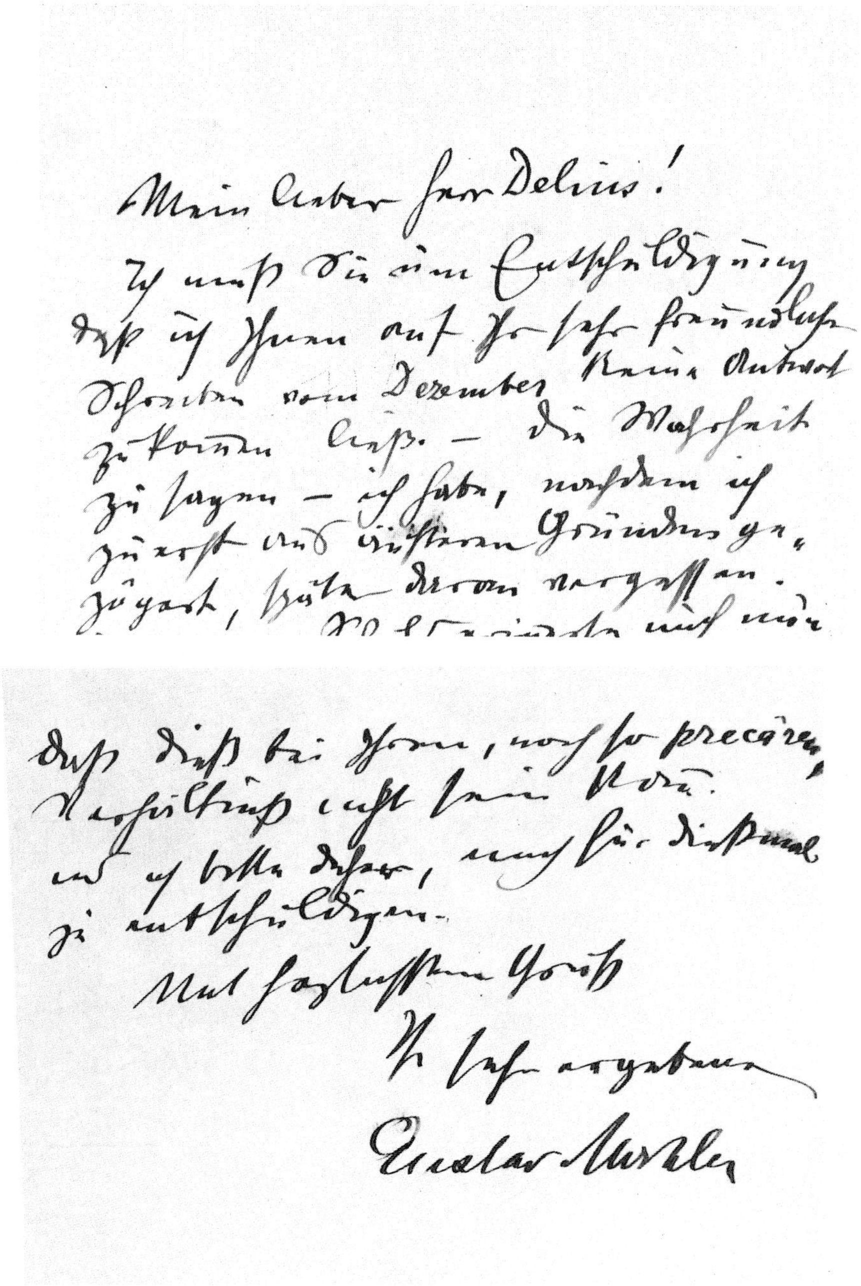

PLATE 3   Extracts from a letter from Mahler to Delius, May 1909
(see p. 25).

PLATE 4   Frederic Cowen.

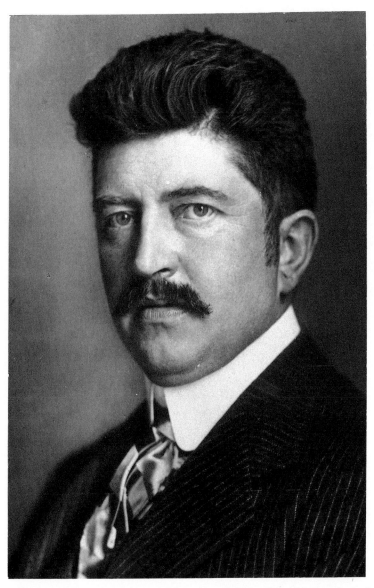

PLATE 5   August Schmid-Lindner. (*Coll. Familienarchiv Schmid-Lindner.*)

PLATE 6   (a) Oda Krohg, c. 1905, by Christian Krohg; (b) Ethel Smyth;
(c) Clare Delius Black with her son.

PLATE 7   Hans Haym and Delius with the score of *A Mass of Life*, Elberfeld,
12 December 1909.

PLATE 8   Zoltán Kodály and Béla Bartók.

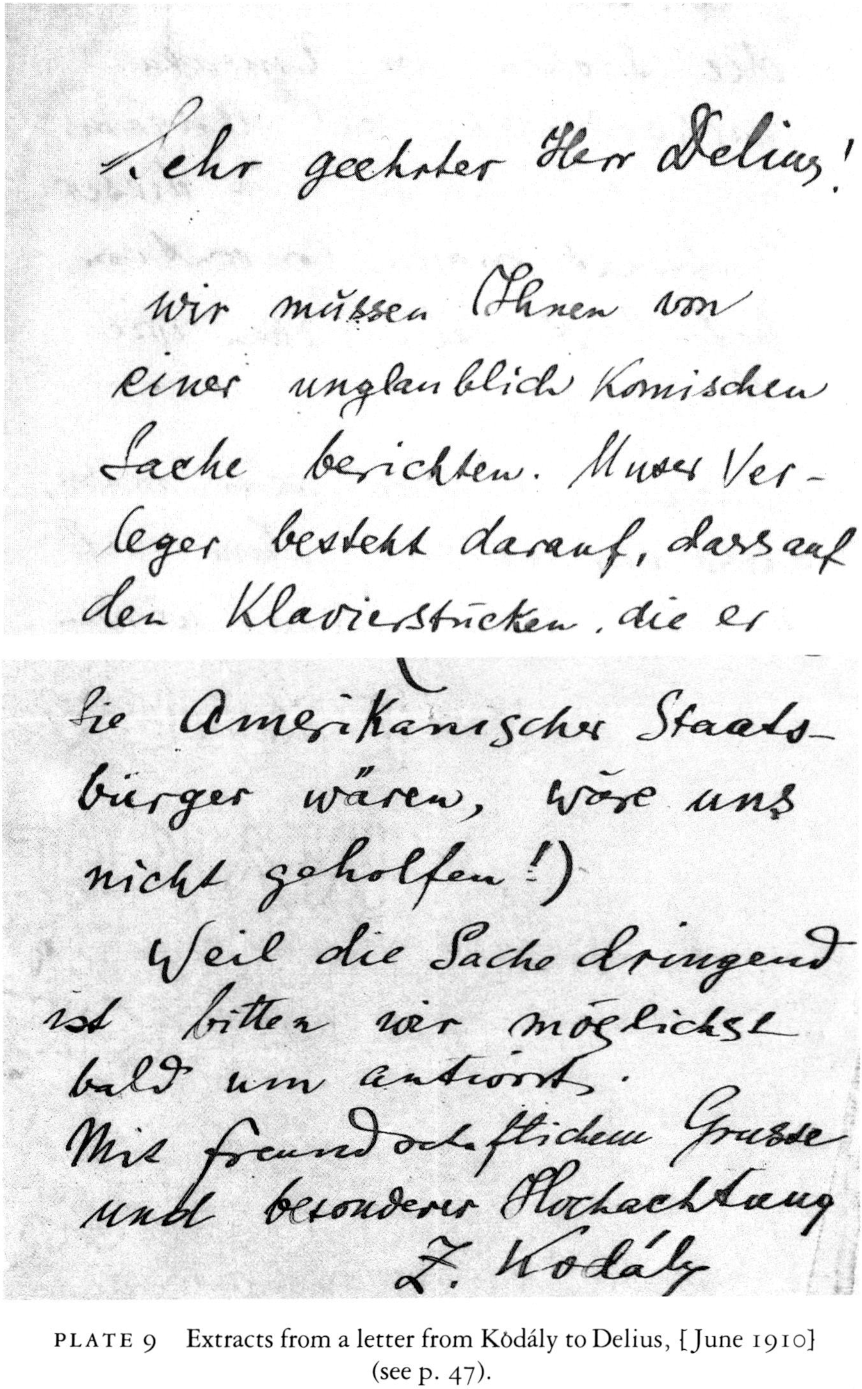

Sehr geehrter Herr Delius!

wir müssen Ihnen von
einer unglaublich komischen
Sache berichten. Unser Verleger besteht darauf, dass auf
den Klavierstücken, die er

sie Amerikanischer Staats-
bürger wären, wäre uns
nicht geholfen!)
Weil die Sache dringend
ist bitten wir möglichst
bald um antwort.
Mit freundschaftlichen Grüsse
und besonderer Hochachtung
Z. Kodály

PLATE 9   Extracts from a letter from Kodály to Delius, [June 1910]
(see p. 47).

PLATE 10   Percy Grainger and Nina Grieg.

PLATE 11   Frederick Delius, 1912, by Ida Gerhardi.
(*Gerhardi/Steinweg Collection.*)

PLATE 12   Frederick Delius, 1914.

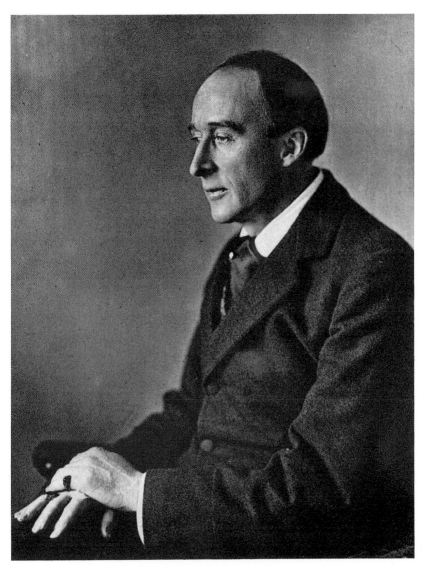

PLATE 13   Frederick Delius, 1914.

PLATE 14   Delius, Jelka, and Ida Gerhardi at the home of Consul Esser, Elberfeld, March 1914. (*Gerhardi/Steinweg Collection.*)

PLATE 15   Robert Phifer, from a portrait by Robert Brydon Jr.
(*Coll. Averett College, Danville.*)

PLATE 16   Thomas Beecham.

thing seems so sketchy – Besides, one cannot unite successfully Theatre & Concert performances –[1]

I am enjoying again excellent health – quite my old self again. I finished "Niels Lyhne"[2] a few days ago –

I shall probably come to England for the performance of the "Village Romeo & Juliet" – which Beecham is going to give again – as the last performance was given under such bad auspices – No piano scores, no text books etc – Old fashioned Regisseur. I shall however not stay more than a week & then go to Germany – Berlin & Leipzig – Vienna where they do the "Mass of Life" & then Tunis or Cairo for the rest of the winter – If the performance of R & J came off towards Xmas, I should of course come & see you & hear the Concerto.[3] I had a visit from Mr Burlingham Hill[4] of Boston who told me they were doing your "Omar" in Boston this winter – I was delighted to hear it –

My Editor only sent me 1 Score of Paris & Brigg Fair but I shall see him in Leipzig & try & get another one out of him for you –

What a mistake that the Committee of The Musical League decided not to give a Festival in 1911. The aim of the Society is to give a Festival every year & encourage Local Orchestras – If we dont give a Festival every year the whole thing is a failure –

How strange that all English Artistic undertakings turn out a failure – The wrong people get hold of it at once – However "tant pis" I have something else to do than to stir up English Apathy   I should so much like to read the Controversy between Newman & Bernard Shaw.[5] Send it me if you have it. I will return it to you faithfully –

With best love to you both
I remain

Yours ever
Frederick Delius

Autograph letter, signed and dated. Envelope addressed: Monsieur/Granville Bantock/Broadmeadow/Kings Norton/nr Birmingham/Angleterre. Postmark: GREZ 26 -10 10.

The original is in the Delius Trust Archive.

1   Delius's vice-presidency of the Musical League and his swift rise to fame in England since the performances late in 1907 of his Piano Concerto and *Appalachia* had brought about some unexpected offers. On 22 August, the music critic H. Bonnaire wrote from London: 'May I ask if you will be so good as to let me know whether you have any objection to acting as a member of the provisory Committee of the British Society of Composers which we have founded for the purpose of obtaining performing fees for composers?' There was another letter on 23 September outlining the possible composition of his committee and disclaiming any connection with the Society of British Composers. Two days later Delius wrote to Bantock: 'Who is Bonnaire? & the

British Society of Composers?' And two days later Bantock replied: 'The present members of the Committee appear to be Theatre & Music Hall Conductors & Composers, such as Paul Reubens, & Lionel Monckton. So I am not having any of it.'

There had been a similar proposal earlier in the summer, as we learn from a letter to Jelka, written when Delius was recuperating at Mammern: 'I got a letter from Manchester – informing me that a new Society had been formed to promote the performance of Modern music & that they had unanimously elected me a President.' It took him a day to decide, and he wrote to Jelka on 30 June: 'I am refusing the Presidentship of the Manchester Society – I have nothing to do with local musical affairs.'

2 *Fennimore and Gerda*: 'hear you have nearly completed your "Nils Lyhne,"' Bantock had written on 27 September.

3 Bantock had written on 27 September: 'I have put your Piano Concerto down for performance at the School at Xmas by one of the members of the Teaching Staff, who is a capital player.' There was to be no revival of *A Village Romeo and Juliet* until 1920.

4 Edward Burlingame Hill (1872–1960): American composer. A Harvard graduate, he taught piano in Boston as a young man, and at Harvard from 1908.

5 Correspondence conducted in the columns of *The Nation* on the subject of Strauss's *Elektra*.

(348)
Frederick Delius to Roger Quilter

Grez sur Loing
(Seine & Marne)
Oct 30 1910

Dear Quilter.

Many thanks for your kind & sympathetic letter[1] which gave me ever so much pleasure. I am so glad you liked "Brigg Fair" & that it was well done – I knew nothing of this performance – Who conducted? On the 7th of November you will hear "Sea-drift" – Kapellmeister Karl Schuricht – I should so much like to come but I am afraid that it is quite impossible. I shall most likely be in Germany end of November & if I am anywhere near Frankfort of course I shall come & join you & be present at Percy Grainger's concert –

My wife & I both send you our hearty greetings.

Sincerely yours
Frederick Delius

Autograph letter, signed and dated.

The original is in the Delius Trust Archive. Two other letters from Delius to Quilter are also preserved. The first is dated 19 April 1908, and the second was written in October 1929.

Roger Quilter (1877–1953): English composer, best known for his songs. He studied with Ivan Knorr in Frankfurt, where he was a contemporary of Gardiner, Grainger, O'Neill and Scott. He became a devoted friend of the Deliuses, but the relationship is scantily documented.

1   Quilter had written from Frankfurt to tell Delius of this unexpected performance of *Brigg Fair* which was conducted by Ludwig Rottenberg.

(349)
Béla Bartók to Frederick Delius

Budapest, Teréz-körút 17.IV.23.
[December 1910]

Dear Mr. Delius,

I would never have imagined that you would be ill again and in a sanatorium. Is this still a continuation of your illness in the summer? $2\frac{1}{2}$ years ago Kodály was in the same sanatorium, which he did not find very much to his liking – the atmosphere was not free enough for him. However he did not go because of any illness, but simply to build up his strength.

I hasten to send you some of our Rumanian tunes; perhaps you will get them while you are still in Dresden? Please keep this copy. I am curious to know what impression this distinctive music will make on you. Of course, many things ought to be heard either in the original or at least imitated in order to get the right mood. The tunes on the bagpipes in particular lose a lot of their grotesque individuality if they are only read. But then you may have already heard the bagpipes quite often, and so will easily be able to supply what is missing in the transcription.

I wonder whether you will be well enough to come on an excursion into the countryside if you come to Budapest in March? It would be a pity if we could not manage this, but on the other hand you must take too much care of yourself rather than too little.

Please write and give me news soon of an improvement in your health. This is something I wish for you.

Best regards,
Bartók

I will send the score to the address you gave me.

German typescript, undated, in the Delius Trust Archive.

On 4 November Delius left Grez for Frankfurt to hear Schuricht give *Sea Drift* on the 7th. From there he travelled to Cologne to meet Gerhard Tischer, who together with his wife joined Delius and Jelka at Elberfeld for a further performance of *Sea Drift* on the 12th, conducted by Haym. The Deliuses then left for a sanatorium at Weisser Hirsch, near Dresden, and Jelka wrote on 9 December to Tischer: 'Since we saw you and your dear wife in Elberfeld, we have been here the whole time for the cure and must still stay for some time, as my husband's nerves need a thorough rest.' This was a gloss on the real circumstances, as a recently discovered medical report written at Dr Lahmann's Sanatorium and dated 7 December 1910 describes some of the symptoms of tertiary syphilis and confirms that Delius had the disease. Jelka's brother Felix (who had spent a few days at Grez in the autumn) visited them at Dresden one day during the Christmas holidays to consult with Jelka on the best course of action, and advised her to take Delius to Wiesbaden and put him in the hands of a doctor there. A few days later Jelka wrote to another of her relatives: 'he is always suffering – up and down & I myself in great anxiety all the time . . . we have not really got any further than before . . . I myself do the cooking for him – as I have been doing all year in Grez . . . I have to conduct all the correspondence, to nurse him, walk with him, read to him – There is not much time left over for myself –'. She resumed the letter after a week, 'because Fred got shingles which pained him dreadfully for a whole week and still pains him. – Yes, I am terribly worried – and cannot think of anything else at all – This cure has only made him even thinner & more miserable.' After a seven-weeks' cure at Weisser Hirsch and a further stay at a nearby hotel, Delius left with Jelka for Wiesbaden around 21 January.

1911

The beginning of the year found Delius still in Dresden and still unwell. Friends were worried and pessimistic about his condition, and Joe Heseltine, in Marlotte, wrote to tell his nephew Philip in the spring that Delius was unlikely to live very long to enjoy his fame. Leaving the sanatorium, he stayed for a while in a hotel and then moved to Wiesbaden, where his condition gradually improved during February. He was not fit enough to travel to Berlin for a performance by Nikisch of *Brigg Fair* (Fritz Steinbach had conducted it in Cologne on 10 January), nor to Vienna, where *A Mass of Life* was given twice. However, much more important was that on 22 February he was able to write to Tischer from Wiesbaden: 'I am *much* better now & we are thinking of returning to Grez soon.' The return was effected on 7 March, and visitors to Grez later that month included Fritz Cassirer and then Thomas Beecham, who brought with him Lady Cunard.

In April Delius was 'putting the finishing touches' to *Fennimore and Gerda*. *Paris* had been given in London and Birmingham and *Sea Drift* in London, confirming that his major works were rapidly becoming common musical currency throughout Europe.

It was a lovely spring, and during the months of April and May much time was spent working and relaxing in the garden, a poignant contrast with the recent terrible winter months of chronic invalidism. Beecham came out to Grez again at the beginning of June, and on the 10th Delius travelled with him to London by car. He became ill on the journey, but recovered to undertake the social round in London, and to attend on 16 June Beecham's concert of his works at Queen's Hall, when he first met Philip Heseltine.

In the middle of July, the Deliuses travelled to Norway, staying for several weeks in the Rondane and Gudbrandsdal regions, Jelka painting, while her husband went walking. It was probably around the end of August that they returned to Grez. There was a brief visit to Elberfeld in October to hear Haym give the *Mass* for a second time. Even more ambitious plans were evidently discussed with Haym, as is clear from a letter that Philip Heseltine, newest and youngest of Delius's disciples, wrote to the composer on 25 November: 'I am looking forward immensely to the coming production of *A Village Romeo and Juliet* at Elberfeld. I shall attend every performance if I can, as I have long known and loved the piano score of it.' Nothing, unfortunately, came of this project. After Elberfeld, the rest of the year was spent at Grez. *An Arabesque* was completed (according to the manuscript dating) in the autumn; and *The Song of the High Hills* was then begun: 'I am working on a new choral work', Delius wrote to Heseltine on 4 December. This new friendship resulted in Heseltine's painter uncle Joe being invited over from Marlotte to dine with the Deliuses on New Year's Eve.

Fennimore and Gerda, opera (RT I/8). Completed, but further revision later.

'Chanson d'automne', song (Verlaine) (RT V/27).

Summer Night on the River, for small orchestra (RT VI/19).

An Arabesque for baritone solo, mixed chorus and orchestra (J. P. Jacobsen) (RT II/7). Autumn.

The Song of the High Hills, for orchestra and wordless chorus (RT II/6). Begun.

(350)
Thomas Beecham to Frederick Delius

Sunday
Jan. 15/11
Ritz Hotel,
Piccadilly,
London, W.

Dear Delius

I should have written long ago but until the end of the season I was over-whelmed with work. Then, unfortunately, during the last week, I fell very ill and have been in bed ever since in this hotel, as my house is in the hands of decorators and cleaners. I am feeling a little better now but shall not be really well again for some weeks. From a public point of view the last opera season has been a failure the audiences being absurdly inadequate – that is really the reason why I decided against reviving "The Village Romeo" this autumn:[1] I feel most strongly that a work like that needs everything in its favour for success – proper time for production and sympathetic audience. I think during the present year things will look up a little: all during the last, everything was under the shadow of old Edward's decease.

I am delighted to hear "Fennimore" is now finished and that you have dedi-cated it to me – it is very kind of you, old man, and I fully appreciate it. We will produce it here during this the coming season[2] – de luxe – with the real cast of singers for the job – I am picking them up by degrees – Whitehill I find to be excellent and I have a wonderful little soprano with a lovely voice, perfect style, (and a splendid musician) who sings everything, your music included, at sight – Maggie Teyte – she was formerly at the Opera Comique, Paris. I gave "Brigg Fair" twice at my concerts this Autumn and the Piano Concerto. In the Spring, I am doing the Mass of Life again, the Dowson Cycle and some of the other works I have already played.

It is possible that in April I may go to Paris with my orchestra – you should hear the beggars play *now* – the other day I did the "Heldenleben" of Strauss and at the first rehearsal they read the whole thing from beginning to end without a stop or any palpable slip whatsoever. They make "Brigg Fair" sound quite divine.

Yesterday I had a visit from Bantock who came to me as ambassador from Birmingham and all it's wealth of musical resources with a proposition which, when I am able shortly to tell you about it, will, I am sure, be of some amusement to you. It is a complete reversal of the state of things existent there in 1907, it now being a case of "come over into Macedonia and help us".[3] Well I do hope, old fellow, you will now get rapidly better and cease to worry any longer your anxious friends here – Love to your wife and self from us here.

Affectionately yours
T. B.

Autograph letter, initialled and dated, written on headed notepaper. Envelope addressed: Frederick Delius Esq/Villa Hohenzollern/Weisser Hirsch/Dresden/ Germany. Postmark: LONDON. W. JAN 16 11.

The original is in the Delius Trust Archive.

1   Beecham had announced his intention on 27 August 1910: 'I have included your "Village Romeo & Juliet" in the repertoire for the coming season at Covent Garden.' He hoped to give it in November and was anxious to repeat it, 'as I am convinced the *more it is* heard the *more it will be appreciated*.'

2   In fact Beecham was never to give *Fennimore*. He simply did not like the work.

3   Bantock was to write to Delius on 15 February: 'We had a capital performance of "Paris" under Beecham at our last Philharmonic Concert in Birmingham, and you will be glad to hear that Beecham will be our Conductor next season.'

(351)

Percy Grainger to Frederick Delius

Veendam. 26.1.*1911*.

My dear friend

I cant say how grieved I am to hear you are seedy   You are so precious & it is
so miserable to think of you wasting your time being ill. Do get nice & well &
let us have *lots of joyeous meetings* in London in the spring. I so long to see &
hear you again.

I never told you my deep delight at & thankfulness for your dedication of
Brigg Fair to me. I had no idea you intended doing so & I am overdelighted &
proud to see my name above that glorious poetic work.

I took the score with me to Mengelberg[1] the other day but was glad to hear
that he knew it well already.

God bedring[2] is the heartfelt wish of your

fond friend
Percy

Autograph letter, signed and dated, written on the headed notepaper of the Victoria
Hotel, Amsterdam. Envelope addressed: Herrn Frederick Delius/Hotel Guisisana/
Wiesbaden/Duitschland. Postmark: VEENDAM 26.1.11.

1   Willem Mengelberg (1871–1951): Dutch conductor. An early champion of
Mahler, he was, from 1895 to 1941, conductor of the Concertgebouw Orchestra,
Amsterdam. See letter 388, note 1.

2   Danish: *Get well soon*. Delius was now in Wiesbaden, where his health was gradually improving.

(352)

David Josef Bach to Frederick Delius

Arbeiter-Zeitung
Zentral-Organ der österreichischen
Sozialdemokratie   *Vienna*, 11 February *1911*

Dear Sir,

I have the honour to inform you that your work "Messe des Lebens" is to be
performed in Vienna on the 18th February this year in the large Musikvereins-
saal, and in fact before an audience of workers, who will come with the best
will in the world and free from all prejudice, so as to be readily receptive to
new artistic experiences.

If you would like to attend this performance in person, it would be a great pleasure to your audience, and perhaps to you too, in the satisfaction you would get from appearing before a responsive audience.

Yours faithfully
for the Committee of the
Workers' Symphony Concerts
Dr D. J. Bach

Typed letter, signed and dated, written in German on headed notepaper.

The original is in the Delius Trust Archive. It is the only letter from D. J. Bach to Delius that is preserved.

David Josef Bach (1874–1947): Austrian musicologist and critic. He instituted the Workers' Symphony Concerts in 1905 in Vienna, and wrote for the *Arbeiter-Zeitung*.

(353)
Béla Bartók and Zoltán Kodály to Frederick Delius

[Vienna, 18/19 February 1911]

We are about to return home to Budapest from the performance of the "Lebensmesse" which made a deep impression on us.[1] We all send you most sincere greetings.

Z. Kodály (& wife whom you met among others in Zürich)
Bartók

Autograph picture postcard: *Wien. Stefanskirche*, signed and undated, written in German; the pencilled message (in the hand of Kodály?) is signed by Kodály and Bartók. Addressed: Monsieur/Frederick Delius/Grez sur Loing/Département Seine et Marne/France. Readdressed: Frankfurter Str 16[?]/Wiesbaden/Allemagne. Postmark obscured. Receiving postmark: GREZ 20 -2 11.

The original is in the Delius Trust Archive.

1   So much so that Bartók was inspired to write an article (on Delius's use of the wordless chorus) in *Zeneközlöny*, Budapest, 14 (1911), pp. 340–2. (In English in *Béla Bartók Essays*, selected and edited by Benjamin Suchoff, Faber & Faber, 1976, pp. 449–50, as 'A Delius Première in Vienna'.)

(354)
Béla Bartók to Frederick Delius

Budapest, Teréz-körút 17.IV.23.
[27? March 1911]

Dear Mr. Delius,

Would you believe it, immediately after my return from Vienna I fell ill; and then something even worse happened to me: I was asked to play Liszt's E flat major concerto here — I had to practise again, and had to make my fingers come to life again after many months without practising. It is all over now — so I can write and tell you what it was that moved me most in the Mass. It was "der alte Mittag" and "O Mensch! gieb Acht". I wonder if you feel the same way. In their simplicity and poetry both these sections are intensely moving. Then the wordless choruses interested us greatly. We have heard nothing like it before. I think you are the first to have tried such an experiment. I think a lot more of this kind of thing, quite original effects, might be done. A pity that the Vienna Choral Society's planned concert in Budapest came to nothing. I heard that Brigg Fair was given rather a confused performance here. In this respect conditions here are quite impossible. Just now some of us are endeavouring to establish a permanent first-class concert orchestra. — For as things are here now, we can never get a decent orchestral performance.

If our plan does not succeed, I must resign myself to the fact that I shall not hear my things (those I intend to write) performed for many years — for rather no performance at all than a discreditable one which says nothing either to the public or to the composer. I have now begun a difficult task — that is to say a one-acter.[1] I have never written songs before — you can imagine how much and how often — at the beginning — the text bothered me. Now things are already going better. And I think the music is the sort you will like. This summer I am going to Paris (around 20 June). I wonder if you will still be at home then? How I should like to show you this work of mine!

I have not yet sent the 2nd Suite to Elberfeld. I have a new orchestral work (in 2 movements).[2] If you should still be in France when I arrive, I would very much like to discuss with you which of these might be the more suitable for Elberfeld.

And how are you? Have you found the tranquillity necessary for your work? And what are you working on?

I am so afraid that you will reply to me from a sanatorium again. Please set my mind at ease as soon as possible.

With best wishes

Yours
Bartók

German typescript, dated, in the Delius Trust Archive.

1   *Bluebeard's Castle*, op. 11.

2   *Two Pictures*, op. 10.

(355)
Jelka Delius to Adine O'Neill

Grez sur Loing
S. et M.
28.3.1911

Deares[t] Adine –

Yes it is awful and horrid that I did not write before to thank you for your dear long letter and nice article on Paris and all your papers – You see, I meant to write *not* a card but a nice letter and never could get leisure. Your card dated 21st only left London on the 27th and I just received it.

We are back here again since 7th of March, and Fred is now very much better – but still he needs constant care and looking after and I am by nature so anxious for him – I engaged servants from Wiesbaden by announcing in the papers of Seine et Marne and without seeing them. So I have a ménage, and they seem quite satisfactory, but I had to teach all our way of cooking, serving etc; and so was constantly busy. The cure in Dresden only made Fred worse – awfully thin and haggard and he only picked up in Wiesbaden and everybody thinks he looks very well now. He is working again and we take nice walks. He had quite overrated his nerves with all those beastly performances and I was quite glad that Beecham did not do an opera of his this winter – and he could rest. –

The Cassirers came the other day on their way back from Birmingham, where he seemed to have been very successfull.[1] They had heard that Beecham was so ill – but I suppose he is better, as he wrote from Paris yesterday and is coming out here on friday.[2] My friend Miss Gerhardi is in London and heard Sea-Drift and thought it went rather well. Did you hear it? It was a concert of english Composers I suppose? I see they also did something of R. Quilter's. And how are you both? Flourishing – I hope – and you looking charming in tight pretty little dresses. I shd love to see you in them! I have not been able to think of clothes at all, in all this trouble, and cannot go to Paris before this woman is safe with the cooking. Tant pis! It does'nt matter here. Otherwise we live so alone that we know nothing and can only hope for another dear letter from you. And Beecham may tell us some news. I hear he is engaged for all Birmingham Concerts for next winter!! Cassirer was trying in vain to grasp the "dessous" of the Birmingham Musical politics. And how about Manchester? Whom will they take as a chef d'orch?

How is Balfour? Is he back again? Please give him our love –

That wretched Mrs Stoop did not engage you for an at home – as I wanted her to –

Freds Mass of life was given with great success in Vienna twice, the second evening Populäres Konzert, every seat was taken. He is now correcting the proofs of the Dowson Cyclus, edited by Leuckart and called Songs of Sunset. I translated the poems into german – which was fearfully difficult. His "Summer Garden" is also in print. Susan Metcalfe sang his songs at the Stoops the other day. Is she good?

Best love and wishes for all success, dear girl – and make the most of the Sunshine – always. Many kind messages to you and Norman from Fred and me.

Yrs affe ly
Jelka D.

Excuse horrid blots.

Autograph letter, signed and dated.

The original is in the Delius Trust Archive.

1   The last extant letter from Cassirer to Delius is dated 20 March: he was seriously considering giving up conducting to become a writer (and was indeed soon to do so), but nonetheless had an engagement to conduct in Birmingham in November.

2   Beecham asked to bring 'a friend and the most complete admirer of your music, Lady Cunard', in a note written to Delius from the Hotel Campbell, Paris, on 27 March.

(356)
Frederick Delius to Granville Bantock

Grez sur Loing
11 April 1911

Dear friend – I was so glad to hear from you again & learn something of the English affairs – I am very glad that you are going to conduct "Appalachia" in Manchester & I am sure you will give an excellent performance of it – So they are going to have an International Congress in London! This is the first I hear of it & if it is in the hands of the well known English Genii – Parry, Stanford – MacKenzie & Co – It will no doubt be a great success & will *interest* the foreigners. I advise them, however, to provide tea & buns – The musical League I suppose is dead, & will only live on in the salary of the undersecretary McNaught's son – No! I am afraid artistic undertakings are impossible in England – The country is not yet artistically civilized – There is something hopeless about English people in a musical & artistic way, to be frank, I have entirely lost my interest & prefer to live abroad & make flying visits – I shall be over in June for the "Mass of Life" & then I hope to be able to run up to Birmingham & see you – or perhaps you will come up to London to me[1] – This time, if you can, you must hear the "Mass". I am putting the finishing touches to Niels Lyhne – My choral work of Dowsons Poems – "Songs of Sunset" is being published by Leuckart – I passed a rotten winter in a Sanatorium, eating only an apple for breakfast in the morning – starving & walking about naked in the snow – needless to say I composed nothing & got very thin & weak – I am much better now, thank goodness! – I only possess 1 copy of Paris or should have sent it you long ago – Leuckart is very mean – I will however, write & try to get another copy for you – What is your new Choral Work? Write me soon again – My wife joins me in sending you both our best love –

Ever yours
Frederick Delius

Remember me kindly to Newman –

Autograph letter, signed and dated. Envelope addressed: Granville Bantock Esq/ Broadmeadow/Kings Norton/near Birmingham/Angleterre. Postmark: GREZ 12 -4 11.

The original is in the Delius Trust Archive.

1 Bantock records in his diary that he met Delius in London on 16 June, and attended the all-Delius concert given by Beecham that evening. Two days later he lunched with Delius, Beecham and Tcherepnin at the National Liberal Club.

(357)
Philip Heseltine to Frederick Delius

Eton College
June 17th, 1911

Dear Mr. Delius,

I feel I must write and tell you how very much I enjoyed your concert last night,[1] though I cannot adequately express in words what intense pleasure it was to me to hear such perfect performances of such perfect music. I hope you will not mind my writing to you like this, but I write in all sincerity, and your works appeal to me so strongly – so much more than any other music I have ever heard – that I feel I cannot but tell you what joy they afford me, not only in the hearing of them, and in studying vocal scores at the piano (which until last night was my only means of getting to know your music), but also in the impression they leave, for I am sure that to hear and be moved by beautiful music is to be influenced for good – far more than any number of sermons and discourses can influence.

It was extremely kind of you to see me in the interval, especially as you had so many friends to talk to. I am most grateful to you for allowing me to make your acquaintance, and I shall value it very highly.

If you would be so kind as to do me the honour of a visit in Mr. Beecham's motor, as you suggested, I should be overjoyed to see you and Mr. Beecham any Tuesday, Thursday or Saturday afternoon, this or next month, and I will show you everything you may wish to see in Eton and Windsor.

I was immensely struck by Mr. Beecham's magnificent conducting: I have never seen him conduct in a concert hall before, though I was lucky enough to hear him do all three Strauss operas. I am so glad the concert was such a success.

I cannot thank you enough for allowing me to meet you and for the most glorious evening I have ever spent.

Believe me,

Your very sincere admirer
[Philip Heseltine]

From Cecil Gray: *Peter Warlock: A Memoir of Philip Heseltine*, London, Cape, 1934, pp. 39–40. This would appear to be the first letter of a substantial correspondence between Heseltine and Delius.

Philip Heseltine (1894–1930): English composer, critic and author, later known as Peter Warlock. He was at this time a schoolboy at Eton, where he was studying music – in particular any scores of Delius that he could lay his hands on. During May he had spent much of his time transcribing *Brigg Fair* for two pianos. Family letters of 1908 show that he was already then aware of Delius; and by fairly early in 1910, at the age of fifteen, he had developed an interest in and appreciation of the composer's work through studying scores. On 18 June 1911 he wrote to his mother after hearing Delius for the first time played by an orchestra: 'the recollections of that music and the impression they made haunt me, and the more I study the score of *Songs of Sunset* the more wonderfully beautiful they seem to me – standing absolutely apart from any other music in their loveliness.' For most of his life he was to remain Delius's most ardent – and helpful – disciple.

1   On 19 May Beecham had announced to the composer his plans for the all-Delius concert of 16 June: he would give the *Songs of Sunset* (first performance), *Appalachia*,

Paris, and the Entr'acte from *A Village Romeo* ('I will give the "Mass" a little later on'). And writing from Paris on 28 May, shortly before visiting Grez, he told the composer: 'I shall probably include the Dance Rhapsody in the Programme.' While Jelka took the train to London for the concert, Delius travelled in Beecham's car. Ida Gerhardi, also in London, went to fetch him some time after his arrival: 'He had already become ill early on in the journey, dragged himself with his last reserves of energy into the car and into the house, straight to bed.' (Letter to Lilli Gerhardi, 11 June 1911.)

(358)
Frederick Delius to Philip Heseltine

9, HANS PLACE,
S.W.
[20 June 1911]

Dear Mr Heseltine

Let me thank you for your appreciation & sympathetic letter which gave me the greatest pleasure – If it is possible to arrange it I will come down to Eton this week with Mr Beecham. If I should not be able to do so I should be delighted if you would visit me in Grez[1] – Please remember me very kindly to your mother &
Believe me

Very sincerely yours
Frederick Delius

Autograph letter, signed and undated, written on headed notepaper. Envelope addressed: Philip Heseltine Esqre/ c/o H. Brinton Esqre/Eton College/Windsor. Postmark: London N.W. Jun 20 11.

The original is in the British Library. It is the first in a collection of over two hundred communications written by Delius and Jelka to Heseltine until the year of his death, 1930. (Add. MSS. 52547/8/9.)

1   Philip would be able to stay with his uncle, Arthur ('Joe') Heseltine, in Marlotte, a neighbouring village. In October 1909 he had written to his uncle to ask for Delius's autograph.

(359)
Béla Bartók to Frederick Delius

[Paris, mid-July 1911]

Dear Mr. Delius,

I very much fear that I have arrived here too late and that you will no longer be in Grez.[1] However, if you are, please write to let me know whether I can come out to visit you on Friday or Saturday. My address in Paris is:

Hotel des Voyageurs, 93 B^d Strasbourg.

I have found out about trains from the timetable; but I need your exact address to be able to find your house.

However, if this letter should find you no longer at home, please write a few lines to me at my own home (My address is no longer Budapest etc., but *Rákoskeresztúr nyaraló, Hungary*) to let me know how you are, how things went in England, where I hear your opera was performed.

I was too busy to get away before the middle of July; in spite of all I did not manage to finish the compositions I wrote to you about recently; so I came to Paris empty-handed. Until we meet again, perhaps quite soon.

With best wishes

Yours
Béla Bartók

German typescript, undated, in the Delius Trust Archive.

1   Bartók was indeed just too late: the Deliuses sailed on 15 July from Antwerp for a holiday in Delius's 'dear old Norway'.

(360)
Thomas Beecham to Frederick Delius

Hotel Belmont
FORTY-SECOND ST.
AND PARK AVENUE
(OPPOSITE GRAND CENTRAL STATION)
New York
Sept 19th/11

Dear Delius

Here I am, a curious pilgrim in this extraordinary country – Up to the present I cannot for the life of me understand what all this din and talk about the United States means – Everything moves twice as slowly as elsewhere, the people appear to be doubly as barbaric and to make matters worse, one pays twice as much for every trivial necessity or comfort – There are no buildings worth looking at, not a single first-rate picture in the art-galleries, and generally an impression of vast waste of time, energy and resources –

What particular field there may be for my endeavours, I do not yet know – But there is just a possibility of my returning here in December and conducting some Concerts and Opera performances in New York, Boston and Chicago. I should like to do something here, as I feel I could stir them up a bit, but it must be under satisfactory conditions – I have arranged my season in Paris next May, and think that it should be in every way successful – (I give several concerts as well –) I have also recently accepted another post at Cardiff and Swansea where they have an orchestra of ninety – Still, none of these plans give me very much pleasure either in anticipation or fulfilment – It is not that I am tired of making them, but in the present very imperfect state of musical civilisation, there has to be so much alloy mixed up with a very little genuine gold. I am leaving here on September 30th and shall be in London again on Oct. 6th. I was so disappointed at not being able to come to Norway,[1] but I have had the most harassing business affairs to attend to all the Summer – I am feeling much better than I was when I last saw you – Then I was and for some time previous I had been in a very indifferent state – I hope all is well with you and your wife – Love to you both

Ever yours
Thomas Beecham –

Autograph letter, signed and dated, written on headed notepaper. Envelope addressed: Frederick Delius Esq/Grez-sur-Loing/Seine-et-Marne/France. Postmark: GRAND CENTRAL, STA. N.Y. SEP 20 1911. Receiving postmark: GREZ 1 -10 11.

The original is in the Delius Trust Archive.

1   The Deliuses spent several summer weeks in Norway at Lauvaasen Høifjelds-Sanatorium and Golaa Høifjelds-Sanatorium in Gudbrandsdalen. They had corresponded with Nina Grieg, who looked forward to entertaining them at Troldhaugen around the middle of August – a plan which had to be abandoned when Beecham announced, around the beginning of August, his imminent arrival in Gudbrandsdalen. This was for the purpose of discussing a projected London performance of *A Mass of Life*, but the visit was shortly called off, Beecham having after all to stay in England. Delius's health was much improved: 'I take long walks paa Vidderne & find it wonderful,' he wrote to Nina Grieg on 26 July; Jelka was painting and the weather was splendid. He hoped, writing later, to take 'a little tour' in the Jotunheim mountain region. It seems not to be recorded whether he and Jelka did stop as planned in Thisted, Denmark, on their way home at the end of August or early September, 'where my wife wants to make some sketches for the scenery of *Niels Lyhne*' (letter to Percy Grainger, 11 July 1911).

(361)

Frederick Delius to Philip Heseltine

Grez-sur-Loing
S & M
26 Nov 1911

Dear Mr Heseltine

I return you by the same post your transcription of "Brigg Fair"[1] – I have looked at it carefully again & find it exceedingly well done – In several places there are notes missing – & at times you might have made it rather fuller – With 2 pianos one need make no restrictions   One ought at times, I think, to interpret rather freely in order to try & regive the orchestral effect – Let me know how you are getting on & what the professors give you to do – I suppose they are still teaching in the old, old fashion[2] – Never lose your own criticism & dont be *imponirt*[3] & above all write as *much as possible* –

Sincerely yrs
Frederick Delius

Autograph letter, signed and dated. Envelope addressed: Monsieur/Philip Heseltine/ pr adr Fräulein Bussius/Brüsseler Str 98/Cologne/Allemagne. Postmark: GREZ 26 -11 11.

The original is in the British Library.

The Deliuses had made a further major excursion from Grez since their Norwegian holiday. This time it was to Germany, where they attended, from 20–22 October, the Centenary Festival of the Elberfeld Choral Society, an event which also commemorated the fiftieth anniversary of the foundation of the Elberfeld Concert Society. *A Mass of Life*, conducted by Haym, was the main work of the opening concert, by all accounts receiving an inspired performance.

1   See note to Letter 357; the unpublished manuscript is now in the British Library (Add. MS 57966).

2   Heseltine had left Eton in the summer and was now spending the autumn studying music at Cologne.

3   German: (*over-*)*impressed*.

(362)
Frederick Delius to Philip Heseltine

Grez sur Loing
S & M
4 Dec 1911

Dear Mr Heseltine

Thank you so much for your warm & sympathetic letters which gave me the greatest pleasure – I am so glad you like the sound of Brigg Fair & am sorry you did not hear it conducted in a better way[1] – What you say is perfectly correct – One must beat one in a bar – 3 makes me shudder – Then again the slow section can scarcely be taken slow enough – The maestoso section must be taken solemly & not hurried – In other words it seems to have been a miserable performance! It would interest me to read Clutsam's articles if you possess them.[2] I do not believe in any music constructed knowingly on any Harmonic Scheme whatsoever. All the people who write about the Harmonic system or try to invent other systems quarter tones etc. Dont seem to have anything to say on Music – Systems are put together from the compositions of in-spired musicians   Harmony is only a means of expression which is gradually developing – I dont believe in learning Harmony or counterpoint – There is no piano score of the "Summer Garden" as yet or of the "Dance Rhapsody"[3] Do one of them for 2 pianos – & I will hear it when I next come to Germany – perhaps in March – Send on the pieces you have orchestrated & I will be very glad to help you – You have a great talent for Orchestration – that I could see from the 2 pieces you showed me – We should be delighted to come & see you in Wales & we will try and arrange it for next September – or August – I should just love to see Wild Wales again & of course you must be there to shew it me – I think it is absurd that your teacher only gives you finger exercises – I would simply tell him you did not come to Cologne for that purpose – If I were you I would go to the best Theorist in Cologne & learn what you can from him – As a writer & critic it may be of some use to you, as a composer none whatever – It is of no importance whether you write at the piano or not – As long as you *feel* you want to Express some emotion – *music is nothing else –*

I am working on a new choral work[4] – You must have thought very much about Brigg Fair – as on the 25th I was quietly reading in my room when, suddenly, I could only think of Brigg Fair & I was obliged to get up & play it thro & the rest of the evening it quite haunted me – Telepathy![5] Write me soon again

& Believe me

very sincerely yours
Frederick Delius

Autograph letter, signed and dated. Envelope addressed: Herrn Ph. Heseltine/p.a. Frl Bussius/Brüsseler Str 98^{III}/Cologne/Allemagne. Postmark: GREZ 5 -12 11.

The original is in the British Library.

1   Heseltine heard *Brigg Fair* in Coblenz on 24 November: 'it is absolutely marvellous!' In his letter to Delius of the following day (reproduced *in extenso* in Gray: *Peter Warlock*, pp. 40–43), he nonetheless queried faulty tempi in the performance.

2   Gray does not include the original reference to Clutsam, who was music critic for *The Observer* 1908–18.

3   Heseltine had proposed making a piano score of *In a Summer Garden* or 'any other work' that Delius might suggest.

4   *An Arabesque* is dated Autumn 1911 in manuscript; the published score, like that of *The Song of the High Hills*, bears the date 1911.

5   'As a matter of fact,' ran Heseltine's reply on 10 December, 'I spent the whole evening of the 25th writing my first letter to you which . . . contained my description of the Coblenz concert . . . I think it was undoubtedly telepathy, in which I believe very strongly.'

1912

News came from Grainger at the beginning of the year: 'It was lovely to hear a lot of schwärmerei for your works in Frankfurt & to learn what a fine performance the Rühlsche gave of S-Drift.' Delius in his turn was able to secure for his friend a concert engagement in Elberfeld in March. Meanwhile, *In a Summer Garden*, in its recently revised form, was performed by Stransky on 25 and 26 January in New York at Philharmonic Society concerts. Delius himself, declining an invitation to hear Bantock perform *Appalachia* with the Hallé on 25 January, was evidently preoccupied with his work on *The Song of the High Hills*. 'I have been very busy with a new work,' he wrote to Heseltine on 24 February. 'I suppose the new choral work will be ready soon,' was Heseltine's response four days later. However, more travels intervened. The Deliuses left Grez on 12 March for Berlin, where Oskar Fried was to give *Paris*; they continued to Munich and thence to Venice, holidaying there for part of April. The principal reason for the visit to Munich was to see Jadassohn and to come to some sort of arrangement with the publishing firm of Harmonie, with whom Delius had for so long been in dispute. Arriving for the agreed meeting, Delius found that Jadassohn had left for Berlin. Delius angrily arranged another appointment, which would necessitate his stopping off again at Munich on his way home from Venice. This time he arranged for his Berlin accountant also to be present. Again Jadassohn disappeared before the agreed meeting, and after examining some of Harmonie's books in relation to the company's dealings with Delius, the accountant agreed that Jadassohn was probably a swindler and advised Delius to go to law. The composer turned to his legal kinsman in Berlin, Franz Heinitz, and the wheels of justice started slowly to turn. Jadassohn did not respond to Heinitz's letters, but by the time steps had been taken to bring him to court, the war had begun and the matter, like so many others, fell into abeyance.

Meanwhile, what Delius had missed in England was a London performance, conducted by Balfour Gardiner on 13 March, of the *Dance Rhapsody*. This was given at the first of a series of four spring concerts sponsored and part-conducted by Gardiner, concerts which were largely devoted to unfamiliar works by British contemporaries. Wherever possible, the New Symphony Orchestra was conducted by the appropriate composer.

The Deliuses were back in Grez on 24 April, and before long composition of *The Song of the High Hills* was resumed: 'I am at work on a new work Chorus & Orchestra' was the message to Bantock on 10 June. Jelka, meanwhile, was painting.

On 8 August Delius informed Theodor Szántó: 'The Universal Edition has taken over all my works published by Harmonie.' And on the 15th the Deliuses travelled to Arcachon, on the Atlantic coast, where they stayed for nearly a month. On returning to Grez a temporary indisposition caused Delius to postpone for seven days a trip to London originally scheduled for 22 September. He was nonetheless in England in time to hear a performance of *Sea Drift* at the Birmingham Festival, soon followed by the *Dance Rhapsody* and the Piano Concerto in London. He was puzzled about the 'persuasion' Wood had apparently needed to use on the Festival Committee to get *Sea Drift* performed, and wrote to Bantock on 3 June: 'When, I wonder, will they give the 'Mass of Life' at an English Festival – They are even giving it in several American towns next season & in Berlin, Munich – Hagen & Hamburg – Oh! my Country!' He was back in Grez on 12 October, only to be off again a month later, this time to Germany, where Fried was to give the newly-revised *Lebenstanz* in Berlin. Settled once more in Grez in mid-December, Delius told Heseltine: 'I cannot tell you how glad I am to be back here again . . . I want to work now so am afraid I shall not be in England before the "Mass" is given.' Heseltine himself had begun his labours of love; he had arranged, at Balfour Gardiner's request, *In a Summer Garden* as a piano duet. And by October he had made a piano arrangement of *Lebenstanz*.

The year had also seen the final parting of the ways of Delius and his Florida plantation. On 22 January Solana Grove was sold to Hans Haym (whose son Rudolf was to try his hand at farming it), with Delius and Jelka signing a warranty deed in Paris before the American Consul-General.

The Song of the High Hills (RT II/6). Completed.

Lebenstanz, symphonic poem for large orchestra (RT VI/15). Revised.

On hearing the first Cuckoo in Spring, for small orchestra (RT VI/19).

(363)
Thomas Beecham to Frederick Delius

Feb 9/12
32, UPPER HAMILTON TERRACE,
N.W.

Dear Delius

I have been so busy lately or would have written to you before – I am[1] giving the "Entr'acte" from "Romeo" at Birmingham – next Wednesday, and on March 7th, the "Dance Rhapsody" at Manchester. I have done the Piano Concerto twice this season, and on both occasions it was a great success. Last December I gave "Brigg Fair" at Liverpool, and everyone was very pleased with it – All this to let you know that I am not forgetting you – I shall be giving either the "Dance Rhapsody" or "Paris" in a week or two in London –

I have just floated a new opera scheme for the coming Winter about which I will write you later – It is on a better and larger scale than anything I have yet attempted – All musical affairs here are very bad, – less with me however than with others – I do not see how most of the existing institutions can possibly continue – I am giving a work of Grainger at my next concert (Sunday) – it is scored for the orchestra in the most abominable way you can possibly imagine –[2]

I shall be passing through Paris on my way to Italy about the beginning of April, and will come to see you then –

I am in better health now than I was last year. Stronger and more tranquil – I have been with Lady C–[3] today and we talked a good deal about you –

Love to you both

Yours
T. B.

Autograph letter, initialled and dated, written on headed notepaper. Envelope addressed: Frederick Delius/Esq/Grez-sur-Loing/Seine-et-Marne/France. Postmark: LONDON.N.W. FEB 10 12.

The original is in the Delius Trust Archive.

1   The original has *have* for *am*.

2   *English Dance*.

3   Maud, Lady Cunard, née Burke (1872–1948): American-born society hostess and patron of the arts. She married Sir Bache Cunard, a grandson of the founder of the shipping line, in New York in 1895, from which time she lived mainly in England. Long an intimate of the novelist George Moore, she became Beecham's mistress in 1911, the year of her separation from her husband. She changed her Christian name to Emerald in 1926.

(364)
Percy Grainger to Frederick Delius

[London] 18.2.12.

My dear Delius

Beecham did your entr'acte music to "Romeo & J" today just before my piece.
I never loved anything more in my life. You are certainly the greatest living
genius & one of the greatest & most adorably touching souls that ever lived.
I find that stuff of yours *perfect* in every deepest sense. Beecham did my thing
like a *God*.[1] Lots of it is imperfectly scored, but lots comes off well.

Your loving & thankful friend
Percy

Autograph letter, signed and dated.

The original is in the Grainger Museum.

1   'As for Beecham,' wrote Grainger, just three days earlier, 'he is a *genius* from top to
toe in my English Dance just as he is in your adorable things. He would do it *perfectly*
if only the orchestral parts were not so badly copied.'

(365)
Frederick Delius to Tischer & Jagenberg

Ebereschenallee 7
Westend – Berlin[1]
20.3.1912

Dear Herr Doktor,

In reply to your kind letter I sent you both my scores by registered post today
& ask you to acknowledge receipt by postcard *at once*.
    I would really very much like to have my works published by you, but as I
said, I must have a good fee now, as my works are, after all, now being played
everywhere.
    I therefore require a sole payment of 5000 Mk for the "Dance of Life"[2] &
4000 for the Arabeske. If you want to have the 5 songs too, then 1000 Mk for
these.
    I consider the "Dance of Life"[2] really to be my best orchestral work. I have
had it in my file for some years now, as the ending did not quite satisfy me;
but at last I have found what I was looking for & it is now a fully mature work.

Please let me know your decision as soon as possible, for I have taken no other steps as yet.

With best wishes from both of us to all of you

Yours
Frederick Delius

Letter in the hand of Jelka Delius, signed by Frederick Delius, dated, written in German.

The original is in the Delius Trust Archive.

1   The Deliuses left Grez for Berlin on 12 March, '& shall be away about 18 days' (letter to Heseltine, 11 March). They subsequently visited Munich and then travelled to Venice, where they stayed at the *palazzo* rented by Lady Cunard. A postcard written to Tischer on 19 April indicates that Delius was about to leave Venice and return to Grez.

2   The original has *Tanz des Lebens*.

(366)
Frederick Delius to Philip Heseltine

Grez sur Loing
(S & M)
April 28 1912

Dear Heseltine –

Your letter was forwarded on to me – I received it in Berlin some 3 weeks ago where I had gone en route for Munich & Venice – Whilst in Berlin I heard "Paris" excellently given by Oskar Fried – your letter gave me the greatest pleasure & I am so glad that you look upon me as a real friend – long acquaintanceship means nothing whatever – You are just going thro' what I have also gone thro' & I own that until I had become an entire disbeliever in any Life here-after I was constantly in a very unsatisfactory state of mind – Read *Nietzsche* – the "Anti Christ" – "Beyond good & evil"[1] – Christianity is paralysing – If one is sincere it utterly unfits one for Life – If hypocritical one becomes hateful to oneself – And thenceforward one can only live amongst similar hypocrites – England & America have, I believe, the monopoly of such   The moment you chuck all this rot over board Life becomes interesting – wonderful – & one gets a great desire to make something of it – *to live it to its full*   One enjoys things more thoroughly – *one feels Nature* – there is no reason whatever for any doctrine or religion. Savages have superstitions which they form into a sort of religion & perform certain rites & we have nothing more with the exception that Priests invented a System to rule over Kings & the Kings used the system & the Priests to subdue the masses – the superstition often remains even when the belief in the System is gone – See table turning & spirit rapping etc – Be free – believe in Nature – it is quite enough & by far the most satisfactory standpoint – there is a great deal we do not understand – Every day one understands more – in a thousand years they will be considerably farther altho' I do not believe that certain things will ever be understood & why should they? – I cannot stand the moral atmosphere of England & therefore I live here – to send missions to China or Canada is merely ignorance & stupidity. – When I come to see you in September we will talk about these things – I am but a poor writer – I stayed 12 days in Venice at the Palazzo of Lady Cunard & enjoyed my stay altho' the weather was icy – The arrival at Venice at night & being fetched from the railway station in a gondola made a great impression on me – The celebrated paintings in the Churches & galleries with one or two exceptions I did not care for – I infinitely prefer modern painting to these old buffers with their saints, Jesuses & Virgin Marys – May I never see their faces again! I except a painting of the Crucifixion by Tintoretto – Musical Criticism is another fraud – Our critics are nearly always composers who have failed & who have become bitter – Every musician of genius brings something which belongs entirely to himself & cannot be criticised by miserable failures who have stuck fast & crystalised   Write to me soon again. I love receiving your letters – Our garden is too lovely just now & we were so happy to get back to Grez again   We arrived last Wednesday   Perhaps you will come over here in the summer   we should be delighted to see you here again. I remain, with best love, your sincere friend

Frederick Delius

Autograph letter, signed and dated. The date appears to be written 1911. Envelope addressed: Philip Heseltine Esqre/Chadlington/Oxfordshire/Angleterre. Postmark: GREZ [28 -4 12?]

The original is in the British Library.

1   Delius returned to the theme in a letter to Heseltine dated 23 June 1912: 'I consider Nietzsche the only free thinker of modern times & for me the most sympathetic one – He is at the same time such a poet. He feels nature. I believe, myself, in no doctrine whatever & in nothing but in Nature & the great forces of Nature – I believe in complete annihilation as far as our personal consciousness goes.'

(367)
Frederick Delius to Clare Delius Black

Grez sur Loing
S & M
21 May 1912

Dearest Clare –

You would do me the greatest favor by *not* giving a recital of my songs in
London –[1]

Firstly the songs are quite old – then a recital of songs in London only ought
to [be] undertaken by a quite first-class artist – You know very well that you
are only an excellent amenteur – & that the chief interest in the concert would
be that you are my sister – Which makes the whole affair ridiculous – & I am
quite sure that the less kind part of the Press will draw attention to this. If you
wish to take up singing professionally – which I think is a mistake as it is too
late – do so by all means – but do not try to "battre monnaie" by being my
sister & singing my old songs – I am not a song writer – Dont be hurt at what
I say – I have always liked you better than the others:– Please let me continue
to do so & do not do something which I should never forgive you for –

your affectionate
Fred

P.S.
It is the sort of "reclame" I loathe

Autograph letter, signed and dated.

The original is in the Delius Trust Archive. It is the fifth of fourteen communications
from Delius and Jelka to Clare, written between 1900 and 1934, that have been
found. An undated postcard from Delius postmarked 6 -9 12 is in the Jacksonville
University Library.

1   Clare mentions the episode in her book on her brother: 'I can give an illustration of
his meticulous conscientiousness where his music was concerned from my own experience. It was rather disappointing. I had been singing my brother's songs in the
West Riding with some success, and the proposal was made to me that I should give a
concert in London. Delighted with the prospect I wrote to Fred and told him what was
afoot. This was in 1912. By return of post I received a communication from Grez'
(Clare Delius: *Frederick Delius*, p. 177). Clare did sing some of her brother's songs at a
recital in Bradford on 3 December 1913.

(368)
Frederick Delius to Philip Heseltine

Grez sur Loing
S & M
27 July 1912

My dear Heseltine –

I had such a lot of work to do – correcting proofs etc – that I decided not to go to Norway this summer[1] – It would have been too late & I have not yet finished correcting proofs. We have hired a villa at Cap Ferret near Arcachon (on the coast) – from the 20th of August & we shall stay there, no doubt, until the end of September when I come to England for the Birmingham Festival.[2] Now, should I come to see you before the Festival or After? Which would suit you the best? Sea-drift is on October 3rd & I must no doubt be in Birmingham about the 30th of Sept or Oct 1. for the last Rehearsal – Referring to your last letter I want to tell you that Jesus – Nietzsche & Co are really the same natures – Earnest, ardent & sincere natures protesting against human fraud & humbug: & destroyers of doctrine – Neither of them had any system; both were destroyers – These sort of intense natures seem to appear periodically – & in all parts of the world – Jesus, coming at the time of the great Roman decadence – preached naturally the negation of life – Nietzsche, coming at the end of the Roman Catholic & Protestant church systems based on the negation of Life – preached Optimism & the affirmation of Life – When this has had a good innings something else will crop up – I do not find it depressing at all to look upon death as complete annihilation   It harmonises perfectly with my outlook on Life & I am an optimist & I love life in all its forms   What do you believe? I dont mean – what do you want to believe – but what you *really* believe – So many people either deceive themselves or never dare to think the matter out to the end – All that has been said about reincarnation – The higher spheres etc is simply childish – Our soul is simply our brain & nervous system & can be entirely destroyed before death – However enough of the subject – try to be yourself & live up to your nature – Be harmonious – Whatever ones nature be one ought to develop it to its utmost limits & not be constantly trying to become someone else or be constantly trying to cork up ones nature: this leads to continual dissatisfaction & to failure –

I shall stay here until August the 19th & then we go to Cap Ferret. The garden is lovely – but we are having quite a number of thunderstorms this summer –

Affectionately yrs
Frederick Delius

_____

Autograph letter, signed and dated.

The original is in the British Library.

1   Delius had indeed been busy: 'I am at work on a new work for Chorus &
Orchestra,' he wrote to Bantock on 10 June; and on the 23rd he told Heseltine: 'I am
working hard on a new Choral & Orchestral work & am already far advanced.' In the
same letter he announced his holiday project: 'At the end of next month I intend going
to Norway for a 3 weeks walking tour in the mountains – Doesn't it tempt you? I love
Norway & the Norwegian peasants.'

2   Henry Wood wrote on 24 May: he was pleased that he had been able to persuade
the Birmingham Festival committee to include *Sea Drift* in the programme. A week
later he asked '. . . would it be possible for you to direct the work in person, as
I should love you to give your own interpretation of it?' Letters to Bantock early in
June indicate that Delius was anxious about the order in which the works were to be
performed: 'On the Programme I see they have put it on the 4th day morning at the
very end of a 4 hours Concert – Who is responsible for this friendly act?' *Sea Drift*,
'unknown in Birmingham', he wrote, should be earlier in the programme: 'Brahms
Requiem – Beethoven Symphony   Scriabines Prometheus & Sea-drift – so it runs.'
The programmes were duly changed, *Sea Drift* being given on the third evening with
the Verdi Requiem.

(369)
Frederick Delius to Philip Heseltine

Villa La Brise
Cap Ferret
par Arcachon[1]
(Gironde) 22/8/1912

My dear Heseltine,

I am looking forward immensely to my visit to Wales. The scenery you
describe must be beautiful & I love that sort of scenery – I was born on the
Yorkshire moors & the love of the rough & solitary moorlands clings to me
still. I shall try to be with you about the 23rd or 4th of September – If it is
possible I should prefer to travel right thro' the same day: I dont care how early
I leave Paris – We shall stay here until the 14th or 15th of Sept & then return to
Grez – My wife will stay in Grez as she wants to paint a good deal this
Autumn – the summer has been abominable – The weather here is a little
better but very unsettled – The place is lovely – Our Villa is situated on the
bay of Arcachon in a pine forest & we have only to cross a strip of pine covered
land to reach the Atlantic ocean & sands running to the horizon on both sides
– There are no people here & we are entirely alone & undisturbed – Arcachon

is 10 hours from Paris & from Arcachon one has to take a boat (a small steamer) to Cap Ferret, a journey of another hour – so you see we are quite isolated – Bernard Shaw seems to me to be very much influenced by Nietzsche – Nietzsche seems to have given him the start – to have made him fruitful – But Nietzsche is ever so much deeper & ever so much more poetical & ever so much more daring – Bernard Shaw has a wonderfully clear mind but not much *feeling* – He is superficial like nearly all Irishmen – He is a clever – very clever polemist – Journalist – & what he *really* wants to do is to surprise you or make you laugh – or shock the "bourgeois" just enough to avoid being put in prison – And then again *he is no artist whatever* – He is the "Richard Strauss" of litterature – As soon as the problems his plays are written about are solved – or the abuses bettered – his plays will instantly become most uninteresting & worthless[2] – The *preface* is by far the best part of his play. I know nothing of his conception of Man or of the Life Voice[3] – Nietzsche does not want to reduce the lower order of mankind to slavery – They are in slavery & always have been in slavery, & will remain in slavery in spite of all theories to the contrary – The whole history of the world is the history of a few *individuals* – Coming back to our old subject let me assure you of one thing, & of this you may be *perfectly certain* – In the year 2200 your self conciousness will be in exactly the same state as it was in 1820 – *your ego* – I believe in the Eternal recurrence of nothing whatever – Eternal change of matter is more likely – Let me know all about the trains – & believe me

yrs affectionately
Frederick Delius

P.S. I should certainly like to enjoy good health & live for 3 or 400 years at least – Life is so interesting to me –

Autograph letter, signed and dated. Envelope addressed: Philip Heseltine Esqre/ Newbold Pacey Vicarage/Warwick/Angleterre. Postmark: ARCACHON GIR-ONDE 23 -8 -12.

The original is in the British Library.

1   'We travel on the 15th inst to Arcachon,' wrote Delius to Szántó on 8 August.

2   Heseltine would appear to have questioned his friend's judgment, as Delius, some three weeks later, took a careful step backwards: '. . . consider that I have a fairly good opinion of Shaw to compare him to Strauss – Strauss is a wonderfully clever musician & has left his mark on his epoch – He is wanting in Soul & poetry & so is Shaw – They both interest me very much & I think Shaw extremely amusing, witty & clever – But I would not compare him to Ibsen or Nietzsche – I know lots of Englishmen who would like to be compared with Strauss.'

3   Presumably 'Life Force'.

(370)
Frederick Delius to Philip Heseltine

Grez sur Loing
S & M
24/9/12

My dear Heseltine —

Your 2 letters & the Musical Standard arrived this morning — I have just got up & feel much better[1] — but am afraid that I shall not be able to leave here before next Sunday — I feel terribly disappointed that I could not come to Wales & walk about the moors with you — I might perhaps be able to come for a day or 2 after the Festival if I feel alright — We will talk about it in Birmingham — Your Article on Schönberg[2] is very good & fair — I know nothing of his music & am very keen to hear or see something — *Bring what you have to Birmingham* & we will go thro' it together — Bring also your arrangement of "In a summer garden", which I want you to lend me for a short while   I want to hear it & also to lend it to a musician in Frankfort who wants to play it. I like your attitude towards music so much; your mind is so open — Of course the attitude of the critics is always stupid — Critics as a rule are musicians who have failed   I know no exceptions. Clutsam is a man who for 25 years has tried to imitate every musician of repute & every style — Hoping by so doing to have a success — He has imitated from an American Coon song up to the 2 popular Composers Debussy & Strauss & music of all description — But he himself (Clutsam) is a dead failure & he knows it — I mention Clutsam because he is an intelligent composer — the others are merely rotters — English rotters — which means rather more rotten than any other country's bar American — In no other country is there such talk about British composers etc. British music as a rule wont stand crossing the Channel — Music is a matter of temperament — Emotional music will be understood at once by emotional people — Intellectual music will be liked & understood by intellectual people & so on & soforth — I dont believe in the music you have to get accustomed to — That is what puts me out about Schönberg — you say yourself you cannot make head or tail of it — The attitude of reserving ones opinion vis a vis a new form of art is not always the best one, altho' it is the wisest one — we have to thank "the reserving ones opinion attitude" for some of the most idiotic expressions of art — *The Futurists & the Cubists.* The public have become funky about giving their opinion — because the critics have made such terrible blunders — & quite a number of sensation seeking — opportunistic artistic rotters are taking advantage of it — I never once remember having made a mistake vis a vis a new work of music[3] — When I first heard Chopin as a little boy of 6 or 7, I thought heaven had been opened to me — When also as a little boy — I first heard the Humoresken of Grieg — a new world was opened to me again – When at the age of 23 I heard Tristan – I was perfectly overcome – also when I heard Lohengrin as a schoolboy. Beethoven always left me cold & reserved – Bach I always loved more – it seemed to me more spontaneous – Brahms I never liked much & never shall – it is philistin music – altho' some of the chamber music is good – But to have to get accustomed to music is a fearfully bad sign – The sort of people who get accustomed to music are the unmusical & when once accustomed to it they will hear no other – All the music critics have got accustomed to music – to their great composer – I shall leave London for Birmingham on Oct 1ˢᵗ morning: I go to the Queen's Hotel & hope to see a lot of you –

Remember me to your mother most kindly
Believe me

Affectionately yours
Frederick Delius

Autograph letter, signed and dated. Envelope addressed: Philip Heseltine Esqʳᵉ/Cefn-Bryntalch/Abermule/Montgomeryshire/Angleterre. Postmark: GREZ 24 -9 12.

The original is in the British Library.

1   Shortly before leaving Arcachon, Delius told Heseltine: 'Our stay here has been very successful' – an unlikely line had he been feeling unwell. It would therefore seem likely that he fell ill soon after his return to Grez on 12 September.

2   Heseltine's first published article on music, 'Arnold Schönberg', appeared in *The Musical Standard* (pp. 176–8) on 21 September. Delius had written to him on 11 September: 'I should very much like to hear Schönbergs music – He seems to be very *Academic* à rebours – He writes after a system – He is perhaps the first musician who ever consequently wrote after a system that is perhaps why it sounds so awful – No musical genius ever wrote a treatise on Harmony.' He returned to the subject when writing to Heseltine on 27 December 1913: 'A friend in Vienna sent me Schönbergs Harmonielehre I have read some of it & it is by far the most intelligent Harmony I ever read – His theories are *alright* it's his music that is wrong.'

3   This early self-confidence is confirmed by John Foulds: 'Wilhelm Bauerkeller, of whose quartet I was a member in my youth, told me a story of Delius, to whom he taught the violin when the composer was a lad ... Being set to learn a trifle of Dancla, "I can make better music than that *of my own*," said the boy, and promptly began to improvise, beautifully.' (*Music To-day: Its Heritage from the Past. and Legacy to the Future*. London: Ivor Nicholson and Watson, 1934, p. 308.)

(371)
Frederick Delius to Jelka Delius

London & North Western Railway.

QUEENS HOTEL
BIRMINGHAM, 2.10 *1912*

Dearest Jelka —

I just have a little time so I will write a letter — Beecham was just the same as ever & we were together the whole time in London[1] — He gives the "Mass" on Dec 7th & he wrote to engage Kraus for 2 Concerts — for the "Mass" on Saturday afternoon & also for his Sunday Concert — It was good that we met again   He wrote to Kraus whilst I was there & he might have put it off until too late — Last night I heard the "Musik Makers" Elgar[2] & the Symphony of Sibelius — Elgars work is not very interesting — & very noisy — The chorus treated in the old way & very heavily orchestrated — It did not interest me — Sibelius interested me much more — He is trying to do something new & has a fine feeling for nature & he is also unconventional — Sometimes a bit sketchy & ragged   But I should like to hear the work again — He is a very nice fellow & we were together with Bantock before & after the Concert[3] — Today I tried to hear the Mathew Passion but could not stand more than 40 minutes of it — I see now definitely that I have done for ever with this old music. It says nothing whatever to me — Beautiful bits — Endless recitations & Chorale   My goodness! how slow! Heseltine & his mother are here — He is so nice & so enthusiastic — We played "In a summer Garden" for 2 pianos this morning & he has done it really very well — I shall stay at the Kensington Palace Hotel — Room 8/6 in the Kensington Gardens when I return to town — The Cecil is too big & noisy — I got a Cardigan jacket 31/6. They have knocked Prometheus out of the programme[4] so I shall leave on Friday morning with Balfour for 2 or 3 days & arrive in London on Monday next — Just as I arrived in Folkestone a tremendous gale began —

With lots of love —

your affect[e] Fred —

Kind regards to Ragnhild

I will write you what Hotel I stay at as it is not yet decided —

Autograph letter, signed and dated, written on headed notepaper. Envelope addressed: Madame/Jelka Delius/Grez sur Loing/Seine & Marne/France. Postmark: BIRMINGHAM OCT 2 12.

The original is in the Grainger Museum.

1   Delius left Grez on 29 September, calling on an old friend, the artist Achille Ouvré, in Paris en route to London. Beecham met Delius unannounced on his arrival at Charing Cross and took him by taxi to the Cecil Hotel. The object of the visit to Birmingham was to hear Wood conduct *Sea Drift* on 3 October.

2   This was the first performance of Elgar's *The Music Makers*, conducted by the composer. It seems that he and Delius saw each other at the Festival but avoided speaking to each other (cf. Percy M. Young: *Elgar, O.M.*, .p. 227).

3   Bantock was one of Sibelius's early champions in England (Sibelius's third symphony being dedicated to him). The Finnish composer stayed at Broad Meadow during the festival, and Bantock, Sibelius and Delius sat together to listen to *The Music Makers*. The Sibelius symphony played was the 4th.

4   A pity for Delius: 'I am looking forward to Scriabine's "Prometheus" as all novelties interest me,' he had written to Heseltine on 11 September.

(372)
Frederick Delius to Philip Heseltine

[Grez, 21 October 1912]

My dear Heseltine

I received your letter & card in London – Many thanks – The Concerto was magnificently played by Szantó – I left the day after (11th) & am here since last Saturday week & at work again   I was so glad to have seen something of you – We motored to Oxford & looked over the Colleges – We nearly got killed in the motor car. The steering broke – luckily we were in a village & going slow – otherwise my career would have ended abruptly – With love

    yrs ever
    Frederick Delius

Remember me most kindly to your mother

Autograph postcard, signed and undated. Addressed: Philip Heseltine Esqre/Cefn Bryntalch/Abermule/Montgomeryshire/Angleterre. Postmark: GREZ 21 -10 12.

The original is in the British Library.

Delius's visit to England had indeed proved eventful. *Sea Drift*, conducted by Henry Wood, with Thorpe Bates as soloist, 'went off very well' at Birmingham on 3 October, as he reported to Jelka two days later. He had also been able to hear, on the previous evening, Bantock's *Fifine at the Fair*: 'really very good – the best thing he has done,' he told Jelka on the 3rd, adding: 'I am very well – The air is so bracing' – a surprising comment on industrial Birmingham. A part of the weekend following the festival was spent at Balfour Gardiner's Ashampstead home and included a trip to Oxford, Delius returning to London in time to hear Beecham give *A Dance Rhapsody* at the Sunday Concert of 6 October. There was a happy reunion, at this concert, with Nina Grieg, who was delighted at last to hear some of Delius's music again. Then, on 8 October, the composer visited Elise Delius, now living in Datchet, near Windsor: 'I think my mother and me were like Aase & Peer Gynt today,' he told Jelka. On the 10th there was lunch with the O'Neills, and then a London performance of the Piano Concerto, with Theodor Szántó as soloist. The following day Delius left for Paris, where, joined by Jelka, he stayed briefly before they returned to Grez together.

(373)
Thomas Beecham to Frederick Delius

Dec 26/12
DEVONSHIRE CLUB,
ST. JAMES'S, S.W.

P.S. Write always to
this address.

My dear Delius

I am so sorry I could not come to Grez after leaving Berlin but I had to get back here in order to arrange for my Opera Season. I gave my Second Concert there last Saturday and the audience was more enthusiastic than ever – Everyone tells me the whole affair has been the greatest artistic success ever achieved by a foreign organization in Germany –

Richard Strauss was present at the Second Concert and we had a long talk afterwards. He was immensely impressed and interested in *"Paris"*, which he had not heard before. He was also quite delighted with the Entr'acte from the "Village Romeo" and said he would give it at one of his concerts in Berlin –[1]

I am arranging a Tour for next October and November in Germany (i.e. the last week in October) when I hope to really carry the old flag to victory –
Tell me, does Gmür of Weimar know the part of Zarath(r)ustra?[2]
All love

Yours
Thomas Beecham

Autograph letter, signed and dated, written on headed notepaper.

The original is in the Delius Trust Archive.

In mid-November there had been another major excursion, with Delius leaving Grez on the 12th for Berlin, Frankfurt, Wiesbaden and Cologne. He returned just a month

later, writing to Heseltine on 14 December: '"Life's dance" was given in Berlin on
Nov 15ᵗʰ at the Philharmonie – Oskar Fried – wonderfully well . . . My new Music
drama "Fennimore" will be performed at the beginning of next season at Cologne or
Frankfort.' Although his last opera is generally thought to have been fully composed
between 1909 and 1911, he was to write to Heseltine rather more than two months
later – on 21 February 1913: 'I am working hard at the end of "Niels Lyhne".'

1   Beecham gave his first Berlin concert at the Hochschule on Monday 16 December:
'Your Brigg Fair and Dance Rhapsody went splendidly and had a great reception,' he
wrote on the 18th. *Paris* and the Entr'acte (*The Walk to the Paradise Garden*) followed
on Saturday 21 December. The orchestra was the Beecham Symphony Orchestra.

2   See Letter 268 and note.

1913

The beginning of the year found Delius revising the ending of *Fennimore and Gerda*. But travels that were frequently to interrupt the course of his work during 1913 started in the middle of January, when the composer left Grez on the 16th for Munich, to attend a performance of *A Mass of Life* there on 20 January. He returned home on the 22nd to resume work on *Fennimore*. The next excursion came in early March to London, for the *Mass* again, this time given by Beecham at Covent Garden. Beecham and Lady Cunard had by now laid down a wide path to the higher ranks of London Society for the Deliuses, who found themselves lunching at 10 Downing Street, with the composer lionized wherever he went. The second season of four Balfour Gardiner Choral and Orchestral Concerts was under way, but as in 1912 Delius could not manage to be in London when his own works were given. On 25 February Gardiner had conducted the New Symphony Orchestra in the first British performance of the revised *Lebenstanz* (already taken up in Germany by Steinbach and Schuricht), and on 18 March the same forces were joined by Evelyn Suart for the Piano Concerto.

In mid-March the Deliuses were back at Grez, where they were joined for a few days by Heseltine. Work was resumed, to be interrupted again later in May when the Diaghilev Ballet attracted Delius to Paris and when he apparently attended the first night of *Le Sacre du Printemps*. From Paris he continued to Cologne and then on to the annual Tonkünstlerfest, held this year at Jena and at which *In a Summer Garden* was conducted by Fritz Stein. While on this trip Delius discussed plans for *Fennimore and Gerda*, due to be given in Cologne in the near future.

A special excursion to Paris came in June, when Beecham gave *Appalachia* at the Châtelet Theatre with the Colonne orchestra on the 22nd. Emil Hertzka, the director of Universal Edition, came from Vienna, and Delius regretted that he had had to hear such a 'pitiful performance'. Hopes that Hertzka and his wife could then join the Deliuses on a Norwegian holiday were not realized, and Delius alone left for Norway early in July. Jelka stayed in Grez to work 'intensively' on sketches for the decor of *Fennimore and Gerda* for Cologne before taking, on 30 July, the sea route from Rotterdam to Bergen to join her husband. She signalled their return home in a letter to Hertzka dated 9 September: 'We have just returned to Grez after a splendid trip.' Delius immediately started work on his Requiem. With *An Arabesque* shortly to be published, Delius urged Universal Edition to procure a performance in October: he was anyway going to hear Nikisch give the first performance of *On hearing the first Cuckoo in Spring* and *Summer Night on the River*, in Leipzig, on 23 October. Meanwhile, Henry Wood wrote to Delius to tell him of the 'splendid success' of the Piano Concerto, given with Szántó at a Promenade Concert. And on 7 November Chicago heard the first American performance of the revised *Lebenstanz*, given by the Chicago Symphony Orchestra under Frederick Stock. A month after his visit to Leipzig, Delius again travelled east, this time to Vienna. And again, his hopes for *An Arabesque* proved ill-fated, the scheduled first performance of the work having to be postponed. He stayed on in Vienna for the small consolation of a recital of his songs on 1 December. The end of the year saw him back at work in Grez on his Requiem.

Fennimore and Gerda (RT I/8). Revision/addition of new ending.

'I-Brasîl', song (Fiona Macleod) (RT V/28).

Two Songs for Children, for chorus with pianoforte accompaniment (Tennyson and May Morgan) (RT V/29).

Requiem, for soprano and baritone, double chorus and orchestra (Heinrich Simon) (RT II/8). Begun.

North Country Sketches, for orchestra (RT VI/20). Begun.

(374)
Frederick Delius to Philip Heseltine

Grez sur Loing
S & M
11/1/1913

My dear Heseltine

Your letter interested me very much indeed[1] – & I may tell you once for all that I take the greatest interest in you & your career, & shall always be only too happy to help you in whatever way I can – You ask me for advice in choosing between the civil service – for which you seem to have no interest whatever – & music, which you love – I will give it you – I think that the most stupid thing one can do is to spend ones life doing something one hates or for which one has no interest — In other words it is a wasted Life — I do not believe in sacrificing the big things of Life to anyone or anything — In your case I do not see why you should sacrifice the most important thing in your life to your mother: you will certainly regret it if you do later on — Children always exaggerate the duty they have to their parents — Parents *very seldom* sacrifice anything at all to their children — In your case your mother has certainly not; since she married again — In other words followed her own feelings — &, of course, did entirely right in so doing & I should advise you to do the same — I was entirely in the same position when I was your age & had a considerably harder fight to get what I wanted — I chucked up everything & went to America. One has every chance of succeeding when one does what one loves & I can tell you that I personally have never once regretted the step I took. The greatest pleasure & satisfaction I have experienced in Life has been thro' music — In making it & in hearing it & in living with it — I should advise you to study music, so that you will be able to give lessons in Harmony, Counterpoint & orchestration. You can always become a critic. I think that you are sufficiently gifted to become a composer — Everything depends on your perseverance — etc etc. One never knows how far one can go — I will find out where you can receive the most modern & best musical instruction — Perhaps in Paris — perhaps in Berlin — The opportunities for hearing music are infinitely greater in Berlin — & I have friends there who might be very useful to you — Emerson says in one of his Essays something that resembles the Arthur Symons quotation[2] — He says something to this purpose —

"A man who works with his Whole soul at anything whatever — will make it a success before he is 50." I believe this to be perfectly true — Ones talent develops like muscles that you are constantly training — Trust more in hard work than in inspiration — I am getting ready to go to Munich for the "Mass of Life" 20th Jan — I leave here on the 16th — & shall be back here again on the 22nd — Beecham gives it in Covent Garden in February[3] — Write me again & tell me what you have decided to do. I have already written a song to words by Fiona MaCcleod I-Brasîl[4] — I think it is good — Have you a copy of the "Mass of Life"? If not I will give you one —

your affectionate friend
Frederick Delius

Autograph letter, signed and dated. Envelope addressed: Philip Heseltine Esqre/Cefn-Bryntalch/Abermule/Montgomeryshire/Angleterre. Postmark: GREZ 11 -1 13.

The original is in the British Library.

1   In a long letter written to Delius on 8 January (quoted *in extenso* in Gray, pp. 49–52), Heseltine asked for advice: should he devote his life to music or should he take up

a more conventional career? 'When I was with you in Grez, nearly a year and a half
ago, you advised me to abandon all other pursuits, and to devote myself to music. I
was a fool not to do so at once, I suppose.' He speculated on whether he might have
the talent and confidence to become a composer – or perhaps a critic or writer on
music. Failing that, he might copy orchestral parts or make piano transcriptions. He
might, on the other hand, learn to play an orchestral instrument, or 'after years of
patient study I might attain to the position of pianist to a cinematographic theatre.'
His reliance on Delius's advice seemed to be total: 'there is no one to whom I feel I can
turn at the present moment, sooner than to you', and he added: 'I cannot tell you what
a help, what a relief it is to be able to turn to you and ask your advice at a time like
this. If you still advise me to devote myself to music, I can assure you that nothing on
this earth shall prevent my doing so.'

2   Heseltine quoted, in his letter of 8 January, from Symons's introduction to
Dowson's poems: 'For, there is not a dream which may not come true, if we have the
energy which makes or chooses our own fate. We can always, in this world, get what
we want, if we will it intensely and persistently enough.'

3   Postponed to 10 March.

4   Heseltine had sent a book of poems by Fiona Macleod (pseudonym of William
Sharp) to Delius for Christmas.

(375)
Frederick Delius to Universal Edition

Grez sur Loing
S. et M.
24.1.1913

Dear Herr Doktor[1] –

I have just returned here. I am *very* sorry too that we were not able to meet in
Munich. So now we shall have to try to discuss everything in writing. It is a
pity that you did not hear the performance of the Mass, which was a really fine
& heartfelt one; although the orchestra was not of the first rank, the choirs &
soloists were so wonderfully good that altogether they made a thoroughly fine
ensemble.[2]

I had read Busoni's announcement in the "Signale", but heard in Munich
that he suddenly cancelled his concerts. In respect of what you say about
Fennimore, I would like to give you *my* opinion. As regards an effective
libretto, we may perhaps be looking at things from quite different viewpoints.
You seem to be setting out from a theatrical-dramatic viewpoint & I from a
musical dramatic. I reject the former as unsuitable to my art.

In my opinion Fennimore as a libretto is dramatic and effective throughout
with a slowly increasing dramatic interest; whatever is purposely not expressed

in words, in order to avoid the notorious longueurs, is made complete by the music. The text is simply there as the basis & situation for the music and *must* in consequence absolutely not give the impression of being something complete in itself. The whole of modern opera literature has this defect: that is, theatrically effective libretti which in themselves are quite complete as stage plays & do not need any music at all. The *theatrical*-dramatic situation does not require any music at all & is diminished by it, while on the contrary the *musical*-dramatic situation comes into its own only through the music. I hope that you are enough of an artist to understand this, for herein lies the whole future of music drama. The same goes for A Village Romeo and Juliet though not yet quite so surely expressed as in Fennimore.

The successes enjoyed by certain modern operas have nothing whatever to do with their music & in consequence these compositions must soon disappear again. Their music *can* only be inferior, because a really sensitive artist could not possibly set such superficial libretti to music. It is only where text & music spring from the same source that a harmonic and living work of art can result.

When I chose Niels Lyhne as a subject I selected from it 2 episodes, namely Fennimore and Gerda. The only thing in Fennimore which made me hesitate was the gloomy and unresolved ending & it has been because of this that I have been occupying myself again in recent weeks with my Gerda music & have become convinced that the "Gerda" episode is necessary after all to round off the opera. I have therefore added just 3 short scenes. 1.) A short scene of Niels L. after he has returned to his father's estate & is recuperating by working in the open air. 2) Scene in spring, when Niels goes to see his neighbour the Kanzleirat, whose four young daughters playing in the garden he watches from the window   The eldest, seventeen-year-old Gerda, is being teased by the others on account of her adoration for Niels. The scene ends with Niels coming into the garden and declaring his love for Gerda; father & sisters at the end etc. The third & final scene shows us Niels walking in the fields with his young wife and showing her home to her. It ends with a happy love scene and closes peacefully.[3]

As far as the publication of the work is concerned, I do indeed have another offer & could have it published immediately   I would, however, of course prefer to have it published by you so as not to have my compositions in so many hands.[4] I would I think prefer to give the first performance to Cologne. Under no circumstances would I have the material produced myself.

With best wishes

Yours
Frederick Delius

P.S. I heard repeated complaints in Munich that other works of mine that people wished to buy were unobtainable there & could only be ordered from Vienna (esp. Seadrift)

Letter in the hand of Jelka Delius, dated, written in German.

The original is in the Universal Edition archives. It is the second item of a large correspondence beginning with a letter from Delius dated 10 January 1913 and continuing – apart from a break of some three and a half years during the war – for the rest of the composer's life.

1   Emil Hertzka (1869–1932): Austro-Hungarian music publisher. He became managing director of the recently-founded house of Universal Edition in 1907. He was noted for his championship of many younger, experimental composers, often securing them for Universal long before they became established, and promoting their work as often as not as a personal friend. Among his composers were Bartók and Kodály, Schönberg and Schreker, Berg and Webern, Schillings, Weill, Milhaud and Malipiero. Among the journals he published was, from 1919, [*Musikblätter des*] *Anbruch.*

2   This Munich Choral Society performance was conducted by Eberhard Schwickerath; the soloists were Mientje Lauprecht-van Lammen, Adrienne von Kraus-Osborne, Matthäus Römer and Felix von Kraus.

3   Delius's three projected scenes for the 'Gerda' episode were shortly to be reduced to two.

4   Delius found it necessary to defend *Fennimore and Gerda* still further, writing to a clearly-unconvinced Hertzka on 30 April: 'I see . . . that you have no faith at all in the work & that your object is an immediate popular success – That is simply not the case with me. People will come back to my works, even if they have not had an initial success with the public – I do not write occasional music – Likewise A Village Romeo & Juliet will appear again, in spite of conductor Bruno Walter's opinion.'

(376)
Percy Grainger to Frederick Delius

5.3.13.
31^A KING'S ROAD
SLOANE SQUARE
S W

My dear friend

I rejoice to see that Beecham is giving your "Mass of Life" on March 10, but at the same time gnash my teeth, as I am in Switzerland that date playing.[1] Alas I have no luck with your big choral works, so far. Beecham has done many thrilling & perfect performances of your lofty & adorable things of late, & I have been there & relished. It is a great joy to follow the progress of your works in this country *within the last year*. You are written of & spoken of in quite another tone now, & *tower* above the other British composers more & more in *all sorts of people's minds*. Folk in this country want hammering away at, & the much that dear Beecham & the little old Balfour has done in the last year have together got home. Of course things move slowly, but by all I can see, as far as I can judge you will not lack *appreciation on the broadest possible lines* in this country if things go on as at present, & not merely a "bewegung" as abroad, with one party for & another against, but a sort of "unassailable position" with a *united* admiration. It fills us all with such joy to see your power here growing in this steady way, & all who adore your work must feel ever so much love & thankfulness for the way Beecham has performed you here, both as to *oftenness* & as to the *touching glory* of the excellence of his performances. He is a ripping genius. I have heard him a lot of late, in all sorts of programs, & in Rosen-kavalier, Elektra, Salome, etc & I admire him & feel affection for him beyond words. He has also been doing my little "Mock Morris" in the most perfect manner. The last year has been a kind one to me indeed. I have come forward wonderfully as a composer, have received the *most just & intelligent* (even when adverse) criticisms on my stuff in the papers & the country at large (provinces, etc) has taken to my stuff generously, & quite a batch of things are going like hot cakes.

Still better I have had some of the actual experience you always so wisely urged upon me, & have learnt enough to know that I want to fairly radically alter my whole style of composition, though I am quite satisfied with several isolated things of mine as they stand, all the same. I *do* wish you had in print some piece for not *too big* orchestra (4 horns, 2 trumpets, no strange wood-wind, nor too many strings required) & not too wildly hard, that orchestras such as those at *Bournemouth Belfast*, etc could perform it, a piece that could be performed with an hours or $\frac{3}{4}$ hours rehearsal & then form part of general repetory.[2] In all these towns they are conscious of your greatness & growing British fame & long to do something but are held back for want of instruments or fear of a difficultness beyond their powers.

Is the "Romeo & J" Entr'act published seperately? That is one of *the* most gorgeous & touching of all your things. A thing like that (if in the right pub-lishers hands here) ought to go right thro the country if not for instruments lacking in usual bands.

Mother will be here March 10 & is wildly looking forward to the "Mass". I wonder are you coming over. If so, I hope you'll still be here on March 13, when I return. Maybe I'm back March 12, even[3]

Very much love from your

fond admirer
Percy.

Autograph letter, signed and dated, written on headed notepaper.

The original is in the Grainger Museum.

1   Like Grainger, Delius received scant notice of this performance of the *Mass*. Beecham wrote to him on 2 March inviting him to attend: 'If you can manage it, try to arrive for Sat 8ᵗʰ – Rosenkavalier – Send me a wire – Lady Cunard wants you to come to Venice again in April.' The Deliuses arrived in London on the evening of the 6th, staying at 9 Hans Place again. Jelka reported on the concert to Ida Gerhardi on 11 March: 'Fred said that, apart from the singers, in this performance his orchestra was for the first time just as he had conceived it, & Munich & Elberfeld so bad that he had had doubts about the quality of the work. Afterwards we were with Lady C & Beecham in the Ritz Hotel quite alone together & in Lady C.'s room. It was delightful ... All the ladies, particularly the older ones, love Fred. I heard the Minister's wife, sitting next to him, say to Lady C afterwards: Oh, but he is a *darling* (very precious accent). All these people are such delightful hosts and so natural.' Jelka was much taken by the social circles in which she and her husband were moving. They had lunched at Downing Street at the Asquiths'. King Manuel of Portugal was, she told Ida, 'enchanted' by the *Mass*, the Prince of Serbia 'excited'; and the German Ambassador's wife had even gone so far as to plead illness in breaking another engagement in order to attend the concert. The Deliuses left for Grez on 14 March.

2   Grainger annotated a copy of this letter: 'This request led Delius to compose his 2 pieces for small orchestra: "On hearing the first Cuckoo in spring" & "Summer Night on the River".' This particular claim would not appear, at least, to be borne out by the dates on the printed score (1912 and 1911 respectively), although in a letter to Tischer on 24 June 1913 the composer wrote: 'One piece is ready, the other not yet.' On the other hand, in his memoir 'About Delius' (Warlock: *Delius*, rev.ed., p. 172), Grainger claims to have written 'around 1910' asking Delius to write 'some short pieces for small orchestra'. Delius's next letter 'told that he had taken my advice'.

3   Grainger was certainly back in London in good time to hear Evelyn Suart play Delius's Piano Concerto. Rose Grainger (who, unlike her son, had been able to attend the performance of the *Mass*) wrote to Delius on 19 March: 'We enjoyed yʳ Concerto last night, but I think it requires a man's power in the loud parts. Percy is practising it at this moment, & it suits him well, he has so much real strength.'

(377)
Frederick Delius to Adey Brunel

Grez sur Loing
S & M –
27 April 1913

My dear Mʳˢ Brunel –

I was very pleased & astonished to receive a letter from you – I almost thought you had gone to join Jebe in the South Sea Islands or the "hereafter"! So you really received news from our dear old Jebe! I need not tell you how much this interests me; & would it be too much to ask you to send me the letter so that I may be able to form an idea of how he is & has been faring – Jebe is the only man I ever loved in all my life & I would fair believe that he has passed entirely out of my life[1] – He seems to be making a reality of his life & living all the music that he has in him – With me it is just the contrary   I am putting everything into my music – all my poetry & all my adventures   I was so glad to hear that you are again enjoying good health – How is your son?[2] I had some unpleasant bilious attacks which lasted over several years – but that is all – With kind remembrances from us both –

I am

always sincerely yrs
Frederick Delius

Send the letter at once – I will faithfully return after perusal –

Autograph letter, signed and dated.

The original is in the collection of Christopher Brunel.

Francesca Louisa Brunel (1865–1946), née Adey. She married and later separated from Reginald Brunel-Norman, who as 'Norman-Concorde' organized Delius's 1899 concert; and her friendship with Halfdan Jebe dated from around that period. As Adey Brunel she taught elocution and gave recitals, adopting that name for the rest of her life. There is evidence that around 1905/6 Delius suggested she might write for him a libretto for an opera. Extensive drafts of the libretto of *Poppy Land* are still extant, in the collection of Christopher Brunel, her grandson. The first page is headed 'Ideas for the Opera Delius is going to write with me'. When it came to a decision, Delius found the work 'drenched [in] nostalgia', according to Adey's annotations, and Jelka's view of *Poppy Land* – as 'not having the elements of a good opera' – was evidently sufficient to turn the scales against it. Adey had personally delivered a synopsis of the first act, together with a number of lyrics, to Delius at Grez. A partly-obscured note would seem to indicate that it was Jebe who had been charged with returning the MS to her.

1   In fact occasional news was still sporadically to arrive from Jebe, although none of his later letters has survived. Writing to Adey Brunel on 19 January 1921, Jelka tells of Delius hearing twice from his old friend: 'He wrote to Fred from Panama in November and told about his assault and subsequent illness and that he wanted to work his way to N. York as a stoker. He really did, and then wrote again from N.Y. that he was now perfectly well and that the heat of the engine quite cured his lungs and rheumatic pains and he had bought a violin and was now going to work southward again playing in Hotels etc.'

2   Adrian Brunel (1889–1958), known as Adrian Brunel-Norman in his youth, when he trained to become an opera singer, was to become a film producer and director. He published in 1949 a volume of memoirs: *Nice Work: The Story of Thirty Years in British Film Production.*

(378)

Frederick Delius to Jelka Delius

HÔTEL OXFORD ET CAMBRIDGE

13, RUE D'ALGER

(*Corner*) RUE St HONORÉ

PARIS

[23 May 1913]

Dearest Jelka – I am afraid I have no better memory than you but luckily you sent me my shaving things & they arrived just as I was getting up & in time – I went to the Princess[1] & we both went together to see Egusquiza[2] who was awfully pleased to see me – On my return from Germany I shall dine with him – He has got very old – I had a splendid fauteuil d'orchestre at Astruc's [3] & met a lot of old friends – Ravel – Schmitt – d'Humieres – Blanche[4] – Stravinsky & Klemperer. After the theatre we all went to De la Rue & had supper – Diagileff & Nijinski I also met – I will tell you all about it on Sunday. I was disappointed with the music of Boris Godounov altho' there are good things & some very dramatic moments. The scenery is also rather disappointing   one or two are good – The Costumes are splendid   Baksts scene rather disappointed me (N° 4) the others are by another artist – The princess will take you to Boris on June 3 & take you also to dinner.

I go tonight to the Oiseau de feu – Astruc gave me a libre entré for the whole lot – I can go in when I like & stand in the stalls or take a seat if there is one –

With love
Fred –

I got to bed at 3 this morning but slept until 6½ & then right up to 9.30 & got up at 11. I have a nice quiet room

---

Autograph letter, signed and undated, written on headed notepaper.

The original is in the Grainger Museum.

1   Almost certainly the Princesse de Polignac.

2   In spelling this name, Delius's hand is ambiguous. The *Bottin Mondain* of 1914 lists, however, a Roger de Egusquiza, living at 32 rue Copernic (near l'Etoile). References to him in *Delius: A Life in Letters*, Vol. I, should therefore be amended from Equsquiza.

3   Gabriel Astruc (1864–1938): Diaghilev's Paris impresario.

4   Jacques Emile Blanche (1861–1942): French painter. He made portraits of Proust, Debussy, Stravinsky and Nijinsky, among others.

(379)
Frederick Delius to Igor Stravinsky

Grez sur Loing (Seine et Marne)
27.5.13

Dear Monsieur Stravinsky, —

I am afraid it is quite impossible for me to come to the final rehearsal to-morrow, but I shall certainly come on Thursday as I insist on hearing your work:[1] only as I haven't a ticket I shall call for you at your hotel to go in with you as I did last time: if there are any difficulties please send me a line at 13 rue d'Alger, Paris. Your music interests me enormously, something I cannot say for most of the music I have heard for a very long time.

Very cordially yours,
Frederick Delius

From Eric Walter White: *Stravinsky: The Composer and his Works*, p. 550. Text in French. It is the only known item of correspondence between Delius and Stravinsky.

1   The first performance of *The Rite of Spring* took place at the Théâtre des Champs-Elysées on Thursday 29 May. Delius does not refer to this performance in any other letter, and there is no record of his initial reaction to the work. (Cf. p. 108, note 1.)

(380)
Frederick Delius to Philip Heseltine

Grez sur Loing
S & M
[28 June 1913]

My dear Heseltine —

It is a long time since I wrote to you but my time has been pretty well filled up & I had little time for correspondence. The Jena Festival[1] went off very well or very badly if one thinks of the miserable quality of the novelties performed — The "Summer garden" was very well given & seems to have been quite a success. Of course it sounded very light & airy against the background of "Schwere Musik". All the pieces were also so fearfully long — Max Reger's Römische Festgesang was noisy Bier musik. A piece by "Rude Stephan"[2] was the best — but far too long — Last Sunday "Appalachia" was played in Paris — Beecham conducted — The Orchestra was 2nd rate & the Chorus awful & Beecham seemed to be entirely out of his water & made nothing of the

Orchestra or Chorus – Next Saturday I leave for Norway – sail from Antwerp & go straight up to the mountains – My wife joins me a month later & we then go up to the Lofoten Islands. I am looking forward immensely to the trip – If you care to join me about the middle of July we might have ten days or a fort-nights tramp together amongst the finest mountains in the world – Write me here – or Post Restante – Kristiania Norway – which will always find me – I could not come to England as I was hard at work on something new[3] & did not want to break off. Write me soon how you are & what you are doing –

   With love

   yrs ever
   Frederick Delius

Autograph letter, signed and undated. Envelope addressed: Philip Heseltine Esqre/Didbrook Vicarage/Winchcombe/(Glos)/Angleterre. Postmark: GREZ 28 -6 13.

The original is in the British Library.

1   The 1913 Tonkünstlerfest of the Allgemeine Deutsche Musikverein took place at Jena, 4–8 June. Delius travelled first to Cologne on 30 May. 'I wonder how the Fest Musik will strike you after Stravinsky,' wrote Jelka on 1 June. Delius replied three days later: 'The Concert came off very well – & Stein did it [In a Summer Garden] really remarkably well & so did the Orchestra – the woodwind was rather weak – But an ex-cellent performance   It sounded lovel[y] – & of course made a great impression on the musicians – The public received it warmly but I fear did not understand much – The other things were simply wretched – The old, old schwere Deutsche geist – Nothing whatever new or poetical ... I am very well & it is quite amusing to see all these people again.' He intended to be in Cologne on Sunday 8 June, when Mahler's 8th Symphony was to be given at the Lower Rhine Music Festival; and would return to Grez on 9 June. In the event he wrote to Jelka from Jena on the 6th: 'I have heard so much bad music that I can hear no more – Tomorrow I leave for Weimar & shall visit Frau Förster Nietzsche', adding 'My piece seems to have been the great success.'

2   Rudi Stephan (1887–1915): German composer, considered a forerunner of German Expressionism. The piece performed was his Music for Orchestra. Martin Cooper has suggested that as a composer Stephan was influenced by Delius (cf. The Daily Telegraph, 17 December 1977).

3   North Country Sketches?

(381)
Frederick Delius to Edvard Munch

[Grez, 30 June 1913]

Dear friend – I have received your card – I leave Antwerp next Saturday 5th &
arrive in Kristiania on Tuesday evening. I shall be staying at the Hotel Westminster – & would be very pleased if you would pick me up on Wednesday at
12 or 1 o'clock so that we can be together. I am staying until Thursday or
Friday & then am going on to the Jotunheim.[1]

Best wishes
Frederick Delius

Autograph postcard, signed and undated, written in German. Addressed: Herrn
Edvard Munch/Kunstmaler/Grimsröd/pr Moss/Norvège. Postmark: GREZ 30 -6
13.

The original is in the Munch Museum. The previous recorded communication
between the two friends dates from March/April 1908.

1   Delius spent some three weeks touring until Jelka joined him at the beginning of
August in Bergen, where Nina Grieg was expecting them to stay with her. Following
this they apparently went on to Lofoten. For Delius it had been a combined mountain
walking and fishing holiday, starting off on the Hardanger Vidde and taking in Gol,
Kongsberg, Gjeilo, Aurdal, Fagernes, Tyin, Maristova and Laerdalsøyri. 'I feel
marvellously well,' he wrote to Tischer.

(382)
Frederick Delius to Universal Edition

Grez sur Loing
20.9.13.

Dear Herr Direktor,

I have just received a letter from Eug. d'Albert,[1] President of the Wiener
Tonkünstler-Verein, who invites me to have half a concert of my own music
on 1st December. I will of course accept. Kindly try to make arrangements for
the performance of the Arabesk to take place at this time. I am trying to
arrange for Nikisch, too, to postpone his first performance & give it at the
same time. When is the Mass coming off in Munich? If all this could only be
combined! I am working on quite a big new composition (a choral work)[2] &
must absolutely keep a quiet working period to myself.

At the Vienna concert I would very much like among other things to have my Entr'acte from Romeo & Juliet performed (between the last but one & the last scene) which is played so often in London. For that purpose it would be necessary for you to have it prepared at once for concert use &, if anything has to be done with Harmonie[3] in this connexion, to take appropriate steps immediately. Furthermore I would ask you to let me know who is the conductor of the Wiener Tonkünstler Verein & if he has a *good* choir? Also I would like to know when the performance by Schuricht of the Mass is to take place in Frankfurt?

With kindest regards from us both

Yours
Frederick Delius

Letter in the hand of Jelka Delius, dated, written in German.

The original is in the Universal Edition archives.

1   Eugen d'Albert (1864–1932): Scottish-born composer and pianist. In 1907 he succeeded Joachim as director of the Berlin Hochschule für Musik. Of Anglo-French parentage, studying in London, Vienna and Weimar (under Liszt), marrying (as second of his six wives) the Venezuelan pianist Teresa Carreño, living in several European countries, and dying in Riga, in his cosmopolitanism he perhaps rivals only Delius among composers. His letter to Delius has unfortunately not been preserved.

2   Heseltine, staying with his uncle in Marlotte, reported on the new work to Viva Smith: 'On Sunday I walked over to Grez and saw Delius: he has just returned, in great form, from a two months' sojourn in the Norwegian mountains, and is working hard at his magnificent *Requiem* (which will be the first atheistical requiem in musical literature): the text is a wonderfully lovely prose-poem by a modern German poet . . . I wish you could know Delius: he is so wonderful' (Tomlinson: *Warlock and Delius*, p. 16). Heseltine would work late at night on his piano transcription of *A Dance Rhapsody*.

3   Harmonie were the original publishers of *A Village Romeo and Juliet*, from which the entr'acte *The Walk to the Paradise Garden* was one day to be issued separately – a publication that Delius (and his friends) had long been urging.

(383)
Frederick Delius to Ernest Newman

Grez sur Loing
S & M
10th [Oct] 13

My dear Newman –

A question! If you had to characterise the 4 principal religions in music – which religious melodies used in the several religious ceremonies would you choose? – In other words – what themes do you consider would characterise the best the Christian – Mahomedan – Jewish & Boodhist religions?[1] If you can help me out I should be very grateful. My new Musik drama "Fennimore & Gerda" 2 Episodes taken from J. P. Jacobsen's Niels Lyhne – will have its first performance in Cologne next March & I hope you will be able to come. I should very much like to read your Contraversy with Shaw about "Electra" – I wrote more than a year ago to Bantock to send it me – but got no answer – Can you lend it me for a few days? Should you come to Paris I hope you will come out to Grez; we can always put you up as our house is big –

With kindest remembrances from us both to you & your wife –
I remain

Sincerely yours
Frederick Delius

Autograph letter, signed and dated 10th Nov 13. Envelope addressed: Ernest Newman Esqre/c/o The Birmingham Post/Birmingham/Angleterre. The correct date is confirmed by the postmarks: GREZ 10 -10 13 and BIRMINGHAM OC 11 13.

The original is in the Delius Trust Archive.

1   Delius was continuing to work on his Requiem. Newman's reply has not survived, but Delius wrote to him on 12 November: 'Many thanks for your letter with the 2 tips: Do you not think that "Ein feste Burg" is rather typically protestant? It is so entirely german.' On 27 December in a letter to Heseltine Delius commented: 'I am working at my requiem.' He combined, in the second movement, the chants of 'Hallelujah' and 'La il Allah'.

(384)
Frederick Delius to Jelka Delius

[Leipzig, 22 October 1913]

Your card just arrived. I shall leave here on Friday morning or evening but in every case I shall be in Paris Saturday night – When I arrived at Cologne there was no direct Schlafwagen to Leipzig, but only to Magdeburg & I should have had to change at 6. am so went to the Dom Hotel & had a good nights rest – leaving next day 8.36. This morning Wed. was the Hauptprobe – ausverkauft.[1] Nikisch played the 1st piece (Spring) much too slow – but very expressively the 2nd He played most beautifully – perfect – I asked him to play the 1st one faster at the Concert so I hope it will go off alright[2] – Orchestra splendid – Muriel Foster[3] staying at Hotel Hauffe & so am I, as I could not get in at Sedan – Mr & Mrs Goetz left this evening – I am supping at Lamprichts – Leipzig all decorated & looking very ugly – I took a long walk in the Rosenthal this afternoon – it was lovely weather – Leipzig scarcely to be recognised again but certain quarters are the same. I will make you a present of the pearl neckless to compensate you for the dress I do not like. I am so glad you are getting one from Felsland – Love from

Fred.

Autograph postcard, signed and undated. Addressed: Madame/Jelka Delius/Grez sur Loing/(S & M)/Frankreich. Postmark: LEIPZIG 22.10.13.

Within two months of his return from Norway the composer was off again, this time to hear Nikisch give the first performance of *On hearing the first Cuckoo in Spring* and *Summer Night on the River*, the two new pieces dedicated to Balfour Gardiner. The concert in which they featured was at the Leipzig Gewandhaus on 23 October.

1   German: *final rehearsal – sold out.*

2   'Nikisch gave a beautiful performance of the 2 pieces –,' Delius wrote again to Jelka on 24 October. 'The first he took rather too slow – The public seemed to like it the best – altho I like the 2nd best.'

3   Muriel Foster (1877–1937): English mezzo-soprano. She sang in the earliest performances of several of Elgar's oratorios, including *The Music Makers* in Birmingham on 1 October 1912. (See letter 371.)

(385)

Percy Grainger to Frederick Delius

Grand Hotel   *Helsingfors, den* 12.11.1913
FENNIA
HELSINGFORS
FINLAND

Darling Delius.

We rejoiced unspeakably to hear your "Lebenstanz" *gloriously* performed by Schneevoigt here two nights ago.[1] I love it more each time. What genius in *every* line   I think Schneevoigt a *ripping* conductor for your works. He did it with leib und seele. I think he would be a good man when you have a choice of conductor for a performance somewhere. He schwärms for you, performed the Lebenstanz in Sweden also & is doing it in Riga tonight & I'm sure you'd make him very happy if you'd send him a gruss & tell him you'd heard from me how splendidly he did it.

   Hr Kapellmester Georg Schnéevoigt
   Helsingfors, Finland

will reach him.
   He asked me to greet you.
   I've just finished a wonderfully successful tour of 60 concerts in Norway Russia & Finland. Helsingfors is *delightful*
   In great haste, hoping you are very well & with tons of love to you both from mother & me

   Yrs ever
   Percy

Autograph letter, signed and dated, written on headed notepaper.

The original is in the Grainger Museum.

1   Georg Schneevoigt (1872–1947): Finnish conductor and cellist, noted for his performances of the music of Sibelius. Delius replied on 18 November to thank Grainger for the surprise news: 'I at once wrote a few words to Schneevoigt.' Coincidentally the work had just had its first American performance, by Stock in Chicago.

(386)
Frederick Delius to Jelka Delius

Hotel Residenz
Ludwig Domansky   *Wien, den* 25 [November] *1913*
Wien, I., Teinfaltstrasse 6.

Dearest – You will have seen by the telegramm that must be lying in Grez
that the Concert is postponed until 26th January[1] – Charmant! to have come
all this fearful way for nothing – However I shall try to settle everything with
Hertzka – The Chorus & Solist are giving me a rehearsal on Friday next very
probably. They all seem enthusiastic about the work – The reason of postpone-
ment was rotten orchestral parts of a work by Weigl – Schrecker[2] told me that
the parts of Eine Arabeske were almost as bad & he had to send them back
again – This after all I have been saying to Hertzka – However I am going to
give him a serious talking to – for if this occurs also with "Fennimore" it
would be terrible – I write you a few lines in haste – I am just off to the Universal Edition – I dined yesterday out at Hertzka's   His wife is very nice &
natural & regretted very much that you were not with me – It is quite wrong
to put terreau[3] with roses – It was right to have dug out the tuffe[4] but we
ought to have put back the common garden earth. Terreau is too light – They
have lovely hot houses – We sent you some earth from here – It looks very
much like our earth – Lehmig[5] – I like Wien very much. The people are nice
& friendly the coffee superb – The water quite excellent & also delicious beer –
   Au revoir ma fille bientôt – I shall write again tonight – I dine with
d'Albert today – Whether I stay or not I do not yet know –

   your loving
   Fred

later –

It was too late for the morning post so I continue – Have just dined with
d'Albert who was exceedingly nice – we were quite alone & had a good talk – I
go on Friday to tea to meet Weingartner. This morning I went to the Kaiserl
Bibliotek to see rare old manuscripts – was introduced thro' Hertzka & was
very warmly received by 2 Musical Doctors who shewed me interesting manuscripts of Mozart   Hayd[n] – Beethoven & Monteverdi   But the most wonderful of all was an old Codicis (illuminated from 1460) Pleinchant with
perfectly wonderful illustrations & illuminations – also extraordinary erotic
things in between the illuminations – I am now off to a "conference" with
Hertzka about business – Harmonie etc   Will write you tomorrow result

   Fred –

Autograph letter, signed and dated '25 *1913*', written in English on headed notepaper.

The original is in the Grainger Museum.

1   Delius left Grez for Vienna on 20 November in order to attend what was to have been the first performance of *An Arabesque* six days later. 'Instead of the Concert,' he wrote to Jelka on the 27th, 'we had a box at the Opera   Die Königin von Saba – Goldmark   Gregor gave us a box – The music has really good things in it – but only when "das Jüdische hervortritt" – otherwise it is Wagner & Meyerbeer – I have made the acquaintance of Loewe & of d'Albert – Loewe has the Tonkünstler Orchester & is giving "Lebenstanz" next season. He has also the Orchester in Munich & gave Brigg Fair.'

2   Franz Schreker (1878–1934): Austrian composer and conductor. He studied and subsequently taught in Vienna, and founded in 1911 the Vienna Philharmonic Choral Society, of which he was conductor. It was in Vienna later in 1912 that he conducted *Sea Drift* and *Paris* in the same concert.

3   French: (*vegetable- or leaf-*) *mould*.

4   French, properly *tuf*: *bed-rock*.

5   German: *loamy*.

1914

'I am working so successfully at present,' Delius told Heseltine on 2 January. His health was good and the year seemed to hold marvellous musical promise. *On hearing the first Cuckoo in Spring* and *Summer Night on the River* duly received their first British performances at Queen's Hall on 20 January. Wood gave *A Dance Rhapsody* on 14 February. George Bernard Shaw, whom Delius was to meet at least twice during the summer, was there to hear it. But the Deliuses themselves had gone to Germany, where over a period of a month a number of the composer's works were given in his presence. Delius was to hear the *Mass of Life* at Wiesbaden on 16 and in Frankfurt on 23 February. If the Wiesbaden performance was a fine one, that at Frankfurt was better still – a great success, as he later reported to Hertzka. Moreover it was now planned that Frankfurt should see *A Village Romeo* the following season. In March came further good news: Gustav Brecher in Cologne was anxious to engage singers for an autumn production of *Fennimore and Gerda*. This was soon followed by news from Bradford: a full-scale Delius concert, to include part of *A Mass of Life*, was down for 27 November. Like so much else this year, this was not to materialize.

Philip Heseltine was again in Grez by the end of March. He stayed for some weeks, helping Delius in various ways. He began, too, to collect material for, as he himself put it, 'a little book about Delius'. In May Delius heard that Paul von Klenau was hoping to give *A Village Romeo* in Freiburg. On 21 June the composer travelled to London where Beecham was to give more of his music. For a few days towards the end of the month he and Heseltine stayed with Gardiner at Ashampstead; otherwise Delius was successively O'Neill's and Beecham's guest in London. The season was at its height, with Beecham very much at the forefront; and Delius, 'very fit with all this', plunged into a glittering world of operas, ballets, concerts, receptions – a world which again opened up immediately to accept him. 'Un vrai Gotha!' was Jelka's reaction to the letters describing the circles he moved in for nearly three weeks. In July came word that the first performance of *Fennimore* was fixed for 10 October, Jelka duly making preparations to travel to Cologne towards the end of the month in order to advise on the decor and scenery.

It would be almost impossible to exaggerate the promise that London alone

– and the highly influential friends it was providing – now held for Delius and his music. Beecham and Wood, among others, were asking for his latest works; there was a proposal that Nijinsky dance the *Dance Rhapsody*; and publishers were pressing for his compositions. 'I do hope War will not break out & knock all Art and Music on the head for years,' wrote Delius anxiously to Heseltine on 30 July. But, of course, it did. Three weeks of July spent in the summer garden at Grez quietly at work on the Requiem were followed by an August of unease, with the countries of Europe at war. *'Take my advice,'* wrote Grainger on 30 August, *'dont remain in Grez.'* He urged the Deliuses to leave for England and then cross to the United States. Caught up in the general panic caused by the German advance to the Marne, the Deliuses had to leave Grez on 5 September. They got as far as Orléans, where they stayed for a week before at last deciding, as better news came in, to return home and to sit things out. In October Beecham proposed that the Deliuses come to England, where they would be free to stay at either of his houses in London or Watford. Delius accepted, and in mid-November he and Jelka moved over to England.

The composer joined Beecham for a short trip to Manchester, where two orchestral pieces from *A Village Romeo* were given on 3 December. The playing of Beatrice and May Harrison, at that same concert, of the Brahms Double Concerto enthralled him. An introduction to the sisters was effected and he promised to write a double concerto for them. Returning to London, he and Jelka next installed themselves in Beecham's newly-leased house in Watford. The pre-war social and musical life of the metropolis had largely vanished.

North Country Sketches (RT VI/20). Nos 3 and 4 completed.

Requiem (RT II/8). Continued.

Sonata No. 1 for violin and piano (RT VIII/6). Completed.

(387)
Frederick Delius to Philip Heseltine

Grez sur Loing
S & M
2 Jan 14

My dear Philip – I need not tell you that your long letter interested me in the highest degree – I thank you for the confidence you bestow upon me in writing me so thoroughly & frankly all about your life, thoughts & doings – It is a letter from a real & loving friend – I shall be just as sincere & frank with you[1] – Not everyone falls really in love – only few men & few women are capable of a great & real passion – But in my opinion it is of enormous importance for an artist to have had a great passion – It is that which gives that extraordinary depth of emotion to his work – 2 never love each other at the same time or scarcely ever – The woman when she sees she is the object of a great passion often gets inspired by the lover to something almost equivalent – The man either loves or does not. When he does not – he takes & enjoys & that is all – Women are never blind when they love. Men nearly always – Your friend[2] knew you loved her a good deal sooner than you did – Women are very much wilier in these things than men think. Men always take women to be so innocent, in these things, forgetting that they spend most of their life thinking about them – Men think, on the whole, little about them – & when they do think it is mostly in a purely sexual way – When love awakens in them it mostly awakens in an astonished child who will innocently fall in to the most obvious trap or be led on to anything by the most commonplace guile – I have had a very similar experience to you – I was madly, passionately in love when I was 21,[3] & with evidently a very similar sort of woman – She was, however, not ten years older than me – but just my own age – My opinion of your friend is the following – She does not love you but is flattered at being the object of such a great passion & wants to make it last as long as possible – Most women have the idea when they do not love – that as soon as they let the man obtain what he wants – or satisfy his desire – His love will stop & the whole thing will be over – The only possible way of bringing her to the point is the one you have taken – to see her no more – If she wants you *she* will come to you & then you might enjoy the one thing that is absolutely necessary between a man & a woman before they can be true friends. I am afraid your friend is cold – all you tell me about her lying naked with you before the fire points to a very self-possessed & cold nature – quite impossible in France & Germany – Only possible in England & America – It is very cruel – If she meant well by you she ought not to exasperate your senses when she does not intend to satisfy them – Indeed if she had real tenderness for you she would behave quite differently – It is unhealthy & enervating & no wonder you feel depressed & in an unsatisfactory state of mind – The whole affair is much simpler than you imagine – You see everything now thro' those wonderful eyes of love – such wonderful colors & it really does not matter a bit who you do love, or wether she is worthy or not of your passion – for me the important point is that you are *capable* of a great passion; that sets a mark on you which elevates you greatly in my eyes. She is of course afraid of getting a child like all women who are not in love are – This touches, of course, on the old question of convention & Society which I will not touch on here – Everybody must settle that for himself – You have done well in fleeing & getting out of that atmosphere for the present. I had just as bad a time of it as you & almost identical. She would not give herself. Probably what occured to me will happen also to you – 7 or (or) 8 years after she came to me of her own accord – but I was no more in love with her & then she became madly in love with me – but all in vain – I had another dear & charming friend who had given herself to me without compunction & I had learned to appreciate what a fine & real woman was – Love is a thing one must snatch at & hold & keep & enjoy as long as it lasts – for *it does not last* – but friendship does & that very often follows on love & gives place to something more lasting & gentler & more sure & healthier. A man who is in love can never be brutal & take a woman by force – Only a man who is not in love can do that – But the sort of woman you speak of is destined either to never get a man – or be forced by a man she does not even like – or get married to a perfectly indifferent person who can support her in a so called respectable way. When she writes to you that at the right time her love will be active enough it really means that she is incapable of a love sufficiently great to become active. If a woman has not loved before 27, or 30 I very much doubt whether she ever will – Now to another subject – To become a music critic is to become nothing at all – The only possible attraction in music is to be a musician You could write criticisms when you felt like it & also do something else – I could, of course, help you in several ways & should do so as soon as you wanted it – But *critic* is no career – Do not be in a hurry. Go into an office if it must be & gain time & money that way – You would be able to make a little money making piano arrangements etc. but what is that? mere drudgery – To start with: work at any subject you fancy to get into a calmer state of mind: It will not be lost. Harmony, Counterpoint or anything that attracts you – Write to me as often as you feel like it – I will always give you my advice which you can take for what it is worth – but it might be of help to you. I have so much more experience – The world will presently be obliged to adopt methods to prevent over population & also the procreation of children by diseased people – A good syringe never hurt anyone & is used by every clean woman on the continent – Cundums are not as healthy for the woman – I have already heard of "Karezza" but do not agree with any of those methods – That sort of thing might be all very well for the woman but for the man it would be very unhealthy & would shatter his nerves ultimately – The one real natural & healthy way to enjoy a woman is the natural one – with emission – & even this not to be abused especially when one is doing brainwork – Prolonged virginity for women is always very bad – they simply dry up & often become entirely sterile at a comparatively early age – 30. 35. There are many works on this subject: I do not interest myself enough in it to read them – They are mostly medical – Kraft Ebing & Havelock Ellis I believe also write on this subject Christianity might be entirely condemned by its *morals* alone – Ignoring sex & the very source of life & Bringing forth generations of onanizing men & women: both becoming hysterical & impotent & disatisfied – The womans question in England & America especially is one of enormous importance. The suffragettes are nearly all menless women Sex is at the bottom of it all & they will ultimately carry the day & perhaps change entirely & revolutionize sexual life – In Germany &

the North (Scandinavia) girls are beginning to live entirely free & enjoy men whilst they are quite young & before they get married – they want to live – Very few people now really believe in any life hereafter & they want to, at least, get something out of this one – The next ten years will see enormous changes – I received only *one* volume of "Love poems" by D. H. Lawrence – I do hope the other volume has not been lost – When did you send it off? – I have not had time to read the poems yet as I am working hard just now & scarcely read at all – I thank you heartily for the poems & am looking forward to them. How foolish of your mother to take the pianola away – Well! Well! parents still seem to be the same – but abroad there is a decided change taking place – much more so than in England – In your piano score of the Song of the high hills, the chorus must of course be on separate lines – When necessary also use 3 systems (lines) instead of only 2 for the piano – Why is it impossible to work in the quaver accompaniment to the melody on Page 7. Put it on a 3rd line perhaps – you see the effect must be attained some way or other – otherwise one gets a wrong impression of the work – the quavers there are important – I am eagerly awaiting Leuckarts' answer – I should put all the work I possibly can in to your hands, of course, but I have not always the power – as the editor buys the works outright from me & has them arranged by his own man – I can advise him, of course, but he may not always take my advice – We will see now what Leuckart does[4] – I will send you the parts of the "Song of the high hills" & should be very thankful if you would correct them for me[5] – I am working so successfully just at present that it would be of great help to me – Who is conducting my 2 orchestral pieces at the Philharmonic?

Now, dear boy, write me soon again – your letters always interest me –

your affectionate friend
Frederick Delius

I hope you can read this scribble.

Autograph letter, signed and dated. Envelope addressed: Philip Heseltine Esqre/ Cefn-Bryntalch/Abermule/Montgomeryshire/Angleterre. Postmark: GREZ 3 -1 14.

The original is in the British Library.

1   As long ago as 11 March 1912, Delius had written to Heseltine: 'If ever you want some advice from someone who really likes you & feels real interest in your welfare you can come to me without the slightest restraint – On any subject or question whatever I will tell you what I really think & I can assure you that very few people ever tell one what they really think – When they do they are always invaluable.'

2   Olivia (Viva) Smith, of Didbrook, Gloucestershire. Heseltine fell in love with her while staying in the village in 1913, and some hundred letters he wrote to her are preserved in the British Library (Add. MS 58127).

3   In 1914 Delius was still under the impression that he had been born on 29 January 1863; and little more than a month after his '21st' birthday he was on his way to Florida. This remark, therefore, may refer to an American love affair; alternatively, with some licence, to Camilla Jacobsen, whose name follows his in the register of the Leipzig Conservatorium and whom he subsequently visited in Norway.

4   Delius was trying – in vain – to interest Leuckart in Heseltine's piano arrangements of *Brigg Fair* and *A Dance Rhapsody*.

5   Delius wrote to Heseltine on 18 January: 'All the corrections you sent me "Song of the High hills" were right – It is wonderful how one oversees mistakes – You seem to have an eagle eye.'

(388)
Frederick Delius to H. Balfour Gardiner

[Grez, 18? January 1914]

Go & hear my 2 pieces for small orchestra – I hear Mengelberg is doing them on the 20th or 21st at the Philharmonic[1] – We are having glorious weather, hard frost & snow & sun

Fr. Delius

Picture postcard: *GREZ-SUR-LOING – Vue sur le Loing*, signed and undated. Addressed: H. Balfour Gardiner Esqr/7 Pembroke Villas/Kensington/Londres W. Postmark: GREZ 18[?] -1 14.

The original is in the collection of John Eliot Gardiner. It is the only communication from Delius himself to Gardiner that has been found. See also Letter 487.

1   Willem Mengelberg conducted the first performances in England of *On hearing the first Cuckoo* and *Summer Night on the River* at a Philharmonic Society concert on 20 January, having just given them in Amsterdam. 'He told me he *loved* them,' wrote Grainger from Amsterdam on the 25th, 'and all tell me that it was a ripping performance & made a *deep impression*. Am trying to get hold of the critiques which I hear were splendid.' On 3 March Fritz Steinbach was to give the two pieces in Cologne.

(389)
Frederick Delius to Universal Edition

1st March 1914
Adr. bei Herrn Max Esser
Göbenstr
Elberfeld

Dear Herr Direktor,

I have just received a letter from the pianist Percy Grainger. He would like to play my Piano Concerto often on his concert tours in England and is unhappy to find this quite impossible for him to do, because 5 pounds Sterling, that is 100 Mk, are asked for *each performance*. That is quite out of the question when the circumstances of the provincial English societies are taken into account.

Now what do you suggest? Can you not find a practicable alternative? Can you not provide him with material he can use always? That would be of the greatest importance in getting my Piano Concerto played widely, as Grainger gives concerts all over Europe, particularly Scandinavia   Holland   etc.

Can you not prevail upon Harmonie to issue a new edition including the corrections?

You might e.g. arrange with Grainger for each Concert Society to pay Mk 50. This Concerto is just the sort of work that could become so popular, but *everything* is in its way – the high price which scares everybody away & the lack of a proper material.[1]

With kind regards
Frederick Delius

Letter in the hand of Jelka Delius, dated, written in German on notepaper headed *Dom-Hôtel   Köln   Domplatz.*

The original is in the Universal Edition archives.

1   Dealings with Universal Edition took up a great deal of Delius's time during the first months of 1914, from reminding Hertzka on 5 January to print the dedication '*Halfdan Jebe* gewidmet' on the title page of *An Arabesque*, to asking him on 19 June not to 'give away' first performances of his work without first asking for permission to do so (*An Arabesque* had already been promised to Wood, preventing Beecham from giving it as he wished to do in July). Both parties – Delius and Hertzka – had been feeling their way in January towards acceptable terms for a contract, and Hertzka was taken aback by Delius's 'extraordinary caution' and 'lack of trust'. In reply Delius pointed out that it was only sensible to get matters properly sorted out – and in considerable detail at that – at the outset of a business relationship. He trusted Hertzka, but a well-founded contract could not be based on trust alone. What would be the point of transferring all his works from Harmonie to Universal if for example Hertzka

were to disappear tomorrow and 'a second Jadassohn' were then to take over the direction of Universal? In March and April Delius was to complain to Universal about deficiencies in the newly printed orchestral parts of the *Mass*, just as he had recently complained about the mistakes the company had allowed to get through in *An Arabesque*.

(390)
Frederick Delius to Philip Heseltine

GREZ-SUR-LOING
Seine et Marne
March 11 1914

My dear Philip —

I only returned here last night[1] — We have been away in Germany just 1 month — Heard the "Mass of Life" at Wiesbaden & Frankfurt — The two Orchestra pieces in Frankfurt & Cologne — & Songs of Sunset in Elberfeld[2] — It gave me the greatest possible pleasure to hear you liked the 2 pieces so much — I have since written 3 more shortish Orchestra pieces[3] — On my return here I found the whole material of Fennimore awaiting me — Wont you come here & correct it for me? or help me? When do your holidays begin? We brought 2 servants with us back from Germany — I heard Schönbergs Kammer Symphonie in Cologne — it is very dry & unpoetical & entirely intellectual — but did not sound bad at all — At times quite like Strauss in Heldenleben — & sometimes quite interesting — But what sometimes sounds very bad on the piano — sounds quite tame on the Orchestra — I agree with every effort of the young school to do something new — but I disagree with music becoming a merely mathematical, & intellectual art — Be careful Philip!! Be Careful my boy!! you live in a bourgeois world — Take care of yourself & of your friend. Do not travel about with her yet — Come here to me alone — I have lots of things to tell you — Dont break with your family — Come here as soon as you can — Of course you can now stay with us here —[4]

your affectionate
Frederick Delius

Autograph letter, signed and dated, written on headed notepaper. Envelope addressed: Philip Heseltine Esqre/Christ Church/Oxford/Angleterre. Postmark: GREZ 12 -3 14.

The original is in the British Library.

1   From Frankfurt, Delius had written to tell Hertzka that he would return to Grez on 11 March. On the 10th the Oriana Madrigal Society, soloist Thorpe Bates, conductor Charles Kennedy Scott, gave *Sea Drift* in London – '*gorgeous performance*,' wrote Grainger to Jelka the following day. Also on the programme was *On hearing the first Cuckoo*. Another Delius work given in London, a little before this, was *A Dance Rhapsody*, on 14 February. Heseltine and Balfour Gardiner were present, and Heseltine reported to a friend: 'Henry Wood did the Delius *Dance Rhapsody* disgracefully badly', adding that Wood 'has no ideas whatever, where D is concerned.' (Tomlinson: *A Peter Warlock Handbook*, 2, p. 83.) The first London performance of *In a Summer Garden* followed on 27 March, with Geoffrey Toye conducting the Queen's Hall Orchestra. This was in the work's revised form.

2   Delius wrote on 13 March to his sister Clare, telling her that in fact he and Jelka had attended in Germany '7 concerts where works of mine were played'. The Elberfeld concert, on 7 March, was notable in that the work given, *Songs of Sunset*, was performed by its dedicatees, the Elberfeld Choral Society, conducted by Hans Haym. The soloists were Ilona Durigo and Sydney Biden. Haym had earlier written to Ida Gerhardi, on 21 April 1913, commenting on the work: 'a risky thing. For this is not a work for a wide public, but rather for a smallish band of musical isolates who are born decadents and life's melancholics at the same time. He mustn't write anything like this again. For even if in parts of it there is much that is movingly atmospheric and of the greatest beauty, it cannot work as a whole, as it lacks contrasts.'

3   It is not clear to which pieces Delius is referring: probably individual movements of his *North Country Sketches*.

4   Heseltine was at Grez by the end of March, correcting the parts of *Fennimore and Gerda* and translating the text of *An Arabesque* into English. He returned to England in time to begin, on 24 April, his final term at Oxford University. 'We both enjoyed your stay immensely,' wrote Delius on the 24th, '& hope you will repeat it.'

(391)
Frederick Delius to Matthew Smith

Grez sur Loing
S & M
10th April 14

My dear Mr Smith

I was very glad to receive news from you and learn where you were. We had a most lovely winter. 6 weeks with nothing but hard frost and sunshine – for days together not a cloud. Since I am in Grez I never enjoyed a winter so much. In February the bad weather came and we went for 5 weeks to Germany and attended a number of concerts. On the 12th of March we were back here again and the weather was cold and rainy – But since a few days it is lovely

again and real spring. Our garden is lovely with spring flowers. I intend remaining here even until June when I may go to London for a fortnight. Have
you found anything to paint down there? We both send you and Mrs Smith
our kind regards

Sincerely yours
Frederick Delius

Autograph letter, signed and dated.

The original is in the collection of Mrs Alice Kadel. It is the only item of correspondence between Delius and Smith that has come to light.

Matthew Smith (1879–1959): English painter. A great colourist and influenced by the
Fauves, he lived in Grez for a time in 1912–13, and was to return there frequently
between 1918 and 1922 and occasionally too in later years. Eric Fenby remembers him
as 'a most delicate and charming man'.

Alden Brooks relates how he himself met Matthew Smith (who was later to paint a
portrait of him) late in August 1912, 'thanks to Joe Heseltine who came over from
Marlotte deliberately and to introduce us and our families to each other'. He continues: 'Smith first met Delius on the afternoon of October 7th, 1913. I had wanted
for some time to introduce him to Delius, but he had always shied away. However he
had now met Lloyd Osbourne at the local inn, and the Osbournes were going to a tea-
party at the Deliuses, and Lloyd urged him to come along, so Smith rushed over to me
and got me to come as a second escort. Smith was of course an admirer of Delius, but
he remained always . . . well, not frightened of Delius, but nervous, ill at ease in his
presence. Though, as my wife says, who didn't remain so?' (Typescript dated 29
August 1960 supplied by Sophie Royde Smith.) Another link was through Guy
Maynard, American expatriate painter and friend of Delius at Grez; he had met Smith
in 1908/9 while painting in Pont-Aven.

(392)
Jelka Delius to Auguste Rodin

Grez sur Loing
28.4.1914

Dear Maître,

I had just written to tell you that we have had to put off our trip to Paris –
when your telegram arrived.[1]

I am glad to know that you are nearby, and that you too can see this delightful springtime countryside –

If your friend the doctor has a motor car perhaps it would not be impossible
for you to pay us a visit when you are passing this way? We are in the house

before the church at Grez. The garden is quite full of lilacs and my husband
and I would be *delighted* to see you here!

With my most affectionate regards I am ever

Yours
Jelka Delius
nee Rosen.

Autograph letter, signed and dated, written in French.

The original is in the Musée Rodin, Paris. It is apparently the last letter that Jelka
wrote to Rodin.

1   Jelka had written to Rodin on 26 April to propose a visit: 'I am really sorry that
you were away on your travels the last time we called on you. Could we not come to
see you next Thursday at about five o'clock – if not Thursday, perhaps Friday?' Early
on the 28th she wrote to tell him: 'We are very sorry to have to put off our trip to
Paris.' Rodin's telegram, which arrived a little later that day, has not survived.

(393)
Frederick Delius to Percy Grainger

GREZ-SUR-LOING
Seine et Marne
29 April 14

What pleasure your letter gave me, dear friend![1] You are always the one who
sends me good news from England – I love your impulsive letters – they are so
entirely yourself & just like your music which you know I love so much. I feel
we have an enormous lot in common & that you understand better than anyone
what I am trying to do – I was so happy to hear of your success in Torquay. Do
you know that in Bradford they are giving a whole concert of my works. I proposed you should play the Concerto – It is on Nov 27th & I do hope you are not
engaged.[2] Szanto arranged the Klaviersatz most beautifully – & made it much
more effective[3] – Cant you come over here & pay me a visit with your mother.
The spring has been simply divine – The garden is full of Lilacs & Laburnums
in full bloom – Try & come – I have 2 new Orchestra pieces – In June we come
to London for a fortnight – you must either come before or come back with me
– you will love it here – it is out of the world –

Ever so much love to you & to your mother –

your loving friend
Frederick Delius

Autograph letter, signed and dated, written on headed notepaper. Envelope addressed: Percy Grainger Esqre/19 Cheniston Gardens/Kensington/London W/ Angleterre. Readdressed: 7 Pembroke Villas. Postmark: GREZ [date illegible]. Receiving postmark: KENSINGTON.W 30 AP 14.

The original is in the Grainger Museum.

1   Grainger wrote on 26 April to tell Delius about the recent Torquay Festival, where on 16 April he had for the first time performed the Delius Concerto, 'which was a great success, & in which I felt very happy. It is a work one loves more & more as one knows it longer ... I very much want to play it *everywhere* I can. You are now getting so universally loved & honored everywhere & the time seems to me just ripe for the lovely Concerto to come into its own.' He continued: 'Above everything I am in love with your adorable "First Cuckoo", that goes to my very heart ... The mood of it & lots of the Dance Rhapsody feel closer to me personally than my own work does, it utterly voices what I most inwardly long to hear expressed or to express.' Delius had already had a report from Beecham, who wrote on the 20th: 'Percy Grainger played your Piano Concerto and it went fairly well in performance, and most successfully with the Public. Percy was good in the "forte" passages, but made far too much noise in the quieter bits, rather to the poetic detriment of the work. The "Dance Rhapsody" was also an immense favourite with the Public, who greeted *most* of the novelties with the stoniest silence.'

2   'I have already signed for it,' wrote Grainger on 6 May.

3   Grainger had complimented Delius – and Szántó – on the piano part.

(394)
Thomas Beecham to Frederick Delius

June 14/14
THE COTTAGE,
8^A HOBART PLACE,
S.W.

Dear Delius –

I am delighted to hear you are coming here soon – You must try to arrange to stay in London until the end of the first week in July as I am organising a concert of your works for July 7th or thereabouts. I want to make it very interesting and pleasant, and can do so on this occasion as I have two opera choruses at my disposal and some first-rate singers. Do you think you could send me at once the scores of the "North Country Sketches" and the "Arabesque", as I might include one or both of them in the Concert if you wish it.[1] But if so, I must have the music at once as I presume you have not yet got the orchestral parts ready. You can safely send them to this address as I am now permanently lodged here.

We have a concert on June 26th at the French Embassy (a very nice affair) when I play your "Dance Rhapsody" and the "Village Romeo" Entr'acte (*or* the 2 pieces for smaller orchestra). There are two other concerts where I am playing some of your pieces of which I will tell you when we meet. I shall look forward immensely to "Fennimore" and will give it in 1915 at Drury Lane. We are having a most successful season, the London public having gone perfectly mad over these Russian Operas. I don't blame them, as most of the works are simple, unaffected and refined, and a great relief after all this German blather and vulgarity. Strauss is practically "finished" in London, though his Ballet, (produced here on the 23rd) will provide the usual sensation of the moment – welcomed as a masterpiece and relegated next year to the dust-bin. You know, he is the modern Meyerbeer and will in ten years be written of as such –

I thought that for your concert, the following Programme would do –

Brigg Fair
In a Summer Garden
Village Romeo Entr'acte
Arabesque
Dance Rhapsody
Songs of Sunset (certain numbers to be selected)
Selection from Koanga
North Country pictures
and some Songs.

Why don't you come here to stay for a few days about the time of the concert. It is a pretty house, with a garden.

Please let me have a line at once about the new music. I do not want to be rushed this time.

Always yours
T. B.

Autograph letter, initialled and dated, written on headed notepaper. Envelope addressed: Frederick Delius/Esq./Grez-sur-Loing/Seine-et-Marne/France. Postmark: LONDON 14 JU 14.

The original is in the Delius Trust Archive.

1   Universal Edition had already promised the first performance of *An Arabesque* to Wood. On 1 August Universal wrote to tell Delius that Wood had waived his claim, and that Beecham was free to give the work – information that did not reach the composer, as the postcard was held up by the postal authorities and returned to Universal on the outbreak of war.

(395)
Frederick Delius to Jelka Delius

4, PEMBROKE VILLAS,
KENSINGTON, W.
[23 June 1914]

Dearest – I had a fairly smooth passage – The sandwiches were very welcome at
Folkstone – Beecham met me at the station – just as nice as ever & full of plans
– He drove me on to O'Neills & stayed talking for quite a long time with the
cab waiting at the door to take him back – Yesterday afternoon I went to the
Répétition generale of Strauss' – Joseph[1] – Everybody was there – from Lady
Cunard to Bernard Shaw I also spoke to Ernest Newman who looked very well
& who I shall soon meet again –
Joseph is absolutely the worst that Strauss has written & the whole ballet, is
long & awfully dull – nothing going on whatever with a most banal sort of
music going on, one wonders why, & Having nothing whatever to do with the
ballet – Then, again ones eye is not pleased with anything – The costumes are
a sort of Beardsley Venetian style – & the scenery much too mastock[2] Heavy
columns looking like an Egyptian temple & not suiting the rest of the picture
– In other words the whole thing dull & slow & very pretentious – Neither
Ballet or music of the slightest interest – In the Evening I went to the
Borodine Opera "Prince Igor" – which pleased me *very much* – Lovely scenery
& charming – sincere music full of poetry & colored with russian & Tartar
folklore – The work of a man of genius & delicate poet – the 3rd Act – the
Tartar Camp – simply lovely – & so simple as scenery. Huge Kirgise tents in
purple & red – on the banks of some lake or river – with the steppe & all
so simply done – After the Opera, Lady Cunard & Nancy[3] drove to a ball in
Grosvenor Square & dropped Beecham & me at his little house where we had
supper – Lady C suddenly turning up again & chatting with us until 2.30.
Then they both took me home to O'Neills – Nancy looks now quite lovely – &
sends you her warmest love as does also Lady C. Beecham thinks of giving a
concert on the 7th July at a small Hall. Everything will be arranged today &
then I will let you know – Beecham wants me to stay with him next week –
His house is quite lovely – & he lives there all alone – He seems to be rolling
in money again – His father has just been made a Baronet – so Lady C – who
has brought it of course all about, is exultant – I met also the Duchess of
Rutland & Lady Diana[4] who looks quite lovely – Lady Ripon – Lady Randolph
Churchill – Cambon – Me Jules Cambon the Berlin Ambassador's wife[5]
Bernard Shaw – M^r & Mrs Legge – Holbrooke Diagilew & many others whose
names I cannot remember – But it is really very amusing for a short time –
Beecham is going to get Nijinski to dance the Dance Rhapsody[6] – With heaps
of love –

your
Fred

Remember me to the girls – Has Elaine appeared yet?[7]

I shall probably want the parts of Koanga – II Act but will telegraph

---

Autograph letter, signed and undated, written on headed notepaper.

The original is in the Grainger Museum.

1   In a letter to Jelka written from Ashampstead on 26 June, Delius sketched in the events of the evening of the première, on the 23rd: 'On Tuesday I went to the Première of "Joseph" Everybody was there – First came "Thamar" which I had not seen before – The music is in parts splendid: altho' as a whole I liked 'Igor' better – In Lady Cunard's box were heaps of people – It is the royal box of Drury Lane – Lady Islington, M[r] & Mrs Asquith, Nancy – Count Benckendorf the Russian Ambassador – Chaliapine – who I spoke with & liked very much – I shall send him "Niels" when edited – Lady Diana Manners – who is very nice – & spirituelle – the Duchess of Westminster came in also.' Delius also attended, on 26 June, the première of Rimsky-Korsakov's opera *Nuit de Mai*.

2   French, *mastoc: heavy, lumpish.*

3   Nancy Cunard (1896–1965): English writer and poet. She was to become much associated with intellectual and artistic circles in Paris in the 1920s. Daughter of Maud, Lady Cunard, it was almost inevitable that with her strong left-wing political sympathies Nancy would break with her mother and with the particular social world that she represented. Like Delius she, too, was to sit for Henry Clews, who sculpted a bust of her.

4   Lady Diana Manners (1892–1986): artistically gifted daughter of the eighth Duke of Rutland. She married in 1919 Alfred Duff Cooper.

5   Paul Cambon was French ambassador in London from 1898 to 1920, his brother Jules French ambassador in Berlin from 1907 to 1914.

6   Although nothing was to come of this project, Delius had apparently laid plans rather earlier, as a letter from Heseltine to Viva Smith on 10 April indicates: 'I am to visit Nijinsky in London, at the first favourable opportunity, play him my four-hand arrangement of Delius' *Dance Rhapsody* . . . and endeavour to get him to perform it with his company' (Tomlinson: *Warlock and Delius*, p. 17). He was to take with him a letter from Delius to Nijinsky.

7   Hilma Brooks was expecting a child.

(396)
Frederick Delius to Jelka Delius

ASHAMPSTEAD GREEN,
PANGBOURNE,
BERKS.
[28/29? June 1914]

Dearest –

I hope you sent off the parts – I go on Wednesday to "The Cottage" 8ª Hobart Place – to Beecham. He is not doing "Songs of Sunset" but perhaps the 2 part songs by Symonds[1] The Programm will probably be – Brigg Fair   Dance Rhapsody – Summer Garden   Koanga – Aria, & Finale of R & J. If you dont come I shall leave for Grez on the 10th. But if you have the slightest envie to come, do so of course – I went to the French Embassy after the Opera – It was too full of people – Beecham did the Entracte of R & J. *very well* & it was a great success[2] – Then they Acted "La Damoiselle Elue" about 30 girls of the Aristocracy stood up on a sort of Escalier platform – hideously dressed à la Rossetti & sang. In the middle, on the top, stood a very beautiful young woman, Phillis Terry[3], dressed in a gold gown & holding a lily & looking very aesthetic – They all were too heavily dressed   Afterwards at supper, I said to the Duchess of Rutland – "who on earth invented those awful costumes" & she pointed to Lady Diana sitting opposite me & said Oh, Diana did them! I did not attempt to make things good again – but simply said, I think all those lovely girls ought to have had less on. There were some just too lovely women there & décollté? down below the waist at the back & as low as possible in front, with nothing over the arms & shoulders & their hairs taken away under the arms. But real beauties. Lady Curzon is really quite lovely. I met Lady Elko[4] again & her lovely daughter. I see Nancy nearly every night but she looks as if she were not happy. I met George Moor[5] at the Embassy. He loved R & J. I have not yet had time to go & see my mother, but will try on Thursday or Friday next. When did she say she was leaving for Germany? I have not got her letter here – It is a fearful life to lead for anyone having anything serious to do – Nancy & Lady C. went to a ball at the Duke of Argyle's, after the reception at the French Embassy So that they got home every night at 5 & 6 in the morning. I am feeling very fit with all this. Today I am here & enjoying the lovely weather. Tell Hilma that *Eileen* is even prettier than Elaine.

With love your
Fred.

Autograph letter, signed and dated, written on headed notepaper.

The original is in the Grainger Museum.

1   *On Craig Ddu* and *Wanderer's Song*, to words by Arthur Symons.

2   Following the première of *Nuit de Mai*, there was a midnight reception, with music, at the French Embassy.

3   Phyllis Terry (1892–1977): English actress.

4   Lady Elcho, Countess of Wemyss, a patron of the arts.

5   George Moore (1852–1933): Irish novelist and memoirist, and an intimate of Lady Cunard.

(397)
Frederick Delius to Jelka Delius

THE COTTAGE,
8ᴬ HOBART PLACE,
S.W.
[2 July 1914]

Dearest – I received all your letters & am glad all things are going on so well in Grez.¹ Here it is tropical 88 in the shade fahrenheit I came here yesterday & am very comfortable. The Concert is not yet announced – If I can get him to give it in November instead I shall – I have just come from a grand reception at Grosvenor House – Duke of Westminster. A french exhibition is there – The one where our Gauguin was to appear – The Queen Alexandra & the Ex Empress of Russia were there & all the high pots of England – I lunched with Rodin & Comtesse Greffulhe at Lady Cunards² day before yesterday – Lord Londsboro was there & sat next to me – He seems to love my music. I sat next to the French Ambassadress in Berlin Mᶜ Jules Cambon who is very nice – Rodin is a senile old idiot – running about to all these lords & Ladies with Comtesse Greffulhe & Miss O'Connor He asked after you very kindly I said we should come & see him soon – He said he was in the country but in a month he would be in Paris again – However we must let him know beforehand. The pictures are splendid but so badly lighted that one cannot see them – Rodins best things are there – But what was very interesting was the wonderful collection of paintings in the Grosvenor House wonderful Rembrandts & Gainsboroughs – God gracious what a collection – also the old Dutch – Teniers – Rubens – but many – We had tea afterwards – I met also Annie Morgen – Lady Randolph Churchhill – !! Tomorrow I dine at Lord Howard de Waldens & go to Dylan³ after – I ought to have dined last night at Lady Elcho's to meet Balfour again – but I was too tired & it was too hot – so I put it off – I forget the names of all these Dukes Lords & Ladies that I am intro-

duced to & I am about sick of it now I met Bernard Shaw again – Tonight I go
to the Opera again Le Coq d'or. Excuse these scribbling letters – I write them
like a "Cinema" when I have a moment to spare – I met also George Moore
again & Isadore de Lara – Karsavina was at Lady Cunards lunch – a lovely
creature – like an objet d'art & real russian – I had a long talk with her & she is
really sympathetic. In haste & with love – your Fred –

Autograph letter, signed and undated, written on headed notepaper.

The original is in the Grainger Museum.

1   Apart from village and household gossip, Jelka had told Delius of her continuing
work on sketches for the scenery of *Fennimore and Gerda*.

2   It is to Lady Cunard's legendary hospitality, at 20 Cavendish Square at this period,
that we owe a sensitive pen-picture of Delius, drawn by another guest – Osbert Sitwell
– on just such an occasion as this: 'I do not know that his looks precisely interpreted
his nature. He was rather tall and thin, possessed a high, narrow forehead, an aquiline
nose, delicately cut, and a finely-drawn face, of the Roman intellectual type. Though
it is true that his head showed every sign of distinction, he might, from his appearance, more easily have been a great lawyer than a great composer. In talking – and he
was a voluble and delightful conversationalist – his tongue betrayed, not an accent,
exactly, but a slight foreign stress and lilt, attractive, and personal enough to make a
contrast with the theories and speculations of which his soliloquies were full: for he
loved abstract ideas with the passion of a Latin for them – the English hate them –
and, though he formulated them with all a clever Englishman's love of paradox, there
was, nevertheless, a certain stringency pertaining to them. The most gifted of English
composers living at that time, head and shoulders above his bumpy buttercup-and-
daisy confrères, a musician of the world, he found himself somewhat of a stranger in
London.' (*Great Morning*, pp. 252–3.) Eugene Goossens remembered a later occasion
when Lady Cunard gave a lunch party at Carlton House Terrace: 'I remember Lord
Balfour, Herbert Asquith (whose régime of war-time premier had just given way
to the coalition of Lloyd George), the Duchess of Rutland, Lady Diana Manners,
Duff Cooper, Sargent the painter, Yeats, Delius, Beecham, and Eddie Marsh (Mr
Churchill's secretary) all seated at an enormous table presided over by the picturesque
Emerald herself. However large the gathering, the querulous voice of Delius always
managed to make itself heard over a general conversation, and this occasion was no
exception to the rule. Even England's two senior statesmen lapsed into silence when
the Delius tones were heard asking why it was that the British public displayed such
abysmal ignorance of opera as compared with other European peoples. "Don't talk like
that," answered Beecham. "Just you wait till we produce *A Village Romeo and Juliet*.
That'll disprove what you say." "Bah," said Delius. "The public here doesn't know a
note of my music, and cares less!" "Perhaps," slyly observed Eddie Marsh, "that's
because they don't like it." "Don't like it? Don't like it" shouted the irate Delius.
"Tell me what they *do* like!" A quiet voice interrupted with: "*Dear* Mr Balfour, *do* tell
us how the Lloyd George coalition is working," and Maud Cunard had steered the
conversation into safer channels.' (*Overture and Beginners*, London, 1951, pp. 126–7.)

Although Goossens remembered this luncheon as taking place at the beginning of 1917, the Delius letters give no indication that the composer left Grez at all that year.

3   Delius had written to Jelka on 26 June: 'I lunched on Wednesday at Lord Howard de Walden & sat on Lady Walden's right hand . . . of course the de Waldens wanted me to be present at the "premiere" of Holbrooks opera "Dylan". So I am dining there on July 4th & going to Dylan with them.'

(398)
Frederick Delius to Jelka Delius

8[a] Hobart Place
[3 July 1914]

Dearest – The Concert is fixed & advertised[1] – Brigg Fair. 3 Verlaine Songs. (good Frenche singer Madame Gilles.) – "In a Summer Garden" – The last scene of Koanga (when he rushes off into the swamps) – Entre acte & Finale of R & J. with Agnes Nicolls & an excellent Tenor[2] who I heard in Dylan (the rehearsal) I forget his name – & Dance Rhapsody I went to see Coq d'or – which is about the best thing Rimski has done – & the arrangement of Diagilew combining the ballet & a chorus & solo singers doing the singing part is quite genial & certainly saves the work which would otherwise be too long & tedious. The Costumes are simply marvellous – as is also the scenery – & Karsavina!!! I was introduced to the Grand Duke Alexander uncle of the Tsar a nice sympathetic looking man – I meet old Cambon almost every night – He is really very nice – Prince Troubitzkoi & his wife are also very nice – He is a painter & brother of the Sculptor – Wife American – in fact there are a tremendous lot of American women in the English Aristocracy now & also in the German – French & Russian – I am rather tired of meeting these people now – they are pretty well all the same – I hope to leave here on the 10th & travel thro – I bought the print for the girls. 16 yds – pink & white stripes 8 $\frac{3}{4}$d a yd – Got also a nice holdall – This is the Silurian paper they gave me in a big packet Isnt it too thick? Lady Diana looked lovely at the Opera – Coq d'or. She was in our box – & had a lovely chinese cloak on – red with gold & an enormous dragon on the back. She told me that she was not responsible for those costumes – They had overthrown her ideas of color entirely & a costumier had done it – I quite believe it as she has really good taste & is very sensual in everything – She looks lovely, & I am sure n'a peur de rien real race – They made up a night boating party – to go straight from the Opera at 12, up the river in a Steam launch – Luckily I & Beecham & Lady Cunard did not go but came home & had a nice supper & chat – The young men must have been shewing off & playing the fool & perhaps drinking too much – One of them a young Baronet Sir W. Anson – suddenly sprang into the river & the current carried him away – One of Beechams Orchestra (they had taken music with them) sprang in after him & was also carried away by the strong Current – Then young Count Benckendorf – sprang in to save them & would also have gone – but they threw him a life belt & he was saved – I hear Lady Diana looked quietly on & said – What does it matter – 2 human lives are nothing at all – perfectly unmoved[3] – Nancy got home at 6. a m & had to be put to bed quite hysterical – Nice goings on eh! They go it strong here in this lot – I can tell you – M^{rs} ONeill has seen a pied a terre for us – lovely – but it costs 80 pounds! I am going to see it presently – I spoke with Henry Wood who wanted the "Requiem" I arranged to let them have it *if it is done* – He was very nice – The performance of the "Arabeske" is postponed – Speyer has lost a fearful lot of money They were bringing up a Chorus from the North – It may however be given a month later "Next April" Write soon –

With love – yrs ever
Fred –

Autograph letter, signed and undated.

The original is in the Grainger Museum.

1   This all-Delius concert was given on 8 July at the Duke's Hall, Royal Academy of Music. 'I never heard Beecham play my things so wonderfully,' wrote Delius to Jelka immediately after it was over, 'and indeed, I am sure, my music has never been played as well by anyone . . . Beecham has real genius, he feels every bar of my music like no one else.' The Duke's Hall evidently held out fewer attractions to Society than did Covent Garden or Drury Lane: 'There were not many people present but those that were there were very enthusiastic.' The excerpt from *Koanga* was dropped from the final programme, as were the Verlaine songs, and the *First Cuckoo* and 'Danish Songs' (Agnes Nicholls) were substituted.

2   Frank Mullings.

3   The incident was widely noticed in the press, and Margot Asquith's diary entry for 31 December 1914 highlighted it as part of what she saw as the pre-war 'frightfulness' in England, itself partly mirroring the departure of the Germans from the 'Spirit of Christ': 'We observed . . . pleasure people watching a man they loved drown, while incapable of either feeling or showing mourning for him.'

(399)
Frederick Delius to Philip Heseltine

Grez sur Loing
(S & M)
30 July – [1914]

My dear Heseltine –

Your letter gave me immense pleasure   It means a great deal to me that you appreciate so greatly what I have done[1] – It was also a great pleasure to me to have seen you a good deal whilst I was in England – I looked out for you after the Concert as I wanted to take you home with me to dinner – I spent the evening purposely all alone – & went into Hyde Park & up to the Marble Arch, where I listened to several discussions – In one *I took part*   It was awfully interesting & you ought to have been there – Have you finished "An Arabeske"? The editor wants it now – please send it me as *soon as possible* – I do hope War will not break out & knock all Art and Music on the head for years[2] – I am working at my Requiem –
    Write soon & send the poem –

    your affectionate friend
    Frederick Delius

Autograph letter, signed and dated. Envelope addressed: *Please forward*/Philip Heseltine Esqre/Cefn Bryntalch/Abermule/Montgomeryshire/Angleterre. Postmark: GREZ 30 -7 14.

The original is in the British Library.

Delius returned to Grez on Friday 10 July, excusing himself from a lunch invitation to the French Embassy so that he could take a morning train. 'Thank goodness I am now back again in Grez & enjoying the quiet & our lovely garden,' he wrote to Adine O'Neill on the 16th.

1   'I must write you just a few lines to tell you, however inadequately, what a wonderful and overwhelmingly beautiful experience last Wednesday's concert was for me, and to contribute my tiny share – however futile – to the debt of gratitude the whole world owes you for such superb, such glorious music. No words could do it justice; it is too magnificent. It transcends everything – not only all other music. For me it is the greatest thing in life.' Heseltine to Delius, 10 July (Gray, pp. 57–8).

2   Jelka to Delius, 30 June 1914: 'What an affair of the Serbs again this Serajewo murder.'

(400)
Thomas Beecham to Frederick Delius

EWANVILLE,
HUYTON,
NEAR LIVERPOOL.
1st. October 1914.

My Dear Delius,

Many thanks for your letter: You must have had a very interesting and exciting time during the German advance. I read your letters to Lady Cunard dealing with your adventures on the road to Orleans, and I am delighted to know
that you are back again at Grez, as tranquil as ever. From what one can make
out of the War reports, you are not likely to be troubled again, as there seems
to be no doubt that the neck of the German attack has now been broken. Of
course, for years to come any kind of rapprochement between this country
and Germany will be out of the question, and I think that on the whole it will
be a splendid thing for us, for this means the actual end of the long German
influence and domination here in musical matters, which is bound sooner or
later to produce a healthy re-action in our own people.[1] It is not as if Germany
had still something vital and first-rate to send us: on the contrary, in music,
and most especially in thought, she is a bankrupt Nation. Several of us have
been aware of this for some time, but I do not think anyone was prepared for
the recent self-exposition on their part of strange miscalculation and childish
ineptitude in organization. Not a single thing they confidently anticipated has
yet happened, and it is more than a little refreshing to be able to say that for
these emergencies the English were perhaps the most prepared.

I am afraid it is not possible for me to come over to France at present, as
I have a multitude of things here to attend to. I am going to make use of the
present situation to put in hand a great many things that have hitherto been
difficult because of old prejudice here and the consistent opposition on the part
of German Jews to any serious endeavour made by an Englishman. With the
exception of my projected tours on the Continent, I am in no way altering my
plans. Concerts are going on here as usual, and I look forward to another
Opera Season next Summer. What about 'Niels Lyhne'? I should very much
like to see it with a view to working it in to one of my Seasons. You will now
have to seriously consider the question of having it played in some other language than German, and I think it should play fairly well in French, even
though some of the sentiment be lost thereby.

Next week I am conducting a Concert at Bradford with the "Halle
Orchestra", and am giving your two short pieces, which they have specially
asked for. I should very much like to see your "Requiem" as there will be a

good chance of giving it somewhere this Winter if you should so wish it. Perhaps you could find some way of sending it over to me.

With love

Affectionately yours
T. B.

P.S. Please excuse this "type-written" letter, but I have hurt my hand a little – T. B.

Typed letter (with handwritten postscript), initialled and dated, written on headed notepaper.

The original is in the Delius Trust Archive.

Some background to the events of September is supplied by friends and neighbours. Hilma Brooks wrote to Matthew Smith's wife on 8 September: 'Is there really any chance of there being conscription in England? Delius has some friend who has left for America on that account. Every one who can has left Grez – we are you see in the military zone. The Deliuses were going to stay like us to the bitter end but they noticed there was a good deal of ill feeling about them, perhaps because his wife is German or because he writes so often to Germany. In fact the Gendarmes came to see about it. He sent a manuscript off on the 25th and war was declared on the 1st, so of course was denounced as a spy – of course it is perfectly absurd and was only done by someone who has a grudge against them. So they thought it wiser to leave, but had to leave their poor servants behind as they are Austrians.'

On 1 October, Guy Maynard wrote (from Concarneau) to Matthew Smith: 'The Delius's, after enraging Chadwick by jeering at him for "running away", finally decided to run themselves. But after a journey of fifteen hours to Orleans, and a night spent on a bench in a railway station they decided to spend fifteen more hours in going right back home again. Probably constrained to this course by the authorities, who, if they allowed them to remain out of a concentration camp while in Grez, doubtless objected to promiscuous traveling on their part. Their house is gay with the flags of all nations, and they themselves have suddenly become Danish.' The Deliuses' 'Germanness', of which some of their friends suddenly became more aware, is obliquely referred to in a further letter from Maynard to Smith of 18 February 1915: 'Have you ever encountered the Delius's in London? Perhaps, however, they are not in London. I heard something, I don't know where, of their going to America. Though it seems rapidly becoming as unhealthy for Germans there as everywhere else.' (From transcripts supplied by Sophie Royde Smith.)

Additional background to the events of early September is given in a letter from Delius to Norman O'Neill, written from Grez on 15 September and included in Lewis Foreman's *From Parry to Britten* (pp. 64–5).

1 Heseltine's attitude to the music-making of the day showed none of Beecham's optimism: 'Music is, of course, at a low ebb, and I fear it will suffer greatly during the next few years, though there will be some consolation for the flood of patriotic filth that will be poured forth, in the fact that those composers who resist the force of the

mob's passion will stand out in the greater relief and pre-eminence ... I have been to various Promenade Concerts, but as a whole the programmes have been worse than usual, and the audiences – as a result – proportionately larger. It is difficult to escape Walford Davies' *Solemn Melody* or Gounod's *Hymne à Sainte Cécile*, or some such tosh, which invariably gets encored. Whenever the organ is used the Britisher applauds, presumably because it reminds him of Church! Your two little pieces were mangled in the most execrable way; the strings played just anyhow, and the cuckoo came in at the wrong moment nearly every time – as for the rendering of the second piece ...!!'
(Letter to Delius dated 18 October, quoted in Gray, pp. 96–7.)

(401)
Thomas Beecham to Frederick Delius

MIDLAND
HOTEL
MANCHESTER   Oct. 25/14

Dear Delius

Thanks for your interesting letter of the 17th – Yesterday I gave your two little pieces at Liverpool – I send you the Programme – I want to give a New work of yours at the Philharmonic Concert on Nov. 24th – What could you let me have – The "Arabesque" or the "North Country Sketches" or the new Orchestral Dance –?[1] Please wire me as soon as you receive this, and I will send Herbert over to Grez for the music – A rapid decision is here necessary – Now I will tell you what is the best thing for you to do – You ought to come to England in about three weeks time – I am taking a beautiful little place in the country about sixteen miles from London where you can settle yourselves, and write and paint at your complete convenience. When you wish to go to London, you can both stay at 8.a. Hobart Place, which will also be kept going through the Winter – you will thus be spared the expense of any household cares, and I can arrange for one or two musical societies to pay you fees for the performance of your works that I shall give, that will keep the "pot-a-boiling" for some months to come. I am sure you will understand that in making these suggestions I am doing so only by reason of the stringent nature of the times. I hope you will be able to see your way to accepting these proposals of mine, as I think it would be a great pity for you to interrupt your work in order to go to America or take up professional work. But if you come over here, as I suggest, and continue your work quietly and without outside worries, I shall have no trouble in arranging for fees with different societies, but of course you would have to be present at each concert, *not* necessarily to conduct, but simply to be in evidence as an "English" composer! Only you ought to come here without much further delay – please do not leave it until too late – it ought to be sometime during the next two or three weeks – And please let me know *at once* about the new work for the "Philharmonic" on Nov. 24th – also your opinion of what I have suggested and whether you will come here or not –

It is, believe me, much the best thing to do, as I think there is an indication of affairs musical brightening up a bit –

Always yours
Thomas Beecham

P.S. I enclose a description of my new house in the country –

Autograph letter, signed and dated, written on headed notepaper. Envelope addressed: Frederick Delius Esq-/Grez-sur-Loing-/Seine-et-Marne/France. Postmark: MANCHESTER 25 OC 14.

The original is in the Delius Trust Archive.

1 Presumably the 'Dance' movement from *North Country Sketches*. In the event Beecham gave 'Dance at the Fair' and 'The Walk to the Paradise Garden', both from *A Village Romeo*.

(402)
Frederick Delius to Philip Heseltine

GREZ-SUR-LOING
Seine et Marne
[26 October 1914]

My dear Phil –

I was very glad to receive your letter: We have been having very exciting times here – During the German advance there was an ever growing panic here caused, no doubt, by the refugees from Belgium & the North of France streaming thro' Grez – The high road to Nemours was a terrifying sight & we sat for hours watching this terrified stream of humanity pass by in every sort of vehicle possible – We had hundreds every night in Grez & they told terrible tales of german atrocities – On Sept 5th it got too much for us & we also could hear the booming of the canon (Battle of the Marne) so we decided to get out also, so we left for Orleans in a cattle truck with 50 or 60 others. We took $16\frac{1}{2}$ hours to go 75 kilometers & arrived in Orleans at 3–30 in the morning & as there was not a room to be had in the whole town we spent the rest of the night on a bench on the boulevard near the railway station – We had the great luck to get a room at night so we decided to stay there & await further developements – We had a most interesting & exciting time in Orleans watching the soldiers going off to the front & the wounded coming back – trainload after trainload – this was awful – Some of the poor soldiers, carried on stretchers, with one or both legs shot off – As soon as we heard of the great Victory of the allies we quietly returned to Grez & found everything as quiet & peaceful as ever – Your uncle had gone off the same day as we did with his 2 servants en route for Guernsey – At Havre he got a steamer for Cherbourg & had a most fearful passage in a miserable little dirty boat. On arriving in some port or other they were fired on 3 times, it appears, as they had no flag up. I nearly died with laughter when Joe told me of his adventures – We are thinking of going to America until all this is over[1] – I am entirely sick of it – We shall leave about Christmas probably from England – I may come to London a fortnight or 3 weeks before sailing & then I should just love to roam about London with you – I am glad you have not enlisted[2] – I hate & loathe this german militarism & autocracy & hope it may be crushed for ever – but I can get up no enthusiasm whatever for the war. My sympathies are with the maimed & slaughtered on both sides. My North Country sketches are ready & also my "Requiem"   I shall take them with me to America & perhaps conduct them myself – I shall have to make some money over there in some way or other. Music will be dead in Europe for a year or more & all countries will be ruined – It makes one despair of humanity – Lloyd Osbourne & his wife[3] were here thro' the panic – They were seized with it 24 hours before we were & left for Nantes but they returned a fortnight ago here to Grez & are now on their way to London. We had great fun burying our best wine & silver – I would not have missed this experience for anything. The world has gone mad – Write me another long letter as soon as you can & tell me all you are doing & your experiences –

With love – your friend
Frederick Delius

Autograph letter, signed and undated, written on headed notepaper. Envelope addressed: Philip Heseltine Esqre/54 Cartwright Gardens/Londres WC/Angleterre. Postmark: GREZ 26.10.14.

The original is in the British Library.

1   This was very much due to Grainger's encouragement. He had left, as he expressed it, 'for a short trip' to America, in the company of his mother on 1 September. '*Take my advice, dont remain in Grez,*' he wrote to Delius two days before departure from London, adding: 'Dont wait for a panic near you. Leave *now* for England & from here to U.S.A. Her er heller ikke godt at vaere mere [Danish: It's no good staying here any longer either].' On 16 October, Rose Grainger wrote: 'We wish you were both over here, now. We like New York & Boston very much.' Grainger returned to the charge on 11 November, writing from New York: 'I cannot help feeling that your presence here (in this elsewhere barren period) might wake up the handling of your works

splendidly. I dont think your things are being pushed here at all.' He had written to Damrosch, who was 'much interested to know that Mr Delius is coming over'; Damrosch hoped to meet him and 'give some composition of his'.

2   Physically unfit for military service, Heseltine had entered London University, studying English, Latin, German, Mathematics and Logic until early in 1915, when in February he started work as a musical journalist.

3   Lloyd Osbourne (1868–1947): American author. He was stepson of Robert Louis Stevenson; and it had been in Grez-sur-Loing in 1876 – where in the company of his American mother Fanny Osbourne and his sister they were staying with artist friends after the break-up of Fanny's marriage in California – that the initial meeting with Stevenson occurred. After divorcing her husband, Fanny married Stevenson in San Francisco in 1880. Osbourne collaborated with Stevenson on a number of books and stories, the best-known being *The Wrong Box* (first published in 1889), *The Wrecker* (1891), and *The Ebb Tide* (1893). He went on to publish many books of his own. His marriage to Katherine Durham took place in 1896. How and when the warm friendship between Osbourne and Delius began is uncertain.

(403)
Frederick Delius to Philip Heseltine

Dear Phil – We are coming to London about the 14th or 15th – A new work of mine will be given at the Philharmonic on the 24th – North Country Sketches[1] – We must wander about London together – We shall first stay 8^a Hobart Place S.W. and afterwards in the Country.[2] With best love –

affectionately
Frederick Delius

[Grez] 3 Nov. 1914

Autograph postcard, signed and dated. Addressed: Philip Heseltine Esqre/54 Cartwright Gardens/Londres WC/Angleterre. Postmark: [unfranked]. Receiving postmark: LONDON W.C. NOV 6 14.

The original is in the British Library.

1   *North Country Sketches* had in the event to wait for its first performance till 10 May 1915.

2   The Deliuses stayed initially at Beecham's London home. Frederick spent a few days with Beecham in Manchester, 'an awful place', at the beginning of December, attending a Hallé Concert performance on 3 December of '*Village Fair and Dance*', *leading to Intermezzo* – '*The Walk to the Paradise Garden*' (from *A Village Romeo and Juliet*). After the concert, Samuel Langford, music critic of the *Manchester Guardian*, introduced him to the cellist/violinist sisters Beatrice and May Harrison, who had just played the Brahms Double Concerto. He immediately proposed to write a double con-

certo himself. Returning to London on 5 December he continued direct, with Jelka, to Grove Mill House, Watford, the home 'in the country' which Beecham had offered them – and where they were to stay until the beginning of July 1915.

(404)

Frederick Delius to Universal Edition

Grove Mill House
Watford
Herts
England
[early December? 1914]

Dear Herr Direktor,

I obtained your address through Dr Ethel Smyth. I was *very* pleased to know that you are well and that you did not have to go into the morasses of Poland. We have been here in London for just a fortnight, up to then we stayed in Grez, where the war goes unnoticed. For the next 2–3 months the above will be my address. Concert life in England goes calmly on as if nothing had happened. Beecham intended to give my Arabesk already at the last Philharmonic Concert, but he could not get any material. Could you not send it here via Holland. Score & parts, then I will listen to it here & it can then finally be printed together with the English translation. I think it best if you send it to Th. Beecham Esqre 8A Hobart Place London S.W. If possible please send me also 1 copy of the corrected score & parts of my Piano Concerto.

How do matters stand with my Fennimore & Gerda in Cologne? I have already asked my friend H. Suter in Basel to write to you about it. I am *very* worried that the entire material of this opera is in Cologne. I no longer have a copy *at all*. So if Cologne should be bombed & the theatre burnt down, my work would be irretrievably lost. Couldn't you get back at least *one* full score & one piano score. Beecham would like to give the work here in London; for that, however, I must have the text translated and so need the piano score.[1]

Let us hope that this dreadful war will soon come to an end & that you and your company do not have to suffer too much from the results of this situation. I should very much like to know how Brecher[2] is? Is he in the war? And Fritz Cassirer – Berlin? Dr. Siegel?[3] Dr. Cahn-Speyer?[4] And all other friends. We are worrying about them all. And how is friend Schreker? please remember me cordially to him & his wife, also to your nephew? I just hope that he has not had to enlist!

With kind regards & best wishes for your continued well-being

Yours
Frederick Delius

Letter in the hand of Jelka Delius, signed Frederick Delius, undated, written in German.

The original is in the Universal Edition archives. Communication apparently ceased in July and was resumed in December.

1   On 23 December Delius again told Hertzka of his wish to have *Fennimore* translated into English as soon as possible so that it could be given in England and America.

2   Gustav Brecher (1879–1940): German (Bohemian) conductor, composer, and writer on music. After studying in Leipzig, he conducted opera successively in Leipzig, Vienna, Hamburg and Cologne. Later active in Frankfurt, he was to conduct there the first performance of Delius's *Fennimore and Gerda*.

3   Rudolf Siegel (1878–1948): German composer and conductor.

4   Rudolf Cahn-Speyer (1881–1940): Austrian musicologist and composer. There is some evidence that in the summer of 1914 he was preparing to conduct a performance of *Songs of Sunset*, presumably in the autumn season.

1915

The Deliuses, whose exile from France was to last just over a year, were now settled at Watford. Apart from excursions into London, Delius himself made two further trips to Manchester with Beecham, the first of which, late in February, was to judge a singing competition in which *Sea Drift* was the set piece, as well as to be present on 24 February at the first performance of his Violin Sonata No. 1, and on the following evening at a Hallé Concert performance of part of Act 2 of *A Village Romeo and Juliet*. The second in mid-March was to hear the Piano Concerto played by R. J. Forbes, and *Sea Drift* sung by Hamilton Harris, the competition winner, at another Hallé concert. For a while at Watford, as Beecham remembered, Delius had 'remained in a highly nervous and agitated state, with small inclination for anything but restless inaction' (*Frederick Delius*, p. 172). Within a month or so he had, it seemed, regained much of his composure, writing on 9 January to Hertzka: '. . . all goes well & I am working very much here as we are living in the country. In the next few months a good number of my works are to be performed here. I hope this terrible war will not last too long.' Beecham recalled work at Watford on the Requiem, some further work on *An Arabesque*, and first sketches of *Eventyr* being put on paper.

During the first two months of the year Delius was to reproach Hertzka for not having established a stock of his music in London. Now nothing was available – not even songs – and just at a time when demand for his music was virtually at its greatest. Moiseiwitsch's enormous success with the Piano Concerto, given in London by Beecham on 8 February, pointed to many more performances of the work in the near future and Delius urged Hertzka to bring out a new and corrected edition of the piece. After making some song settings, the composer turned in the spring to his Double Concerto, frequently calling in on the Harrisons in London to work through freshly composed passages. A setback in his health, after a long period with seemingly little worry on this score, occurred later in April, and he and Jelka spent some three weeks in London where he underwent physiotherapy. Meanwhile, Beecham and Heseltine were preparing works for publication – works which Beecham 'bought' from the composer and handed back the copyright at the same time: a generous device, enabling the Deliuses to live a little more comfortably at a time when income, particularly from German and Austrian publishers, and indeed from other sources, was rapidly drying up.

The last month or so in England was spent back at Watford, before the Deliuses left, on doctor's advice, for Bergen on 6 July. By the end of the month they were 'high up amongst the Snow Mountains' on the Nordfjord, with the war a very distant echo. Persistent bad weather obliged them to move on to Gjeilo where they at last found sunshine. Before leaving Norway they probably spent about a week in Christiania, en route to stay with their friends the Schous in Juelsminde, Denmark, where they arrived on 9 October. Delius was feeling very well. On 20 November, having taken in a few days in London en route, they finally returned to Grez, determined to stay put for the duration of the war.

Meanwhile, Grainger's Delius campaign in America was bringing results: notable first performances there were of *A Dance Rhapsody*, given in Minneapolis on 5 November, and the Piano Concerto, with Grainger himself as soloist, at a New York Philharmonic Society concert in Carnegie Hall conducted by Stransky on 26 November. Then came *Summer Night on the River* and *On hearing the first Cuckoo in Spring*, given at a New York Symphony Society concert in the Aeolian Hall on 28 November. And new and influential American friends, the sculptor Henry Clews and his wife Marie, began to play a role in the life of the Deliuses, who spent a fortnight with them in their beautiful Paris home in December.

Four Old English Lyrics, songs (various authors) (RT V/30). Nos 2–4 completed.

Concerto for violin, violoncello and orchestra (RT VII/5).

Air and Dance for string orchestra (RT VI/21).

Eventyr ('Once upon a time', after Asbjørnsen's folklore) for orchestra (RT VI/23). Sketched.

(405)
Nina Grieg to Frederick and Jelka Delius

Holmenkollen Sanatorium
nr. Christiania 27–1 1915

Dearest friends,

As you write to me in such good Norwegian, dear Fru Delius, I think it best to spare you my bad English, and use my own honest language – I cannot say mother tongue, as my mother was Danish. Good heavens; what haven't you been through! To me it would seem impossible ever to get over such experiences, as if one could never be one's own self again. Indeed, I had never thought I would live to see such horrors, advanced in years as I now am and it is as if I cannot grasp that Edvard has passed on from it all.[1] It would have been so much easier to endure if he had still been here. You can of course say that I am staying up here in a haven of peace and cannot imagine what war is really like *there* where it is being fought out. That may be true, one of humanity's imperfections is that people always must *experience* everything before they really can get it into their heads, but we have the feeling of *here*, too, standing on the brink of an abyss, and if we are to plunge into it, then we want to share in our dear old country's fortunes, good or bad, and that is why we are staying here at home this winter and waiting for what may come. I am still at the stage where I believe that life is *not* without meaning, and that is why I constantly wait for a higher power to come along with its veto. Well, well, dear Delius, I know very well that you smile sympathetically and shrug your shoulders, but people are after all so very different both inwardly and outwardly. I am glad to know that you are in England, and it was really kind of you, dear Fru Delius, to write and tell me about everything you have been through. I wonder if all your lovely things now will remain buried at Grez until the war one day comes to an end. I have heard that life goes on as usual in London, so I can well believe that a lot of English music gets played. The fact that you want to hold an exhibition also shows that the war has not killed people's interest in the arts. Here foreign artists are now beginning to get used to giving concerts again; luckily people are easygoing, and soon fall into the old ways. The Halvorsens are well, he is busy with the theatre and enjoys his work. It seems to be his intention to stage two operas by Schjelderup in the spring, if all goes well. Here at Holmenkollen we really are in the middle of winter, everything is white, forests and fields and all roads, the weather is fine and the air fresh and pure.

But it doesn't feel like home here, far too many people. I have a little room in another house, all to myself, with a piano thank God.

I suppose we shall stay here till the spring, till we go back to Troldh. Nice that Beecham plays Grieg.

Fare well, both of you, and do please send me a line now and then.

Tonny[2] sends many good wishes.

Autograph letter, unsigned and dated, written in Norwegian on headed notepaper.

The original is in the Delius Trust Archive.

1 Grieg had died in 1907.

2 Antonie (Tony) Hagerup (1844–1939): Nina Grieg's elder sister.

(406)

Frederick Delius to Philip Heseltine

[Watford]   Monday [26 April 1915]

Dear Phil – I have not yet received the Score of the North Country
Sketches   Beecham is clamouring for it & I have to have it bound –
In the Biographical Programme for the Festival[1] see that *my parents* are left out
of it this time –

   In haste
   Fr. D.

Autograph postcard, initialled and undated. Addressed: Philip Heseltine Esqre/34
Southwold Mansions/Maida Vale/W. Postmark: WATFORD 26 AP 15.

The original is in the British Library.

The first few months of 1915 were passing relatively quietly. There were excursions to
concerts, visits by friends to Watford, and the two trips to Manchester. Heseltine, as
ever, was making himself helpful in various ways, doing some work on *North Country
Sketches* and correcting the parts of *Sea Drift*. 'Spring, the sweet Spring' was composed
in February, while 'So white, so soft' and 'To Daffodils' followed in March. By April,
work had started on the Double Concerto, which was finished in June. Moiseiwitsch
played the Piano Concerto on 8 February at Queen's Hall, and the Epilogue from
Koanga was given at a Royal Philharmonic Society concert on 13 April; both concerts
were conducted by Beecham. Heseltine, temporarily music critic for the *Daily Mail*,
attended and reviewed Delius performances whenever possible. After lauding the
Piano Concerto, he looked forward to the time when 'the public wakes to the fact that
in Frederick Delius they have the greatest composer England has produced for two
centuries.' And Catterall and Forbes gave the first performance, in Manchester, of the
new Violin Sonata. Having apparently spent a few days in London in mid-April,
Delius then suffered (in Jelka's words) 'a perfectly horrid bilious attack', and his health
must have been giving cause for some concern again at this period, with the composer
writing to Heseltine on 1 May from Hobart Place: 'We are staying here for 3 weeks as
I am undergoing a massage treatment.' On 10 May Beecham conducted the first performance of *North Country Sketches* at Queen's Hall.

1   The British Music Festival was held in London in mid-May. Beecham conducted
Sea Drift, with Herbert Heyner as soloist, and the London Choral Society and London
Symphony Orchestra. Arnold Bennett's journal of Wednesday 12 May notes: 'Festival
of British Music at Queen's Hall last night, alone. I dined at R.T.Y.C.   O'Neill and
Bantock and Holbrooke music (Humoreske – Fifine – The Bells) rotten. But Delius'
Sea Drift very fine.' (*The Journals of Arnold Bennett*, II, 1911–1921, ed. Newman
Flower, London, Cassell, 1932.) On 13 May, two days after the performance of *Sea
Drift*, Evlyn Howard-Jones played the Piano Concerto at the Festival.

(407)

Frederick Delius to Universal Edition

THE COTTAGE
8^A HOBART PLACE
LONDON S.W.
[early May? 1915]

Dear Herr Hertzka,

I have just received a letter from Percy Grainger who is in America   Address: Antonia Sawyer,[1] 1425 Broadway, New York City. He wants to play my Piano Concerto in America, where he has had great successes, & he would of course appreciate the same conditions as before; please contact him *at once*. America is of great importance for the future of my music, but I hear from various people that, in the 1st place, *nowhere* do they have my compositions in stock over there, neither at Breitkopf & Härtel's nor at Schirmer's & 2nd that the price of the performing material is simply prohibitive considering American conditions. In these circumstances it is quite out of the question that my music can be made widely known. Even R. Strauss is *very* rarely played there on account of the prices   The public is perfectly content without these new compositions & the conductors who would *like* to play them are obliged to abandon the idea because of the cost. I should greatly appreciate it if you would also inform Herr Leuckart & Tischer & Jagenberg of this. E.g. the two small pieces for orchestra are quite unobtainable in New York & if they could be bought there at a reasonable price they might often get performed. Besides, I must always remind you that composers & artists would anyway like to buy such scores for themselves.

Here, of course, where there is the greatest demand for all my works – it is impossible to get them anywhere, as it is now forbidden to import them. But America on the other hand is a neutral country & entirely open to your trade; I advise you to establish over there a depot for all my works.

I hope you are all keeping well!
With kind regards

Yours
Frederick Delius

Letter in the hand of Jelka Delius, signed Frederick Delius, undated, written in German on headed notepaper.

The original is in the Universal Edition archives.

1   Grainger's American agent.

(408)

Thomas Beecham to Frederick Delius

May. 22/15

Frederick Delius Esq

8 a. Hobart Pl.

S.W.

THE COTTAGE,

8^A HOBART PLACE,

S.W.

My dear Delius –

I write to confirm the arrangement proposed in my letter to you of April 29th last and since accepted by you which I here set out again –
That I buy from you

> The Sonata for Violin and Piano (£300)
> The Legende for Violin and Orchestre – (£150)
> The North Country Sketches – (£250)
> Three Songs (£200).

The total amount payable to you will be therefore £900 to be disbursed by me over a period of three years in equal payments of £300 per annum – After the expenses of publication are cleared off, I will hand over to you the copyright of the above works to be your own property.

You can accept this letter as binding upon me and as the equivalent of a written contract – If you write me formally an acceptance of this, the matter will be in order –

Yours
Thomas Beecham

P.S. Having already paid you £50 (per letter of the 29th last) on account of this agreement, the remaining sum due to you is £850 –

Autograph letter, signed and dated, written on headed notepaper.

The original is in the Delius Trust Archive.

(409)
Percy Grainger to Frederick Delius

N.B. permanent
c/o concert Direction
Antonia Sawyer
Aeolian Hall. W 42 St
New York City. U.S.A.
June 19.1915.

My dear friend

Lovely to hear from you, & thank you a million times for your sweet kind words & all your kindness. Have heard from Universal-Ed that they give me the same terms as last years (hearty thanks that you wrote them)   I have also written, visited & shaken up Breitkopf & Haertel in N. York, your agents over here. A boat was sunk containing your music, but they have ordered more. In the meantime I wrote to Walter Damrosch, conductor of N. York Symphony orchestra expressing my feelings about "Cuckoo" "Summer night on river" & presenting him with the scores. He replied:

"Many many thanks for the fascinating Delius scores. I shall most certainly do them next winter and am glad of the opportunity of introducing them to New York."

Now I must see to place "Dance Rhap" with him or Stransky for next winter & also chivvy Stock (Chicago)[1] & others when I see them or write. If you could happen to spare me scores of Dance Rhap & the 2 Stimmungsbilder[2] I could use them well; also any other orchestral scores.

Quite apart from my efforts, I can see there's going to be a boom in Delius here anyhow. People ask me about you & talk about you fifty times more than they did 6 months ago.

But *dont* risk your life coming across the seas *any*where till the war's over. What is a year sooner or later compared with the preciousness of your life? In the meanwhile your stuff, etc, will be paving the way.

Earlier in the winter I did speak of you as "Anglo-German" but will not do so any more, & have written to interviewers etc to omit it if not already printed.

I agree with you, B & H seems to ask quite fair performing fees over here.

I have the most *marvelous* winter before me. *Shoals* of engagements & great big fees.

Love to you both from us both

Ever fondly
Percy

I am again overwhelmed by the beauty & touchingness of the Dance Rhap. What a summing up of life's varied moods, what Bach-like tender & subtle flow of undercurrents, what exquisite details too!

Typed letter, signed and dated.

The original is in the Grainger Museum.

1   In Chicago, Stock had already given *Brigg Fair* on 19 February and *Lebenstanz* on 9 April.

2   *On hearing the first Cuckoo in Spring* and *Summer Night on the River.*

(410)
Frederick Delius to Philip Heseltine

[Norway, 16 July 1915]

Dear Phil – Here we are in this glorious country   We decided to come here instead of Cornwall[1] – We had a rough crossing over the North Sea – How are you & where –? Send me your address to Post Restante *Molde* Norway   We are travelling slowly about & making our way to the Mountains inland[2] – One does not feel the war here at all – Norway is quite pro-Allies – there are no tourists this year which makes travelling very agreable –
With love from us both, yrs ever

Frederick Delius

Autograph postcard, signed and undated. Addressed: Philip Heseltine Esqre/c/o J Allinson Jun Esqre/4 Spanish Place/Manchester Square/London. Readdressed: The Bungalow, Crickley Hill/n^r Cheltenham/Glos. Postmark: BERGEN-NEWCASTLE 16 VII 15. Second postmark: LONDON.W. 20 JUL [15].

The original is in the British Library.

1   Jelka wrote to Heseltine from Watford on 29 June: 'We went to [Dr] Byres Moir today and he wont at all allow Fred to go to the sea, and absolutely advised us to go to Norway . . . Norway is Fred's land, and it will make him feel well and it is a country "not at war".' Plans to holiday with Heseltine in Cornwall were, in consequence, 'entirely upset'.

2   Delius wrote on 8 August the last of his letters that was to reach Universal Edition until the war was over. He was at the Hotel Gloppen, Sandene, on the Nordfjord, where he intended to stay for a few weeks so as to get some work done. Asking again after Schreker, he expressed the hope that neither he nor Hertzka would be drawn into military service.

(411)
Frederick Delius to Percy Grainger

Gjeilo
Hallingdal
Sept 26th 1915

Dear Percy

Your letter, newspaper cuttings & "Impress of Personality"[1] arrived here safely & gave me immense pleasure. What a devoted friend you are to boom me & my music in America & get me all those performances[2] – Need I tell you how delighted I am! It will, of course, be of enormous benefit to me with my editors – I shall send you my Sonata Violin & Piano as soon as it comes out – I am expecting the proofs every day – It has been heavenly here all September – Not a cloud, no wind & hot sun all the time We are in the Højfjeld – 3000 ft – the fjeld is simply a marvel of colors, russet gold & scarlet & down below where the forest begins the woods are in their brightest autumn tints – This morning I woke up in the middle of a snow landscape. 3 inches of snow on the ground & trees & snowing! In a few days we leave for Kristiania & then Kopenhagen where we intend staying a month with the Skou's at Palsgaard – Juelsminde & also in Kopenhagen – What we shall do after we dont yet know – We have a great longing for Grez – The Germans will *never* get to Paris or anywhere near it any more – I firmly believe. I cannot work in Hotels & private houses & want to get back home again; however we have settled nothing as yet – We may risk the North sea in November[3] – I was greatly impressed by your "Impress of Personality" – it is quite excellent & the most lucid thing I have read since years on the subject – *My firm belief is* that when the Intellect outweighs the Instinct in all art – *especially music* "then the trouble begins" As long as the instinct has the upper hand everything sounds *right & rare*. That is why the discords of primitive savage music sound so strange & wonderful – & right & as soon as the intellect gets hold of the idea & *systematises* it – it *sounds wrong* & *is wrong* & is not rare – since it runs around like the measles & one finds every Tom, Dick, Harry & Louisa doing it – & especially every little Jew musician who sees his opportunity in the new fad or the rising stocks & shares of art in other words – I admit that one man can come along & see everything in Cubes – He may have something the matter with the lense of his eyes, but I dont admit that several thousand at once see everything in Cubes – otherwise than thro their intellect which has less to do with art than one likes to think. I should love to come out to America again, I feel sure there is a lot of good informed stuff out there & less prejudice; but I will take your advice & keep over here until you think it would be wise for me to come[4] – I might try & get my Drama, Fennimore & Gerda on in New York – The war will last at least another year – Conscription is coming on apace in England but I dont think they will take me.[5] I am 52 already – It was a splendid move to come here to Norway – The Country agrees with me like no other. I feel well & strong & up to every sort of devilment – The air is too wonderful here – Give my love to all the *real sorters* over there – Who is Marion Cook?[6] what you say sounds awfully good – I am just longing to here the Clef Club[7] –

Now fare well, dear Percy, & write soon again – We both send our united love to you both –

your devoted friend
Frederick Delius

I picked these flowers on the Fjeld –

Autograph letter, signed and dated. Envelope addressed: Percy Grainger Esq[re]/c/o Concert Direction/Antonia Sawyer/Aeolian Hall/W42 Street/New York City/ N.Y./U.S.A. Readdressed: The Southern/Mad. Ave. & 62 St.   Postmark: Gjeilo 26 IX 15. Receiving postmark: NEW YORK N.Y. OCT 8 1915.

The original is in the Grainger Museum.

1   Percy Grainger: 'The Impress of Personality in Unwritten Music', *The Musical Quarterly*, 1, 1915, pp. 416–35.

2   The indefatigable Grainger had sent the score of *A Dance Rhapsody* to Stokowski: 'I have arranged to do Delius' Dance Rhapsody on Oct 29–30,' wrote Stokowski in return, and Grainger gave Delius the good news in a letter dated 18 August: 'He is the conductor of the Philadelphia Symphony Orchestra, one of *the most* gifted men here, a young Pole born in England, full of temperament & skill. He did not know your work & I felt sure he would love it. He is a big bug here. I play the Grieg Concerto with him 2 or 3 times in various towns next season. Some other season I shall hope to do your Concerto with him ... Damrosch (N.York Symphony) giving your "Stimmungsbilder", & the N.York Philharmonic & I doing the Concerto. Now I shall write Stock (Chicago Symphony) & enthuse to him about "Dance R" & "Stimmungsbilder" & send him scores, too.' On 2 December Grainger was able to report to Delius: 'Your Piano Concerto went *magnificently*, both Stransky & I were at *our very best*, & the public success was *just as great* as if for an old war-horse like the Tchaikovsky Piano Concerto!!' Stransky wanted to give the Concerto again in 1916.

3   Delius wrote to Heseltine on 17 September: 'We have decided to stay here a few weeks longer – We read in the paper that a German Submarine had stopped a Norwegian passenger boat & taken off an English passenger!!' The Deliuses planned, after visiting Denmark for a few weeks, to spend the winter in Norway.

4   Grainger had begun to have reservations: 'I would not advise you to come here *yet*,' he wrote on 18 August. 'Let us pave the way *thoroly* this season. I will keep you well posted. Next year (winter 1916–1917) would be far more advisable than this coming season, I feel.'

5 Grainger referred to the possibility of general conscription in his letter of 18 August: 'If "Almene Vaernepligt" should be introduced into England, it might be awkward to live in France, England's ally; one might get inveigled into some sort of "war work" not as suitable to you, nor so *benificial to your country's welfare*, as your superprecious creative work.'

6 Will Marion Cook (1869–1944): American black composer. Having studied in Ohio, Berlin (under Joachim) and New York (under Dvořák), he composed a ragtime opera, *Clorinda*, given in New York in 1898, and a string of popular hits.

7 The Clef Club Orchestra, a black American band, was founded by James Reese Europe in 1910. Grainger was to retain a lively interest in ragtime and jazz throughout his life.

(412)
Frederick Delius to Philip Heseltine

GREZ-SUR-LOING
Seine et Marne
24 Nov 1915

My dear Phil

We arrived here last Saturday after a long & tedious journey[1] – I received your letter[2] – California is a far better climate than Florida – My orange grove has been left to itself for 20 years & is no doubt only a wilderness of gigantic weeds & plants – The house will also have tumbled down – Even if the house had been habitable I should not have advised Lawrence to live in it – The place is 5 miles from any house or Store. Life is frightfully expensive on account of the isolated situation – One lives entirely off tinned food & a servant costs 1 dollar 50 cents a day. In the South of California – there are nice little towns – The climate is devine & living far less expensive – I should have loved to be of use to Lawrence whose work I admire – but to let him go to Florida would be sending him to disaster – I am so happy to be back here again in our own house & amongst our own things – & the food is all so good – What a pity you did not come to Pagani's after the Concert – I should so much like to have seen you again. Send me my Score as soon as possible – *Insured* & let May Harrison[3] have the piano score of which she will have a copy made – We shall not leave Grez now until the war is over: travelling is really too difficult – Write to me soon & tell me how things are going with you – How about Suroaadj's[4] servant? With love from us both

your affectionate
Frederick Delius

We have found an awfully good french servant who cooks splendidly

Autograph letter, signed and dated, written on headed notepaper. Envelope addressed: Philip Heseltine Esqre/ 12^A Rossetti garden Mansions/Chelsea/Londres SW/Angleterre. Postmark: GREZ 25 -11 15.

The original is in the British Library.

1   Writing from Juelsminde, Denmark, on 21 October, Jelka told Rose Grainger: 'We shall stay here till the end of the month, then 14 days Copenhagen and then back to France via Bergen-Newcastle-London. We cannot bear being away from home any longer'. In fact they probably spent no more than five days in Copenhagen and three in Bergen en route to London. Delius himself wrote to Grainger from Grez on 21 December: 'We shall not budge from here until the war is over.' It is interesting to speculate whether Delius may have met another notable composer during his stay in Denmark, speculation prompted by an unexpected reference in a letter from Nina Grieg to Jelka, dated 8 February 1916: 'We are both well, Tonny and I, Carl Nielsen is in Norway. I wonder if Delius knows his new symphony [No. 4] and what he thinks of it?' This was in reply to a postcard from Delius that has not been found among the Grieg papers.

2   Heseltine had written from London on 16 November: 'This evening I met and had a long talk with D. H. Lawrence. He can stand this country no longer and is going to America in a week's time. He wants to go to Florida for the winter, since he is, I am afraid, rather far gone with consumption. I write this hurried note to ask whether it would be possible for him to go and live in your orange grove. He has nowhere definite to go in Florida and is very poor. His last book [*The Rainbow*] – a perfectly magnificent work – has just been suppressed by the police for supposed immorality(!!)

He begged me to write you at once and asked whether anything could be arranged about living at the grove, but I told him that you probably had very little control over affairs out there now. However, it would be splendid if he could go there. He is such a marvellous man – perhaps the one great literary genius of his generation, at any rate in England.' (Gray, p. 106.)

3   May Harrison (1891–1959): violinist sister of the cellist Beatrice Harrison. Delius wrote his Double Concerto for (and dedicated it to) them. Heseltine had made a piano score of the work.

4   Kaikhosru Shapurji Sorabji (b. 1892): English-born composer, pianist and writer. A friend of Heseltine, self-taught, he began composing in 1915. His late work for flute quintet, *Il Tessuto d'Arabeschi*, commissioned by Norman Gentieu for the Delius Society, Philadelphia, and dedicated to Delius, received its first performance in Philadelphia on 2 May 1982.

PLATE 17   (a) and (b) Delius in Elberfeld, 1914; (c) Mask of Delius, 1916,
by Henry Clews: 'Frederick Delius, whose mask so strongly brings to mind
the noblest works of Houdon' (Hubert Dhumez); (c) Frederick Delius, 1919,
by William Rothenstein: 'W. Rothenstein wrote to me; he wants to do a
drawing for the Music-paper you are writing the article for. I'll pose for him
on my return to London' (Delius to Heseltine, 19 September 1919).

PLATE 18   Igor Stravinsky. (*Photograph Robert Regassi, Lausanne.*)

PLATE 19   (a) Adey Brunel (*coll. Christopher Brunel*); (b) Maud, Lady Cunard; (c) May Harrison; (d) Margaret and Beatrice Harrison.

Lieber Freund – Deine
Karte habe ich erhalten.
Ich reise nächsten Samstag 5-ten
von Antwerpen & komme
am Dienstag Abend
in Kristiania. Ich
werde Hotel Westmin-
ster wohnen – & wirde
mich sehr freuen wenn
Du mich Mittwoch um
12 – oder 1 Uhr abholst
so dass wir zusammen
sein können. Ich bleibe
bis Donnerstag oder Frei
tag & dann reise nach
Valenhennen. Herzlichst
Frederick Delius

PLATE 21   (a) Philip Heseltine (centre) with friends in France, about the time of his visit to Delius in September 1913. Poet Alan Seeger (left) was to be killed in the Great War (*coll. John Bishop*); (b) Emil Hertzka (*coll. Universal Edition*); (c) Gerhard Tischer.

PLATE 22   Delius and Henry Clews at Grez.

PLATE 23   Jelka, Delius and Henry Clews at Grez.

PLATE 24   (a) 'Grandfather', by Jelka Delius, Sennen, Cornwall, summer
1919 (*coll. Bradford City Art Sallaris*); (b) Bertha Stoop, 1910, by Ida Gerhardi
(*coll. Karl-Ernst-Osthaus-Museum, Hagen*).

PLATE 25   (a) Helge Rode, 1908/9, by Edvard Munch (*coll. National Museum, Stockholm*); (b) Jappe Nilssen, 1909, by Edvard Munch (*coll. Munch Museum*).

PLATE 26   Henry Clews, Delius and Jelka at 82, rue d'Assas, Paris, in
1916.

PLATE 27   (a) Adrian Allinson's design for Act I of *A Village Romeo and Juliet*, London, 1920; and (b) the same scene, as designed by Karl Walser, photographed at Berlin, 1907.

PLATE 28   (a) Delius and Jelka at 'The Waffrons', 1921; (b) A walk in
Surrey, 1921: left to right, Evlyn Howard-Jones, Delius, Jelka, Beatrice
Harrison (*coll. Margaret Harrison*).

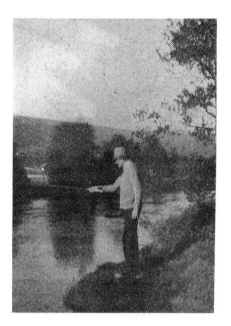

PLATE 29   (a) Delius and Jelka in Norway, 1921, photographed by
Kenneth Spence (*coll. Lionel Hill*); (b) Delius fishing in Norway, summer
1921.

PLATE 30   (a) Delius with Samuel Midgley, Bradford, October 1921;
(b) Delius, 1920, by Edvard Munch (*coll. Munch Museum*); (c) Delius, 1922,
by Max Beckmann.

PLATE 31   'The Composer Delius at Wiesbaden', 1922, by Edvard Munch
(*coll. Munch Museum*).

PLATE 32   (a) Matthew Smith (*coll. Eric Fenby*); (b) C.W. Orr (*coll. Lewis Foreman*); (c) Kaikhosru Sorabji (*coll. Alistair Hinton*); (d) Adrian Boult.

(413)
Frederick Delius to Philip Heseltine

GREZ-SUR-LOING
Seine et Marne
21/12/15

Dear Phil –

Your letter interested me in the highest degree. All you say about music in England is entirely true; it is just the same with the other arts – but, of course, music is nearer to our hearts. I, of course, have been aware of this for many years & I have no hopes that it will ever become better, but when I work I forget everything &, as you know, I only write for myself – Every artist ought to have just enough to live on – The real tragedy begins when he is obliged to earn his living: for the more he concentrates upon the earning the worse his art seems to become – The greater the artist the greater the tragedy & the greater the difficulty of being understood – The great artist has not only an entirely uncomprehensive public – but he has all the mediocrities of art against him or when not against him, absorbing the attention of the public as soi-disant great geniuses – Then again he has the charlatan at his elbow & the officially not understood original genius – who has cribbed certain peculiarities of an individual & works them up logically into a system so that he also adds to the confusion in the brains of the otherwise well disposed public & as a rule passes off as the real thing – I wont talk of critics since they really dont alter things one way or the other – They simply dont count except to "embêter l'artiste" – Embêter him with their condemnation or embêter him with their praise – I am most eager to see Goossens quartet[1] & also the song of Whitaker[2] I shall write as soon as I have made myself thoroughly acquainted with them – My dear Phil – I would not advise you to go to America or to Tahiti except for *adventure* & to get out of a groove[3] – You are only 21. I went to Florida at your age & had not yet become a musician – Dont get despondent & desperate – The conditions of art in America are far worse than in England – If you dont feel sufficiently gifted to become a composer why not become a powerful writer – not a critic – but a writer on artistic things – on music – Why not, with your pen, try to help on Goossens & Whitaker & try to persuade the public at least to try & understand them – It would be a great work to discover the gifted musicians & help them out into the light so that they dont become mouldy – If you went to Tahiti I am afraid you would stay there for good & gradually lull yourself to sleep under the coco palms & in the arms of the lovely "Waheenees" (Vahinés) Very few Europeans who go out there ever come back again – You must have a real fight with life before you give at up & there is some satisfaction to be got out of surmounting difficulties – By force to overcome the bourgeois! To lift oneself by degrees over the mob &

feel ones powers – Dont let yourself be crushed by masses of inferiority &
phrases of catchwords – Dear old pal! you are on the brink of being in love
again – a phrase in your letter seems to tell me so – I have been in love twice
myself – the 2nd time by far intenser than the first – in fact it gave the direction
to my life – Perhaps you will get your direction that way – You are very much
like I used to be –very much – If you can – come over to me here in Grez & stay
with me awhile & we can talk it over together – I suppose the authorities will
allow you to take your Xmas holidays in France – In any case I want to see you
before you go out on adventures & mind, that is the only thing to go out on –
to tramp the highroads of the world & sail the great seas – to hear languages
one doesn't understand & see strange customs & not always come home to five
o'clock tea – to sleep with a revolver under ones pillow – I have done it for
months – All that is splendid & colors ones life – If I were not such a music
scribbler I would come with you – I simply love travel & adventure & the
country in which I found it the least was England – old Roast Beef, Yorkshire
pudding England – I remember when I was only 7 trying to find it by running
away from home over the moors – Write me soon again or, better, come &
spend Xmas with me –

your affectionate friend
Frederick Delius

Please leave the copy of the Concerto with Miss Harrison – 51 Cornwall
gardens, Gloucester R^{d} & ask her to have it copied – Many thanks for doing
it[4]

Autograph letter, signed and dated, written on headed notepaper. Envelope
addressed: Monsieur/Philip Heseltine/13 Rossetti Mansions/Chelsea/Londres S
W/Angleterre. Postmark illegible.

The original is in the British Library.

1   Eugene Goossens (1893–1962): English composer and conductor. As a violinist he
played from 1911 to 1915 in Sir Henry Wood's Queen's Hall Orchestra, after which
in 1916 he became assistant conductor to Beecham. He subsequently became best
known as a conductor, notably in England, the United States and Australia. His
String Quartet No. 1 was composed in 1915.

2   William G. Whittaker (1876–1944): English composer. He was at the time on the
staff of Armstrong College, Newcastle upon Tyne, the city of his birth, and was a fine
teacher and scholar. As a conductor he promoted in particular the work of his English
and French contemporaries.

3   Heseltine had written from London on 15 December: 'I have never yet lived at all,
and that is why I am going away – to Florida, Tahiti, anywhere – to have at least a
year or two of real life to try and make something out of . . . Now do write, when you

have time, and tell me more about Florida, and about Tahiti – which I myself favour personally ... Is the orange grove entirely impossible? Couldn't we by any means rejuvenate it with the aid of niggers?' It seems odd indeed that Delius had still not told Heseltine of having sold Solana Grove to Haym in 1912.

4   Heseltine was also at work correcting the proofs of the recently composed Violin Sonata.

(414)

Jelka Delius to Marie Clews

GREZ-SUR-LOING
Seine et Marne
23.12.1915

Dearest Mrs Clews

This is to wish you both the happiest Xmas and the most glorious new year and to tell you that we think *ever so much* of you and long for you both terribly in the evening – Why, every evening in your dear house was a special and most enjoyable little fête, and when on the last evening you came down as a true Madonna and with your halo, that was the crowning of it all! –[1]

In the silence here I love to think of the God of humour-mystics with the wreath of strange heads and the wonderful intense "Penseur".[2] You have given us something so new and so entirely personal, dear Mr Clews – and it is so splendid that you let us see it all and gave us this new joy.

The rain is dreadful; happily we found splendid letters here from Percy Grainger and other American friends: the Piano Concerto has been a huge success in New York and Damrosch has also given the 2 small Orchestra-pieces "On hearing the first cuckoo in Spring" and "Summernight on the River". Everybody seems to love them and Damrosch will therefore do them again soon. I wish he would whilst you are in America! –

How are the Robinets?[3] Ours in the Kitchen suddenly leaked fearfully, and the reservoir overhead had just been pumped full. We had to catch the water in pails and tubs and I finally succeeded in corking it and then it dripped lugubriously all night. It is perhaps an astral combination that affects all robinets.

Fred has begun work again and he sends you all his love and wishes!

Affectionately yours
Jelka Delius

Autograph letter, signed and dated, written on headed notepaper.

The original is in the Delius Trust Archive. It is the first item of a major correspondence, preserved either as originals or in photocopy or typed transcript form, consisting of some 130 communications from the Deliuses to the Clews, dated 1915–35, and presented in 1972 to the Delius Trust by Mr David Colton, trustee of the Henry and Marie Clews estate, and his wife Katheryn. The return correspondence unfortunately has not survived.

Henry Clews, Jr. (1876–1937): American sculptor and painter, born in New York. Son of a banker, he was educated at Amherst College and Columbia University, and also studied at the universities of Lausanne and Hannover. He worked briefly for the family banking firm before becoming an artist, making his home in France from 1914, by which time no less than seven exhibitions of his painting and sculpture had already been held in New York. His second wife, Marie Elsie Clews (1880–1959), was a wealthy Philadelphia heiress and socialite. Her father was Henry Whelen, Jr., a founder of the Philadelphia Orchestra. Beecham suggests that Delius first met Clews in Venice in 1913 (*Frederick Delius*, pp. 169 and 182); Marie Clews, in her unpublished (and highly unreliable) memoirs, states that the meeting occurred in Lady Cunard's house in March 1916! Delius's only visit to Venice seems to have been in the spring of 1912, and the present letter might suggest that the friendship, if already warm, was fairly newly-minted.

1   Jelka reported on this visit to the Clews in a letter to Adine O'Neill, written from Grez on 24 January 1916: 'We spent a fortnight in Paris, staying in the dear old rue d'Assas, right on the Luxembourg with some American friends.' The Clews lived at 82 Rue d'Assas, where the sculptor had his studio. Marie recorded that the Deliuses would come and pass a night in town 'when they had errands to do or Delius wanted to see the doctor'. She had a great love of dressing up, often in medieval/Renaissance-style finery which would enhance her considerable natural beauty.

2   *The God of Humormystics* (1913), a life-size bronze, can be seen in the courtyard of the Château de la Napoule, near Cannes. *The Thinker* (1914), a related bronze, now stands in Brookgreen Gardens, South Carolina.

3   French: *water taps, faucets*.

1916

The early weeks of the year were spent working on the ending of the Requiem. 'I dont think I have ever done better than this,' Delius was to write to Heseltine over two years later. The winter was proving mild, and Delius divided his time between composition and working with Jelka in the garden, which had been much neglected during their long absence. He was 'hard at work & in good form', as he told Heseltine in a letter written on 15 March. Two movements of his String Quartet were finished by late April, and early May found him composing a third. Letters from Jelka to Delius's sister Clare and from Delius himself to Grainger in the summer months stress how well the composer had been and how hard he had been working ever since the return from London. Early in June he was at work on a second *Dance Rhapsody*, and it was about this time that Henry Clews modelled his fine mask of Delius. The summer months saw exchanges of visits with the Clews, one result being a request from Jelka to Marie late in August for the words of Shakespeare's 'It was a lover and his lass', as Delius wanted to set them. He appears to have done this in September.

If Grainger was the first line of attack in America, the Clews were proving to be the second, with Marie using her Philadelphia connections to press for performances of Delius's music there and elsewhere. Delius particularly wanted *A Mass of Life* ('my best work I believe', he wrote on 1 September), *Sea Drift* and *Songs of Sunset* to be given and hoped they could all travel over together if a performance of the *Mass* could be secured. Uncharacteristically perhaps, but wisely enough, Grainger counselled caution: stocks of printed music were depleted in America, so no sales of Delius's music would result – and above all travelling would be highly dangerous. Delius clung nonetheless to his American dream: provided the war was over, he and Jelka would cross the Atlantic the following summer and stay with Lloyd Osbourne in California. And indeed, by the end of the year, letters indicate that Delius had Stokowski and Karl Muck in mind for performances during the American 1917–18 concert season of the *Mass*, *Life's Dance* and *A Village Romeo and Juliet*; and the Clews had agreed to come too.

Late in September the Deliuses spent another few days in Paris with the

Clews, after which Delius immediately started work on a Violin Concerto. In mid-November there was another excursion to their American friends, with whom they stayed for ten days. Jelka had written on 1 November to Marie: 'Fred's work is going so well', an accurate summing-up of a year which ended well for her too: 'I am painting very happily and am quite settled in my winter studio now,' she was to tell Marie on 29 December.

Requiem (RT II/8). Completion of last movement.

String Quartet (RT VIII/8). Three movements completed.

A Dance Rhapsody No. 2 (RT VI/22).

Four Old English Lyrics (RT V/30). No. 1 completed.

Concerto for violin and orchestra (RT VII/6).

Sonata for violoncello and pianoforte (RT VIII/7).

(415)
Frederick Delius to Percy Grainger

GREZ-SUR-LOING
Seine et Marne
Jan 11 1916

Dearest friend – All your cards & the wonderful criticisms[1] arrived safely & we were both overjoyed with your marvellous success – I am also so glad you met the Osbournes – They wrote me a long letter, full of enthusiasm & admiration for you – They also sent me criticisms – Both your letters arrived on the same day – So it was a "jour de fête" with us – I have been working at the "Requiem" & have now completed it & am just longing to shew it to you – When shall we meet again? I do hope it will be soon – Osbournes have invited us to visit them on their Ranch in California – might we not all meet out there? This war is not over by a long way – I have the "Song of the high Hills" The Arabesk & the Requiem & also Fennimore which have never been performed – Perhaps it would be possible to have one of them produced in America – They are all published with the exception of Fennimore   I wish they would perform "Sea-drift" in America – They have got conscription now in England – I wonder what Balfour will do – I dont see him being shot at in the trenches – do you? Your going to America was an inspiration & your success seems to be quite phenomenal – We are so happy to be in Grez again – Our garden was terribly neglected so we are both working in it every afternoon – No gardener is to be had – Otherwise one does not feel the war here whatever – I am reading the Sagas again – Grettir is wonderful – also Howard the Halt. What are you composing now? I hope you will have lots to shew me when we meet. We enjoyed our stay in Norway immensely – The peasants are splendid people – They used to stop me on the mountains to ask me if I were English & all about the war – Their sympathies are violently pro allies – Such a contrast with the Danes – who avoid the subject most carefully & neither write nor talk about the war – they are strictly neutral & one feels that they are all doing splendid business selling their margarine & pigs to Germany – Write me soon again & telling of your doings & successes & plans for the coming year – We both send you love & warmest greetings –

your loving friend
Frederick Delius

Autograph letter, signed and dated, written on headed notepaper. Envelope addressed: Percy Grainger Esqre/The Southern/680 Madison Ave/New York City/NY/ Etats unis d'Amerique. Postmark: GREZ [date illegible].

The original is in the Grainger Museum.

1   Reviews of recent performances in the United States, probably mainly of the Piano Concerto, premiered in New York by Grainger on 26 November.

(416)
Frederick Delius to Philip Heseltine

GREZ-SUR-LOING
Seine et Marne
Jan 22 1916

Dear Phil –

Just a few words to tell you how much I like Goossens quartet: it is the best thing I have seen coming from an English pen & full of emotion – Tell Goossens that I will get it published for him as soon as the war is over – Your Song the "Curlew"[1] is lovely & gave me the greatest pleasure. – Turn to music, dear boy. *There* is where you will find the only real satisfaction – Work hard at composition – There is real emotion in your song. *The most essential* quality for a composer – Whitaker's song I like also – altho' it is, at times, a little précieuse & *cherché*. Is he young? If so, *it is very promising*. I am hard at work on the end of my "Requiem"   I should love to shew it you – Cannot you come & stay with me here for a fortnight & bring the biography you are writing with you[2] – Say in March or April when the weather gets nice & springy – How are your other plans developing – I cannot understand Law-

rence wanting to give up writing[5] – What on earth for? – Surely not for planting potatoes or tobacco. Just fancy neglecting the gifts one has – those most
precious & rare & mysterious things coming from one knows not where, nor
why. My most earnest advice to you is to turn to musical composition at once
& for good – Voilà – Please send the piano score of the double Concerto to
Miss May Harrison, 51 Cornwall Gardens, Gloucester R[d]. Kensington –
Write me soon again

In haste –

your affectionate
Frederick Delius

P.S.
The little dance tune is charming
P.P S
Get the proofs of the Sonata from Forsythes –
Other proofs if the first have gone astray –

Autograph letter, signed and dated, written on headed notepaper. Envelope
addressed: Philip Heseltine Esq[re]/c/o D. H. Laurence Esq[re]/Porthcothan/St Merryn/
Cornwall/Angleterre. Postmark: GREZ 22 -1 16.

The original is in the British Library.

1   'He Reproves the Curlew' (1915), to words by W. B. Yeats; later incorporated
into the song cycle *The Curlew*.

2   Heseltine's biography of Delius was long in the writing, and was not finally
published until 1923. He referred to it in a letter to Delius dated 13 May 1917: 'The
little book about your works which I partially wrote last year, I am rewriting (since a
great deal of it was very crude and stupid) and expanding into an examination of the
condition of music in general at the present day. I hope to have it quite ready by the
autumn.' (Gray, p. 155.)

3   Although no letter from D. H. Lawrence to Delius has been found, Heseltine,
writing from Lawrence's Cornwall address on 6 January, told Delius: 'I asked Lawrence to write you a few days ago, to give you this exposition of our plans. However,
I don't want to identify myself with him in anything beyond his broad desire for an
ampler and fuller life . . . He is a very great artist, but hard and autocratic in his views
and outlook, and his artistic canons I find utterly and entirely unsympathetic to my
nature.' Nonetheless, Heseltine busily sent out pamphlets, written by himself, inviting subscriptions to a privately printed edition of *The Rainbow*. Delius, 'very
curious', immediately agreed to subscribe and induced Alden Brooks to do so too. 'I
think he is best,' he wrote on 15 March to Heseltine, 'in his shorter stories about sex
which I admire very much – The pamphlet you sent me I dont like at all. Why all this
symbolism – There is no need for it nowadays & then Nietzsche says that so much
better & in such a wonderfully pithy & clear language in "The Will to Power"   read

it & get Lawrence to read it.   L. is not yet far enough away from Good & Evil.' *The Rainbow* scheme 'died the death', as Heseltine wrote to tell Delius on 22 April, with just thirty replies received from six hundred circulars: 'My sojourn with Lawrence did me a lot of good, but not at all in the way I had anticipated. Lawrence is a fine artist and a hard, though horribly distorted, thinker. But personal relationship with him is impossible – he acts as a subtle and deadly poison.' (Gray, p. 118.)

(417)
Jelka Delius to Adine O'Neill

Grez   9.2.16.

My dear Adine,

Of course we caught a beastly "grippe" in Paris and I was so bad that I had to stay in bed and therefore only write to-day!

How charming it really is that you have got such a lovely big baby and a girl too, just what you wanted.[1] I am afraid tho' by the time she grows up – if there is another war then – it will be the *women* who will go and fight. We are beginning to do *all* the work now, and I think the men will find it very jolly and get lazier and lazier and we more and more energetic!! But I hope there will be no war and that this little girl will have a splendid time. Fred is very eager to be "godfather".[2] I wonder how you are getting on and I was sorry to hear you had such a bad time, let us hope all is well now!

Paris is much gayer and brighter now tho' the raid got them to darken the streets again. But the shops are frightfully full – The Bon Marché quite madly full and women like tigresses – yet it is only "exposition de blanc". I should have thought nobody would want to buy new sheets during the war.

Everybody is tremendously confident and the soldiers look remarkably well and strong. We went to all the Cinemas, but to see the films from the war you have to go through the most harassing american Drama's Vampyres, New York mysteries, murder thro' dreadful concentrated light-rays – No, I think I like best to be in the country and not in any town during the war – The restaurants in Paris are as good as ever and not much dearer. But somehow there is no real fun in anything now – until this is over –

It is cosy and peaceful here and it is really very lucky that we found such a good "bonne" who cooks all the real french things marvellously well; and is working hard all the time, even whilst we are in Paris. Fred has been working splendidly here and has been very well and that, I am sure, is a lot owing to the french food.

O dear – how little we hear from London – The Paris Daily Mail is also much shorter, than the London one – and on rainy days especially has the habit of not arriving.

Is Norman pleased with his little daughter?

We both send you both all our love and good-will and hope to hear more soon.

Affectionately
Jelka Delius

Autograph letter, signed and dated. Envelope addressed: Mme O'Neill/4 Pembroke Villas/Kensington W/Londres/Angleterre. Postmark: GREZ 9 -2 16.

The original is in the Delius Trust Archive.

1   Yvonne Patricia, the O'Neills' second child.

2   Delius was indeed to be the child's godfather, with Jelka one of the two god-mothers.

(418)
Frederick Delius to C. W. Orr

Grez-sur-Loing,
(Seine & Marne)
26 May 1916

My dear Mr Orr –

Your kind & sympathetic letter reached me safely & gave me the greatest plea-sure – It is always a great joy & gratification to me to learn that my music appeals to a few individuals – I suppose as it is not written for the public it does not appeal to it sufficiently to make the conductors give it very often. You must be a very good musician if you have been able to make a piano score of the "Cuckoo in Spring" – I am just finishing a string quartet – Last year I finished a "Requiem" (not religious) & a Concerto for Orchestra   Cello & Violin which I hope you will hear in the coming season – May & Beatrice Harrison will play it –. Here in Grez we are quite away from the war & living in our lovely garden which lies on the river – The roses are in full bloom as well as all the other summer flowers & the perfume is wonderful – I dont know when I shall come to London – As soon as the war is over perhaps & then it would give me great pleasure to meet you again – We both wish you "good luck" – May the war be over before you get to the front is our most sincere wish –

With kindest remembrances from my wife & me
I remain

Sincerely yours
Frederick Delius

Should you pay Paris a visit when you take a few days leave – Come & see us here; you will be welcome.

Autograph letter, signed and dated.

The original is in the collection of Mrs Susan Pumfrey. Thirteen communications dated 1916–21 from Delius to Orr are in this collection, and one further letter in the series, dated 22 January 1917, is in the Delius Trust Archive. No letters from Orr to Delius have been found.

Charles Wilfred Orr (1893–1976): English composer (mainly of songs) and writer on music. He had introduced himself to Delius, whose music he had grown to love, on 16 June 1915 having heard earlier in the evening the performance in London of the first Violin Sonata given by May Harrison and Hamilton Harty.

(419)
Frederick Delius to Philip Heseltine

GREZ-SUR-LOING
Seine et Marne
11 June 1916

My dear Phil –

I received your song safely & am glad to see you are working at your music – The "Curlew" is my favorite of the 3 altho there are beautiful things in all 3 – I wish you were here so that I might point out little things which strike me as unnecessary & which could be easily avoided – I find No. 3 less spontaneous – I have finished my String quartett – & am now writing a "dance"[1] – which I think is going to be good. How sweet of you to take the trouble to do another piano score of the Concerto for Cello & Violin – Miss Harrison wrote me that she has had it copied. You must be nice & snug up in your new little flat;[2] the description is delightful & it must be quite charming – I hope it will not be long before I visit you there – Keep pegging away at your work. Our garden here is simply lovely. We have done it all ourselves this year & it has never looked as well – I mow with a scythe every afternoon & am now quite an Expert at it. The book "Round the Corner" arrived here safely & we have started reading it. It sounds very good indeed up to the present – Your uncle Joe has turned out an awful old fraud – Just fancy,! whilst we were in England, he spread the report about Bourron & Marlotte, that we had been interned in a concentration camp in England & many other idiotic but treacherous reports about us – What do you say to that? He also said that I had thro my influence prevented you from enlisting – I had such confidence in him that I had written to him to go to my house in Grez & get me a certain book – It appears he

searched the house like a detective & went thro everything – this as a friend
mind you, & told people he found nothing really suspicious – Of course, I do
not want to see any more of him – His excuse may be perhaps that he is a fearful moral coward & has a most tremendous respect for all conventions & he
wants to give himself a certain importance with the social & conventional
people who I have always fought very shy of: in fact I wont associate with that
crowd here & so he found a ready public – But his falseness raises my gorge –[3]
How about the Rainbow – Brooks, next door, wants his copy as soon as it
appears – or has the thing come to nothing altogether – Gardiner wrote me a
long letter from Calais where he is employed reading soldiers letters 7 hours a
day – Sundays included – He enlisted as an ordinary Tommy & had a very hard
time of it drilling in a camp (Hazely Down)   He was lodged in a sort of Hut
with 37 others – fearful discomfort – He got so confused at last that he could
not understand what people were saying to him. However he has been
promoted to Sub Lieut now & has an easier time of it. Write me soon again,
your letters are always so welcome & send me all you compose – I will, if you
like, send you back a comment on the things I do not like –

Believe me ever

your loving friend
Frederick Delius

How about Nichols[4] –
I have still a few books of his with me here –
Have you his address?

***

Autograph letter, signed and dated, written on headed notepaper.

The original is in the British Library.

1   Probably *A Dance Rhapsody* No. 2, although the original score is dated 'Spring 1916 Grez sur Loing'.

2   Heseltine had taken 'a tiny studio attic' at 14 Whitehead's Grove, Chelsea.

3   Alden Brooks also relates how 'when war broke out, Joe took me aside and told me with the utmost seriousness that [Matthew] Smith's painting was only a blind – obviously so – that in fact Smith was an English spy sent out by the British General Staff, of which his brother-in-law was a member, in order to keep an eye on Delius, who though he pretended to be Danish, was actually of German extraction.' (Alden Brooks to Francis Halliday, 29 August 1960; transcript supplied by Sophie Royde Smith.)

4   Robert Nichols (1893–1944): English poet. He had befriended Heseltine at Oxford in the autumn of 1913, and he served in France from 1914 to 1916. Much later he collaborated with Fenby in selecting words from Whitman for an imaginative resetting, in Delius's *Idyll*, of some of the music from *Margot la Rouge*. His wife, Norah, whom he married in 1922, was a niece of Roger Quilter.

(420)
Thomas Beecham to Frederick Delius

Aug 14/16
E3, ALBANY CHAMBERS,
PICCADILLY, W.

My dear Delius

I have deferred writing to you until now because it is only during the last few days that I have known definitely whether I could be numbered among the "mice or men". In plain words whether or no until after the war I was to remain in a state of temporary pauperdom or no. You have rightly imagined that there have been lively times over here and for over three months my interests hung badly in the balance. On March 31st last the Government forbad the importation of certain articles – parts of machinery, manufactured wooden goods and other things that are vitally necessary for the carrying on of our various businesses including the one at St Helens. Indeed had I not obtained special concessions (only a week ago) we could not have gone on after Xmas next. Our big motor industry in which I hold the controlling share, would have had to close down next month. Luckily I have been able to obtain favoured treatment so that everything is now flourishing as before.

I have paid two instalments for you into the Bank which takes us up to the New Year, and your publications are going apace. The "Legende" is out and the others are on the point of appearing. So that from now on you need not have the smallest worry about material matters – I have had a very strenuous and harassing year, and am beginning to feel a little tired. I should like to see you very much but I am not allowed for the moment to leave the country. My various musical doings are too long for correspondence, but during the past year I have given forty consecutive weeks of opera (this for the first time in English musical history) and have directly and indirectly been responsible for over eighty concerts. Doing this in the midst of business annoyances has been rather a strain, but I have now got over that, and will be as fit as can be in a week or two[1] – Love to you both

Affectionately yours
T. B.

Autograph letter, initialled and dated, written on headed notepaper.

The original is in the Delius Trust Archive.

1   Lady Cunard (none of whose letters to the Deliuses has unfortunately been found) had recently written to Jelka, who quoted her to Marie Clews on 16 August: 'Thomas is delightful but so nervous that he must go alone to the country to have a fortnight's rest cure.'

(421)
Frederick Delius to Percy Grainger

October 5th. 1916
GREZ-SUR-LOING
Seine et Marne

My dear Percy –

I was overjoyed to receive your wonderful letter & printed cards[1] & hasten to reply – Firstly let me tell you how glad I am to learn that in spite of tremend-ous practical work, you have composed such a lot of new things – & let me thank you, dear friend for the dedication of your new orchestral work "The Warriors" – I need not tell you how I am longing to get to know it & all your other new things. I entirely agree with you about the American trip & shall follow your advice[2] – I am invited to stay with Osbourne on his ranch in Cali-fornia next summer – so, if the war is over & I believe it will be, I shall come over next summer & be there for the Concert season 1917–18 – I have not yet heard from Schirmer or B & H. The new works I would like published in America are a double Concerto for Violin, Cello & Orchestra. a string quartet & Dance Rhapsody *No 2*. What price, do you think Schirmer would pay? I sell my pieces outright. Leuckart gave me £200 each for my Orchestral pieces & Tischer £250 for "Lifes dance". I am going to practise conducting all the winter. I have already conducted the Dance Rhapsody – "In a summer garden" & Appalachia. I am now writing a "Violin Concerto" which I shall also bring with me to America – Tell Kreisler when you see him as I should love him to play it if possible. What I should love to do would be to conduct my piano Concerto with you. I could practise it with you when we meet in New York: I cannot tell you how I appreciate all you have done for me & what a rare & won-derful friend you are. Grez is very quiet & one feels the war very little indeed – I shall not budge from here until I take the boat for America   My wife re-ceived your mothers letter & is writing – Whenever you have time let me hear from you & tell me of your new triumphs – We both send you & your dear mother our love –

  ever your friend
  Frederick Delius

Autograph letter, signed and dated, written on headed notepaper. Envelope ad-dressed: Percy Grainger Esqre/'The Southern'/680 Madison Avenue/New York City/NY/Etats Unis d'Amérique. Postmark: GREZ 5 -10 16.

The original is in the Grainger Museum.

1   On 14 September Grainger wrote and enclosed publicity material he had recently had prepared, including 'a postcard printed on your Concerto'.

2   Grainger had counselled care: 'Personally I would advise you *not to budge* from Grez
while the war lasts. It is the duty of us all to try to preserve such a genius as yourself
from danger ... As long as the war lasts & it is so difficult to get music over the
benefit to you would be so small.' Influential friends of the Clews were also busily
tilling the ground on Delius's behalf in the United States, one result being a letter
dated 25 September from Stokowski, conductor since 1912 of the Philadelphia
Orchestra, to Andrew Wheeler, Secretary of the Philadelphia Orchestra Association:
'Many thanks for your letter and quotation from Mrs. Clews' letter. I know most of
the scores of Delius's orchestral works. You will remember that last season I had
planned to do his Dance Rhapsody, but unfortunately, owing to the war, we were
unable to get a baritone oboe from Paris in time for the performance. It is strange that
you should write to me of this composer, as for the last week I have been studying his
"Messe des Lebens." This is a work planned on an enormously large scale and interests
me very deeply. Unfortunately I have not been able to obtain a full score of this work
and have only so far been able to study it from the Klavierauszug. Of course such a
monumental work as this would need a great deal of preparation, as I only would do it
if it were given a performance of the highest quality, and as you know with all the
plans I have for next season, it would be quite impossible to add a work of such dimen-
sions to the already large list of new works I am producing. Percy Grainger and I have
often discussed Delius, and I am hoping soon to hear him play his piano concerto.'

(422)
Frederick Delius to Philip Heseltine

GREZ-SUR-LOING
Seine et Marne 15 Oct 1916

My dear Phil –

I was so glad to receive your news; not having heard from you for so long I was
beginning to think you had been "conscripted." Your enthusiasm is always so
refreshing – Now to your idea of regenerating music in England, especially the
musical drama – I entirely agree that realism on the stage is nonsense & that
all the scenery necessary is an "impressionistic" painted curtain at the back
with the fewest accesories possible – Even furniture ought mostly to be
painted – but one requires a real artist to have thoroughly understood the
Drama & then to paint the scene after his own conception. In Germany this
has been already tried with success   The Village Romeo was performed like
this for the first time & the scenic part was a great success: The theatre was
awful & no music could be heard in it – The orchestra therefore – *the chief thing*
– dropped into the 3rd plane. They gave the Fair quite simply with a painted
curtain – it cannot be left out as it is so important – & the walk thro' the fields
& woods to the "Paradise Garden" would have no contrast. I entirely agree
with all your ideas about the music drama – they are also mine & all my works

are written in this spirit. I have not much hope for English music or music
Drama in the near future for the following reasons – the English have very
little imagination & therefore are very hard to appeal to – I have experienced
the press & public acclaiming Electra as one of the greatest masterpieces of the
world – a work which has already died a natural death – which it deserved – &
the Village Romeo was declared undramatic. It is one of the most dramatic &
emotional works ever written & in years to come will be constantly played
everywhere – Beecham's production was from a scenic point of view perfectly
mediocre & insufficient – He used old Covent Garden scenery – now a scene
out of the Gotterdämmerung again one out of some other opera. The singers
were nearly all bad & insufficient & none of them could act. I know no English
singer who can act or who is capable or willing to show any emotion on the
stage & mind, dear Phil, this is going to be one of your great stumbling blocks
– the English are an unemotional race & wallow only in the worst & most
obvious sentimentality. I quite agree that The Village R ought to be given in
a small theatre but there must be an orchestra of at least 60. The piano Idea
does not smile to me – My orchestra is too all important & almost the whole
action on the stage is indicated in the Orchestra – To tell you the truth I have
no desire to have any more of my dramatic works given in England for some
years – *There is no public* – mark my words – Even if there were – I dont think
that anything ought to be undertaken before the war is over & the people have
calmed down a bit. In itself the idea is excellent & your friend Gray[1] unique
with his enthusiasm to pay for such a highly artistic undertaking – *Wait a bit* –
prepare – gather works – look out for singers & teach them to act & then open
up in a small theatre a highly artistic & original repertoire – you may form
gradually a public – but dont open before March 1918. I believe in the english
youth under 25 or 30. After this age he is hopeless. The war will have changed
much – people will have suffered – many will have realized the *rot* – that has
been going on – the hollowness of patriotism & jingoism & all the other isms –
Politicians & diplomats & experts of all kinds have been making & continue to
make such fools of themselves that the wiser folk will, perhaps, look for a little
truth in art & the artists – & perhaps find some satisfaction in that rare event
– *A really artistic & emotional performance*. I should like to come over for the
quartet[2] – but everything is so difficult – It takes 10 days or more to get your
passport in order & the journey across the channel is dangerous – I should just
love to talk with you about all these things & help you if I am able – at the
beginning of a London Season 1915 I went to see "Deidre of the Sorrows" by
that remarkable writer Synge – It was an artistic affair – a good ensemble & a
remarkable play – The theatre was not half full – quite a small theatre.
Nobody cares! – The Russian ballet, because it was new – sensational, very
artistic & tremendously boomed – & fashionable, drew full houses – otherwise
only a low style of entertainment succeeds in London – Barker no doubt en-
deavoured to do something – but did he succeed? could he exist? & then it was

not music drama. You see you must be able to keep at it in order to form a public – one season is not enough – it must be followed up by another season equally good & for this purpose you only ought to begin such an undertaking at a favorable moment – Why not begin by a series of concerts in a small hall with a small orchestra – giving only rare & excellent works – Some of which you have named. The Mime drama[3] you sketched for me would only have an effect with 3 great artists – Which at present do not exist in England & It might turn out simply ridiculous　Nijinski, Karsavina & Fokine might do it – I have written another Elizabethan Song. "It was a lover & his Lass" from 12th night – I am writing a Violin Concerto now – When you start your Scheme you must absolutely make it a success or it will again fizzle into nothing like all artistic attempts in London – including Beecham's & that makes the public more & more sceptical – Practise conducting – if possible, take an engagement at any theatre simply to get a little routine – even if you have to conduct musical comedy – What you write of Van Dieren[4] interests me exceedingly – cannot you send me something? Can I not help him in some way? Does he want a publisher? I am going to publish with Schirmer now. Is Van Dieren a dutchman? Write soon again　We both send you our love

　your affectionate friend
　Frederick Delius

Autograph letter, signed and dated, written on headed notepaper.

The original is in the British Library.

Heseltine had met Cecil Gray earlier in the year; they were now planning, as Heseltine wrote to Delius on 11 October, to give in a small theatre the following spring a short season of opera and concerts. A *Village Romeo and Juliet*, 'one of the loveliest operas in existence', as Gray was later to describe it, would be produced, freed of realistic conventions and, in Heseltine's words, 'not buried beneath a mass of stage properties and theatrical misconceptions ... What you have achieved in this work – and it is a great and unique achievement – is a drama in which the various emotions, brought into play by various contingencies and circumstances, are the real protagonists. But they are not *personified* in the old allegorical "morality" style. They are far too subtle. They are presented, typified, in certain individuals who appear on the stage. But it is not these individuals that really absorb us. The work grips one, entrances one and carries one away because these individuals are so shadowy, so unrealistic that they become symbols of the pure emotion they are feeling'. (Gray, pp. 131–3.)

1　Cecil Gray (1895–1951): English musicologist and composer. A friend (and, subsequently, biographer) of Heseltine, Gray first got to know Delius when the latter came to live in London late in 1918, and was in close contact, as he claimed in his *Musical Chairs*, 'whenever he was in England or I in France'. He was to stay in the house at Grez 'on several occasions'.

2   The first performance of Delius's String Quartet in its original three-movement version was given by the London String Quartet, leader Albert Sammons, in the Aeolian Hall, London, on 17 November.

3   'I have sketched out a little mime-drama . . . It is called *Twilight*,' Heseltine had told Delius, whose reaction seems appropriate enough: Columbine, Harlequin and Pierrot were apparently to spend most of the fifteen minutes sitting in armchairs 'as though waiting'.

4   Bernard van Dieren (1887–1936): Dutch-born composer, domiciled in England from 1909. He had been introduced to Heseltine in June by the sculptor Jacob Epstein. His music at once made an enormous impression on Heseltine and, according to Gray, the latter's subsequent 'clear and vigorous part-writing' and 'contrapuntal discipline' were direct results of van Dieren's influence. Heseltine had at this time been hoping to secure publication of van Dieren's 'Chinese' Symphony.

(423)
Frederick Delius to Philip Heseltine

GREZ-SUR-LOING
Seine et Marne
Nov 6th 1916

My dear Phil,

I want to lay before you, very precisely, my point of view with regard to artistic &, especially, operatic enterprise in England – I am so fond of you & admire your whole attitude so much that I wish you to thoroughly understand my attitude towards artistic undertakings in England – I know of no artis-tic(tic) musical dramatic undertaking that has *ever come off* in England. The great success of the Russian Ballet was, firstly, it was boomed by a fashionable clique – 2^{ndly} no Englishman had anything whatever to do with it – bar financing – It came to London entirely ready to ring up the curtain. Every other enterprise has been a failure & often a miserable failure – Where there has been enthusiasm amongst the promoters there has been amateurism & in-experience & inefficiency which has just as thoroughly ruined the whole affair – Electra came to London from Berlin – with singers scenery & stage managers – a finished work. The attempt to mount the Village Romeo with English sing-ers, Chorus & stage manager was a miserable failure – inefficiency & inexperi-ence bursting out from every crack – The only good point was the splendid english Orchestra & Beecham conducting. Beecham however knew nothing about the stage & how the singers ought to behave & therefore the whole was a failure – Now here you come & want to mount the Village Romeo once more & under worse auspices – Firstly – an inadequate orchestra   2nd singers who are an unknown quantity   I know of *no English* singer who can act – & cer-

tainly of no 2 singers who could act Sali & Vrenchen – Especially thro the love
scenes – A love scene between 2 English singers is a farce which only one who
know[s] what a love scene ought to be can appreciate – The English singer is
by far too self possessed, he & she is afraid to show emotion & especially
passion – you should have only seen Mr Hyde – Sali   & Ruth Vincent – Vrenchen – kissing each other!! & when at the end in the great love scene on the
Hay boat they ought to possess each other whilst the boat gradually sinks they
were both reclining gracefully side by side on the hay – as if they were out for a
boating tour on the Thames at Maidenhead – Mr Hyde pulling a left hand oar
– you tell me Mr Gray, you & Mr Van Dieren will entirely control the music
& dramatic direction – Tell me which of you 3 has any experience whatever? –
Every gesture of the actors in my work must be controlled & ordered by the
Conductor – for my music is conceived in that spirit – Only thus can the
whole be made comprehensible to the public – an old actor stage manager will
be no good whatever – for he will make the singers act from the stage & not
from the music – Dont you see, dear Phil, that you are all going towards disaster with the best intentions possible & that is what seems to me so hopeless
in our own country – With no experience whatever you are going to undertake
one [of] the most difficult of tasks & you want to begin at once with one of the
most difficult works – Why at least dont you give the "Village Romeo" in
your 2nd season – It is the Dardanelles – & Mesopotamia over again – I again
advise you to begin in quite a small way – in order to gain experience –. The
Russian ballet did this – it began in a barn in the slums of Petrograd with old
cast off costumes & gradually acquired the wonderful perfection which we have
all admired – Tell Gray he has the opportunity of doing quite a *unique thing* &
it would be a terrible mistake to spoil the whole affair by a too ambitious
opening – Feel your way & whilst you are so doing you will gradually be ac-
quiring valuable experience – My whole heart goes out towards your undertaking & for this reason I write as I have done – It would be better & less
harmful for the future of art in England not to begin this undertaking than to
do it badly & fail – there have been *too many* such failures in England & already
the public only really believe in what comes from abroad –[1]

  your affectionate friend
  Frederick Delius

Autograph letter, signed and dated, written on headed notepaper.

The original is in the British Library.

1 Perhaps fortunately, the whole scheme was abandoned – even though many arrangements had already been completed – with Gray's trustees insisting that the
venture be postponed until the war was over.

1917

'Fred is writing a wonderful new Orchestra-piece and hard at work; only the unsettled plans for our future worry us a good deal.' Jelka's remark, in a letter to Marie Clews dated 20 January, is the first to refer to *Eventyr*, as the work was eventually to be known. The 'unsettled plans' related to Delius's desire to leave for America in the spring, a project very soon postponed to the autumn. Meanwhile the winter weather was to Delius's taste – crisp, fairly cold and sunny. 'We have been in Grez all the winter & I have done a lot of work –' he wrote to Heseltine on 27 May. 'It is a great thing to be able to isolate ones self completely: altho' not very practical.' In point of fact there had evidently been visits to Paris, as Delius added: 'I have rewritten my string quartet & added a scherzo – I heard it in Paris.' And late in May there was a visit to stay with the Clews.

However, a change for the worse in Delius's health came quite suddenly. Within a month of the early days of June spent actively in the open air, he was, on his doctor's recommendation, at a spa in Normandy, scarcely able to walk. There had been an innocuous-sounding message from Jelka to Marie Clews on 20 June: 'Fred wants to go off for a little trip to Normandy . . . He wants a change and to get away from his piano for a bit.' He left Grez on 6 July, according to Jelka 'much more depressed about the future since he has stopped working'. After beginning the bath treatments he was able to tell Jelka: 'The numbness persists still in hands & feet but legs & knees stronger', and before long he could report taking on the afternoon of 24 July a ten-kilometre walk with only occasional pauses. By early August he was well enough for Jelka to join him on a holiday in Brittany.

During the autumn, visits to the Clews would be arranged to coincide with appointments with his doctor in Paris, and by the end of the year Delius was considerably better. The winter weather, however, had grown bitterly cold, and coal – a dire necessity at Grez – was unobtainable. Once again, a move to London seemed to be the answer in all current circumstances, and the Deliuses began laying plans accordingly.

To be sung of a summer night on the water, two unaccompanied part songs (wordless) for mixed voices (RT IV/5). Late spring.

String Quartet (RT VIII/8). General revision, and Scherzo added.

Eventyr (RT VI/23). Completed.

(424)
Beatrice Harrison to Frederick Delius

Hotel Wellington
SEVENTH AVENUE
FIFTY FIFTH AND FIFTY SIXTH STREETS
New York, January 11th 1917.

Dear Mr Delius,

Thank you so much for your last letter. Mrs Lanier[1] has been so charming & kind, it was so very good of you to introduce me to her. We went to see her yesterday after the big concert given by the "Friends of Music", & we talked so much about you & your wonderful music, & every one over here is most excited about your beautiful Double Concerto & Mrs Lanier told me to ask you to send over the Score of the Double Concerto at once, & the Conductors want to see & study it, & she does want it by the spring, & she does hope she can fix it up for us to play it next year at the "Friends of Music". The Boston Symphony Orchestra is most anxious to have it I hear, also the New York Philharmonic, every one is thrilled about it. I do hope you will be able to come over to England this summer, & May and I will work & study it, & get it as one instrument, as I think we really do understand your exquisite music a little bit, & I think you know how we love it.

With love to dear Mrs Delius & you from Mother & me,

y^{rs} ever sincerely
Beatrice Harrison

Autograph letter, signed and dated, written on headed notepaper.

The original is in the Delius Trust Archive. It is the only item of correspondence preserved from any of the Harrison family, having been found among the Clews papers deposited in the Archive in 1972.

Beatrice Harrison (1893–1965): English cellist. She studied in London and Berlin and was to be particularly associated with the Elgar concerto. Two of Delius's works for cello were dedicated to her, the Sonata and *Caprice and Elegy*.

1   Mrs Lanier, who ran the Society of the Friends of Music, was a prominent patron of music in New York at this time. Jelka hoped to hear from her soon, according to a letter she wrote to Marie Clews on 20 January: 'Fred has written to Thomas ages ago to beg him to send the Mass of Life, but as usual *no* answer. Maybe we shall hear from Mrs L. about it. I really do not know *what* we ought to do? The programmes for the winter season are generally made up in the spring and early summer and Fred wants so much to go to N.Y. then, firstly to get his new works published, and secondly to arrange for as many performances as possible for next winter. But where to be all summer? The Osbournes have very kindly invited us to spend the summer with them on their Californian ranch, where I should paint some more portraits of Mrs Osbourne

But of course the journey out there is terribly expensive and uncomfortable, fatiguing beyond words and once one makes it one ought to be flush with money, so as to go about comfortably and see all there is to be seen. To spend the summer on our own in and near New York we *could not* afford. It seems to me it would be so much better if we only went to N.Y. in the autumn If the Mass of Life could be given in several places and Romeo be put on at the Metrop. that would of course make it worth-while, especially if we got our travelling expenses paid.' She added: 'I hope you will look at it with clear fresh eyes and tell us candidly what you think.'

(425)
Frederick Delius to C. W. Orr

GREZ-SUR-LOING
Seine & Marne
April 10th 1917

My dear Mr Orr –

I received your two letters & also the 3 songs which greatly interested me – I find you have what to me is the most important quality in music "emotion" There is a warm feeling over your music & I should certainly advise you to devote yourself entirely to it & work very hard – Especially if you have sufficient means to live without gaining your living by music – You see "cleverness" counts for very little in my opinion – the french composers are all far too clever when young your technique ought to develope with your ideas – Debussy wrote his best things before 30 & got gradually more superficial & uninteresting – The same with Ravel who is even cleverer than Debussy but even more flimsy & superficial – But their chief idea is to startle & be brillant – Eugene Goossens is also far too clever altho' he is gifted & I hope, will do something – Debussy's best work is "L'après midi" – an early work. Parts of Pelleas are also very fine & there is great dignity in the work – I consider Pelleas & L'après midi Debussy's works which may live – but none of the others – Of Ravel the string quartet is one of the best & also a piano piece in "Gaspard de la nuit" called "le Gibet" – But without Debussy Ravel would not exist. – The other young frenchmen dont count – they all resemble each other – You amused me very much by your description of the English "aesthetes"   it has always been thus – English artists are always imitating something foreign & if possible "outré" – Go by all means to the Guildhall school of music for a while & see how you profit by it – But do not get hold of a professor who teaches you little 4 or 8 bar counterpoint exercises & little harmony exercises – Trust your own ears & try to express your emotions in any way you can[1] – I dont know who the teachers are in that establishment. I know Landon Ronald to be a good & progressive musician. I know all Dostoievsky & am a great admirer of his works – Do you know "The Idiot" – perhaps his best? I corrected the last proofs of my Violin Sonata yesterday so it will be out in a fortnight – I may come to England this summer & hope to see you, otherwise, you must come & see me here when you come abroad. It is still wintry here altho' the garden is full of Daffodils & I saw a solitary swallow yesterday – I find you are influenced by "Tristan" in "Mary Magdalene" the song I like the best – But it is a good influence & you will work out of all that – But mind, if you devote yourself to music, there is only one way to attain anything at all – I mean any originality – & that is by *work* – Work right thro' all your influences – Everyone has been influenced at first & you will only find your real self after getting rid of great masses of other people –

With kindest regards from us both – I remain

Very sincerely yours
Frederick Delius

Autograph letter, signed and dated, written on headed notepaper.

The original is in the collection of Mrs Susan Pumfrey.

1   Delius had written on 22 January, when he replied to a question from Orr: 'You ask me whether I found composing difficult when I began – It is rather a difficult question to answer. I found learning theory very difficult & sterile – I may say I am entirely auto didact – I always found intense pleasure & satisfaction in composing & found doing theoretical exercises a fearful drudgery – I dont even now know whether doing this drudgery has ever been of any use – *But work* if you feel you have something in you to express – You will gradually acquire a technic of your own – It is the only way to acquire one of any use – Simply work as much as possible on Composition – studying the scores of the works you love – Never mind about the music you dont like, however clever it may be'.

A little later, on 27 May, Delius wrote to Heseltine: 'There is really only one quality for great music & that is "emotion" – Look with what ease hundreds of young composers are quietly expressing themselves in the so called "new idiom". Otherwise the wrong note system – Hundreds of painters are seeing in Cubes – But it all means nothing more than a fashion – & merely intellectual when at its best.'

(426)
Frederick Delius to Jelka Delius

VILLA JAVIN   PENSION DE FAMILLE
TESSÉ-LA-MADELEINE
STATION DE BAGNOLES (ORNE)   [7 July 1917]

Dearest – I arrived here half an hour ago – Everything crammed with people –
The 3 big Hotels requisitioned for the military – I got in here for 12 francs a
day pension – a small room – the etablissement des Bains is closed on Sundays
– so that I cannot follow Dr Bas' indications exactly – I shall have to take 6
baths running 4 for 10 minutes & 2 for 15 & then take a repos – Otherwise I
should have to take 2 days of repos – I dont know what to think of the weakness in my legs – When I arrived in Paris there was no taxi to be had & I had
to sleep at The Palace Hotel – The train went from les Invalides direct to
Bagnoles. I could scarcely walk this morning on getting up – Have never felt
anything like this before – Probably I exerted myself getting in & out of the
train with my things – Should I consult a doctor here or simply wait & see? I
do hope I shall not become like Heinrich Heine! Dearest I miss you terribly –
Even standing on my legs I feel tired at once – I travelled 1st class I felt so miserable 27^{frcs} 2nd it costs 18 francs – If I feel too miserable I shall telegraph
you to come here – There is scarcely any room to be had anywhere & frightfully bourgeois looking people – How shall I last 21 days? Dont get frightened
at this letter – I write just as I feel – I may feel better tomorrow. In every case
you will have to come to Brittany to join me –
   Write at once – dearest

   ever your
   Fred

Autograph letter, signed and undated, written on headed notepaper.

The original is in the Grainger Museum.

This letter, from a Normandy spa, gives the first indication of another breakdown in
Delius's health. The spring and early summer had, it appears, brought no problems.
Work on composition had continued busily during the first months of the year, and
the earlier part of the summer saw the Deliuses preoccupied with their garden. On 8
June he was able to write to Henry Clews: 'I have been working on my vines all day
yesterday & today & have not yet finished – I work entirely naked in the sun & enjoy
it'. And five days later, Jelka wrote to Marie: 'We are working in the garden and
picking lovely strawberries; it is tremendously dry, but hot and lovely, and we spend
the evenings up on the roof. How delightful our days in Paris with you both were!'
The idyll seemed set to continue, with Delius planning to make a tour of Brittany at
the end of the month and inviting Clews to join him. But on 23 July Jelka reported to
Marie: 'He was really not at all well lately and so Dr Bas advised him to take the baths

at Bagnoles (Orne) and he went there. He always forbids me to say that anything is the matter with him, so I did not write. He felt so very weak and low and depressed – and I hated to let him go alone but it is all so expensive and he has been so good and staid in that rotten place and taken his baths ferruginous-radium and says they are marvellously good, and he feels much better.'

(427)
Frederick Delius to Jelka Delius

VILLA JAVIN   PENSION DE FAMILLE
TESSÉ-LA-MADELEINE
STATION DE BAGNOLES (ORNE)   [25? July 1917]

Dearest – Your letter enclosing Marie's just received. How nice about the sugar – Please bring 1 copy of my Sonata for Violin – It is in my music cupboard on the right, as I want to send it with a dedication to May Harrison – Our room is engaged at Val-André Hotel de la Plage for Thursday August 2nd – If you like to leave on the 2nd you will arrive early on the 3rd [1] – I arrive at 10 p m 2nd August – Lamballe is the station – Bring all the money & my rings & jewels – only for safety – One does not know what will happen before the Autumn – Tell Clews where we are going & try to get them to join us – We can stay with them on our return in September – I stay 40 minutes in my bath now & it does me a lot of good – 45 minutes tomorrow – I rest all the time & really have improved wonderfully Eat well & sleep well – Bring also a casquette – Your train leaves at 20–10 & 20–20 or at 7–30 in the morning Gare *Montparnasse* – Bring painting things & dont tire yourself carrying things – Take cabs & go 2nd Class – Dont try to save: Lets have a good time in Brittany regardless – Russia is rotten & I dont see any issue as things are – I walk very little & loll about resting a lot in a chaise longue – The Pleigne[?] lady (proper spelling) is very nice but terribly bourgeois – The rest of the crowd is awful – one woman shrieks for hours at the piano every afternoon – The Doctor will cost about 60 francs – it appears – It is the tax – whether one consults him twice or twenty times – He told me on his last examination in my bath que j'avais une belle santé & the tiredness in my legs was varicose veins – inflamed by sun baths – The country is lovely around here & the weather beautiful – Some ladies took me a long drive in their Auto the other day The country resembles Britanny & England – We saw some lovely Chateaux – I hope you sent me the 50 francs – Goodbye dearest –

ever your
Fred –

I leave here Thursday at 12 noon

Autograph letter, signed and undated, written on headed notepaper.

The original is in the Grainger Museum.

1   Jelka was to join her husband for a holiday in Brittany. Delius sent a postcard on
28 July: 'Beecham has paid in £150. so we are rich – Take *first class* & have it comfortable – especially if you travel at night.'

(428)
Frederick Delius to C. W. Orr

Grez-sur-Loing
(Seine & Marne)
29th Dec 1917

My dear Mr. Orr –

Many thanks for your kind letter & good wishes   We have decided to come to
London about the 20th of January – as we find the life here very lonely & there
is scarcely any music in Paris – I am bringing my new works with me & hope
to hear them during the season – We should so much like to hire a little furnished house or flat – Do you know of anything? I should be very grateful to
you if you would look out for something for me – Perhaps one of your friends
might wish to let his house or flat. I dont care in what district it is situated.
The weather has turned arctic & we have the greatest difficulty to heat our
house – Coal is not to be had & we are heating with wood.
    I am, of course, a great admirer of Dostoievski   Do you know "The Idiot"?
it is wonderful – Write me as soon as possible & let me know about the house,
should you hear of anything.
    I am looking forward with great pleasure to meeting you again –
    We both send you our hearty new years greetings

    Very sincerely yours
    Frederick Delius

Autograph letter, signed and dated.

The original is in the collection of Mrs Susan Pumfrey.

The Deliuses had spent a quiet autumn at home, punctuated by short visits to Paris,
where they probably stayed with the Clews. It would seem that Delius himself had
been fairly well since his return from Brittany, although Jelka wrote to tell Marie on
27 October: 'He is not yet quite up to the mark – it is always such a difficult season,
when autumn turns into winter!' Early in December they tried to find an apartment to
rent in Paris, but without success. Delius turned his eyes to London; Jelka wrote to

Marie Clews on 31 December: 'We cannot keep the house warm without coal and even the enormous provision of wood will soon be burnt up . . . . The cold has been simply terrifying.'

(429)
Frederick Delius to Norman O'Neill

Grez-sur-Loing
(S & M)
[Dec] 31 1917.[1]

A happy new year to you, dear old pal, & the same to Adine & the children – I was delighted to receive news from you & learn that everything is well, so far as it can be in these rotten times. If we can get Balfours house we shall be very relieved as I hear it is difficult to hire flats or furnished houses   We are thinking of hiring a house in London & living there most of the time – I am thirsting for music & there is none here & very little even in Paris & then nothing of interest – I am making efforts to get a pass via Calais or Boulogne as I rather wish to avoid the long night passage via Havre – Southampton – They will also not allow us to bring our bonne – which is a great drawback as she is so excellent – However I have appealed to my influential friends in London & am awaiting their answer – I think England owes me a "safe conduct" by the safest & shortest route! I am bringing 7 manuscript works with me – If I cannot get the pass we may probably go to Switzerland for a couple of months & they will produce one or 2 of my new works there – But we are quite "en l'air" & have decided nothing – Balfour's House would probably turn the balance – I want to edit[2] my works in London as I now have to earn some more money   As soon as we get back our sequestered fortune we shall furnish a house in London   Is Beecham giving interesting music in London? I shall approach him when I see him in London about my new works. For the last 16 days we have had arctic cold & cannot keep our house warm, as we only have wood to burn – I have just finished a new work "Eventyr" after Asbørnsens fairy tales for Orchestra & have rather tired my eyes – I am just longing for a change & *Music*.

Good bye & au revoir I hope soon

Ever your friend
Frederick Delius

Autograph letter, signed and dated. Envelope addressed: Monsieur/Norman O'Neill/ 4 Pembroke Villas/Kensington W/Londres/Angleterre. Postmark: GREZ 31 -12 17.

The original is in the Delius Trust Archive.

1   The original has Jan 31 1917.

2   It should be remembered that Delius commonly spoke of editing when he meant publishing.

1918

Josef Stransky, in New York, remains the principal champion in America of Delius's orchestral music, framing the year with Philharmonic Society performances of *In a Summer Garden* (11 January, with two further performances in February), and *Life's Dance* (12 and 13 December). As for Delius himself, very little was achieved during the first two months of the year. London was in view for February: 'We shall no doubt stay until the end of this awful war,' he wrote to Orr on 14 January. 'I may perhaps have a class or take a few pupils for composition & orchestration.' But his health again took a turn for the worse and later in January he entered briefly a sanatorium in the Parisian suburb of Rueil. His nervous condition slowly improved on his return to Grez, although the enemy bombardment of Paris meant that any tonic visits to the Clews would have been unlikely. Indeed, Henry and Marie Clews, together with their infant son and maidservants, descended on Grez for a short visit in the early spring, and although they returned briefly to Paris, they soon left for the south and La Napoule, which from mid-1919 was to be their home for the rest of their lives. Jelka had earlier, on 15 March, signalled Delius's gradual recovery: he seemed much better and was at work again, probably on a new composition, *Poem of Life and Love*. April saw his improvement maintained, and by the beginning of May the decision had been taken to spend at least part of the summer at Biarritz, no doubt on his doctor's recommendation. Home had already lost much of its quiet attraction, with large numbers of French and American soldiers now quartered on Grez and Bourron respectively.

The Deliuses arrived in Biarritz, where they were to spend over two months, on 5 June. Delius himself embarked on a course of baths; he also hired a piano and got down to composition. Before long came bad news: their house at Grez had been requisitioned and was occupied by French officers. At least all was well at Biarritz: the *Poem of Life and Love* was completed by the end of the month, as was the little *Song before Sunrise*, both orchestral works, and Delius seemed fully restored to vigorous health. Deepest dismay, however, resulted on their return to Grez in mid-August. The house had been vandalized and left in a shameful state by its temporary occupants and there had been much petty thieving. Another temporary setback was that Beecham, now in

considerable financial difficulty, could not for the present fulfil the remainder
of his contract with Delius. The decision was taken to leave, with their French
maid, for London, where they rented Henry Wood's house in St John's Wood
for the month of September, before taking a furnished apartment in Belsize
Park in October. A Promenade performance by Henry Wood of the first *Dance
Rhapsody* in September was probably the first chance Delius had had to hear
any of his orchestral music since 1915. Friends and enthusiasts were program-
ming more of his works in the autumn. The war ended; only in December did
Delius learn that a nephew, his sister Clare's son, had been killed on active
service shortly before the Armistice.

By the end of the year the attraction of London had faded considerably. He
was not composing. Musical and artistic life was little more than a pale reflection of the life that had prevailed before the war, and the Deliuses' spirits were
as damp as London's dull and cold weather. Nonetheless an element of surprise
is supplied by the composer's attempts to found in London yet another concert
society, undaunted by the failure of his two efforts of some ten and twenty
years earlier. More and more one is drawn to wonder how and why there came
into being the mystifying and indeed misleading legend of the composer-
recluse who never lifted a finger to further the performance of his own, still
less of other people's music.

―――――――

A Song before Sunrise, orchestra (RT VI/24).

Poem of Life and Love, orchestra (RT VI/25).

Sonata No. 3 for violin and piano (RT VIII/10). First movement sketched.

(430)
Henry Wood to Frederick Delius

APPLE TREE FARM HOUSE,
CHORLEY WOOD COMMON,
HERTS.
16th Jan. 1918.

My dear Delius,

Delighted to receive your note of the 8th and to hear that there is some chance
of seeing you over here again soon.

"Brigg Fair" was a great success both at the Promenade and Symphony Concerts: I also played the Dance Rhapsody in Birmingham a short time ago, but
I have no longer a good bass oboe player, as the original man Horton, has been
called up.

I do hope you and Mrs. Delius will run down to Chorleywood and see us: it is only 35 minutes from Baker Street. Our little London house, 4, Elsworthy Road, N. W. has just been vacated by its last tenants: how would it suit you?

With kindest regards, in which my wife joins,

Sincerely Yours,
Henry J. Wood

─────────────

Typed letter, signed and dated, written on headed notepaper.

The original is in the Delius Trust Archive.

Good news from London, but unfortunately Delius's health was to take a turn for the worse; by the end of the month he was in a sanatorium at Rueil, depressed, and surrounded by nervous cases. Only shortly before this, he and Jelka had spent a happy week at the Clews in Paris, but symptoms of the present nervous disorder became evident soon afterwards. He stayed only briefly at Rueil and then steadily recuperated at Grez during the rest of February. On 15 March, Jelka reported to Marie Clews: 'I think Fred is so much better and he is working: his eyes are wonderfully much better.'

(431)
Frederick Delius to Henry Clews

4 Rue Gardague [Biarritz]
20 June 1918

Dear friend –

I received your two cards – The last one convinced me that in spite of what "Pessimists" affirm – Idealism is not dead. – Marie's letter arrived this morning & gave us great pleasure – We are glad to hear you are both so well & having a good time – Here it has been cold, windy & raining for the last ten days – Much colder than in Grez & I dont see this at all as a Winter resort – the baths are, however, excellent – I feel sleepy all the time & could doze all day & all night. – The people here, of course, that one sees on the beach & on the streets are a terrible crowd & what it will be in July & August I can well imagine! – The nouveaux riches en masse & then any quantity of Cocottes & petites femmes from Paris – the gayest possible toilettes – Very little mourning to be seen here! – In other words not my place at all – When we have both done our baths – I think we shall clear out to some quieter place – either on the coast or in the mountains – Schvan[1] sent me a letter with his new colonisation project. – I have already in mind 3 such plans which all failed miserably – He seems to forget that Tahiti belongs to the french & therefore he will, to start with, come up against the french administration; then the missionaries are pretty active out there! – Jack London (in the Voyage of the Snark) after a prolonged visit, sums up the people of Tahiti something like this – "The less said about the inhabitants of Tahiti the better, they seem to consist of robbers & thieves" – The climate must be devine & the women wonderfully beautiful, luxurious & entirely immoral (Christian standpoint) this of course is the great asset. However I wish him all success – I should love to go on a visit – but should never think of settling too far from a *big orchestra & chorus* & also not too far from my beloved Norway & the light summer nights & all the poetry & melancholy of the Northern summer & the high mountain plateaus where humans are rare & more individual than in any other country in the world; & where they also have deeper & more silent feelings than any other people – No! I dont see myself making part of any community or any reform colony of any sort – I am sure he will gather together around him a most tedious crowd – consisting of Vegetarians   Christian Scientists – Neo Spiritists – Free sexologists & Eugenic polyandrists – However I wish him luck & success & I believe in everyone following his own fancy. Look around & see if you cannot find a small house or appartment for us – I have hired a piano & am working a little at my new Symphony.[2] We go at nights to a cinema & see the most stirring drama's & Terrible Crimes enacted – We should love to see your daughter, tell her to write us when she can come to tea so that we are in – We take our meals at home & also in Restaurants – Wonderful Jelka cooks delightful fish meals & we have it very cosy, but not elegant: eating off oilcloth in the kitchen –

We both send you our love –

Ever yours affectionately
Frederick Delius

P.S.
Enclosed a few tit-bits & a picture postcard[3] whereon I seem to recognise Netta – P.P.S our house in Grez has been requisitioned & occupied!!! Ugh! We know no details as yet – I sent you a postcard of our beloved Edward VII. God bless his memory. I knew you would like to see him – We sometimes walk over the very ground where he used to walk – just fancy!!

Autograph letter, signed and dated. Envelope addressed: Monsieur/Henry Clews jr/Hotel du Cap d'Antibes/*Antibes*/Alpes Maritimes. Postmark: BIARRITZ 21 -6 18.

The original is in the Delius Trust Archive.

The Deliuses originally planned to leave Grez in May for a summer stay at Biarritz. Lady Cunard wrote, however, to say that she had found a prospective buyer for their Gauguin canvas, *Nevermore*, and someone was to be despatched to Grez to fetch it. 'The eventual 2000 Guineas are not to be dispised just now,' wrote Jelka to Marie

Clews on 28 May, 'and so we are waiting here – poor old Fred trying to be good but *terribly* impatient at heart.' Nonetheless, Jelka was glad so far to have avoided the bombardment of Paris – on the night they were originally to have stopped there, en route to Biarritz, there had been two air-raid warnings and bombs were dropped. Lady Cunard's man having failed to appear (the sale having in fact fallen through), the Deliuses left Grez by train on 4 June, travelling by way of Tours and Orléans in order to avoid Paris.

1 August Schvan, mutual friend of Delius and Clews, is referred to a number of times in their correspondence. A sculpture of him by Clews is in the Ringling Museum, Sarasota, Florida.

2 *Poem of Life and Love.*

3 A newspaper clipping 'Goethe Statue Painted Yellow', datelined Chicago, May 8, a poem 'Ira Dei' by Edith M. Thomas, an item from the *New York Times*, 'Will pray for animals', and a comic sea-side postcard.

(432)
Frederick Delius to C. W. Orr

4 Rue Gardague,
Biarritz
(Basses Pyrenées)
[June/July 1918]

My dear Mr Orr –

Forgive me for keeping you so long before thanking you for the Elgar score[1] which you so kindly sent me – We had rather an anxious time of it as the german offensive seemed very menacing & we were preparing to move on. We arranged our house for all eventualities & came down here for a month or two to await events. I am afraid I am not as enthusiastic about the Symphony as you are – But that means nothing whatever – Music is entirely a matter of temperament & taste. The first movement I like the best – I find Elgars musical invention weak – Whenever he gets a good theme or nice harmonies they remind me of Parsifal or Brahms – He never seems to have outlived his admiration for the "Good Friday magic music" He has it also in Gerontius. His manner of composition is that of Brahms & also his orchestration which is thick & clumsy, as is also Brahms', & then the symphony is very long & the musical matter in the 2. 3rd & 4th movements very meagre. I heard the Violin Concerto in London & found it very long & dull – Sammonds played it – In every case Elgar is a very earnest musician & sometimes gets hold of a good tune Pomp & Circumstance What have you been writing lately? For goodness sake dont do what most of our composers have done for years –

Write oratorios & dull symphonies – Try your hand in the shorter forms at first & also the freer ones – & dont become scholastic – We have just begun "Mary of the Winds"[2] & I will write you later about it as I want to read it at my ease – The language is quaint & delightful – We have hired an appartment in Biarritz & so live very quietly – We are taking the Briscous baths here which are excellent. I am also working – How are food conditions now? We hope to come in September if all's well.

Let me thank you once more for the score & dont let my criticism alter your opinion in the least. Always stick to your likings There are profound reasons for them –

Ever yours sincerely
Frederick Delius

Autograph letter, signed and undated.

The original is in the collection of Mrs Susan Pumfrey.

1   Orr had spoken highly of Elgar's first symphony in a letter to Delius. 'I only know of Elgar the dream of Gerontius & the Apostles', replied Delius on 11 May, '– both of which I thought very dull – Gerontius very much influenced by Parcival – I know nothing else but some trivial marches – I should not, however, like to do Elgar an injustice & should very much like to see the score of the Symphony you speak so highly of –'

2   Delius wrote to Orr on 11 May: 'the book [arrived] this morning – Very many thanks I shall read it with great interest –'

(433)
Frederick Delius to Philip Heseltine

4 Rue Gardague
Biarritz (Basses
Pyrenees)
[3 July 1918]

My dear Phil –

Your long & interesting letter was sent on to me here where we have been since June 5th. Our house has been commandeered & is full of officers – Grez is now in the War Zone. After spending a few weeks here we shall probably go to London – All what you wrote me of Van Dieren makes me wish to get there as quick as possible – So that he, himself, may make me acquainted with his music & that I may yet be able to help him. I will certainly do all in my power both in England & America for this unfortunate genius – God help a genius

without money & influence anywhere, but most of all in England – I again got
a whiff of the London musical atmosphere on reading Van Dieren's description
of the "Audition" at his own house – almost the same scene has been enacted
by myself in bygone years – I know, also, what it is to pass, for years, as a sort
of musical idiot & be patronised by 4th class musicians & dilettants interested
in young modern composers – You ask me about the mental processes of my
own work. I dont believe in the possibility of conceiving an entire work in all
its details instantaniously – Especially one in several movements – I, myself,
am entirely at a loss to explain how I compose – I know only that at first I con-
ceive a work suddenly – thro' a feeling – the work appears to me instantaniously as a whole, but as a feeling – The working out of the whole work in
detail is then easy as long as I have the feeling – the emotion – it becomes difficult as the emotion becomes less keen; sometimes I am obliged to put the
work aside for months – sometimes years – & take it up again, having almost,
or entirely, forgotten it, in order to bring back my first feeling. You see the
two most conventional people in Europe are the English & the French because
they have the oldest culture – Italians, of course, have simply lived off Rome –
until the Renaissance – & have been paralysed ever since – The french have
never got over the eighteenth century in many forms of art – & look at their
architecture today – An old race seems to have greater difficulty in inventing
new things or adapting themselves to new conditions. You see an individual or
genius is always dangerous – The bourgeois feels it instinctively – He feels
that an individual is going to alter his tastes & habits – & the individual does
alter them – that is why the new has such a lot of enemies, especially in old
countries – America is a better country for a genius than either France or
England or Italy – In America they have no very old preconceived ideas & welcome something new even if they dont understand it – It, at least, amuses
them – They dont get angry & abuse you. England had music, before Handel
came over & gave them the Oratorio – this formed their taste for generations.
Then came Beethoven, & Mendelsohn – & then Wagner came along & had a
devil of a time, – then he formed their taste. In the meantime England had
been turning out – Sterndal Bennets – Fields, Stanfords, Barnbys, Mackenzies
& Elgars – Not one of whom has any very real personality & all based on one of
the greater composers from abroad – France the same – & Beethoven is to this
day the most popular composer in France – The french are quicker witted,
however, & cleverer than we are – Debussy came along & formed a precieux
school – He himself by far the most gifted of the lot – But not profound or
capable of any great developement & so he fizzled out, into a manneristic composer & chef d'ecole   The head of a clique of clever musicians who have
nothing to say or very little – but try to impress one by very suggestive &
picturesque titles – Debussy the most gifted encountered also the most opposition[1] – In England we have again the french equivalents – always very much
weaker & slower – You know who I mean – the Scotts etc –

The people here in Biarritz are a terrible crowd of nouveaux riches – & as soon as I have finished my briscous baths we shall clear out – Women in short dresses & silk stockings, very much powdered & rouged walking in 3^s & 4^s with 1 immaculately dressed man along the esplanade – Where have the intellectuals hidden themselves? They seem to have disappeared until the end of the war – I am thirsting for music & shall endeavour to have all my new works given this winter – How long shall you stay in Ireland? cannot we meet in London? I should love to have long talks with you & hear about all your experiences since we last met. I could also shew you my new works – I am looking forward to Van Dieren's Symphonie, & can assure you that when I believe in anything I am capable of putting forward considerable energy & persuasive powers – Especially when it is someone elses work – Write me at once, whether we shall meet in London – I will write you again as soon as we have decided when we shall go. This is the noisiest & loudest place in the world – I am trying to work & thro' the open window I hear a blanchisseuse singing at the top of her voice – a parrot is shouting Go away & Papa – & a trumpet is playing variations on Gounod's Faust.

With love from us both – ever your affectionate

Fr. Delius

Autograph letter, signed and dated. Envelope addressed: Monsieur/Philip Heseltine/ 28 Upper Fitzwilliam Str/*Dublin*/*Irlande*. Postmark: BIARRITZ 3 -7 18.

The original is in the British Library.

1   The subject of Debussy had been touched upon in a letter of 11 May to Orr: 'One must not forget that altho' Debussy's originality dwindled into a mannerism & that he did not develop, it was perhaps not capable of development – But it was for all that great originality.' Only a few days later, on 19 May, Delius returned to the charge in a letter to Heseltine: 'You know my opinion on Contemporary music. For me "music" is very simple – It is the expression of a poetic & emotional nature – Most musicians by the time they are able to express themselves manage to get rid of their poetry & all their emotion – The dross of Technic has killed it or they seize upon one little original streak & it forthwith develops into an intolerable mannerism – Debussy & Ravel.'

(434)
Frederick Delius to Edvard Munch

[Biarritz, 9 August 1918]

Dear friend, I hope that all goes well with you. We have been here for 2 months taking sea-baths.[1] I hope to see you in Norway next year – Best regards from us both

Frederick Delius

Autograph picture postcard: *BIARRITZ. -Vieux Mendiant Basquais*, signed and undated, written in French. Addressed: Monsieur/Edv. Munch/(Maler)/pr adr/H^r Blomqvist/Kristiania/Norvege. Readdressed: 'Ekely'/pr. Sköien. Postmark: BIARRITZ 9 -8 18.

The original is in the Munch Museum.

1   'Fred is seabathing with me every day,' wrote Jelka to Marie Clews on 30 July, 'and it does wonders for him. He gets so strong and hardy and enjoys it so immensely.' She added: 'Fred has been working splendidly and has quite finished his Symphony. He calls it "A poem of Life and Love", and it really is that, so emotional and warm and flowering forth so wonderfully! He has also done another short piece for small orchestra, a Song before Sunrise which is quite charming too – Oh, how I wish you could see him so well, his eyes so *entirely* alright again. It is the greatest blessing.'

(435)
Frederick Delius to Henry and Marie Clews

Grez-sur-Loing
(S & M)
21/8/18

Dear friends –

"Maya" everything is illusion. We thought we lived in a fairy dell called Grez & we returned to a filthy barrack – All transformed by a few filthy humans & evidently reflecting the real state of their souls. Well! the place is spoiled for me for ever & I shall try & sell out as quick as possible & try & find another spot where we can finish the rest of our lives in our own atmosphere – I hope no one will ever again talk to me about the vandalism & thieving of the "Boches" – I doubt whether they would have taken so much away with them as our allies. Luckily we had locked up our most valuable things in my study & the summer bedroom – But they opened several locked cupboards & took things taking care to lock the cupboard again – A box of Havanna cigars had been taken also – & all the jam eaten   But I wont go into details – The house was *filthy & is so still* – We cannot clean it – However we leave for London on the 29th – leaving Paris on the 31st. The only regret I have in leaving the country is that we are putting more kilometres between us & you. We returned just in time to save the wine cellar – They had burned up most of our wood which was piled in front of the door & the cellar door was already exposed to view – If you had been in Paris we should have loved to stay 48 hours with you in order to leave France with the happy harmonious feeling we always have when we are together. Henry's card amused us very much & the description of the place where you are living made us wonder whether we should not try & find something near you[1] – Biarritz was a wonderfully bracing place &

very invigorating – & we bathed in the sea every day & I am bathing now here in the river. But it is no place to live – much too mondain. Maud Cunard wrote me yesterday – Beecham is in great financial difficulties – the estate of his father cannot be wound up for 2 or 3 years & he seems to be without money entirely & of course he cannot fulfil his contract with me – We are taking the Gauguin to London in order to try & sell it – If we dont succeed I shall have to try & make a loan. When you return to Paris perhaps you might like to take some of my wine off my hands. It could be easily managed as a wagon goes regularly from Nemours to Paris – Maries letter just arrived. We were so happy when we saw the well known hand writing & we read & re-read it. – It was a delightful awakening & day-beginning – I am so sorry to hear of poor Mrs Baldwins death – how sudden –! She was much more sympathetic than her daughter who I once met at your house – Even now the garden here has a charm about it – Everything has run wild: Enormous sunflowers, hollyhocks & Roses everywhere in a great tangle, as if they were all trying to give us a last beautiful impression. In fact everything that humans have touched is defiled & filthy & the garden even in its disorder is pure & lovely – We spend our evenings on the roof – We have a great yellow harvest moon now. Our address in London until the end of September is 4 Elsworthy Road N.W.[2] I wonder if we could leave our Rodin statuette with you in Rue d'assas. Nothing is safe here – Jelka will write from England as she is terribly hard at work packing & hiding things. We are trying to get a family to live for nothing in order to look after the house – Is there no chance of your coming to Paris for the 29th– 30th? If we may put our Rodin in your house please wire us here[3] – Ever so much love to you both from me & Jelka

Frederick Delius

What is Shvan's address?

Autograph letter, signed and dated.

The original is in the Delius Trust Archive.

1   The Clews had bought in the summer a considerable property on the Mediterranean shore, not far from Cannes: the Château de la Napoule, a largely-ruined medieval fortress which they were to spend years in restoring.

2   The Deliuses were to take Henry Wood's house in St John's Wood.

3   They were indeed able to visit the Clews en route; and took the opportunity there in Paris to draw up forms of will, with their friends as witnesses, on 31 August. Executors were to be Gardiner, Grainger and Heseltine. In the event of their simultaneous deaths, everything the Deliuses possessed was to be channelled into the foundation of a trust to help young English composers: awards of £200 a year – for up to three years – would go to the composers chosen by the executors. Both wished their remains to be cremated in England.

(436)
Jelka Delius to Marie Clews

4 Elsworthy Rd
N.W.
[19 September 1918]

My dear Marie,

We only saw Lady C. yesterday   she was out of town till then. She is just the same as ever. She is so wonderful she is getting everybody into a perfect fever about the Gauguin and I really think she'll sell it. She will get people so hypnotized about it that they will all think they *must* possess it. On Saturday we are going to lunch with her, and then I'll write and tell you more. We are so dreadfully busy hunting for a house for the winter, at least, rather a flat[1] on account of the coal difficulties.

Our journey was perfectly normal and I understand now why your friends all slept during the crossing: we were *so* tired out with standing in line and going through so many formalities again and again, that we sank entirely ex- hausted into our births and only really were conscious again when we were reaching the english coast. The Landscape was quite changed   few meadows now and beautiful cornfields everywhere and endless vegetable patches all along. –

I begin to get accustomed to the food regulations. They are most trying at first. When we arrived we could get nothing at all until we had made a pil- grimage to a distant town hall, where they gave us our food books. One gets very little butter and meat – even cooking fat is rationed and one has to buy all these things only in one certain shop where one is registered. If one sees a nicer chicken or better bacon somewhere else, one cannot get it. The bread is very good and there are lots of biscuits and *cakes* shortbread, scones and tea- cakes   hardly any jam. It is all less cheap than the Daily Mail says. Very few women in uniform to be seen – *no* short dresses, few taxis, a great sim- plicity in clothes, but most of our friends are out of town.   T. B. is in the North. *Very few American uniforms* to be seen.

We heard Freds Dance Rhapsody in the Promenade Concert (Wood)   it was delightful! They had played his "Brigg Fair" the day before our arrival[2]

We were at Selfridges yesterday with Lady Cunard. She at once introduced us to a head man there, as most important persons and so we obtained a pot of jam without standing in line. It was killing the way she cross examined this chef de rayon as to *how* she could give her luncheon parties on only 4 meat coupons at 5[d] each per week. "But what are my friends to *eat*. You *must* find something, etc. Oh, but I *must* give luncheon parties." We shall see on Saturday at lunch – what she has hypnotized him into procuring.

Fred looks very well and has been running about a great deal and seen some of his music-friends at last. He will write to you soon and so shall I, as soon as we have a flat. I am so very tired looking at all these houses. I shall only begin to live when we are settled for the winter.

We are most anxious to hear from you. I hope you are back at La Napoule, and that you were not in the Paris air-raid yesterday?

Have you been able to get the house. Lady C. would love you both to come over here and so should we! Do come! Do come!

Most affectionately yrs
Jelka Delius

Autograph letter, signed.   The date '19 Sept. 1918' is added in pencil in another hand.

The original is in the Delius Trust Archive.

1   By early October the Deliuses had moved again, this time into a large furnished flat with 'a beautiful Bechstein grand' at 44 Belsize Park Gardens, London N.W.3. 'At the Woods it was so chilly and trees right in front hiding the sun and whipping against the windows in the night,' Jelka complained to Marie Clews, in a letter dated 7 October.

2   More performances were planned, as Jelka wrote to Marie in her letter of 7 October: 'Wood is going to perform one of Freds new works, the one called "Once upon a time" inspired by the Norwegian Fairy tales, end of this month, so that is something to look forward to. Another conductor, Hamilton-Harty is going to do "Paris" and "On hearing the first cuckoo". The orchestras were rather depleted but are doing well now with lots of women playing in them ... We also saw the Harrisons and Beatrice is going to bring out Fred's new Cello Sonata quite soon. A singer also wrote today that he is going to sing Fred's songs in a concert in November; I feel that everything is beginning to stir and that makes me happy.' On 31 October Beatrice Harrison and Hamilton Harty gave at the Wigmore Hall the first performance of the Cello Sonata.

(437)
Frederick Delius to Universal Edition

Address: Augener Ltd.
18 Great Marlboro' Str
London –
[November/December 1918]

Dear Herr Hertzka,

At last the war has come to an end and it is now possible – thank God – to resume our relations. Above all I would like to hear how you have fared during this long time?

I am now sending you the final proof of the score & parts of the "Arabeske" and the excellent English translation, so that the work can now be published.

How do things stand with Fennimore and Gerda? I hear that Brecher is now in Frankfurt.

I have *many* enquiries from America; just like here my music has not been obtainable over there for a long time now. It is of the greatest importance to have a good agency in both countries. For London I recommend Augener rather than Chester. As Augener has published a Violin Concerto & a Double Concerto of mine he will be far more interested in getting things circulated than Kling. There is to be a centenary festival in America for Walt Whitman (the poet of Sea-Drift). The Boston Publishing Company want to publish an American edition of Seadrift. What is the position with Harmonie now? In this matter we must arrive at a final arrangement. As you know I have not yet got a single penny for all these works: Appalachia   Seadrift, Mass of Life, Piano Concerto, A Village Romeo & Juliet, 5 Songs. Also there must be no delay in bringing out a new edition of the Piano Concerto. Everybody wants to play it & no material is to be had.

Trusting to have good news from you soon
With kind regards

Yours
Frederick Delius

Letter in the hand of Jelka Delius, signed Frederick Delius, undated, written in German.

The original is in the Universal Edition archives.

(438)
Percy Grainger to Frederick Delius

New address
309 WEST 92 STREET
NEW YORK CITY, U.S.A.
Dec. 15, 1918.

To Frederick Delius.

Beloved friend,
Stransky[1] and the New York Philomonic gave your "Lifes Dance" last Thursday and mother and I were there. It was an inspired performance and had a great and genuine success. The *whole press* treated it big and liked and admired it and acclaimed you as a genius, as you will see from the enclosed clippings, which represent the entire press, so far. By all this you will see that the

moment is absolutely ripe for you over here, as soon as you care to come after the war. We both long for your coming, tho I, naturall[y], hope it will not be until I am out of the army and able to play your Concerto, etc. I have no idea when I may be discharged, maybe quite soon, but more likely in 3 or 6 months time, or later. My work in the band (I am assistant bandleader now, am practically in charge of a band of about 50 pieces, and do a lot of teaching and coaching on various instruments) is still as sympathetic to me as ever, in fact more so than ever, for I have ceased to be a guesser and amateur as regards wind instruments, and would learn to score *really well* for wind instruments if my present work kept on for another year or 18 months. Never the less I am longing for the time when I can take up concert work again, so that I can *earn enough money* to give chamber and choral-orchestral concerts in New York, etc. The war has taught me the shortness and unreliability of life. I now long to earn quick so that I can quickly realize the wishes of the immediate moment, and strike quick blows for the art I love (my own and others's) while it is still new from the composer's pen, still part of the musical wave of the *present*. What my earning capacity is going to be I cannot accurately foretell, of course. But if I earn as I wish, this is what I want to do: To give occasional big concerts of the new works I like best, orchestra, chorus and chamber, much as B. Gardiner did, only – with this difference; I shall plan to do only the works I *personally* like best, without any national considerations and without any feeling of artistic *duty* in the matter. It is difficult to get a good chorus in New York, perhaps impossible, but some kind of chorus it must be possible to get hold of. Your works, Cyril Scott's and my own are the compositions I am most interested in. I would love to bring out things of yours like: Song of the High Hills, The Dowson work, Sea drift, Dance Rhapsodies, and, of course your new works. I shall begin shortly to think out my programs, so as to be good and ready *in case* I do earn enough within a year or two to give one or several such concerts. Would you therefore, dear friend, kindly send me a list of all the things of yours you would like to see performed, stating whether they are still manuscript or printed (giving publisher). Should I be successful and able to give the concerts in the way I plan I would terribly like you to be over here for them, to enjoy all that musical fun with you and to give the publishers the chance to acclaim personally the genius in the flesh as well as in the works. Americans love the presence of the *man*, and it would all be a glorious glorious time. You could conduct your own things yourself, or let me take them, just as you wished, and you could conduct your Piano Concerto while I play it, etc. But much as I long for you and your dear wife to be here for my concerts (if they materialize) I do not, even in my own mind, wish you to wait till then. I think the time will be ripe for you next season (winter 1919–20) if peace is fixed up by then and peace is truly in the air. They are just ready for you now and I believe you would meet with a ripping reception if you came then (next season). I enclose a "Metronome" article[2] in which I had the pleasure of alluding to you several times. I have made an invariable point of hammering Delius into them in every article or interview I have had in this country, and that has also played its little part in the gradual readiness for you which I now observe, alongside the great influence exerted by your evergrowing fame in England and that greatest of all the factors – the towering greatness of your genius, and the consciousness of it filtering thru to every nook and cranny of the earth.

It was exquisite to hear "Lifes dance" again and I enjoyed it, if possible, even more than I did under the hands of that glorious Finnish conductor Georg Schneevogt, when we heard it in Helsingfors, in 1913. What sadistic passion, what agony of bliss; and what a glory in the horn theme smashed out near the end! Everyone I know who was present (folk of the diferrentest kinds) were struck all of a heap. Try and come here next season, unless there is some good reason for not so doing. Mother and I just yearn to see you and your dear wife again, and are hungry to hear all your new things. I have also several things I badly want you to hear.

Please let me have the list of your things if you can, also any copy of any new-published score of yours that I havent yet seen. Let me know if Grez is no longer the safest address to find you. Mother joins me in affectionate love to you both. Words can never tell you how I love your music and what it means to me.

I just love my life here; have never been so happy, hopeful and satisfied anywhere. I became a full American citizen last June, and am full of a happy impatience for my future here. This country is today, compositionally speaking, where England was some 10 or 12 years ago; coming out its shell and realizing what itself signifies musically. In 5 or 10 years time it will be in full blast compositionally. John Alden Carpenter and Howard Brockway are real geniuses, to my mind, and there are 3 Negro composers of the real stuff in smaller forms: W. M. Cook, Dett and Diton.

Once more with lots of love, and forgive this ragged letter – I am in a tearing hurry, but cant wait to write you,

Ever worshippingly
Percy

Typed letter, with MS amendments, signed and dated.

The original is in the Grainger Museum.

1   Josef Stransky (1872–1936): Bohemian conductor. He studied both medicine and music at Prague, Vienna and Leipzig. Having conducted widely in Europe from 1898, he succeeded Mahler at the New York Philharmonic Society in 1911.

2   'Possibilities of the concert wind band from the standpoint of a modern composer'. *The Metronome Orchestra Monthly*, 34 (11 November 1918), pp. 22–3.

(439)

Jelka Delius to Marie Clews

44 Belsize Park Gardens
20.12.1918   N.W.3

Dearest Marie,

This is to send you both our heartiest Xmas wishes – Oh, I wish you were here
with us. How good it would be to be all together and discuss the state of
affairs! I so loved your letter with the description of Paris in the armistice.[1] It
was very much like it here. Riotous joy and triumph and flags and Motor-
lorries of drunken dominion-soldiers and crowds and crowds. the whole quiet
north emptied itself into the inner town   no getting back – and these enormous distances here, that one *cannot* tramp on foot. I was quite overcome with
joy that the fighting was over – a sort of relief – but I never had sympathy with
the great rejoicings. It seemed to me so entirely out of all proportion – after
the terrible catastrophe we have traversed – the wonderful grandeur of Germany's downfall – all these upheavals – Nobody seems to seize the enormity of
it all – The insipid press – well, we will talk of that, when we meet! I wonder,
when that will be. It is lovely that you bought the place you love and where
you feel you can be happy. Towns are so depressing – nothing makes one feel
as lonely as the *crowds* of uncongenial people around one in towns – and the
terribly superficial babble of the Society people – the freedom of the Seas, the
boycott of german trade, the repatriating of all germans here are subjects that
really become rather stale.

I think Fred is rather disappointed with the artistic London – There is
hardly a public for beautiful things. However Fred is doing a lot and really
wakes them up a bit. He is creating a new Concert Society, which is to give
only quite few Concerts, but with really fine programmes beautifully executed. He has found some people to finance it, and it is almost constituted.[2]
The new orchestral work inspired by the Norwegian fairy tales "Once upon a
time" will be given on Jan. 20th and others are to follow.

We have not seen very much of Lady C. – she has a terrible crowd there
always – Checo Slovac – Polish – Jugo Slav Representatives – peculiar people,
her Russian attache with the big teeth is a fixture   the conversation perfectly
grotesque. Lady C says: Oh, I have been *so* busy, I am just sending an army to
Omsk – and all approve in chorus. They say T. B. is also going into politics
now. He was nearly bankrupt and all his furniture was sold at Christies. We
have not seen him. She says he does not "wish to see Musicians just now. Oh,
but he must meet *you* Delius, he wants to spend an evening with you". I feel
sure she herself for some wonderful reasons keeps them apart. *She* is helping to
run his Opera scheme "on a proper financial basis". They play mediocre operas
and give them mediocre performances   The seats are awfully expensive –
absurd –

Oh, we went to a De Lara-Concert – that was the most grotesque of all – suddenly between the music a dancing scene out of one of de L.'s operas   He himself most sentimentally at the Piano – awful music – one harp and one flute and the dancer making her desperate antics all alone and always towards de L – who looked "pâmé". Then he conducted some dreadful female singers called the Prima Donna Chorus; dreadful hopeless creatures and it ended by "God save the King" sung by these horrible women in sort of pale blue silk housemaid's dresses and De Lara in the middle his head thrown back in an emotion of overwhelming patriotism – bellowing the anthem at the top of his voice – (They say he wants to become a "Sir"!!!)

Little Phil Heseltine has made such a terrible mess of his life   he's gone and married a model who got a baby, which he thinks is his – If he *liked* the girl – but he doesn't – there he is in a small flat a-quarrelling with her – pitiful – He looks so pale and miserable that I think he takes drugs. –

We have just received permission to write to our bank asking them to get our American dividends sent here!!!? But of course we dont know if they can.

Sunday 22^d It is one of those *dreadful* english sundays, drizzling rain and dark at 3 p.m. Fred has gone to speak about his concert-Society, so I have leisure to finish my letter to you. As he does not work here at all, he keeps me pretty busy all the time. I do not think he could ever compose seriously living in a town, with constant distractions, visitors, phone-calls etc. The future lies so in the dark. I had always hoped we could live in Grez part of the year so that he could work – as he always worked so wonderfully well there and *all* he has created, *almost* all, he has done *there* – But if he cannot live there any more we must find something else somewhere. Grez before the war had the enormous advantage of being so very near Paris and so central, and near England, Holland, Switzerland and Germany, where his music called him so often. I suppose in an airship or an air plane it would only be 2 hours from there to London.

Here in England the climate is really prohibitive – This dark damp cold; – and the dullness of the people!!! However, we must let the world calm down again and I am already contented that he is so well – he walks wonderfully fast and eats and sleeps well –

We met Dhiaghileff the other day and he gave us seats for the Russian ballet, "The midnight sun" but it was very poor and uninteresting, a rustic Russian scene with the red and gold costumes and a nice decor of red suns with big faces, rows of them on a dark blue background. – But nothing interesting otherwise. And it is only one number in a common smoky music-hall programme in a big high dingy theatre, the Coliseum. I had never seen Diaghileff, but in that english musical party I spotted him out at once. He has his hair parted in the middle and it is grey on one side and brown on the other and the soft and melancholy-eyed young Miassine at his side, with beautiful eyelashes and pale, languid movements – No, those two were not english looking! I do not know if you ever met Mrs Gordon Woodhouse, such a charming little woman, with enormous "style" who plays so beautifully on the harpsichord? We go there rather often, she has such a charming milieu. Poets, musical people – les jeunes y vont. She is not young, and not got up "young"; but just dressed and to her fingertips in harmony with her delicate, dainty old instruments and her whole person.

Fred also met a Mr. Zogheb once, a Syrian, very intelligent. Is that your friend? He was with Dr Dillon³ who has written a wonderful book about Russia: *The Russian eclipse*

Now I must really stop at last, dear friends, excuse me for indulging in the pleasure of chatting to you *so* long. Freds best loves and X greetings –

Affly
Jelka

Autograph letter, signed and dated.

The original is in the Delius Trust Archive.

1   Only the day before writing this letter, Jelka had written to Clare Delius Black with commiserations on the death on active service shortly before the armistice of her son, Delius's nephew, adding: 'It *is a blessing* that the german militarism has been smashed so completely.'

2   Little evidence has so far come to light of this further attempt by Delius to found a concert society – a surprising idea when remembering his less-than-successful efforts to achieve something similar following the Norman-Concorde concert in 1899 and with the Musical League a few years later. Jelka touched on the subject again, in a letter to Rose Grainger on 14 January 1919: 'Fred would like and probably will found a new Concert-Society – appealing to a more democratic public, as they certainly seem to appreciate music more than the Society people; they are deadly.'

3   Emile Joseph Dillon (1854–1933): Irish-born journalist and author; special correspondent of *The Daily Telegraph*. He wrote many books on political subjects, and his *The Eclipse of Russia* was published in 1918.

(440)
Frederick Delius to Henry Clews

44 Belsize Park Gardens
London NW3.   25/12/18

Dear Friend. I send you & Marie my warmest Christmas greeting & regret that we are not all together. We have quite settled down in our flat & feel quite comfortable (materially)   I suppose I have lived too long abroad ever to accustom myself again to the english intellectuality – if it may so be called – There is still one God[1] awaiting to be immortalised by you, my dear Henry, the one reigning over this country – the *God of Dullness* & Indifference to all things artistic. After being here a few months one begins to realise that one is up against something entirely new to our living in Europe or even – must I say it – in America – An utter indifference to things artistic – Even the artists are not curious, eager or enthusiastic – there is a certain well bred indifference reigning everywhere – The only real interest, or curiosity seems to exist in the middle & lower classes – The milieu of our mutual friends is of an appalling frivolity – a certain pretence to artistic interests. Certain catch words à la mode go the round, just as do certain à la mode – dernier cri artists – Their Amour propre is to be "up to date"   I have almost ceased to see M.C[2] & her clique. I could not stand it – So I am gradually retiring, as much as possible, without wishing to appear rude – If you had been here we might, at least, have got some fun out of it – There is one really artistic salon – M[rs] Woodhouse – a real artist – who plays the Harpsichord most beautifully & plays us all the lovely english music of the 15th & 16th centuries – also Bach & Scarlatti – Many of my new works will be played here in the next 6 months – I have also started some really good Concerts (Orchestral)   I am trying to gather around me all that is hopeful in London – the quite young are the nicest – those that have been in the war & suffered & those that refused to go to war & also suffered. When you go down to Cannes look out for something for us – I think we shall have to join you down there before very long – One evening I saw real enthusiasm – I was taken to a great international boxing match at the Albert Hall & saw Jimmy Wilde knocked out by Mike O'Dowd!!![3]

My love to you, dear friends
Frederick Delius

Enclosed a couple of rather good things out of a paper called "Common Sense"[4]

Autograph letter, signed and dated.

The original is in the Delius Trust Archive.

1   Apart from the major work *The God of Humormystics* (1913), Clews sculpted other imaginary deities such as *The God of Spiders* and *The God of Flies* (both 1914), bizarre human heads with traits that hinted at characteristics implied in the titles the artist gave to them.

2   Maud Cunard.

3   Further evidence that Delius was still prepared to look into various matters well outside the expected range of his interests is furnished in a note to Heseltine dated 30

December. Heseltine was not to come to visit them on Thursday evening as 'we are going to a labor meeting at the Albert Hall – It may be interesting.'

4   Two newspaper clippings: an unsigned poem 'A virtuous Minister's thoughts after winning the Election', and 'Mr Bernard Shaw on the bitter comedy of the War'.

The Memoirs of Marie Clews

Some interesting sidelights on Delius's character are supplied in the unpublished memoirs of Marie Clews (which are preserved in the collection of Mrs Katheryn Colton of Sarasota, Florida). Marie remembered gatherings in Lady Cunard's house in Grosvenor Square, where her husband and Delius, 'brilliant talkers', would indulge in keen verbal duels. The most entertaining of these discussions would normally occur in the presence of relatively few intimates, such as Maud Cunard herself and Beecham, for Marie pointed out that Delius was 'shy and diffident in social life, and the acidity and irony of his conversation when he did speak was often repellent to lion hunters'. She regretted not having made notes during some of the memorable evenings the Deliuses spent with them in Paris, again recalling the composer as a brilliant conversationalist, talking with Clews for hours until the exchanges might, on occasion, grow 'dangerously overheated'. The shared antipathy, almost to the point of obsession, was the bourgeoisie, and in particular the English bourgeoisie, the seeds of Delius's disaffection having been sown in his childhood. He told the Clews of how as a child he would be dressed in a black velvet suit with a lace collar, 'like Lord Fauntleroy', and then made to show off his dexterity with the violin 'to those terrible bourgeois who didn't know a violin from a tennis racket. I think I began to hate the bourgeois then and my hatred has only increased as I grow older.' Marie went on to recall an occasion during a visit to Grez when she had found Jelka in tears in her studio, in desolated reaction to an incident which had led the 'often very short-tempered' Delius furiously to condemn his artist wife as 'a bourgeois with the soul of a bourgeois'. To Jelka, there could scarcely have been a more hurtful charge.

Marie Clews also remembered the sheer delight when her husband and Delius would meet again after a long absence. There would be 'some hours' of sparkling conversation until at last 'they could not resist taking a nip at each other's sensibilities', the edge of their talk becoming cutting; tempers would grow short, and the encounter would necessarily have to be limited by the wives leading their respective husbands outside until ardours cooled. 'They were too much alike, these two, to get on together for long at a time, their nerves were too keen, their perceptions too acid, their scorn too deep . . . Jelka would coax Fred into the garden, where he would go grumbling and mumbling to himself and pull his hat down over his ears.' Yet the friendship easily survived such encounters, and Marie recorded Clews's later reaction to them: 'He is a grand old fellow. I love his rages and his violence. He is a great artist and what can one be more than that?' (The sculptor Jacob Epstein, who knew Delius – no doubt through Philip Heseltine – in the early 1920s, also crossed swords with the composer on the subject of art. Delius was, he wrote in his autobiography, 'argumentative, cranky and bad-tempered, and we had many a set-to'.) Another point of dispute between Delius and Clews is noted in a diary of Marie's that has been preserved, describing a dinner party at the Château de la Napoule on 17 February 1933, when Beecham and Lady Cunard were among the guests. The subject of conversation turned to Delius, and Clews talked of his 'constant quarrels with Delius about Nietzsche, as he claimed that Delius was incapable of understanding Nietzsche whatsoever. This would send Delius into paroxysms of rage as he claimed ... the *Mass of Life* was a transcription of Nietzsche's spirit.'

Some doubt about the accepted dating of the Clews mask of Delius is raised by Marie Clews in her memoirs, never the most reliable source of information on dates or time-sequences. She relates that the composer 'sat unwillingly for his bust to Clews in the studio' during the Deliuses' visit to La Napoule in 1923. And furthermore she identifies the piece as the mask of Delius, cast in bronze by Valsuani, with which we are familiar. 'He was restless and jittery as a sitter, jumping up constantly and walking around and trying to pick a quarrel with Clews about nothing, about everything, just out of irritability and overwrought nerves ... Clews could not get Delius to sit long enough to do a bust of him, so he had to be satisfied by a mask of that medieval face with its long sentient nose and mobile lips.' The claim follows that with the mask just cast in plaster, Clews removed 'with a fine steel instrument' his subject's 'keen and vivid eyes', having suddenly felt that Delius 'had no eyes, no eyes at all'. Marie then affirms that 'at that moment Delius's eyes were bright and strong, and he was able to write his orchestral manuscripts with no fatigue', something that makes nonsense of this particular chronology. The alabaster version of this mask (see Carley and Threlfall: *Delius: A Life in Pictures*, p. 70), eyeless like the plaster and the bronze, is clearly incised '1916'. Whatever bust Clews purportedly attempted to model late in 1923 was never executed, one must assume, and in penning some of the pages of her memoirs, an elderly Marie Clews's memory was at fault, with time as well as place occasionally transposed. At all events, with the Clews' side of the Delius correspondence presumably gone for ever, we must be grateful for the few perspectives of the composer and his relationships that these memoirs afford us.

Music in England During the War

It also seems appropriate to interpolate here one of Delius's rare excursions into print, in the form of a short memoir originally published in *Musikblätter des Anbruch* (Vienna), 1, No. 1 (November 1919), pp. 18–19:

I was in France when the war broke out and in November 1914 I left for London, where I spent a year. I then went back to Grez-sur-Loing and stayed there, returning again in September 1918 to England where I have since remained.

Musical life has been exceptionally active in England. Perhaps the one most gratifying thing during the war has been to see how little affected musicians and the great concert-going public have been by chauvinism. An attempt to boycott all German music, including Wagner, was completely unsuccessful. When the usual Saturday Wagner evenings in the Queen's Hall Promenade Concerts were replaced by another programme the hall stayed quite empty, with the result that the management were obliged to put on a Wagner programme the following Saturday and the hall was sold out.

Living German composers have, however, not been performed; but I know that Strauss's Rosenkavalier is to be given in London next season.

Just a few of our mediocre composers made a great deal of propaganda for all-British music and British programmes, but the public showed not the slightest desire to follow their lead.

Serge Diaghileff, the Russian ballet master, who had a very successful season at the Alhambra Theatre in London with his ballet, distinguished himself by some very silly newspaper articles against German music in which he reproaches the English for being thoroughly "pro-Boche" in music. Whereupon Ernest Newman, the distinguished English musical writer, put him in his place with a few well-written, very logical and sarcastic articles. Diaghileff's reproach was doubly unwarranted, since an enormous amount of purely French and Russian music had been performed; so much so in fact that the public had eventually become satiated with it, and it became obvious that the content of this music was not on its own substantial enough to capture and hold the attention of the public.

The performances of opera in English, which through Sir Thomas Beecham's initiative have periodically taken place in London, Manchester, Birmingham etc. with ever-growing success, have greatly enriched English musical life. I myself attended a very good performance of Tristan in London when the house was sold out.

In summing up I should like to add that neither musicians nor audiences in England will tolerate nationalism and chauvinism in music in spite of all the agitation in the Press.

1919

For the first five months of the year the Deliuses were to remain at Belsize Park Gardens. After attending the first performance of *Eventyr*, given at Queen's Hall on 11 January, Jelka wrote to tell Rose Grainger how things stood with musical friends at this period:

'Things here looked rather dull when we came – Only dear old Wood was valiantly doing his Prom's. But Beecham has entirely thrown up Concert-conducting – He only cares for his opera-schemes – and there even he is more Impresario than conductor. He has Pitt young Goossens and Harrison as conductors. As they give all the dull old operas it is really not very interesting. He is also not conducting at the Philharmonic any more – He was too erratic and the Public became less and less. Now Norman O'Neill has made a great effort to reconstruct the Phil. Balfour Gardiner has helped financially and they have Geoffrey Toye Landon Ronald and Boult as conductors. Boult is to conduct Fred's new Violin Concerto there on the 30th Jan – Sammons playing it . . . Balfour G. is still in Wales, guarding a Prisoner's camp; I hope, tho' he wont be very long now. They are woodcutters and he does not dislike the work – walking far thro' the woods to look after them. He came to see us here and was awfully nice – so sincere and real – Cyril Scott we met once at Lady Cunards he looked rather tired, but seemed quite alright. The O'Neills are bringing up their new baby. Austin is in the Beecham Opera, Bax has inherited no end of money from his father and Geoffrey Toye also lots from a brother officer.'

The Deliuses were not so fortunate as Bax and Toye: a significant part of their funds was still tied up in Germany, with the result that performance and publication of the composer's works took on a more pressing importance than usual. And for the present, Beecham clearly could not be relied on: he was 'in terrible financial difficulties', as Jelka wrote to Marie Clews on 4 February. At least the first performance of the Violin Concerto was a public success. The revised String Quartet was given for the first time in London two days later, on 1 February. And there was a rare Paris performance, when Beatrice Harrison played the Cello Sonata on 6 June at the Salle Gaveau. But on the whole the few months in London do not appear to have been productive compositionally;

something of the almost febrile creative effort of the war years had gone – with those long periods spent relatively quietly in one location or another, and without the diverting social round to be undertaken. Delius's restlessness for the remainder of the year was to allow even less time for composition.

At the beginning of June a week was spent in Sussex; then followed a few days in a Kensington hotel before the Deliuses took themselves off to Sennen in Cornwall. Delius hired a piano from Penzance and Jelka took up her painting again. After six apparently rather chilly weeks at Land's End the lure of Norway proved too strong for Delius, in spite of worries concerning the expense of travelling and living there. He was rejoined in London around the end of July by Jelka, who had had to make a short trip to Grez in connection with assessing recent damage to the house there, and after a few days they left once more for Scandinavia. They stayed on a saeter in the Valdres region for a month, before going on to Christiania on 20 September, where they renewed acquaintance with Edvard Munch. Meanwhile good news began to come in from Germany and Austria of performances of his larger works due in the forthcoming season. The most important of these was to be the production of *Fennimore and Gerda* at Frankfurt, initially scheduled to open in September, but actually first given on 21 October. The Deliuses made their way there late in September and stayed with their friend Heinrich Simon, editor of the *Frankfurter Zeitung*. They attended every rehearsal they could and were delighted with the work's reception on the first night, the composer being called forward some eight or nine times at the curtain. Glowing with this success the Deliuses returned to Grez on 25 October. Balfour Gardiner came and stayed for a few days. In the middle of November they were in London again, as Beecham was preparing a fresh production of *A Village Romeo and Juliet*. In the event the composer managed to have what was evidently an ill-prepared venture postponed until the following year. A busy fortnight was nonetheless spent in the city going to the opera, seeing friends, lunching with Lady Cunard and the Princess of Pless and dealing with the Public Trustee over the matter of sequestered funds. And Delius posed for the artist Will Rothenstein. They had initially asked Heseltine to book them into a cheap and central hotel. 'London quite impossible to get a room,' wrote Jelka to Marie Clews a few days after their return to Grez in the company of Balfour Gardiner; 'we lived in a funny little Restaurant and Hotel in Soho, where rather amusing artists frequented and discreetly disappeared upstairs with veiled femmes du monde!!'

The end of the year was spent quietly at Grez. Delius pleaded with Hertzka to come to a long-delayed agreement with Harmonie. The death during the war of Franz Heinitz, Delius's legal adviser, had meant that many papers relevant to the matter were lost. On Christmas Day the composer wrote to ask Hertzka for piano scores of the *Mass* and *Sea Drift*: he had sent his own copies to Stokowski during the war.

'Avant que tu ne t'en ailles', song (Verlaine) (RT V/31). Sketched.

Dance for Harpsichord (RT IX/6).

(441)
Frederick Delius to Percy Grainger

44 Belsize Park Gardens N W. 3
16th Jan 1919

Your letter, dear old pal, arrived here like a flash of sunshine & I cannot tell you what pleasure it gave me. I was delighted to hear that "Life's Dance" was so well performed by Stransky & his Orchestra & also so well received. Wood gave the first performance of my new Orchestral Ballad – Eventyr (Once upon a time) after Asbjørnsen – He gave a ripping good performance & took no end of trouble with it[1] – I have a wild shout in it (20 men behind) which came off very well. I shall bring all my new works to America when I come – Your letter encouraged me very much to come out next season 1919–20 – Say in October or November – My new manuscript works are –

1) Requiem (in memory of all young artists fallen in the war. –) (*Not religious*)
      for
    Baritone & Soprano solo
    Mixed Chorus & Orchestra
2) Concerto for Violin, Violoncello & Orchestra
3) Violin Concerto
4) Eventyr (once upon a time)
    (after Asbjørnsen)
5) Sonata for Violoncello
6) Dance Rhapsody No 2.
7) Poem of Life & Love
    Orchestra

all manuscript.
Then there are several works published, but awaiting a first performance –

1) Song of the high hills
    published by F. E. C Leuckart, Leipzig: Orchestra & chorus
    (small)
2) an Arabesk (J. P. Jacobsen)
    Baritone Solo, Chorus & Orchestra
    published by the Universal Edition Vienna –

It would be splendid if some of these works could be produced whilst I am in America. Your energy & enthusiasm is so wonderful & such a contrast to these dull countrymen of mine   Oh! how dull & unresponsive this country is – I am just longing for a bit of American alertness & vivacity – I also want to visit California & have a look at the Pacific Ocean. We are both just longing for a change of climate & scenery & surroundings –

I forgot 1 new work – quite short –

    8)   Song before Sunrise
          for small orchestra

& my Violin Sonata has not been played in America – & then there are 4 Elizabethan Songs, published by Winthrop Rogers & 2 à capella Chorus's
To be sung a summer night on the water –
My wife is writing to your dear Mother & telling her all the news – I am looking forward hugely to being in America with you   What a time we shall have – I ll conduct the Concerto & you play it – Hurrah!!

Ever your loving friend
Frederick Delius

Autograph letter, signed and dated. Envelope addressed: Percy Grainger Esq/309 West 92 Street/New York City./U.S.A. Also enclosed, a letter dated 14.1.1919 from Jelka to Rose Grainger. Postmark: HAMPSTEAD NW 16 JAN 19.

The original is in the Grainger Museum.

1   Wood had indeed taken considerable trouble. 'The Queen's Hall Orchestra have tried your work & I think it will come out *very well indeed*', he wrote to Delius on 2 January. There was to be an extra string rehearsal (which Delius attended). 'There will be no other novelty & I have arranged my programme so as to devote as much time as possible to your work.' On 10 January, the day before the concert, Jelka wrote to Heseltine: 'Wood came yesterday and certainly has studied the new score most carefully; he seems to enjoy it, so I hope he will do it *well*! Anyhow it is a blessing to get into an era of first performances again after these weary years.' In her letter of 14 January to Rose Grainger she related: 'There was an enormous audience and the piece was awfully well received – I felt as if I was at last throwing off the war – breathing the Queen's Hall rehearsal-atmosfere – then the public, the enthusiasm and all quite thrilled me.' On the other hand on the same date, Heseltine wrote to let his friend Colin Taylor know that 'the first performance of a new Delius work had left me cold and disappointed!'

(442)
Frederick Delius to Ernest Newman

> 44 Belsize Park Gardens
> NW3
> Jan 31st/19
> phone 879 Hampstead

Dear Newman. Many thanks for your letter; we were both greatly surprised & grieved to hear of the death of your wife; When I last saw her she seemed so young & strong. What was the cause of her death?

I thought there must be something wrong with the mental state of Brian & therefore postponed writing to him until I heard from you. But what on earth can I say to him? How is one to help such a man? It would be just the same if he came to London & in what capacity is he to come?[1] We came to England for 6 or 7 months & shall return no doubt to Grez in May or June. We had to evacuate our house twice during the war before the german push, but luckily they were stopped before they got to Grez. During the war I wrote a great deal, almost incessantly; I completed my "Pagan Requiem" A Concerto for Violin, Violoncello & Orchestra. A Violin Concerto — A Cello Sonata — A ballad for Orchestra Eventyr (once upon a time) after Asbjørnsens folklore – A Dance Rhapsody (N° 2) – A string quartet – A Poem of Life & Love for Orchestra – A Song before Sunrise for small Orchestra – 4 Elizabethan songs 2 a capella partsongs – I should be very glad to see you again & have a talk about music in this country – Let me know a day or 2 before you come so that we may have a good day of it.

My wife joins me in sending you our kindest remembrances

Yours ever
Frederick Delius

Autograph letter, signed and dated. Envelope addressed: Ernest Newman Esqre/ Casalini/Moseley/Birmingham. Postmark obscured.

The original is in the Delius Trust Archive.

1   Delius had broached the subject of Havergal Brian with Newman on 21 January: 'I received the enclosed letter a few days ago. Is the man mad or what's the matter? Perhaps you will be able to enlighten me: How should I answer such a letter?' What this missive may have contained is not clear, but Brian had been going through emotional and financial problems of some severity and his letters to other friends were at this period often disturbed and confused.

(443)
Frederick Delius to Henry Clews

44 Belsize Park Gardens
London N W 3.
Febr 4th 1919

My dear friend – I have got rather a bad cold so I will use the opportunity to write you a few lines – Since I came to England I have had four first performances of works completed during the war – First came my Cello Sonata then my Orchestral Ballad "Once upon a time". Then last Thursday my new Concerto for Violin & Orchestra was given at the Philharmonic[1] & last Saturday my new string quartet was given by the London String quartet – The success has been ever increasing & was quite enormous when the Violin Concerto was given last Thursday – Everybody musical in London was present (a very big audience) & it was really quite an event. Albert Sammons[2] the violinist played it most beautifully – Even the criticisms are splendid – Am I becoming popular!! beware! beware! However what is really nice is that we are hearing a lot of music & a lot of my own music & I am realising that the war was not a barren & lost epoch for me – In between these concerts we have been attending labor meetings & hearing Shaw & Ramsay Mcdonald & Henderson & Mrs Snowden speak – We are coming to it old boy, & it is coming to us! as I told you once in Paris – Bolschevism. – We have heard an audience of 10,000 people Hiss Lloyd George & cheer Trotski to the Echo – the same 10,000 cheered our german brothers – It has been all most intensely interesting & I deeply regret you are not with me here – this is perhaps the most interesting time of the whole war & something stupendous is going to happen – I can only hope that a real brain will reveal itself, a *real leader*   Is it Wilson? Very likely – He is certainly the strongest man on the Horizon – Bernard Shaw is most amusing & wonderfully clear headed – but not an artist – They are talking of confiscating Capital & making everybody work – See! (Shaw) We are having strikes – Yesterday & today the tubes – they threaten to turn off all Electricity on Thursday! & it may become very unpleasant – I am afraid the rich russian land owners many of whom are in London will never see their land & wealth again – There is an unfortunate Attaché always at our friends M.C. who is constantly clamoring for intervention – but even he is beginning to lose all hope. I see very little of our friend as the other side of London Life is so much more absorbing & interesting & then music took up the rest of my time – We are thinking of coming back about the end of March. The question, in short, is this: "How long shall you & I be able to live the lives we do now?" I am afraid Art is going to disappear, to be eclipsed for several decades! It looks horribly like it – The mob here is alarming! but there is a great mass of middle class, common sense, sort of people who may save things from going Russianwise – The upper classes are just as light headed & frivolous as ever & dont

seem to real(s)ise what is coming – They do not even protect art in this country or take any real interest in music painting or sculpture – There is a public
for music – (middle class & lower) but none for painting or sculpture – All our
most gifted litterateurs are occupied & absorbed by the social question – Perhaps France will be the last country where the artist will be able to live a while
– altho', I am not sure – I have seen George Moore once – He was not very interesting & has got very old. He remarked that Cologne ought to be dynami-
ted into a heap of ruins & left "tel quel" as a warning to people who intend
sinning against Christian morality. How are things Parisian? What do you
think of the "Peace Congress"? I met here a certain Dr Dillon – an irish man –
very interesting – who has been many years in Russia with Witte & also in
Austria & the balkans – He is now in Paris for the Daily Telegraph – try to get
at him – He considers Russia absolutely hopeless – Get his book *The eclipse of
Russia.*

Love to you both from your friend

Frederick Delius

Autograph letter, signed and dated.

The original is in the Delius Trust Archive.

1   In a letter of the same date to Marie Clews, Jelka wrote of the 'most beautiful
Violin-Concerto. It is so perfectly lovely, all in one movement and everywhere the
most fascinating music – instead of the habitual runs and meaningless flourishes. The
slow middle part is quite wonderful and the orchestra harmonically so rich, yet it is so
beautifully orchestrated that throughout the work the Violin is always well heard . . .
it made a wonderful impression and the applause was tremendous, and after the
Violinist had appeared they all shouted for Fred, who was tremendously cheered. I am
just aching to hear Kreisler play it in America.' To Rose Grainger on 18 February she
reported: 'Augener's immediately undertook to publish the work.'

2   Albert Sammons (1886–1957): English violinist. Mainly self-taught, he was
picked by Beecham as leader of the Beecham Symphony Orchestra and was for some
years first violin of the London String Quartet. By now he was considered to be the
leading English solo violinist, and was particularly associated with the Elgar concerto.
He was later to record the Delius Violin Concerto, which the composer dedicated to
him.

(444)
Frederick Delius to Adrian Boult

44 Belsize Park Gardens NW 3.
Wednesday [5 February 1919]

Dear Mr Boult

Many thanks for your letter: Since the Concert I have been confined to the house with a cold (not influenza) but am almost well again.

Do come up & have tea with us one afternoon – say at 3-30 – 4? the changes of tempo can easily be marked in the score

The Concerto received quite a wonderful reception, most gratifying to me & I should like to thank you again for the care & sympathy you gave to the work – What a pity the Philharmonic can not repeat it during the season; We might then attain a quite perfect performance – I suppose a repetition is impossible! Sammons was splendid –

Do come & we will have a talk about things musical in London –

Sincerely yours
Frederick Delius

Tel 879 Hampstead

Typed transcript in the Delius Trust Archive. Two further transcripts of letters from Delius to Boult are in the Archive; they are dated 10.2.28 and Feb. 22. 1932 (qv).

(445)
Frederick Delius to C. W. Orr

Treeve Lodge,[1]
Sennen (Cornwall)
[July 1919]

My dear Orr

Many thanks for your nice letter. We are having a very good time here & like it ever so much. The weather has been sunny but windy. However it agrees with us both. The sea & coast are quite beautiful. I was glad to hear you are practising the Concerto[2] with the Harrisons & hope the first performance will come off early next season; altho' if you go to Mentone middle of October you may miss it: but, no doubt, another opportunity of hearing it will come. I think 12 francs a day, as things stand, is very reasonable – We, no doubt, shall be down there in the course of the winter & shall hope to meet you in that lovely vicinity – The intelligence of Florent Schmitt is rather simple – I have known him now for over 25 years – I dont quite understand why anyone attaches any importance to what the french clique in Paris think or say about English music & composers – They are so narrow that they only like what resembles their own Lollipops. Casella is nothing at all – A few years ago he was composing a sort of bad imitation Wagner – now he imitates the Paris clique. I am glad you are satisfied with Dent – go at it as hard as you can. It is certainly rather funny that the English Concert in Paris did not include Elgar, inasmuch as the programme was made by English musicians in London – aided, no doubt, by Edwin Evans; Schmitt wrote to me saying they did not consider me as English, but as *Neutral*! It all amuses me very much.[3] You do well to stick to your likings, it shows that you *really have* likings, & the more one can love the better: one is all the richer for it. We shall be back in London beginning of August en route for France & I hope to see you then. Remember us both most kindly to your mother – With kindest regards from us both – I remain

Yours ever
Frederick Delius

Autograph letter, signed and undated.

The original is in the collection of Mrs Susan Pumfrey.

The Deliuses stayed at the Belsize Park Gardens apartment until the end of May. Some time before they left, Jelka wrote a short letter to her sister-in-law Clare: '... the French officers billetted in our house in France have broken into the rooms where we stored all our valuable belongings and many things are stolen. We therefore had to spend all our time taking steps – consulate, foreign office, etc. and may be called to France at any moment to have the thing investigated.' To Marie Clews she wrote at about the same time: 'I must go and make lists of all that is missing. I am afraid all our houselinen and copper and aluminium kitchen things are gone. The rest I'll have to see ... we are so depressed about it all.' For some reason Jelka was for the moment denied a visa to travel, and the Deliuses instead spent a week 'with friends in Sussex'. Returning to London, they stayed for a few days at the British Empire Hotel in De Vere Gardens, and then left for a holiday in Cornwall, arriving at Land's End on 14 June. 'Penzance is our nearest town and Fred got a Piano from there,' Jelka wrote to Marie Clews on 30 June, 'and I am painting an old man by his fireside with a lightest blonde little boy called "Charles-Thomas", very sturdy and eating "saffron-cakes" their national dish all the time ... We live here in the english way, lodging in a house with some nice people who do our work for us and cook.'

1 Now Churchtown House, adjacent to 'The First Inn' at Land's End.

2 The Double Concerto.

3 In an undated letter from Sennen, Delius told Heseltine: 'English music continues

to be dull – They gave a Concert of English music in Paris last April & took care to leave my name out of the program – Why? The real Britishers were all there. This is all very amusing – of course! I dont claim to be a British composer.'

(446)

Frederick Delius to Philip Heseltine

July 17th. 1919   Treeve Lodge   Sennen
                                                           Cornwall

My dear Phil

We have again been obliged to alter our plans: my wife has now to go to Grez to make a list of the things stolen by the french officers for the Conseil de Guerre; I shall stay on here for a few days longer – Jelka leaves on Monday & I on the Monday following.[1] Jelka will join me in London on her return from Grez & then we shall either go to Germany (if we can) or to Norway for a few weeks for Mountain air. I like it very much here but the sea has been too cold for us yet to bathe. The air is bracing & invigorating. I am sorry about the "Sackbut"[2] your circular made such a good impression everywhere. You would have done better if you had followed my advice & waited until you had the funds – Dont begin to think, dear Phil, that luck is against you because the real reason is that you do not push your ideas to their materialisation with sufficient energy & "Suite dans les idées". You would succeed at anything you take up if you would concentrate on it & not diffuse your energies on so many things. (I am not booming Pelmanism !!!) Stick to one thing just for fun for 2 or 3 years & see if I am not right. I think you are admirably gifted as a writer – you would succeed either as a writer on music or as a composer if *you stick to one* & push it thro' regardless of everything. I vouch that you would have the most influential & powerful paper in London if you started one & stuck to it. Why not get Newman to join you   I read his articles & they were splendid. Altho' I cannot understand why anyone gives such importance to what a russian ballet master & a few french miniaturist composers think about English music & composers. Ravel is the only one who has any talent whatever & he has absolutely no emotion & they have established for themselves entirely false values which they want everyone to accept. Stravinsky at his best is a musical acrobat. I shall write you before arriving in London so that we may meet. Volkert[3] has not written me yet about the Requiem   If he does not take it, I know Leuckart will – or the Universal. We both send you much love.

Ever yours affectionately
Frederick Delius

Dont think I want to preach at you but I am so fond of you that I would like to see you become something & assert yourself as I know how gifted you are & what possibilities are in you. It annoys me to see fools succeeding all around us

---

Autograph letter, signed and dated. Envelope addressed: Philip Heseltine Esqre/35 Warrington Crescent/Maida Vale/London. Postmark: SENNEN 17 JY 19.

The original is in the British Library.

1 Delius left Cornwall on 28 July.

2 Heseltine was proposing to launch a new musical journal.

3 Charles G. J. Volkert (1854–1929): German-born music publisher. He joined the firm of Schott, in Mainz, in 1872, moving to the company's London house in 1873. He became London manager of Schott & Co. in 1881 and was, from around 1905, also associated with Augener Ltd. A naturalized British citizen, he did a great deal to introduce modern British music, publishing the works of Grainger, Cyril Scott, Norman O'Neill, John Ireland and the younger Elgar, among others. Jelka told Rose Grainger on 17 July 1919: 'Old Volkert only heard the Harrisons rehearsing the "Double" with a piano and immediately took it.'

(447)
Frederick Delius to Norman O'Neill

Fosheim Saeter
Røn
Valdres
Norway
26th Aug 19

Dear Norman,

I have just received a letter from F. E. C. Leuckart   Salomon Str 9, Leipsic asking me how many Doublier Stimmen (Orchestral Parts) and how many Choral Parts will be required for the London performance of the Song of the High Hills. Please answer direct to Leuckart and at once, in order to save time. I think the later the performance takes place the better.

   We are having a lovely time up in the mountains here. Any amount of good things to eat – Butter milk   Cream etc. all in profusion, and heavenly air and view.

   The Uraufführung of my last music-drama Fennimore and Gerda takes place in Frankfurt a/M in October – I have just heard and in September we have to go there for the rehearsals. I have also just received news that the Arabesque, Appalachia and the Mass of Life are to be given in Vienna this winter.[1] They are spending more money on music in Germany than ever.

They have sent the Scene instructeur from Frankfurt to Denmark to make studies for the Scenery and "Milieu" for my opera and all will be painted quite new (11 Scenes). A wonderful country! My Publisher (Universal Ed. in Vienna) whom I had asked, whether he suffered very much, these last years answered *"Nur seelisch"*. I lunched with Beecham before I left London. He is doing the Village Romeo in his next season; and also Fennimore and Gerda next summer season.

I am having the Full Score of the Song of the High Hills sent direct to Coates[2], who I saw before leaving London. We wonder where and how you are and if you are away on a holiday too.

Jelka rushed over to France before going here and arranged all about the Cambriolage. They were all very polite and all is to be refunded. We leave here on the 9th September. Write to poste restante Kristiania. Letters take 5 days from London here, at least. Best love to Adine and her mother and a kiss for Yvonne with love to you both

Yrs always
Frederick Delius

Letter in the hand of Jelka Delius, signed Frederick Delius, dated.

The original is in the Delius Trust Archive.

After a brief visit to London, which took in lunch with Beecham at Lady Cunard's, the Deliuses were travelling again, this time to Bergen. 'Here we are after a very rough voyage', wrote Delius to Heseltine on 10 August.

1   'These are the things they always postpone in London and New York as being so expensive to do!!!' wrote Jelka to Marie Clews on 18 August.

2   Albert Coates (1882–1953): English conductor. After studying at Leipzig he conducted opera widely in Germany and then at St Petersburg, and occasionally too at Covent Garden. Beecham engaged him in May 1919 as senior conductor and artistic co-director of the English Opera.

(448)
Frederick Delius to Edvard Munch

Untermain Kai 3
c/o Dr H. Simon[1]
Frankfurt a/M.   10 Oct 1919

Dear friend – We arrived here safely & find everything very interesting & stimulating – plenty of enterprise – a much more interesting spirit than before the war. I see a lot of Swarzenski.[2] A fine new museum for Modern Art has been built here & Swarzenski is very keen that you, especially, should be represented with 2 or 3 of your best pictures. He has asked me to write to you & to put the matter near to your heart – Can you not send 4, 5, pictures so that he can choose. Of course he will pay all the expenses. There are some wonderful things among the modern pictures. e.g. Dr Gachet by Van Gogh – One of the finest Renoirs & several Manets etc. Have you seen my Gauguin yet? Tell Jappe I would like to hear what is happening about it.[3] Write soon

Your old friend
Frederick Delius

The first performance of my opera takes place on the 18th & I am in the midst of rehearsals –[4]

Autograph letter, signed and dated, written in German.

The original is in the Munch Museum.

The Deliuses left Norway on 20 September, travelling by way of Copenhagen and Hamburg to Frankfurt. 'We have had a lovely time up in the Mountains,' wrote Delius to Heseltine on 17 September from Voksenkollen, '& now we are at a lovely place right above Kristiania with a heavenly view.'

1   Heinrich Simon (1880–1941): Editor of the *Frankfurter Zeitung*. He became a close friend of the Deliuses, printing an extensive review of *Fennimore* in his paper. He was later to write a sensitive appreciation of Jelka after her death (see Redwood (ed.), *A Delius Companion*, pp. 131–4). Like many Jews he was to flee Hitler's Germany, but – tragically – the Nazis had him murdered in Washington on 6 May 1941.

2   Georg Swarzenski (1876–1957): director of the Stadelsches Kunstinstitut, Frankfurt. He purchased two paintings by Munch, probably in 1921.

3   As an influential art critic, Jappe Nilssen was trying to find a buyer for Delius's *Nevermore* in Norway.

4   Delius wrote to Universal Edition on 30 September to tell Hertzka that the plan was to give *An Arabesque* (another J. P. Jacobsen-based work) 'as an opener' before the opera. At some stage the idea was dropped.

(449)
Frederick Delius to Philip Heseltine

Grez-sur-Loing
(S & M) – Oct 27
19

My dear Phil –

We arrived here day before yesterday – The performance in Francfort was very good – Singers excellent & the regisseur the best I ever knew. I had 9 Orchestral rehearsals – No trouble or expense was spared   I am satisfied with the work & it is certainly a step in a new direction – perhaps the only direction where "Singspiel" has any future – There are no tedious moments. – The drama plays wonderfully well & is clear to the public – Almost every word is heard. Brecher was not as good as I had thought – but gradually got into the spirit of the whole – I send you a criticism of Paul Becker[1] – It has now to be translated – Hertzka of the Universal offers 2000 Kronen – it is not much translated into £ sterling but if you leave it in Vienna it will go up – Hertzka will supply you with any music you desire – also for the 70 Mark he still owes you – Life in Vienna is cheaper than anywhere else in Europe. It would be the place to go to. The opera is excellent: & the Concerts excellent & numerous. There is absolutely no feeling against the English in Germany or Austria & Hertzka has any amount of translating work for you to do, which would be sufficient to keep you. I spoke to H. very warmly of Van Dieren & his piano pieces – tell Van D. to send them at once. I am sure he will take them after what I told him. I knew nothing of The Village R. performance in London but have written to Beecham.[2] My wife has not yet made sketches. Try & see what Allinson is doing.[3] I told H. to send you the piano score of Fennimore: it is only provisoire – & there are many mistakes, also bars missing. Write as soon as you get this & tell me about the trunks.[4] With love from us both –

    ever affectionately
    Frederick Delius

The Universal Edition is also going to publish my new works. North Country Sketches, Dance Rhapsody – etc. etc. Please send North Country sketsches to me here – Insured as I want to revise it.

Autograph letter, signed and dated. Envelope addressed: Philip Heseltine Esq/35 Warrington Crescent/Maida Vale/Londres/Angleterre. Postmark: GREZ [date illegible].

The original is in the British Library.

1   Paul Bekker (1882–1937): German musician and writer on music. Trained as a violinist, he was also a proficient conductor. He was highly influential as music critic from 1911 to 1923 on Heinrich Simon's daily, the *Frankfurter Zeitung*. In 1927 he was to present *A Village Romeo and Juliet* at Wiesbaden, where he was Intendant at the opera (See Letter 514). Among his writings on Delius, there is a very short review in *Die Musik*, 9, No. 18, of *Brigg Fair* in Zürich in 1910, a detailed review of *Fennimore* in *Musikblätter des Anbruch*, 1, No. 2 (November 1919), pp. 60–63, 'Delius/Zu seinem 60. Geburtstag' in the *Frankfurter Zeitung* of 13 March 1923, and articles in the *Frankfurter Zeitung* of 15 March 1923 and 30 January 1927.

2   On 5 December Jelka wrote to Marie Clews: '. . . we were summoned to London as Beecham intended giving the Village Romeo and Juliet – and Fred thought it necessary to be on the spot, and actually postponed the performance – it was all too hurried and they could not get the music over in time – so it was a good thing we went – he also arranged for the publication of all his new scores etc and saw the Public Trustee once more about our financial affairs . . . In London we had a very good time, We heard Parsifal and the Covanchina at Covent Garden, and Lady Cunard runs the whole show now, was as amusing as ever, tremendously décolletée . . . Freds Village Romeo will now be done at Covent Garden in February   We heard very good reports from Francfort about Fennimore and Gerda which continues running.'

3   Jelka had of course long since made sketches for the scenery of *Fennimore and Gerda*, and in December she was at work designing the cover for the Universal Edition piano score – at the same time as Heseltine was working on his English translation of the libretto. In fact the designs for Beecham's 1920 production of *A Village Romeo* were made by Adrian Allinson. Six of his scene designs are in the possession of Bradford Grammar School.

4   The Deliuses had left in London two trunks 'full of our warm clothes and things' which they needed for Grez and had asked Heseltine if he could find someone who was travelling to Paris who might bring them over.

(450)
Frederick Delius to Percy Grainger

Grez-sur-Loing
(S & M)
17 Dec 1919

My dear Percy

We have just returned here from London[1] where Jelka received a letter from your mother asking me to write a work for piano & orchestra for you. If I can only get to work again in peace I would try & do so: We have been rushing about for the last 4 months – First to Norway for 6 weeks – Then we read in

the Danish papers that my last music drama "Fennimore & Gerda" (Niels
Lyhne) was going to be given in Francfort on the 18th October – so after much
difficulty, what with passes etc, we went to Francfort for the rehearsals & first
performance & were there a month – It was all wonderfully interesting & they
gave themselves endless trouble. – All the scenery entirely new for the occasion & the performance was excellent & came off on October 21st – I was called
8 or 9 times – There is no feeling whatever against the english or Americans –
We spoke english in the streets, tramways & restaurants & only encountered
politeness. There is more music in Germany than before the war & great interest in all the arts. I think defeat has done Germany good.[2] In February we
go to London again for the first performance of "The Song of the high hills".
The double Concerto & the Pagan Requiem.[3] I will write you all about it –
I send you the Frankfurter Zeitung with an article on "Fennimore & Gerda".
Write me soon all about yourself & doings. When shall we meet again? I did
not receive the batch of criticisms your mother speaks of – Where did you
address them to? Balfour Gardiner came back with us here from London &
spent a few days here; he is now in Ashampstead again & very contented –
Write soon & give me all the news – With love to your dear mother from us
both –

  I remain
  ever affectionately

  your friend
  Frederick Delius

Autograph letter, signed and dated. Envelope addressed: Percy Grainger Esqre/309
West 92nd Street/New York city/N.Y./Etats Unis d'Amérique. Postmark: GREZ 18
-12 19. Enclosed, a clipping from the *Frankfurter Zeitung*: 'Frederick Delius:
"Fennimore und Gerda".'

The original is in the Grainger Museum.

1   In fact evidence points to the Deliuses already having left London for their return
to Grez on 29 November. They had stayed for a fortnight in a small Soho hotel, the
Tour Eiffel, at 1 Percy Street.

2   Busoni too was in London during the autumn, playing at the Wigmore Hall, and
in a letter to his wife dated 23 November, he echoed his old friend's sentiments:
'Delius has come back from Frankfurt, full of enthusiasm. He is the first to bring good
news from Germany. His "Niels Lyhne" was performed there at great expense and
with much care ... It was a relief to hear something good about Germany for once.'
Two days later he wrote again, this time with a more enigmatic reference to Delius: 'I
met Delius and his wife in the street yesterday. At his wish, we arranged to meet for
dinner. As he was going, he turned round again, as if he had forgotten some form of
politeness. 'I like the Sarabande best' [from Busoni's *Sarabande and Cortège*], he said in

a consoling voice. I turned my back on him. And in the taxi, I let myself go: I was obliged to cry.' (Ferruccio Busoni: *Letters to His Wife*, p. 289.)

3   Of the three works, it was the Requiem that had to bide its time – for a further two years in fact. Delius was confident of its quality, writing to Hertzka at the beginning of December: 'I have made a sacrifice in entrusting the Requiem to you, as I am convinced that it is a work which will achieve the greatest significance in Germany.'

1920

The sequestered funds abroad still remained a source of worry to Delius at
Grez during the first weeks of the year. However, Jelka could at least write to
Marie Clews on 8 February: 'Happily Fred is working very regularly again at
his music. That is so splendid because it keeps him at least from worrying over
these things all the time.' There were to be more discussions with the Public
Trustee, as well as with bankers and solicitors, when Delius travelled to Lon-
don on 18 February for a stay of more than a month. He put up at the
O'Neills' and attended rehearsals and the first performances of the Double
Concerto and *The Song of the High Hills* on 21 and 26 February respectively. A
few days were spent with Gardiner at Ashampstead before Delius returned to
London around the middle of March in order to attend rehearsals of Bee-
cham's second production of *A Village Romeo and Juliet*, opening on the 19th at
Covent Garden. The composer returned to Grez on 22 March. It is clear that
fairly soon he was sketching out the work that was eventually to be known as
Songs of Farewell: 'I am now busy on a new choral work,' he wrote to Universal
Edition on 15 May. Composition of this, however, soon had to be put aside.
For one thing he began to feel nervous and unwell, abandoning a planned mid-
summer holiday in Brittany; for another, there came in July from London an
urgent commission – would he compose for impresario Basil Dean incidental
music to James Elroy Flecker's play *Hassan*? At about the same time came the
welcome news that Elberfeld intended to give the *Mass of Life* again next
season. However, it may have been Haym's retirement that prevented this.

In August Philip Heseltine came to stay for a while at Grez. Delius meanwhile was already at work on *Hassan*, and it was agreed that he would send his
pencilled drafts to London for Heseltine to make a fair score from them.
Delius's hand was growing shaky, and more and more of his letters were
written by Jelka. She had anyway for many years herself written a good proportion of his business letters and could imitate his signature faithfully. A
September holiday in the Basque country was cut short because of bad weather
and Delius was back at work on *Hassan* later in the month, despatching his
work as agreed to Heseltine, who at the time was also correcting proofs of the
Requiem. A few days early in October were spent in Paris, where among other

things Delius renewed acquaintance with Theodor Szántó – who was planning to give the Piano Concerto in Budapest in January. Then on 15 November Delius travelled to Frankfurt-am-Main for the winter, Jelka joining him at the end of the month. She told Heseltine 'we are looking forward immensely to all the good music, theatres and friends over there.' They stayed at the Carlton Hotel until the end of the year, when they moved to an apartment overlooking the river.

Songs of Farewell, for double chorus and orchestra (RT II/9). Sketched.

Hassan, incidental music to James Elroy Flecker's drama in 5 acts (RT I/9). Begun.

(451)
Frederick Delius to Jelka Delius

4 Pembroke Villas
Kensington W
[22? February 1920]

Dearest Jelka –

I received your card, letter & also Tischer's – Tischer had already sent me his estimate direct to London – The Concerto went wonderfully well[1] – The girls played superbly & Wood surpassed himself – It was enthusiastically received – The house was crowded – the best of the season – Wood gave himself endless trouble – I enclose an interview of the "Daily Mail" Where they got that awfull picture I do not know – The evening I arrived they telephoned for an interview – I shall hear a choral rehearsal of "The song of the H.H." to-morrow afternoon & will write you all about it[2] – I sup with Mrs Woodhouse tonight – Zogheb was in the Concert too – I lunch with him on Wednesday. He was very enthusiastic about the double & also about the Violin Concerto – which appears had a wonderful reception – Things seem to be going well here at last!! The O'Neills are very kind & do everything to make me comfortable – I may have to stay a little longer – The V. Romeo, it appears, comes off in first half of March. I saw Allinson at the Concert. I shall try & see Beecham tomorrow. How are you, dearest? I do hope you are beginning to feel the good effects of Dr Bas' treatment. Rest as much as you can – I shall write soon again –

Much love –
Fred

Autograph letter, signed and undated.

The original is in the Grainger Museum.

Delius travelled to London on 18 February, while Jelka, rather unwell for a time, stayed at home in Grez: 'The journey is frightfully expensive now:' she wrote to Marie Clews on 8 February, 'they have just raised it by 100 frs. and our funds are at the very lowest.' They were in fact still waiting for American funds to be released and Jelka, in particular, had long been engaged in a voluminous correspondence with German publishers and others, attempting to obtain large sums owing from German sales and copyrights.

1   The Double Concerto was given its first performance, under Wood, by Beatrice and May Harrison at Queen's Hall on 21 February.

2   The first performance of *The Song of the High Hills* took place at Queen's Hall on 26 February; Coates conducted at this Royal Philharmonic Society concert, with the Philharmonic Choir. Delius wrote to Norman O'Neill, who was drawing up the programme notes, from Grez on 10 February: 'I want the note on The Song of the h. hills to be as short & simple as possible – I have tried to express the joy & exhiliration one feels in the Mountains & also the loneliness & meloncholy of the high Solitudes & the grandeur of the wide far distances. The human voices represent man in Nature; an episode, which becomes fainter & then disappears altogether.' Whilst in London, Delius also took in on 27 February a performance of *Tristan*, conducted by Beecham at Covent Garden.

(452)
Frederick Delius to Jelka Delius

4, PEMBROKE VILLAS,
KENSINGTON, W.
[1 March 1920]

Dearest Jelka

I received your 2 cards & letter at the same time – Thank goodness the strike is over – I am anxious about your cough & cold – Are you keeping warm enough? You ought to stay in bed as much as possible – When the shares come lock them away in my drawer & dont go out until quite better – I saw a solicitor today, who sang in the Chorus – He is going to establish our claim for me & then I am to send it to a big pot in the Treasury   friend of Lady C. who will push it thro' for me – Lady C arranged it – There will be 3 performances of the Village R – on the 17th, 23rd & 29th – I shall stay for the 17th [1] – On Saturday I go out to Balfour's for a few days;[2] on my return I shall probably stay at the Langham Hotel[3] – Adine will get you the stuff for the dressing gown & the silk – Most of the other things I have already bought – I got another £250.

from Volkert – royalties in advance on North Country Sketches & 2nd Dance Rhapsody – not so bad! Dont save now on anything – Keep the warm & have Madame Creuset as long as you can. I shall only bring the clothes back – You forgot to pack my dress trousers & waistcoat – On[ly] the smoking jacket was here – I went in my blue serge trousers – no one noticed it – I better buy a few more shirts – the new cuffs are fluffy & get dirty in one wearing. The documents for America must also be signed by you. That paper we had done in Grez is no good for England or America – Where are the Union Pacific I wonder?

ever your loving
Fred

Autograph letter, signed and undated, written on headed notepaper.

The original is in the Grainger Museum.

1   The first of the three performances in fact took place on 19 March. The others followed on 25 March and 5 April. The parts of Sali and Vreli were sung by Walter Hyde and Miriam Licette, with Percy Heming as the Dark Fiddler. Delius left London on Sunday 21st, arriving at Grez the following day. On 16 April Heseltine wrote to tell Delius 'how utterly marvellous the *Village Romeo* seemed to me. I can honestly say that no music that I have heard has ever moved me more profoundly or given me such a satisfying sense of absolute perfection of expression . . . I was amazed at the way in which the whole work came off dramatically – it is such a wonderful whole, as finely balanced and proportioned as a symphony, unrolling inevitably from the first bar to the last.

I had no idea, from merely reading the libretto, that it would play so marvellously (even with the handicap of bad acting and misconceptions of character) and that it would convey such a sense of cohesion and unity' (Gray, p. 205). Heseltine was now writing an article on the subject for the first issue of his journal *The Sackbut*, due to appear on 15 May.

2   Delius stayed with Gardiner at Ashampstead from 6 to 15 March.

3   In fact, after a further night at the O'Neills', Delius spent his last few days in London at the Rubens Hotel.

(453)
Frederick Delius to Philip Heseltine

Grez 24.3.20

Dear Phil, I am very sorry I saw so little of you in London – but of course I was over head and ears in rehearsals, you will understand that. I left early on Sunday and had a lovely passage. On my next visit to London you must arrange for me to hear something of your friend Saradji[1] – it would interest me very much.

Strangways[2] sent me his magazine for Jan. and April with a long dissertation on Vaughan Williams, *the Great English Genius*!!! Get him to send me Febr. and March! Up to now a spirit of dullness pervades these magazines; certainly what Mr Strangways writes is the essence of dulness – I had already judged him at the Concert where you introduced him to me. If he turns out anything interesting *ever*, I shall be a very astonished person.

I hope you have sent Fennimore and Gerda off to Vienna. I am now correcting the Double Concerto. As soon as I have finished I shall send it to you and beg you to correct once more, and then hand it on to Augener's.

In haste, Ever your affectionate friend,

Frederick Delius

Love from Jelka –

Letter in the hand of Jelka Delius, dated.

The original is in the British Library.

1 Sorabji.

2 A. H. Fox Strangways (1859–1948): English writer on music. He was music critic of *The Times* from 1911 to 1925, and founded the quarterly *Music and Letters* in 1920, editing it until 1927. Delius wrote to Heseltine on 10 April: 'The article on Elgar in Music & letters by Shaw is worthy of the Pink 'un or The Tatler . . . What an article on Vaughan Williams God! "We do not classify Matterhorns, we accept them" catches my eye as I peruse it again – & it exposes its author, the editor, to ridicule.' Delius's 'Harpsichord piece for Mrs Woodhouse' (Dance) appeared in the first issue of *Music and Letters*, before being published separately.

For an account of the first meeting, in November 1919, between Delius and Fox Strangways, see Foreman: *From Parry to Britten*, Letter 99.

(454)

Frederick Delius to C. W. Orr

Grez-sur-Loing,
(S & M)

May 16th 1920

My dear Orr – Your two letters gave me the greatest pleasure & I should have written before had [I] not been very busy at my work – I spent 6 weeks in London – the "double" went off very well indeed – of course Beatrice outweighs May: She has more passion & vigor – May is very good but rather cold

& unimpassioned – Wood conducted beautifully – The "Song of the High Hills" also went off well – especially the chorus – Coates evidently did not quite know what to do with my music – It was unfamiliar to him & I am afraid he had not occupied himself sufficiently with the score – However, no doubt, he will give a better rendering of it on the 2nd of June when it is to be repeated. The "Village Romeo" went off as well as could be expected & much better than 10 years ago – Beecham & his orchestra were perfectly splendid Hyde unimpassioned as usual The black fiddler was good – Vrenchen – fairly good – Manz & Marti good – the two children also good – Scenery by Allinson not particularly good – The last scene was very good – If you have the criticisms I should like to send them to my editor who wants them – & of course, will return them to you when done with. I hear there was a good one in the Spectator.[1] I am always happy to receive your news altho' I am afraid I keep you waiting for an answer – however, dont mind that. We intend spending the whole of next winter in the south – were you pleased with Mentone? Was Hotel de Turin good? We intend coming south in October or end of September. We may stay on the Riviera or go to Spain – Our garden is looking lovely again & it will be a great fruit year. I am working on another choral work[2] – Write soon again & remember us both most kindly to your mother

Yours ever
Frederick Delius

Autograph letter, signed and dated.

The original is in the collection of Mrs Susan Pumfrey.

1   In a postcard to Heseltine dated 22 May, Jelka corrected the error: the article had appeared in the *New Statesman*.

2   *Songs of Farewell*.

(455)
Frederick Delius to Philip Heseltine

Grez-sur-Loing
(S & M)
29 June
20

My dear Phil –

I am leaving for Parame or Roscof in Brittany about July 11th [1] – I hope you will be able to join me there later or if not come & stay with us here in Sep-

tember for a couple of weeks. One of the abuses in the English music world is
the "first performance craze" – There are many others which I will indicate to
you when I have a little leisure – You ought also to have a column in the
Sackbut of enquiries – for instance – We should like to know why so & so etc
– Let us say, as an example – "We should like to know why none of the works
of Delius were included in the Programms of the so called British Music
Festival." Here we have the clique abuse again – You ought also to have a sort
of review of the musical criticisms on a new important work – Especially to
draw attention to anything especially inane or idiotic – Ernest Newman could
be held up to great advantage every now & then – Some of his articles are really
nothing but words – a sort of writing Diarrhoea – Such a review would at once
make the critics more careful – It would perhaps raise the standard – What are
more useless or idiotic than Kalisch's notices in the Daily News! Newman
wrote an especially stupid notice on my "Double Concerto" as time will show
– There is no Concerto where the solo instruments blend so well with the
Orchestra or where there are fewer unnecessary passages – Write soon again

Ever affectionately
Frederick Delius

P.S. I've not read or heard a thing about that Welsh Festival and should like so
much to know how the Arabesk went?[2]

Autograph letter, signed and dated. Postscript in the hand of Jelka Delius. Envelope
addressed: Angleterre/Philip Heseltine Esq[re]/35[a] St Georges R[d]/Kilburn/Londres
N W 6. Postmark: GREZ [date illegible].

The original is in the British Library.

1   Delius had written to Heseltine on 22 June encouraging him to come to Brittany.
But on 14 July he was to write: 'I have decided to stay here until I go to Spain in September. Brittany was so overfull I could get in nowhere.' A month earlier, however,
Jelka had told Heseltine: 'He has not been so very well lately and this constant anxiety
about the money makes him so nervous . . . do not mention anything about his not
being very strong; as he hates me to say so. But I cant help it, I get so anxious about
him.' In the event Heseltine came to spend part of August at Grez with the Deliuses.
Hassan, for the first time, was a topic of conversation. The English impresario Basil
Dean had visited Grez on 15 July ('He wants to shew me a play!! Who is he?'). Much
later, in an undated (1935) letter to Dean, Jelka recalled the occasion: 'I shall never
forget how you came here and read the whole Drama to us. It was so thrilling to see
how Delius gradually got more and more interested.' The result was that the composer
began to sketch incidental music for the first and second acts of the play. A week or
ten days later, Hellé Flecker, the poet-playwright's widow, made a special visit to
Grez to see Delius ('a bundle of quivering and spasmodic nerves', as she described him)
to discuss the music required. Heseltine, after talking about the work with Delius,
agreed to write out the full score from the composer's pencilled drafts, which would be
sent to him in London. Heseltine was also able to report that he had made an agree-

ment with John Lane to publish the biography of Delius on which he had – at intervals – been working for some years.

2   *An Arabesque* was conducted by Arthur E. Sims at the Welsh Musical Festival at Newport on 28 May.

(456)
Frederick Delius to Henry Clews

Grez-sur-Loing
(S & M)
22/9/20

My dear Clews.

Should you happen to be at the La Napoule railway station when the Paris train arrives sometime in the middle of the day you will notice an elderly young man in a brown hat & golden spectacles looking rather weary & care worn step down from a first class compartment on to the platform: you will, no doubt, go up to him & raising your hat exclaim, Frederick Delius I believe – He will then raise his hat an[d] exclaim Henry Clews, I presume. Whereupon they will fall into each others arm[s]. You will then, no doubt, conduct him to the waiting room where he will be received by the Mayor & the Conseil Municipal: whereupon they will form into a procession & with the Fanfare de La Napoule at the head wend their way to the Chateau de la Napoule amidst admiring & enthusiastic crowds –!! –

I hope to leave Paris on the 9th November at 8. something p m arriving at La Napoule somewhere about 1 I believe[1]

Am looking forward immensely to my visit. Love to you both. Jelka is writing to Marie –

Ever yours
Frederick Delius

Jelka comes a little later.

Autograph letter, signed and dated.

The original is in the Delius Trust Archive.

Delius had left Grez early in September for a holiday at Hendaye, on the French/Spanish border, where Jelka was to join him on the 11th. Subsequently they debated whether to continue to Spain or to Italy, but with the weather breaking, disappointed, they returned to Grez around 22 September.

1   The visit did not materialize.

(457)
Frederick Delius to Edvard Munch

> Grez sur Loing
> Seine et Marne
> 23.9.1920

Dear Munch,

I wrote to Jappe Nilsson and asked him, if he could not get 28 000 Kroner for my Gauguin, to send the picture to

Hr Marchant
  Goupil Gallery
5 Lower Regent Str
  London.

It is a good month or 6 weeks since I wrote and so I sent a telegram and received no reply. I am afraid therefore that he has not received my letter.

Will you be so kind, dear Munch, and look into the matter and let me know what is happening.

When are you coming down to visit us here?

We both send you our warmest greetings

Your friend
Frederick Delius

_____

Letter in the hand of Jelka Delius, dated, written in Norwegian.

The original is in the Munch Museum.

(458)
Frederick Delius to Edvard Munch

> Grez sur Loing
> Seine et Marne

13.10.20

Dear Munch,

Won't you come and stay with us out here for a few days?[1] It is so lovely here now with the autumn atmosphere, and then we can chat together a little and drink some of the wonderful bottles of wine we buried during the battle of the Marne. There are 2 good trains a day 10.50 a.m. and 5.45 p.m. from Gare de Lyon to Bourron St. Couldn't you come on Saturday, you must not dash off without us having seen you. We both look forward so much to seeing you again.

Please send a telegram telling us when you will arrive as we have to book a driver to fetch you at Bourron.

Best wishes from us both

Your old friend
Frederick Delius

Letter in the hand of Jelka Delius, dated, written in Norwegian.

The original is in the Munch Museum.

1   Evidence seems to point to a meeting between Munch and Delius about this time, and the artist's first lithograph of the composer would very likely have been sketched then. (See John Boulton Smith: *Frederick Delius and Edvard Munch*, pp. 122–3.)

(459)
Frederick Delius to Jappe Nilssen

1 Dec. 1920   Carlton Hotel
                                               Frankfurt a/M
                                               Tyskland

Dear friend

Your letter has been forwarded to me here, and I am quite astonished and sorry that you are still without your money.

The same day as I got your letter of 27 October I sent instructions to my Bank in London (National Provincial and Union Bank of England   208–209 Piccadilly) to send you 180 Kroner 90 øre, the sum you had been so kind as to lay out for me. What has happened I do not know, I have today written again to have the sum sent to you *immediately*; and to ask what happened to my first letter.

Marchant wrote to tell me that the picture has now arrived[1], but was so badly packed that it got 2 "skratches"[2] on the varnish and that it would be for the insurance company to pay for it. But I do not know the insurance company's name and must therefore ask you to make the claim for me. The company must then send a representative to Goupils, 5 Lower Regent Str London and assess the damage, and then pay for it. It was a pity of course that the case disappeared. It had been specially made and cost £3 and was *"tin-lined"*[2]

We are both very sorry to hear that you are so poorly, and we sincerely hope that there will soon be an improvement!

We plan to stay here for two months and then travel to London.[3]
Please tell me right away whether you have now received the money.

Yours sincerely
Frederick Delius

Letter in the hand of Jelka Delius, dated, written in Norwegian.

The original is in the University Library, Oslo. Only one other communication from Delius to Nilssen is recorded: a postcard of 15 or 16 October 1900.

Jappe (Jakob) Nilssen (1870–1931): Norwegian author and art critic. He was an intimate of Edward Munch and had long been acquainted with Delius.

1   Jappe Nilssen had sent Delius's Gauguin canvas *Nevermore* to London, where at last it was soon to be sold.

2   In English in the original.

3   After debating, in mid-October, the merits of London or the Riviera for the winter, the Deliuses settled for Frankfurt. Delius left in the middle of November and Jelka followed a fortnight later; they took a suite at the Carlton Hotel 'till after Xmas', Heinrich Simon's brother lending a grand piano to the composer.

(460)
Frederick Delius to Philip Heseltine

91 Schaumainkai
Frankfort °/m
26th Dec 20

My dear Phil – It is a long time since I heard from you & I hope that things are going well with you – I received the November Sackbut & was very glad to see an article on Bartok by Gray – You never let me know how the concerts went – Van Dierens' quartet – my songs – Sorabji's Sonata etc[1] – When you have a little leisure sit down & let me have a little news – I hear nothing about English affairs here – Did you hear the Harrisons play my double Concerto at the Sunday Concerts Dec 12th? When can I have the copy of Hassan – I should like to work on it here as soon as possible – Life here is very agreable   Lots of music & operas & excellent plays at the Schauspielhaus – They are playing again a good deal of my music in Germany[2] – amongst other things – the Violin Concerto – on Febr 21 & 22nd   The Mass of Life at Elberfeld – Next tuesday 5 of my new Tischer Songs here – Life for us is cheap & we have hired a lovely appartment on the Main & feel very comfortable – the food in Restaurants is excellent – Prices for German's terribly dear – We shall stay here until we come to London – Did you hear Sammons & Felix Salmond[3] play the double? Write soon – A happy & lucky new year to you my boy –

ever affectionately
Frederick Delius

Autograph letter, signed and dated. Envelope addressed: Philip Heseltine Esqre/ 122 Cheyne Walk/Chelsea/London S. W. 10/England. Postmark: FRANKFURT 27.12.20.

The original is in the British Library.

1   Two *Sackbut Concerts* had been organized on 18 October and 2 November.

2   Writing to Emil Hertzka on 30 December, Jelka reported continued interest in Delius's music, both in Frankfurt and in Germany generally. Furthermore, Schuricht had recently called on Delius and was seeking an opportunity to give *A Mass of Life* in Berlin.

3   Felix Salmond (1888–1952): English cellist. A member of the London String Quartet, he gave the first performance, in 1919, of the Elgar Cello Concerto.

1921

The Deliuses were enjoying their stay in Frankfurt, where they intended to remain until the middle of March before spending the rest of the year in London. Their evenings were spent in the concert hall, opera or theatre, and there were recitals to attend that included Delius's own works. Heinrich Simon was organizing a concert of Delius's chamber music to be given before an invited audience on 15 March; but the composer was unable to hear this, as he and Jelka had by then left for London, in time to attend a very fine Philharmonic Society performance of *Appalachia* conducted by Albert Coates. They took an apartment at 21 Lancaster Road (now Grove), Swiss Cottage – only a short distance away from their earlier home in Belsize Park Gardens: 'Broadwoods have put me a beautiful piano in.' Delius began work on his Cello Concerto almost right away, dividing his time between the old Surrey farmhouse at Thames Ditton, where the Harrisons were now living, and the London apartment. He was still 'completely absorbed' in the concerto at the end of April, which took him another month to finish. A hearing of *Le Sacre du Printemps*, on 7 June, provided a contrast; 'an Anti-musical pretentious row' was now his judgment on the work. With the *Hassan* rehearsals due to begin in August and the first night due in September, the Deliuses saw an opportunity for a holiday in Norway, made easier as funds blocked since the early war years at last began to be released. The financial prospect certainly seemed brighter: Cologne had put forward feelers about *Hassan*, and it was clear that Delius saw the possibility of an American production, for he stipulated that any income from the work in England or America should be paid to him by Universal Edition in pounds or dollars; he was not prepared to accept German or Austrian currency.

On 17 June, then, the Deliuses left for Norway. They made their way to the village of Lesjaskog, in the valley of Gudbrandsdal. The Hotel Mølmen was 'the nicest little place we've ever been in – quite patriarchal – the family running the Place,' as they told the Clews on 4 July, with Jelka adding: 'Fred is doing a little trout fishing.' It was during the course of this holiday that they decided to have a small chalet built on a hill slope above the village, with magnificent views over the valley. While they were in Norway, Kennedy Scott and the Oriana Madrigal Society gave the first performance of the two un-accompanied part songs, *To be Sung of a Summer Night on the Water*, on 28 June in London; and news came that Wood was to give *Life's Dance* in August. At the same time, Hassan was further postponed. For a time Delius had high hopes that Jelka would be able to undertake the German translation of the work until he heard from Simon in September that a translation already existed. He pointed out to Universal that some of the numbers in *Hassan*, especially an 'Oriental Dance', might sell well if published singly. He was distinctly annoyed with his publishers over the matter of the high prices they demanded for scores and performances of his works. He had seen a number of projected performances abandoned because of their pricing policy: English – particularly provincial – musical organizations simply could not afford to put them on.

'I am longing to get back to work again in Grez,' Delius wrote to Heseltine early in August, and around the 20th of that month he and Jelka left Lesjaskog and started out on the return journey to England. The composer spent some time with Beatrice and May Harrison, who wanted to give the Double Con-certo in Vienna – and perhaps too in Prague and Budapest – later in the autumn. Delius told Universal to press for a first performance of the Cello Concerto at one of the Philharmonic concerts while Beatrice was in Vienna. The Deliuses returned to Grez at the beginning of September. For the com-poser himself there was to be one more excursion abroad this year – a nostalgic (and indeed final) trip to his native city of Bradford, for a performance of *Sea Drift*. He was away for about a week at the end of October. Some good news arrived in November: the Requiem and *Sea Drift* were down for performance in April in Frankfurt; in January Grainger was to give the Piano Concerto twice with the New York Symphony Orchestra; and Heseltine expected to complete his book on Delius by the end of the year. Furthermore Grainger was anxious to make, without fee, a two piano arrangement of the first *Dance Rhapsody*. On the other hand there was dispiriting news concerning *Hassan*: the London production was again postponed, to September 1922 at the earliest.

For the Rosen family 1921 had certainly been a year to remember: for several months Jelka's brother, Friedrich, had served Germany as its Foreign Minister.

'Avant que tu ne t'en ailles' (RT V/31). Some revision?

Concerto for violoncello and orchestra (RT VII/7).

Hassan (RT I/9). Original version completed.

(461)
Frederick Delius to Philip Heseltine

91 Schaumainkai
Frankfurt ª/M

Jan 7. 21

My dear Phil — I received your letter 2 or 3 days ago & the score of Hassan yesterday — Many thanks for the copy which saved me a lot of tedious work & strain on my eyes — I have not received the December Sackbut[1] — To what address did you send it? I should very much like to have it — If you possibly can, hold out with the Sackbut — No one wants anything at first, but they will begin to want it — Try & hold out until I can help you with money — which I hope wont be long. Dont go to Paris for a long stay   it will entirely unfit you for any more work in London — Especially the Life in Montparnasse which is very agreable but which also breeds endless ratés. I never quite approved of the Sackbut Concerts — The Sackbut is quite sufficient & will absorb all your energy to run it successfully — The start is excellent, but you must keep at it & not give way if success does not come at once — you must make it a success & now that you are rid of Rogers[2] you are no longer hampered — Gray is a valuable asset — You ought, of course, to review new works & first performances — naturally in a different way than the daily press. We shall probably come to London in March & hire a flat or small furnished house. I shall have to be in London most of this year — I should like a piano score with vocal part of Hassan & as soon as I have finished it I will send you the complete score —[3]

With love from us both

ever affectionately
Frederick Delius

P.S
One ought to be able to read in the Sackbut what is going on in the musical world —

Autograph letter, signed and dated. Envelope addressed: Philip Heseltine Esqre/122 Cheyne Walk/Chelsea/London S W 10/England. Postmark: FRANKFURT 7.1.21.

The original is in the British Library.

Life in Frankfurt continued to be agreeable to the Deliuses, Jelka writing to Marie Clews on 2 January: '. . . we have a very good time, going to the Opera and Schauspielhaus, where they send us tickets whenever we like, also concerts all the time. They are playing quite a lot of Delius-Music in Germany again now and they want to play all his new works, so we shall probably stay a couple of months yet.' Max von Schillings called on 13 January, wanting a piano score of *Fennimore and Gerda*. And on 20 January, Jelka wrote to Heseltine: 'We are very comfortable here, we heard

D'Albert last night; he played a lovely Ballad by Grieg – but has gone off a bit upon the whole. We also heard the 2ᵈ Mahler Symphony.'

1 Still more reminders went to Heseltine, until: 'What has become of you?' Delius wrote irately on 14 February. 'I have never seen the December number of the Sackbut in which you published my souvenirs of Strindberg – I should at last like to read it!! I have written several times for it without result. Are you ill?'

2 Winthrop Rogers, London music publishers originally associated with *The Sackbut*.

3 Basil Dean was to write to Delius on 18 January: he wanted to come over to discuss *Hassan* as soon as the composer returned to Grez.

(462)
Frederick Delius to C. W. Orr

91 Schaumainkai,
Frankfurt ª/M
7ᵗʰ/2/21

My dear Orr –

I was so glad to receive your long letter which I hasten to answer at once. We have been here for some time now & had the good luck to find a beautifully furnished appartment right on the river where we are very comfortably settled & intend staying here until we go to London middle of March. The Requiem will not be given this season but very probably in the Autumn – Hassan has also been postponed until the early Autumn: so you will no doubt hear both – Our affairs are progressing as well as possible considering the idiocy of our rulers & treaty makers – I have seen my Berlin banker & he assured me that they have done & will continue to do everything in their power to have my affairs speedily settled – We are now awaiting the pleasure of the Public Controller – Our American securities are still held by the American Public Controller who writes that as I am a British subject I shall not receive them until reciprocal rights have been granted to American subjects by England – It appears at the outbreak of the war Securities & funds belonging to American subjects were sequestered by the British government as they were deposited in German banks in London – It really is stupendous! Your description of the South & the balmy weather makes me long to be just there as the weather here is cold, windy, & rainy – The people would not bother me much as I can always keep them at arms length – Hotel life is hateful & I can never stand it for long, neither can my stomach. We go quite often to the theatre here both opera & Drama – We heard Peer Gynt the other night with Griegs music –

We also go to Concerts – They play a good deal of Mahler in Germany at present & we have already heard 3 Symphonies – I find them dull pretentious & unoriginal – I heard my Violin Sonata beautifully played by a yong russian violinist the other night also a lot of my latest songs – those which are edited by Tischer & Jagenberg – 4 Verlaine songs, I Brasil, The Nightingale has a lyre of gold etc – They are playing my Violin Concerto a good deal in Germany – I have a grand piano here & have been working at Hassan & also another Verlaine Song   The little Chinese poems are beautiful especially the "Cutting Rushes". Have you been working at your Counterpoint, or at some more ambitious work? We are also going to hire a flat in London & keep it so as to have a comfortable home there. Part of the Winter we should like to spend abroad in Spain or Sicily – So it is pretty sure we shall meet in London in April, how nice it will be to exchange our impressions of the last 2 years –

Write soon again. With warmest greetings to you & your mother from us both

I remain

Yours ever
Frederick Delius

Autograph letter, signed and dated.

The original is in the collection of Mrs Susan Pumfrey.

(463)
Frederick Delius to Universal Edition

21 Lancaster Road
Hampstead
London N.W.3

23.3.1921

Dear Herr Director,

We have just moved in here & this is now our address.[1] I would like to begin on the orch. arrangement of Appalachia right away, but do not have a score here.[2] Please send me one *immediately*. Coates has just given a quite wonderful performance of this work at the Philharmonic & with the Philharm. Choir. I was present   it was very enthusiastically received. The concert before an invited audience that Dr Simon organized in Frankf. was very well reviewed in the Press. A pity that I had already left!

Cordially

Yours
Frederick Delius

Letter in the hand of Jelka Delius, dated, written in German.

The original is in the Universal Edition archives.

1   Shortly before the middle of March, the Deliuses left Frankfurt; their intention
was to spend the rest of the year in London.

2   Prompted, apparently, by Dr Hertzka, Delius had informed Universal Edition on
7 March: 'I think the idea of arranging Appalachia for orchestra alone is a good one,
and I will do it when I have the opportunity. Seadrift is however a choral work &
cannot be played without a chorus.' By 10 May he had changed his mind: 'After careful consideration I am afraid I just cannot see how I can arrange Appalachia for orchestra alone without spoiling the work.' There is no reference in the surviving Delius
correspondence to the death on 15 February of the early champion of these works,
Hans Haym.

(464)
Frederick Delius to Philip Heseltine

6.4.1921   21 Lancaster Rd
                                                                 Hampstead N.W.3

My dear Phil,

Many Thanks for your two nice letters which interested me very much. I
know what the near Orient is. I was at Tangiers once and just as disgusted as
you with all this picturesqueness got up for the stupid Europeans.[1]

I have finished Hassan and am now just waiting for you to do me the Piano
Score. I am at present working at a Violincello-Concerto. We have a nice little
flat very near where we were before in Hampstead, only smaller and nearer
Swiss Cottage. Broadwoods have put me a beautiful piano in.

The rehearsals of Hassan begin in August and it is to be produced in
September.

Please give my kindest regards to Bartok[2] and to Hertzka. I hope you'll
thoroughly enjoy the rest of your trip.

Ever aff^ly yours
Frederick Delius

Letter in the hand of Jelka Delius, dated.

The original is in the British Library.

1   After seeing another issue of The Sackbut through the press, Heseltine suddenly left
for North Africa; he wrote of his disappointment with the region in a letter to Delius
that was penned in Biskra on 28 March, adding: 'We leave here to-morrow for Tunis

and cross thence to Naples by sea. From there we make a wild rush up to Budapest where we shall be able to visit Béla Bartók. We shall arrive there about April 7th and stay five or six days.' After a few days in Vienna and Munich he would be home some time late in April.

2   Writing from Budapest, Heseltine told Delius: 'Bartók is quite one of the most lovable personalities I have ever met.'

It was perhaps during this stay in London that Delius met another young composer, presumably through Heseltine, their mutual friend. The occasion was recalled in the spring of 1932 by Jelka, and immediately recorded in a letter from Cecily Arnold to her husband, Eric Marshall Johnson: 'She told me that some time ago when they were in London, William Walton came to see them, & he sat for 2½ hours & never said a word in spite of all her efforts – he was so shy!'

(465)

Jelka Delius to Marie Clews

Mølmen Hotel
Gudbrandsdalen   *Lesjaskog den* 31.7.1921
Norway

Dearest Marie,

It was indeed delightful to see your dear handwriting again and hear from your warm kind letter all about you both. You can imagine how we are with you in thought and appreciate the thrill of the creation of the Drama.[1] Those periods always stand out in one's memories as the loveliest times. Fred says he is longing to hear the Drama, and so am I, of course, and I hope by the time we come it will be far advanced or almost completed.

Our plans are to sail back to England 24th August, spend a few days only in London, and go on to Grez where we shall stay until we are called to London for the rehearsals and Première of the Drama by Elroy Flecker for which Fred has written very beautiful incidental music. It was to have been given early in September but the strike and slump in everything in England made them postpone it. Our idea is to go from London after that Première to Rome and spend a few wintermonths there. On our way to Rome we should love to call on you. The Director of the theatre[2] has promised to let Fred know as early as he can about the dates and as soon as we know you shall hear. I cannot tell you how I long to see you both again   The only light spot in all the years of the war is your friendship! And how unforgettably dramatic all the last times were! The airraid, the cellar, your arrival in Grez fleeing from big Bertha! And how we studied those maps!

Now I will tell you what we did after Francfort: We went straight to London and found a little furnished flat there, up in Hampstead again – rather an incomplete little place, but with a very cosy large sittingroom to the south. Broadwoods sent Fred a lovely piano and he began composing at once and never stopped for over 2 months. He wrote a beautiful Concerto for Violincello and Orchestra there; it was quite heavenly how the beautiful music streamed out and seemed to make everything so lovely – even our rotten little household with an idiotic Irish servant and all the little bothers. – During that time we saw hardly anybody but when he had finished an avalanche of Engagements, friends, business and concerts broke in upon us, and we lived in a perfect whirlpool. – first of all the Osbourne's came to London after a trip round the world and it was really delightful to have them, as they thought about the war and the world as we do and we had such a jolly time together – having lovely little dinners en partie carrée in Restaurants, and also at our little place, and jolly outings in Motor cars. They *are* such kind, sweet-charactered people. –

They were quite disgusted with America and American War-and hatred-propaganda; they went back to California but are coming over to get a little house in London next year. Lady C had been in Paris all winter, I think mostly at the Ritz with T. B. whose affairs in London were from time to time in the papers. He is in bankruptcy; which does not mean much as he has an enormous yearly income, and the capital was not left to him, so he cannot lose it. He will simply have to make an arrangement to pay of[f] so much a year for his debts. Meanwhile he has stopped *all* his musical activities in England – disgusted with their indifference and ungratefulness – So there was *no* opera and the Concert-Season pretty dull also. They gave a few very good performances of Delius Orchestral works, especially Appalachia with Chorus, which went off most brillantly conducted at the Philharmonic by Coates, who after the endless enthusiastic applause and many callings-out of Fred embraced him before the whole orchestra and hall. Coates is such a big strong healthy robust creature and he was like a great big bear and Fred looking all spirituality in contrast quite disappeared in this embrace. In Germany they are giving his Music again everywhere and are going to do the new Opera Fennimore and Gerda at Cologne and his great Choral work The Mass of Life at Dortmund in the Coming winter. At Francfort they gave a Delius Concert and are going to do his "Requiem" in the Winter, also in London. We managed to arrange our affairs rather well during our stay there. Those dreadful publishers[3] who swindled Fred have now sold all his works to a very big and active Firm Universal-Edition Vienna who has also bought up nearly all his works from other german Publishers and is now starting a much more active boom and advertisement and has efficient branches in London and New York.

In October there will be a Musical Festival in Bradford, where they will do *Seadrift* and want to specially feast Fred, who was born there.

I think the music for the Drama "Hassan" is lovely – I am awfully curious about all that and how it will come off. We have influenced the manager and drawn his attention to the old beautiful coloured persian designs, and illustrations of the original Persian Arabian Nights. In style and simplicity they are just perfect – and just what you want for the stage, costumes, movements and all and yet unused – whilst that claptrap vulgar stage-oriental stuff is simply sickening.

Thro' the English Public Trustee we have received a first instalment of the money due to us and a first payment has also been announced of our American Dividends thro' Kuhn Loeb. So we feel much more safe and hopeful – As to the Correspondence about all this, and the Signatures before Consuls in *all* countries and Affidavits – it would fill a volume were I to describe it all.

The greatest miracle of all is that in Grez the French Government has refunded us quite decently for our losses thro the military occupation of our house and the burglary by the french Officers who were lodged there.

It made me truly happy, as it was due entirely to my management of that affair and that *I* was able to obtain it under the circumstances is really a satisfaction; Especially as none of the other claimants in Grez have been paid at all yet!!

I read this thro' and I laugh at myself – such a long letter, will you ever have time to read it? I suppose people like myself who do not talk very much have a special delight in being list[e]ned to in writing.

And I yet forgot to tell you about Nancy Cunard who has published a volume of poems, that are said to be very good, very weird, very pessimistic.[4] She has of course long ago entirely discarded her stupid little husband whom she had moreover discovered having an intrigue with her best friend. She lives in a little flat in Paris.

T. B. we also met again in London. I had not seen him since 1915 and we fairly hugged one another on meeting again. He had no side on whatever and was really delightful – he and Fred and I sitting on a big Sopha in an upstairs room at Lady C. who was receiving her habitual tributees downstairs. Then he came to dine with us up in Hampstead too and was most awfully nice too.

Lady C. had a young italian Sculptor (Secessionist from Rome called Riccardi) and she got him to make a bust of Fred.[5] It was really awfully fine and full of character and I am very curious to see it again in plaster or bronze on our way thro' London.

This place is lovely, cool to cold and sparklingly fresh – lovely hills and sunny slopes with flowered meadows.

I am painting a bit and we live off our own cows, drinking fresh milk, eating calves-cheese and butter – it agrees so well with Fred, who was dreadfully thin after the milkless stay in Germany. He dreams and does nothing and I shall send you a photo I made of him fishing – a poet fishing, not an excited sports-fisherman. Also he catches no fish –

Now, my beloved friends, I *dare* not go on!

All our love to you both – Jelka

I wish you could send us photos of the Chateau de N. and the courtyard with the God of H. M. and all you have done!

Autograph letter, signed and dated, written on headed notepaper.

The original is in the Delius Trust Archive.

The Deliuses left London for Norway on 17 June. Jelka wrote from Lesjaskog to Marie Clews on 4 July: 'We are up here in the high mountains in the most heavenly sunshine and fresh snow-mountain air. After London's strenuous season this is perfectly delicious . . . Fred is doing a little trout fishing and we wander about in the lovely birch and pinewoods gathering lilies of the valley.'

1 Henry Clews was writing his play *Mumbo Jumbo*.

2 Basil Dean.

3 Harmonie Verlag.

4 Nancy Cunard's first volume of verse was published in 1921.

5 Eleuterio Riccardi's bust of Delius is now in the Cartwright Gallery, Bradford.

(466)
Frederick Delius to Jelka Delius

12 Oak Avenue [Bradford]
Tuesday – [25 October 1921]

Dearest. Altho' when I left Paris & the Daily Mail prophesied a very rough passage, I had a very good one: the wind had entirely dropped before arriving at Boulogne. Midgley & Halliday[1] met me at the station & we had a chorus rehearsal the same evening – The chorus seems very good   tomorrow we have a rehearsal with Orchestra & Chorus – There were no slippers in my sack when I opened it – Midgley lent me a pair & in London I shall buy a pair – I will let you know all about the dinner & Concert – I leave on Friday for London – In haste

  lovingly
  Fred

Autograph letter, signed and undated, written on the headed notepaper of the 'Bradford Liberal Club, Bradford, Yorks.'

The original is in the Grainger Museum.

The Deliuses left Norway on 24 August, stayed for a few days in London, and returned to Grez on 2 September. During the virtually unbroken autumn sunshine of September and October the composer was preoccupied with proofs of *Hassan* and the Double Concerto. After working through his papers Delius wrote to Heseltine on 14 October: 'I have lost half of the poem of Life & Love & dont know whether I shall be able to complete this work. The lost part is just the new part & the best. I ought to be over in Bradford for October 26th Musical Festival when they are giving Sea-drift but I have not the courage to go.' In the event, he was to be able to write of his Bradford visit (in what was to be the last letter he penned to Jelka, from London on 28 October): 'I saw a lot of old friends & it was quite fun.'

1   Samuel Midgley (1849–1935): English pianist and writer on music. He instituted a series of chamber concerts in his home town, Bradford, soon after having spent a year at the Leipzig Conservatorium (1873–4), and is best remembered for his establishment, in 1911, of an annual series of six Free Chamber Concerts which continued for 14 seasons. The very first concert included songs by Delius and Mendelssohn. Midgley, at whose home Delius stayed from 24 to 28 October, had known Delius as a boy and had taught one of his sisters.

Ernest Halliday was at the time President of the Bradford Old Choral Society, whose centenary the present festival was celebrating.

1922

January 1922 was a bad month: 'his weakness came on gradually in the course of a month,' Jelka was to tell Adine O'Neill on 2 July, 'after he had for some years been more or less weak in his limbs.' He was sixty. A year later, in a letter to the Clews', she was to recall: 'He grew so weak last January.' However, it is clear that he started composition of his second Violin Sonata. And, as ever, his finished music led, of course, its own independent life, noted as news came in of proposed forthcoming performances of *Sea Drift*, by Schuricht at Wiesbaden, of *Fennimore and Gerda*, now scheduled for Easter at Cologne, and of the Requiem, to be given in March in London and in April in Frankfurt. Grainger, meanwhile, had played the Piano Concerto at a New York Symphony Society concert on 8 January. It is doubtful whether the composer was well enough to attend a recital given on 25 January in Paris by his friend Evlyn Howard-Jones, which included the Dance for Harpsichord. Before long, the decision was taken to go to Wiesbaden for a cure, and the Deliuses packed their bags early in February and set off. After a week there Delius felt that he needed to stay for two months; but after two weeks he estimated three months. He was too unwell to continue correcting proofs of the Requiem material, only just begun, too unwell to travel as intended to London for the first performance of that work, too unwell to visit the director of the theatre at Darmstadt to discuss *Hassan*. He was not permitted to walk and was under orders to rest completely. Late in March he asked Heseltine to correct the proofs of the Cello Concerto for him: 'I am as yet quite unable to do it myself, as I cannot write.' At the beginning of the month he had had a visit from Otto Klemperer, conductor at Cologne, who clearly did not favour *Fennimore*, and who proposed *A Village Romeo and Juliet* for Cologne in its place, although this would have to be given rather later in the year. Some weeks later Delius took pains to ensure that Klemperer had the latest corrected edition of the *Village Romeo* vocal score and he reminded Universal of how frequently Beecham had given orchestral performances of excerpts from that opera: these had been very effective and should as soon as possible be published as individual numbers.

By the middle of April he had clearly made some progress, and was able to check proofs of the Requiem. There were visits by Lloyd and Ethel Osbourne and, later, by Edvard Munch; and the Deliuses made a short stay in Frankfurt for the performance of the (slightly-postponed) Requiem conducted by Oskar von Pander on 1 May. Jelka found the work 'quite splendid', and it was received with enthusiasm and emotion by the Frankfurt audience – in contrast to the lukewarm reception London had accorded to it on 23 March. Max Beckmann's lithographic portrait of the composer possibly dates from this period. In mid-May the Deliuses left Wiesbaden for Wildbad in the Black Forest, where Delius was to take the waters. On 19 June came a visit from Heinrich Simon. He had been preparing a short biography of Delius, which was to be published by Piper Verlag, in Munich, by the following January. It was to include portrait drawings by Max Beckmann and Edvard Munch. Delius wrote to Universal to ensure that Simon was lent a number of scores to help him in his study. After this, oddly, all trace of this projected book disappears completely. 'The cure here has done me a lot of good,' Delius wrote to Hertzka on 20 June, and just two days later he left, on doctor's advice, for the mountain air of Norway.

Jelka had meanwhile spent a few days in Grez preparing the house for its summer guests, the Osbournes. By the end of June the Deliuses had moved into their newly-built chalet at Lesjaskog with their Austrian maid Senta Mössmer, and had arranged to hire a piano. Writing to Adine O'Neill, Jelka indicated that finances were a 'great source of anxiety to us both'. Evidently, over a third of the year spent on cures, the construction and furnishing of their chalet, and the lack of an anticipated royalty income from *Hassan* were all factors contributing to this anxiety. Delius pressed his friends and his publishers to secure performances for his works. He was an invalid still, walking only with the aid of sticks, but he was gathering strength and informed Universal that he was ready to correct proofs of both the full and piano scores of his Cello Concerto; and he could tackle anything else too as in Norway he now had a piano, time and the inclination. News had come from Simon that *Hassan* was to come out at Darmstadt at the beginning of September and in London probably shortly before Christmas. A visit from Balfour Gardiner was expected early in September, and on the 7th the Deliuses left Lesjaskog for Grez, via Oslo (where there was a reunion with Grainger), Hamburg and Cologne, arriving home around the 14th. The Osbournes were evidently still in Grez, for when Delius made a new will there on 27 September, leaving everything to Jelka, the two witnesses were Lloyd Osbourne ('author, 38 Grosvenor Gardens, London S.W.I.') and his wife Ethel. After a period seemingly quietly spent at home, the Deliuses abandoned Grez once more late in November for Frankfurt, where they intended to spend the winter months.

Sonata No. 2 for violin and piano (RT VIII/9). Begun.

Five Piano Pieces (RT IX/7). Begun.

Three Preludes for piano (RT IX/8). Begun.

(467)
Frederick and Jelka Delius to Helge Rode[1]

Dear friend, This is to wish you and your wife a very happy and prosperous
New Year. We read and reread often your delicate and beautiful poems which
we love; and also your interesting dramas.[2] Thanks so much for your last
envoi! splendid! – Let me hear how you both are and believe me   Affly yours

  Frederick Delius
  Jelka Delius

  5.1.1922

Picture postcard: *GREZ. – Vue sur l'Eglise et le Vieux Donjon.*, signed by Jelka Delius
and dated, written in English in the hand of Jelka Delius. Jelka adds to the caption
'Grez sur Loing   Seine et Marne. Are'nt you coming to see us?' and also indicates 'our
house-'. Addressed: Hr/Helge Rode/p.a. 'Politiken'/Copenhague/Danemark. Readdressed: Allegade 4.F. Postmark: GREZ 5 -1 22.

Photocopies of seven communications from Delius to Helge Rode were passed to the
Delius Trust in 1984 by John Boulton Smith, who had received them from the
author's son, Mikal Rode, of Copenhagen. The originals, two of which lack final
leaves, are variously in the collections of the Rode family (3) and the Royal Library,
Copenhagen (4). Apart from the present postcard (the last in the series), all are
autograph letters of Frederick Delius. The first is dated 4 November 1897.

1   Helge Rode: See Vol. I, pp. 130–2.

2   Early in 1914, Rode had sent Delius a number of books. Writing on 10 March
that year Delius praised Rode's poems highly, but was even more impressed by the
play *Greve Bonde og hans Hus* (1912): 'I know no modern drama which I consider so
strong & so fine – Every character is so alive & worked out to its very last consequence
– Since Ibsen I have read nothing that made so deep an impression upon me.' Having
immediately interested Heinrich Simon in the play, to the extent of his agreeing to
arrange for it to be given in Frankfurt, Delius proposed that Jelka ('I know no better
translator') should make a German translation, if indeed one had not already been
made. The outcome is not recorded.

(468)
Frederick Delius to Universal Edition

7.3.1922   Hotel Quisisana
                                                           Wiesbaden[1]

Dear Herr Direktor,

I am today returning the galley proof of the Requiem corrected once more in accordance with your questionnaire & I will also send these proofs separately to Goodwin & Tabb. I learn from the Philharmonic Society that they have the right to only *one* performance, so Coates evidently plans to give the work again with another Concert Society.[2] You must therefore get in touch with Coates direct concerning the return of the material. I very much hope that the wind parts will now arrive in London fully and accurately corrected, so that there are no mistakes at all in them.

Some days ago the conductor Otto Klemperer[3] came to see me here. After quite a long discussion I became more and more convinced that Klemperer would much rather perform A Village Romeo and Juliet. He does not think Fennimore and Gerda so suitable for the Cologne public. On the other hand he clearly expects Romeo & Juliet to be a great success. In these circumstances I would strongly recommend you to alter the contract accordingly. If such a work is not approached with complete confidence and enthusiasm, nothing will come of it. Besides, it would really be a fine opportunity to launch A Village Romeo & Juliet at last and the fact that this opera has already been performed several times & with great success at Covent Garden will have a great effect on the English public there. Please go ahead; Klemperer himself will write to you on the subject.

By the way, I was astonished to learn that the theatre in Cologne had received neither the scenery nor Brüggemann's directing instructions, so that they were *quite at a loss* as to the kind of staging and production, the easy arrangements for scene-changing etc. For these reasons alone I would absolutely refuse to allow such a performance of the work. I do not understand why you do not help the theatres in these matters. We are talking about a quite new art form & not a routine opera & the theatre directors still have no idea of all my intentions and the way in which they were realized in Frankfurt. Also, why is the score not engraved? Klemperer complained of having received a completely illegible copy of the score.

With kind regards from us both

Yours sincerely
{Frederick Delius}

Letter in the hand of Jelka Delius, dated, written in German. The signature has been detached.

PLATE 33   (a) At the piano at Grez; (b) and with Lloyd Osbourne.

PLATE 34   Delius in the garden at Grez.

PLATE 35   (a) Jelka in the garden at Grez (*photograph* C.W. Orr); (b) the living-room at Grez in the early 1920s.

PLATE 36   (a) On the veranda at Høifagerli; (b) Høifagerli, Lesjaskog,
looking out over Gudbrandsdalen (*coll. Grainger Museum*).

PLATE 37   (a) With Balfour Gardiner at Høifagerli; (b) a meal is served on the veranda by Senta Mössmer, the maid (*coll. Grainger Museum*).

PLATE 38   Grainger and Delius, Frankfurt, 1923. (*Coll. Grainger Museum.*)

PLATE 39   Violet and Sydney Schiff (the novelist Stephen Hudson).

PLATE 40   (a) With Henry Clews at the Château de La Napoule; (b) The
Château de La Napoule during its reconstruction by Clews.

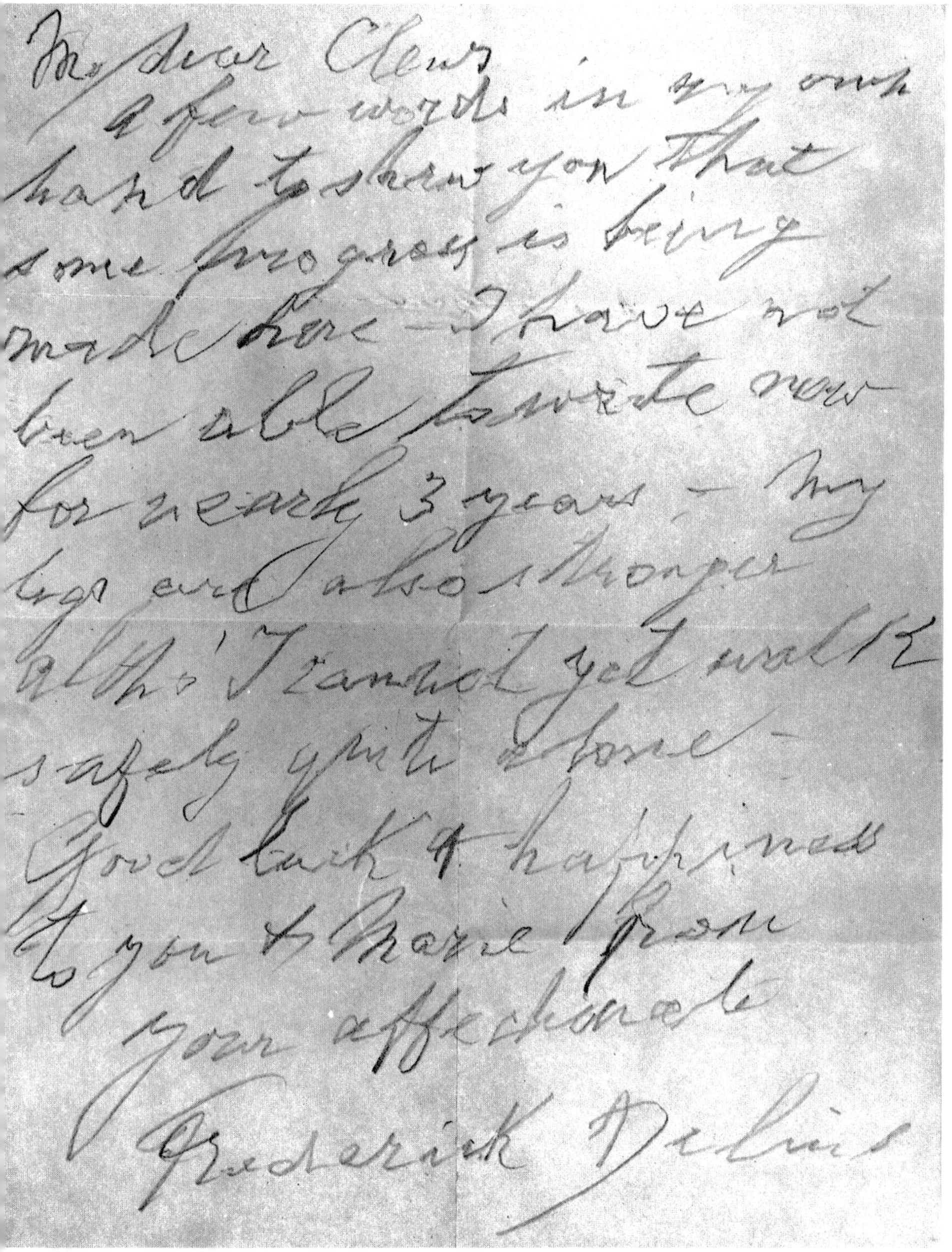

My dear Clews
    a few words in my own
hand to show you that
some progress is being
made here — I have not
been able to write now
for nearly 3 years — My
legs are also stronger
altho' I cannot yet walk
safely quite alone —
Good luck & happiness
to you & Marie from
    your affectionate
    Frederick Delius

PLATE 41   Letter from Delius to Henry Clews, [20 December 1924], almost
certainly the last letter in Delius's own hand (see p. 295).

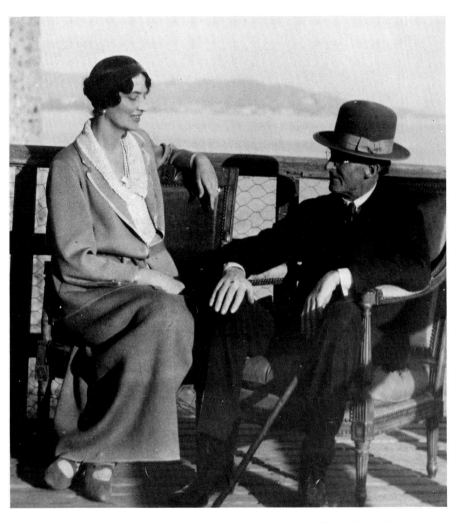

PLATE 42   With Marie Clews at the Château de La Napoule.

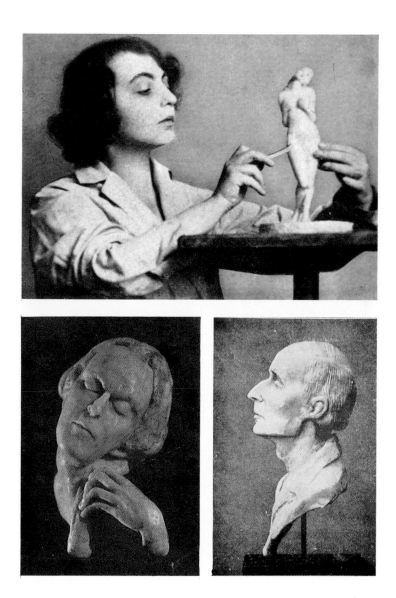

PLATE 43   (a) Catherine Barjansky; (b) Alexandre Barjansky, wax bust by
his wife; (c) Delius, 1925, wax bust by Catherine Barjansky: 'Another portrait
of a soul, that of the composer Delius, contemplating, from under lowered
eyelids, an inaccessible world' (Colette).

PLATE 44   On the Loing, 1925: Barjansky, Jelka and Grainger. (*Coll. Grainger Museum.*)

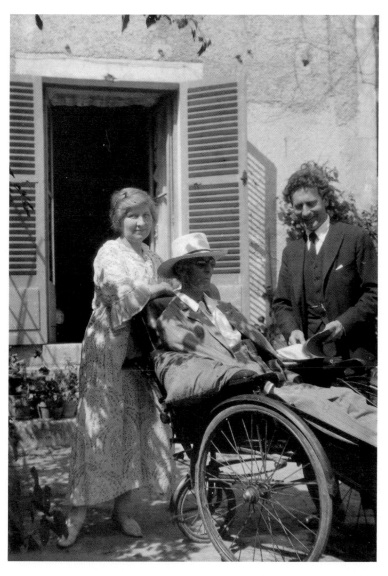

PLATE 45   Jelka, Delius and Grainger, Grez, 1925. (*Coll. Grainger Museum.*)

PLATE 46   Adine O'Neill. (*Coll. Mrs Derek Hudson.*)

PLATE 47   (a) Cyril Scott, Roger Quilter, Percy Grainger and Norman
O'Neill, 1929 (*coll. John Bird*); (b) Charles Kennedy Scott (*coll. John Kennedy
Scott*); (c) Paul Bekker: a sketch dating from the mid 1920s.

PLATE 48   Philip Heseltine, c. 1929.

The original is in the Universal Edition archives.

1   The Deliuses left Grez around 6 February for a cure at Wiesbaden.

2   'The London performance of the Requiem is on the 23rd March,' wrote Delius to Hertzka on 24 January. He understood that Coates intended to conduct two perform- ances, but he did not know when the second was to take place. Evlyn Howard-Jones, he added, was to play the Dance for Harpsichord in Paris on 25 January. The première of the Requiem, on 23 March, was at a Royal Philharmonic Society concert at Queen's Hall, with the Philharmonic Choir, and with Amy Evans and Norman Williams as soloists. Delius had originally intended to be present, but ill health precluded this. A further performance of the work, initially scheduled for April, took place at Frankfurt on 1 May, and this he *was* able to attend.

3   Otto Klemperer (1885–1973): German conductor and composer. He was at this time conductor at Cologne. 'There is a question in Cologne,' wrote Delius to Hesel- tine on 28 March, 'whether they will not first do the Village Romeo and Fennimore only later, but nothing is settled yet.'

(469)
Frederick Delius to Charles Kennedy Scott

Wiesbaden,
Villa 'Mon Repos,'
Frankfurter Strasse.
[mid-March 1922]

My Dear Kennedy Scott,

I have been here at Wiesbaden for the last month undergoing a very severe treatment. My legs had suddenly gone very weak and for the present I am for- bidden to use them and am being wheeled about in a bath chair. I shall there- fore be unable to come to London for the performance of the *Requiem*.[1] You will understand *how disappointed* I am. Please write and let me know how it went off.

Thanking you most heartily for all the trouble I am sure you will have had with the work,
I remain,

Very sincerely yours,
Frederick Delius

From Peter Warlock: *Frederick Delius*, revised edition, 1952, p. 168. Seven letters from Delius to Kennedy Scott, dated 8 August 1917–5 November 1929, are reproduced as an Appendix to this edition.

Charles Kennedy Scott (1876–1965): English choral conductor. He studied at the

Brussels Conservatory, founded the Oriana Madrigal Society in 1904 and the Philharmonic Choir in 1919.

1   In an earlier letter to Kennedy Scott, of 8 August 1917, Delius listed works he had completed since the beginning of the war, and wrote: 'I have a *Requiem* (something for you).'

(470)
Frederick Delius to Tischer & Jagenberg

20.3.1922   Wiesbaden
Villa Mon Repos
Frankfurter str 6

Dear Herr Doktor,

I have just received a letter from the English conductor Albert Coates, who on the 23rd March next gives the first performance of my "Requiem" in London. I quote from it the following passage:

"I was going to do your 'On hearing the first cuckoo in Spring' in Rome on April 5th and the Roman management were very keen on my doing it. I had however a bitter disappointment because Goodwin and Tabb inform me this morning, that your publisher's will not allow this material to be *hired*. I know that the Roman management would not be willing to buy it, just for one performance and I therefore have had, to my great regret, to substitute another work. I wish you would write to your publishers and tell them, that this is a very foolish policy of theirs."[1]

The letter from Goodwin & Tabb was enclosed with this letter and I learn from it that the material costs £8 to buy. In the first place this price is *much too high*   £4 would be more than enough for this short piece. But I must say that it is quite incomprehensible to me that you feel unable to make this material available on hire through Goodwin and Tabb, a really first-rate and utterly reliable firm, for around £2 per performance. In England it is simply not the custom to buy such material; it is always hired. In this way you let slip any number of performances and harm your interests and mine.

Anthony Bernard[2] was another who wanted to do the piece in London, and only now do I understand, on hearing this, why nothing came of it.

That such a work should, in the hands of Goodwin and Tabb, be further hired out & performed without authorization, is *completely out of the question*

When am I to receive settlement of my account? As you see from the address we have moved.

With kind regards to you and your wife

Yours
Frederick Delius

Letter in the hand of Jelka Delius, dated, written in German.

The original is in the Delius Trust Archive.

1   In English in the original.

2   Anthony Bernard (1891–1963): English conductor, pianist and composer. He founded the London Chamber Orchestra in 1921, and conducted with the British National Opera Company.

(471)
Frederick Delius to Edvard Munch

Dear friend, We have arrived here in this delightful place; it is almost like Norway. Everything is very cosy, nice old hotel with excellent food, one can also inhale here and I shall do that and get rid of my cold   It is sheltered and warm here, a much better place than Wiesbaden, lovely smell of pine trees. I took my first bath today. We shall stay here for perhaps a month or 6 weeks.
    It was nice to see you![1]

Your old friend
Frederick Delius

Greetings from Jelka

Hotel zur Post
Wildbad
Schwarzwald
17.5.1922

Postcard in the hand of Jelka Delius, signed and dated, written in Norwegian. Addressed: Herrn/Edvard Munch/Hotel Kaiserhof/Wiesbaden. Readdressed: Kunsthaus/Zürich. Postmark: [WILDBAD] 18.5.[22].

The original is in the Munch Museum.

In later March, the Deliuses moved from the Hotel Quisisana in Wiesbaden to the 'Villa Mon Repos' in the Frankfurterstrasse; and on 12 April the composer was able to tell Hertzka: 'At last I am beginning to feel *a little* better.' Alden Brooks visited him around this time, and wrote from Paris on 6 May to Matthew Smith: 'I left him in Wiesbaden in a wheelchair, improved from the condition he had fallen to on leaving Grez but still unable to walk. However, it is all nerves with him and I think he will shortly be able to walk again.' There was also 'a most delightful visit' from Lloyd and Ethel Osbourne, who were to stay in July in the Deliuses' house at Grez. Back in Wiesbaden, after hearing the Requiem in Frankfurt, Jelka wrote to Hertzka on 5 May: '. . . the work really is *quite magnificent*   the enthusiasm & the emotion of the audience was quite touching.' And Delius himself told Hertzka a day later: 'The performance of the Requiem was very good, orchestrally it could have been better still with more rehearsals, but the choir was excellent.' On 15 May the Deliuses moved to Wildbad.

1   Munch visited Delius at Wiesbaden in April, en route to Berlin and Zürich, and while there he made his lithographic portrait, *Delius at Wiesbaden*.

(472)
Jelka Delius to Adine O'Neill

Mølmen Hotel   Adr:
                                                          LESJASKOG   2.7 1922
                                                              Gudbrandsdalen
                                                                      Norway

Dearest Adine,

I got your letter on arriving here, and thank you very heartily for your kind words. It seems to me as if you thought Delius had had a stroke or seizure, but that is not the case. It is rather a physical breakdown, mentally he is as fresh and vivacious as ever, but his legs and arms are so very weak and might, if we had not begun a cure immediately, have been paralysed altogether.

As it is they are decidedly better, and if only we can spend an agreable summer up here and not be continually harassed by these dreadful worries about the Clearing House he would perhaps get stronger and stronger. A stroke comes suddenly but his weakness came on gradually in the course of a month, after he had for some years been more or less weak in his limbs. We have hired a piano for up here and he is to play a little all the time, he plays better than at Wiesbaden now. And I shall try to get him to write a little Dance for Yvonne.

Our finances are of course the great source of anxiety for us both. And I do hope and wish you would do all you can to have his works performed. It is his 60th birthday on the 29th of Jan. and Dr. Simon is writing a short biography with some splendid etchings of Fred which is to be brought out by Piper in Munich very artistically. For that occasion they wish to arrange a Delius concert at Francfort. They have a new conductor there named Scherchen.[1] Could not the Philharmonic also give a Delius-Concert? They might do Seadrift with the Philharm Choir. The Cello Concerto will also be ready by then. The Double Concerto is out now (score and all). North Country Sketches will also be ready at Augener's.

The Arabesque (Baritone Solo and Chorus and Orch.) has never been given in London. And no end of other things. Of course Fred does not know I am writing this, and *must never know*. But something in the way of a boom must be done otherwise, how *shall we live*? What we get from german publishers is practically worthless now. But as all the works are brought out now, re-edited by Universal-Edition who has bought up all Leuckarts works and Augener's are bringing out all the rest and have brought out all the Piano Scores, he would get quite a lot by the Sale if there were some sort of boom. The Osbourne's are going to Grez now. We are quite delighted with our little hut up here – it was a tremendous moment, when we saw it standing quite finished on the hillside, after we had only designed the plan before leaving last year. What honest people they are here. I managed to get Senta through by writing and explaining the whole situation to the Norweg. Minister in Berlin and she turned up in Hamburg and is a splendid help. I feel already quite rested, we are staying in the little hotel till our things for the hut have arrived. Senta helps Fred to dress and to-day even shaved him and he was awfully pleased!!! To-morrow the pianino we hired in Kristiania has to be pulled up the steep hillside by 2 horses – it will be an awful affair and they are first going to take up a big trunk and the Kitchen stove as a sort of rehearsal. There is a lovely big Verandah in front of our hut and the view all round is perfectly exquisite and ever changing – and the absolute stillness up there. But there are english Fishermen coming to the hôtel and they will come up and see us and bring trout, I hope!! Senta is sewing all the towels dusters and sheets, making herself a sack of straw to sleep on; carrying up things etc, and planning all the good things she will cook for Fred. The piano is spending the sunday standing in its case outside the railway station in the landscape in the pouring rain with a canvass over it and an admiring crowd around!!

How strange about Mrs Grainger, but what was the real reason of her killing herself?[2] It must be so frightful for Percy.

How splendid about Norman's music for the M. of Venice. Let us hope it will be a huge success, and I am sure he will enjoy the trip!

Next time you want to come to Germany you shd come to Wildbad in the Black Forest when we are there. It is quite near Freudenstadt and you can take Motor trips to all the old places you are so fond of and take the baths, which have a rejuvenating effect and make one's skin so sleek and elastic. It is a *much* nicer place to be in than that overfull cheating, hateful Wiesbaden. We were so disgusted there and in Wildbad they are all so honest and the hotel zur Post *so good*!

Best love, dear old girl.

Ever aff ly yours
Jelka –

Love to Norman
and a Kiss for Yvonne!

Autograph letter, signed and dated, written on headed notepaper. Envelope addressed: Mrs N. O'Neill/4 Pembroke Villas/Kensington W/London England. Postmark: [obscured] 2 VII 22.

The original is in the Delius Trust Archive.

The Deliuses left Wildbad on 22 June, travelled by way of Karlsruhe and Hamburg, and arrived in Christiania on the 25th. Jelka had felt able to write on 15 June to the O'Neills: 'He is better upon the whole and can now walk about 10 minutes on my arm, sitting down 3 or 4 times in between, he can not dress himself nor do anything really without help . . . But if only he gets a bit better, the doctors think after all this cure the good air and calm up there [at Lesjaskog] will do a great deal for him, so we *must* struggle on.'

1   Hermann Scherchen (1891–1966): German conductor. He had recently become conductor of the Frankfurt Museum Concerts.

2   On 30 April Rose Grainger, mentally disturbed, had committed suicide by jumping from a window in New York.

(473)
Frederick Delius to Norman O'Neill

| Hoifagerli | | Lesjaskog |
| (the name of our hut) | 20.8.22 | Gudbrandsdalen |

Jelka amanuensis

Dear Norman,

Since the end of June we have been up in our hut in the high mountains and altho' the weather has been wet and cold lately our stay is a great success; we love our hut which is beautifully built and in a lovely situation   I am walking about with 2 Sticks now out of doors and with one stick in the rooms, which is quite a great improvement and I hope my legs and arms will continue to get stronger gradually.

Would the Philharmonic like to give the 1st performance of my Cello Concerto with Beatrice Harrison? Perhaps in March? Universal Edition is publishing it and I have just corrected the proof of the full score and piano Score. Why not give the Song of the High Hills again with that lovely Kennedy Scott chorus? And why not "Paris"? It has not been heard for a long time in London. All these belong now to the Universal-Edition Vienna, Karlsplatz 6.

Please tell Adine that I have just written a little prelude for Yvonne for her

Album and will send it to her in a few days. We leave Kristiania for Grez on
Sept. 9th

With love to you both

Aff yours
Frederick Delius

Letter in the hand of Jelka Delius, dated.

The original is in the Delius Trust Archive.

(474)
Jelka Delius to Edvard Munch

Dear friend, We leave here tomorrow, Thursday for Kristiania Victoria Hotel,
where we will be on Friday & will leave Saturday towards midday on the
Condor for Hamburg.[1] Should you come into town, it would please us *so much*
to see you.[2] Of course I have to go to the Consulate etc. but Delius will probably stay in the hotel, please telephone first!

Tak for sidst![3]

Sincerely yours
Jelka Delius

Lesjaskog 5th Sept 1922

Autograph postcard, signed and dated, written in German. Addressed: Edvard
Munch/Villa Ekely/Skoien/pr Kristiania. Postmark: LESJASKOG 6 IX 2.

The original is in the Munch Museum.

In spite of all, it had been a trying time at Lesjaskog, and Jelka wrote to Heseltine on
2 September: 'all these months I have been busy *only* for Fred, to read to him, to help
correcting, correspondence, in fact to keep him from depression etc. in this lonely
place! I am grieved that I had quite given up my piano playing. I have now to stumble
to it again with the greatest difficulty and out of sheer devotion so as to help him, as
he has such difficulty about using his hands. Ah! if only you had been able to come
here! We expect Balfour G. to-night and we leave on the 7th and hope to be in Grez on
the 14th.' In Christiania they were able to meet Grainger again and hear him play; he
was to give 31 performances during the course of a recital tour in Norway during
September and October.

1   After Hamburg, Delius proposed to stop off in Cologne on 12 September to see
Otto Klemperer. 'Do you know dates yet,' he had asked Hertzka on 14 August, 'for

the Cologne perf. of Romeo & Juliet?' He was still asking, on 12 December: '*When* is it in Cologne? I would like to be present at the rehearsals.'

2   As Munch was in Christiania at the time, it is likely that he called on Delius.

3   In Norwegian in the original; literally: *Thanks for the last time.*

(475)

Frederick Delius to Percy Grainger

Domplatz 12
Frankfurt
16.12.22

Fred dictates:

Beloved friend,

I was deeply touched by your letter and that you had gone over to London specially to hear the Song of the High Hills. I think it is one of my works in which I have expressed myself most completely[1] – When you tell me that on hearing it your great sorrow was appeased, then I feel that that is the highest appreciation possible.[2]

Of course I want to give you the full score and have already written to Vienna for it.

I cannot tell you how we are looking forward to your coming to Francfort and being able again intimately to exchange our thoughts, and then to become acquainted with all your later works and especially "*The Warriors*".

As soon as the Song of the H. H. arrives I will forward it on to you.

I am ever your devoted friend

Frederick Delius

Letter in the hand of Jelka Delius, signed Frederick Delius, dated. Envelope addressed: Hrrn Percy Grainger/Joh. Verhulststr. 163/Amsterdam/Holland. Postmark: FRANKFURT 16.12.22.

The original is in the Grainger Museum.

The Deliuses left Grez late in November for Frankfurt, where they were to stay for some months.

1   'In fact it is without doubt one of my best works,' wrote Delius on 12 December to Hertzka, asking for a copy of the score to be sent to Frankfurt so that he could inscribe it to Grainger. The piece had been given by Coates at a Philharmonic Society concert on 7 December.

2   Grainger had been abysmally depressed since the suicide of his mother.

1923

Comfortably settled in Frankfurt, the Deliuses looked forward to forthcoming performances there: a Delius chamber concert on 29 January and a Delius orchestral concert on 1 March. And on 8 January, Grainger came to the city to stay for some time (until early summer in fact). Like other friends, he would come to play to the composer in his home, an unalloyed pleasure for Delius. On that date too Delius wrote to tell his publisher that the Zürich Festival had enquired after *A Village Romeo and Juliet*: how much it would mean to him to see this work, based after all on Keller, performed there! Another letter, of 20 February, told Szántó that *Hassan* was to open at nearby Darmstadt on 15 March (it was in the event soon postponed to June) and that *A Village Romeo* would be given in Cologne before the season was out (a project which never came to fruition). Around the beginning of April, a few days before leaving Frankfurt, Delius met the conductor Hermann Scherchen, who proposed to give *An Arabesque* in Frankfurt and in Switzerland.

The next destination was Bad Oeynhausen, not far from Hannover, and Delius began yet another course of baths. He and Jelka stayed at this particular spa for some two and half months. On 30 May Jelka was able to tell Beatrice Harrison: 'Our beloved Delius is progressing so well now in spite of the atrocious weather here.' During this period though there was a volatile correspondence with Tischer & Jagenberg, who did not seem to be playing fair in the matter of royalty payments. Better financial news came in the person of Basil Dean, who visited Bad Oeynhausen in May with the information that his long-delayed production of *Hassan* was definitely to open in London in September. More incidental music was, however, required before then. The Deliuses left Bad Oeynhausen on 21 June and made their way by easy stages to Lesjaskog once more, arriving on the 29th. Once settled into their Norwegian home the composer tackled *Hassan* again, mainly by dictation to Jelka. Further help arrived however on 21 July in the shape of Percy Grainger, who during his three-week stay at Lesjaskog fully composed a 'General Dance' to be incorporated – anonymously – into Delius's final *Hassan* score. Poor weather led the Deliuses to leave, rather earlier than intended, in mid-August. The 17th found them en route by sea from Christiania to Antwerp and they arrived

back in Grez on the 21st. Delius was deeply depressed about his state of health
– the stay at Lesjaskog had done less to improve it than hoped. However, in
three weeks or so they were on the move again, this time to London to attend
the final rehearsals and opening night of *Hassan*. They were kept extraordinarily busy during their nine days in London and saw one further performance of the play before returning to Grez. The show was evidently going
to be highly successful, and the appearance of Heseltine's biography ('quite
excellent', thought Delius) helped focus public attention in England on Delius
to a degree he could scarcely have experienced before. But again his publishers, he felt, were letting him down. He wrote to Universal a few days after
his return, complaining bitterly about the continual overpricing of his printed
music – people simply could not afford to buy the piano score of *Hassan*,
among other works.

Now the Deliuses bought a car, much enjoying excursions into the surrounding countryside. They began to look for a permanent chauffeur/handy-
man. At the same time Delius began working again, albeit slowly, 'and has
almost finished a violin sonata', Jelka informed Grainger on 14 October.
There were visits, too, from Beecham and Lady Cunard, and we find Philip
Heseltine and his musicologist friend Cecil Gray in Grez at the beginning of
November. Delius was now taking short walks and had made some progress
since the Norwegian trip. Soon the decision was made to take the car and
travel south for the winter, renting Gordon Craig's villa in Rapallo. All this
owed much to Balfour Gardiner's generosity: in November he bought the
house in Grez from the Deliuses, on the understanding that they should live
rent-free there for the rest of their lives. First, though, there was work to complete, and on 29 November Jelka told Grainger – who was back in America –
that she had just finished making fair scores of the new Violin Sonata, of a
Tennyson part song, and of the *Two songs for Children* of 1913, all of which
Delius had now 'greatly overhawled' and finished; she had duly sent them to
London. Grainger had meanwhile sent news that he was to conduct two performances of *The Song of the High Hills* in America in April 1924. Jelka
promised that she and Delius would come over to hear him and would arrive in
time for rehearsals; they would probably sail direct from Italy in the spring.

In London there had been an autumn first performance, with Wood giving
the *Dance Rhapsody* No. 2 on 20 October at the last night of the Proms.

Once more the Deliuses left Grez, this time for the south by easy stages, on
7 December. Their maid Senta left later by train. They were reunited with
Henry and Marie Clews, and stayed almost a week with them at the Château
de la Napoule, before motoring on to arrive at Rapallo around 20 December.
Compared to La Napoule they found it cold and lonely there. Jelka wrote to
Adine O'Neill, hoping that the O'Neills might soon join them for a holiday:
'Fred is rather disappointed after the French Riviera.' Meanwhile, well set on
its long run, *Hassan* was bringing its composer a steady income of £25 a week.

Five Piano Pieces (RT IX/7). Completed.

Hassan (RT I/9). Final version completed.

The Splendour falls on Castle Walls, unaccompanied part song for mixed voices (RT IV/6).

Sonata No. 2 for violin and piano (RT VIII/9). Completed.

Three Preludes for piano (RT IX/8).

(476)
Jelka Delius to Henry and Marie Clews

Domplatz 12
Francfort o/M
23.1.1923

My dear friends,

We were so delighted to receive your wire of New Year-wishes; it followed us here, where we are staying for the wintermonths. –

I have been silent so long. We have had such terrible times and I was too depressed to write about it: Fred has been seriously ill the whole dreadful year of 1922. Now at last he is greatly improving. He grew so weak last January, that he could hardly walk and we rushed off to Wiesbaden and spent the year making cures. He is now in much better general health and can get about in the room alone, but cannot walk more than 200 yards out of doors. For him who is so energetic this is a great bereavement, but it looks as if he would *slowly* and gradually get better and better if only he goes on as well as he is now.

We went to Norway in summer and had let the house in Grez to the Osbourne's and now we are here in quite a medieval house just under the Cathedral for the wintermonths as there are quite a number of Delius performances coming on. Especially a Delius-concert on March 1st and Elroy Flecker's Drama "Hassan" at Darmstadt with Delius' musique de scène.

On the 29th of this month he will be sixty[1] and we are surrounded here by delightful and friendly musicians, poets and also Beckmann, a great german painter:[2] They are giving a chamber-music concert on that day as a surprise at the house of a great friend. Percy Grainger is here and will play some of his things New Songs will be sung, Binding the Poet[3] has translated a Verlaine song most admirably, all this will be heartwarming for him. I believe, that all this genial companionship is excellent for him; because in my mind there is no doubt, that all the harassing cares of the war and the endless after war period (our sequestered money is not all paid back yet!) contributed very much to this breakdown of his.

Now we are greatly worried about this new law the french are introducing about foreigner's holding landed property in France. You have surely read about it, — it is also to act retrospectively and we shall all have to apply for permits to continue owning our property in France. If they then should refuse the permission the place at Grez might be sold "d'office" far too cheap. Please be so angelic and write what you know about it and how you are going to act etc. —

We want to sell the place, but under present circumstances no foreigners would want to buy it and the french would not pay enough. What should we do?

Fred looks on at present events with very pessimistic forebodings. The French have achieved *one* thing certainly: to unite all Germans in a passionate resentment, which has done away with all party feeling.

Dear friends, *how* we should love to see you once more! Have you been in U.S.A. or all the time at La Napoule? Marie, dearest, sit down and write one of your charming letters so that we feel a bit near you again and tell us what Clews is working at? We are *so* interested!

Are we ever going to forget the friendly Rue d'Assas and those lovely discussions and the bombs, the cellar and all?

Fred sends you all his love and messages of good will and friendship

Ever affectionately yours
Jelka Delius

Autograph letter, signed and dated.

The original is in the Delius Trust Archive.

1 Heseltine had not yet made his discovery, through Somerset House, that Delius was, oddly enough, one year older than everyone had thought. Earlier biographical/musical dictionaries all give the date of birth as 29 January 1863.

2 Max Beckmann (1884–1950): German Expressionist painter. Born in Leipzig, he studied at the academy at Weimar before taking a studio in Berlin, where while in his twenties he exhibited at the Cassirer galleries. He settled in Frankfurt in 1915, and his fine lithographic portrait of Delius was executed there in 1922. There is evidence that Beckmann had it in mind to make another portrait of the composer, in a letter written to the artist by the publisher Reinhard Piper on 2 September 1922: 'Simon told me you intended to do another etching of Delius from the life for his paper. Has anything come of this? If not, you could still do it, of course, from the surely very strong mental image you have of him already.' (*Reinhard Piper: Briefwechsel mit Autoren und Künstlern*, ed. Ulrike Buergel-Goodwin and Wolfram Göbel, München/Zürich, Piper, 1979.)

3 Rudolf Binding (1867–1938): poet and novelist who was born in Basel and spent much of his life in Frankfurt.

(477)

Frederick Delius to Sydney Schiff

30.1.1923   Domplatz 12
                                                                   Francfort o/M

Dear Schiff,

I was so very glad to get your letter and so very interested in all you told me. I was so touched by your and Mrs Schiff's kind appreciation of my music and the Song of the High Hills. I am happy that you heard it.

I am afraid all your forebodings about the future of Europe will come true only too quickly: Things are getting worse and worse here every day and it is inconceivable to me how the middle classes and the "Intelligentia" live. As to the lower classes they are entirely demoralized. They are convinced of the uselessness of saving their money and eat and especially drink up everything as fast as they get it. Prices are soaring up. The cheapest meat is Mks 2000 per Lb; Butter 5000 – a loaf 1000, Milk 1500 a liter, but hardly obtainable at all. I fear it can only end in rioting and bolchevism. Since the Ruhr-occupation it has got ever so much worse and there is a fanatical hatred against the French. The passive attitude of England and America seems incredible to anybody living here; for in the coming catastrophe, which is inevitable England will go down with the rest. Englands policy seems extraordinarily short-sighted. Of course our European civilization is at its last gasp, but I believe that the United States of Europe may rise out of the ruins.

Our own life here has been extremely agreable, and we are surrounded by artistic and interesting friends. We give them a little supper every week and they always play to us most beautifully.

Yesterday on my 60th birthday the Simons gave a reception and about 100 people of the Musical Francfort were present and the enclosed programme[1] was performed. It was entirely a surprise for me and most enjoyable. Afterwards the Intimates stayed to supper. The Germans are really very great for "Festlichkeiten" and make a great deal of such events and our rooms are full of flowers. Our servant Senta came in in the early morning with a wonderful self-baked birthday-cake and 60 candles alight.

Percy Grainger is here now   he is a most delightful personnality and quite a genius. I expect great things from him. What a pity you and Mrs Schiff are not here also. I am sure you would enjoy it. On March 1st a concert of my works will be given here:

North Country Sketches
Cello Concerto
Song of the High Hills.

In the beginning of March the Darmstadt theatre (quite close to Francfort) will produce Elroy Flekker's "Hassan" with my music

Let me soon hear from you again and accept both our affectionate greetings to yourself and your dear wife

from your friend
Frederick Delius

P.S. My health is gradually improving, altho' I cannot walk much yet.

Letter in the hand of Jelka Delius, signed by Frederick Delius, dated.

The original is in the British Library (Add. Ms 52,917). It is the third of forty-seven items of correspondence sent by the Deliuses to the Schiffs between 12 December 1921 and 6 May 1932 that are preserved. No envelopes have survived, but postcards are addressed to 18 Cambridge Square, Hyde Park, London. No letters from the Schiffs to the Deliuses have been found.

Sydney Schiff [pseudonym Stephen Hudson] (1869–1944): English novelist. A close personal friend of Marcel Proust, to whom he dedicated *Richard Kurt*, he only started writing seriously around the age of fifty. Most of his novels, which were particularly remarked on for their conciseness, clarity and simplicity, centre around one group of people, with Richard Kurt as the principal figure. They are concentrated studies of human character and motivation. Schiff was also a wealthy art collector and connoisseur.

His wife Violet (née Beddington) came from a musical family and was a younger sister of Ada Leverson, the novelist. Among a range of artistic pursuits she taught singing and translated novels from the French. A perfect partner to Schiff, she helped make their home a place of welcome and encouragement to many young artists and writers.

1   The full programme is given in Carley/Threlfall: *Delius: A Life in Pictures*, p. 78.

(478)
Frederick Delius to Philip Heseltine

26.2.1923

Domplatz 12
Francfort o/M

Fred dictates:

My dear Phil,

Forgive me for not answering your kind letter of congratulations and acknowledging your charming serenade,[1] which I received early in the morning on my birthday to my greatest surprise and pleasure   I like it very much indeed; it is a very delicate composition of a fine harmonist. Composition is your true vocation and I cannot tell you how happy I am that you are now following it and have left the Polemic of the Sackbut behind you.

Percy Grainger and Alexander Lippay[2] played me the Serenade several times from the Score and they all liked it. – Just at present I am in the midst of rehearsals and very busy indeed as the Delius-Concert is to take place on March 1st with the following programme. North Country Sketches – Cello Concerto and Song of the High Hills. Barjansky[3] played me the Concerto at the house yesterday; and he is wonderfully good; a Russian; he played it with great success in Vienna on Jan. 31st. I shall write you again and tell you all about the concert when I have a little time. I had an awful lot of parts to correct, also those of Hassan. The 1st perf. takes place on March 15th at Darmstadt.

Life is extremely agreable here in spite of the Chaos of the Ruhr. – I think Europe is at its last gasp and does not seem to react to anything any more.

Give my kindest regards to your mother and thank her for her kind birthday wishes.

Percy Grainger had 2 orchestral rehearsals of his Warriors, a very strong, vital and rhythmic piece, dedicated to me – very interesting indeed. Lippay conducted – by far Graingers greatest thing. He is indeed a wonderfully gifted musician and a most lovable personality.[4]

Ever affectionately yours
Frederick Delius

Letter in the hand of Jelka Delius, dated.

The original is in the British Library.

1   'I'm writing a Serenade for strings in three movements now,' wrote Heseltine to Colin Taylor on 19 December 1922. It would seem that only the first movement was finally composed: *Serenade for string orchestra*, dedicated 'To Frederick Delius on his sixtieth birthday'. Among other works dedicated to Delius was the piano piece, *Summer Valley*, composed in 1925 by Heseltine's friend, E.J. Moeran. Moeran's *Nocturne* for baritone solo, chorus and orchestra, to words by Robert Nichols and inscribed 'To the Memory of Frederick Delius', was published in 1935.

2   Alexander Lippay was conductor at the Frankfurt Opera. Quite possibly introduced to the Deliuses by Heinrich Simon, he is mentioned only rarely in the Delius letters but was evidently considered a good friend. Before long, he was to leave Germany to conduct in the Philippines.

3   Alexandre Barjansky: Russian cellist. Possessed of the deepest of insights into Delius's music, he is remembered by Eric Fenby as playing it with an unparalleled verve and authority. He was a close friend of d'Annunzio, in whose drawing-room in Paris he often gave recitals. Barjansky was the soloist in the first performance of the Delius Cello Concerto, under Ferdinand Löwe in Vienna on 31 January. 'Barjansky said old Löwe, who conducted it in Vienna, after being rather diffident of "modern

music", said in the second rehearsal: "Ja, wer das nicht sieht, dass das ein Meisterwerk ist, der tut mir leid."' (Jelka Delius to Adine O'Neill, April 1923.)

4   Grainger's stay in Frankfurt (he was living for a while in Holland) came about through Jelka sending him a telegram asking him to rehearse the chorus there for the Delius Concert which was to take place on 1 March. He came on 8 January and took part in the Delius birthday recital given at Heinrich Simon's home on the 29th. His presence in the city was a source of great pleasure to Delius, who after one particular visit by Grainger wrote, on 28 March: 'Do come again soon and play me a lot more Grieg, some of which I do not even know and some more Bach – I got such a thrill over the Bach the other night and Jelka loved it so much too!'

(479)
Jelka Delius to Beatrice Harrison

Francfort o/M
19.3.1923

Dear Beatrice, I send you to-day piano score of the Cello Concerto marked very carefully with Metronome marks. Please copy them into your copy and send me this one back.

Barjansky a russian Cellist, has played the Concerto here in a concert of Delius's[1] works given in honour of Delius's[1] birthday (60th). The Cello Concerto is perfectly lovely and had an enormous success. Hertzka wants you to play it in Vienna next winter; he came over for the Concert. With orchestra the Concerto is too beautiful for words – and the Solo instrument never covered, I have never heard such a poetic combination before. Hertzka said you were going to play it in London in April[2] and several friends have asked me about it, so please let us have the date of the Concert! Who is going to conduct it? I do so wish we could hear you play it!

The Delius Concert has been a great success. It was perfectly lovely and the audience quite spellbound. von Klenau,[3] a Dane, conducted awfully well. They also did "North Country Sketches" and the Song of the High Hills.

Unfortunately none of our friends from abroad could come. They do not give visas, thro' the occupied zone, and that is all round Francfort –

We should love to hear how you all are and what you are doing and planning.

Fred is slowly getting stronger. At last we have a bit of Sunshine! the winter was so wet and nasty. It reminds me of 2 years ago when we went to see you at the Waffrons[4] on good friday. How delightful that was.

With all affectionate messages to you All from us both

Yrs always
Jelka Delius

Autograph letter, signed and dated.

The original is in the collection of Miss Margaret Harrison, which includes a considerable number of letters from the Deliuses to the Harrisons.

1   In each case Jelka crossed out 'my' and substituted 'Delius's'.

2   Beatrice was to play the concerto in London, with Eugene Goossens conducting, on 3 July; this was its British première.

3   Paul von Klenau (1883–1946): Danish composer and conductor, and brother-in-law of Heinrich Simon. He conducted at Stuttgart 1908–14, after which he devoted considerably more of his time to composition in Copenhagen. Throughout his life he remained a champion of Delius's music.

4   'The Waffrons', at Thames Ditton, near Surbiton, Surrey, was for a time the home of the Harrisons.

(480)
Jelka Delius to Adine O'Neill

Domplatz 12
Frankfurt a/M
30.3.1923

Dearest Adine, I posted seven little piano pieces to you yesterday. Fred wants me to tell you that he composed them each one, so as to make an easy piece for Yvonne, but they always grew too difficult, but the seventh one, we think is quite easy; should anything be too wide stretched for her hands it can be arranged by giving it to the other hand, I think.

Fred is rather diffident about the pieces and begs you to see if you think *all* of them should be published, or some left back. He leaves it to you to see. They are my début as an amanuensis – as he can not write and has to dictate it all to me and I find it pretty difficult. He has also composed a Violin Sonata, which is nearly finished and an a capella chorus.[1] We have not attempted anything for orchestra yet.

We are soon (in a week) going to leave Francfort for Oeynhausen where Fred is to make a cure of 7–8 weeks and from there straight to Norway. I am sorry the winter here is ended, we had such a delightful time. Percy Grainger is with us a lot and a delightful friend. Also several other young musicians and composers from here were awfully nice and spent many evenings here – and on the 1st of March they gave a Delius Concert. North Country Sketches, Cello Concerto and Song of the High Hills. Klenau conducted and Percy had prepared the Chorus. It was beautiful and very stimmungsvoll, altho the Symphonic Orch here is 2^d or even 3^d rate. The Public was most enthusiastic right to the end and made great ovations. I wish the Philharmonic would do North Country Sketches   Augeners   next season. All musicians think it is one of Fred's finest works – and it really has not been heard in London; Beecham did it once, but with hardly any rehearsals and it was inadequate entirely. It is a most lovely work. Then there is also the Cello Concerto which he composed spring 1921 in London, a most lovable piece delightfully written for the Cello, impulsive and beautiful sounding. Barjansky played it, a young Russian, and really most beautifully. Beatrice Harrison I am sure, knows it to perfection   she would love to play it in London. They said she was going to play it in London in April; but I have written to ask her where, and have had no answer. If she played it now in London the Phil. could do it with Barjansky, who is sure to have a huge success. He looks extraordinary when he plays, so extatic, with a delicate, sensitive face and hair like an italian Primitive – People would love him. He stays at Vienna and Universal-Edition who has published the Concerto runs him. He would not be expensive either.

We have not heard at all how the Piano-Concerto fared with Cath. Goodson at the Phil?[2] And Seadrift with Kennedy Scott? How I wish we could have been there!

Fred is so grateful to Norman for his advice about "Reandean"   he acted accordingly and the matter is still in discussion.[3]

We were awfully sorry Balfour did not come. But the Ruhr occupation makes travelling awfully difficult. I do not know what to do either; I have to go from Oeynhausen to Grez and I asked Cook's in Paris for the best route Paris-Hanover and he advised to go by Strassburg thro' Bavaria and Berlin. Oeynhausen is quite near Hanover, and on the direct line Cologne-Berlin so, *what* a round-about. It really disgusts one to see them bringing on war conditions again. Francfort is all cut off from West, south and North – only the route to Berlin and the east and south-east open. In Mainż there is neither phone, telegraph or train-communication with Francfort, neither in Wiesbaden   To go to Paris from here one has to go to Mainz on a motor-lorry and then take the train run by the french where there are daily big accidents, as the Germans refuse to work the railways and the signals etc. are all upset and the French do not understand them.

I read this to Fred and he thinks Beatrice Harrison ought to play it if the Philharm. gives the Concerto.

I must rush this to the post. I hope you have a lovely easter holiday!

Affly Jelka

Here it is heavenly weather since 2 weeks – no fires, quite warm.

Autograph letter, signed and dated. Envelope addressed: Mrs Norman O'Ne[ill]/4 Pembroke Villas/Kensington W/London/England. Postmark: FRANKFURT 31 3. 23.

The original is in the Delius Trust Archive.

1   The sonata was the 2nd, and the chorus: *The Splendour falls on Castle Walls.*

2   Katharine Goodson, considered one of the finest English pianists of her time, performed the Delius concerto a number of times. 'We were delighted to hear the Piano Concerto was so beautifully played by C. Goodson!' wrote Jelka to Adine O'Neill in April.

3   'Please tell Norman the contract with Reandean [Basil Dean's company] is concluded,' wrote Jelka in April, 'and *almost* entirely as he suggested.'

(481)
Frederick Delius to Henry Clews

near Hannover

Bad Oeynhausen
Hotel Königshof
10.4.1923

Tears, idle tears, I know not what they mean
Tears from the depth of some divine despair
Rise from the heart and rush to the eyes
On looking o'er the happy autumn fields
And thinking of the days that are no more.
How sad, how strange, the days that are no more.

I have no Tennyson with me and I quote from memory, so this may not be quite correct, but it is the emotional and artistic way of looking back on the past. We luckily forget all the unpleasantness, the vileness etc etc that was mixed up in it all and therefore perhaps we become unfair to the present and exaggerate. It seems to me in your preface to your play[1] you are also unfair to the present. You speak of the chivalry of the times of old and forget the ceintures de chasteté which the knights locked on to their spouses and Lady-loves before leaving for the Crusades. You forget the horrible injustice and tyranny of the high lords, the dungeons, the tortures and the oubliettes. I prefer to be press-ridden, than priest-ridden with their horrible tyranny and the terrors of the Inquisition. The press has never bothered me and I ignore it. But you could not ignore the church and their priests in those days. To a great extent I agree with you in what you say of industry and its result. I cannot give a final judgement yet on the Russian revolution and Lenin and Trotzky, having heard too many conflicting opinions from both sides. It seems to me that Lenin is the only big man that the war has produced and as far as the terrors, cruelties and injustices of the Bolschevik régime go, they seem to be very much the same sort of thing as under the Zar's régime; they have only got into other hands.

After reading the play somehow or other I could not help regretting you had published the foreword in front of it. It hardly wants a foreword. Shaw's forewords are all better than his plays, whilst your play is so awfully good that it requires no preface.

I think your satirical play is certainly *the best one* that has been produced in our time and one of the most scathing. I was going to say *the best*, that has been produced since Molière, but I am not sufficiently erudite to go so far back. But Jelka and I are both quite enthusiastic and delighted. Jelka would love to translate it into German. I am sure it would be played everywhere here.

But concerning the past, dear Clews, let me remind you that not only you, but I would have been long ago "supprimé" under the old régime, or languishing in dungeons, so let us both be thankful to the present régime, which has allowed us to practise our art in peace and protest as much as we like.

I am still pretty weak on the legs and am taking the baths at Oeynhausen near Hanover.[2] After 6 or 7 weeks here we go to Norway for the summer to our little Châlet in the mountains; then from the end of August till middle of October we intend to be in Grez, and then we intend spending the winter in the Italian Riviera or Sicily and shall very likely knock at your door in the end of October.

With love to you both
I remain

Your affectionate
friend
Frederick Delius

Best love to you both from Jelka

Letter in the hand of Jelka Delius, dated.

The original is in the Delius Trust Archive.

1   Delius is discussing in this letter Clews's extraordinary and highly eccentric satire on the art establishment, *Mumbo Jumbo*, just published by Grant Richards. The preface is almost as long as the drama.

2   The Deliuses had just moved to the spa town of Bad Oeynhausen. 'I at last have quite a rest,' wrote Jelka to Adine O'Neill shortly after their arrival there. 'I only realize now how much I needed it. Fred had pains all the time in Francfort the last weeks and I think it came from the swed. Massage. Here he has no massage, and no continuous guests and has become much more tranquil and the pains have stopped. I am disgusted with the stupidity of almost all doctors . . . Fred is too nervous to walk alone if people are about, but out of doors he walks quite 5 minutes at a time without a stick, only he always looks careful and anxious. He will not use his hands at all and of course it makes them stiffer and stiffer and I must force him to make little exercises.'

(482)
Frederick Delius to Tischer & Jagenberg

Hotel Rose[1]
Bad Oeynhausen
14.6.1923

To Dr Gerhard Tischer
Verlag   Cologne

Dear Sir,

In reply to your letter of 6.6.23 I inform you of the following:

I am returning the cheque which you sent to me for Mk 8372 in respect of the annual account for 1922 and indeed under the strongest protest.[2]

I know that in the present chaotic state of Germany there still exists no direct legislation for the protection of authors.

It seems to me all the more regrettable that a self-respecting German publishing firm does not acknowledge its obvious obligation to send appropriate compensation to the composer whose work it has exploited. On 6.6.1923 Mk 8372 was worth about 6 pence in English currency. On the same date you explain to me that for a single copy sold in England my 50% net profit comes to 4 pence. According to your statement 2 scores of the small orchestral pieces, 13 piano arrangements, 1 set of orchestral parts   9 "Five Songs" were sold abroad in 1922. Not counting sales in Denmark[3]

That you think it enough to send me 6 pence for this year is quite incomprehensible to me! I will carefully preserve the relative documents among my papers for the edification of Posterity, also I will not fail to publish the matter shortly in a German musical paper, in order to give something of a surprise to our contemporaries.[4]

Furthermore the judicial decisions in most analogous cases have *not* been arrived at according to the letter of an antiquated law but in accordance with a moral sense of justice, so that I would have nothing to fear from a court case. I have already won one case against Harmonie Verlag before the war, although Harmonie had not demonstrably offended against the Law and our contract, on the grounds that their business methods in my case were immoral and unethical.

As concerns the accounts for 1919, 1920 & 1921, I am now awaiting the immediate remittance of Mk 182,220, the amount still due to me under our agreement. At the same time I want a clear assent in writing to my proposals for settlement. If you should delay any longer, you will force me to raise my demands according to the rate of exchange even up to 4 times as much.

I note from your letter that you agree to my separate proposals concerning the *old songs*; with the exception of the clause concerning the bill for expenses. These expenses according to my expert adviser should not exceed 5% (five per cent) of the gross receipts. If I am to have anything to do with a new edition, I should require an exact account as to costs and the number of copies

Lebenstanz   You acquired this work by purchase before the war for 5000 German Goldmarks. So apart from the purchase price I get nothing from you, while during my lifetime and for *thirty years after my* death you are able to exploit this work gratis and for your sole benefit. Your reasoning by which you will not pay me in full the last instalment of 1000 Goldmarks still due after the 40th performance lacks therefore all logic and is quite untenable.

In the case of both of the small orchestral pieces, piano arrangements and songs, for which I remain entitled to a royalty on sales, it is different and they can and should be sold at the peacetime price, multiplied by the official index figure of the music firm.

On reflection you must surely agree that the case is quite different here from that of a work obtained for one outright payment, like "Lebenstanz". That the last instalment is only to be paid after the 40th performance was purely a concession to you, protecting you against any risk, for if an orchestral work is performed 40 times, its future is assured.

With regard to your remarks about the 1922 account I would point out that I did not mean orchestral sales but *all* sales, and that your account of 6.6. does not agree with the one previously presented, even in the number of copies. What special pleasure you wished to give me by sending me an annual account which yields me a grand total of 6 pence, certain expenses apart, is not clear to me. Also the 6 pence have today already gone down to 3 pence!!

I will forgo my claim to the immediate payment of the smaller sums in foreign currency if settled quarterly and not converted into Marks, which I strictly veto and which you must prevent. Larger sums in foreign currency are to be paid to me immediately in accordance with your own proposals.

As a permanent address I give you

Westminster Bank

106 Finchley Road

London N.W.3, with the proviso that if I am in Germany when the time for payment is due I will let you know my address there in order that you may send it on.

Yours faithfully
Frederick Delius

P.S. I have received with thanks the payment of 18 Danish Kroner for 1923.

F.D.

I am here until the 21st inst. after which my address is:
Lesjaskog
Gudbrandsdalen
Norway,

where I request you to send the account for the 1st 6 months of 1923. Enclosed cheque for 8372 Mk.

F.D.

Letter in the hand of Jelka Delius, dated, written in German.

The original is in the Delius Trust Archive.

1   Jelka wrote on 29 April and explained the recent change of hotel to Grainger: 'we have left the Koenigshof. It was like this: the food there was the beastly meaty fatty, tasteless, ever-alike-tasting german hotel food and Fred quite lost his appetite. Meanwhile we had discovered that Professor Dr. Frenkel, of whom we had heard since years as *the* great authority in these illnesses is here in Oeynhausen and of course I went to see him and got him to treat Fred. There are fearful feuds, tyrannies, hatreds and intrigues among the many doctors and hotels here, and the patients are the prey they are fighting for.

Frenkel is on such bad terms with the proprietor of the Königshof that they would not let him enter the place. So of course we had to find another hotel . . . . . Frenkel is an intelligent little hunchback, very quaint and mostly goes about in a bathchair himself . . . There was atrocious music in the Königshof. Fred always fled from it. He heard some people saying as he hurriedly left: Ach ja, die Engländer sind doch so unmusikalisch!!'

2   Delius's correspondence with Tischer had gradually become embittered as 1923 wore on. An uneasy compromise was finally reached in July; it nonetheless still left Delius highly dissatisfied with his dealings with the company.

3   This sentence was added at the foot of the page in a second hand.

4   No record has been found of any such publication by Delius.

(483)
Jelka Delius to Marie Clews

Hoifagerli
Lesjaskog
Gudbrandsdalen
Norway

4.8.1923

Dearest Marie,

Please forgive my not writing sooner. I *did* get your first letter, sent on to me here, and the second one late last night.

I had to help Fred composing[1] as he can not write the small notes and dictates them all to me and then I had to copy the whole orchestra score here: 52

big pages. It was additions to the Drama "Hassan" and they were waiting impatiently for them in London, so that I had to sit at it all day long when I was not busy with Fred. So I postponed all letters till this was done last night; it is, thank God, going off to London to-day. We only arrived here on the 29th of June and your dear friendly letter welcomed us here.

We did not know at all about your husband's father's death and I can fully feel with you, what a sad and difficult thing it all was for you both – those great and sad Landmarks in one's existence!

All you said in your letter about Fred and Clews's friendship for him, and the great place it has taken in his heart, filled us with that great affection and friendship, which we both always have for you both splendid, dear people. And we really must meet and see you this autumn.

Fred's health is *so so* delicate, and after a fortnight's lovely summer weather it has been chilly, cloudy, rainy and changeable and most trying; so much so, that we think of leaving quite soon and going back to Grez, before we go to London.

Fred had begun to walk so well at Oeynhausen, but in this damp cold weather and without any good flat road, he cannot keep it up. The dreadful thing is that our maid, without whom we cannot travel has sent her passport to Germany to the Besetzte Gebiet[2], where evidently the French have got hold of it, and it does not come back; and I am again writing in vain to all consulates to get her permission to travel with us; How terribly difficult all these things are! We have the visit of Percy Grainger, who is such a dear and delightful friend, and so devoted to Fred. Just fancy, what he did: Fred was *longing* to go up the mountain side and up a high mountain back of our hut, because there is a heavenly view on the High Snow-mountains and a great solitude with no human trace up there. So Percy arranged a chair and two poles thro it and straps and ropes for us all three, Percy in front, Senta and I at the back,[3] all strapped in like horses and so we carried Fred up to the top and down again. With wraps and overcoat, our lunch etc. to carry it was an awfully heavy job. But we could not get any Norwegians to do it. It took us $7\frac{1}{2}$ hours, as we had to rest so often and we had to go over stones and rocks, up the steep mountain, thro' snowfields, rainclouds, bogs, becks – a tremendous job. I cannot boast for myself as Percy and Senta had the heaviest carrying; but being quite out of training I found it all I could do. But we came home in triumph at 9 p.m. having been watched from below with telescopes and marvelled at by the inhabitants, Fred very cold and tired, but all the better for the beloved mountain-air and sight and we all rather stiff but alright next day.[4]

I am delighted that Mancha wants me to translate the book[5] and I shall start it straight away as soon as I have got my correspondence in order and if I feel I cannot do it, I shall let you know quite soon. Of course, from the practical side, I am afraid we have very little to expect just now, owing to the terrible ruin of german money. But I will write to some competent friends in Germany and hear which is the best way of setting about the publication.

We have quite made up our minds to spend the winter somewhere, where it is warm. We think of first going to the Riviera, and should we not find anything suitable there, go further south. Maybe you know of nice places, where we could winter? I suppose Italy is cheaper than France? We should so love to be within reach of you!

Fred sends you Both all his love, and all I have said is from him too. I could write volumes more, but want this not to miss to-days post, so that you forgive me.

Ever affectionately yours
Jelka Delius

P.S. I want to translate first the Drama and as soon as that is done, and I am well in my subject, I shall translate the Preface, which is, of course more difficult; but I feel as if I could do it, and give it the right flavour in German. How I do hope I shall succeed!

Autograph letter, signed and dated.

The original is in the Delius Trust Archive.

1   Ola Mølmen of Lesjaskog remembered in 1968: 'He still had some movability in his fingers and could sit in his wheelchair and clunk a little at the piano while his wife wrote notes for him as he went along.'

2   German: *Occupied Territory*.

3   Ola Mølmen remembers otherwise: 'Together with lector Ola Nordsletten from Lesjaverk and the maid Senta, [Grainger] carried Delius ... all the way up to Liahovda'. The climb was from 750 metres above sea level to 1150 metres.

4   From 21 July Grainger spent nearly three weeks with the Deliuses, helping in particular by composing a short dance movement required urgently by Basil Dean to supplement the *Hassan* music. Jelka wrote to him from the ship taking her and Delius back from Christiania to Antwerp, telling him about the homegoing descent from the cottage at Lesjaskog: 'Øverli and Senta carried Fred down, Øverli could hardly manage to do it, and Senta had to take the front and he the lighter back!!! So without your glorious energy and devotion Fred would never have been taken to the top ... How we missed you at Hoifagerli! How delightful it was to have you – We do belong together all three, and Fred loves you and your music so intensely, as nobody else's.'

5   Jelka undertook to translate *Mumbo Jumbo* into German. She was to spend a great deal of time and trouble on the work, but all her efforts to get it published failed. 'Mancha' was Henry Clews's pet name: he had long seen himself as a modern equivalent of Don Quixote, tilting against society's established attitudes.

(484)

Frederick Delius to Universal Edition

Grez sur Loing
S. et M.
28.9.1923

Dear Herr Direktor,

We have just returned from London, where we attended the final rehearsals[1] & the première of "Hassan". The whole thing was splendidly staged & the press marvellously favourable. The music is *very* good, orchestra as well as choruses, & the various new interludes & the newly added ballet[2] were magnificently done. It was the event of the season & we may hope that the drama, which is interesting & in every respect artistically staged, will have a reasonably long run, something which will greatly help towards making the Delius music accessible to a wider public.

The piano score is being sold in the theatre, but it is a pity of course that it is at present incomplete. Heseltine will now arrange the additional pieces for piano immediately & also make a number of passages which are technically difficult more easily playable. It is now in your & our interest to publish the piano score in this form as quickly as you possibly can.

Today I received a letter from Pathé frères Pathéphone asking for permission to bring out a selection from the Hassan music on the gramophone. What am I to answer on this matter? What are the usual conditions?

Furthermore I heard in London that Hassan is to be produced in Swedish in Stockholm this coming winter, the drama has been translated by a Swedish Prince.[3] I would therefore ask you to get favourable terms for my music for this performance, which is surely possible after this success. For your information let me tell you that I get £25 per week in London & £12.10–0 per week in the provincial towns.

Moreover I would not give the music free of charge again in Germany; & should also have more of a guarantee that the drama be staged complete & really well, which *was not the case* in Darmstadt. The band was very mediocre & the whole of the last scene, the best of them all, was omitted.

The general complaint in London was that it is impossible to get hold of my music. My colleagues there thought it incredible that *you*, just like all the others, do not have this music on sale in London's music shops.

Curwen does nothing for it. The Sackbut, under the management of Miss Ursula Greville, has sunk to such a low level that nobody reads it any more. Curwen has no shop. At Chester's, Augener's & Goodwin & Tabb's people ask in vain for it.

In view of this new interest, now would really be the time for a good firm, like Chester, or Goodwin & Tabb, to have this music permanently in stock &

displayed for sale. I am talking of *all* my published works. Many people have wanted to buy the Cello Concerto for performance in its piano arrangement, but when it comes to getting it for when they need it, at Curwen's they try in vain. If it is all so difficult, people simply give up.

Please send to:

Mr Karl D. Kinsey
Manager
Chicago Musical College
624 S. Michigan Ave
Chicago, Ill. U.S.A.

| (free Copies)[4] | Song of the High Hills ———— Appalachia ————————— Requiem ————————— | } Full score & piano score |
| | Messe des Lebens ———————— | Piano score |

Percy Grainger has warmly recommended these works for the Evanston Musical Festival to be held in the spring. There will probably be a whole Delius evening, which I may possibly attend & the matter is of the greatest importance for me. At the same time send a list of all my orchestral works published by your firm.

I enclose some reviews.

Sincerely yours
Frederick Delius

Many of the music reviews have not yet come out.

———————————

Letter in the hand of Jelka Delius, dated, written in German.

The original is in the Universal Edition archives.

The Deliuses returned to Grez from Norway on 21 August. They travelled to London around the middle of September so as to attend the final rehearsals of *Hassan* at His Majesty's Theatre. Dean's production opened on 20 September with a star-studded cast, the orchestra being conducted on the opening night by Eugene Goossens and subsequently by Percy Fletcher. An instant and fashionable success, it was to have one of the longest runs in the history of the West End theatre, and it spawned innumerable sideshows: 'I helped Sybil Thorndike (a decent creature) to judge the costumes at the Hassan Ball,' wrote Arnold Bennett, who had attended the première, to Frank Swinnerton the following February.

1 'Never shall I forget that last dress rehearsal; Delius, carefully tended by his wife, sitting wrapped up in the stalls, hearing the music played for the first time by a special orchestra conducted by Eugene Goossens, with brother Leon playing the oboe and Sidonie the harp; and many other instrumentalists of the foremost rank in the orchestra. So well I remember Delius' high-pitched expostulations when, because we

were a little slow in changing the scenery, Eugene, obeying the instinct of an experienced theatre conductor, filled in the vacant time by repeating one of the interludes. Here and there in the shrouded theatre little knots of distinguished people sat about watching the proceedings. Hellé Flecker, the poet's widow, was with J. M. Barrie in the stalls; other authors and musicians were in the dress circle. Galsworthy looked in for a short while, I remember, although he was cross with me at the time, because he did not approve of the selection of Delius to compose the music. There was about the theatre a sense of great occasion.' (Basil Dean: 'Memories of "Hassan"', *Radio Times*, 31 October 1952.)

2   Choreographed by Fokine.

3   Prince Wilhelm's translation was published by Norstedt, Stockholm, in 1923. The Swedish Crown Prince Gustav Adolf was present at the London first night, together with his future queen, Lady Louise Mountbatten.

4   In English in the original.

(485)
Frederick Delius to Percy Grainger

Grez sur Loing
Seine et Marne
Fred dictates: 29 Sept. 1923

Dear Percy,

Your welcome letter with all the good news I received just before leaving for London for the production of Hassan; so I could not reply to you before now.

If Mr Karl Kinsey would give some of my works at the Evanstone Festival it would be splendid. Of course I should prefer those works to be given there, that have never been done in America   "Song of the High Hills" "North Country Sketches" "Eventyr" and of course Seadrift and Appalachia and Mass of Life above all. I have already ordered all those of Universal and complete catalogue to be sent to Mr Kinsey and shall also have North C. Sk.   Eventyr and the Concertos sent from Augener's. I am writing to Kinsey by this same Mail.[1]

We were both so awfully glad that your affairs are so prosperous in America and that you feel happy in your old home. You have no idea how we missed you after you left.

We were 9 days in London and attended 2 rehearsals and 2 performances. The whole show is really magnificent, wonderful scenery, lighting and costumes and I understand now that there really was too little music before I had written the additions, especially for the last 2 scenes, where music goes on almost all the time. The leaving of the Caravan, the gradual disappearing made a wonderful effect and was beautifully realized by the chorusses on and behind the scene. In fact all chorusses were excellent. *Our* ballet piece was a *great success* and brought just a vigorous contrast to the rest. The serenade sounded *very well* pizzicato and a muted violin playing the melody. It is then sung later on with the tenor voice and orchestra. I have discarded the Piano altogether. Afterwards it comes once more as an entr'acte for full orchestra – also very good. But of course a real artistic atmosphere is unobtainable as the public chats, drinks tea, eats chocolates as soon as the curtain drops and the actors insist on coming out after every scene, instead of only after the big acts. The piece, tho', seems to have been a very great success and the advance-booking has beaten all records of London theatres.[2]

We spent one evening with Balfour, altho' there was no question of his getting a place at the theatre for weeks to come.

We are now back in our quiet home in Grez; lovely summer-weather still and we are sitting in the boat on the shady river writing this letter.

If I feel strong enough I shall of course come to the Festival at Evanston, but I cannot quite decide that now.

We have just received the beautiful book about your dear mother,[3] and need not tell you how we cherish it and how it brings her dear presence freshly to our memory. With love from us both

Your ever affectionate friend
Frederick Delius

P.S. In the ballet you brought in that rhythmical vigour which contrasted so well with the first part. I wish you could have heard it. It really came off splendidly.

Letter in the hand of Jelka Delius, dated. Envelope addressed: Percy Grainger Esq/ 7 Cromwell Place/White plains/U.S.A. Postmark: GREZ 29 -9 23.

The original is in the Grainger Museum.

1 'It appears,' wrote Jelka to Grainger on 29 November, 'that U.Ed. sent the music too late for this year's programmes, so Mr Kinsey wrote to Fred. What a pity! Let us hope he will put some on the programmes for next year!'

2 In fact Jelka had already written a brief preliminary report to Grainger, from Cox's Hotel, Jermyn Street, on 23 September: 'Hassan was brought out truly beautifully. Orch and Chorusses *very good* excellently trained, all the additions so lovely the Ballet [Grainger's contribution being the 'General Dance'] most splendid sounding gorgeous.

Most artistic scenery and light. Up to now it seems a huge success . . . I am sure it will do Fred's fame a lot of good. We have been besieged by reporters; and Fred bore up very valiantly during the long rehearsals . . . The only thing that marrs the Hassan performance is the chatter of the audience during the tender and delicately beautiful interludes, when the curtain is down and the actors appear before the curtain and are applauded – which is truly shameful O, England!'

3   *Photos of Rose Grainger and of 3 short accounts of her life by herself, in her own hand-writing reproduced for her kin and friends by her adoring son Percy Grainger – also table of dates, & summary of her cultural tastes.* John Bird (p. 182) relates how Grainger had several thousand copies of this 'touching and gruesome' production made and shipped to White Plains. It ended with a photograph of his mother in her coffin. He had supervised the production of the book while in Frankfurt, and gave away large numbers of copies to his friends.

(486)
Frederick Delius to Philip Heseltine

Italia   Villa Raggio[1]
21.12.1923   San Ambrogio
                                                                         Rapallo

Dear Phil, We just arrived here at this lovely place after a very long and tiring but really beautiful trip in the car.[2] We were very well driven by our young french chauffeur, but the days are so short it took us 8 days to get to Rapallo. We stayed nearly a week at La Napoule with the Clews' our american friends. It was perfectly lovely, right on the sea in an old fortress chateau, the sea beating against the foundations all around. The weather was warm like in May and the snow mountains high above the blue mountains too beautiful in the bay of Cannes.

I received the contract from Hawkes but should very much like to know something about this firm before signing. Are they a new firm? A big firm? Honest? Have they a good reputation? You know how dreadfully I have been cheated already. What, for instance, would happen, if this firm went bankrupt? One has no control over publishers, so one must try to get hold of really honest ones.

I have immediately written again to Hertzka to send you the £10 at once and hope you will receive it.

I told the Copyright Society to forbid any cuts to be made in my records[3] but I am very grateful to you for telling me about the Dance Rhapsody. I am writing to them again about it.

From the Oxford Press I have not heard yet, neither have I received a contract or the money.[4]

We have only just arrived and are very busy starting our house-keeping and getting eatables. We do not know Italian so it is quite a job to get going[5]

We both wish you a very happy Xmas and New year.
Kindest regards to your mother if you spend Xmas with her

Ever aff^{ly}
Frederick Delius

Letter in the hand of Jelka Delius, dated.

The original is in the British Library.

1   The Deliuses were renting the house of the theatre designer, Edward Gordon
Craig (1872–1966).

2   Jelka wrote from Grez on 27 October to Marie Clews: 'We have decided to always
keep Grez as headquarters and have bought a little Motorcar which *does* make living
here delightful . . . Delius loves it . . . Fred is rather better now, after being a bit less
well in and after Norway . . . We had a short visit from Beecham and Lady Cunard,
who came in a motor car and spent an hour on the river with us.' Heseltine and Cecil
Gray were other visitors around this time.

3   'The music for Hassan is being recorded by the Gramophone Co and Fr. has
become a member for the Copyright protect. Soc.,' Jelka informed Grainger on 14
October.

4   On 3 March 1925 Jelka was to tell Heseltine: 'The Oxford U.P. wrote again about
the small orch. piece and I am keeping it in mind; but Fred cannot look it throu' now
on account of his eyes; but I do hope.'

5   The first week or two had proved trying: 'It has been so dreadfully cold here, and
in the house also so icy that we felt we were cast out of Paradise after leaving you where
we were so happy,' they wrote to the Clews at Christmas. There were sixty steps up to
the house, which meant that Delius had to be carried each time. The garden was 'a
vertical precipice', and although there were comfortable armchairs and sofas and the
Craigs had left them all their books, there was little else: 'They must be very poor.'
New Year's Eve was spent in the company of Max Beerbohm and his wife.

1924

By the middle of January Delius had hired a piano and before long was at work on an (unspecified) orchestral score, 'a very good sign', as Jelka reported in mid-February. Life was quiet, even lonely, but there were occasional visits from Balfour Gardiner and Arnold Bax, and from the Deliuses' near neighbours at Rapallo, Max Beerbohm and his wife. Excursions were restricted as the Deliuses did not enjoy the noise and traffic of the coast road, 'so we mostly sit on our terrace.' At the end of February a specialist from Germany came to stay with them for a week, as a consequence of which it was determined that Delius should undergo a cure at Cassel in the spring. So the American trip in April was off – Delius was not strong enough to undertake it. The orchestral work still preoccupied Delius in early March, but was put aside when the time came to leave Rapallo on the 16th. Later the following day the Deliuses arrived back at La Napoule, taking a villa close by the Château – where they spent much of their time in the company of the Clews – for the next five weeks. Delius declined to throw himself wholeheartedly into the social life of the Château – an invitation from Henry Clews to meet the Vendômes brought the response that the composer no more wished to meet them than he wished to meet Lenin – but it seems that he did meet another intimate of Clews, André Maurois. Jelka meanwhile was still busily engaged on making a German translation of her host's play. The end of April saw the Deliuses back in Grez. It seems they were in Cassel by the middle of May. Unhappy with the poor conditions at the sanatorium itself, they moved after ten days to a hotel nearby. Once again, Delius's condition gave Jelka cause for some anxiety, but from the beginning of June he began to improve as a consequence of the cure. The news that Kennedy Scott's choir was to sing the *Mass of Life* in London in the forthcoming season brought with it the composer's determination to attend the performance. A rare break for Jelka came at the end of June when she went 'to see some very great [German] friends of mine for a few days'. Furthermore they expected a visit soon from Delius's sister Clare.

The Deliuses were back in Grez on 12 August. The composer, happy to be home again, felt very much better and was delighted with the results of the cure. His eyesight was better than it had been for some years. Evlyn Howard-

Jones and his wife came to visit in September. Delius had just finished his *Five Piano Pieces* and Howard-Jones was anxious to have the first performance, hoping to give it as part of a planned recital of Delius's chamber music in the Wigmore Hall on 8 November. Before this, Howard-Jones was to première the second Violin Sonata in London with Albert Sammons on 7 October.

Clare Delius Black, who had been staying in Grez, left on 6 October. Her hosts were relieved – likeable she may have been, but she was distinctly unpractical and no help about the house at all. Compounded with this were servant problems, something that was to be a distinct feature of the last decade in Grez. Nonetheless it is clear that Delius was busily at work on composition during much of October. There was heartening news, too, of forthcoming performances: the *Mass* was down for Wiesbaden, Berlin, Vienna, Prague and London, *Sea Drift* and *Songs of Sunset* for Germany, and *The Song of the High Hills* for Leeds in a year's time. And *A Village Romeo and Juliet* was officially (if again abortively) announced for Cologne. *Hassan*, oddly, had been a complete and unexpected failure in New York. The decision was taken to resume the beneficial cure in Cassel, rather than to spend another winter on the Mediterranean, and around the middle of November the Deliuses were there once more. Jelka was glad to see her husband under the renewed care of Dr Heermann, as Delius had recently begun to have some trouble with his left eye. Nonetheless she was cautiously optimistic when writing to the Clews on 20 December, and enclosed a short note written by Delius himself. This is Delius's last-known letter in his own hand. After Christmas he gradually lost his appetite and began to grow weak.

A Late Lark, for tenor and orchestra (W. E. Henley) (RT III/6). Begun.

Fantastic Dance for orchestra (RT VI/28). Sketched?

Sonata No. 3 for violin and piano (RT VIII/10). Sketches for second and third movements.

(487)
Jelka Delius to H. Balfour Gardiner

[Rapallo, 14 January 1924]

Delighted to see you & Bax here beginning of Feb. The weather is heavenly now and we are sitting in the sun on our verandah. We are quite comfortable and have at last found a piano   an old, old little Broadwood – but Fred needed one to work with. Best love from us both   Aff Jelka.

Senta climbed an enormous mountain yesterday and came back with torn boots and very happy.

Autograph picture postcard: *Rapallo – Panorama de la levante*, signed and undated. Addressed: H. Balfour Gardiner / Esq / Ashampstead Green / Pangbourne / Berks / Inghilterra. Postmark: RAPALLO 14.1.24. Jelka has indicated 'Savoia', 'Hof Europa' and 'our house' on the photograph.

The original is in the collection of John Eliot Gardiner.

(488)
Frederick Delius to Percy Grainger

Villa Raggio
San Ambrogio
Italy   Rapallo
23ᵈ· Jan. 1924

Fr. dictates

Dear Percy,

We are sitting in the Sunshine on the terrace of our Villa overlooking the beautiful bay of Rapallo and talking of you; and we were wondering, whether *ever* any other Composer had met with a Colleague and friend like you, so devoted and interested in his friend's work and understanding it thro' his own genius. Your résumé of The Song of the High Hills is perfectly splendid for the Programme-book – and I have nothing to alter or add. It seems to me it might be advisable to open the concert with a short orchestral piece to get the audience settled down, or to begin with the North-Country Sketches and play the Song of the High Hills after?[1] But I leave that entirely to your own judgement.

We have not got the Heseltine-book here, so cannot quite judge – do as you feel about it.

Our near neighbours here are Mr and Mrs Max Beerbohm, such delightful people. I know you love the work of Max Beerbohm, he is really quite a genius in his way.[2] Otherwise we see no one. It has taken us about a month to get a piano – and at last we found one in an Antiquity-shop. It is very bad – a true antiquity. Even in Genoa there are no pianos on hire.

We travelled right down here in our car it was a lovely trip on from Lyon, Avignon, the Provence, and along the coast from Cap Fréjus on. We stayed 7 days with the Clews at La Napoule near Cannes and then it took us 2 more days to Rapallo. Of course we did not go fast on these bad roads and our peasant-boy-chauffeur did extremely well.

I am awfully pleased that you have done the Two Piano-arrangement of the Song of the H. H's and most eager to hear it or see it . Your arrangement of the Dance Rhapsody is so wonderfully good. I am very keen therefore, to hear the effect of this one. I am also so pleased to hear of your continued and ever growing success in the States.

Ever your loving friend
Frederick Delius

Letter in the hand of Jelka Delius, dated.

The original is in the Grainger Museum.

An accompanying letter from Jelka told Grainger: 'Fred is looking well and is getting on quite well ... The Dance Rhapsody, Brigg Fair and Hassan are recorded on the Gramophone now.'

1   Grainger was to conduct the New York Philharmonic Orchestra and the Bridge-port Oratorio Society on 28 April in Bridgeport, Connecticut, and two days later at Carnegie Hall in New York; in this way *The Song of the High Hills* and two movements from the *North Country Sketches* were to receive first performances in the United States, and works by Grainger, Grieg and Rachmaninov to make up the programme. 'Fred wants me to tell you,' wrote Jelka early in April, 'that in the score of the Song of the H. H. only *two* drummers are marked. But that is a mistake, there ought to be three drummers to give the right effect.' Delius reaffirmed the point in a letter of 13 April, adding: 'Let all their entrances be slightly accentuated.'

2   Max Beerbohm (1872–1956): English critic, caricaturist and essayist. He and his wife Florence made their home in Rapallo from 1910, the year of their marriage. 'Our only solace here are the Beerbohms, delightful people,' wrote Jelka to Marie Clews on 17 January. 'He is a very subtle Satirist and both are refined and kind.'

(489)
Jelka Delius to Percy Grainger

Villa Raggio
San Ambrogio
Rapallo
Italy
[24 February 1924]

My dear Percy,

Your letter of Febr 14th (in the train) came to-day, but the one posted the day before has not yet come. It is always such a pleasure when we see your hand-writing. I answer the questions *at once*. Delius has no jewish blood at all, not a drop; no jewish relatives and he knows his ancestors from Philip Melanchton's time (the reformator's) whose friend one of his ancestor's was. Delius says: Please deny this of the jewish origine wherever you can; altho I have no antipathy to the Jews. Music indeed would be in a very bad way without them. They have always done *a lot* for Delius' Music. Here again Haym, Buths, Beecham are *not jews*, no more are *you*. F. D.   Lippay also not a jew

Now I must tell you about a german doctor in Cassel, of whom I heard and who is alleged to treat all Lähmungen Geh-Störungen[1] etc so successfully. I wrote to him describing Freds whole state and antecedents. He wrote back rather hopefully; As it is too cold for us to go to Germany at once we have arranged for him to come here to see Fred, begin the treatment and tell us exactly what to do. He has greatly bettered and almost cured resembling cases. Now it will depend upon what *he* says whether we can travel to America. I know dear Percy, best of friends, that if his cure must be done first and this journey postponed to next year – you will understand. If he could be relieved it would be such a true blessing. With what difficulty he is dictating me an orchestral score, his mind so active and bright, and he so hampered by his invalid limbs.[2] The Doctor is coming in a day or 2 and going to stay with us and it will be a great thing really to hear all about this new cure and be fixed what we have to do. I shall let you know as soon as a decision is come to.

It would be so lovely to stay with you and hear all this music and hear you conducting. Well we must see.

Balfour was here with Bax, they were both very nice – but stayed rather far away on the other side of the Rapallo bay, so that thin little Bax always looked exhausted when they got here – Balfour doing exercise on principle.[3]

Otherwise we see nobody, except the dear Beerbohms. Mrs B, an American is one of the kindest and most lovable women I have met. The days run past us – I trying to copy Fred's very pale pencil score in the morning; then at noon he comes down and when the sun shines we read and walk etc. on the Verandah; from 4 – 6 working at the Piano – reading at night. When we think of how *you* live in the midst of activity   dashing railway trains and concerts!

It was so angelic of you to send some money to Lippay. We also sent him a little. But the greatest pity is that he is really wasted; that he cannot conduct etc. etc. And I fear in Europe it will be hard to find something for him. –

Fred sends you his best and fondest love. We shall remain here only until March 17th, so please address your next letter to Grez, from where it will always be forwarded to us. Probably we shall stay a week or so with the Clews' at Cannes; but of course *all* depends upon what the Doctor Heermann says.

It is quite dark and I close in haste with
love and all good wishes

Ever affectionately
Jelka Delius

Autograph letter, signed and undated. 'Postmark Feb 24, 1924' added in Grainger's hand.

The original is in the Grainger Museum.

1 German: *paralyses* (or *lamenesses*), *difficulties in walking*.

2 'He has set to work on an orchestral score, begun before his illness,' wrote Jelka to Marie Clews on 17 February, 'and for me it is a very good sign that he feels like tackling it. It gives me a lot of hard work tho, to copy and arrange parts of it etc.'

3 'We have had Gardiner's and Bax's visits,' Jelka told Marie Clews on 17 February. 'They are now in Siena and Pisa and coming back once more to-morrow. It poured with rain all during their stay.'

(490)
Frederick Delius to Philip Heseltine

"Les Brisants"
La Napoule
Alpes Mar.
France

23.3.1924

Fred dictates:

My dear Phil

We left Rapallo on the 16th in the car and spent the night in San Remo. From there we went next day to La Napoule lunching at Mentone where we met Orr in the street who looked very well. We are now in a Villa in La Napoule where we intend to stay till the end of April.[1] Then we go to Cassel in Germany, where there is a wonderfully good doctor who cures my sort of trouble. We shall probably spend a month or 6 weeks in his Sanatorium. This doctor came from Cassel to see me in Rapallo and spent a week with us, examining my case and beginning preliminaries for his cure.

Which is the best Gramophone, as I want to get one; but of course, I want absolutely the best. Have you heard all my things, Hassan, Brigg Fair, the cuckoo and how do they sound?

Schiff seems awfully anxious to arrange concerts of my works in London. I should so much like the Mass of Life, Songs of Sunset, the Arabesk and the Requiem to be done again. Schiff takes great interest in this and can evidently command a good deal of backing and would like to see you again and talk things over. What have you got against him? He seems to like you very much and always asks so kindly after you. I should so much like the few friends I have in London to be in harmony with one another.

Please write me here soon and tell me what you are doing and what is going on.

I enclose a cheque for £5-0-0 which, I surmise will be useful to balance your budget.

With love from Jelka

Ever aff^{ly}
Fr. Delius

Letter in the hand of Jelka Delius, dated.

The original is in the British Library.

1   Jelka wrote to Sydney Schiff on 25 March: 'We are to get a piano from Cannes to-day and then we shall go on with the new orchestral work that Fred has so at heart!' They intended to go to Cassel on 1 May. (She also informed Schiff that the Clews kept fourteen servants at La Napoule.)

(491)
Frederick Delius to Percy Grainger

26.5.24

Schlosshôtel
Wilhelmshöhe
bei Cassel

Fred dictates:

My dear Percy,

It was a great joy to receive your news about the concerts at once after the performances, your true impressions untainted by other opinions.

As you know, criticisms good or bad have always affected me very little – knowing, as I do, the sort of musician the critic is. Mr Fink's[1] criticism is certainly a very kindly one. When I heard that over a hundred people had come to you after the concert I was very much surprised and also gratified on my own account and also on yours. I generally reckon that there are about five people in a hall who are specially impressed. And judging by this concert, the American public is certainly more easily impressed than an English one.

What I do thoro'ly regret is that I was not present at the concert, not only to hear my own works, but your Song of Democracy which I do not know properly and which must have made a great impression. And *how* [I] should have liked to hear the beautiful singing of the Br. Choir which must have been magnificent. I hope this will reach you before you leave for Australia – but dear old friend – we both wish you the happiest and most successful journey. I place Finck quite apart from musical critics; for a man who can enthuse over a genius like Grieg is much more than a musical critic: He is a music-*Lover*. I feel that you did splendidly as a conductor and brought out the best that was in the works – as I know how exacting you are with yourself and how high your aims are.

I do not feel very tangible results of my cure yet, but the doctor feels quite hopeful. We removed from the Sanatorium as the food was too bad and I was absolutely undernourished, which kept me from getting stronger. In this hotel, beautifully situated in the lovely park everything is good and comfortable.

Frederick Delius
his first signature since 2 years

Letter in the hand of Jelka Delius, signed (with a postscript) by Frederick Delius, dated. Envelope addressed: Percy A. Grainger Esq / 7 Cromwell Place / White Plains / New York / U.S.A. Postmark: CASSEL WILHELMSHÖHE 27.5.24.

The original is in the Grainger Museum.

The Deliuses left the Riviera around 24 April, the journey to Grez taking them a leisurely four to five days. Jelka's painter's eye was evident as they motored through Provence: 'I marvelled all the way about the trees. Our whole trip has been a revelation about trees. Those great thumping heavy entirely trimmed off plane trees, like fantastic elephants-limbs stretching to all sides – The miracle of leaves coming out of this grey oldness! Avenues and avenues and then the Cypress trees in groups, the willows (old as from the middle ages all forming a sort of chalice). No, it is too wonderful.' (Letter to the Clews, Châlons sur Saône, 27 April). They stayed only briefly in Grez, as it is clear they were in Cassel quite early in May. By the end of their stay in Cassel it seems that Jelka had completed her translation of Clews's play – although the preface still remained to be tackled.

1   Henry Finck (1854–1926): American author and music critic. Alive to and appreciative of many of the trends in modern music, he had been a champion of Wagner, Grieg and MacDowell, among others. He was music editor of the *New York Evening Post* for forty years.

(492)
Frederick Delius to Philip Heseltine

Grez-sur-Loing.
18–9–24.   S. et M.

Dear Phil.

I was very glad to hear from you again.

We returned here a fortnight ago[1] – from Cassel, where I underwent a 3 months' treatment, with a wonderfully clever Doctor.[2] His treatment (mostly electrical) has really done me good; altho' I can walk a little alone for five or ten minutes, I walk mostly on Jelka's arm, when I can go for twenty or twenty five minutes. I am also beginning to write again. The whole trouble has been nervous, caused by the tremendous strain & anxiety of the War.

Many thanks dear Phil for the Score of the "Curlew", which I only received on my return to Grez; it having been forwarded here from La Napoule. I think it is a very delicate piece of Music, but I think – if I may make a criticism – that you have spun it out a little too much – It seems to me that your Song "The Curlew" was more concise, & therefore more effective; but, on no account must you get disheartened about your Music, keep hard at work, & you will eventually do something fine & great –

The Philharmonic are giving "The Mass of Life" on 2^d April, & of course – we shall come over – I *do hope* they will engage a really good & impressive singer, for the Baritone-part.

Won't you come over here & stay with us a week or two – We should so much like to see you.

Remember me kindly to Agustus John[3] when you see him.

Ever your affectionate
Frederick Delius

Letter in an unknown hand, signed in pencil by Delius, dated.

The original is in the British Library.

1   The Deliuses had in fact been at Grez already for five weeks.

2   The first few weeks in Cassel had a depressingly negative effect on Delius's condition. However, after moving from a particularly ill-equipped sanatorium to the Schloss-Hotel, Wilhelmshöhe-Cassel, the cure began to take effect, with his legs gradually growing stronger and his appetite virtually returning to normal. Jelka's faith in Dr Heermann, who had diagnosed multiple sclerosis, was complete. On 12 August the Deliuses returned from Wilhelmshöhe to Grez.

3   Augustus John (1878–1961): English painter. An intimate of Heseltine, he presumably met Delius on one or other of the composer's visits to London. In 1929 he was to execute at least two pencil drawings of Delius during the last such visit. In earlier days his sister, the painter Gwen John, had sat as model for Ida Gerhardi in Paris.

(493)
Frederick Delius to Percy Grainger

[Grez, 20 October 1924]

Dearest friend

Just a few lines in my own hand[1] to tell you I sent off to your address the full score of Eventyr, 3 preludes for piano & 4 Songs, words by Nietzsche – Many thanks for all the cuttings – We are again in Grez & longing for further news of the homeward voyage

With love from us both

Frederick Delius

20.10.1924[2]

Autograph letter, signed and dated. Envelope as for Letter 494.

The original is in the Grainger Museum.

1 Delius also penned, on 17 October, a short letter to Norman O'Neill.

2 The date was added by Jelka.

(494)
Jelka Delius to Percy Grainger

Grez sur Loing
Seine et Marne
20.10.1924

Dearest Percy,

Fred wrote you a few words which I am glad to send you. We think you must be back now and it is good to feel you are not *quite* so far away. Fred is getting on quite well[1] and is composing a bit every day (dictating to me) The rest of the time we are out walking and driving alternately. He does 45 minutes walking daily, sometimes 15 or 20 minutes at a time. He certainly plays the piano better. But I want him very much to return to Dr Heermann to continue his cure; and perhaps later on to the Riviera.

I think I told you that the Mass of Life will be done in London at the Philharmonic on April 2[d]. We hope to be able to go there. Klenau will conduct and the Philharm. Choir under Kennedy Scott will sing. Un. Ed. also wrote that the Mass of Life will be done in Vienna   Prague, Berlin and Wiesbaden. Isn't that fine? I do not know dates or details. Songs of Sunset will be done at Hagen in December.

Fred's second Violin Sonata has just been brought out by Hawkes & Son. Sammons and Howard-Jones played it. They are giving a Delius Chamber-music concert at Wigmore Hall, London on Nov 8th. The 2 Sonatas (violin & piano) the Cello Sonata, Songs, the 3 Preludes and 5 little M.S. pieces for piano, played by Howard-Jones, who is so very enthusiastic about Delius. He came here with his wife and played it all for us. The 5 new piano pieces will be published by Un. Ed and Curwen for England.

Grez is in its touchingly beautiful autumn mood now, yellow poplar trees, soft skies, autumnal russet fields – last apples in evening sun; Everything so mellow and harmonious – a most lovable landscape. We both send you our love and hope to hear from you soon.

Yrs ever affly
Jelka Delius

Autograph letter, signed and dated. Envelope addressed: Percy Grainger Esq/7 Cromwell Place/White Plains/New York/U.S.A. Postmark: GREZ 21 -10 24.

The original is in the Grainger Museum.

1   On 6 October, Jelka confirmed her husband's continuing improvement to Marie Clews: 'Certainly Fred is *much* better in every way, can walk better, eat better, play the piano better looks so much better. Yet he has not quite got his balance yet and that is what ought to be obtained. His eyes are ever so much better. He does not wear his glasses any more and uses weaker glasses for reading than he has used for 5 years. We had several visits from friends, who saw him last in London last autumn and find him wonderfully improved.' One visitor from England had been his sister Clare. Jelka continued: 'I am rather happy that my sister-in-law has left us to-day. She is very nice but a great disappointment as a help with Fred and house. In fact she disturbed me very much with her chattering and we both found her to be – not of our world – at all.' On 17 October she wrote to Adine O'Neill: 'He is composing all the time, dictating it to me, which is rather a difficult task, but he has got quite accustomed to it.'

(495)
Jelka Delius to Henry and Marie Clews

Hotel zur Post
Cassel
20.12.24

My dear friends,

This is to send you a little letter Fred wrote you. I am sure it will give you pleasure to see how well he can write again now. Last year at this time he was absolutely unable to hold a pencil.

We are quite comfortable here and have had such splendid sunny weather all the time that we are out for hours daily   Dr Heermann is making wonderful cures all the time, and I only wish Fred's progress were as sensational as some of the other's. *But he is progressing.*

I was so pleased to get your delightful letter Marie, dear. But what an awful fellow Grant Richards must be! I only hope you have a proper contract so that you can attack him. Fred is constantly swindled by publishers and one cannot be careful enough.

It is about a year ago that we landed at La Napoule in our car. We take the greatest interest in the new Gate and Gatehouse. Cant you photo it with the sculptures? I should love to see it.

M.J Preface progressing.

Would you like me to send you a typewritten copy of the Drama?

We both send you our heartiest Xmas and New-Year's wishes!

Ever devotedly yours
Jelka –

Autograph letter, signed and dated. Envelope addressed: Mrs Henry Clews/Chateau de la Napoule/Alpes Mar-/Frankreich. Postmark: CASSEL 22 12 24.

The original is in the Delius Trust Archive.

The Deliuses left Grez some time in November for a further stay in Cassel. 'Everybody finds Fr. very well looking, only his eyes are troubling him,' wrote Jelka from there to Marie Clews on 23 November.

(496)
Frederick Delius to Henry Clews

[Cassel, 20 December 1924]

My dear Clews

A few words in my own hand to shew you that some progress is being made here – I have not been able to write now for nearly 3 years – My legs are also stronger altho' I cannot yet walk safely quite alone –

Good luck & happiness to you & Marie from

Your affectionate
Frederick Delius

Autograph letter, signed and undated.

The original is in the Delius Trust Archive. It is the last known letter in Delius's own hand.

1925

This was to be the year that brought to a close all the long travels in search of a cure. By the end of 1925 Delius had largely lost the use of his limbs and was a sightless invalid. Mentally his faculties were unimpaired, and from around the middle of the year until his death nine years on he was effectively to stay in this state, his physical condition deteriorating very slowly – almost imperceptibly – until near the end. His mental powers were to fade very little. The months at Wilhelmshöhe/Cassel were not without interest. Delius wrote to Universal Edition on 18 January to commend Adrian Boult to Emil Hertzka. Boult had conducted an excellent performance of the Cello Concerto with Beatrice Harrison in Birmingham on the 11th and now wanted to give the work – together with some more Delius – with her in Vienna (and indeed in Germany). The composer asked Hertzka to see what he could do. And later in January Delius learned that Schuricht had conducted the Piano Concerto in Wiesbaden with the Swiss pianist Hans Levy Diem. By February he was weak and depressed. 'We are having a very lonely time here,' Jelka told Heseltine on the 14th. Again, and not surprisingly, she was beginning to worry about the expense of the cure, and asked friends in England on Delius's behalf to look into the matter of some unpaid royalties there. But *Sea Drift* had been given in Cassel: 'It did Fred good to hear it.' The next event was Schuricht's 'magnificent performance' on 16 March of the *Mass* in Wiesbaden, where the Deliuses made a short stay. Schuricht had long since assumed the role of champion and prime interpreter of Delius's music in Germany and Jelka wrote of Delius as having been 'uplifted' and 'animated' while in Wiesbaden. Indications of renewed interest in the *Mass* poured in from Hagen, Barmen, Cassel, Duisburg and Dortmund. Welcome visitors to Cassel at Easter were Gardiner and Kennedy Scott. Gardiner was correcting proofs of the full score of *Fennimore and Gerda*; and some two weeks later Delius told Universal that the condition of his eyes would not permit him to correct other proofs. Other visits looked forward to early in May were those of Frederic Austin and of the Philharmonic Society's special representative, Gerald Cooper, who came to Cassel to present Delius with the Gold Medal recently awarded to him by the Society. Visitors at the end of May were Alexandre and Catherine Barjansky, and the Deliuses returned to Grez, rather disillusioned with Dr Heermann, shortly after this.

From now on Delius was largely confined to the village of Grez-sur-Loing, and to hear live music he had to rely on the visits of his friends. Among the first to come was Philip Heseltine, who brought to Grez in July a composer friend, E. J. Moeran. The Barjanskys arrived on 26 July, spending the rest of the summer at the little Pension Corby in Grez. Howard-Jones came next for a few days. Percy Grainger probably stayed for as long as four weeks in August, his visit being the most eagerly anticipated of all. He was joined by Balfour Gardiner and together they played to Delius Grainger's newly-made transcription for two pianos of *The Song of the High Hills*. Although Delius pressed Universal to publish this 'outstandingly beautiful' version of the work, it was not to appear in print. The summer music-making season closed with the Barjanskys' departure in mid-September; there may have been a visit, too, by Heinrich Simon.

It must have been a higher might that decreed that at this stage of Delius's life wireless broadcasting should begin its golden era. It seems little short of miraculous that his close friend and neighbour Alden Brooks should have installed a radio set and that Delius should have been able to hear in September compositions of his own direct from the Three Choirs Festival. There was no electricity as yet in their own house, and until it was put in the following year there could be no question of a radio. But the Deliuses did next buy a gramophone and so were able to listen to a wide range of music, as well as to those few works of Delius that were up to now recorded. Gardiner came again early in November for a few days and was particularly delighted with the machine. Perhaps it was his advice that caused Delius to arrange for a lawyer from nearby Nemours to come to Grez to assist with a more formal *testament*, drawn up in the dining room with three local people of Grez as witnesses on 10 November, and again leaving everything to Jelka.

In the autumn, Barjansky played the Cello Concerto in Wiesbaden. Jelka had also proposed that he should arrange an evening of chamber music in Lüdenscheid, Ida Gerhardi's home town. This he did, and to the ailing Ida's joy, she was enabled once more to hear the strains of Delius's music. News came from Grainger that he was to conduct *The Song of the High Hills* in Los Angeles next year. Before then he conducted the first performance in America of the Cello Concerto, with Herman Sandby as soloist, at the Aeolian Hall in New York on 29 December. And the *Mass of Life* continued its triumphant progress: on 18 December it was given in Coblenz. At Christmas, Gardiner and Kennedy Scott came for the holidays. Among other things they practised Grainger's arrangement of *The Song of the High Hills*. 'We gave old Fred two performances of it, & he was delighted.'

No serious composition was undertaken this year, nor during the following years until 1929.

(497)
Jelka Delius to Sydney Schiff

Cassel. 22.1.25.

Dear friend,

My letter had to wait until I got time to buy some big envelopes.

We have taken Fred to the Doctor, for the first time after a week, and I think it did him good, altho he was rather tired.[1] His state is much the same. We are going to have the visit of a young checoslovak Composer from Frankfort for the week-end, and that, I hope, will brace him up a bit. Unfortunately our maid and help is becoming more and more unpleasant. Hotel life and gossip are so bad for her. I am afraid we shall have to send her away. This is a step I have always been very reluctant about; for one never knows where one will get. On the other side I realize, that a bad-tempered, moody person is no good at all for a patient like Fred.

Is not this world strange   Here are Delius and myself, two superior people, and *one* a great artist, buffetted about by an uneducated servant and the victim of all her whims and all her unrequited sex-instincts. For that is the reason of the perversion of her character, I feel sure. But tho' I understand it all so well, I cannot alter it or better it. I must rush this to the post now.

With much love from us both

Yrs affly
Jelka Delius

Autograph letter, signed and dated.

The original is in the British Library.

1   'He is going thro some sort of crisis ... eats very little and feels weak,' Jelka wrote to Schiff on 6 January.

(498)
Frederick Delius to Universal Edition

Schlosshotel Wilhelmshöhe
Cassel
20.3.1925

Dear Herr Direktor,

We have just returned from Wiesbaden, where we attended a magnificent performance of the Mass of Life. Unfortunately it will be quite impossible for me to undertake the long journey to London for Klenau's performance, although I should have *really loved* to do so. You will meanwhile have received Gardiner's translation of the Introduction by Dr. Haym & let us hope that copies of this will be *plentifully* available in London. They were dreadfully hard to come by in Wiesbaden; they were all already sold out by the final rehearsal, then a few more copies arrived which sold out *immediately* on the day of the performance. I was told that many hundreds could have been sold. My wife & good friends could not get any. As the publisher, you really ought to have taken care over such matters.

It was only at the last minute that I learned that Schuricht, who, by the way, devoted himself to the work with great love, had undertaken certain alterations in the choral parts & also in the instrumentation. I am sorry to say that he did not ask my advice beforehand. The alterations in the choral parts are not of great consequence, and they do make it easier for his still new choir. However I could hear at once that the orchestral alterations diminished the orchestra too much & affected the timbre, something which I told Schuricht immediately. Also he had left out the 2nd Tanzlied completely – just one of the best parts of the work. The work seemed rather too short. Yet I think the work might be too long without any cuts at all, have therefore asked Klenau to omit "Süsse Leier" & maybe something else in London.

I felt however very distressed that the general opinion seemed to be that my work was really only "finished" by Schuricht's arrangement. I enclose an article from the Wiesbadener Tageblatt (Doorn) which gives a terribly errone-ous impression. Some people who had read it and who had also attended the Vienna performance were quite taken aback and thought the Mass had been much better in the original version in Vienna.

I hope you will understand my dilemma. The splendid Schuricht took enor-mously great pains, is so enthusiastic, the success was unbelievable, enthus-iasm etc. He now wants to repeat the Mass in May & then do the Tanzlied, too, & for then do away with many of his orchestral alterations. But if the other conductors think the Mass may be done in Schuricht's "arrangement" only, this would do me a great deal of harm. I can absolutely not permit this arrangement to be used for other performances. My work stands as it is and came through the test of fire long ago. Scheinpflug, Weisbach & probably also Sieben will perform it next season; Weisbach in Hagen & Barmen – Please therefore see to it that they do it to my original score. I have already told Schuricht this myself when I said goodbye. Please keep an eye on the press too and if this notion about the arrangement should find its way into the press & also into the music journals, you as the publisher will have to deny it firmly. *As long as I live, alterations, cuts etc. may only be made with my permission.*

I am sorry to say that the old material is full of mistakes, as everyone tells me. It is therefore *urgently necessary* to correct the material conscientiously for the many forthcoming performances, so that it is faultless and to produce a flawless new edition of the orchestral material as soon as possible.

I will look the Fennimore proof over soon.

Kindly let me know something about the Vienna performance of the Mass, also reviews, which I shall be glad to return.

Please send me 1 Dance for Harpsichord, which I have promised to a young pianist here.

With best regards from us both

Sincerely yours
Frederick Delius

P.S. What have you now arranged with Curwen concerning the price of the piano scores?

When are the 5 little Pieces coming out? Has Howard Jones corrected them yet?

F.D.

Letter in the hand of Jelka Delius, dated, written in German.

The original is in the Universal Edition archives.

(499)
Jelka Delius to Percy Grainger

Schlosshotel
Wilhelmshöhe
bei Cassel
28.3.1925

Dearest Percy,

What a great blessing your dear letter of March 12th is![1] Oh, *do* come in August! Any time you can arrange it we shall be in Grez awaiting you with open arms. Freds face beamed with joy, when he read your letter. Arrange just as you best can. All these last weeks I have just been longing for you, but of course you are *so* busy, and I did not dare to hope you would come. I do feel so lonely in my dreadful responsibility about Fred – and I feel so tired sometimes that my resources in keeping up his spirits are so minimized. We have really had a dreadful time and Fred has grown weaker and weaker and the doctor as helpless as myself to stop it. Can he have eaten poisoned meat? Since about Xmas he has no appetite at all and an unquenchable thirst. He is a *little* better since we came up to Wilhelmshöhe, but still his stomach is quite out of order. Last week I felt so in despair I told Dr Heermann we *must* consult a stomach specialist. I think that was a good move; he gave Fred an exact diet, trying little by little to nourish him more.

On April 2d the Mass of Life is being done in London by Klenau with Ken. Scotts Chorus at the Philharmonic.[2] We had *so* looked forward all the time to going there – but we had to realize that it was quite impossible to undertake the difficult journey over the sea in his present state.

So I took him to Wiesbaden instead to hear the work done by Schuricht. It was an excellent performance and really Fred enjoyed it ever so much; and the whole thing – the atmosphere of music – quite took him out of himself. The Chorus was absolutely first rate. They took splendid tempi, most rhythmic and precise in the quick sections and softest pppp where needed.

The work made a most wonderful impression on me. Surely it is more beautiful than anything else – and there is no flaw in it. There is so much variety of mood, too. Altho' I myself *love* those sustained elegiac Delius-moods, I realise that a great public is *too* far removed from them, and that a work, also containing grand strong chorus'ses full of Life, animation and rythm appeals more to it. That first chorus: "Oh du mein Wille" Then the Dance Song Das ist ein Tanz über Stock u. Stein and in the 2^d part Herauf herauf Du grosser Mittag and also the last with the Mitternachtslied and that heavenly final climax were perfectly wonderful and never impressed me quite as much. I must not even begin to tell you of "On the mountains" and all those tender-sad soft endings, Der alte Mittag schläft etc etc -. Fred was a touching figure, sitting in the middle of the hall in his bath-chair, listening so intently. The applause was wonderful – no clapping at all between the sections – and at the end by a sudden impulse of reverence the whole audience rose and turned towards Delius and bowed to him and then only the enthusiastic applause began.

The Orchestra wanted to lift him on to the platform carriage and all – but that seemed rather risky, so at last we were taken out thro' a side door into the artists room. But the audience simply did not leave and when we at last came out crowded round Fred and many went right to the hotel door with us. The Chorus gave Fred a most lovely enormous bunch of flowers. They want to repeat the work in May, and very much want Fred to be present again; it will then be a sort of Musik fest. The dress rehearsal was public too and both performances were sold out. We were so uplifted – it seemed like exile to return here – and see noone, but a grumpy nurse.

Balfour is to come and see us, but you know his combinations. *He has* to be in Munich to hear Frankensteins[3] Opera and *has* to visit some little towns from the middle ages on his way. There will be but 2 or 3 days for Fred. Ida Gerhardi would help me if she only could, but she is *so* delicate herself and I really have noone I could apply to, and talk things over with. I feel it a terrible responsibility, apart from all the distress and anxiety. I say all this so that you feel *what it will mean to me* if you come! How I long to show you dear old Grez and for you to go thro' Fred's works with him, and all the rest of your enlivening and sympathetic presence.

We read with great interest all you sent us about the Boston Concert, and are delighted with the warm reception of your works. All you say about your Chamber Music plans etc. is perfectly splendid and you are quite right not to wish to appear a Delius-maniac. People *must* have time to ripen up to him. Enclosed a cutting from the Daily Telegraph, which the publisher Hawkes sent Fred. He is very pleased with the Sonata evidently.[4]

I must at last stop, dear friend and with one united love

Yrs always
Jelka Delius

P.S. Just now your Strathspey and Reel has been sent from Schotts   It looks a nice edition and Fred will read it, as soon as he can, and we must get Balfour to play it on the piano
Those jolly Francfort rehearsals!

Autograph letter, signed and dated. Envelope addressed: Percy Grainger Esq/7 Cromwell Place/White plains/New York/U.S.A. Postmark: CASSEL WIL-HELMSHÖHE 29.3.25.

The original is in the Grainger Museum.

The winter months had seen a gradual deterioration in Delius's condition. Around the beginning of February they moved once more to the Schloss-Hotel, Wilhelmshöhe, 'to have the purer and more bracing air', as Jelka wrote to Heseltine on 14 February. She continued: 'Fred has naturally been very depressed about his health and especially as he wants ever so much to go to London for the Mass of Life on April 2^d ... We are having a very lonely time here – The only event was the performance of Seadrift here at Cassel the other day. The work sounded so beautiful ... It did Fred good to hear it. On Febr 23 and 24th the Mass of Life is to be done at Vienna, on March 16th at Wiesbaden and on March 26th at Berlin.'

1   Grainger's letter has not been found.

2   Jelka had told Heseltine on 19 March: 'I heard that the Vienna performance was very fine and made "einen gewaltigen Eindruck"   Klenau is a fine musician; he loves the work.'

3   Clemens (Freiherr) von Franckenstein (1875–1942): German composer and conductor. While studying under Knorr at Frankfurt, he became a friend and associate of Gardiner, Grainger, O'Neill and Cyril Scott. He conducted frequently in London in the early 1900s, moving to Wiesbaden, Berlin and, from 1912, Munich, where he had first studied. He composed several operas, including *The Emperor's Poet (Li-Tai-Pe)*, which Gardiner travelled to Munich to attend.

4   The second Violin Sonata had recently been recorded.

(500)
Jelka Delius to Sydney Schiff

Schlosshotel
Wilhelmshöhe
30.3.1925

Dear Sydney,

We have read "Myrtle" with great interest. It is a very original way of treating the subject. We love Myrtle – Nanny at once is delightful – Marcel most sympathetic, but it seems to me the best is "Kurt". Sylvia is so good and true too!

I read it all to Delius. After a little while I want to read it again alone. Fred wishes me to tell you that he feels very happy and gratified that you felt like dedicating to him so intimate a work.[1]

We are so sad we cannot be in London for the Mass of Life on thursday. It is a sore disappointment, and snow, sleet and rain, a grumpy nurse, the muddy Park the hum-drum daily routine here make it more difficult to bear.

Perhaps we feel this more keenly after our trip to Wiesbaden, which really was delightful and most enjoyable.

I am so glad we went. The performance was excellent, the Chorus studied to perfection and drilled, as perhaps only Germans allow themselves to be drilled: 40 rehearsals and some of them extended till over midnight. There was a public last rehearsal and the performance both packed full. The audience was wonderfully enthusiastic and after the glorious end, through peculiar feeling of reverence the whole audience stood up and turned towards Delius who sat in his bathchair in the middle of the Hall. It lasted quite a little moment and then the clapping etc began. They presented him with the most beautiful flowers and really it was a unique and wonderful "Stimmung", only possible in these little german towns – people followed us right to the hotel, just to see the last of the Composer.

Wiesbaden is quite itself again: the avalanches of grasping french families who swarmed there during the german inflation have all left again and there are only those *officially* there. We breathed the delicious atmosphere of orchestral rehearsals – questions about the score, corrections of mistakes, talks about music – etc. Schuricht the conductor consecrated every free moment to his "geliebte Meister" and was so exhausted after the performance that we waited for him in vain; but when we were safely in bed he came with his young wife and the leader, a very black little man and said he could not go to bed before having hugged the master and we spent a charming hour together.

Naturally I was made the confidante of all poor Schurichts matrimonial troubles and indeed they would be an admirable subject for a book – the solution not yet arrived at. Both wives, the resolute helpful old one, and the pretty, callous new young one – His best friend now married to the old wife –

but both of them, husband and wife, so absolutely devoted to Schuricht that they linger on at Wiesbaden – the child from the first marriage – a 5 months terrible illness of the little new wife – her desire for Dances and amusement, her jealousy, the old one's unerring motherliness to Schuricht, the unpractical phantastic rather megalomaniac little man! Always wavering between the two!

Delius seems to be doing just a wee bit better. I had consulted a specialist for his stomach and I ardently hope be will get his appetite back thro' this treatment.

Please thank dear Violet for her kind words
and with love from us both

Yrs always
Jelka

Autograph letter, signed and dated.

The original is in the British Library.

1   Schiff had evidently told the Deliuses of this dedication some time earlier. 'My husband thanks you most heartily for your kindness in dedicating your new book to him,' wrote Jelka on 28 September 1924.

(501)
Frederick Delius to Philip Heseltine

30.4.1925   Schlosshotel
                                                 Wilhelmshöhe
Fred dictates: bei Cassel.

Dear Phil,

Your letters giving me so much news about the rehearsals and performance of the Mass gave me the greatest pleasure. From all sides I hear it was a wonderful performance and *I was* sorry that I could not be present, but it would have been impossible in my present state of health.

The book you tell me of, which you are preparing seems to me to be an excellent idea and I hope you will be able to bring it out soon.[1] We shall go back to Grez in about a fortnight or 3 weeks and I shall be able to look at it there.

Balfour Gardiner and Kennedy Scott paid me a very pleasant visit here.

The Royal Philharmonic Society is presenting me with its Beethoven Gold-Medal and Gerald Cooper will come this week to hand it to me personally.[2] –

3.5.25. We could not finish this letter the other day, and now your last letter has arrived. We shall be delighted if you come to Grez as soon as we are there, which will be so delightful and we can go thro' all the indications and tempi. It is a splendid thing you have written this little book, it will prove most useful. We are only waiting for permission from the french authorities for a german male nurse we have engaged – to enter France – and we are most eager to get back.

We expect Austin's visit here in a few days[3] and are looking forward to seeing him – it is so monotonous here. I have seen a very excellent eye specialist and he thinks, as Jelka always did, that the whole trouble comes from my general weakness and cerebral anemia and I hope we shall be able to better that in Grez.

As soon as our departure is fixed we'll let you know.[4]

With best love, dear Phil,

yours affectionately
Frederick & Jelka –

Letter in the hand of Jelka Delius, dated.

The original is in the British Library.

1 Apparently Heseltine was preparing a 'more or less technical study' of Delius's music for the Oxford University Press. It was not published and was presumably never completed.

2 Gerald Cooper (1892–1947): English musicologist. He became the Royal Philharmonic Society's Honorary Secretary in 1928. Elgar, too, was awarded the Society's medal in 1925; the previous Gold Medallist was Cortot in 1923, and the next was to be Beecham in 1928. Several of Delius's works were given their first performance by the Society, beginning with *In a Summer Garden*, in 1908; there followed *On hearing the first Cuckoo in Spring* and *Summer Night on the River* (1914) (these being first English performances), the Violin Concerto (1919), *The Song of the High Hills* (1920) and the Requiem (1922).

3 Frederic Austin's visit was confirmed in a letter from Jelka to the Schiffs on 7 May. He was due to leave the following day.

4 The Deliuses probably left Wilhelmshöhe for Grez at the end of May or early in June.

(502)
Jelka Delius to Marie Clews

FREDERICK DELIUS
Grez-sur-Loing
S. & M.
31.8.1925.

Dearest Marie.

Your card just arrived. I have thought of you often, but I thought that all the world knew of Fred's sad state: *he can not see at all*. We have passed a terrible winter in Cassel, trying to save his eyes and seeing them get worse and worse, trying all specialists etc, at last we came back here end of May and since then his general state is *slightly* improved, but not the eyes. He therefore cannot walk at all. We have a man who carries him up and down,[1] and he lies most of the day in the garden on his chaiselongue. That lovely garden all full of flowers and he cannot see it! His mind is as lucid and as active as ever and of course to keep him from depression I read to him a tremendous lot.

But best of all, a few weeks ago Balfour Gardiner and Percy Grainger came together and played to him on 2 pianos and also the great Cellist Barjansky came to Grez to spend the holidays and we had wonderful concerts every day. It seemed to do Fred wonderfully much good, only just these last days the change of weather pulled him down again, and perhaps *some* fatigue too. Percy is leaving today for Denmark then U.S. He has been delightful.

It was so horrible, all this illness in an hotel room and unsympathetic surroundings and I cannot tell you how comforting it was for me to come back here and be able to make Fred physically comfortable at least and cook little meals to tempt him; to get the freshest eggs, the best chickens and all the luscious fruit for him; to be able in rainy weather to carry him to other rooms, to make him breathe the sweetest air – and the young man we have is very good-natured tho' not brilliant, but well educated, so that he can also read to Fred. Howard-Jones the pianist also came to play to him.[2] We shall not be able to go away for the winter and all the Music friends will try and come over alternately from time to time to play to him.

His optic nerve is not dead and, could Fred be really strengthened it could possible improve again. It is very shrunken and impoverished, Dr Heermann was utterly helpless and could not help at all. The strange thing was, that with the beginning eye-trouble Fred got an unquenchable thirst and a disgust for all food, especially meat. Dr H. thinks that the whole comes from a disorder of the "Hypophyse" a little gland at the base of brain.

We are so tired of Doctors – and certainly Fred is better without them.

Meanwhile, my poor youngest brother, Professor Rosen age 62 of Breslau has been murdered, as is believed, by his housekeeper, whom he had since

24 years, and whose daughter he had adopted. You may have seen it in the papers, a most disgusting crime.[2] He was a sweet, good, unpractical scientist and 24 years ago tried as a true Don Quixote to save a prostitute, nursed her sick child back to life and took her into his service. Finally he adopted the child, tho' she was not his. He had long grown to hate the woman, but could not get rid of her. He lived in a villa, where mother and daughter and the latter's husband had all the good rooms and he only a small bare bedroom and tiny mansarde as a study. Noone of us were ever allowed to visit him – he received my brother in his University Laboratory. They tormented him until he adopted the daughter but he absolutely refused to marry the mother. After all these years they murdered him, so as to inherit *at once*. Can you see these dreadful people planning to kill the man who only did good for them and kept them all those years. Miserable! It grieved me terribly. He was just completeing an important work on the beginning of all organisms, on which he threw quite a new light.

In all this trouble it has been quite impossible for me to finish the translation of the Mumbo-Jumbo preface, or to try actively to place the Drama. However all who read the translation think the Drama extremely good; only it seems to them too long for the stage. Dr Simon kept it a long time and has now handed it to Dr Hartung, who is just taking over an important theatre in Berlin. Hartung was at Darmstadt before and brought out many interesting novelties there as f. ex. Hassan. Simon will probably come here for a few days in September and I hope to hear about it then and shall let you know.[4]

I have also sent the Play to the Direktor of the Theatre at Leipsig but have had no reply so far.

It is a pity that all these theatre people in Germany are Jews and they resent these wonderfully true revelations.

Please dearest Marie, let me hear from soon. Fred also would love to hear from you both! After our stay at La Napoule we can place you so well in your "Castle in the Sea" and all about *it* and *you* interests us greatly.

Ever devotedly yrs:
Jelka –

How is Mancha and has he written a new work?

Typed transcript, dated, in the Delius Trust Archive.

1   Described by Jelka in a letter to the Schiffs dated 13 July as their first 'religious Bruder'.

2   'Howard-Jones came for a few days before Balfour and Percy, and played a lot too,' wrote Jelka to Heseltine on 16 August. She continued: 'They are all so devoted to Fred and it is a great consolation to me that he has all you friends!'

3 Evelin Gerhardi remembers well the interest aroused by the murder of Felix
Rosen: 'In the summer of 1925 our mother and we three children spent our school
holidays by the sea and every day read in the paper about "Mordfall Rosen". His
housekeeper was suspected to have murdered him for sheer greed. She was tried and
defended herself by saying that the murderer came into the house and she saved herself
by letting herself down from the upper floor by means of knotted bedclothes. But
when the bedclothes were brought to the court the knots were quite loose. No grown-
up person could have let herself (or himself) down without pulling the knots tight.
Apparently there was not enough evidence for a sentence so they had to let her go.'
(Letter to L. Carley, 20 June 1984.)

4 Gustav Ludwig Hartung (1887–1946): German theatre director. After a period
spent directing plays in Bremen and Frankfurt, he became Intendant (and subsequently General-Intendant) of the Hessische Landestheater, Darmstadt, from 1920 to
1924, and again from 1931 to 1933. He also worked in the 1920s in Berlin. A
devotee and leading exponent of Expressionism, he abjured the star system and
cultivated the ensemble. Under his direction, Darmstadt became one of the foremost
theatres in Germany. Having acquired the rights to the first performance of *Hassan*, he
brought the play out there on 1 June 1923. Whatever he may have thought of
Mumbo-Jumbo we do not know, but there was to be no production.

(503)
Jelka Delius to Percy Grainger

FREDERICK DELIUS
Grez-sur-Loing
S. et M.
12.9.25

My beloved Percy,

I hope this will yet catch you at Kristensen's.[1] Needless to say we missed you
terribly; I thought *I* missed you most, but Fred missed you so much too – and
Barjansky was quite disconsolate and little Filippa Brooks[2] has quite lost her
heart to you and blushes when your name is mentioned. She gets up early and
does her own room because *you* did. Mme Stecher thanks you *so* much for your
message and is devoted to you.

After resting for a few days Fred was quite alright again and it is absolutely
certain now that this great festival of friendship and music did him no end of
good. He even once or twice has *seen* some little movement, or a figure going
by like a shadow.

There are no words that could express my gratefulness for this beautiful gift
of your precious time you so generously gave us. No help could have been
better or more welcome! It has been one of the beautiful things in life!

This was already begun early this morning and then your dear letter came   It is a great wonderful thing for me to have such a dear friend, who understands the *aims* of my nature. With all your help and encouragement we must try and go thro' the winter without letting Fred feel too dull.

Yesterday Heseltine had written that the Gloucester Festival concert would be broadcast. They were doing "On hearing the first cuckoo" and 2 Elizabethan songs   "To Daffodils" and "Spring the sweet spring" of Freds. Also a Song of Roger Quilters (very charming and well sung). So the Bruder drove Fred to the Brooks' to hear it.[3]

We *actually heard it*, only unfortunately a polka of Radio-Paris (about the same Wave length) was well audible at the same time, especially during soft parts. Still it was a miracle to be in Gloucester and hear the applause etc. The songs we heard better only hardly a note of the piano part. The voice comes out best. After the songs there was enormous applause, so much so, that "Daffodils" was repeated – the only encore of the evening! It was really enjoyable to hear – as if one were there, how Fred is beloved of the public in England – and that: a provincial public!! Reed[4] conducted the cuckoo and took it too slow. On the 17th there will be a London programme of Phil Heseltines works. The Serenade dedicated to Fred, another small orch. piece and Songs sung by John Goss.[5] We must go to hear that too. Brooks was too nervous, he will do better when he does not change his screws all the time.

Fred and I are delighted about your conducting the S. of the H. Hs at Los Angeles! Especially as to-day Robert Nichols, the poet, who is in California wrote such a delightful letter, telling all about the performance of the Dance Rhapsody in a natural Amphitheatre in the Californian hills before a huge audience of 25 000. He said the work sounded incredibly beautiful in those surroundings and made a very great impression on the audience (conducted by Wood) and they "caught on to it" immediately, and that the Californian coast is demanding more Delius.

I'm sure it must be lovely in Denmark and so fascinating to collect more folk-songs with your friends! We enjoy the Taylor[6] records you so kindly sent us immensely. They are splendid. I often play them to Fred at night. Barjansky sends you his love. They will be leaving in a few days.[7] All affectionate blessings accompany you from Grez to White Plains   Always devotedly yours

Jelka –

P.S. Fred has had neither wine nor Champagne since the day before you left and certainly is better for it. He drinks lemonade, English ale and Eno's fruit-salt, which latter seems to agree with him quite wonderfully.

Autograph letter, signed and dated, written on headed notepaper.

The original is in the Grainger Museum.

1   Evald Tang Kristensen (1843–1929): Danish collector of folk-music and folk-tales, whom Grainger considered 'the greatest genius known to him amongst folk-song collectors anywhere in the world' (Bird, p. 137). Grainger went to Denmark on a number of occasions between 1922 and 1927 to collect folksongs with him.

2   Daughter of Alden Brooks.

3   'Our neighbour Brooks has a fine wireless now. Should there be anything of special interest, please let us know and we can get Fred to hear it there,' wrote Jelka to Heseltine on 5 September. She had apparently heard that Heseltine was to write occasionally for the *Radio Times*.

4   William Henry Reed (1876–1942): English violinist, conductor and composer. Leader of the London Symphony Orchestra from 1912 to 1935, after which he became the orchestra's chairman. He was particularly associated with the Three Choirs Festival (held in 1925 at Gloucester) and was a close friend of Elgar.

5   John Goss (1894–1953): English baritone. He was particularly noted for his performances of the works of English composers, and was closely associated with Heseltine, who had commended his voice to Delius.

6   Joseph Taylor (1833–1910): the venerable folk-singer from Lincolnshire, whose singing Grainger had recorded on cylinders and who subsequently – in 1908 – made a number of records for the Gramophone Company.

7   On 8 December, Jelka told Grainger of some Barjansky performances: 'He played the Cello Concerto with Orch. in Wiesbaden, where he also had a Kammermusic Abend.' She went on to give news of an old friend: 'And then he gave a Kammermusik Abend in Lüdenscheid and so Ida Gerhardi at last had the immense joy of hearing it, especially Fred's cello Sonata. For her and her family this was of course an *enormous event* and she wrote most touchingly about it. As I had conceived the idea I was rather anxious, but Ida's brother had written in the papers and the Hall was "Ausverkauft" and a most enthusiastic Audience. A friend of Ida's took the piano part and played gratis and also invited B. to stay at his house. The Gerhardi's gave a little supper!'

1926

Delius's condition appeared to be more or less stable and the household at Grez was beginning to conform to the regular patterns of behaviour that Eric Fenby a decade later was to describe so vividly in his *Delius as I Knew Him*. For Jelka the only release from her duties came in the form of the once-weekly drive to Fontainebleau, to shop for food in the market. The car was also used on most days to take Delius for a drive. Jelka's letter of 20 January to Adine O'Neill indicates little if any abatement in interest in Delius's music generally, and on 14 February she reported the success of the *Mass* in Hagen to Philip Heseltine. Then Kennedy Scott conducted *The Song of the High Hills* in London, and Gardiner, in a letter to Grainger on 20 March, commended Grainger's beneficial influence: 'A further result of this arrangement of yours, you will be glad to hear, is that CKS, having had the advantage of studying & discussing it at Grez, gave a good performance of it in London a couple of weeks ago.' Jelka was perplexed that Oxford University had offered Delius an Honorary Doctorate but could not award it to him as he was unable to travel to Oxford to accept it in person.

Following the wiring of the house for electricity, the Deliuses tried various radio sets in the spring. For use with their gramophone Grainger sent a batch of records, including his own performance of Chopin's B minor Sonata: 'splendid – *awfully good*', Delius told him on 20 May. 'We enjoyed it ever so much.' A few days later, Jelka wrote to Adine O'Neill: Delius was 'getting on fairly well'. There had been visits in the spring by Arnold Bax, by the Howard-Joneses and Barjansky; and a surprise came in the visit of an older friend and colleague, Fritz Cassirer, last seen before the war. In July, 'quite a lot cheerier and better', Delius tried to dictate a little music to Jelka. Summer visitors reaffirmed the concert-giving tradition in the Deliuses' own home: they included Barjansky, Howard-Jones, Norman O'Neill and Balfour Gardiner. C. W. Orr was another visitor. Heseltine was expected, but had still failed to appear when Jelka wrote to him on 8 September: 'I read in the paper that the B.B.C. are planning 12 big concerts at the Albert Hall. We have a very good wireless set now and *I do hope* they will do some of Fred's things. It seems all to be the Elgar-clique and official celebrity-conductors ... I wish you could push in Fred's direction a bit   It would do him so much good to hear some of his bigger works again. He needs stimulus . . . He must not be allowed to stagnate and "Les absents ont toujours tort." They give mighty little of his music in England now.'

On 10 September Jelka recorded in a letter to the Schiffs that they had lost the girl who had been their servant, and furthermore that the Bruder had been taken away and replaced by another. Later in the autumn there came the special pleasure of a visit from Edvard Munch, in Paris at the time. He was impressed to find in the invalid the 'optimistic good humour' that he remembered from the days of their comparative youth. December brought news of Fritz Cassirer's death, so soon after the happy reunion at Grez. Jelka penned a brief and touching reminiscence for the *Frankfurter Zeitung*.

(504)
Jelka Delius to Adine O'Neill

FREDERICK DELIUS
Grez-sur-Loing
S. et M.
20.1.1926

Dearest Adine,

Thanks for letter, nice bookmarker Calender and enclosures. I wonder if you could go to the L.O.S. concert? I am so delighted, Beecham gave "In a Summer Garden". Did I tell you that the Mass of Life was given on Dec. 18th with greatest success at Coblenz, on Febr. 4th it will be done at Hagen, later on at Duisburg and in May by Schuricht in Wiesbaden and Francfort. The Song of the High Hills is down for perform[ance] in Athens! Sea drift at Gotha   "Paris" was just done in Vienna bei Knappertsbusch[1] from Munich   The Cello Concerto with *great success* with Barjansky at Wiesbaden. It always breaks my heart that this beautiful work had such an unfortunate first performance in London – so slow that it took 9 minutes too long! (Goossens)

Our neighbours here have the Radio; Sunday we heard Fred's Cello Sonata played by Barbirolli[2] – not very well played – but we heard it perfectly. So if you broadcast again, do let me know in time.

Paul Cassirer who killed himself is the Cousin of our Fritz Cassirer and was formerly associated with Bruno Cassirer, Fritz Cassirer's brother. Bruno fell in Love with Paul's beautiful 1st wife and a divorce and deadly feud ensued. Then he was long the lover of this very gifted but "vicieuse" actress, whom he later must have married. Fritz Cassirer – he lives in Munich now – brought out

Koanga (Elberfeld) and The Village Romeo in Berlin; but he has given up conducting. You must be tremendously busy and I wish all success. If you write in your french musical paper still, you might put in something about Fred as there is a scheme "in embryo" to do his Mass of Life in Paris with Klenau and Philharmonic choir. But do not mention this scheme – it is far too vague yet.[3] Fred is not too bad and has a good appetite now. I have to make oyster patties, lobster, Irish stew etc etc.

Ever affly with love to Norman
Jelka

Autograph letter, signed and dated, written on headed notepaper. Envelope addressed: Mrs O'Neill/4 Pembroke Villa's/Kensington W/Londres/Angleterre. Postmark: GREZ [?] 1 26.

The original is in the Delius Trust Archive.

1   Hans Knappertsbusch (1888–1965): German conductor. Born in Elberfeld, he was from 1913 to 1918 opera director there (a post earlier held by Fritz Cassirer), and so would have been well aware of the Delius tradition of his native town. Particularly renowned for his interpretation of Wagner and Strauss, he was at this time opera director at Munich.

2   See Letter 516, note.

3   Nothing was to come of this promising scheme, of which Jelka had written to Grainger on 8 December: 'A french friend of ours has offered 25 000 frs if we can organize a Delius-Concert in Paris. It will be a most difficult thing, especially as Fred wants the Mass of Life with the Philharmonic Choir and Klenau conducting. I have written to Klenau, who is most willing.' In fact Klenau paid a visit to the Deliuses in Grez in February, no doubt to discuss the project.

(505)
Jelka Delius to Percy Grainger

FREDERICK DELIUS
Grez-sur-Loing
S et M
20.5.1926

Dearest Percy,

It is a wonderful living joy, all this splendid news about your Los Angeles Concert.[1] It is the greatest Test for a work if one loves it more and more the more one lives with it. Your beautiful letter gave Fred the greatest pleasure –

(me too)   It must have been a wonderful performance and I only wish we could have been there. And now you are going *still further away*. I do wish we could have you nearer. The Gram. Records are so splendid – I put them on a number of times   I do love that Strathpey reel. The brother was quite scared at all that liveliness

I think if you saw Fred now you would find him ever so much better. He eats quite normally and is so much more lively and sits up longer at night, sleeps less in the day. He has not had a drop of wine, only his light beer at lunch, which he will not give up. But he has knocked it off at night and takes "Surmelk"[2] instead, a great improvement. Only his eyes do not seem much changed. It is true we have had the most trying cold wet spring and only now it is beginning to be better. We have made a lot of essays with wireless sets and have an expensive english one on trial now. It works very well for the big english Station Daventry but we fail to obtain the shortwave towns in the north and on the continent. Germany has generally beastly programmes. But the smaller english towns excellent ones. As it is we had a lot of pleasure: frequent performances of Grieg – Songs, Piano and orch Suites, yesterday the whole 2^d act of Götterdämmerung from Covent Garden which was absolutely perfect and just as if one were in the theatre, singers and orchestra equally audible. We had "Molly on the Shore" several times and often madrigals (old engl) and Folk Songs – I must get a good set.

We have had visitors quite often. Fred protests beforehand every time and then enjoys it thoro'ly and is often quite amusing. We had the Howard-Jones's and Barjansky; they played the double conc; Barjansky plays it gloriously. The other day the Cassirers came (the man who conducted Fred's Opera's in Berlin and Elberfeld). Fred was tremendously "aufgeregt."

Beecham was going to give an English Festival in Paris and Kennedy Scott was to conduct The Song of the High Hills   They were bringing over the Philharmonic choir and London S. Orch. But the strike came – and Beecham has new lawsuits and has vanished again – so it is all off. I am terribly disappointed – as we were to hear it.

The Scheme to do the Mass of Life with Klenau in Paris (bringing over the Philharmonic choir and with a Paris orchestra) was *nearly* right. All Orch. advertis. in fact all Paris expenses were guaranteed. But it was to cost 700£ to bring over the Choir. Of this 400£ had been guaranteed, but the rest could not be got. Perhaps it was lucky as the strike would have upset it too![3] But I have emptied my inkbottle in vain over all this – and as it is now it is terribly difficult for me to write – If I only had the faculty of doing 2 or 3 things at a time like you do!

I must stop, dear friend Percy, I was writing at dawn and now the sun has risen and I must to work. The Simons from Francfort are coming to-morrow to spend the Whitsundays – very jolly.

Did you read "Inland Far" by Clifford Bax?[4] A nice book!

I wish you all possible good things in Australia and always love to hear from you

Ever aff^{ly} yrs
Jelka

How kind of you about Schirmer's – but I am afraid it is no good! We received a most enthusiastic letter about your Los Angeles Concert from Robert Nichols.

Autograph letter, signed and dated, written on headed notepaper. Envelope addressed: U.S.A/Percy A. Grainger/Esq/7 Cromwell Place/White Plains/New York. On reverse: 'Kindly forward'. Postmark: GREZ 20 -5 26. A letter in Jelka's hand from Delius is also enclosed.

The original is in the Grainger Museum.

1   Together with his own works, *Marching Song of Democracy* and *Father and Daughter*, Grainger conducted Delius's *The Song of the High Hills* at Los Angeles on 30 April – the fourth anniversary of his mother's death.

2   Norwegian: *sour milk*.

3   That his major works were virtually never heard in Paris was ever a source of disappointment to Delius. On 8 September he informed Universal Edition that Koussevitzky planned to conduct *The Song of the High Hills* there. No evidence is to hand of such a performance taking place, but Koussevitzky certainly did give the work in Boston, Massachusetts, in March the following year. In August Delius asked Hertzka to put the work forward for the 1928 Tonkünstlerfest in Essen.

4   Published by Heinemann in 1925, *Inland Far* would have particularly interested the Deliuses for its author's account of a holiday in Barcelona and Mallorca with his brother Arnold, Gustav Holst and Balfour Gardiner (pp. 211–44). Arnold Bax had in fact paid a call on the Deliuses in April. On his return to England, he wrote his *Romantic Overture* for small orchestra with piano, and dedicated it to Delius.

(506)
Jelka Delius to Philip Heseltine

FREDERICK DELIUS
Grez-sur-Loing
S. et M.
[July 1926]

Dear Phil. I was delighted to hear from you and the little pamphlet¹ with your good photo gave us great pleasure. Fred said: I am doubly glad Phil is getting on so well, as I always encouraged him to keep to his music. I wish we could have heard the concert with Goss. We have a very good Radio now at last   Yet it is not easy to get English towns, except Daventry, London Cardiff, Bournemouth; the latter by no means always. But I get Munich, Francfort, Barcelona – But just now programmes are abject. We keep the Radio-Times.

Fred is really quite a lot cheerier and better, tho' his eyes do not change much. But his general status and food assimilation are much improved and he is much more his old self. It would be jolly if you could come. Balfour G. is coming on Aug 16th for 8 or ten days.[2] You had better come after that – or if more convenient, *before*. Please stay with us if you come alone.

We have gramophone records of the Cello Sonata Harrison-Craxton[3] and "Daffodils" Columbia, the latter sung by Brunskill[4] (a contralto-dragoon!)! Twilight Fancies (Princessin) and Venevil have also been done by H.M.V. Could you perhaps go and hear it somewhere? If it is no better than Daffodils it is no pleasure for Fred to hear it. Fr. has dictated a few bars twice the other day and *I do so* hope he will go on with it. The difficulties are so great as he cannot see what he has written, I mean: dictated. But I can play it to him. *It could be done* and it would be so good, and he would think about music again. Barjansky is in Grez again.[5] Best love from us both – dear friend

Ever aff[ly]
Jelka.

Autograph letter, signed and undated, written on headed notepaper.

The original is in the British Library.

1   Probably the essay by Moeran: 'Peter Warlock', published by Chester in 1926.

2   Balfour Gardiner continued to be supportive: 'Mr Gardiner is in the process of correcting Appalachia & then will also look over Sea Drift', Delius told Universal Edition on 20 November. A little later he sent Gardiner's 'thoroughly corrected score' to Hertzka for engraving, reminding him that Gardiner was waiting to receive a *Sea Drift* score for the same purpose.

3   Harold Craxton (1885–1971): English pianist. Known as a fine accompanist, he taught at the Royal Academy of Music from 1919 until his retirement in 1960.

4   Muriel Brunskill (1900–80): English contralto. At this period she was singing with the British National Opera Company.

5   'Barjansky and 3 Americans played him, Delius, his Quartette in the Garden, where it sounded quite lovely', wrote Jelka to Heseltine on 8 September. 'The London String Quart. never understood it.'

(507)
Jelka Delius to Edvard Munch

Gare Bourron   Grez sur Loing
depart Gare de Lyon   S. et M.
                                                      Sunday 31.[10.]1926[1]

Dear Munch,

Delius was so indescribably glad to hear from you from Paris! But both your
letters arrived together only this morning & I have telegraphed immediately to
ask if you would not visit us. Please, please do so, we would so much love to
see you again, and you know how bad my husband has been, although he has
been better again during the last few months, but he can hardly see at all.

　　You have a good train 10.43 & would then be here for déjeuner, taxi at
Bourron. There is also a train at about 4 o'clock in the afternoon. Should you
not be able to tomorrow, please come, *whenever you like*　we are always here of
course & would be happy to see you.

　　Yours ever
　　Jelka Delius

P.S. You can also get here direct from Paris by car, just take a taxi, 69 kilometers, via Fontainebleau

---

Autograph letter, signed and dated, written in German.

The original is in the Munch Museum.

1　The original has 31.11.1926. A letter from Jelka to Sydney Schiff dated 10
October records that a visit from the Schiffs on 12 October was also much looked
forward to.

(508)
Edvard Munch to Frederick Delius

[Oslo,[1] November/December 1926]

Dear friend Delius

I am so glad that I have seen you and your wife again[2] – And it makes me especially glad to see that you looked so well and that you have kept your fine
cheerful voice – That you [have kept] your optimistic good humour which I
have so often envied you – He who has this strong inner self is happier than so
many others –

This year I saw a lot of old friends again in Paris too – I went and visited old haunts. – I thought of the poor but beautiful time when I had my studio in the rue de la Santé – I remember the times when I wanted to sell old wine bottles so as to get something to eat – And I could not even get 10 centimes for them. In those days, you remember, I would often dine at your place – would drink fine wine and you would cheer me with your good humour – Then you also took me to Mollard where they were so kind to me – All our acquaintances had indeed become very old – Molard was an old man – I also met Ouvrés[3] the printmaker (that is his name isn't it?) – But he looked just the same as before – Jappe Nilssen is very poorly and ailing   My good friend also complains a good deal about life – I think it cheers him up a bit to take a swipe at the young painters – He does that pretty well too – But otherwise quite a number are dead – But I do meet old friends of yours – I cannot understand why one does not hear more of your music – Everyone talks of how in other countries and especially in England you are reckoned one of the greatest – I and Jappe Nilssen believe that it comes from the fact that you were always modest about your own things – and that you always took an interest in the rest of us –.

Draft autograph letter, unsigned and undated, written in German.

The original is in the Munch Museum. No evidence that a fair copy was sent has been found.

1   The city of Christiania officially reverted in name to its original 'Oslo' on 1 January 1925.

2   The actual date of Munch's visit to Grez has not been established.

3   Achille Ouvré.

1927

The year started brightly with an enjoyable visit from Annie Harrison with her daughters Beatrice and Margaret (as well as Gerald Moore) who played to Delius. 'Fred certainly is stronger and better in many ways' was Jelka's message to Philip Heseltine on 9 January. A few days later Delius was to learn that the Wiesbaden Staatstheater intended to give *A Village Romeo* during their next winter season; and in February came news of plans to perform the *Mass of Life* at Darmstadt. One result of recent strictures by Beecham on what some took to be the 'shameful neglect' of Delius's music in England came in the form of a visit on 15 January from a correspondent of the London *Evening Standard*. Jelka took the opportunity of the interview to castigate Oxford University for having declined a year earlier to confer *in absentia* an honorary doctorate of music on Delius. 'Delius is indifferent to such things,' she wrote to Annie Harrison after the journalist had left, 'but in my heart it made me wild that in such an exceptional case they could not break their silly old rules!!! So pedantic!!'

There were several visits from Beecham later in the winter, on one of which he was accompanied by a doctor from London. Spring brought news of performances by Koussevitzky in Boston of *The Song of the High Hills* and by Beecham in London of *Sea Drift*. The summer brought less consolation: 'we have been rather lonely,' wrote Jelka to Marie Clews on 10 August. She might have added 'depressed', which they unquestionably were on hearing the news of Ida Gerhardi's death on 29 June. The Deliuses were touched by Nadia Boulanger's pilgrimage to Grez on 9 August and delighted, later that month, with the arrival on loan of a Duo-Art piano together with a selection of piano rolls. The end of the summer brought Gardiner, together with Percy Grainger. Soon after this visit, Oskar Fried came to see them; he came again in December, with the information that he was going to perform some Delius in Russia and that he was keen to record some of Delius's music.

Meanwhile the *Mass* had been given in the autumn in Berlin and Frankfurt, and *A Village Romeo* revived, if in an indifferent production, in December at Wiesbaden. Furthermore, the riches of Europe's concert halls were regularly available on the radio. Balfour Gardiner and Frederic Austin came to Grez for

Christmas, celebrated in the house with a party which was joined by Alden
Brooks and his family.

(509)
Jelka Delius to Percy Grainger

GREZ-SUR-LOING (S & M)
[station] BOURRON
30.3.1927

Dearest Percy,

Both your letters, March 11th and 14th have arrived –

I am so happy that you have found this wonderful swedish girl[1] – it will put
quite a new colour into your life, and I am sure she must love you too. Your
life was becoming too strained, and I hope she will help you to think more of
yourself and to allow yourself more leisure, not *all the year* round these deadly,
lonely Concert-journeys – all those gushing faces of people, who, after all, give
you nothing – And then some real happiness, if you only could have it! – I *do*
so want it for you, dear friend. And has not perhaps some sunny, deep-hidden
feeling come out in your present piano playing? You may not realize it
yourself.

Dear Fred has been patiently thro' the wintermonths; he looks tolerably
well – really *very* well – and is lively and ever improving tho very little.
Beecham paid us several visits. He also brought a London doctor over to see
Fred and he advised a Paris Doctor, whom we went to see. I do not think,
tho', that he was very hopeful about bringing about a great change. He
seemed very thoughtful and wise and told me, it was rare to see a man with
Fred's illness, so calm, reposed-looking and especially so entirely clear headed
and it would be a great mistake to risk a very drastic treatment that *might* get
him infinitely worse and into a state in which he could not enjoy life as much
as even now he did. That is my feeling too: Let us make him as happy as
possible and not ruin him with Medicine-poisoning etc. The London doctor
had rather frightened me by suggesting, he should go to some Sanatorium for
a prolonged treatment. That would have made Fred miserable.

I suppose you have heard about the B.B.C. Concert given in the London Studio for Fred's birthday End of Jan. Geoffrey Toye conducted Brigg
fair, Violin-Concerto, Summer Garden, 1st Dance Rhapsody. (Sammons
fiddled)   It was quite good upon the whole, Summer garden better than the
other 2 works; we heard really quite well, and they addressed a little speech to
Fred, which seemed so personal and extraordinary; he enjoyed it all. Of course
on the other hand it is shameful, that they have given 11 big broadcast

Concerts in the Albert Hall, without giving a note of Delius – it is really extraordinary. Beecham does not hate them for nothing. The Harrisons came here to play to Fred and played really beautifully.[2] Beatrice plays his Concerto splendidly now and the younger sister Margaret the Violin Concerto with great style and purity Fred was delighted with their playing (That little Russian in Francfort quite travestied the Concerto)[3] Beatrice is going to America in October – and she would have loved you to give her some introductions etc; but of course you will not be there when she is. But you can perhaps hear her in London. The Harrison's are devoted to Fred, and did much to bring about that B.B.C. studio Concert. They also got them to give us the excellent Loud speaker and a first rate H.M.V. Gramophone (Useful devotion!!!) We have not seen Balfour for ages. The Philharmonic did Fred's Violin Concerto; but it appears Frank Bridge[4] conducted – and not well at all. Beecham is conducting a lot again. He conducted in Prague and Vienna and had great success, and is going again in the autumn

Dear Percy, I have a terrible feeling as if I had written you all this before – I cannot quite remember. Please forgive me, if it is so –

We are expecting your visit with love and impatience.

Yrs devotedly Jelka.

P.S. We have a friend, Kenneth Spence,[5] who has been much to the Hebrides and has been humming to Fred their beautiful songs, shearing – milking, reaping etc. all doing something songs. It made me think of you.

The Barjansky's are on their way to Sweden, after an exhib in Brussels, where Mrs B.[6] made the portrait of the Queen of Belgium.

Do you hear from Lippay? We have not for ages.

Fred sends you all his love again, and that your new plans are wise, and you are to store some money, and not give it all away.

I have quite finished my Mumbo Jumbo translation. I must say I had a lot of fun over it. I tried to render Clews' expressions and train of thought, alliterations, puns, nonsense-poems etc. These intellectual gymnastics are most agreable and exhilarating. Only I regret that he has not eliminated more and repeats himself so much. It could have been more pithy, if shorter.

Excuse this rambling letter.

Jelka.

P.P.S. "She" had to be a Scandinavian, of course!

Autograph letter, signed and dated, written on headed notepaper. Envelope addressed: Percy Grainger Esq/7 Cromwell Place/White Plains/N.Y./U.S.A. Postmark: GREZ [date illegible].

The original is in the Grainger Museum.

1   Ella Viola Ström (1889–1979): Swedish artist. Grainger became acquainted with her on board ship from New Zealand to Honolulu late in 1926. Less than a year later, he proposed to her, and they were married on 9 August 1928.

2   Gerald Moore came with the Harrisons early in January and stayed overnight at the Deliuses' (cf. *Am I Too Loud? Memoirs of an Accompanist*, pp. 71–2). He accompanied the sisters, playing the Cello Concerto and Sonata with Beatrice and the Violin Concerto and Sonatas with Margaret.

3   An extraordinary statement, considering that otherwise the Deliuses' frequently reiterated opinions of Barjansky's playing were always highly complimentary.

4   Frank Bridge (1879–1941): English composer. A violinist by training, he also played the viola, and conducted frequently in England. As a teacher he was to exert an important influence on Britten. As a composer, his harmonic language was not dissimilar to Delius's. No evidence has been found to suggest that the two men met. The performance of the Violin Concerto took place on 24 February.

5   Kenneth Spence was a wealthy English schoolmaster, with a keen and influential interest in rural preservation, who had first met the Deliuses by chance while on a walking holiday in Norway in 1921. A music-lover, he was, according to Eric Fenby, a great admirer not only of Delius, but also of Arnold Bax, and of Bax's orchestration in particular. He became a frequent visitor to Grez, and Delius always enjoyed his company. (Cf. Lionel Hill: 'Kenneth Spence 1887–1944', *The Delius Society Journal*, 83 (July 1984), p. 19.)

6   Catherine Barjansky, née Konstantinovsky (1890–1965): Russian-born sculptress. In her *Portraits and Backgrounds* she was to publish a sensitive pen-portrait of Delius during his last years. She also modelled a small wax bust of the composer.

(510)

Jelka Delius to Percy Grainger

GREZ-SUR-LOING (S & M)
[station] BOURRON
2.7.1927

Dearest Percy,

Our dear friend Ida Gerhardi died on the 29th of June. After terrible sufferings she died of exhaustion quite quietly.

I have been so anxious, so unbelievably in revolt against this long impending blow and I feel this loss of such a unique wonderful angelic, spirited, all-understanding gifted friend of my whole life – I feel it as an immense sorrow – a void.[1] It makes me think of you when you lost your dear mother, your greatest friend!

She was so overjoyed when you had written that you would go and play to her — it is too late — alas. You have given her so much pleasure with your letters etc. in her long and weary illness.

I was prepared for her death — but I could not, *would* not believe it, and had no heart to do things; or I should have written to thank you for all you have so kindly done re Steinway and the hope about the Duo-Art.[2] Fred would enjoy that *immensely* it is such a wonderful invention and it is so glorious of you to have recorded his own things — dear kind Percy.

You do not say when you are leaving? Will this catch you yet? Fred was happy reading all you wrote about N.C.Sk. and Brigg Fair and I played it for him on the Gramo, and he looked happy. I thought he loved it. He is fairly well, greatly looking forward to seeing you again.

Fond love from us both, dear kind friend, and "au revoir"

Ever affly
Jelka

Autograph letter, signed and dated, written on headed notepaper. Envelope addressed: Percy Grainger Esq/7 Cromwell Place/White Plains./New York/U.S.A. Postmark: GREZ [date illegible].

The original is in the Grainger Museum.

1   Barjansky heard the news from Jelka and wrote to Ida's family: 'Mrs Delius's letter is one of utter despair. Delius and she feel forsaken, everything is quite empty for them.' Bertha Stoop also wrote: 'How she worked for others, for Delius. Mrs Delius is quite desolate.'

2   Discontented with their Ibach piano, Jelka wrote to Grainger on 26 April: 'Would it be quite impossible for you, dear Percy, to induce Steinway to let Fred have one of their pianos? ... In view of all this great publicity that has been made about the neglect of Delius, might you not get them to let Fred have a piano all the time? Numerous great conductors like Beecham, Klenau, Schuricht etc etc; numerous composers, virtuosi etc come here constantly and it would really not do for a man of Fred's standing to have to buy pianos.' Grainger's efforts bore modest fruit, the Aeolian Company lending Delius later in the summer a Duo-Art piano, together with a selection of piano rolls, including some recorded by Grainger, Ignaz Friedman and Paderewski.

(511)
Jelka Delius to Marie Clews

FREDERICK DELIUS
Grez-sur-Loing
S. et M.
10.8.27

My dear Marie, Thanks for your kind letter. No, I have heard nothing at all from Bismarck.[1] I am writing to him by this same post.

If he fails us the best thing would certainly be for the Publisher of your new book to make arrangements with a german firm for the Publication of M. Jumbo in German. (as I suppose Grant Richards is no good?)

A woman writing like that and from France too – simply means Paper-Basket.

I shall yet try, of course but – ??

We should love you both to come and see us, could make you quite comfortable sleeping in the Hotel with all the "comfort moderne".

Fred has been very upset by a beastly tooth-root-inflammation – caused naturally by the dentists who fix such heavy gold work on to teeth, that they can not stand it. He is better now; we have been rather lonely, but yesterday we had a delightful surprise visit of Nadia Boulanger[2], a very gifted french musician, who was the love of Raoul Pugno the great Pianist. She brought 2 young American composers and a music stud. girl along. They played their compositions and played some of Fred's compositions most beautifully – they knew and adored much of his work. Nadia Boulanger possesses the Score of his Mass of Life and adores it. They all hung on Fred's lips and the great calm of the garden with its touching central figure made a great impression on them.

With love and all good messages from Fred

Yrs affly
Jelka

Lloyd Osbourne is a very nice man. He often comes to Grez en passant and we see him with pleasure. They have a villa at Antibes   Mrs O. is perhaps rather a Social climber. They make a very good thing out of the R.L.S.-rights, films, stage, manuscript sales etc.

Autograph letter, signed and dated, written on headed notepaper.

The original is in the Delius Trust Archive.

1   A friend of the Rosen family, the Prince von Bismarck was busily trying to find a German publisher for Jelka's translation of Clews's play. He wrote to her on 17 August: two publishers had turned it down and the manuscript was now with another

in Munich. So that he could press the matter further, he asked Jelka to send him some of the favourable reviews (from both England and America) the piece had received on its publication: 'I will do all I can to place the book.'

2   Nadia Boulanger (1887–1979): French composer, conductor and teacher. She studied with Fauré, and became the teacher of many distinguished American and European composers.

(512)

Frederick Delius to May Harrison

GREZ-SUR-LOING (S & M)
[station] BOURRON
3 [?] Nov 27.

Delius dictates

My dear May, It was so delightful to hear from you and I am so pleased you are going to play my Sonata. I have not forgotten how beautifully you played it 1915 with such pure intonation and poetic conception   How splendid that Bax is playing it with you. You could not have found a better partner.

Please let us hear how it went and try to play it for Daventry once. I have not heard it for such a long time.

We are delighted to hear of Baba's success in U.S.A.[1] Your mother sent a Boston cutting; but we know no details. Please send them my love and do come to Grez to see us whenever you can

Ever aff^{ly} yrs
Frederick Delius

Letter in the hand of Jelka Delius, dated, written on headed notepaper.

The original is in the collection of Miss Margaret Harrison.

1   Beatrice Harrison had brought out both the Cello Concerto and the Cello Sonata (the latter with Margaret Harrison as accompanist) in America. The conductor at the New York Philharmonic Society concerts at Carnegie Hall on 23 and 25 November when she played the concerto was Mengelberg.

(513)
Jelka Delius to Adine O'Neill

FREDERICK DELIUS
Grez-sur-Loing
S. et M.
15.11.27

My dear Adine,

We listened to your playing the other night and it came thro' very well. Fred liked the Scarlatti best. I enjoyed it very much! We both admired your pearly technique

I see in the papers that Fried is conducting thursday night at the Phil. He is a wonderful conductor and he always gets so much more out of an Orchestra than any one else thro' his wonderfully good rehearsing. Please tell Norman to engage him for some Delius next time. He did "Appalachia" admirably in Berlin with so much life in his rhythm contrast, precision. Appalachia has not been done for ages in London[1]

He was here to see us a few weeks ago and can tell you the latest news. (He is a card!!)   He also did "Life's Dance" and "Paris" in Berlin.

I suppose you heard of the unexpectedly great success of the Mass of Life in Berlin beginning of October. Schuricht did it and the Philharmonie was "ausverkauft". To-morrow it is to be done at Francfort; I think by a man called Temesvary. The Village Romeo is being done at Wiesbaden Staatsoper on Nov 27th.[2]

Fred is not doing too badly, he is eating oysters all the time and that seems always to do him good. He is taken for a drive in spite of the cold every day – and we read all the time. Fred is always furious about the Radio, but enjoys it all the same. We hear England best of all (France is abject). Francfort, Stuttgart, Hamburg, Vienna, Rome, Cologne – as there is a lot of variety. I suppose you are as busy as ever. Do let us hear sometimes.

Much love to you all three!

Ever affly yours
Jelka

What do people say about the Beecham Opera scheme?

Autograph letter, signed and dated, written on headed notepaper. Envelope addressed: Madame O'Neill/4 Pembroke Villas/Kensington W/Londres/Angleterre. Postmark: GREZ 15 -11 27.

The original is in the Delius Trust Archive.

1   Fried's menu on 17 November was Weber, Brahms and Liszt. He was to conduct
one more Philharmonic Society concert, on 3 April 1930, a more adventurous occasion
featuring the first performance of Holst's Concerto for Two Violins as the only English
work. No Delius.

2   'I find it terribly hard not to be able to go there –,' Jelka wrote to Marie Clews on
8 November, 'but Fred can not bear the idea of my going away for a single night.' In
the event, the first night at Wiesbaden was postponed to 4 December.

(514)
Frederick Delius to Paul Bekker

GREZ-SUR-LOING (S & M)

14.12.27

Dear Herr Bekker,

I have received your telegram and letter, which delighted me enormously &
would like to thank you with all my heart for all the love and care which you
have devoted to my work. As you can imagine, it was awfully hard for me not
to be able to be present.

Today I was sent by friends a programme containing your marvellously
sympathetic Delius-essay & introduction. Please accept my heartfelt thanks for
everything!

The criticisms you promised to send have not yet arrived.[1]

I would also ask you to express my sincere thanks to all who took part, but
particularly to Vrenchen, Sali, the Dark Fiddler.

In addition, special thanks to Herr Zulauf.[2]

I am sorry this letter comes so late, as my wife, to whom I always dictate my
letters, has just had a bad bout of influenza. She herself takes a most fervent
interest in the performances & would much like me to have the opportunity to
hear it on the radio.

With kind regards to your wife

Sincerely yours
Frederick Delius

Letter in the hand of Jelka Delius, dated, written in German on headed notepaper.
Jelka crossed out the symbol for 'railway station' and BOURRON in the original
heading. Envelope addressed: Herrn General-Inten/danten Paul Bekker/Opernhaus/
Wiesbaden/Allemagne. Postmark: PARIS MONTARGIS 15 -12 27.

The original is in the Library of Congress, Washington D.C. It is the only known
letter from Delius to Bekker.

Paul Bekker: See Letter 449, note 1.

1   As reports of the production came in, the Deliuses registered disappointment at
the fact that it had, after all, proved 'middling'. Jelka wrote to Grainger on 27
December: 'The Kapellmeister "nüchtern" u. "ordentlich". The Scenery and stage
management rather without taste or intimate fitness for the subject. Had we only been
able to be there for rehearsals, much could have been improved. It is tragic to have to
leave a work like that in more or less rough and clumsy hands.'

2   Ernst Zulauf (1878–?): German conductor. He studied at Leipzig, joining the
Frankfurt Opera in 1901, and conducted opera at Cassel from 1903.

(515)
Frederick Delius to Universal Edition

FREDERICK DELIUS
Grez-sur-Loing
S. et M.
29.12.27

Dear Herr Director,

Many thanks for your letter of the 14th.[1] I agree with your opinion regarding
the over-large stage. Just as in Berlin, this needs to be reduced in size & in fact
in Berlin it was very beautifully done so that each scene respectively was seen
through a frame which remained for all the scenes. In this way the decor was
also simplified considerably. A painted backcloth behind – the greatest simplicity, which of course the work very much needs. In this way the fair scene
made an excellent effect too, there was just a small merry-go-round & the
shooting-gallery – the rest was splendidly simulated by the painted backcloth.
In the scene in the hut the dream of Sali & Vrenchen was very well represented. The stage was darkened & at the same time the wall of the little hut
was drawn aside to reveal behind it the wedding ceremony of the couple in
church with wedding guests   priest etc. with singing & bells. It is a great
mistake to omit this, because the music is made for this scene & clearly
demands it. – The penultimate scene during the incidental music is also just a
curtain & the couple are seen wandering towards the Paradise Garden, while
behind this the last scene is being prepared. I am afraid all that was rather too
clumsy, too realistic in W[iesbaden]. Also the fair must not be out of the style
of the whole; not too many walkers-on & people. The few dancers, vendors
etc, who come on & sing are perfectly sufficient.
    Regarding your plan to reduce the orchestra. I am not opposed to it in prin-
ciple. But everything depends on this being done by a talented musician who
is truly capable & who has a real feeling for my music. Before agreeing de-

finitely I would also like to know a few more details about it. How large is a Mozart orchestra?

You see, if there are, as in Hassan, 26 *solo instruments*, then something can be done with them, but if just an indifferent arrangement with the same number of players is made, the whole can be ruined. Please let me have more details about this. Such an arrangement is no easy matter.

Hoping to have more details from you & with best New Year's wishes from us both

I remain

Cordially yours
Frederick Delius

P.S. You may know that the Mass of Life is to be given in London on the 16th May.

verte

Mr Gardiner[2] is waiting impatiently for the final proof of Sea Drift.

Please do not on any account have a foreword printed which has not first been checked by myself or one of my English friends. There are some bad mistakes in the Appalachia foreword & grammatical howlers too. It is a failing of the Germans always to think that they have a complete command of foreign languages. Before printing any further copies, please submit them for checking.

F.D.

Letter in the hand of Jelka Delius, dated, written in German on headed notepaper.

The original is in the Universal Edition archives.

1   Hertzka had written to tell Delius of his visit to one of the performances of *A Village Romeo and Juliet* at Wiesbaden. Musically, he felt, it had been excellent, but the direction and decor had 'not quite satisfied' him. The huge Wiesbaden stage had robbed the work of its intimate and lyrical character. If the opera were to have a future, there would be far better chances for it on smaller stages and, consequently, with a reduced orchestra. Would Delius consider having a sympathetic conductor make a greatly reduced score for a Mozartian-scale orchestra?

2   Gardiner came again for Christmas. 'We have just spent a few delightful days with Balfour & Fred. Austin,' wrote Jelka to Grainger on 27 December. Gardiner and Austin had played to Delius during their stay. Oskar Fried had paid another visit, too, probably a little earlier than this.

1928

'We are alright, so far; living our calm and almost posthumous existence, and longing for spring!' Thus Jelka to Marie Clews on 22 January. During the winter the radio represented the most important link with the outside world, and earlier in the month a letter from Delius congratulated May Harrison on her broadcast performance of the first Violin Sonata with Arnold Bax, given on 3 January. Geoffrey Toye's fine performances of three of Delius's orchestral works were welcome additions to the record collection; and the Duo-Art piano continued to play its tunes. In February, Oscar Klemperer wrote to report on a discussion he had had on a visit to Czechoslovakia with the director of Prague's Municipal Theatre, who in consequence became greatly interested in the possibility of producing a Czech version of *Hassan*. Delius asked his publisher to press the matter. Having wrestled so long with her translation of Clews's play, Jelka was still trying in the spring – without success – to find a German publisher; she hoped too that Clews might get André Maurois to translate it into French. Later in the spring Dr Heermann from Cassel came to spend a week at Grez in order to examine and prescribe further treatment for Delius. The summer drifted slowly by: 'My health is a little better and I am enjoying the sunshine in the garden,' he told Heseltine. He had recently taken up once more his *Folkeraadet* music, the *Norwegian Suite* from 1897, and now hoped that Ralph Hawkes would publish it in London. One of the summer visitors was C.W.Orr.

Much the most significant event of the year, though, was the arrival around the beginning of June of an enthusiastically appreciative letter from a twenty-two-year old English musician, Eric Fenby. Delius was touched. There was an exchange of correspondence and the result was that at the end of August Fenby heard that Delius had accepted his offer to come to Grez in order to help Delius complete those compositions of his that lay unfinished. Fenby arrived on 10 October and soon found himself playing piano accompaniments with visitors Barjansky and Gardiner. Some time after Gardiner's departure the first attempts at composing by dictation to Fenby began. Although marked by extraordinary difficulties at the outset, the working partnership was under way. On 21 November Jelka pointed out to May Harrison that there would be no need for her to bring a pianist when she next came to Grez: Fenby was 'very gifted' and '*very* musical'.

As for Delius, he was in fairly good form: 'The wonderful summer, months and months of uninterrupted sunshine has been a godsend to him. Even now he is out every day, unless it pours.' May was to play the second Violin Sonata with Bax in London on 23 November. Bouts of pain, compounded by a bitterly cold winter, restricted Delius's efforts to work with Fenby for the time being, but May Harrison did indeed come to Grez and Fenby did join her in playing to Delius. The Howard-Joneses arrived for Christmas, and the end of the year found Jelka nursing higher hopes. She wrote of Fenby's arrival to Marie Clews: '. . . he has come here out of sheer devotion to Delius to help him to do any musical jobs. He has already made himself very useful and also plays the piano parts for any Virtuosi who come . . . Dear Fred is quite lively and in good form and begins to think of his music again.'

(516)
Frederick Delius to John Barbirolli

GREZ SUR LOING (S & M)
[station] BOURRON
7.1.1928

Dear Mr. Barbirolli,

I was very much pleased with the way you conducted my music last night. I heard it fairly well. The treble of the strings I heard better than the bass, which sometimes I could not hear. I heard Sammon's solo perfectly, but not always the orchestra, as if they were playing too softly.

Your tempi were perfect, just as I want them and I felt you were entirely in sympathy with the music for which I thank you most heartily.

Yrs sincerely
Frederick Delius

Letter in the hand of Jelka Delius, dated, written on headed notepaper.

The original is in the collection of the Royal Academy of Music. It is the only known letter from Delius to Barbirolli.

John Barbirolli (1899–1970): English conductor and cellist. He was in 1926 appointed conductor at the British National Opera Company, and was to conduct and record a range of Delius's works. Barbirolli's first experience of Delius was of hearing *A Dance Rhapsody*, 'the most beautiful music I'd ever heard', at Queen's Hall in 1914.

1   Barbirolli had conducted for the BBC on 6 January a concert of music by Delius, including the Violin Concerto played by Albert Sammons.

(517)

Frederick Delius to Geoffrey Toye

[Grez, February? 1928]

Dear Toye,

The records are splendid and I am delighted with the way you conducted them, all three.

Your interpretation of these works is most poetical and understood entirely; I am very grateful to you for having made these records.

Please thank the orchestra from me for having played so beautifully.

These records can now be sold as the only ones authorised by me.[1]

Yours ever,
Frederick Delius

From an unattributed and undated press clipping in the collection of Felix Aprahamian.

Geoffrey Toye (1889–1942): English conductor. He studied at the Royal College of Music and conducted largely in the theatre, including for the Beecham Opera Company and the D'Oyly Carte Opera Company. He was to be managing director at Covent Garden from 1934 to 1936. The fine waltz from his music to the ballet *The Haunted Ballroom* is frequently heard today. The Delius works he recorded were *On hearing the first Cuckoo*, *Brigg Fair* and *In a Summer Garden* with the London Symphony Orchestra, and *Summer Night on the River* and *The Walk to the Paradise Garden* with the New Symphony Orchestra.

1   'Naturally I trust you will now withdraw the old "Brigg-Fair" and "Cuckoo",' wrote Delius to The Gramophone Company on 22 February.

(518)
Frederick Delius to Universal Edition

FREDERICK DELIUS
Grez-sur-Loing
S. et M.
1.4.1928

To Universal-Edition
Vienna

Dear Sir,

I received your letter of 27/3 & am very sorry indeed that I have again to reply in the negative regarding the introduction to "Sea Drift".[1] I find the introduction to the music lifeless and without interest. It cannot help anyone to an understanding of the work. I do not like such introductions at the best of times. As far as the English & French versions are concerned, they are *absolutely impossible*

I have already told you so many times that a German, no matter how well he speaks English and French, can never translate anything into these languages faultlessly. It is simply impossible; the Germans are known for always making these impossible translations.

I will pick out just one passage as an example
Florida (United States of America) where Delius spent his young years to cultivate an orange plant. Literally in German "wo Delius seine jungen Jahre verbrachte eine *Orangenpflanze* zu kultivieren." In his earlier version Dr P had written that Delius was considered an *Englishman* because he had had a plantation in *Florida*. Of course that sounded as if Florida were in England. Now here he writes Florida, (United States of America); which is entirely superfluous. Also an Englishman & American would never write it out in full but put U.S.A. All these are usages that simply do not run in a foreigner's blood.

I cannot go into all the other errors here. Also I would ask you not to forward my letters to Dr P., to whom I had to send a long explanatory letter recently. If you are set on printing an introduction just put down date and place of birth & where I live at present. And then print the text in English, German & French. It will convey the mood of the work better than all these explanations. E.g. it is nonsense that "the harps are particularly prominent". Evidently Dr P. has never heard the work & with the best will – which I am ready to concede – cannot describe it. In Germany only Schuricht – Wiesbaden or someone similar could do so – and it would then have to be translated by English & French experts on music. So please leave it out altogether.

I would further like to point out that it is absolutely useless to emphasize nationality quite so much in these explanatory notes. Please omit this. In England the mention of German parents only makes an unfavourable impression on the masses, just as in France. I was born in England & am an English-man, as my parents were already naturalized when young. All this is best passed over in silence – we heard enough of it during the war.

At any rate, I forbid this introduction to be printed. Also the introduction to Appalachia, which was published without my knowledge, must be removed before a new edition appears.

You will be pleased to hear that in his concert at the Paris Opera House tomorrow eve. Sir Thomas Beecham will also conduct one of my orchestral works.[2]

Yours faithfully
Frederick Delius

Letter in the hand of Jelka Delius, dated, written in German on headed notepaper.

The original is in the Universal Edition archives.

1   Delius had already told Hertzka on 11 February: 'Mr Gardiner is now correcting the Seadrift proofs. However, he has sent me the introduction, as it is quite impossible to correct. Among other things it says that Delius lives in Germany, but *is considered an English composer, because he received his impressions in Florida on an orange plantation.* But Florida is not in England & furthermore oranges do not grow in England!' Other errors were pointed out, and Delius asked that there be no foreword to the edition.

2   The work was *The Walk to the Paradise Garden*. Delius had reported to Universal Edition on 11 February that Beecham had recently played the work (as well as *Paris* and *On hearing the first Cuckoo*) on tour in America; and he pressed Universal to publish it as a separate piece, as it was now so popular, not just in its original orchestral setting but in a piano arrangement too. On 25 February Universal's reply was that the work really demanded too large an orchestra for it to secure many performances, but that they were thinking about having it arranged for 'salon orchestra' instead. After a period of silence Delius was to take up the matter again, on 5 September: he wanted, he insisted, to see the piece published just as it stood.

(519)
Jelka Delius to Percy Grainger

FREDERICK DELIUS
Grez-sur-Loing
S. et M.
11.5.1928

My dear Percy,

We talk so much of you and your approaching marriage of which we received the "so to speak": broadcast news. But of course we always hoped for some word about it from you in real ink. I hope when at last you are united Ella will let us hear; and we *do so* hope that you will both come and stay with us on your way to Iceland. I hope you know and feel what a great place in our hearts there is for you and those dear to you, and especially *The One* dearest of all to you.

It was lovely that you heard Beecham conduct,[1] he must have done the Delius beautifully, judging from 2 Gramophone records he made for Columbia, and which are just out: Interlude Village Romeo and Cuckoo. They are so fluid and balanced and suave. – He gave 2 concerts in Paris and did the Interlude in the first one, but it was very severe weather and we could not go there.

You sent Fred such an excellent roll of the "Warriors". I put it on several times and Fred thinks it very good indeed; but he says it is rather different to the version you played for us at Francfort. Is that so? Or does his memory trick him?

We have had a weeks visit from Dr Heermann from Cassel and he has tested and observed Fred most carefully. His general impression was very good as regards looks appetite, well-being, digestion. He has a marvellous way of Diagnosis and he is convinced that Fred's eyes are not blind but the optic nerve is not nourished with blood, as it should be. The circulation behind the eyes is entirely disturbed. If at certain moments there is the least influx of blood, Fred can see a little. He is trying to treat this – but it is, of course terribly difficult. The veins are hardened and should be rendered active again. He has succeeded in several cases of impaired vision from the same causes, even when it had been so since childhood. The treatment we are doing seems to make Fred more active, more inclined to dictate letters, less sleepy; he also sleeps more quietly at night. We have had a most uncertain treacherous spring, and such constant changes are always very trying for Fred.

Dear Percy, Are you aware that we have not yet received the real rolls of Brigg Fair and North Country Sketches or *any* of Dance Rhapsody?[2] and Fred would so much love to have them soon, as they might fetch away the D.A. Piano. Anyhow he longs to hear them, and so do I. You are so terribly busy that you may not have had time to see about it. I wrote the letter you had so kindly sketched for me to the Aeolian people ages ago.[3]

Mrs Stoop has died quite suddenly on the Riviera.

We often hear things of yours on the Radio and I enclose a few programmes, which I had kept.[4]

Fred sends you most affectionate message, and should love you to come here! We shall be with you in thought at the Hollywood Concert: Let us hope it will be a great success.

With all my love

Yrs
Jelka

Toye has also made excellent records H.M.V. Summer Garden, Brigg Fair & Cuckoo.

Autograph letter, signed and dated, written on headed notepaper.

The original is in the Grainger Museum.

1   Beecham conducted a dozen concerts between 12 and 30 January in New York, Boston, Washington, Baltimore and Philadelphia. He took three Delius works with him: *Paris*, *On hearing the first Cuckoo* and *The Walk to the Paradise Garden*, playing at least one of them at each concert.

2   *Brigg Fair* and *North Country Sketches*, in four-handed versions played splendidly by Grainger and Ralph Leopold, had been published as piano rolls; but not the *Dance Rhapsody*.

3   This was a letter from Delius to the Aeolian Company, praising the Grainger/Leopold recordings, which the composer had been loaned for a short time.

4   Three clippings from *Radio Times*.

(520)
Frederick Delius to Charles Kennedy Scott

Grez-sur-Loing (S-et-M),
31.5.1928.

Dear Charles,

I thank you so much for your letter and the criticisms. I hope you know what I think of music critics. It is only *now* they begin to see there is anything in my music at all. The enthusiastic letters I received from England from all different quarters have convinced me that the performance must have been wonderfully good.[1] And I have more faith in the music-lover than in the music critic. Every one of my works has at one time been damned by the London critics – from *Sea-Drift* to the *Mass*. I am just longing to hear the *Mass* again, and if you repeat it next year I will come, even if I end up in an urn at Golders Green.

Stick to your conducting. Don't let either friend or foe dishearten you. You will see that one day every one will see what a good conductor you are. For where there is such great and understanding love for a thing, there are also the necessary qualities.

Do come and visit us here if you can possibly do it this summer. We should so love it!

With all affectionate messages from Jelka,

Ever your friend,
Frederick Delius

From Warlock: *Frederick Delius*, revised edition, 1952, p. 169.

1   Delius wrote concerning this London performance of the *Mass* to Kennedy Scott on 21 May: 'I thank you from the bottom of my heart, dear Charles, and I am grieved indeed that I could not hear it. I do so long once to hear this work again and sung by your wonderful chorus!'

(521)
Frederick Delius to Eric Fenby

GREZ-SUR-LOING (S & M)
[station] BOURRON
9.6.1928

My dear young friend,

Your sympathetic & appreciative letter gave me the greatest pleasure.[1]
    I am always so glad when I hear that my music appeals to the young!
    I know Scarborough quite well; when a school-boy I used to spend my summer holidays at Filey and my memories of all the happy days on that coast are still very green.
    Most likely the Philharmonic choir will give the Mass of Life again under Kennedy Scott next year, when perhaps you may be able to hear it.
    With warm greetings I remain

Sincerely yours
Frederick Delius

Letter in the hand of Jelka Delius, dated, written on headed notepaper. Envelope addressed: Eric Fenby Esq/12 Mayville Avenue/Scarborough/Angleterre. Postmark: GREZ [date illegible].

The original is in the Delius Trust Archive. It is the first of 141 letters and postcards from the Deliuses to Fenby until shortly before Jelka's death in May 1935. None of Fenby's letters to the Deliuses appear to have survived.

Eric Fenby (b. 1906): English musician, teacher and writer. Largely self-taught, he trained as an organist in his native Scarborough before leaving England in October

1928 to become Delius's amanuensis. Among his later achievements he was to become celebrated as an interpreter – conductor and pianist – of Delius's music.

1   'It was in . . . a mood of intense gratitude for all the loveliness Frederick Delius had brought into my life that I first wrote to him, in the hope that it might give him pleasure to know that his music had meant so much in the life of a very young man.' (Fenby: *Delius as I Knew Him*, p. 5.)

(522)

Frederick Delius to Eric Fenby

GREZ-SUR-LOING (S & M)
[station] BOURRON
29.8.28

Dear Mr Fenby

I am greatly touched by your kind and sympathetic letter and should love to accept your offer.

Come here by all means as soon as you can and see if you like it before deciding anything.

How old are you? And would I not be taking you away from your profession? What is your occupation? How much of a musician are you?

You know, this is a lovely little spot, just a quiet little village and our house is in a big garden going down to the river; but of course we live very much alone.

Should you not have travelling money, please let me know at once and I will send it to you.

Perhaps the best way for you to come would be to travel from London during the night; for instance by Newhaven-Dieppe, leaving Victoria at 8.20 p.m and arriving in Paris at 5.25 a.m. There you have to taxi to the Gare de Lyon, where you can get nice breakfast in the Café of the station and you take the train at 9.10 to Bourron, our station, where you will be at 11. and where we will have you fetched if we know when to expect you.

With kind regards from my wife I am yrs sincerely

Frederick Delius

. We live very simply here – No grand clothes needed.

Letter in the hand of Jelka Delius, dated, written on headed notepaper. Envelope addressed: Eric Fenby Esq/ 12 Mayville Avenue/ Scarborough/ Angleterre. Postmark: GREZ 29 -8 28.

The original is in the Delius Trust Archive.

Fenby had become obsessed, as he himself put it, with the idea that he might be able to help Delius finish several works which he had begun but, because of his illness, could not complete. Finally the obsession conquered him and 'getting up in the middle of the night, I took pen and paper and wrote to Delius offering my help for three or four years.' Delius accepted, Jelka writing three further letters to Fenby before he left.

(523)
Jelka Delius to Eric Fenby

[Grez, 21 September 1928]

Dear Mr Fenby,

I wonder, whether you have heard that Delius's Sea-drift, a beautiful choral work will be given at the Leeds festival in the quite near future. It would be nice if you could go and hear it. But we do not know the date.[1]

Hoping to hear from you soon. Yrs sincerely

Jelka Delius

Kind regards from my husband

Autograph postcard, signed and undated. Addressed: Eric Fenby Esq/12 Mayville Av^ue/Scarborough/Angleterre. Postmark: GREZ 21 -9 28.

The original is in the Delius Trust Archive.

1 The performance was on 2 October. Fenby, who travelled to Leeds specially for it, writes: 'owing to the stupidity of a minor official on the door I was not allowed even to pay to stand at the rear of the Town Hall, every seat being booked long in advance. Beecham was furious when I told him at our first meeting at Grez in the following year, and said he would have "put me on the platform" had he known!' Fenby left Scarborough on 9 October and arrived at Grez the following day; Balfour Gardiner was due to arrive on the 20th, and Fenby found that his first task was to finish Gardiner's arrangement for two pianos of Poem of Life and Love, so that they could play this and other duets to Delius. Carefully optimistic, Jelka wrote later in the year to Heseltine: 'Balfour G. will have told you that we have a young musician here and that Fred is trying with his help to complete his last orchestral work and also to make an orchestral Suite of the Hassan Music.

Young Fenby is very sensitive and adaptive, but, of course, it is very difficult for Fred to control f.ex. his orchestration.'

(524)
Frederick Delius to Edvard Munch

GREZ-SUR-LOING (S & M)
[station] BOURRON
19.11.1928

Delius dictates:

Dear friend,

Your kind letter gave me great pleasure, & I also hear from Jappe that you are getting on so well, & that pleases me very much.[1]

My health is on the whole a little better & I am less weak & can eat a little more. I should always be pleased if you visited me; your room is always ready here.

Although it is quite autumnal I go out in my wheel-chair daily. We have had a wonderful summer & for months I have been always out of doors.

Sadly my Jotunheim days are over, something I miss very much.

I am happy to hear that you continue to have such great success with your art. You know how I love and understand your work —

Please write to me again soon, everything that concerns you interests me. And please, do not fail to visit me when you next come to Paris.

Your old friend
Frederick Delius

Letter in the hand of Jelka Delius, dated, written in German on headed notepaper.

The original is in the Munch Museum.

1 Munch's letter has not been found; nor, for that matter, has any letter from Jappe Nilssen dating from this period.

(525)
Jelka Delius to Edvard Munch

GREZ-SUR-LOING (S & M)
[station] BOURRON
19.11.1928

Dear Munch,

You gave Delius great pleasure with your kind letter.

When I look at him, I always have to think of *you* for I always feel that *no-one* could make a picture of him as *you* could. He is now so beautiful, so expressive; particularly when he listens to music he is fantastically absorbed, serene, quite unique. You could paint or draw that so splendidly.

Please, please, when you are anywhere near us again, do come & paint him.

Here you have peace, a studio & good red wine and the two of us, your loyal friends.

We have a new gramophone, a work of art, not mass-produced, but hand-made. We have a number of Delius's orchestral works, which sound really magnificent on it; much better than on the big famous gramophones, which are much more expensive.

But *you must paint* the picture of the sick Delius. You will make a masterpiece of it.

Yours ever
Jelka Delius

Autograph letter, signed and dated, written in German on headed notepaper.

The original is in the Munch Museum.

1929

'I am longing to take my beloved Delius to London, if as is so repeatedly proposed, there will be a Delius Concert or festival in Spring.' Jelka's hopes, as expressed to May Harrison in November 1928, were to be affirmed in February, when we find Delius writing to tell Universal Edition of Beecham's plans for a Delius Festival in London in October, and urging Universal to give full co-operation. Meanwhile, with Delius feeling well enough, work had begun in January, with Fenby, on arranging an orchestral suite from the *Hassan* music. More recognition came the composer's way on 21 April, when Nevile Henderson, British Minister Plenipotentiary in Paris, came to Grez to invest him with the order of Companion of Honour. From the end of winter, meanwhile, visitors came thick and fast: Barjansky, Gardiner, Roger Quilter, Heinrich Simon, Edward Dent, Heseltine, Anthony Bernard, among others. With Fenby's help, the unfinished *Cynara* and *A Late Lark* were completed in the summer, in order that they could be premièred at the Festival in October. In June, Grainger and his wife Ella, wed the previous summer, came to stay for a week or so. Gardiner, too, was again in Grez at the same time. Then the Howard-Joneses came, taking a cottage in the village until the beginning of September. Also Norman O'Neill, whom Delius ever held in great affection. It should also be recorded that Florent Schmitt occasionally paid visits to Grez during Delius's latter years: 'Schmitt was a welcome visitor,' writes Fenby. 'I always just missed him.' Meanwhile Delius dictated to Fenby a new opening to the work which was to become *A Song of Summer*.

In London Beecham and Heseltine were devising the programmes, which, in consultation with Delius, were to make up the festival, and a 'Preliminary Announcement' was published: 'The committee of the present Festival desires to give the public an opportunity of appreciating the fact that in Frederick Delius England has produced not merely a great British composer but one of the greatest composers of all time ... Such an event is without parallel in the history of music in England.' Delius's music, ran the panegyric, was 'an oasis of pure and ageless beauty'. Inevitably, there was much correspondence throughout the summer on various arrangements for the festival: programmes, artists, travel, accommodation.

The beginning of September saw changes: Fenby left on the 7th for home and a well-deserved holiday; the Erard piano which had been used by Howard-Jones at Grez was bought and moved into the house; and Karge, Delius's male nurse, left too, a new 'Bruder' arriving to take his place. Karge was one of a series of nurses recruited from a religious organization in Germany. Eric Fenby remembers them regularly saying their daily prayers: they were 'almost like lay clerics'. Beecham himself called several times during the first week of the month. By the end of September Jelka wrote to tell Heseltine: 'We are overrun with the strangest visitors.' On the 16th Brooks had brought along a correspondent from the *New York Times*, and much of this unusual traffic was itself brought about by articles on Delius and the forthcoming festival which had begun to appear both in European and American papers. (Barjansky, in Grez for a week, had played his part in this by helping Jelka to send out material to various German contacts.) Jelka wondered whether Heseltine might find further financial support for the festival by getting in touch with Edgar Simon, manufacturer, an old schoolfellow of Delius's who had come to visit him at Grez; as well as with Sydney Schiff, and with Frank Stoop, who had only just called. Jelka took advice from Delius's Paris doctor, who came to see his patient on 3 October, 'and strongly advised Fred to travel.'

On 9 October they arrived at the Langham Hotel. Among the greetings was a welcoming note from Elgar and a bouquet of roses and carnations from Roger Quilter. Delius, fêted – hero-worshipped, even – as never before, remained with Jelka in London for the duration of the festival, only returning to Grez a few days after the final concert (*A Mass of Life*) at Queen's Hall on 1 November. Fenby stayed on in England for a further three months.

The remainder of the year was fairly uneventful. The new Bruder proved to be very slow, and Jelka found herself having to spend much more time than usual reading to Delius. Beecham was expected for Christmas, but did not come. All was anti-climax. 'We were quite alone at Xmas,' Jelka wrote to Fenby.

Arrangement of *Hassan* suite for orchestra. Begun January, completed May.

Cynara (RT III/5). Completed.

A Late Lark (RT III/6). Completed.

A Song of Summer (RT VI/26). (Revision of *Poem of Life and Love*).

(526)
Jelka Delius to Edvard Munch

[Grez, 2 February 1929]

Dear friend; Just in case you now have a radio please listen to a Delius concert on the London Radio Friday 8th Febr 9.35 pm Engl. time.[1] It is conducted by Sir Thomas Beecham, the best conductor in England & a very fine programme. As the last item: "Eventyr" Ballad for Orchestra after Ashbjørnson. We have a new set now & hear splendidly, it is a Ducretet & is French. Delius is not too bad. We have had a real winter with snow.

Yours ever
Jelka Delius

Autograph postcard, signed and undated, written in German. Addressed: Mons/ Edvard Munch/Skøyen/Oslo/Norvège. Postmark: GREZ 2 -2 29.

The original is in the Munch Museum.

1   The concert included *Paris*, *On hearing the first Cuckoo in Spring* and *Summer Night on the River*, *Dance Rhapsody* No. 2, Songs with orchestra (Dora Labbette), *The Walk to the Paradise Garden* and *Eventyr*. As Jelka subsequently wrote to tell Beecham, the performances were splendid, with the Kingsway Hall sounding better than a studio; Beecham's witty remarks, also broadcast, were enjoyed and Delius had sat up for it all until 'God Save the King': '. . . you are a genius.' (Letter from Jelka Delius to Beecham, dated 9 February 1929, sold at Sotheby's, 11 May 1977.)

(527)
Edvard Munch and Jappe Nilssen to Frederick Delius

[Oslo, February/March 1929]

Dear old friend Delius

I was delighted to receive a letter from you – and above all that things are going well with you – you have indeed a rare ability to look life bravely in the face

– It was not possible for me to make a connection with London – I spoke to the Radio office here but was told that a connection could not be made

– On the other hand he was interested in the possibility of a concert on the Radio here – How should one set about it

Dear friend!

I shall be writing a letter to you in a few days. Munch is here at home with me and wants me to improvise a letter while sitting beside me chattering away at the top of his voice.

So this is only a short greeting that I send you.

With my regards to your wife I give you a firm handshake

Yours
Jappe Nilssen

Autograph draft letter, undated. Munch's portion, unsigned, is written in Norwegian; Jappe Nilssen's, signed, is in French.

The original, which was not sent, is in the Munch Museum.

(528)
Edvard Munch to Frederick Delius

[Oslo, March/April 1929]

Dear friend Delius

I wrote you a letter as long as a month ago   But then I see that I wrote it in Norwegian – and so didn't send it – I usually need 3 weeks to write a letter so it is delayed.

I thank your wife very much for her letter. Unfortunately it was not possible to hear anything from London here –

Perhaps it could be arranged sometime that we could hear something of yours on the radio here

I have been thinking of making a short trip to Paris – but not until summer   But it is not certain –

– It was to visit you and other friends –

I would have painted you then   It would have been a very beautiful picture. I was very glad that you are fairly well   You have what I envy you for very much   a wonderful optimism and you are strong-minded – I am convinced that you can also see – Really one sees not just with the eyes alone but with the whole body

Do you remember how we – you, Helge Rode and I talked in Aasgaardstrand over 30 years ago about things to come   We talked about the transparency of the body and telepathy – It was what we have now X-rays and radio and the wonderful waves which connect the whole world and the whole stellar system with us –

(Do you know that Helge Rode has become quite religious, and writes books on religious subjects?)

Haven't you ever thought of writing your memoirs – ? I have myself written a kind of spiritual diary for 40 years and am now at work arranging it.

It is very interesting –

All best wishes to you and your wife

Your old friend
Edvard Munch

Autograph draft letter, signed and undated, written in German.

The original, which was not sent, is in the Munch Museum. There had in fact been a second draft of Letter 527, and this is also preserved in the Munch Museum. So Letter 528 represents a third attempt to respond to Jelka's invitation to listen to the broadcast concert of 8 February. It is quite clear that some of the Munch/Delius correspondence has not survived, so it is just possible that a fourth attempt actually got into the post . . .

(529)
Frederick Delius to Thomas Beecham

GREZ-SUR-LOING (S & M)
[station] BOURRON
10.3.29

Dear Thomas,

I was overjoyed by your letter about the proposed Festival etc. What good news! What life & enterprise you have and what would musical England do without you? I do believe they are at last beginning to see, what they have got in you.

I am quite delighted with your last record "Summernight on the River", which has just been sent to me. It is lovely and so delicate. The three best records of my work are your Cuckoo, Summernight & Walk to the Paradise garden.

By the way: Keith Douglas[1] has arranged this latter for a rather smaller orchestra, 2^s and not 3^s of Brass and woodwind. He sent it straight to my publisher's, the Universal-Edition-Vienna and they seem to have accepted it. But I am telling them to send you a copy of the score *at once*, and I beg you to look at it. Of course I do not want this version to be played when a bigger orchestra is available.

I received a command to attend the Investiture to be held by the Pr. of

Wales on March 26th. Of course I can not go and have replied that my physical state made it impossible for me to attend, and I begged to be graciously
excused. For this distinction[2] they have bestowed on me I owe all thanks *to
you*, dear friend!

Since some months I have a young Yorkshireman, Eric Fenby staying with
us as my musical secretary. I am making an orchestral Suite of Hassan and also
completing an orchestral work upon which I was at work before I became
ill.[3]

I got Fenby to write a letter to the Times[4] to contradict the nonsense that
has again been circulated about me in the "United Press" and also in a great
big book "A Musical Pilgrimage in Yorkshire" by one Dr Sutcliffe Smith, in
which every statement about me is false: He enumerates 3 of my orchestral
works calling them "dramatic works" and then goes on to say that I write my
numerous songs under the pseudonym of "Peter Warlock". (!!!)

When you come *do* try to stay a few days. I should so much love to have you
here again and have a good talk. The Spring sunshine and balmy mild air is
lovely now.

I wish *you*, who so thoro'ly understand my music and who are the one
authority as to how it should be played – would re-edit my music as you are
planning. Nothing would please me better.

With love from us both

Yrs affectionately
Frederick Delius

Letter in the hand of Jelka Delius, dated, written on headed notepaper.

The original is in the Delius Trust Archive.

1   Keith Douglas (1903–49): English conductor, concert promoter and musicologist. He was the nephew of Charles Stuart Douglas, whose parents were near neighbours of the Deliuses in Bradford, and who had travelled to Florida with Delius in
1884, jointly to manage Solana Grove. While at Oxford University, Keith Douglas
had become president of the Oxford Musical Union. Returning to Bradford he was
extraordinarily effective in revitalizing the city's musical life, founding (and conducting) the Bradford Philharmonic Concerts, the Bradford Chamber Music Festivals and
the Bradford Music Club. Forceful and energetic, he also found time to compose some
fifty works. He began corresponding with Delius around the mid-1920s (although one
letter only, from 1934, survives in the Delius Trust Archive), with the intention of
producing a festival of the older composer's works in Bradford, but he was unable to
take up Delius's standing invitation to Grez until June 1929, when he came for a day.
Fenby remembers Delius as having been unusually agitated, even anxious, at the
prospect of this visit, which in the event passed smoothly and enjoyably. In 1932,
succeeding Gerald Cooper, Douglas became Honorary Secretary (until 1947) of the
Royal Philharmonic Society, and in 1933 Honorary Secretary of The Delius Society

(the first society of that name), formed to promote recordings of Delius's music. His (orchestral) arrangements of *The Walk to the Paradise Garden* and the *Waltz* from *A Village Romeo and Juliet* were published in 1934 and 1939 respectively by Universal Edition. In an article published after his visit to Grez in 1929, he was to write of Delius as 'the greatest musical genius since Wagner'. Among the works of Delius that he conducted in Bradford were *The Walk to the Paradise Garden*, the Cello Concerto, the first *Dance Rhapsody* and *Appalachia*.

2   Companion of Honour. 'Fred would have refused a knighthood,' Jelka wrote on 8 April to Marie Clews. 'It has made us have a terrible lot of correspondence and old friends and ancient schoolfellows have turned up or written.

There were also fearful faked interviews in the Press, saying this made Fred the happiest man in the world. – Of course quite untrue – and just about the last thing Fred would say or think. –

No, he has kept his aloof dignity – in fact he has now a calm beauty and serenity that are quite wonderful. When the people of the world sit near him gushing they look like horrid caricatures and so much older, pleated and yellow than he does that I am amazed at their courage, talking nonsense to him.'

3   *A Song of Summer*, using material from *Poem of Life and Love*. On 27 August Jelka wrote to Grainger: 'Since your departure Fred has written quite a new opening to the Orchestral piece and Fenby did remarkably well in helping him.'

4   Eric Fenby writes: 'My letter was published in the Yorkshire Post, and dated March 6.'

(530)
H. Balfour Gardiner to Frederick Delius

21.3.29

Dear Fred,

My proposals for making a concert suite out of the Hassan music are as follows:
Use the existing material and existing instrumentation as far as possible, and arrange the suite for *small orchestra*, *small chorus*, and *soloists*. There is a large quantity of most attractive music, and there ought to be no difficulty in making a suite that would be a useful addition to the répertoire of small choral societies.

I should proceed thus:
(1)   Get Eric Fenby to play over the whole of the music in its existing form, and first pick out the numbers that will stand by themselves: these can form the backbone of the new suite
(2)   You will then have to consider questions of contrast, alternating long numbers with short ones, instrumental numbers with numbers in which the chorus is employed, quiet with noisy ones and so on.

PLATE 49   Delius is read to by Karge, his male nurse.

GREZ-sur-LOING (S & M)
BOURRON

9. 6. 1928

My dear young friend,
    Your sympathetic &
appreciative letter gave
me the greatest pleasure.
    I am always so glad
when I hear that my
music appeals to the
young.
    I know Scarborough
quite well; when a schoolboy I used to spend my
summer holidays at
Filey and my memories
of all the happy days
on that coast are still
very green.
    Most likely the Phil-
harmonic choir will

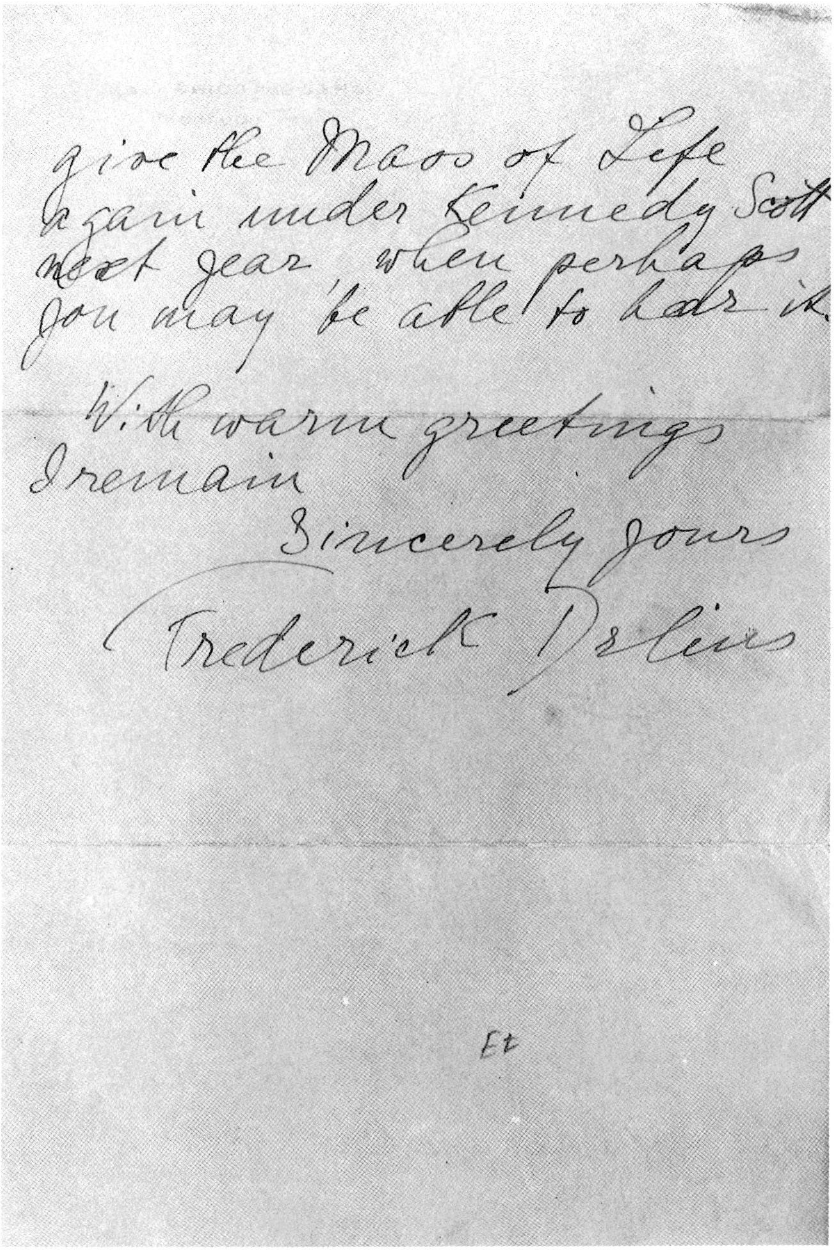

give the Mass of Life
again under Kennedy Scott
next year, when perhaps
you may be able to hear it.

    With warm greetings
I remain
         Sincerely yours
      Frederick Delius

51

PLATES 50, 51   Letter, in the hand of Jelka Delius, from Delius to Fenby,
9 June 1928 (see p. 337).

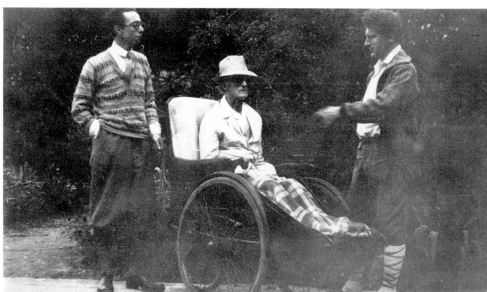

PLATE 52 (a) The Deliuses with Percy Grainger and his fiancée Ella, Grez,
1 July 1929 (*coll. Grainger Museum*); (b) Fenby, Delius and Grainger, Grez,
1 July 1929 (*coll. Eric Fenby*).

PLATE 53   (a) Roy Henderson, c. 1932 (*coll. Roy Henderson*); (b) John Barbirolli; (c) Lionel Tertis; (d) Geoffrey Toye, a caricature.

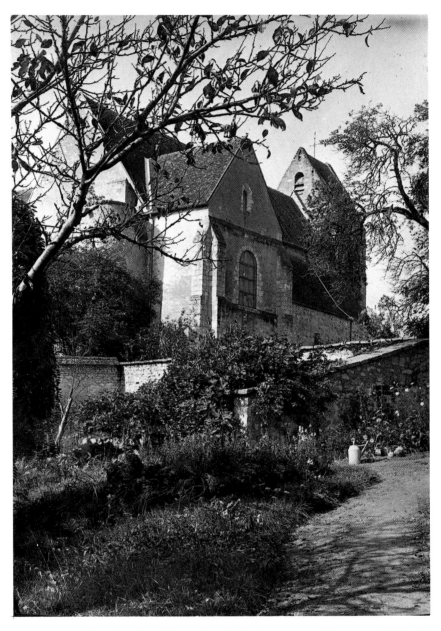

PLATE 54   The church at Grez, from Delius's garden. (*Photograph Philip T. Oyler.*)

PLATE 55   The high street at Grez, with Delius's house on the left.
(*Photograph Philip T. Oyler.*)

PLATE 56   (a) Dr Friedrich Rosen, brother of Jelka Delius; (b) the Rosen
home in Berlin.

PLATE 57 (a) Evelin Gerhardi in the garden at Grez, 1932, photographed by Cecily Arnold; (b) 'Réunion de famille': Alden Brooks (left) and family (Corinne, centre, and Filippa, standing right) in Paris, June 1932, photographed by Evelin Gerhardi (*Gerhardi/Steinweg Collection*); (c) Cecily Arnold.

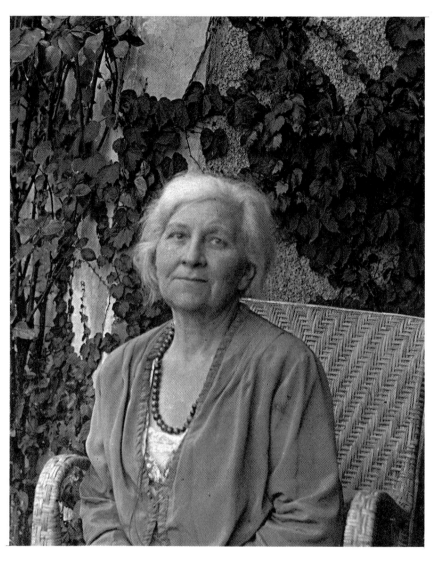

PLATE 58   'Madame Delius'. (*Photograph Philip T. Oyler.*)

PLATE 59   (a) Eric Fenby, sketched by James Gunn, Grez, September 1932;
(b) On the bridge at Grez: Hubert Thieves and Eric Fenby, 1933 (*coll. Eric
Fenby*).

PLATE 60   Elgar leaves for Paris, 28 May 1933.

PLATE 61   Edvard Munch in the 1930s.

PLATE 62   Delius, Grez-sur-Loing, 30 September 1932, study by James
Gunn.

PLATE 63   Jelka: a last photograph.

PLATE 64   The burial procession at Grez.

(3) The problem may then arise of joining up small sections in order to make a sufficiently long movement.

(4) When the suite is arranged, a new score should be written out, eliminating all the errors in the old one

(5) A new version for piano must then be made: it will be possible for the publisher to use many of the existing plates, thus saving the heavy expense of engraving fresh ones

(6) Printed parts for the chorus probably exist already, and if that is so, all that will be needed is to use the old plates but alter the title and binding

(7) Fresh orchestral parts will have to be made and carefully corrected

(8) Negotiations will have to be undertaken with the publisher regarding the new suite, performing rights and mechanical reproduction rights not being forgotten.

I think that is all.[1]

Yours ever
H.B.G.

Autograph letter, initialled and dated, written in pencil.

The original is in the Delius Trust Archive.

1   Jelka was able to report to Norman O'Neill on 24 April: 'Fred has just made a glorious orchestral suite with Chorus of the Hassan Music, with the aid of Eric Fenby.'

(531)
Jelka Delius to Philip Heseltine

GREZ-SUR-LOING (S & M)
[station] BOURRON
[May 1929]

My dear Phil, It was so delightful to hear from you yesterday so promptly about the recording of the N.C.S.'s and the little string piece.[1] I hope they will send us test-records as soon as possible, as Fred is very keen to hear it. It is a great pleasure to him that you have such a high opinion of the N.C.S. as he evidently knew it was one of his best works, and yet it was hardly ever played.

Further I think it is splendid that you are to to help Beecham plan the Delius Festival. I read Fred your letter; as you foresaw he was not very much for performing the early pieces. At least not yet, while there are several things he has never heard yet, and which he considers among his best things, notably the Arabesk, Songs of Sunset (not heard in England since 1912 or 13.) the A capella chorusses. When Beecham unfolds his plans to you you will see what a lot of works he has already. – I myself, however am inclined to think like you, that there may be much that is lovely, young, fresh in those early works and I will keep your idea in mind and speak to him when a favourable moment presents itself.

For instance, *I* think that if he could hear the Norwegian Suite he might decide to have it published or possibly to make some alterations. At least then one could decide.

One must be very careful. I was so annoyed at all the stupid things Newman told us last night about the Delius Music on the wireless. Among other things he said, that Delius never had a gift of adapting words to music. This, he said, was in part because Delius was really not english at all, but quite international. Moreover, he said that in Seadrift, for example, as in other works he composed the words in German, thinking of probable German performances and then the thing had to be translated back to the english words laboriously. Not a word of truth in that, and God knows I had to exert all my powers to give an adequate german rendering fitting in with the music; and how I tried to render in the german some of the colour and emotion of the english words! You will remember that the same thing was said about the Village Romeo. Here, of course, it was in a way easier to get the german, as I had Keller's novel as a guide. But Fred wrote the whole libretto in English. What can be more english in feeling than Brigg Fair, North Country, in fact, most of his works? Fred's idiom is english, his language is English. Apart from the exceptionally beautiful Zarathustra, german poetry has never appealed to him, as you know. No german poem could have appealed to him like Seadrift and Dowson did. In the case of the Arabesk and Fennimore, of course, the german resembled the danish more and he had *me* as a translater and was sure I would try to retain the whole flavour. I write all this because when occasion comes you might put these erroneous notions right.

I think these Music Critics do all that *can* be done to hinder the listeners from understanding Delius, when they *could* and *should* help them; in fact they seem rather annoyed that so many people insist on liking his music.

When next you come to France, and you could stay here a few days, I should so much love you to go thro that M.S. Music. Please give my love to your friend Barbara[2]; I am afraid she must have bored herself here; had I but known that she was *your great friend*, I should have taken her to my heart at once. Well that is for another time.

Please let us hear developments with Beecham. Fred must go to England for the Festival. I think it can be done, if all goes well.

Love to Bernard[3] and blessings for his fine conducting.

Ever aff[ly]
Jelka

Autograph letter, signed and undated, written on headed notepaper.

The original is in the British Library.

1   *North Country Sketches* and *Air and Dance*. According to Fenby, the records were not issued because of trouble over the scratch orchestra which had been assembled for the recording. Anthony Bernard, the conductor, also recorded *Sea Drift* (on 29 May), with Roy Henderson, an unnamed chorus and the New Symphony Orchestra. Fenby wrote home to his mother on 30 July: 'The gramophone records of "Sea-Drift" were very poor indeed. A bad orchestra, a miserable little chorus and faulty singing by Roy Henderson, the soloist, and a poor reading by the conductor, Anthony Bernard. Delius did not recognize much of it.' This seems to have been the reaction to the performance as broadcast. Fenby remembers that when the records arrived at Grez, they 'sounded somewhat better on the gramophone'; so much so that on 14 August Jelka wrote to tell Heseltine that they 'greatly enjoyed' the recording!

2   'A very quiet, attractive girl', according to Fenby, 'quite different from Phil's usual types.' Heseltine had visited around end-April/beginning of May.

3   Anthony Bernard.

(532)
Jelka Delius to Thomas Beecham

Grez 14.8.29

Dear Thomas,

Fred received your delightful letter and it quite relieved him of his anxieties about the singers[1] and he is greatly looking forward to seeing you on your way back.

It is all too wonderful about the Festival and I can not tell you how much it means to us – and then your delightful and generous invitation to stay so comfortably at the Langham!

And then all those glorious Gramophone records the Columbia is bringing out!

Then there is your great idea about the Delius-Edition!!

Fred has no works published on a profit sharing scheme. They all belong to the publishers and Fred has a royalty, varying for every work. But quite a number of works he has sold outright and so gets no royalty. They are chiefly the ones Leuckart had bought, and which Univ. Edition bought up. They are: "Dance Rhapsody 1" "Paris", "In a Summer Garden" "Songs of sunset", "Brigg Fair", "Song of the High Hills".

Cuckoo, Summernight and the Songs at Tischer & Jagenbergs are all on a Royalty system; so are the works at Augener's.

It will be a difficult thing to arrange and we must talk it over. How glorious to see you so soon!

I have written about the Arabesk on a separate sheet[2] and will rush it all to the post.

Our hearts are ever with you!

Ever affectionately
Jelka Delius

I hope the glorious mountain air has made you quite well again —

Autograph letter, signed and dated.

The original is in the British Library.

1   Delius had pressed the claims of Roy Henderson, as opposed to John Goss and Dennis Noble, in a letter to Heseltine on 6 July.

2   Jelka wrote out the Jacobsen poem in the original Danish, with English translation beneath, and explained the poem's meaning.

(533)
Frederick Delius to Ernest Newman

GREZ-SUR-LOING (S & M)
[station] BOURRON
Aug 19th 1929

Dear Newman,

An announcement made in the Radio-Times about one of my Shelley-Songs: "To the Queen of my heart" rather annoyed me.

The notice said that the song was "a setting of a German version of Shelleys poem": Of course I composed the song in english and only reluctantly allowed a translation to be printed at all.[1]

This naturally has nothing to do with you, only it brought back to my mind certain statements you made in one of your musical talks on the BBC some months ago.

You said that many of my works were written to a german translation and afterwards "Laboriously retranslated into English". You specially mentioned "Seadrift" as an example of this.

I composed "Seadrift" in English and could not have done otherwise, as the lovely poem inspired by music. Owing to the entire lack of interest in my music in England at that time I was compelled to give it to a german Publisher and to have it performed a number of times in Germany before it was given in England. My wife therefore translated it into german (and a very arduous job it was, too, fitting the german words to my music).

A similar mistake went thro the English Press about my Village Romeo and Juliet the words for which I made myself and in *English*, of course. This work also was first performed and published in Berlin, and my wife then translated it into German to the music. This time her task was easier, as she had Keller's novel, which gave her the characteristic dialogue.

You know how difficult it is to translate to music. This is the reason why in composing "Fennimore and Gerda" and the "Arabesk" – to avoid a language like Danish, which has no public – I composed to german words. German is so very similar to Danish that much of the original wording of J. P. Jacobsen could be retained.

All my Danish Songs and also the Norwegian ones were first composed in their original language.

My wife and myself are always battling against the publishers, who wish to print the words in their own language over the others, even if they are translated words. If certain editions have been put on the market like that it is entirely against my will.

In the hope of meeting you agaìn in London *if* I manage to get over for the Festival[2] and with kind regards from my wife

Yrs sincerely
Frederick Delius

Letter in the hand of Jelka Delius, dated, written on headed notepaper. Envelope addressed: Ernest Newman Esq/c/o 'The Sunday Times'/London/Angleterre. Re-addressed: Polperro./Epsom Lane./Tadworth. Surrey. Postmark: GREZ 20 -8 29.

The original is in the Delius Trust Archive.

1   On 23 August Jelka wrote to Heseltine: '. . . a notice said that this song was composed to a *german version* of Shelley's song. We immediately sent a wire about such an absurd idea to the BBC, and I took the occasion to write to Newman about the Seadrift being composed in German, which is of course preposterous.'

2   Jelka wrote to Grainger on 27 August: 'Yesterday we had the Paris doctor here again and he thinks we can attempt the journey if all is done for Fred's comfort regardless of expense. It will be a tremendous undertaking tho' all the same.'

(534)
Jelka Delius to Philip Heseltine

FREDERICK DELIUS
Grez-sur-Loing
S. et M.
3.9.1929

Dear Phil,

I am so glad you got thro' so well with your conducting of the Capriol,[1] I am sure you will conduct again too. I am so glad too, that the Cello Concerto went so well.

I will answer your questions:

Fred is not averse now to the "Nightingale" being sung with the new words. *It is the first song he ever wrote*; that lends it a special interest, also there is that wistful feeling about it that afterwards became so characteristic of his music.[2]

Debussy

Fred did not know and would very much like to hear what Debussy wrote about his Danish Songs.[3] Fred himself was not at that concert. (I was there.) Fred said he really heard nothing of Debussy's before Pelleas, 1st performance, spring 1902 in Paris. He said: "I liked it, I thought it very good. I noticed a certain similarity in our outlook. Before, I had only heard a piano piece 'Pagodes' (1897 played to Fred by Ravel), which struck me as being much influenced by the Java music and Dancing, which made such a great impression in the Paris exhibition of 1889." Fred heard "l'Aprémidi" only *years* later, I think in 1909 in a Prom, in England. I said to Fred "were you with Ravel, Schmitt and that 'bande' at the 1st perf. of Pelleas?" No, he went quite alone. I may mention that we had vaguely discussed the possibility for Fred to write an Opera on the same drama Pelleas, or another Maeterlinck drama. But he was never quite keen on Maeterlinck; whom he even then thought anaemic.

Now Fred's journeys to Germany. He thinks he was 6 or 7 when he first went there with his mother by Cologne to Bielefeld, where everybody called him: "Der kleine Engländer". After that he went with both parents and 2 sisters when he was about 16 one summer a journey along the Rhine, Francfort etc. then Nürnberg Stuttgart etc. His next big journey was in 1881 when he went to Sweden and Norway. In summer the Delius family always went to Ilkley or Filey. They were so many that they hired a Saloon-car.

We remember now about the Verlaine-Orchestrations.[4] And please send what Debussy wrote.

With love from us both (in sweltering heat)

yrs ever
Jelka D

Autograph letter, signed and dated, written on headed notepaper.

The original is in the British Library.

1 Heseltine had conducted his *Capriol* suite at the Proms.

2 On 23 August Jelka had told Heseltine: 'Fred had written to Beecham the other day that he would prefer 3 of the songs *not* sung. They are *Nightingale* – Welhaven (the first song he ever wrote) *Spielleute Verborgene Liebe*. Of course these are not very good and he dislikes them. But if it upsets Beechams plans, let them be sung. Only in that case they must be retranslated, as the english words are so terrible. Fenby and I are trying to do it.' She wrote again on 9 September: 'you are probably right and the H{ans}. A{ndersen}. song {"Zwei braune Augen"} was possibly the very first one.'

3 Debussy's somewhat uncomplimentary review, including the memorably dismissive 'very sweet songs, very pale, music to lull convalescent ladies to sleep in the rich quarters', was published in *La Revue Blanche* (Paris), 24, No 188, 1 April 1901 (p. 551). Jelka wrote coolly to Heseltine on 9 September: 'Debussy, I think, has a rather absurd way of criticizing: but it is interesting, of course.' In fact, as Oscar Thompson has pointed out, Debussy used almost these identical words in a later review to describe a song by Grieg, a composer he described as no more than a clever musician, 'more concerned with effects than with genuine art'. The phrase could equally be used to describe Debussy as critic, for his early articles in *La Revue Blanche* often sought to amuse and to mock (*Debussy: Man and Artist*. New York: Dodd, Mead & Company, 1937, p. 184 et seq.).

4 Jelka had asked Heseltine on 23 August: '*The 3 Verlaine Songs* that Kate Winter sings {in a concert shortly to be broadcast}. Fred says: Who has orchestrated them? He does not remember having done so.' The Deliuses listened to the present concert: '. . . the orchestra seemed in a jolly mess. Yet Kate Winter was quite good. Fred really thinks them better with piano.' (Jelka to Heseltine, 9 September.)

(535)
Jelka Delius to Philip Heseltine

FREDERICK DELIUS
Grez-sur-Loing
S. et M.
28.9.1929

Dear Phil

We are expecting Mr Angus Wilson from Columbia this afternoon[1] and will concoct a letter. It is amusing how H.M.V. come out with their advertisement *now*!!

"Eventyr" is not based on any particular story of Ashbjørnsen; it is a resumé-impression of the book. I remember reading the book in Norwegian to him; the spirit of Asbjörnson is opposed to that in the Arabesk, as A. is not at all erotic; his are rather the old legends still quite alive with lonely peasants, hunters and mountaineers. These people have a naïve belief in the "Underjordiske" (the Underearthly ones) Trolls, Heinzelmännchen, hobgoblins; who either help the humans or, if provoked, become very revengeful. A boy alone in a forest would imagine he heard them trotting after him, and get very frightened. At a wedding or Xmas meal a little dish of cream porridge is put on the loft for these underearthly ones, or else they might be offended – they have been known to fetch girls away (even the bride of a wedding) in such cases and dance with them furiously till they fall down unconscious. A hunters luck would depend upon their good or bad will. In the queer noises at night in lonely huts and woods you would imagine you heard the hordes of these mysterious beings galloping along in the distance.

Perhaps this may give you an idea of Ashbjørnson. The dead girl in the Coffin would surely be in Grimm's fairy tales. I think Schneewittchen must be lying in such a coffin of glass, looking lovely and the 7 dwarfs watching her. I will try to find it and write to-morrow.

As to the Photos, what really ought to be done is to get a really artistic photographer to make a Studio portrait of Fred at once on his arrival in London. Here I could not get one; and nobody seemed to know one in Paris. But you will be able to find out in London. Elliott & Fry are abominable and they forced Fred to smile and look imbecile in 1923.

I have no photo of my portrait of Fred and no-one here has a good enough Camera to do it. But a little pastel-portrait of Fred by Geo de Monfreid, Gauguins friend from about 1892 to 95 is in London at the O'Neills. It has great charm and the right character, as he was then and the hand on the piano is beautiful. You could get it photographed. But please be very careful as it is pastel. The O'Neills have been keeping it for us and I am going to take it back this time.

I send you a photo of Fred with Dr Haym, probably from, 1903–5 one with Koanga and an early one with mustache, which may be the one you have. But promise dear Phil to restore them to me. I would be miserable if I lost them.

I really can not bring that big portrait over, nearly a yard and a half high.

Fred does not at all care for the idea of getting tributes from german conductors; so you had better cut that out. Anyhow 4 of his principal conductors are dead. Dr Haym, Prof Buths, Fritz Cassirer who brought out the Village Romeo in Berlin and Suter–Basel.

The Entr'acte of the Village R. was composed or changed in 1906 for the Berlin performance   He does not remember who made the first piano Score. The Entr'acte was composed at once after the Mass of Life and just before or in between Songs of Sunset.

A. Wilson was here just now and Fred was very talkative. He also dictated to him the words of appreciation for the Columbia

Fred was particularly pleased about your treatment of his niece!! He said: Ward off all my relations, tell Phil again.[2]

I think it is truly great that Beecham has edited all the works so splendidly. I heard from Hertzka to-day and he is probably going to London for one Concert of the Festival. This would be a very good thing; we could then talk the matter of the Re-Edition over; he also seems to be licking his lips for the new works. Please encourage him to come.[3]

With Barjanskys help I have sent Programmes to all the important german conductors and other important personalities.

Beecham wrote a splendid letter to me yesterday and it had a most excellent effect on Fred, who was very pessimistic about being able to travel.

I did not quite understand about our seats, and I do not like to bother Beecham, who has all these big rehearsals etc. I suppose I am to sit with Fred, and then the Bruder nurse must be there and also Fenby. Fred particularly wants Fenby near him to make him note down anything he may wish to tell him about the music. I suppose it will be alright and that there are 2 seats behind us?

I must get this off at once, so, Goodbye

Ever Affly
Jelka.

I read to Fred, what I had written to you about Eventyr. He said it was quite perfect and expressed exactly what he had meant. So that is quite alright

J. D.

Autograph letter, signed and dated, written on headed notepaper.

The original is in the British Library.

1   The Columbia Graphophone Company was closely associated with the Delius Festival, now causing a great deal of coming and going at Grez. Within a few days of the departure from Grez of the Howard-Joneses on 1 September, Beecham too came visiting. Fenby left on the 7th for a holiday in Scarborough.

2   Heseltine had evidently asked who could be turned to, for the purposes of publicity, for reminiscences of Delius's youth. Jelka warned him on 23 August: 'Fred says: For God's sake, dont let him ask my sisters, they will only tell lies.'

3   Hertzka wrote on 25 September that he hoped to be able, while visiting Paris, to come over to London for one of the concerts. On 10 October he wrote that he still hoped to come to the *Mass of Life*, but on the 30th he wrote to Jelka expressing his great sorrow that ill health had in the event prevented him from travelling. He asked her for a report and reviews.

(536)

Frederick Delius to Edward Elgar

LANGHAM HOTEL,
PORTLAND PLACE,
LONDON, W.I.
11.10.1929

My dear Elgar

Your greeting of welcome gave me the greatest pleasure and touched me deeply.[1]

Should you be staying in London it would give me great pleasure if you came to see me.

Very sincerely yours
Frederick Delius

Letter in the hand of Jelka Delius, dated, written on headed notepaper.

The original is in the Hereford and Worcester County Record Office. It is the first of 16 communications addressed to Elgar by the Deliuses that are known to exist.

The Deliuses left Grez on Monday 7 October, and arrived at the Langham on the 9th. Howard-Jones had booked a room from the 10th at 24 Nottingham Place, Marylebone, for Fenby, who was in the event to spend the remainder of the year in England.

1   This is the first sign of the gradual rapprochement with Elgar, the two composers studiously having avoided each other for most of their lives. Elgar was to write to Bantock the following January asking for Delius's address, which he had mislaid.

(537)

Jelka Delius to Universal Edition

Langham Hotel
2.11.29

To Universal Edition & Dir Hertzka,

I have enclosed a few reviews herewith, but please return them to me *without fail* when you have finished with them.

The whole festival has been a fabulous success.[1] I have asked Barjansky to write a personal report for you today. Do please make as much publicity as possible.

Dr Simon was here for the first concerts & his article should appear any time now in the Frankf. Zeitg.[2] Please watch out for it.

In all the turmoil here it is imposs. for me to write more. We will be returning to Grez within the next few days.

Yours
Jelka Delius

Autograph letter, signed and dated, written in German.

The original is in the Universal Edition archives.

1   The Festival had indeed proved to be a 'great success', as Jelka was to write to Ella Grainger on 27 December. 'Really in a way incredible. I was rather anxious of course, but Fred travelled so well and bore up wonderfully in London too. It was a great experience, Beecham was wonderful and *all* his performances were first rate. I do wish you and Percy had been there! On our return here of course it seemed so calm and uneventful and so I have been reading to him and doing all I can to keep him amused.'

2   Simon also reported on the Festival in *Anbruch*.

(538)
Frederick Delius to Charles Kennedy Scott

LANGHAM HOTEL,
PORTLAND PLACE,
LONDON, W. I.
5.11.1929

My dear Charles,

I cannot tell you how much I enjoyed the singing of your splendid Philharmonic Choir.[1] It is a really and truly great achievement to have trained them as you have. I have never heard my works sung so subtly and with such fine nuance.

Thank you for all the trouble you have taken!

Yours ever affectionately,
Frederick Delius

From Heseltine: *Frederick Delius*, revised edition, 1952, p. 170.

1   On the same date Delius also sent a note to the Philharmonic Choir: 'Let me thank you again for your really magnificent singing of the *Mass of Life*. It was a great joy to me to hear my work so beautifully performed.'

(539)

Frederick Delius to Roy Henderson

6.11.1929
LANGHAM HOTEL
PORTLAND PLACE,
LONDON, W.1.

Dear Mr Henderson,

I want to tell you how delighted I was with your beautiful rendering of
"Zarathustra"

You were entirely in the spirit of the work and you sang so musically and
with greatest understanding. It was a great joy to me to hear this splendid performance.

It is splendid too that you know the part so thoro'ly and are not hampered
by reading from a score.

I should have liked to shake hands with you, but, alas, I had to be taken
home straight-away and I knew you too must be tired.

Yrs sincerely
Frederick Delius

Letter in the hand of Jelka Delius, dated, written on headed notepaper.

The original is in the collection of Roy Henderson. It is the second of four letters
known to have been sent by Delius to Henderson, the first dated 30 May 1928 and the
third and fourth, 4 March and 25 April 1932.

Roy Henderson (b. 1899): Scottish baritone. He studied at the Royal Academy of
Music, where he was later to teach singing. He first came to fame by taking over at
short notice the baritone role in Klenau's 1925 performance of *A Mass of Life*, and was
to become particularly identified with the *Mass*, which he sang no less than fourteen
times, and with *Sea Drift*.

(540)

Frederick Delius to Lionel Tertis

Grez-sur-Loing, 1/12/29.

Dear Tertis,

I have only just heard my 2nd Violin Sonata played by you for the
"Columbia". It is marvellously beautiful, and I am overjoyed. I cannot
imagine it better played. You have got *so* inside the music, and I never

thought the viola could sound so lovely. What a great artist you are! The
Hassan Serenade is also quite beautiful. The few bars you repeat an octave lower
only enhance the piece. Please also thank Mr. Reeves[1] for his excellent col-
laboration.

[Frederick Delius]

From Lionel Tertis: *Cinderella No More*. London, 1953, p. 50.

Lionel Tertis (1876–1975): English violist. He arranged Delius's second Violin Sonata
for the viola, and was to do likewise for the third. Jelka wrote to Heseltine on 2
December about the recording: 'Tertis has really played the Sonata II beautifully.' He
was to play for Delius at Grez in 1933.

Another transcription of Tertis's was the Double Concerto and, after hearing a
broadcast performance of the work some years later, Jelka wrote: 'Tertis was, of
course, the soul of this performance and imparted to it such a wealth of true Delius
tenderness and feeling, carrying May [Harrison] with him quite beyond herself; Boult
at his best where discreet following a master mind is required. – Of course I know that
certain things could not help loosing their effect thro' the deep cello-tone not there.
But as the Cello part is almost all thro' in the high ranges it had not to be changed and
sang out so beautifully in Tertis's supreme playing.' (Letter to Grainger, Grez, 19
March 1935.)

1   George Reeves was Tertis's accompanist in the recording.

1930

'Fred has had pains rather often,' Jelka reported on 15 January to Fenby, to whose return at the end of the month they were greatly looking forward. For a time Delius, unwell and suffering bouts of pain, could do no work, but in March a third Violin Sonata, based on earlier fragmentary sketches, was largely composed. There was a visit from the pianist R. J. Forbes with his two daughters; followed by Bantock's son Raymond who brought his newly-wed wife to lunch. Gardiner seems to have been the first of the older friends to reappear. He came for a few days in April, bringing in tow the young composer Patrick Hadley. Early in May, at Delius's pressing invitation, May Harrison arrived to work through the new sonata with Fenby. She stayed for two weeks, and Delius dedicated the work to her. Another friend, Oscar Klemperer, had been talking to the conductor Albert Wolff who expressed interest in giving one of Delius's works in Paris. On 5 June the composer asked Universal Edition to send scores of *Sea Drift* and *Brigg Fair* to Wolff immediately; at the same time he took the opportunity to ask if Universal were interested in publishing his newly-composed works. Then Fenby recalls the arrival at Grez, at the instigation of one of Delius's friends, of Alex Erskine, a hypnotist who during the course of his two weeks' stay in the village at the beginning of June (during which he treated the composer intensively) effected a surprising improvement in Delius's condition. On his departure, *Songs of Farewell*, the greatest work of Delius's final years, was taken up in its rough sketch form and was fully composed by concentrated dictation to Fenby during the summer. This was the period of composition, too, of *Caprice and Elegy* for cello and chamber orchestra, written as a result of a visit by Beatrice Harrison who wished to have a new work to play during her forthcoming American tour. She also took on tour this year a new arrangement for similar forces of the *Hassan* Serenade.

His work done, Fenby returned to England early in October and was much missed, particularly as after the superhuman exertions involved in the composition of *Songs of Farewell* Delius relapsed into his former condition of pain and nervousness. Domestic problems again came to the fore, in spite of news from Beecham that he was 'going to make a great Delius Offensive in

Germany' (Jelka's words) and that he intended to revive *A Village Romeo and Juliet* very soon. (Another consolation came too in the form of the BBC's efforts to put out Delius's works on wavelengths that were clearly received in Grez.) The present male nurse, who was behaving oddly in the autumn (and who remains unidentified in the letters), would have to leave soon; and cook-housekeeper Marthe Grespier was becoming ever more irascible. Oscar Klemperer came to lunch on Christmas Day, and found a Jelka who was by now overwhelmed by her work and responsibilities. Delius had been going through a bad period, and they were, too, shocked and depressed at the news of the suicide of Philip Heseltine. Jelka's brother Fritz asked her to come to Berlin or Detmold for a rest. Occasional references to the activities of the National Socialists are passing shadows in the correspondence from her brother and sister-in-law. She begged Fenby to come back and was delighted when she heard that he intended to return on 3 January.

Sonata No. 3 for violin and piano (RT VIII/10). Completed.

Songs of Farewell for double chorus and orchestra (Whitman) (RT II/9). Completed.

Caprice and Elegy for violoncello and chamber orchestra (RT VII/8).

(541)
Jelka Delius to Philip Heseltine [Peter Warlock]

[Grez, 12 March 1930]

Dear Peter[1] Fenby brought me the cheque alright, but nobody gave him the Milo's and Programmes[2]; also Gibson promised him to send Koanga-Material *at once* and never did so. I have now written to Beecham as it would be the greatest pity to miss this unique occasion of getting it well done, and under Fred's own supervision.[3]

Your uncle only had a bad abcess in a tooth and went to have it treated in a Fontainebleau Clinique   They sent him back and blood poisoning had evidently set in as he died a few days after in Marlotte after great suffering and Uremia.[4] The Funeral was quite a sad affair, only his wife, the Brooks' Mathew Smith and a protest. Clergyman who could not get away from consoling and advising Mrs H. what to do to get over her terrible bereavement   He was put in a great tiled tomb for three. – Nobody knows who is to be the third. Mrs H. as 2[d] looked gloomily into the tomb in the pouring rain – You know we wrote and wired and wrote again to Gibson ever so many times – and never an answer.

Yrs ever
J. D. –

Autograph postcard, initialled and undated. Addressed: Peter Warlock Esq/101 St George's Sqre/Londres S.W/7. Postmark: GREZ 12 -3 30.

The original is in the British Library.

1   For the first time Heseltine is addressed – by either of the Deliuses – as 'Peter Warlock', the assumed name by which (from 1917) he is remembered as a composer. He wrote later in the year to Delius (on 29 September) telling of the recent death of an immensely rich uncle who had given away 'hundreds of thousands to churches, schools and the like during his lifetime. But never a penny came my way ... After this I resolved finally to abandon all further use of the family name.'

2   Jelka had written to Heseltine on 25 January: 'I wonder whether there are any unsold Milo's with Fred's portrait left? If so I should like very much to buy some, and also some remaining programmes and photos of Beecham and Fred.' She enclosed a cheque for £1. The edition in question of the journal contained a reproduction of a drawing of Delius by Heseltine's friend Augustus John, made at the Langham Hotel during the festival. Fenby, who returned to Grez on 30 January, was asked to call and collect these items en route.

3   The idea was that the lost autograph score of *Koanga* should be reconstructed from the piano score and parts. Henry Gibson, who was to send the material, was Sir Thomas Beecham's music secretary from 1927 to 1932.

4   Jelka had written to Heseltine on 6 March to inform him of the sudden death of his uncle Joe. She was worried about the old man's collection, both of his own paintings and of those by other artists: 'That terrible Maynard is there all the time and he is a man not to be trusted.' Fenby remembers Maynard as being one of the 'rather strange' visitors of Delius's late years. On the other hand Roger Fry's first reaction, in 1921, to this American painter friend of the composer's was that he was 'a most charming creature who knew Cézanne and Gauguin, and tremendously intelligent about art' (D.Sutton, ed., *Letters of Roger Fry*, London, 1972, No. 496).

(542)
Jelka Delius to Percy Grainger

23.4.30.
GREZ-SUR-LOING (S & M)
[station] BOURRON

Dearest Percy

Time is rushing along and I never get to do the things I want to, that is: to write to you.

We were sorry to hear about your having had a real illness; It was so nice of you to send the article by E. Newman[1] – it is very good in its way. Also the news about the Delius music and your own in the former letter gave us *great pleasure*.

You must have been glad to get your beloved Ella safely back, and I hope her little niece is quite well now?

We got thro' the winter alright and Fenby, who has been here since Febr. has worked a lot. They have worked on a new Violin Sonata of Fred's and May Harrison is coming over in a few days to play it to him and to bring it quite up to the mark, as regards phrasing, bowing, tempi expression marks etc. I am *long*ing to hear it; as it seems like a miracle that it has come to life at all.

The great event is that the big orchestral score of the opera Koanga has been found *at last*,[2] after it has been lost since 1915 when Beecham was in money troubles and really bankrupt and had to evacuate the "Aldwych", where he had it then with its entire material. Heseltine discovered the Orch parts at Goodwin & Tabb's last summer and Hadley[3] got them to make another serious search and they found it. English methods, that 3 greatest size bound score volumes which have been enquired after in their library since 10 years and more again and again can escape notice. That they accept valuable manuscripts to keep without labelling or cataloguing or ever taking stock. Fenby is now to copy and revise the whole thing.

We had an amusing visit from Balfour with Patrick Hadley, the young composer, whom we liked very much. Balfour had ordered a little barrel of French wine for us, which he himself was to bottle here with Hadley. I had very explicit instructions: The Barrel had to be placed in the outhouse and so placed, that while bottling the wine they could look into the garden and spring landscape. Madame Grespier was a *picture* when I explained this to her. Balfour sat on a little tree-trunk-sawing-block and filled the bottles and Hadley corked them and Fenby (he so unpractical) wired them with many admonitions from Balfour and me.

Hadley then did a wonderful act of devotion. He extracted from Beecham's secretary all the new scores that he had played at the festival and also the parts of Koanga and brought it all back here straight away. At that time the Score had not been found and Fenby was going to reconstitute the score out of the parts – a frightful work!!

12.5. I'm awfully sorry I could not end this the other day. Now May has been here for about a week practising and playing the new Sonata which is really lovely. It is so limpid and serene, it seems to me quite wonderful that there is nothing of pain and agony, only a peaceful "Ausklang" full of beauty and melody.

The work is now quite finished and May Harrison is to bring it out in the late Autumn with Bax at the Piano. He is no pianist, but he has such great understanding and May loves to play with him, as he is willing to rehearse a lot and the work is not pianistically difficult.

Fred was thinking of offering this Sonata to Curwen for England, Universal for Continent and to Schirmer for U-S. Do you think that is a good plan? The Sonata is in 3 movements, the 2[d] movement begins with a charming little gigue which alternates with a lovely theme with that celtic rhythm, which is in nearly all Fred's last works.

We have as yet done nothing about publishing the other new works. There is

A Late Lark

Cynara (of which I have made a translation to the music, which does not sound like a translation and sings really well.)

"Air and Dance" for Strings.

"A Song of Summer"

The new Orchestral Work now quite ready with a 2 pianos arrangement.

Please advise me, what you think would be best to do? Should we offer the whole lot to Schirmer for U.S.?

It was unfortunate, that, when Balfour was here we did not have these things here to show him. But anyhow he is always so fearfully pessimistic about compositions.

At last I must send this off. I hope you are all well and happy and that you do not have to travel all too much!

With much love and thanks for your letters from Fred

Your old affectionate friend
Jelka.

If possible let me hear re publishing!!

Autograph letter, signed and dated, written on headed notepaper.

The original is in the Grainger Museum.

1   The *New York Times* had recently published a piece on Delius by Newman.

2   May Harrison brought the score with her.

3   Patrick Hadley (1899–1973): English composer. Educated at Cambridge, where later in his life he was to become Professor of Music, and at the Royal College of Music where he taught from 1925 to 1962.

(543)
Frederick Delius to Kaikhosru Sorabji

23.4.1930
GREZ-SUR-LOING (S & M)

Dear Mr Sorabji,

I listened to your "Jardin parfumé" on the Wireless last night and wish to tell you that it interested me very much

There is real sensuous beauty in it.
Believe me very sincerely

yours
Frederick Delius

Letter in the hand of Jelka Delius, dated, written on headed notepaper.

From a photocopy in the Delius Trust Archive.

Kaikhosru Sorabji: see Letter 412, note 4.

(544)
Adrian Boult to Jelka Delius

24th September, 1930

Mrs. Delius,
Grez-sur-Loing,
(S. & M.)
Bourron,
France

[Dear Mrs. Delius,]

Many thanks for your letter. It is most exciting to hear that there is going to be this performance of a new Sonata.[1] We have provisionally come to the conclusion, however, that it would be a more satisfactory broadcast if it could be done from the Studio one evening, when there would be far more listeners than just in an afternoon. We are accordingly getting into touch with Miss Harrison to try and arrange to get her to broadcast the work during the week following the first performance.

Thank you for your suggestion with regard to the Double Concerto. It will give me great pleasure to conduct that lovely work again which the Harrisons play so well, and we must try and arrange it sometime.

It is great news that Mr. Delius has been dictating music this year, and is feeling stronger.

[Yours sincerely,
Adrian C. Boult]

Typed transcript, dated, in the Delius Trust Archive.

Adrian Cedric Boult (1889–1983): English conductor, particularly associated with authoritative performances of his English contemporaries. He taught at the Royal

College of Music and conducted numerous orchestras in the 1920s, then became Director of Music at the BBC and chief conductor of the BBC Symphony Orchestra in 1930.

1   Sonata No. 3 for violin and piano. Completed in March, it was given its first performance on 6 November by May Harrison and Arnold Bax at the Wigmore Hall.

(545)
Jelka Delius to Percy Grainger

4.11.30
GREZ-SUR-LOING (S & M)
[station] BOURRON

Dear beloved Percy,

Your letter gave us both the greatest pleasure and I will, of course, send the photos and dedication as you suggest to both Stoessel and Baer[1]. Fancy, that you had not heard Seadrift before! Fred was delighted with all you wrote about it. It is a most glorious work. Anthony Bernard made a record of it with Decca, but unfortunately they have withdrawn it from sale; I think because Bernard is bound by contract to another firm. I hope that you are raking in money now, so as really to be able to retire from these fatiguing concert-tours. What a blessing that will be!

Now I must tell you about Fred. He has been more lively and active mentally since the great stir of the Festival. It is an everlasting pity that you were not there. Fenby returned to Grez in Febr. and they at once set to to compose Fred's 3^d Violin-Sonata, of which Fred had dictated sketches and snatches and a few opening pages to me in 1923–1924. But he was wonderfully alert, dictating to Eric, correcting, changing, making quite new suggestions. The result (as it seems to me), is a very flowing, melodious Sonata – serene and less wistful than N^{ro} 2. May Harrison came in the later spring and played it for him and he seemed very happy with it and had himself carried up every afternoon to hear it and also the new Orchestral work "A Song of Summer" which Eric had arranged for 2 pianos. He played it with May. It is a lovely short piece now. After the terrible vicissitudes thro' which it went since years, I could never have believed that it would sound so natural. But the crown of all they have done is the Whitman work; you must have seen its sketches. He calls it "The Last Voyage"   It consists of 5 poems, or fragments, all about the Sea and embarking on the last great voyage. It is for Double Chorus and Orchestra (no Solists) and really it seems quite up to the finest of his works.

It was a great strain for him to work all this with Eric and he would sometimes dictate over twenty bars orchestra all of a go. Eric, fever-red, would write it down as fast as he could. Fred kept it up, but when at last it was all done I felt he had to have an entire rest, he was really overwrought. Eric went away to see his people[2] and to-morrow Nov 6th he will be in London to hear May's Recital, where she brings out the Sonata with Arnold Bax at the piano.

Otherwise there have been no musical events, the BBC programmes deteriorating rapidly.[3] Beecham was hidden away all summer and his League of Opera seemed to be going very badly. Now he has suddenly reappeared and is trying to amalgamate the League with the Covent Garden Syndicate.[4] But the public in England is so unresponsive; it is pitiable. B. gave a splendid Concert at the Gewandhaus in Leipsic and we managed to hear it here fairly well, exceptionally well *really* for so distant a station. He gave a heavenly performance of Brigg Fair. It came after the Hebrides Overture, which he gave in a most lively fashion. Then this heavenly calm of the Brigg Fair opening, and a quite celestial clearness and roundness of tone, which, Fred thought, was due to the wonderful Gewandhaus-Accoustic.

We have not seen Balfour since the Spring and I fear he is not very happy. He wanted to sell Ashampstead, and then again not, and now again he has put it in the agent's hands. I think, giving up music like that *entirely*, (and he with no women either) must be so dreary. And planting all these little trees, that may wither again — it does not nourish the Soul; consequently he is not well. I suppose you heard that his grand piano fell thro' the ceiling into the room underneath, and *that*, he said, was the end of music for *him*.[5]

Perhaps, indeed, as you say, there is much more musical Life now in America. It is splendid that they are doing all your best works. Basil Cameron[6] seems to have made a very good start in S. Francisco too.

Fred says he will write to you himself, but en attendant I want to send this to you. How jolly it will be if you come next summer, both of you. Please thank dear Ella for the photo; but it does neither of you justice, you look so black and weird. I should love to see Ella's tiles[7], but most of all I should love to see you both again, so, please, arrange to stay at Grez a little!!

With much love and affectionate messages from Fred

Yrs always and everlastingly
Jelka

Autograph letter, signed and dated, written on headed notepaper.

The original is in the Grainger Museum.

1   Albert Frederic Stoessel (1894–1943): American violinist and conductor, at the time conductor of the Oratorio Society, New York. Grainger had attended a performance of *Sea Drift*, at which the American baritone Frederick Baer had been the soloist, at Worcester, Massachusetts.

2   Fenby returned to England on 8 October.

3   In other words there was too little Delius for Jelka's taste. On 15 May she wrote to
Newman about the recently completed *Song of Summer*: 'If only Beecham could conduct
it on the BBC so that Delius could hear it. But the BBC seems to care only for the
Schönberg-Hindemith and worse music now. I wonder who is responsible for this
overdose we are getting?' She returned to the theme in a letter to Fenby on 19
December: 'We heard Pelleas & M. by Schönberg for a while, but could not listen to
the end. Wagner without inspiration or real Emotion. There is really nothing.'

4   On 22 October, Jelka wrote to Fenby: 'I feel convinced that Beecham is doing the
best that can be done by this merging. If he secures the artistic leadership of this combined opera Company, he will impose his programmes as soon as he has got them into
good working order. I am convinced that people do not understand him or his high
aims at all because they are so earthbound.' And Delius wanted to hear 'what people
say and *know* about T.B.s affairs and the sharks surrounding him'.

5   Here Jelka has crossed out the opening phrase of a new paragraph: 'How jolly
it will be if you' and added in parentheses: 'Please forgive this wrong start after
interruption.'

6   Basil Cameron (1884–1974): English conductor. He conducted the San Francisco
Symphony Orchestra from 1930 to 1932.

7   One of Ella Grainger's many and varied talents was for painting on ceramic tiles.

(546)
Jelka Delius to Eric Fenby

Grez 21.11.30

My dear Eric,

We have just heard from Boosey and Hawkes and I enclose you a copy of their
letter, signed by Ralph Hawkes.[1]
    I think you have most of the works there in London and you would greatly
advance matters by taking them yourself to B & Hawkes 295 Regent Str. You
can probably arrange with Gibson to borrow the 3 works bound together and
take them to Hawkes; as far as I remember we had sent the Air & Dance to
Gibson for that Blind-Performance.[2] You have the Choral work, at least
Beecham has. And finally you have the two little Cello pieces.
    I am sorry indeed to disappoint Gibson about Paxton's,[3] but in Delius's
own interests you must see the great advantage of dealing with a well-known
and established and also experienced firm. Especially as they have just made
such valuable arrangements in U.S.A., where really the most important future
lies. You had better phone to Hawkes and get an appointment. I am writing
them by this same post and announcing your visit with the music. If you could
possibly play the things to them that would be excellent. However I know you
will do your best in Fred's interests, dear Eric. If times are so bad it is all the
more important to grasp a situation speedily.

You will note that I have not mentioned the piano-pieces to Hawkes. I kept them so as possibly to let Paxton have them? What do you think of that? I have not spoken to Fred about them.

In the way of terms Hawkes has offered for the Sonata a royalty of 25% on the published price and 2 thirds of the Gramophone or other mechanical rights. Now I do not know if he will want to pay a smaller Royalty for sales abroad.

The O.U.P. lets Delius have 25% royalty and 20% for abroad and 50% from hired out material. The difference between 25 and 20 being so small I told Fred it is not worth while to withhold from them the Continental rights.

Fred now says he wants to call the work "A Song of Farewell".[4] You can mention that to Hawkes. I had written him about the beautiful words by W. Whitman and you can tell him that a very good translation of Cynara is ready and the others will be translated equally well. – Of course it will be most welcome to Hawkes to have the little Cello pieces recorded. I do hope you will see this thro' at Hawkes's before leaving London on the 26th. You will have to try and restore the 3 works to Beecham before you leave.

I have been in Fontainebleau to-day, and have a lot to do and I must also write to Hawkes, and announce your coming.

So I must hastily close this   Fred is much better to-day. He had 2, nearly 3 bad days. But the Storms, rains and floods are really atrocious.

Much love and a thousand thanks for all your help from us both.

Ever aff^{ly} yrs
Jelka Delius

Autograph letter, signed and dated.

The original is in the Delius Trust Archive.

1   The copy shows that Delius was willing to have Boosey and Hawkes publish the third Violin Sonata if they would also publish *Air and Dance, A Late Lark, Cynara, A Song of Summer, The Last Voyage [Songs of Farewell]* and *Caprice and Elegy*. 'This, to say the least of it is rather a large order,' wrote Hawkes, 'but the whole question is un-doubtedly very interesting to me.' The company's 'Radio connection' in the United States could, he wrote, give Delius's works 'a prominence, which they would not enjoy elsewhere.'

2   The *Air and Dance* was dedicated to the National Institute for the Blind.

3   Gibson had written to Fenby on 16 September, pressing Paxton & Co's interest in publishing some of the more recent Delius works, and on 14 November Jelka had told Eric: 'I would rather give the things to them than the Oxf U.P. They would really be too slow.'

4   The provisional title had for some time been *The Last Voyage*.

(547)
Jelka Delius to Eric Fenby

26.12.1930
GREZ-SUR-LOING (S & M)
[station] BOURRON

My dear Eric,

We were very pleased and really greatly touched by your kind Xmas letter and all you say about the music you have worked on so constantly and efficiently for Fred. Now that this dreadful catastrophe with Heseltine has happened[1] it is still more a blessing that all this is now completed. I thought I had told you that Hawkes has accepted all Fred's conditions and has already sent Draft contracts that only need slight alterations. He is very keen to get all the things *at once* and as soon as ever possible. You know I want *you* for that and I wonder when you could come? You see I am hard pressed. I have written all these masses of letters to nurses, and I seem to have found a good one now, but the contract has yet to be made, then all the difficult steps to be taken with the french authorities.[2] Then I have the translations of Late Lark and Whitman to make, and to adapt them with your help; also Cynara wants slight note changes.

Hawkes wants at once

Sonata III
Air and Dance
Song of Summer
Caprice and Elegy.

Fred says he *must* hear Capr. and Elegy and begs you to get a test record and bring it so that he can give his final consent.[3] Air and Dance is here. Is that quite final; it is in your handwriting. Can I send it to Hawkes at once? Of Cynara I have the P. Score in Phils writing; there is only one bar and a chord after the voice ends, so the later ending is evidently not in   I hardly dare send all these things without your finally looking into them. There would be a fearful unpleasantness if changes were necessary when once they have engraved proofs.

Where is the piano and cello arrangement of Caprice and Elegy?

The third Sonata is here in a good copy, but there is no good separate copy of the solo part. Then if May puts the bowing etc. ought you not to see it again, whether it is quite alright?

O'Neill wrote that you had promised to show him the Choral work on your way through. You must do that; it might be important and if Beecham's scheme with the international fell thro' perhaps the Philharmonic with Beecham conducting would give its première.

I told May to give the Sonata to Hawkes and perhaps then we might let her have our copy, as she is to play it on Jan 15th at the Federation. It is to be ready for the concert of Boosey and Hawkes in February.

Please, dear Eric, write me at once and tell me *when* you think you can come?

I'll quickly rush this to the post. Love from us both

Jelka Delius

Yes, we heard the Sonata very well. It is beautiful.

No time to read through.

———————

Autograph letter, signed and dated, written on headed notepaper. Envelope addressed: Eric Fenby Esq/12 Mayville Av^e/Scarborough/Angleterre. Postmark: PARIS MONTARGIS 26 Dec 30.

The original is in the Delius Trust Archive.

1   Heseltine committed suicide on the night of 16/17 December, although two days later an inquest decided that there was insufficient evidence to decide whether it was suicide or an accident, and simply returned a verdict of death by coal-gas poisoning. He was buried at Godalming, Surrey, on 20 December. In writing to Clews and to Newman, Jelka referred to Heseltine's 'tragic death', and to Fenby she wrote on 24 December: 'the terrible tragedy of Phil H. has really quite unstrung me, and Fred as well. We can think of nothing else.'

2   The search for a new male nurse for Delius led Jelka to write on 4 December to Fenby: 'Now, dear Eric, you know how insufferable these brothers really are. Do you think you could look for a Yorkshireman for us. A nice simple fellow, who has perhaps been an orderly in the war.'

3   The recent HMV recording of *Caprice and Elegy* was conducted by Fenby, with the work's dedicatee, Beatrice Harrison, as soloist.

(548)
Friedrich Rosen to Jelka Delius

27 Dec 30   Berlin-Wilmersdorf
                                                                Binger Strasse 28

My dear Jelka,

Your birthday is coming up again, and we are all thinking of you with loving affection, and thank you at the same time for your very kind Christmas presents, through which you have given us a great deal of pleasure. Among your presents is the third volume of Bülow's memoirs, with me still in debt to you for the first two. For Nina[1] & me it is an extraordinarily interesting book, for of course we were participants in the events described in it and knew Bülow and his wife intimately. It is also very entertainingly written, so that reading it is also a pleasure from an aesthetic viewpoint. I very much admired and respected Bülow, even if I never agreed with his politics, but I am afraid that through his offensive attacks on many of his contemporaries, above all on his master the Kaiser, he has done himself such damage in the eyes of the public that no-one has a good word for him any more. It can be said that morally he has committed suicide and dug his own grave.

For me the book is absolutely indispensable, as I am just now working on my political reminiscences of the years 1901–16. Therefore I am grateful to you for assisting me with my work too.

I am very glad that Fred has been feeling better lately & that he has been able to mark up yet another success with his latest composition. I hope that his condition will soon allow you to visit us again either here in Berlin or in Detmold. And you can stay with us here in Wilmersdorf if you are willing to make do with a small room.

On the whole things have not been too bad with us, except for Nina's suffering an attack of influenza at Christmas & having to take to her bed. But today she is already a lot better. Through me she wishes you many happy returns. Little Fritz[2] also had a mild attack of influenza, but is already well on the road to recovery. Valentina[2] is already a lovely little girl & very sensible too. She has had her first satchel from me for Easter.

With love and affection and with best wishes to Fred.

Your faithful old brother
Fritz

I hope you can make use of the enclosed little hand-mirror, which I send you herewith.
I shall possibly go to London for a few days next week for the Exhibition of Oriental or Persian Art.

Autograph letter, signed and dated, written in German on headed notepaper.

The original is in the Delius Trust Archive. It is among the earlier items in a collection of Rosen family letters dating from around 1930–33. The most frequent writer was Jelka's sister-in-law (and cousin), Nina, whose letters are in English. Friedrich Rosen, represented by some sixteen letters, wrote exclusively in German. There are also a few communications from their son Georg and his children.

Friedrich ('Fritz') Rosen (1856–1935): German diplomat, and brother of Jelka. A member of the short-lived Wirth government, he was German Foreign Minister for some six months in 1921. Otherwise his distinction was achieved through a long and successful diplomatic career and also in the field of oriental studies, in which he was an acknowledged expert. Himself the son of a diplomat (Georg Rosen, 1820–91), he saw his own son, Georg Friedrich (1894–1961), enter the foreign service, and it was while on a visit to the latter, then Legation Secretary in Peking, that he died in China, just six months after the death of his sister Jelka.

1   Nina Rosen, née Roche (1863–1956): English-born wife of Friedrich Rosen. She was not just related to Jelka by marriage, but also by descent, for their common grandparents were Ignaz and Charlotte Moscheles and their respective mothers (Emily Mary Roche and Serena Anna Rosen) sisters. Nina was therefore first cousin to Friedrich and Jelka Rosen.

2   'Fritzchen' and Valentina were the children of Georg Rosen. He also had a second son, Paul.

1931

The year started unpromisingly. Fenby was unwell and had to cancel arrangements to travel to Grez. He was in fact to remain in England for most of the year, spending much of his time in London, amongst other things seeing Delius's latest works through the press. Jelka, who had been making a German translation of *A Late Lark*, now turned to *Songs of Farewell*. The winter's most unsettling event was probably the unexpected arrival at Grez of Halfdan Jebe, who was 'in a terrible state', as Jelka reported to Fenby on 19 February, and had to be taken to hospital at Fontainebleau. Then news came from Paris that *Brigg Fair*, to be given by Wolff at a Lamoureux concert, had to be postponed from 8 to 21 March, as Wolff had either lost or mislaid the parts, fresh ones having to be supplied by Universal. Oscar Klemperer together with Jelka had written a short introduction and analysis of the work for the programme. A visit by Elizabeth Courtauld in mid-March resulted in the confirmation of a performance of *Songs of Farewell* in London in a year's time during a season of concerts sponsored by her industrialist husband Samuel Courtauld. Initially down to be conducted by Bruno Walter, the concert was shortly to be offered to Malcolm Sargent when it was learnt that Walter would after all be unavailable.

Meanwhile Delius had had an uncomfortable winter: 'Fred has had rather much pain lately,' Jelka told Fenby on 7 March, and laid part of the blame on the inadequacies of the new male nurse, Theodor. April saw a gradual improvement in Delius's condition – fortunately, when we learn that Theodor walked out at the beginning of May on hearing that his girlfriend had decided not to marry him. The services of a new man, Richard Göbel, were secured within a short time, and with Gardiner's and Frederic Austin's arrival in Grez in mid-May Delius was in good form, drinking a 'tremendous lot of Champagne', his spirits remaining high through the summer months. Jelka, however, had cause for some unease, as news came in from her relatives about the deteriorating political and economic conditions in Germany and Austria. It was about this time that her diplomat brother Fritz published a volume of reminiscences, and Jelka was soon immersed in it.

May Harrison came again in mid-July. So did the pianists Rae Robertson and his wife Ethel Bartlett; the Deliuses had 'a glorious time' with them, and May & Ethel played the new sonata to Delius. Göbel was reading Nietzsche to Delius and they were delighted with him, even if the consequences elsewhere in the household were unfortunate: 'Mme Gr[espier] has been at her worst and made terrible scenes; jealousy about the man. She is perfectly mad,' Jelka reported to Fenby on 26 July. Links with the Gerhardi family were maintained, Alden Brooks's daughter Filippa leaving Grez for a three months' stay with Lilli (Ida's sister) and her family in Lüdenscheid. In August, Norman O'Neill came for a weekend and found Delius in lively and positive form. Two Americans also called, apparently determined to give *Hassan* another airing in the United States. Charles Leatherbee's company, the University Players, of West Falmouth, in spite of much subsequent planning failed to raise sufficient funds for what was always going to be an expensive enterprise, and the performances scheduled for November had to be abandoned. The early autumn did, however, see two notably successful concerts in England, Henry Wood giving an all-Delius (broadcast) Promenade Concert on 17 September, which enabled the Deliuses to hear the first performance of the new work *A Song of Summer*, and Beecham conducting *A Mass of Life* in Leeds on 8 October. (Beecham, like Henderson in the baritone role, gave the work from memory.) Fenby returned in mid-October, putting the finishing touches to *Fantastic Dance* and a suite from *Hassan* during his six weeks in Grez.

Apart from a painful attack of shingles later in September Delius remained well until at least the middle of December, but towards the end of the year found the cold spell particularly trying. Jelka was again unwell and feeling the strain, and her brother and sister-in-law begged her to come to take a break with them in Germany. This would be made more easy, they felt, if and when Ida Gerhardi's young niece, Evelin, came as expected early in 1932 to help with secretarial and household work. There had been few visitors in the autumn and they were 'quite alone' at Christmas. Moreover, the present male nurse had to leave and was due to be replaced on 1 January.

Irmelin prelude for orchestra (RT VI/27). Autumn.

Fantastic Dance for orchestra (RT VI/28). Completed.

(549)
Edith Buckley Jones to Jelka Delius

Cefn Bryntalch
Abermule
Montgomeryshire

Jan 3rd 31

Dear Mrs Delius

I have long felt I wished to answer your most kind & sympathetic letter on the death of my own dear Phil, but somehow, I just felt I could not, & even now, I cannot believe the awful tragedy has really happened & that my dear boy has gone, with all his wonderful talents silenced for ever, & it seems all so needless he was all the world to me, & I feel quite heartbroken. I know you & Mr Delius sorrow with me, as he loved Mr Delius & his wonderful music. I do hope he is keeping well, & that this terrible blow did not make him worse. Phil was burried in the same grave as his father at Godalming Surrey & many of his good friends came there but the time was so short it was not possible to let them know, otherwise many more would have been there. I cannot believe that it is of Phil I am writing it seems as if it must be an evil dream. Forgive an incoherant letter from Phil's most sorrowing Mother

Edith Buckley Jones

Autograph letter, signed and dated.

The original is in the Grainger Museum.

Edith Buckley Jones, née Bessie Mary Edith Coventon: her first husband, Arnold Heseltine, father of Philip, died in 1897, and she married Walter Buckley Jones, eldest son of R. E. Jones, of Cefn Bryntalch, in 1903. Her family came from mid-Wales.

Jelka wrote to Fenby on 3 January: 'I have had very long letters from Rob. Nichols about poor Phil. Van Dieren also wrote to-day. V. D. is in charge of all the Music and papers Phil has left. He feels it most deeply. He and Nichols have done all they could to keep the details etc. out of the papers and much of what was in the first articles was really crammed with lies from the hysterical neighbours in the house.' (No letters from either Nichols or van Dieren have been found in the Delius Trust Archive.)

Shortly afterwards, Jelka wrote to Sydney Schiff: 'We both feel it very deeply. Such an act gives one a sudden insight into depths of disappointment and suffering – that one cannot bear thinking of, as having been endured by a beloved friend. It is true we were rather separated thro' Phil's latter strange way of living and we lost him bit by bit. But all that is swept away by such a catastrophe. I see constantly the beautiful lovable incredibly intelligent and artistic boy of twenty – and that tragic figure lying in a gas-filled room with his face to the wall in the early morning.

He was almost too critical to create and perhaps at war between the intellectual preference for the ultra-modern in music, and his real innermost love for that aspect of emotional music that Delius represents.'

(550)
Jelka Delius to Herbert and Ada Fenby

GREZ-SUR-LOING (S & M)
[station] BOURRON
12.2.1931

Dear Mr and Mrs Fenby,

These are only a few words to thank you once more for letting us have Eric so long! The work he has done for my husband is absolutely unique and it is almost a miracle that he came at all and then, that he worked so admirably.

I want you to know how deeply we feel and appreciate what he has done. He has always been so steadfast and so painstaking and with his wonderful musical gift added to all those good qualities he has achieved it. It seems so glorious that all these works, that but for him would have remained mere sketches are now actually brought to Life and in the Publishers hands.

We both hope that now Eric will start his own work and achieve great things! I always told him how lucky he is to have such understanding helpful parents. But he knows it well.

I only hope he did not catch a chill on the journey; he looked so specially well when he left. – We miss him very much indeed.

With kind remembrances from Delius to you both and the girls
I remain

Yrs affectionately
Jelka Delius

P.S. Please tell Eric that to-day at last I have received permission for the new nurse to enter France. Lord Tyrrell[1] arranged it all with the french authorities. I hope now to have the new man here in a few days.   J.D.

Autograph letter, signed and dated, written on headed notepaper. Envelope addressed: Mr and Mrs Fenby/12 Mayville Avenue/Scarborough/Yorks/Angleterre. Postmark: GREZ 12 -2 31.

The original is in the Delius Trust Archive.

Fenby was to have left home for Grez on 3 January but was unable to do so, still suffering from the after-effects of influenza. In the event, he remained in England till October – and was given many tasks to do by the Deliuses.

1   British diplomat, ambassador to France from 1928 to 1934.

(551)
Frederick Delius to Eric Fenby

Delius dictates: GREZ-SUR-LOING (S & M)

3.4.1931

Dear Eric,

I received your letter of March 19th and I am glad to learn that everything is going well with you in dear old Scarborough.

I have definitely accepted the Courtauld plan for March 1932.[1] So there is no more question of an early performance and this will give you breathing time and time to continue your own work, which you must, of course, not neglect, especially when the spirit moves you. The thing to do is to copy out *one* set of parts of Songs of Farewell, so that the engraving may be made from your copies. As regards Cynara and Late Lark you should ask Gibson to lend you Beecham's parts of these and let you copy them. I am sure he would be delighted to do so, and it would save much time and work.

That is all nonsense, that I had not answered Hawkes. I answered most clearly.

I consider you now a thoroughly well equipped musician and you have an excellent idea of the orchestra and chorus and I am expecting that you will do something very original. Don't be disheartened if the first attempts do not come off exactly as you want, but go at it again. Dont get tired over a work, but in that case lay it aside and forget it for a while and then take it up again.

Should the spirit move me and I should like to write some more music I shall ask you to come over for a few weeks. In every case, when you want a change or a holyday you are always heartily welcome here.

We both send you our love and kindest regards to your parents!

Believe me yours
affectionately
Frederick Delius

Letter in the hand of Jelka Delius, dated, written on headed notepaper. Envelope addressed: Eric Fenby Esq/12 Mayville Av^e/Scarborough/Yorks/Angleterre. Postmark: PARIS MONTARGIS 4 -4 31.

The original is in the Delius Trust Archive.

In other letters of this period come unhappy echoes of a past friendship, Jelka writing to Fenby on 19 February: 'The norwegian friend from Mexico turned up in a terrible state like the most abject dirty beggar. It affected us very much. His state was so impossible that after 2 days I had to take him to Hospital in Fontainebleau and from there we got him to Paris after the most fatiguing difficulties and we are now sending him back to Norway where he has his brother.' The friend was Halfdan Jebe. Jelka

brought these 'terrible adventures', as she called them, up to date on 7 March in her
next letter to Fenby: 'Our Norwegian-Mexican friend has arrived safely in Oslo – a
great relief for us. It nearly killed me when they handed him back to me at the
Hospital, and I knew I daren't bring him back here. What impossible tasks for me!!'

1   Mrs Samuel Courtauld visited Grez on 12 March. Beecham, to whom Delius had
offered the first performance of *Songs of Farewell*, had failed to respond, and it was in
consequence agreed that the work should be brought out instead at a Courtauld/Sar-
gent concert. Elizabeth Courtauld died later in 1931.

(552)
Frederick Delius to Eric Fenby

[station] BOURRON   GREZ-SUR-LOING (S & M)
                                                              3.7.1931

Fred dictates:

My dear Eric

I am delighted that you have finished the great work of correcting all my
works for Hawkes and I cannot thank you enough for taking all this great
trouble. I am also very glad to hear that you have finished copying out all the
parts of Songs of Farewell. For the 1st performance it will be very handy to
have the score engraved. I am now greatly interested in the progress of your
own Cello Concerto.[1] Whenever you feel like it do come and stay with us;
perhaps in September?[2] Just now there is a tremendous heat wave on and we
have had hot summerweather without a drop of rain all through June. Jelka
drives me out in the evening[3] and we always think of our lovely walks with
you.

    Yes, my dear Eric, you have accomplished a really great work in helping me
so splendidly all these last years. Without you all these works would never
have seen the light.

    With kindest messages to your parents.

    Yrs ever affectionately
    Frederick Delius

Letter in the hand of Jelka Delius, dated, written on headed notepaper.

The original is in the Delius Trust Archive.

1   A number of works either sketched or fully composed in the 1930s, including the
Cello Concerto in question, were later, in a spirit of rigorous self-examination,
destroyed by Fenby. 'I came to the conclusion that I had not the talent for really

original composition,' he notes. 'It is a very salutary thing for a young man to come into contact with genius, and as far as composition is concerned, only genius matters.'

2   As early as 3 April Jelka had written to Fenby: 'Van Dieren wrote very concerned, that he had heard you had left Delius for Good and all. I am writing to tell him that just at present there was nothing more to do, but that you are willing to return, should Delius want to write a new work. That is what Fred says.'

3   Fenby remembers that Delius often said 'drive' instead of 'push', when speaking of Jelka or others pushing his wheelchair.

(553)
Jelka Delius to Eric Fenby

Grez 23.8.31

Dear Eric,

I have read your paragraphs about the three works to Fred and he thinks them excellent and, of course, so do I. I thought perhaps it ought to be mentioned that Song of Summer is a very *short* orchestral work. But Fred said that would be for Hawkes to mention.[1] I think R. Hawkes is back now. He wrote that he could not manage to arrange to give Beecham the Songs of Farewell to conduct in Liverpool, as the only available concert would have been just *before* the Courtauld performance. A great pity!

Will you be going to Leeds for the Mass of Life? Or must you wean yourself of all Delius? Norman said the Philharmonic wants to give it too and that they hope to get Beecham to conduct. They are also doing it at the Hallé with Harty. If one adds to that Schurichts doing it in September in Scheveningen, that is really glorious.

Norman was here last week end, it was just that beastly fête de Grez and the merry-go-round unceasingly energetic. Yet we enjoyed his visit immensely. He is so nice and we spoke so much of you, your ears must have tingled. I showed him all the published works and he really appreciates the wonderful work you have done and all the Labour of correction and piano scores and writing parts. He says he was in Scarborough examining, but only a few hours and had to go on; otherwise he would have looked you up. W[e] had champagne every day and Fred drank the lion's part and was most amusing and chatty. When alone with Norman I told him that I want to take Fred to London once more and that then we would go on our own and take a good little furnished flat, take Hildegard also and keep house, so that Fred gets all his favourite dishes. He seemed very dubious, about Fred's wanting to go. So I broached the subject in the evening, when Fred was in bed and Norman was up there. Fred took it up at once and said he would like nothing better. He would like to stay several months, also stay a little by the sea, eat oysters, take his bath chair in a crate, drive in Kensington Park; Norman would find us a flat etc. etc. Norman was quite amazed at his energy and spirit.[2]

Next evening we heard Tristan from Bayreuth (The 2 first acts from Eiffel-Tower). Fred was most enthusiastic and loved Furtwänglers conducting. He said we ought to go to Munich next summer for the Wagner Festival plays. He would love to hear all the opera's beautifully given, as they do them only in Germany. Then from there we were to go to Detmold, so that I could see my brother and he would prefer coming along, as he cannot bear the idea of my going alone. I said: But all that means long railway journeys? He said: Oh, I do not mind that any more; if you arrange it as comfortably as you can, I trust it will be alright and I'll follow you.

Now isn't that wonderful? What spirit he has! He speaks English with Göbel all the time now, as he does not wish to speak German with him in London. Even if all this never comes to pass, the planning is so lovely. Oh, I do wish T.B. would put on the operas. I told Norman to repeat these conversations to him, and that we have funds to pay our way.

It is gloomy weather still and we see no-one. The Brooks's are $\frac{3}{4}$ the time in Paris. Brooks' father has just died in Boston and he has to go there.

May H. wants to play the Delius Violin Concerto with Barbirolli at the Philharmonic. I spoke to Norman about it and I hope she will succeed. N. said it was up to Barbirolli to present his programme. May says he is very keen on it, so perhaps he will push it through.

I must stop, dear Eric! Fred is resting and may wake up any moment and as it is Sunday I must read the whole afternoon then.

Do tell me how your Cello Concerto is getting on. And are you meditating something else too? If you feel so well and strong up on your moors you must do something great. Mme Grespier is all in a fever preparing for a 5 days trip to the seaside with her husband and a group of others; so I shall be kept busy.

Please give my love to your dear parents and kind messages to your sisters and heaps of love to yourself

Yrs ever aff[ly]
Jelka

P.S. I suppose I told you that Percy Grainger and wife ar[e] at Pevensey. They both came over so as to let the cottage, but have no funds to come to Grez, and Norman said they would not even go to London!! Madcaps!!

Do you sometimes hear from Gibson?

Autograph letter, signed and dated. Envelope addressed: Eric Fenby Esq/ 12 Mayville Avenue/Scarborough/Yorks/Angleterre. Postmark: FONTAINEBLEAU 24 VIII 31.

The original is in the Delius Trust Archive.

1   On 3 September Delius heard that Wood was to give *A Song of Summer* and others of his works at a Promenade Concert on 17 September. Jelka sent Eric an 'SOS' the same day: 'Fred at once said, Oh I am afraid he will take all the wrong tempi like he did in the 2^d Dance Rhapsody. I said: Shall I ask Eric if he would go to London for the rehearsals as Deputy for the Composer? Delius said: I think that would be *splendid* – if Eric will do it? He must hear the rehearsals. Fred would write to Wood that you will happen to be in London just then and any questions arising as to tempi etc, and that having written and edited the work for Delius you know exactly how Delius intends it to be played.'

2   Delius remained in good form, and Jelka wrote to Fenby on 9 September: 'Yesterday we took Fred to Fontainebleau to have ice cream and then there was great trouble because he wanted Ginger-ale after, for which we had to search in all the Pâtisseries and Cafés. At last we got Ginger *beer* and then he had to have Gin to put in. All Fontainebleau was in an uproar, seeing us cruising around in search of these drinks. He enjoyed himself tremendously and was wreathed in smiles and on friday I have to get a great bottle of Gordon's gin, so there will be terrible orgies, I fear.'

(554)
Jelka Delius to Eric Fenby

GREZ-SUR-LOING
SEINE-ET-MARNE
18.9.1931

Dearest Eric,

We listened with the greatest pleasure last night.[1] It crackled a bit, but yet came thro' well and I got it loud, by having all seven lamps. Fred was enjoying himself and looked radiant about the

Song of Summer

"It's a good piece" he said several times. He will write about it himself but as he perhaps will not do it to-day I will send this off first, and try to catch you at your London address. Fred said the Tempi were perfect in S. o. S. and it was surely a blessing that you were there. Fred was very pleased with Orrea P. but disliked Goodson. D. Labbette did not come thro' very well. Was it that the Microphone was not well placed? Brigg Fair sounded lovely. But really S. o S. came through beautifully. I loved it. How different from hearing it on 2 pianos. It sounded so mellow and ripe. Fred was really very pleased with Wood. The applause was thundering on the seven lamps, but was cut off after Brigg Fair, as we had overlapped 12 minutes on the news about "fat porc" etc. Fred sat up till the end, getting *terribly* restless during the Piano Concerto; I stroking him all the time. But calm returned with Brigg Fair. I feel so near to you after all the other memorable BBC performances we have heard together, that I must tell you all details.

Of course we shall love to hear all about your impressions and the friends and people you met etc. Do let us hear about everything. Fred wants me to get some mushrooms for him in the woods, so I am going with Mrs Br. Therefore I must hastily close this

Ever aff^ly
Jelka D.

Could we only have heard the Song o. S. again instead of the P. Concerto!

Autograph letter, signed and dated, written on headed notepaper. Envelope addressed: Eric Fenby Esq/24 Nottingham Place/Londres/Angleterre. Postmark: GREZ 18 -9 31.

The original is in the Delius Trust Archive.

1   Orrea Pernel played the Violin Concerto, Katharine Goodson the Piano Concerto, and Dora Labbette sang Songs with Orchestra. For two nights after the concert Delius was in considerable pain, and his doctor diagnosed shingles. 'Luckily this did not begin one day earlier!' wrote Jelka to Fenby on the 21st.

(555)
Frederick Delius to Eric Fenby

GREZ-SUR-LOING (S & M)
[station] BOURRON
20.9.1931

Delius dictates:

Dear Eric,

I cannot thank you enough for all you have done and I am sure the beautiful performance of the Song of Summer was greatly due to your being on the spot and playing it to Wood beforehand. It came through beautifully and I am really *very pleased* with it.

The mere fact that there were no mistakes in the score and parts shows what care and trouble you have taken with it. I did not like C.G.'s playing, it came thro so hard and she took the 2^d theme of the 1st movement too slow. Anyhow I don't much care for the concerto.

I do not want you to have any expense on your trip to London, and there are always little extras, so I send you £10, which please accept with all my thanks.

There is no hurry about the Fantastic Dance; as you suggest I should like to hear it again before publishing it. So we will postpone it till you have been here again. When you want a little holiday please run over here again and we will crack another bottle of champagne together and we'll both enjoy your visit ever so much.[1]

Your affectionate friend
Frederick Delius

Letter in the hand of Jelka Delius, dated, written on headed notepaper. Envelope addressed: Eric Fenby Esq/12 Mayville Avenue/Scarborough/Yorks/Angleterre. Postmark: GREZ 21 -9 31. A letter from Jelka, dated 21.9.1931, was also enclosed.

The original is in the Delius Trust Archive.

1 Fenby came to Grez again on 15 October and stayed for six weeks before returning to England. Meanwhile Beecham gave a much-acclaimed performance of *A Mass of Life* at the triennial Leeds Festival on 8 October, with the London Symphony Orchestra and with Roy Henderson as principal soloist.

(556)
Frederick Delius to Universal Edition

FREDERICK DELIUS
Grez-sur-Loing
S. et M.
24.11.1931

To Universal Edition
Vienna

I do not know why you or Herr Cranz & C° should think that Sir Thomas Beecham received the complete orchestral material of the Mass of Life & A Village Romeo & J. *from me.*[1] In the first place I never possessed such material, so could not hand it over & 2nd I know perfectly well that in the interests of my publishers I should not do such a thing. Sir Thomas has a large music library & has possibly had these works for years already. You will understand that I cannot interfere in this matter; this can only be done through business channels.

I would urge you also *to handle the matter carefully.* You should always bear it in mind that it is to Beecham that the credit must largely go for having brought my music to a wider audience. He is to conduct the Mass of Life in the Albert Hall in April & proposes to bring out Romeo & Juliet as an opera again at the earliest opportunity. It is only due to him that "The Walk to the Paradise Garden" from this opera is now so frequently played in England & America, & it is thanks to his magnificent gramophone records of this piece that other performances strive to reach his standard. He has also made Brigg Fair tremendously widely known through his performances & gram-records. He alone succeeded in getting the Mass of Life done in that bigoted place Leeds.

He has provided all my works with exact dynamic markings & naturally prefers to conduct from *these scores*, & to have them always at his disposal. Yet another question:

Recently the English texts of the *Fünf Lieder* published by you were printed in the programme of an English lady singer.[2] On top it said translated by Addie Funk.[3] I am told that this is also what is printed in the present edition. There must be an error here. I myself translated the Lieder into English at the time & this translation which is very singable is still just the same as I did it then. I therefore ask you to strike out the name Addie Funk & put Fr. Delius instead & to rectify this in the next edition. How on earth did this happen?

Hassan Suite. I trust this is at the engraver's? Fenby will then read the proofs. Please send them here. I will let you know when he leaves here. No news from the Americans?

Yours sincerely
Frederick Delius

Letter in the hand of Jelka Delius, dated, written in German on headed notepaper.

The original is in the Universal Edition archives.

1   On 20 November Universal wrote to tell Delius that they had heard from Cranz, their London agents, that Beecham had received the complete orchestral material both of the *Mass* and *A Village Romeo and Juliet* from Delius. They asked the composer to remind Beecham that 'for every performance a hire fee and performing fee has to be paid to us.'

2   Cecily Arnold.

3   These four words in English in the original.

(557)
Jelka Delius to Percy Grainger

[station] BOURRON   GREZ-SUR-LOING (S & M)
                                                                  20.12.1931

Dear Percy,

We were so pleased to hear from you. Many thanks! Yes, life does become very difficult and I am sorry you have to overwork like that. It is really too bad. We have not seen any of the English friends and now the pound has sunk so, even Balfour says he cannot travel out of England!!!

Fred is fairly well but often has pains in this his worst time of the year. He had an attack of shingles and felt very unwell, but happily it did not last long.

After that Fenby came and made an orchestral suite of 4 numbers out of Hassan. I think Ross[1] with the New York Scola Cantorum is going to do a Concert version of the whole Hassan.

How nice that you have included Air and Dance and "On hearing" in your programme!

Things are very dull in Europe too, and this letter is dull, but I wanted to send you some affectionate messages for you and Ella from us both.

Yrs ever affectionately
Jelka –

Autograph letter, signed and dated, written on headed notepaper.

The original is in the Grainger Museum.

1   Hugh Ross (b. 1898): English-born choral conductor. He studied at the Royal College of Music. He was based for some years in the 1920s in Winnipeg, and subsequently became New York City's leading choral director. He had visited Delius at Grez in 1928, in the company of the flautist Quinto Maganini, and often included Delius's works in his programmes, most notably *A Mass of Life*, whose first two American performances he conducted in New York in 1938, and *Sea Drift*.

(558)
Jelka Delius to Henry and Marie Clews

[station] BOURRON   GREZ-SUR-LOING (S & M)
                                                          23.12.1931

My dear friends,

It was delightful to have a few words from you and the portraits of Snob and Tory[1] altho' I should have preferred the pictures of Mancha and his Dulcinea!

Yes, do come and see us soon! Come in spring, we should love it. We are struggling along thro' the cold winter.[2] Fred is fairly well   We are going to be quite alone for Xmas. Our english friends seem terrified about the £, it seems. Or do they shoot right past us to the Riviera?

After years and years I was in Paris for 2 days lately. I saw your old house, looking very ragged – and all the memories of the thrilling times there with you both rushed back to me. I stayed with the Brooks' who have built a delightful house Boul^d Arago, opposite the Santé Prison with a convent and gardens behind.

We should love to read the new book and I should love to see the new sculptures; do send snapshots. I could then describe them to Fred. I have now got such a technique in describing things to him that he with his wonderful imagination sees it all. Sunsets and rising moons on the river and the funny people of Grez.

Fred sends you all his most affectionate messages.

Ever yours affectionately
Jelka Delius

Autograph letter, signed and dated, written on headed notepaper.

The original is in the Delius Trust Archive.

1   The Clews' dogs.

2   Jelka was exhausted and felt unwell; her brother Fritz and his wife Nina were growing worried about the state of her health after all the years of ministering to Delius's needs: '. . . you ought to take a real holiday. You ought to come here,' wrote Nina from Berlin on 14 December, adding: 'I think it would be good for Fred in-directly. For it would [be] terrible for him if you broke down again & could not nurse him.' Fritz himself wrote on 20 December: he had long been of the opinion that she should have a real rest. 'It ought to be possible to find a sanatorium for him where he can be well looked after, under medical care and in the company of his sister, while you do something for your own health in the meantime.' They asked her to come to stay in a little apartment on the Bingerstrasse a few doors away from their own home, coming to them for all meals and indeed whenever she liked.

1932

New arrivals in the household were another male nurse, Hubert Thieves, who made a good impression, and Evelin Gerhardi who arrived around the middle of January and who delighted the Deliuses with her cheerful temperament and her willingness to take on all kinds of duties. News from England, however, was not so good: Fenby was suffering from nervous exhaustion. Musically there was special promise in the air, with broadcast performances of the *Mass* in February and *A Village Romeo and Juliet* in May to be looked forward to with conspicuous pleasure. Greetings poured in from all quarters for Delius's seventieth birthday on 29 January. Jelka's present was a smart folding wheelchair which, as she put it, could be lifted 'into cars & railway carriages'.

The first performance of *Songs of Farewell*, a work dedicated to Jelka, took place on 21 March at Queen's Hall. Fenby, recovering well from his illness, was present, and had moreover helped Sargent prepare the performance, which was given by the London Symphony Orchestra and the Philharmonic Choir. Regrettably, the concert was not broadcast. Jelka, still unwell herself, wrote to Fenby on 27 March: 'Fred had several very bad weeks, even the last two months. Much pain, sleeplessness and irritation. These last days he has been better and I too feel better. I was quite worn out with the constant strain.' This brief respite from ill health coincided happily with the visit to Grez of the soprano, Cecily Arnold, accompanied by her husband, the lutenist Eric Johnson. For several days she came along to the house to sing Delius's songs to him, accompanied by Evelin Gerhardi. After her departure, influenza laid virtually the whole household low and Delius was again in considerable pain. Gardiner and Hadley, who were to have come, had to abandon their plans, and Gardiner made a short visit in the summer instead. Presumably the Deliuses were sufficiently recovered to listen to a recital broadcast from Frankfurt on 15 April, when their old friend Heinrich Simon played the third Violin Sonata.

In May came a proposal from Universal Edition to publish, with organ accompaniment, the 'Chorus in the church' from *A Village Romeo* (they had discerned a market for it at weddings!) Delius agreed, and proofs were to arrive in December for correction. Only a week later, Universal, accepting the evidence of press reviews of the recent broadcast that the opera was particularly well suited to radio, informed Delius that they were applying pressure for the work to be given by Frankfurt as well as by American radio stations. Delius recommended Beecham and Schuricht as conductors, adding a word for Hans Rosbaud, and grumbling about the neglect by Universal of *Fennimore and Gerda* ever since its successful production in 1919.

In June there were 'some delightful visits' from Beecham and Dora Labbette. And in July came another honour, with the Lord Mayor and Town Clerk of Bradford arriving at Grez on the 23rd to confer the title of Honorary Freeman of the City of Bradford on the composer. Certainly, by now Delius was once again in good form and enjoying the summer weather that saw Jelka and Evelin Gerhardi swimming in the river. There were short visits from Gardiner in July and from O'Neill in August. At the beginning of August Jelka at last managed to get away for a week to Detmold.

Changes were on the way, with Fenby to return on 1 September and Evelin Gerhardi finally to leave for home a week later. Delius's latest nurse was also proposing to leave before long. And James Gunn, the painter, came to Grez at the end of August to make a portrait of the composer. The main work of the autumn with Fenby was the reshaping of some of the music from *Margot la Rouge* and its magical transformation into *Idyll*, completed in October. After a stay of two months, Fenby left again.

Jelka's health gave cause for increased anxiety. She had X-rays taken at Fontainebleau on 7 November and later had to go for tests in Paris. As for Delius, he had again undergone an experience which was not infrequent during his nine years as an invalid: early in November he had a partial return of vision, even if in the form of little more than shadows. Jelka reported to Fenby: '. . . he had an astonishing spell of seeing lasting the afternoon, evening and next morning.'

In December there were more problems in a familiar area: Hildegard, for some years the maidservant, had to go. Her shouting and cursing were becoming unbearable. A new girl, Anna, a Russian, was engaged. The Deliuses looked forward more than ever to Fenby's promised return.

Idyll ('Once I passed thro' a populous City') for soprano, baritone and orchestra (text adapted from Whitman by Robert Nichols) (RT II/10).

(559)
Jelka Delius to Eric Fenby

FREDERICK DELIUS
Grez-sur-Loing
S. et M.
14.1.1932

Dear Eric,

I have just got your letter and am rather sorry you will not be in London presently. As you know on January 29th is Fred's 70th birthday. It would have been a year later, but Phil discovered in Somerset House that Fred was born already in 1862 and not in 1863 as his mother had always told him. I thought no notice would be taken at all but I saw a little mention of the event in the Paris Daily Mail to-day. The same was also in yesterdays D. Telegraph with this added however: "The BBC is broadcasting a special Concert in Celebration, the works given will be: Caprice and Elegy"!! Now did you *ever*!!! These little pieces were evidently already down on the programme of the 28th and may be played by one of their hopeless Cellists; It is not Baba, for she sent a long wire yesterday asking us to intervene, so that *she* may play these pieces. Naturally we cannot possibly do that; we have never been asked and the whole thing is so absolutely ridiculous. If they cannot do more than *that* they had better not talk of Celebration at all. I write you all this, so that you know what is going on.

As regards the Hassan Suite I feel sure I answered you by return of post, at the same time as writing about it to U. Ed.? Fred accepted the order of the movements as you suggested them. So I suppose U. Ed. will have started engraving the Suite and will soon send you proofs.

It was very nice to get the letter from Harty. I wonder if it will be broadcast thro' the London stations, so that we can *really* hear it?

Yes, I think it would be wise for you to go a fortnight before the performance of the Songs of Farewell. But you had better ask Sargent whether that will suit him, as he seems to be so dreadfully busy.[1]

It is so sad that Mme Courtauld will not be there to hear it after arranging it all. All the most lovely pictures, Gauguins and Renoirs Manets etc. in the French Exhibition in London are lent by the Courtaulds.

I am delighted to hear you are working, and working well at your own music.

I think it is all nonsense about Balfour G. living in France. He only wrote me the other day from Oxford and he even said he could not travel on the continent on account of the bad condition of the £. I am called to read so let me rush this into an envelope

Yrs ever and always
Jelka Delius

Autograph letter, signed and dated, written on headed notepaper. Envelope addressed: Eric Fenby Esq/12 Mayville Avenue/Scarborough/Yorks/Angleterre. Postmark obscured.

The original is in the Delius Trust Archive.

1   Jelka had earlier written to Fenby, on 11 December: 'I am dreadfully anxious about Sargent, but *I think you can get him into it*. It is anyhow a sign of a fine nature that he is so keen to learn and willing. If once he could grasp the delicious lilt in the Delius music, he would get right into it. And *do* take him in hand for the Cello Concerto, this unfortunate work, which is always being murdered.'

(560)
Percy Grainger to Frederick Delius

Copy of letter   In the train, Jan. 29th, 1932.

Darling Fred,

I suppose today is more or less your birthday and I send you my heartfelt loving congratulations and good wishes.

I often think of your birthday in 1923, when we went out on the "Promenade" in Frankfurt with your chair and when you talked to me about your sketches and unfinished works. I should think you must feel very proud of all you have accomplished since then with Fenby, who came like a true angel of art to do what was needful. In 1923 I hoped to do my share, as one of the apostles of your supreme soul-satisfying art, in the years to come. Looking over the 9 years that have passed since then I feel thankful that I was able to give some small impulse to the Delius movement in America, by the concerts I gave in New York, Bridgeport and Los Angeles. But it was all so small, compared with what I would have liked my share to be. What we artists can do, in a really concrete way, is, after all, very limited, since we so seldom possess capital or leisure. You, darling Fred, have had the advantage of some of both, and right nobly you have used whatever small material advantages you possessed in order to lift your art clear above all small and material considerations, thereby providing us with the lovliest and loftiest music of our era.

As a contemporary & as a fellowcomposer I revere and thank you, beloved Fred, for the way you have enriched our world of music by strains that come from your very soul and reach the souls of others as no other music does.

The full measure of my love and reverence for you & your art is not evident when I am with you, because of my annoying ways and manners and my argumentativeness. What I feel is not well expressed in my daily behaviour and particularly has this been the case of late years. For several years I have felt the threat of this present depression coming over the business and musical world and that consciousness forced me to concentrate on my affairs and compositions with selfish singleness of purpose. I felt that certain things had to be accomplished before I was 50 and before the then existing bubble of prosperity burst. I felt that I had to complete certain works of mine speedily yet carefully and I felt that I was obligated to support my publishers in certain definite paths of propaganda & the like. These material duties never touched my soul, of course, but the[y] kept my mind busy and made my actions and moods selfcentered & selfish. All of which you will have devined without my explaining, I feel sure.

I do not mind the poverty that spells mere lack of money and material well-being. But I do resent the lack of leisure that goes with poverty – the lack of time to give to the art & the friends one admires and loves so dearly. Certainly I have never been able to attend to my business duties and my life of art-appreciation & art-friendships as well as I would wish to have. In spite of these shortcomings I wish you to believe, dear Fred, that my adoration for your music & my reverence for your wisdom & philosophy go to the very roots of my esthetic being and mean far more to me than appears in my outward actions & behaviour. The soulful loveliness of your music & the perfection with which you have followed and sustained your inspirations is one of the deepest satisfactions of my life as an artist.

Times are very trying over here at present. Everything costs more effort than usually & the results are hardly worth having. Therefore I have accepted a nice post (Head of the Music Department) at the New York University for next season, at a salary of $5000 (£1000). I am to teach advanced Composition & lecture about music, & I shall enjoy airing my views about your music and other matters.

Ella is very anxious for me to retire from my concert work as soon as possible, and so am I. We have saved money well & if the whole value of money does not change in the near future (& thus alter the value of the Trust Funds I have created for Ella & others) we ought to be able to retire (in a very modest way) in a very few years now. That is what mother and I were longing for ever since I started the hateful virtuoso business over 30 years ago.

We shall not be able to afford any journey this summer except a brief trip to Sweden to see Ella's dear Fosterfather,[1] who is very seriously ill. We both regret keenly that conditions do not enable us to include a trip to Grez to see you both. We will hope for such a treat at some later time, not too far off.

In the 2nd $\frac{1}{2}$ of 1933 we are hoping to be able to pay a long visit to Australia, when I shall hope to be able to introduce all sorts of best beloved Delius works (Dance Rhapsody, Song of the High Hills, Cello Sonata) to various Australian cities. I shall let you know in March how your Concerto goes in Chicago, when I play it there.

With thousands of untold loving and admiratious thots & best wishes

Ever fondly yours
Percy

Typed carbon copy in the Grainger Museum.

1   Ella Grainger's surname Ström was adopted from that of her foster-parents. She was born the daughter of Göran and Matilda Brandelius.

(561)
Jelka Delius to Eric Fenby

Grez 2.2.32

Dear Eric,

We have thought of you so much these days and your last letter brought you again very near. The 29th of Jan. passed very quietly, but Fred was quite touched by the wonderful letters and telegrams he received; and such masses. The young post lady was on the trot here all day, and even then she brought the wires in Batches. Fred felt very well that day and the flow of affectionate and beautiful letters still continues. We played him Beecham's Summernight and The Walk to the Paradise garden records.

Our little german girl[1] is just as nice as one can be. Always gay and pleasant and as helpful as she can be, typing letters   reading to her "Uncle Fred" and gardening and walking out with me, and baking wonderful apple-cakes. Mme G. was most suspicious about this, but Evelin's gay and sweet manner seems to have won her over. As to H[ildegard]. she acts like a real "Berserker" and there is nothing to be done I fear. But having such a nice young thing around I do not worry so much. Evelin is quite an efficient pianist and has a nice little soprano voice. What she lacks as yet, naturally, is musical taste – and when you come next time you must educate her there and teach her the Delius songs. Spring the Sweet – etc. Henley's nightingale – all that would suit her. She seems as yet to prefer horrid old french "Bergerette" songs with many verses.

I am also delighted with our new man; he is excellent and feels quite at home here; he says he loves his life and work here, and we feel that it is true. He is as calm as R. was nervy, extremely cultured and well read and really a companion. – Today Fred has been out for the first time since New Year, as it has turned mild after a cold spell.

Bradford as a town kept absolutely "mum" on the birthday, but the old Choral Society, the Grammar School, the London Old Bradfordians all sent Telegrams, also Malcolm Sargent, Barbirolli, Ham. Harty with the Hallé Orchestra, also a charming one from Elgar. Did you hear the Van Dieren Quartet?[2] How did you like it. They played the Delius beautifully, we thought.

We can hear Northern Region quite well now I found the numbers, so we hope to hear the Mass of Life only it fades often. Did I tell you that old Mrs Chadwick died? She caught Broncho-Pneumonia at Avignon. Monsieur Hazard[3] died too quite suddenly.

I had a very nice telegram from Beecham in which he says that he played Delius on his tour in the North every evening and that he is going to give a Delius concert in Queens Hall in February. But I do not know the date. A few days later I had a delightful letter from him, which made me very happy. He said in it, that he was quite willing to have the BBC. broadcast his concert so that Fred could hear it. He had several interviews with Van Dieren, who really behaved like a brick on Fred's behalf. They all wanted him to get the O.M., but of course all was in vain I suppose and they would probably prefer giving it to Cowen.[4]

I am sending you a beautiful photo of Delius, which the little Photographer in Fontainebleau did.[5] It is marvellous; I worked him up to such a pitch that he quite surpassed himself and was overcome with surprise at his achievement. He did it here in the room too and it was a miracle that a very bright cloud came right opposite the glass door at the moment.

Autograph letter, unsigned and dated. A pressed flower was enclosed.

The original is in the Delius Trust Archive.

1   'Evelin Gerhardi will be here in a few days,' wrote Jelka to Fenby on 10 January. Evelin, the twenty-two-year-old niece of Ida Gerhardi, had agreed to come and live with the Deliuses, helping with the household chores. The new male nurse had already arrived, replacing the recently departed Richard: 'He is a strong square fellow – no nerves, and carries Fred well and carefully.'

2   Van Dieren's String Quartet No. 3, dedicated to Delius, had been broadcast in January.

3   Mayor of Grez.

4   Although knighted in 1911, Cowen was not to be awarded the Order of Merit, a distinction that had been conferred on Elgar as early as 1911. Rumblings over Delius and the Order of Merit had been heard for some years. *The Musical Times* congratulated the composer on 1 April 1929 on becoming a Companion of Honour: 'But we hope it is not ungracious to express the dissatisfaction which we know is felt by most musicians as to the inadequacy of the honour conferred on Delius. Nothing less than the Order of Merit should have been given him.' (In a letter in the May edition one reader wrote that he felt most people had expected Delius to have received a knighthood.) Finally, on 28 January 1932 van Dieren wrote, as a long shot, to Elgar, telling him that all of Delius's friends were convinced that an appeal from Elgar himself to the Prime Minister would 'open the way' for Delius to be admitted to the Order, and appealing for Elgar's 'invaluable' support. Sir Edward replied on 7 February: 'As I said on the telephone I *at once* did what I could; you had better send to The Private Secre-

tary your wishes; this should carry things a step farther.' But this most distinguished of all British civil honours was not to come Delius's way.

5 Esparcieux's effort was to become the best-known photograph of Delius's last years.

(562)

Frederick Delius to Adrian Boult

Grez-sur-Loing,
Seine-et-Marne.
Feb. 22. 1932

Dear Boult,

I listened in last night, and want to tell you that I have never heard a better performance of "Brigg Fair". Everything came through wonderfully distinctly, and you gave me a great deal of pleasure for which I thank you most heartily.

Sincerely yours
Frederick Delius

Typed transcript, dated, in the Delius Trust Archive.

(563)

Jelka Delius to Cecily Arnold

GREZ-SUR-LOING
SEINE-ET-MARNE
25.2.1932

Dear Miss Arnold

Your second letter came to-day and I am sorry I did not answer the first earlier. The difficulty is always, finding the right moment to get my husband's opinion. However I have shown him your translations and they seem to be very good indeed and very singable. We should love you to come here and sing all the songs to us.[1] My husband is constantly asked to listen to his Sonatas but rarely his songs and he would like to hear the newer ones especially. Are you busy in Paris? If not could you not arrange to spend a few days at Grez and sing all these songs to him and discuss all the points you wish to? Saturday

March 26th would suit very well, but if for instance on that day he was not feeling so well your coming would be in vain. It is better to have a little latitude.

Delius says he would like you to sing the new song if Hawkes can let you have it either *ready* or just a proof sheet.[2] He would like you to sing it to him. But how about accompaniments? Do you play your own? We have a young german girl here who is quite an efficient player, tho' very young and inexperienced. But she has played chamber music in public and sings herself and is very intelligent. If you had a morning or so to coach her she would play for you. If you could send a list of the more difficult songs you wish to sing she would practise them now.

There is quite a nice simple little pension here in Grez, where you could stay, (good beds and clean)   As it is just Easter I should have to order your room now. We have a music room which is so placed that one can practise there without disturbing my husband. He is never up in the mornings, so that is the time artists have always practised here.

The new song is not to be translated into english. It is too intimately adapted to the words; but I am sure you sing in french and you could have english words given on the programme.

I enclose you a little timetable. Our station is Bourron, just $1\frac{1}{2}$ mile from here. I have marked the trains. You can also go to Fontainebleau but you would have to take a taxi there (5 miles) and you would hardly get here earlier. If you tell me when to expect you I shall send the man to the station to fetch you.

I can also make arrangements at the pension; it is cheap: about 35 to 40 frs a day with all meals included. I must rush this to the post. So with kind regards from my husband, and hoping to see you here soon

Yrs sincerely
Jelka Delius

Autograph letter, signed and dated, written on headed notepaper. Envelope addressed: Miss Cecily Arnold/41 Lonsdale Rd/Barnes/Londres S.W.13/Angleterre. Postmark: GREZ 25 [-2] 32.

The original is in the collection of the late Eric Johnson. This is the fourth of eleven communications sent by Jelka to Cecily Arnold between 11 August 1931 and May 1935 (the last two being printed cards).

Cecily Arnold (1896–1974): English soprano and musicologist. She studied singing and composition at the Royal College of Music, and married in 1927 the lutenist and former violinist Eric Marshall Johnson.

1   Some months earlier, the singer had listed thirty-two of Delius's songs and then written asking for dates of composition: she was to give a number of them at a recital

at Leighton House on 31 October. In her reply dated 11 August 1931, Jelka told her 'which of the songs he likes best.' These were 'The Nightingale' (Henley), 'I-Brasîl', the Four Elizabethan Songs, 'Chanson d'automne' and 'La lune blanche'. 'Of the older songs he likes The homeward way and Autumn.'

2   Delius's last song, 'Avant que tu ne t'en ailles', to Verlaine's words, was published by Hawkes in 1932.

(564)
Frederick Delius to Hamilton Harty

Grez-sur-Loing
Seine-et-Marne
February 26th, 1932

Dear Harty,

Your kind and sympathetic letter gave me the greatest pleasure. Only one who felt and understood my music entirely could have given such a performance as you did.[1]

And last night, I listened in again to Northern Regional, and you gave again the best performance of "Life's Dance" that I have yet heard. (And I have heard it often in Germany.)

I heard your concerto also for the first time and it seemed to me superbly played by Mr. Barber. After a first hearing the first movement especially appealed to me with its touchingly beautiful second subject.

I hope I shall soon have the opportunity of hearing it again. I like Constant Lambert's "Rio Grande". I think he is the most gifted of the young lot. He has got something to say.

Your grateful friend
Frederick Delius

Letter in the hand of Jelka Delius, dated.

The original is in Queen's University, Belfast.

Hamilton Harty (1879–1941): Irish composer, conductor and pianist. He was conductor of the Hallé Orchestra from 1920 to 1933, and a performance he gave of *A Mass of Life* was broadcast on 18 February 1932. Delius sent a telegram on the 19th, thanking him for his 'splendid performance & perfect understanding of work'. Harty conducted much Delius over the years, the first major work being the Violin Concerto, which he gave with the Hallé (soloist: Sammons) on 18 December 1919, well before taking up the orchestra's principal conductorship. He gave the *Mass* again on 2 March 1933. He was knighted in 1925.

1   Jelka Delius sent an accompanying letter on the same date: 'Delius looked . . . so rapt and happy during the memorable performance of the Mass of Life, from time to time remarking on some special beauty of the rendering. We both enjoyed it immensely, as well as the beautiful performance of "Life's Dance" last night. Those are the glorious moments that lift us over many rather drab times.'

(565)
Adrian Boult to Frederick Delius

The British Broadcasting Corporation,
Savoy Hill,
London W.C.2.
29th February, 1932.

Dear Mr. Delius,

Very many thanks for troubling to write about the performance of "Brigg Fair". I am so delighted to hear you thought it was a good one. We all worked very hard as we thought you might be listening.

We are so much looking forward to the performance of "Romeo and Juliet". Beecham prepared everything before he went off to America, and I hope he will come back to find everything in good order.

Yours sincerely,
Adrian C. Boult

Frederick Delius, Esq.,
Grez sur Loing,
Bourron,
France.

_____

Typed transcript, dated, in the Delius Trust Archive.

(566)
Universal Edition to Frederick Delius

[Vienna, February/March 1932]

Dear Maestro Delius,

It is only today that I learn that you celebrated your 70th birthday some weeks ago, contrary to the date cited in the big Riemann Musik-Lexikon (where 1863 has been given as the year of your birth).

Although late, but no less cordially, I beg you to accept my most sincere and warmest congratulations. May a kind fate bestow upon you a succession of bright and happy years together with your incomparable wife and make it possible for you to enrich the world with new compositions which in a better future will also assuredly receive a better general appreciation than in these wretched present times that are so alien towards art.

It continues to fill me with pride and joy that our publishing house encompasses most of your orchestral works and you may believe me that we are doing our utmost, even with our unfortunately only too modest powers, to ensure the widest possible circulation for your works.

With very best wishes, also to your wife,

Yours very sincerely

Typed letter, signature illegible, undated, written in German.

From a carbon copy in the Universal Edition archives.

(567)
Jelka Delius to Cecily Arnold

[station] BOURRON

GREZ-SUR-LOING (S & M)

9.3.1932

Dear Mrs Arnold,

I ordered your room at the little pension.[1] I chose the one over the kitchen as Barjansky, the Cellist always had it in Spring. There is one very big bed in it but if you wish it an iron bed can be put in.

My husband says you can have the first performance of the new Verlaine Song, if your Concert takes place in April.[2]

Do you think you could bring with you 2 or 3 Gramophone records?[3] H.M.V. have already sent them once by parcel's post and they did not get thro the customs, in Calais. But I myself have brought over quite a number of records in 1929. I simply declared them and paid the duty.

If you drop me a line to say if you can do this I will write to H.M.V. and ask them to send these records to you. The H.M.V. did not charge for them. They were to be a present for the blind composer.

We are all looking forward very much to your visit and our little german girl is practising all the accompaniments.

It is very nice that your husband is coming too and we shall be glad to welcome him.

With Delius's kind regards

Yrs sincerely
Jelka Delius

The Pension is 35 frs a day without wine and 32 frs for a stay exceeding 3 days.

Could you send us a copy of the new Verlaine Song, so that Miss Gerhardi can practise it, please.

Autograph letter, signed and dated, written on headed notepaper.

The original is in the collection of the late Eric Johnson.

1   The nearby Pension Corby.

2   The recital was to be given at the College Hall, Henrietta Street, London, on 12 April.

3   Delius was waiting in particular for records by Kreisler and Rachmaninov, together with *Hebridean Songs* sung by Patuffa Kennedy Fraser, and 'Dancing in the Dark'.

Cecily Arnold supplied graphic descriptions, in letters home, of what it was like to perform for Delius at this time of his life. In a letter to her mother written on the evening of Saturday, 26 March, she wrote: 'I feel as if I had been through ordeal by fire & water – & I am left bereft of words – & Eric feels nearly as bad. We have just come from the Master, & we are sitting over coffee in this little pension. We went to tea with *them* at 4 o'clock – the first meeting – because we missed the train this morning – thanks to wrong information at the hotel, & so arrived at 1.30 instead of 11.30. Mrs. Delius had been here to receive us & had left flowers in our room & a message (our telegram had failed to arrive!!!) We were ushered straight into a pleasant dining room. Mrs. Delius greeted us so sweetly & Mr. Delius was seated in just that ghastly helpless position of the pictures, with a screen round his chair. We had tea & made desultory conversation. And then suddenly he wanted to know when the programme was to begin. I had, of course, not practised with the german girl (she is a dear) & he suggested that we went up & tried the songs over *at once* & he would come up after. I was scarcely prepared, but up we went! She plays very well, but not quite as Kath. Of course – she is very young   Then the attendant *carried* that poor old man up & arranged him in a chair with his screen & rug; & we began – again – I say Gosh! I'll never have a worse audition! However, he liked the first song & only suggested one addition. Then I sang the new one – with what trepidation!!! – He had no single criticism to offer – said it was beautiful & asked me to sing it again – it was just as he would have wished it sung!!!!!!!!!!!!!! Then I sang 'I-Brasil' – he wanted that twice, & 'The Nightingale,' & 'White Lillie'   Then he was tired, & we stopped, but he is looking forward to tomorrow – when I shall have had a better rehearsal with Miss Gerhardi.

After that we walked in the garden & both Miss Gerhardi & Mrs. Delius assured us that I had given him real pleasure & that it was an achievement, because he was very, very difficult to please. Eric was noble – he made noble conversation when I was struck dumb, & turned over & was generally a perfect support.

But oh! can you imagine us in that big room facing that blind, helpless old man

whose musical hearing is so acute & singing almost without rehearsal & without suggestion from him, his own works?'

On Monday evening, 28 March, Cecily wrote to her husband, who had already had
to leave for home: 'We have followed the usual programme – tea & very desultory talk
– then the music room & this time thank goodness everything in the garden was
alright! Evelyn & Mrs. Delius were both making signs of glee after each song! Then
we went for a walk & Mrs. Delius told me he said he was pleased. So we shall do some
different ones tomorrow . . . By the way, I fortified myself with a strong nip of brandy
to-night, before I faced the music. Gosh if only he would say more – but he just sits
there after each song & says 'Yes, that's much better' in his slow old way, & we all sit
silent, not quite knowing what to do next or whether he wants to say any more, &
then just as you are going to start another he may say something – or when you think
he isn't listening, he will make a remark! Never mind – its allright.'

Jelka wrote to Fenby on 27 March to tell him: Cecily Arnold 'is singing all Fred's
songs to him. She really has a great feeling for them.'

(568)
Frederick Delius to Universal Edition

To the   Grez-sur-Loing
Universal Edition   16th March 1932
Vienna

Dear Sir,

I am today sending you a new copy of the libretto of "A Village Romeo and
Juliet". I am glad I asked for proofs, for when looking the old libretto over
I discovered that it has an *entirely faulty text*. What happened was that Sir
Thomas Beecham corrected the complete English text for the first London performance and improved it considerably and made it much more singable. And
this new libretto is the one in the piano score. I have therefore made a fresh
typewritten copy; it will be considerably easier for you to have the text *newly
typeset* according to this copy. It is impossible to correct the old libretto, which
is riddled with all kind of errors. Also I think the print so very ugly, i.e. it is
almost gothic and not nearly so distinct for English people as a text in really
simple Latin type.

As we were in a hurry, we did not copy the title page, but simply corrected
it. Also I leave it to you to have the stage directions set in smaller type.

It would of course be very desirable for the correction of the final proof to
be undertaken *here* – under my supervision, at any rate it must be done by
someone with an intimate knowledge of English.

In haste to get this to the post,

Yours very sincerely
Frederick Delius

Typed letter, signature in the hand of Jelka Delius, dated, written in German.

The original is in the Universal Edition archives.

(569)
Jelka Delius to Percy Grainger

GREZ-SUR-LOING
SEINE-ET-MARNE
17.3.1932

Dearest Percy,

When your second letter came I was just packing up one of Fred's new photo's for you. I hope you will like it. It was made just a few days before his seventieth birthday. I do not know whether you heard the yarn, that Phil Heseltine found out that Fred was really born in 1862 (it is in the registers of Somerset house.)

There was a great outcry and rumpus in England because the B.B.C. which now controls about everything in Music, had omitted to arrange any sort of festival-Concert for the occasion. Beecham waz going to give a special concert in February; but he was called to N. York and so that also fell through. — However he spent the day very happily and serenely receiving masses of telegrams and letters and we had a concert of his works on the Gramophone.

It is delightful that you have played his Concerto with Stock; and that you feel it went so well and that Stock conducted it with love and conviction!

Fred always wanted to answer your first letter himself, and when he does it you shall have it at once. But this winter has been so unnaturally cold and long, that he has been rather low and tormented by pains and bad nights. I feel that when real spring and warmth comes at last and he can be out of doors a lot, he will rally.

I have also not been very well and I do feel the need of a real holiday and change after these 10 years of strenuous striving to help him and take care of him. All the troubles with these nurses of his and the searching for new ones and the ever recurring disappointments seem to have eaten up my nerves.

I have got a little niece of Ida Gerhardi's staying with us now. She helps me a bit and reads to Fred part of my time.[1] She is quite an efficient pianist too, and sings quite well too. Tho' I am afraid she is quite unmusical and has no musical emotions. It is she who is gradually to get to help me in noting down

Fred's sayings etc. Just that which you wrote about is always before me, but it is always more than I can do.[2] Maybe I shall be able to train her gradually. Balfour comes so rarely and then so hurriedly – just a meteor – that one can never do a thing. Then Balfour is in such a state about the £ having sunk, that he dare not leave England on account of the loss!!!

But your thoughtful and deeply affectionate letter went right to our hearts. It is true that in the throes of a real meeting one is often curiously aloof and unmanageable and that in one's solitude often feels so much nearer to those one loves and always *will* love deep down in one's nature. Perhaps if you look at Fred's photo you will see him again in his fine serenity and that rather sad but beautiful resignation that also permeates his music.

We are now all the time thinking of the 1st performance of his "Songs of Farewell" at the Courtauld Sargent Concerts on the 21st and 22d. This work is by far *the crown* of all he has achieved with Fenby. If only the dashy and tempestuous Malcolm Sargent can conduct it right! But happily Fenby is up in London; this work is the apple of his eye and he will do all he can to help Sargent. They are also doing the beautiful Second Dance Song from the Mass of Life with the Philharmonic choir to sing both that and the Whitman work. And Beatrice Harrison will play the Cello-Concerto. All this will not be broadcast, so we *can not hear it*.

I was so sorry to hear of all the difficulties and the beastly state of affairs in U.S.A. All the better that you have taken this post of Librarian; it must be a great relief not to have to count entirely on these nerve-racking Concert-tours.

23.3.
I have waited to hear how the Songs of Farewell went. To-day I received a wonderful letter about it from Robert Nichols. He has understood it so well and has been so impressed that it must be quite beautiful.

At the same time came a touching letter from dear old Lippay from Manila. Perhaps he wrote to you also as with Fred's Summernight and Cuckoo he gave Molly on the Shore and Shepherds Hey in a Concert of the Academy of music there; he is its director. It was all received and appreciated tremendously. And he said that the Orchestra of Filippinos understood the drift of all these pieces at once with quite the right intuition.

How is Ella? please give her my love. Is she going on with her decorative tiles?

You will be glad to hear that we have a very refined and nice man for Fred now. He is not religeous and belongs to no community, so that he is all here. He reads really beautifully and loves to do it. He is from Cologne and I do hope and trust will stay.

With much love to you both from Fred and me

Yrs ever aff.ly
Jelka

Autograph letter, signed and dated, written on headed notepaper.

The original is in the Grainger Museum.

1   Among the books Evelin Gerhardi remembers reading to Delius (all in English) were J. B. Priestley's *The Good Companions*, Clemence Dane's *Broome Stages*, Mark Twain's *Innocents Abroad*, the memoirs of the French diplomat Georges Paléologue; and some Charles Morgan – which Delius found tiresome and lacking in action.

2   On 29 January Grainger had reminded Jelka of 'the desirability of having Fred's sayings & opinions noted down'.

(570)
Jelka Delius to Eric Fenby

FREDERICK DELIUS
Grez-sur-Loing
S. et M.
11.5.1932

My dear Eric,

I was so glad to get your letter to-day but sorry to hear that you are not quite well yet. Really, *what* a winter you have had! If you are really going to London for the Village Romeo[1], could you not run on to Grez? We should love to have a visit from you and from London it is really not far. It has not been a really warm fine spring here either but certainly it is ever so much warmer here and I think if you were to rest here a lot and sit in the sunshine you would pick up in no time. Your habitual room and the music room are just waiting for you. Evelin would love you to come too, and Fred, when I suggested it said so warmly: *Oh yes*, write him at once, get him to come by all means.

It seems an eternity since I have seen you.

I did not write as I imagined you in that lovely country place hard at work. Here too we have been rather worried. Fred had a whole week's spell of ill health and horrible pains. We others all had Influenza at the same time and it was horrible. Our Paris doctor could not come and after much telefoning I got him to send a colleague of his. As a result it was found out that he has some albumine and Dr P. wrote him that he *must* absolutely drink less (not more than one big water glass of beer, wine or Cider for lunch).

Dear Fred was like a lamb and agreed to it. (He drank just double that before.) He is much better since and is also almost quite a Vegetarian, which seems to make him less thirsty. He is sleeping splendidly now. But he has not been able to have his evening walks yet.[2]

I think it was a great triumph that there were 8000 People in the Albert

Hall for the Mass of Life.[3] It gives Fred a new and much larger public and that may have been T. B.'s idea, for the bad accoustic in that Hall is notorious. Did you hear the Meistersinger conducted by Beecham? We listened to a lot of it. Our set went well, but we have had very bad periods and I have ordered a new set on the American system working straight from the main to be brought on trial just those days round the 20th. They are said to be so much more sensitive and pure. They have only 3 very much stronger lamps and the set is contained in the loudspeaker. The question is, *which* mark we should get. A real American one, or the best french one made on the American system and with the marvellous American lamps. In the latter case they would take back our set – at a loss of course.

Brooks could help me, but I distrust him rather. He will get me to go to his merchant and be swindled as he was.

Yes Grez does look lovely now, but all is rather backward the lilac not even quite in bloom yet. The big Appletree is a miracle of blossoms, scent, buzzing bees etc. My little nursling flowers are fearfully late this year. They do not grow. Evelin is now an expert at collecting snails. She looks so well now – she was rather pale and thin when she came. If you come she will sing all the Delius songs with you. And then you will follow her example and grow strong and well looking, eh? Anyhow we will do our best to make you so; you know our great affection for you. It would be splendid if you could help Beecham with his parts and rehearsals. Maybe it *is* all marked as he conducted it from the material he possesses; but perhaps he has become more expert and fastidious with this marking business since 1920, when he did it last. Now then, dear! Au revoir soon. A change of air will do you good. Only you must be tremendously careful on the journey, not stay on deck in rainstorms!! My love to your dear mother and your other dear people.

Ever affly yrs
Jelka Delius

I cannot understand the Universal. They never answer my questions about sending you the Hassan corrections. I fear they have done the correcting there and will then have left mistakes in.

Autograph letter, signed and dated, written on headed notepaper. Envelope addressed: Eric Fenby Esq/12 Mayville Ave/Scarborough/Yorks/Angleterre. Postmark: GREZ 11 -5 32.

The original is in the Delius Trust Archive.

1   The BBC studio broadcast of *A Village Romeo and Juliet* was given on 20 May. Beecham conducted the BBC Orchestra, and Stanford Robinson was chorus master. To Delius's intense pleasure Beecham was now talking of reviving *Koanga*.

2   In spite of Delius's bout of illness, Jelka had written to Sydney Schiff only five days earlier suggesting that she and Delius might go to London again, but only if there were 'some interesting performances'.

3   Beecham gave the *Mass* on 28 April at a Royal Philharmonic Society concert, with the Royal Choral Society and again with Roy Henderson as principal soloist. This was shortly after Beecham's return from a series of Carnegie Hall concerts (from the beginning of March) during which he had given a number of Delius's shorter orchestral works.

(571)

Jelka Delius to Eric Fenby

FREDERICK DELIUS
Grez-sur-Loing
S. et M.
19.8.1932

Dear Eric,

There is an almost incredible heat wave here and whilst this heat lasts Fred will not want to work with you. But of course you can start your work alone here and you are *welcome any day*.[1] Only I am afraid you might find this terrible heat (hottest since 21 years) very trying   Of course a thunderstorm may put an end to it any day, too.

We always have our evening walk with Fred and it is the best part of the day.[2] Norman only stayed 2 nights and one day. He has just written and told me that Beecham is back in London.[3] I thought this might be useful news to you, as you may wish to see him.

Oh, my dear Eric, it will be delightful to see you again. And we will have grand talks!

Much love from us both

Yrs ever affly
Jelka Delius

Autograph letter, signed and dated, written on headed notepaper. Envelope addressed: Eric Fenby Esq/12 Mayville Ave/Scarborough/Yorks/Angleterre. Postmark: GREZ 19 -8 32.

The original is in the Delius Trust Archive.

With Delius feeling much better, Jelka had at last been able to visit her brother and family in Germany for a week from the end of July. After returning to Grez, she wrote on 8 August to Fenby: 'I found Fred in the best of moods, and looking very well.

There was a grand lunch and iced Champagne for my reception(!!!).' 'He deserved to feel so happy,' wrote Nina Rosen from Detmold on 9 August, 'for it was really charming of him to let you come to us, & we feel as grateful to him for sending you, as we feel grateful to you for coming.' As well as O'Neill and Beecham, there were the various other summer visitors to Grez, as Evelin Gerhardi related to Cecily Arnold: 'Mr. Balfour Gardiner, the composer, stayed with us for two days or so, and he always helped me to pick weeds for our nine rabbits or tie up flowers and do all kinds of work in the garden. I suppose you know that he is the composer, or rather – *was* the composer, for he quite turned away from music, never listens to a concert and never writes any music himself any more ... At present, his "hobby" is "gardening", he plants trees, vegetables a.s.o. and really does live up to his name, so to speak.' (13 July.) 'Right now he [Delius] is being painted by an English artist, Mr. Gunn ... and we are sure that the portrait is going to be a masterpiece.' (31 August.) James Gunn was a friend of O'Neill's.

1   Writing to Fenby on 18 July, Jelka told him: 'you can come whenever you like, all is ready for you. It seems to[o] good to be true – from *my own* point of view that more work can be done on Fred's music. For when you had finished everything it made me so dreadfully sad and life seemed so empty.' Fenby returned on 1 September; Evelin Gerhardi left for home on 7 September.

2   Evelin Gerhardi wrote vividly of the institution of the evening walk, in a letter to Cecily Arnold dated 13 July: 'The weather has been so lovely here for the past few weeks, and Mr. Delius went out with us almost every night after dinner. We go up the road towards Marlotte. Then most people sit in front of their doors chatting with the neighbors, and for most of them it is *the* event of the day to see us go by and say "Good evening" or make the same remark about the weather day after day – as the weather is unchanging, too. There is one old couple that gives me a new thrill every night: they seem to pose especially when we come near and then with beaming faces deliver their little speech about the weather and the lovely evening. Both of them, the man as well as the woman, are so extremely short and broad that I call them the "underground" people. It looks as if only their upper ends were sticking out of the ground'.

3   In June the Deliuses had 'some delightful visits from Beecham immensely enjoyable', as Jelka wrote to Fenby on 24 June. 'Beecham spoke so highly of you,' she added. She wrote again early in July: after dinner one evening 'we went to the Music room and B. played the opera and the Singer [Dora Labbette] sang – really her whole part thro'; he filling in Sali as best he could. Her singing in the room was exquisite, and they stayed till almost midnight.' Evelin Gerhardi told Cecily Arnold on 13 July: 'Sir Thomas Beecham came to see Mr. Delius two or three times. It appears he stayed in Paris for a couple of days. One night he was here at dinner and he told us so many funny stories that I kept on laughing for three days afterwards.'

(572)
Jelka Delius to Thomas Beecham

GREZ-SUR-LOING (S & M)
16.10.1932

My dear Thomas,

We follow all your activities with the greatest interest and are delighted at the unanimous great success with your New Orchestra. It is truly wonderful what an amount you can achieve and I am so glad to see that they all begin to appreciate it

Fenby has been here for some weeks.[1] He has made some charming pieces for string-orchestra,[2] easy to perform from the 2 a capella Chorusses "To be sung on the water". They shd become very popular. But the greatest achievement is a New Work for Orchestra, Baritone and Soprano with poetic words.[3] The music is taken from Margot-la-Rouge and all that lovely music is freed from the beastly subject for which it was always much too good and refined. All the knife and murder bits are eliminated and the music really miraculously adapted to the new words, an exhalted Love-poem. (It plays 20 minutes.) We all sighed for The Nightingale[4] whom the Soprano part will suit admirably. When Fenby comes to London he would like to play it to you and Hawkes if you can only spare the time?

Fred had so much hoped that *you* would conduct the Eistedfodd performance of The Mass of Life next year. We fear that Dr Hopkins Evans[5] will conduct it if they cannot secure you. It would be such a great pity if he made a mess of it. This seems probable as no work of this complicated character has been given there in the past. What do you think about it?

Fred is cheerful and frequently finds occasions that have to be celebrated with champagne. Well, when you come again we must have some good bottles together.

Ever affectionately yrs
Jelka D.

Autograph letter, signed and dated, written on headed notepaper.

The original is in the Delius Trust Archive.

1 Fenby left Grez on 1 November. He travelled to London at Beecham's request in order to deal with matters related to publishing with Hawkes.

2 *Two Aquarelles.*

3 *Idyll.*

4 Dora Labbette.

5 T. Hopkin Evans (1879–?): Welsh conductor and composer. He was noted as a choral conductor, and succeeded Harry Evans as conductor of the Liverpool Welsh Choral Union. He adjudicated at numerous festivals, particularly the National Eisteddfod.

(573)
Frederick Delius to Eric Fenby

6.12.32
GREZ-SUR-LOING (S & M)

Delius dictates:

Dear Eric,

Thank you very much for your letter and for the account of the performance of "Songs of Farewell" in Bradford.[1] And I am very glad indeed that it came off so well. Yesterday I received the Ginger-Ale and at once had a bottle for dinner. It is really splendid and the real stuff. No comparison with Schweppe's.

Many thanks again, dear Eric! – We are looking forward to your home-coming. Hubert has manufactured an enormous chessboard for you.

Oyler[2] has been here a few times and we now get our butter from him, which is excellent.

Everything is going on well here and we all send you our best love.

Yrs affly
Frederick Delius

Delighted with the telegram. I have not got Sargent's address so cannot thank him. So pleased about Huddersfield.

Letter in the hand of Jelka Delius, dated, written on headed notepaper. Envelope addressed: Eric Fenby Esq/12 Mayville Av^e/Scarborough/Yorks/Angleterre. Post-mark: GREZ 6 -12 32.

The original is in the Delius Trust Archive.

After Fenby's departure, Jelka had written on 6 November to Lilli Gerhardi: 'Without him of course it is fearfully lonely.' Letters to Lilli Gerhardi in November give clear indications of Jelka's incipient bowel cancer, although consultants both locally and in Paris left Jelka herself to understand that her condition was not as serious as it was eventually to prove. The Paris consultant told her that her illness was almost certainly the result of stress and exhaustion; had he not been aware of her domestic situation, he would have sent her away from Grez for a few months. She was given medicine to counter depression.

1   Malcolm Sargent had conducted the Bradford Festival Choral Society in *Songs of Farewell*.

2   Philip Oyler (1879–1974): English agriculturist. At various times he managed estates in England and France, and in his books *The Generous Earth* (1950) and *Sons of the Generous Earth* (1963) he described aspects of his life and work in rural France, including (in the second) a chapter entitled 'Some Memories of Delius'. He was a frequent visitor during Delius's last years, when he was engaged in managing the estate of a nearby millionaire. He is remembered by Fenby as 'a highly-cultivated gentleman', who at the same time was of great practical help to the Deliuses in many ways.

(574)
Frederick Delius to Eric Fenby

GREZ-SUR-LOING (S & M)

17.12.32

Delius dictates:

My dear Eric,

I dont think I have made myself very plain to you as regards religion and creeds. Personally I have no use for any of them. In introducing you to Nietzsche my intention was to open up new horizons and introduce you to a great poet. I myself do not subscribe to everything Nietzsche said, but I hail in him a sublime poet and a beautiful nature.

There is only one real happiness and that is the happiness of creating.

Here in Grez you can be as free as the winds. We will not influence you and you can entertain your saints if you like[1]

Ever yr affectionate friend
Frederick Delius

Letter in the hand of Jelka Delius, dated, written on headed notepaper. Envelope addressed: Eric Fenby Esq/12 Mayville Avenue/Scarborough/Yorks/Angleterre. Postmark: PARIS [date illegible].

The original is in the Delius Trust Archive.

1   Jelka wrote on the same date: 'And what difference does it make in our affection for you? *None, whatever.* You must follow your heart, and we must follow ours.' Eric Fenby writes: 'He was disappointed in me. He had hoped that in introducing me to Nietzsche I would eventually renounce Christianity completely. I was bored by his constant taunts which had almost become an obsession.'

1933

Fenby was back in Grez. Among the first visitors of the year were two Concerts Lamoureux representatives who came to interview Delius about a forthcoming performance of his Piano Concerto in Paris, and Cecil Gray, who paid a visit on 20 January. Gray was 'quite astounded', as Jelka told Lilli Gerhardi, to see how well Delius looked in the circumstances and how cheerful he was. Lionel Tertis came on 13 February, playing the viola with Fenby in his own arrangements of Delius works. While Jelka's brother Fritz Rosen was immersed in his work on his third volume of reminiscences, Nina, his wife, took the opportunity of paying a short visit to Grez at the end of February. She played duets with Fenby (the *First Cuckoo* in particular) and, like Gray, found Delius in good form; she told Jelka subsequently how much she had enjoyed his 'family tales which were so humorous & witty'. Writing again in June she said: 'people won't believe me when I tell them that Fred was not only very interesting, but positively amusing!' Other visitors who broke what Fenby described as the 'dreary monotony' of the winter were Arnold Bax, Kenneth Spence and Edward Dent, the latter, however, finding that Delius had greatly aged since his previous visit. In April Jelka was injured in a minor street accident. While Alden Brooks's wife helped nurse her to recovery, Fenby had to spend more time caring for Delius. Once matters resumed their normal course Fenby made the decision to return to England, on the understanding that the Deliuses would send for him if really needed.

The event of the year was unquestionably Elgar's visit, on the afternoon of 30 May, serving to establish, so poignantly late in life, a friendship that was at once affectionate and profound. 'I was delighted to see Delius in his home & am glad he allowed me the privilege,' Elgar wrote to O'Neill towards the end of the year, 'although it involved 80 miles in a French taxi; the prospect of seeing him made the journey a light matter.' Inevitably, there were to be other summer visitors, among them Oskar Fried, Oscar Klemperer and Norman O'Neill; and in mid-July came a nostalgic salute from a distant Beecham: 'First visit here since 1908 of cherished memory' – he was in Norway. In July too, Delius's niece Peggy (Margaret Black) arrived to help out, rather as Evelin Gerhardi had helped during Fenby's absence the preceding year. She initially stayed for two and a half months, spending a few weeks in England from around the end of September before returning to Grez in November. July brought a further honour, with Leeds University conferring on Delius *in absentia* an honorary Doctorate of Letters.

'It has been a scorching hot summer here,' Jelka told Fenby on 2 September. But the memories of summer pleasures were quickly to recede, and by the middle of September the drinking bouts and wild behaviour of Hubert, the nurse, were throwing the household into turmoil. It had been decided that he would leave soon, and in fact a new nurse, Wilhelm Engelter, was engaged from mid-October. But by then upset by all the troubles, Delius was 'often tormented by pains', as Jelka told Fenby on 12 October. Some six weeks later she wrote of the 'dreadful nerve pains' that he had been having. The autumn nonetheless had its compensations (including an avid correspondence with Elgar), among them the first performance on 3 October of the *Idyll*, broadcast from the Proms. Wood conducted the BBC Symphony Orchestra, with Dora Labbette and Roy Henderson as soloists (Beecham himself had rehearsed them both). 'I could see that Fred was very pleased indeed,' Jelka wrote to Fenby on 12 October. 'It is really a great achievement.' In November she relayed the news to him that Bronislaw Hubermann, who had just played Delius's Violin Concerto in Prague and Vienna, was coming to Paris and proposed to come to Grez to play the concerto to its composer. For some reason the plan was never realized. Fearsomely cold weather descended on Grez in December and it was fortunate that central heating had – at long last – been installed in the summer. Peggy Black stayed through Christmas, returning to England around the end of the year.

(575)

Frederick and Jelka Delius to Thomas Beecham

GREZ-SUR-LOING (S & M)

9.2.1933

Delius dictates:

Dear Thomas

Your wonderfully delicate rendering of Brigg Fair the other night consoled me for the miserable performance of Seadrift the day before. Roy H. seemed to have no voice and sang a number of wrong notes.[1] Last night I heard a still worse performance of my piano-Concerto in Paris under Wolff with an English pianist I have never seen or heard of before Maud Randle (Lamoureux Conc.) playing like a little schoolgirl.[2]

When will *you* show the Parisians how my music is to be played?
I hope until then they will play no more of my music.
With love

Your ever affectionate friend
Frederick Delius

P.S. I hope you received my wire addressed to Queens Hall after the Manchester Concert?[3]

Love from Jelka

───────────

Letter in the hand of Jelka Delius, dated, written on headed notepaper.

The original is in the Delius Trust Archive.

1   Other broadcast performances from England of particular interest at this period were of *Songs of Farewell* on 5 February and the complete Flecker/Delius *Hassan*, given in two parts on 7 and 10 February. It was the first time that the Deliuses had heard *Songs of Farewell*. 'Delius was very happy,' wrote Jelka to Fenby's mother on 6 February, 'and he called Eric to his bed and thanked him most heartily.' She added: 'I am just writing the german translation into the new work, the Idyl.'

2   Maud Randle wrote to Delius from Birstall Hill, Leicestershire, on 15 January to tell the composer of her forthcoming performance of the concerto with the Lamoureux Orchestra and to ask him if he could possibly attend. 'Am I right in thinking this is it's first performance in Paris? ... I do not feel at all sure of your wishes about the tempi in various places – I wonder if you would be willing to tell me the correct speed of certain parts.' She had recently played the work to an enthusiastic audience in Whitby, with the Municipal Orchestra there: 'It was a real holiday crowd of over 1100 Yorkshire people – & they were thrilled with the work.' Two representatives of the Lamoureux Concerts subsequently came to Grez to interview Fenby about the concerto, but Jelka soon took over. 'I used the opportunity,' she wrote to Lilli Gerhardi on 24 January, 'to tell these people that Del. had not the least interest in seeing this early piece given as the first work of his at these concerts; that we had lived here for over 30 years & nothing had been done, even though D. was regularly performed all over the world, as far as the Philippines, Shanghai & Japan. I had to get it off my chest some time & the little Frenchman was really impressed & quite afraid of me.
      What are the Parisian critics going to think of a 35-year-old piece of juvenilia?'

3   Beecham had given *Brigg Fair* with the Hallé on 2 February.

(576)
Jelka Delius to Lionel Tertis

[Grez, February 1933]

[Dear Mr Tertis]

Your letter with the money reached me quite safely and I am so grateful. I only hope you were not too tired. The remembrance of your masterly and heavenly playing, so full of deepest understanding, is with us all the time, and I hope you will come again when it is not so cold. Delius would love that. It was unfortunate that he had had one of his bad days when you came, and he cannot bear such icy weather. Yet he loved and enjoyed your playing which, he says, is quite *unique*. Kindest regards from Fenby who, of course, loved accompanying you.[1]

[Jelka Delius]

From Lionel Tertis: *Cinderella No More*. London, Peter Nevill, 1953, p. 69–70.

1   Tertis came to Grez on Monday, 13 February. Fenby remembers: 'He was to have been accompanied by Harriet Cohen – but she had to proceed to London from Paris where they had been giving a recital. I had to play instead at short notice without a rehearsal.' Tertis's February tour, which took in Italy, Germany and the Netherlands, also brought him to Paris, simply in order to visit Delius. Believing Grez to be a Parisian suburb, he hired a taxi and after the extreme discomfort of a seventy-kilometre journey through heavy snow he had to borrow the fare from Jelka and Eric on arrival. With Fenby he played his own viola arrangements of the third Violin Sonata and of the Serenade from *Hassan* to Delius. 'It was amazing,' he wrote to Fenby on 18 February, 'how you fell in with all my ways of playing.' During the last week of February he played the sonata in Berlin, The Hague and Amsterdam.

Two days after Tertis's visit, Nina Rosen came to stay for a couple of days, Fenby moving into Oyler's house so that she could have his room.

(577)
Frederick Delius to Ernest Newman

GREZ-SUR-LOING (S & M)
9.3.1933

Delius dictates:

Dear Newman, We were very pleased to get your letter. Like you we had tuned in to hear Seadrift and were disgusted to hear all this political stuff and election Propaganda instead. (Evidently Adolfs orders)   How humanity can again and again cut into such blatherskite from Politicians, not alone in Germany, but everywhere, beats me.[1]

Last sunday your article on Dent's book "Busoni" interested me very much. We had just read the book.[2] I first met Busoni in 1886 in Leipsic. He was then entirely classical and composed in the manner of the Classics. He was Anti Wagnerian, whilst we others were Wagner-Enthusiasts. A few years later he became quite a Wagnerian – always a little too late. In the years following he tried to be modern and encouraged everything modern; but at heart he remained the Classic. The trouble with Busoni was that he was musically entirely unemotional; he composed only with his head. Yet he had emotion, for after hearing Appalachia in Berlin under Fried in 1906 he came into the Greenroom and embraced me bursting into tears. But none of that emotion ever got into his music and that is what made him so unhappy, so unharmonious and so cynically sarcastic at times. And his ambition knew no bounds.

When you next take a holiday come and spend a few days with us here. It will give us the greatest pleasure!

With kindest regards from us both to you and Mrs Newman

Yrs sincerely
Frederick Delius

Letter in the hand of Jelka Delius, dated, written on headed notepaper. Envelope addressed: Ernest Newman Esq/Polperro/Epsom Lane/Tadworth/Surrey/Angleterre. Postmark: GREZ 9 -3 33.

The original is in the Delius Trust Archive.

1   Echoes of a brash, modern world intrude more and more into the correspondence of the Deliuses, pre-echoes indeed of a harsher world they were never to know. Nina Rosen wrote from Berlin on 3 March: 'When I read the Papers here I think we are having a lively time.' She wrote again to Jelka on 18 April: 'Of course one is anxious enough though for one's friends, especially financially, for hundreds or even thousands get sent away. You can imagine what a catastrophe it means for an actor or doctor etc ... to be suddenly out of work ... George is anxious too. The insecurity is terrible. How I wish I could fly over to you & have a chat; one can say nothing in a letter. Not that *my* letters could interest any censor. F. is anxious also. Many who are sent away, get their pensions taken away.' There had been a lighter note on 12 March: 'Yesterday Fritz & I saw Marlene Dietrich (a great film star) in "die blonde Venus". She was excellent.'

2   Edward Dent had asked his publishers to send a copy to Jelka. Dent himself wrote to Fenby on 18 March; he would be in Paris towards the end of the month: 'I would gladly come over one day if you thought it would be a pleasure to him – but I do not want to be a nuisance.'

Fenby remembers an earlier visit (probably that of 1929) by Dent, then still at work on his book: Delius had talked about Busoni, mentioning in particular the 'disgraceful' performance he had given, as conductor, of *Paris*, a performance made even more disconcerting by the fidgeting of Sibelius, distinctly under the influence of drink and sitting next to the composer. At least Sibelius had commiserated with his disappointed colleague and so, unlike Busoni, had been forgiven. The talk over lunch is remembered by Fenby as particularly interesting and entertaining, with Dent being asked to stay on for tea — 'always a good sign for someone who had been asked to lunch'.

Dent's 'English Opera in Berlin' (*The Monthly Musical Record*, 37 (April 1907), pp. 75–6) had dealt with the Cassirer/Gregor *A Village Romeo and Juliet*; and he reviewed the second Beecham production of that opera in *The Athenaeum* of 26 March 1920 (p. 422). In the early 1940s he was to make reduced scores of *Appalachia* and *The Song of the High Hills*.

(578)

Frederick Delius to Edward Elgar

Telegrams   GREZ-SUR-LOING (S & M)
Delius Grez-sur-Loing   18.5.1933

My dear Elgar,

Your kind letter gave me the greatest pleasure and I should like nothing better, than to welcome you here in Grez.[1]

Please, try to make it possible to come out here and lunch with us. Any day will suit us, if only you wire the day before. Letters are delivered too slowly.

The best way to come is to take the train to Fontainebleau from Gare de Lyon. There is one leaving 10.50 and arriving in Fontainebleau at 12.00. From there we could fetch you in our car, a ride of 15 minutes.

In spite of my infirmities I manage to get something out of life and I should love to see you

Yrs very sincerely,
Frederick Delius

Letter in the hand of Jelka Delius, dated, written on headed notepaper.

The original is in the Hereford and Worcester County Record Office.

1   Elgar was shortly to come to Paris to conduct his Violin Concerto, with Yehudi Menuhin as soloist.

(579)

Edward Elgar to Frederick Delius

Marl Bank,
Worcester.
20th May, 1933.

My dear Delius,

This is only to thank you for your letter and to say that I shall hope to be able to accept your kind invitation: I fly over on next Sunday (28th) and will let you know how my time is allotted.

Kindest regards,

As ever,
Edward Elgar.

———

Typed transcript, dated, in the Delius Trust Archive. Ten letters from Elgar to Delius, dated 20 May – 25 December 1933, are preserved in typescript copy in the Archive.

(580)

Edward Elgar to Frederick Delius

Royal Monceau Hotel,
35, 37, 39 Avenue Hoche
PARIS
31st May 1933.

Dear Delius,

Before boarding the aeroplane for England I send a note to thank you and Mrs. Delius for your charming welcome.

It was a great privilege to see you and I was delighted to find you so much better than the newspapers led me to expect.

I shall hope to avail myself of your permission and will write, or dictate, some little intimate account of my visit:[1] this will be a pleasure and satisfaction to me which I hope will send you very many friends and admirers.

Best regards to Mrs. Delius and to you.

Your affectionate friend,
Edward Elgar.

———

Typed transcript, dated, in the Delius Trust Archive.

1   Elgar published his account (reproduced in full in Christopher Redwood (ed.): *A Delius Companion*) entitled 'My Visit to Delius' in *The Daily Telegraph* on 1 July 1933.

Fred Gaisberg, of The Gramophone Company, who was Elgar's companion for the visit to Grez, later recalled that they arrived at Delius's home well after five: 'Delius was sitting in the middle of the room, facing the windows, very upright, with his hands resting on the arms of a big rolling chair. Illuminated by the afternoon sun, his face looked long and pale and rather immobile. His eyes were closed. Mrs. Delius was sitting beside him expectantly waiting for our arrival. Genial, resourceful Elgar quickly established a friendly, easy atmosphere, and in a few minutes they led off into an animated duologue that somehow reminded me somewhat of a boasting contest between two boys. Delius waved his left arm freely; his speech, halting at first, became more fluent as he warmed up to his subject and we forgot his impediment of speech. He seemed mentally alert. From this conversation I gleaned that they were both non-keyboard composers and that both had important compositions under way. Both emphasised the importance of the gramophone to them, and Delius also stressed the wireless. He spoke jestingly of the number of publicity-seeking youngsters who pursued him to his retreat and insisted on giving bad performances of his music. They talked of their Leipzig days as students of Reinecke and Max Reger, of their friends Percy Pitt and Granville Bantock. Delius, recalling his years in America, spoke of frost being the ruin of the Florida orange groves, and told us that the destruction of the forests had changed the climate and brought about the crash of his Florida venture.

Mrs. Delius showed us a photograph of the Royal Academy portrait of her husband, with the comment that to her it seemed expressionless and a libel on the real Delius. They passed on to authors, Elgar extolling Dickens and Montaigne; Delius, Walt Whitman and Kipling. But Elgar's flight to Paris was the crowning achievement that Delius could not match. Still, the idea fascinated him. It offered the sole possibility for a man in his condition to visit his beloved England once more. Finally, in a lordly way, he waved his arm and instructed Mrs. Delius, "Dear, we must fly the next time we go to England." He then brought the afternoon to a climax by ordering a bottle of champagne to be opened, and a toast was drunk all round.'

(Fred Gaisberg, *Music on Record*, London, Robert Hale, 1946, pp. 240–1.)

On 6 June, Elgar wrote to Bantock: 'We talked much of old things including old friends: I said "Granville Bantock" etc. Delius interrupted with "One of the best!" In which I cordially agree.' (P. M. Young, ed.: *Letters of Edward Elgar*, London, Geoffrey Bles, 1956, p. 318.) 'Ever so many thanks', came the reply from Bantock, 'for your kind message from Delius. I was glad indeed to hear such a favourable account from you of his present health. It is sad to think of the bitterness of his affliction – victima nil miserantis Orci.' (Hereford and Worcester County Record Office.)

(581)
Jelka Delius to Eric Fenby

Grez 3.6.1933

My dear Eric, Last night M. Tesson[1] burst triumphant into the kitchen and brought back your passport with an accompanying note that you have nothing to pay. I am delighted too and return it herewith. Perhaps when you write again you might enclose a few words of thanks in English. I have so much to tell; I will begin by saying that I get on quite well with the reading, and that I feel better, my last treatment seems very good. Fred is really very considerate and lets me sit and hold his feet or play the gramophone when I get tired of reading.

Elgar came. It was really delightful; he arrived for tea and stayed till nearly seven. He was accompanied by a little Mr Gaisberg (His Masters Voice Representative) who, Elgar said "is taking care of me". E. was so astonished to find Fr. so fit. At first he constantly telegraphed signs to me, was he tiring Fred,? was he to leave? I negatived, of course. Then they got to chat and Fred grew so lively and jolly. Elgar had a lot of bread and butter with his tea; finally Fred proposed I shd get some champagne and so we all had some and they were more jovial than ever then the little Mr G. said he thought Elgar ought to have something to eat again before leaving so I said – Ham sandwiches? Yes. So I rushed Simone to get ham and quickly made them. E. enjoyed them thoro'ly. He loved Mme G.s tin loaf and ham etc. and ate a whole lot. Mr G. was rather yellow and dispeptic and ate most gingerly. Finally after trying several times in vain to get E. to leave, he got him to go. E. did not look at the garden. He sat most of the time on Huberts little chair next to Fred looking at him with the greatest affection. He said the press was ridiculous, writing about Fred as if he were such a wreck. He is going to write an account of his visit to the papers. Isn't that nice. He was so genial and natural. Mme G. was most impressed that he took such a modest chair, whilst all the Bruders were so discontented with it. To-day we received a little letter of thanks for the Welcome he had received here. (Such a thing as all these ridiculous Mangeots[2] and Perkins[3] etc. would never think of.)

It has been awful weather off and on, but has now turned cloudless and hot for Wh.tide. The Brooks' are here so I hope there will not be a thunderstorm. We are busy consuming strawberries all the time, and Hildegards absence makes itself agreeably felt, in that one can let them ripen. I am still busy planting little pots but I shall soon have finished. The Paeonies are glorious this year and the Canterbury bells just beginning. The Rosebushes in the Garden and on the House simply wonderful. The buds of my carnations are swelling, but inspite of my impatience none have opened yet. Elgar brought Fred a Hugo Wolf Gramophone Album and a Sibelius one. The Sibelius begins with 5th Symphony, beautifully recorded. It is very fine, especially the slow movement with very original phrases always interpolated. Fred thought it very good too. We still have Pojohlas daughter and Tapiola – not played them yet. The Hugo Wolf are the Songs of Wilhelm Meister (Goethe) extremely melancholy and composed with such a depth of despairing sadness, that it quite breaks my heart to think how sad poor Wolf must have been. They are sung superlatively by Herbert Janssen. Every syllable declamed perfectly and with a grave voice and deepest feeling. Truly a wonderful achievement. We have not played the others by Schorr and Trianti yet.

May Harrison wrote: she wanted to come and see us a week-end in June. I wrote back asking her rather to come when you are back, so that we can have some music.

Fred is very grateful for all you have discussed with Hawkes;[4] only he wants to have really first rate singers and as the BBC. employ Haley and Henderson he does not see why they should not be engaged. I have also written to Hawkes to have it put on London Regional, and not National. I think it is very good to have the Organ arrangement of The cuckoo brought out. I read it to Fred and he was not against it at all.

The worst is, dear Eric that I forgot that to send you the passport *registered* I must go into the post, and it is shut now, so I will send you this letter to-day and post the passport as soon as Whit-tide is over. It is safely locked in my drawer.

I hope you'll write again soon and with love to all your dear people and to yourself from Fr. and me

Yrs always
Jelka D.

Autograph letter, signed and dated. Envelope addressed: Eric Fenby Esq/ 12 Mayville Av^e/Scarborough/Yorks/Angleterre. Postmark: GREZ 3 -6 33.

The original is in the Delius Trust Archive.

1   The village schoolmaster.

2   André Mangeot, violinist, was a friend of Heseltine and Anthony Bernard. 'I think he led for Bernard in the *Sea Drift* record' writes Eric Fenby. 'I know he was interested in the "Air and Dance".'

3   Helen Perkin, pianist (and, like André Mangeot, another recent visitor to Grez), was a leading interpreter of John Ireland's piano works, particularly his concerto.

4   Eric Fenby writes: 'I cannot recall the work discussed with Ralph Hawkes. Can it have been the "Fantastic Dance" published in 1933 and first performed by Boult in the following January? Perhaps more likely the "Idyll" also published that year with first performance in October 1933? Ralph Hawkes and Leslie Boosey founded the present company by the merger of the two separate companies. Ralph was a most charming young man fond of squash and sailing. It was he who invited me to be reader

to the new firm to assemble a catalogue of serious orchestral and vocal music to take the place of the Boosey Ballads and the light orchestral stuff used in the silent films and cafés of the day. Hence Ireland's "Piccadilly" (London) overture, Benjamin's "Jamaican Rumba" and Ireland's choral work "These Things Shall Be", and Britten's Variations on a theme of Frank Bridge. I continued until I joined the Army in 1940 by which time a creditable nucleus of works had been published and performed.'

(582)
Jelka Delius to Eric Fenby

Grez 5.6.1933

Dear Eric, Here is your passport. We had a surprise visit from Oscar Fried, the conductor for Lunch yesterday. It was very trying as Fred had a little pain, which of course, got exasperated! I had the unwelcome task to get him to leave again by the 4.33 train.

He has had to leave Germany for good. What a time they are having![1]
To-day I had a letter from Barj., very unhappy and despairing too.
I must quickly register this at the post.

Yrs ever aff^{ly}
J.D.

Autograph letter, initialled and dated.

The original is in the Delius Trust Archive.

1   News from Germany was to grow worse. 'Oh this dreadful Hitler-,' wrote Jelka to Fenby on 2 September, 'what misery he has brought about.' Another great friend, also Jewish, Heinrich Simon, was soon to be driven from his own *Frankfurter Zeitung*, first being obliged to quit his fine home on the River Main for a 'tiny house' on the outskirts of Frankfurt. 'Gardiner's nephew met him on a train,' wrote Jelka to Fenby on 12 September, 'but said he was so aged and altered that he did not recognize him. He said he was carrying on, but must be most careful.'

By contrast, only a year and a half earlier, Jelka's sister-in-law, Nina Rosen, had written in reasonably optimistic vein from Berlin: 'You need not feel anxious about friends. Of course the new people want all the official places. (In that way I feel anxious about George's career!) But in a musical way, the change is not bad. Schillings is again "Intendant der Oper". *He* had been turned out by the democrats some years ago! Some one wanted his place Unter den Linden! Now he has the other Opera in Charlottenburg which is excellent. We live in a queer world but it is very interesting. Such a mixture of parties at present. I sat(e) next to a prominent Nazi at dinner at the house of a lady who is 50 per cent Jewish. The rest of the company was equally mixed. Some Americans came to see us & said their friends in America think they are in great danger here, while they find everyone so kind & are enjoying music enthusiastically.' (Letter to Jelka, in English, dated 27 March [1932].)

(583)
Frederick Delius to Edward Elgar

GREZ-SUR-LOING (S & M)
6.6.33

My dear Elgar,

I want to thank you again for the beautiful Gramophone records you so kindly brought me. It was a pleasure for me to hear really good singing once more. Goethe's words are so fine that it is a special satisfaction to hear them so wonderfully declamed and rendered with such deep feeling and understanding.

Also of Sibelius I get a much better idea than I did thro' the Radio.

I should like to say once more how much I appreciated your delightful visit. I do hope it may be repeated one day!

With kindest regards from my wife I remain

Your affectionate friend
Frederick Delius

Letter in the hand of Jelka Delius, dated, written on headed notepaper.

The original is in the Hereford and Worcester County Record Office.

(584)
Edward Elgar to Frederick Delius

Marl Bank,
Worcester.
8th June, 1933.

My dear Delius,

Thank you for your very kind letter about the gramophone records; I feel that Mr. Gaisberg (H.M.V.) deserves all the credit for conveying them safely to you, but I am truly glad they gave you pleasure.

I wish you would think out (I tremble in making any suggestion) some small composition suitable, as regards difficulty for small orchestras. Your "Cuckoo in Spring" is naturally very much loved and is within the capacity of some of the smaller organisations – we did it in Worcester which, apart from the festival, boasts of no great equipment. I want three movements – any poetic basis you like –? Fontain[e]bleau – Grez – your own surroundings –: you cannot help being a poet in sound and I say no more on this side of the matter. Something, or things, such as I have had the temerity to name, would bring your wonderful art among the devoted people who mean (and do) well in small things and cannot aspire to perform your large works: do not be angry!

I look back to last week with the greatest pleasure – my meeting with you was the 'clou' of my days in Paris: the boy[1] played wonderfully but that is natural to him.

I am snowed under with unreasonable letters and the usual lot of intolerable rubbish which accumulates in one week: so I have not yet been able to write the little account of my pilgrimage to Grez: this I hope to do shortly.

With kindest regards to Mrs. Delius and to you

Your affectionate friend
Edward Elgar.

Typed transcript, dated, in the Delius Trust Archive.

1   Yehudi Menuhin played the Elgar concerto.

(585)
Frederick Delius to Edward Elgar

GREZ-SUR-LOING (S & M)
19.6.1933

Dear Elgar,

I will try to fulfil your wish and write you something for small orchestra.

I have written a piece that might suit, called "Song Before Sunrise", which I will send to you as soon as I have received the score from the Publisher's.

It is an easy work to play.

With hearty greetings from us both

Your affectionate friend
Frederick Delius

Letter in the hand of Jelka Delius, dated, written on headed notepaper.

The original is in the Hereford and Worcester County Record Office.

(586)
Edward Elgar to Frederick Delius

Marl Bank,
Worcester.
1st July, 1933.

My dear Delius,

Thank you for the delightful score of *Song Before Sunrise*, I am glad to have it.

I fear the "interview" – or whatever they will call it – in the D. Telegraph – is as inadequate as anything can be and does not represent you except as the slightest sketch: the thing is cut down[1] but it leaves me free to try further. I am not responsible for depriving you of your "K" and truly sorry the mistake is made.

I still have a vivid memory of Mrs. Delius and you and I hold it one of the few happy events in my life.

Yours affectionately,
Edward Elgar.

P.S. It is wrong to refer to material things – but your home-made *Bread* (I see I have subconsciously given it the Capital initial it deserves) remains a delicious taste – the first Bread I have ever tasted.

Typed transcript, dated, in the Delius Trust Archive.

1   Writing to Elgar on 8 July to thank him on Delius's behalf for the article, Jelka commented: 'How stupid of them to cut out parts of it, and as Mr Gaisberg tells me, just those about our bread etc. that give a truly human touch.'

(587)
Jelka Delius to Ada Fenby

GREZ-SUR-LOING (S & M)
[station] BOURRON
27.7.1933

Dear Mrs Fenby,

It was so kind of you to forward my letter the other day. Please tell Eric that Norman O'Neill was here[1] when the printed piano score of the "Idyll" arrived. He was tremendously pleased with it and thought it very well done and also well brought out.

We are having a dreadful time having Central Heating put into the house, just where we live. So we are sleeping in Eric's room, I in his bed, and we have to have meals brought up to the Music room. It would all not be so bad, if it was not such a terrible heat   It is just like an oven outside and we miss our big cool downstairs sitting room tremendously. The workmen seem to be *everywhere* making holes in all the walls and dropping down masses of old powdered plaster.

Happily my husband's niece "Peggy" arrived some days ago and helps me with the reading etc.[2]

I wonder if Eric is with you? Please tell him the news; I hope his work is going well.

With affectionate greetings to you all.

Yrs sincerely
Jelka Delius

Autograph letter, signed and dated, written on headed notepaper.

The original is in the Delius Trust Archive.

1   O'Neill's visit followed his annual stay at Bagnoles. Shortly before, another old friend, Oscar Klemperer, had paid a visit. And early in August the young Felix Aprahamian was to call, in the company of Ernest Chapman, of Boosey and Hawkes, and Donald Peart.

2   Margaret 'Peggy' Black, daughter of Clare, stayed initially till the end of September; she was back again in November. She was inclined to chatter too much for the taste of the Deliuses, but they were fond of her. And she was helpful at a time when Hubert Thieves, the male nurse, was engaged in devastatingly heavy drinking bouts, something which led to the engagement of a further *Bruder*, who arrived to take over on 12 October. Also particularly helpful through this difficult period was Philip Oyler.

A further note should perhaps be added on the gifted – and ultimately tragic – figure of Hubert Thieves. Although he had actually studied medicine, he preferred to associate with artists and himself experimented in various artistic fields. But he also experimented with drugs, and this had, in part at least, led his young – and at the time pregnant – wife to leave him. He was killed on the occasion of the first bombing raid on Cologne of the Second World War, and his own son was to die later in the war at the age of seventeen.

(588)

Edward Elgar to Frederick Delius

(Nursing Home) [Worcester]
13th Oct. 1933.

My dear Delius,

Thank you and Mrs. Delius for your telegram of good wishes: it gave me great joy to know that you thought of me in this distressful time.[1] I am supposed to be improving and want to share a few more years with you and hear your "brave transluminary things" and to see and talk once more with the poet's mind in the poet's body – you in fact.

Best regards to Mrs. Delius and my love to you.

Yours ever,
Edward Elgar.

_____

Typed transcript, dated, in the Delius Trust Archive.

1 Elgar had entered the nursing home a few days before, for treatment for a gastric condition compounded by sciatic pains. Cancer was to be diagnosed in November.

(589)

Frederick Delius to Edward Elgar

GREZ-SUR-LOING (S & M)
15.11.1933.

Dear Elgar,

We are wondering how you are? We have been thinking of you every day, hoping to hear good news of your recovery, altho' I know that after such an operation convalescence generally takes a long time. If the good wishes which are constantly with you from us both here can help to hasten your recovery, I think you will soon be up and about.

I have had rather a troubled time here too, as we had to get rid of our man who was unfortunately almost constantly under the influence of alkohol – and we were of course so dependent upon him. But we have now got a much nicer, very clean man who is beginning to learn all my little habits and all is more satisfactory.

There is a good book I have just read and which I should like to recommend to you "A Modern Sinbad", a most true and human autobiography.

Here is something that might amuse you taken from a letter of Burne Jones to Lady Horner:

"I heard a nice little tale from Sally Norton. It has to do with overhearing talk through the thin partitions that divide sleeping people on board ship. A poor suffering man could not sleep because this was going on in the next (married) compartment:

He: Do kiss me, Nelly, and make it up.
She: . . . .
He: Kiss me, Nelly; I'm real sorry. Do make it up.
She: . . . .
He: Oh, Nelly, don't be sulky; do kiss me and make it up.
Cross voice from next room: "Oh for God's sake, Nelly, kiss him and let's
        all get to sleep!"

I hope to be able to come to England in the spring and one of the things I am most looking forward to is meeting you again. It was so delightful having your visit here and it is one of my most cherished remembrances.
I remain with all best wishes

Your affectionate friend
Frederick Delius

Letter in the hand of Jelka Delius, dated, written on headed notepaper.

The original is in the Hereford and Worcester County Record Office.

(590)
Frederick Delius to Edward Elgar

GREZ-SUR-LOING (S & M)
19.11.33

Dear Elgar, We were so happy to receive such reassuring news from your daughter[1] to whose kind letter my wife is replying
I can doubly sympathise with you about the sciatica from which I suffer occasionally myself, so I know how painful it is. But then sometimes it suddenly leaves one again and I hope that will also be the case with you.
I was delighted to hear from Mr Gaisberg that he is kindly sending me some Gramoph. records of your works, to which I am greatly looking forward. I wonder whether Falstaff will be among them, as this is a work which I especially love and admire.
On Wednesday I shall be listening to the Beecham B B C. Concert and am looking forward to hearing your Cello Concerto again.[2]
I have got a splendid man now so at last everything is quite satisfactory in

the house. Like that I hope the winter will soon be over. Spring, I feel convinced, will bring you renewed health and vigour and then we must meet again. Perhaps you will be the first to fly over. We shall welcome you with all our hearts!

I remain your affectionate friend
Frederick Delius

Letter in the hand of Jelka Delius, dated, written on headed notepaper. Jelka also sent a personal letter to Elgar under the same cover.

The original is in the Hereford and Worcester County Record Office.

1   Carice (Elgar) Blake.

2   The concert, given in Queen's Hall on 22 November, included a work by Delius: 'I suppose you heard Eventyr,' wrote Jelka to Fenby on the 25th. 'The transmission was not good but yet one could hear what a glorious rendering Beecham gave. How different to Boult's Life's Dance which was quite without the right feeling.' She added: 'We are so distressed that Elgar is so ill. He was so hearty when he was here. Fred is a bit better now with his dreadful nerve pains.' In a letter to Fenby dated 2 December, Delius commented that Beecham's *Eventyr* was 'the best I have yet heard', and that Boult's was 'the worst performance of *Life's Dance* that I have ever heard . . . Unfortunately I see that he is to bring out the "Fantastic Dance" on January 12th and Song of the High Hills on New Years day!!' No mention of Elgar's Cello Concerto is made in the letters to Fenby, but on 2 December Jelka wrote to tell Elgar: 'We both enjoyed thoroughly your beautiful Cello Concerto on the Wireless; it came through very well.'

(591)
Edward Elgar to Frederick Delius

Dictated.

Nursing Home,
Worcester.
Dec. 4th, 1933.

My dear Delius,

You have been too good to me in writing, and I welcome every word that you send.

To refer as shortly as possible to my illness, I will only say that everything goes well as far as the operation is concerned and that the real trouble is still the appalling attack of sciatica. After adding a word of grateful thanks for your sympathy and good wishes, I will avoid this dreary subject.

I am glad to think that you are really coming to London in the spring – I spoke to you very rapturously about flying, and in looking back I have nothing to withdraw as to the rest and pleasure of the journey in the serene and brilliant summer weather, but I have been told in conversation some time ago that the journey can be a very different matter in stormy weather. Of these conditions you will understand I have no experience and I beg you will make all possible enquiries as to the convenience and comfort of the journey in the spring when the weather may be quite a different matter. In any case, I shall look forward to your coming. I always find that our dear friend Gaisberg gives the wisest advice in all matters of travel. It is very pleasant to hear you speak of my works and I thank you sincerely for your good opinion. I have had a few visitors, amongst others that true old friend Granville Bantock who has been able to call and spend a short time with me on two occasions; we have talked much of you and made the old days live again with joy.

In my note to Mrs. Delius, I referred to that very material but unique and gorgeous *Ham* which your resources provided for the refreshment of the Pilgrims from Paris (Gaisberg and myself) to your beautiful home. I am also very glad to hear that you have again an efficient servant and hope that you may be comfortable for the future.

With affectionate regards,
I remain, my dear Delius,

Your true friend,
Edward Elgar.

Typed transcript, dated, in the Delius Trust Archive.

In an accompanying letter to Jelka of the same date, Elgar wrote: 'I am sending a note to Frederick, it was so very kind of him to write and I treasure every word which he sends.' And dictating to his daughter on 11 December he told Delius: 'I cannot write yet but I am able to read everything, and delight in your letters.'

(592)
Frederick Delius to Edward Elgar

GREZ-SUR-LOING (S & M)
10.12.33.

Dear Elgar,

Your beautiful letter gave me the greatest pleasure and I treasure it. Also it made me assured that you are feeling better and are gradually conquering your illness. Last friday Bantock gave us such a good account of your progress on the Wireless – it really delighted us.

I have derived great pleasure from hearing your works on the gramophone. Introduction and Allegro has always been a special favourite of mine and yesterday we had Falstaff. What a magnificent work it is, so greatly conceived, so full of life and in its changing moods so human, vigourous and natural. It is the outcome of a rich nature.

I have a big new E.M.G. Gramophone and really it is so excellent that one imagines oneself in the concert room.

When I hear accounts of all your friends visiting you, how I long to be among them! How I should love to chat with you for a little while, what a pleasure it would be! It is most dreadfully cold just now, I dare not drive thro the garden in my bath chair.[1] The house is well warmed and my wife and my attendant take it in turns to read to me; the latter in German and in so strong a Souabian dialect that it is quite an art to understand him. – Dear friend, with all my heart I wish you continued good progress.

Ever affly yrs
Frederick Delius

Letter in the hand of Jelka Delius, dated, written on headed notepaper.

The original is in the Hereford and Worcester County Record Office.

1   Jelka wrote on the subject to Fenby on 12 December: 'We have the most atrociously cold weather and the whole river is frozen over – a thing I have never seen here in all these years ... all this is dreadfully hard on poor Fred.'

(593)
Frederick Delius to Ernest Newman

GREZ-SUR-LOING (S & M)
13.12.33

Dear Newman,

It was very kind indeed of you to write to me and tell me all about our dear friend Elgar. His visit to me here when he spent an afternoon with me was quite an event in my life. It was the first time that the real Elgar was revealed to me and that I could talk intimately with him and that I had the opportunity of appreciating his fine intellect and affectionate nature.

How I now regret that we were not brought together earlier! How I hope that his improvement will continue and that he will recover his old strength!

I am afraid you are right about the "subman". It is not Nietzsche's philosophic side that I love, but the poetic one. I am afraid in all countries the

Subman has now got hold of the rudder. Elgar sent me through his friend Gaisberg some of his Gram. records. On my most excellent Gramophone (the big E.M.G.) I get almost a concert performance. One of these records is "Falstaff", a work which I especially admire, I think here Elgar is quite on the top of his form.

I should be most grateful to you, if after seeing Elgar again you would tell me how you found him.

My wife sends you kind messages.

Yrs ever
Frederick Delius

Letter in the hand of Jelka Delius, dated, written on headed notepaper. Envelope addressed: Angleterre/Ernest Newman Esq/Polperro/Epsom Lane/Tadworth/Surrey. Postmark: GREZ 13 -12 33.

The original is in the Delius Trust Archive.

(594)
Frederick Delius to Thomas Beecham

GREZ-SUR-LOING (S & M)
17.12.1933

Dear Thomas,

Your superb performance of Eventyr gave me another great thrill. Luckily there was no crackling and it came through wonderfully. I have a new marvellous Gramophone E.M.G. and derive great pleasure from listening to your records of my works. When am I to have the records of Appalachia, Paris, the Idyll and Songs of Farewell etc.? I am just longing to be able to put them on my gramophone. This is now my only pleasure. Don't wait too long, dear friend, or it will be too late for me to enjoy them.

Lovingly
Frederick Delius

Letter in the hand of Jelka Delius, dated, written on headed notepaper.

The original is in the Delius Trust Archive.

(595)
Edward Elgar to Frederick Delius

Dictated.

Nursing Home,
Worcester.
25th December, 1933.

My dear Delius,

Charles Lamb wrote "the birth of a New Year cannot be pretermitted by King or Cobbler". Leaving out all minor matters such as turkeys, Christmas pantomimes etc., there remains the very convenient season for summing up the happenings of the past year. First let me wish Mrs. Delius and you every good thing possible in 1934 and for long after that.

I hope you are well and that the severe weather has not been too trying. I know you will want to know my situation so, in as few words as possible I must tell you that I am still in the Nursing Home enduring incessant pain with occasional outbursts of something more acute; this is sciatica.

Now to something more pleasant; your second consignment (most welcome) of the barley sugar of the holy and sanctified manufacture arrived to-day and it is the most beautiful sweetmeat I have ever tasted; I am so grateful to you.[1]

I am keenly interested in your coming visit to London and scarcely dare hope that I shall be strong enough to be amongst those who will welcome you. I do not know the scheme of the concerts but I wish Sir Thomas would give us "Paris" and the "Mass of Life" again. It has been a matter of no small amusement to me that, as my name is somewhat unfortunately indissolubly connected with "sacred" music some of your friends and mine have tried to make me believe that I am ill disposed to the trend and sympathy of your great work. Nothing could be farther from the real state of the case. I admire your work intensely and salute the genius displayed in it. This recalls an incident which happened to me in New York where I was conducting the inevitable oratorios. Richard Strauss's "Salome" was being given to the horror of some (presumably) ultra moral good folk. A deputation from these astounding people waited upon me and urged me to lead a private prayer meeting, to pray especially for the failure of Richard's Opera. A proposal which was so staggering and so screamingly absurd that I don't think that I have recovered from the shock even now. The mentality of certain "sections" in the U.S. is hard to believe and sometimes to bear.

I do not propose to look back on the past year with any great satisfaction but a few events stand out far apart. My visit to you is still a vivid thing in my memory and is one of the things which will endure. The kindness of Mrs. Delius and you to me lifts 1933 out of the ordinary Anno Dominis.

As I began with good wishes so I conclude.

My kindest regards to you both,

Yours ever sincerely,
Edward Elgar.

Typed transcript, dated, in the Delius Trust Archive.

1   The Deliuses had sent Elgar some barley sugar (sucre d'orge) made to a secret recipe by nuns at Moret-sur-Loing. (See Rachel Lowe: 'Delius and Elgar: A Postscript', pp. 97–8.)

1934

Around the middle of the second week of January, Delius's condition deteriorated. The doctor from nearby Nemours became a regular visitor, and Dr Poirier, a Paris specialist, also came to examine the patient. For a time Delius was largely confined to bed, and Jelka wrote to tell Beecham that it was a matter of kidney or bladder trouble. However, on 25 January she reported that he was much better and – a good sign – had had cider for lunch the day before. Later that same evening, alerted by a telegram from Robert Nichols earlier in the day, they listened to a broadcast performance of *Idyll* from Vienna. On 12 January they had heard the first performance of *Fantastic Dance*, given in London by Boult and the BBC Symphony Orchestra. February was bitterly cold, like the previous month. Norman O'Neill's death, early in March, came as a terrible shock to the Deliuses, saddened as they were by Elgar's passing in February.

By early April, inexorably, Delius's own illness had entered its final phase – 'the most dreadful shooting pains' threatened each night, and weakness and fatigue the following morning. The composer was in no mood to see Arnold Bax, Harriet Cohen and Walter Legge when they called, and Jelka sent them away with little ceremony. Jelka, unwell herself, pressed Fenby to return. On 11 April she wrote to tell him that Delius's kidney trouble was worse and that his pains were continuing. The garden, in all its spring beauty, was a mirage for her: 'I can not get to enjoy it.' In fact Jelka was dangerously ill, and was herself taken to hospital in Fontainebleau on 16 May for a colostomy operation. Fenby, alerted by telegram and letter, arrived back in Grez on the 19th, taking charge of the household in Jelka's absence. Three weeks later Jelka was allowed to return home to be with her husband, who was sinking fast. Just two days later, after weeks of terrible pain, he died.

(596)
Frederick Delius to Edward Elgar

GREZ-SUR-LOING (S & M)
4.1.1934.

Dear Elgar,

It gave me the greatest pleasure to-day to read in the Daily Mail that you are so much better and that you have left the Nursing Home and returned to your own house. This was really splendid news.

The other day a niece of mine, who had been staying with us, went back to England and we gave her a box of Sucre d'Orge to post to you in England, and which, I hope, you have meanwhile received. It was addressed to the Nursing Home.

What you told me about Strauss's Salome in New York and the pious puritans amused me greatly, altho' it did not surprise me. I have seen myself so-called Christians behaving like cruel barbarians and I heard in a small town in Virginia, (where as a very young man I spent some months) a minister declaring from the pulpit:

"If God Allmighty had nott intended the negroes to be slaves, why did he make them black?"

Negroes are certainly the most musical people in America. Sitting on my plantation in Florida on the verandah after my evening meal I used to listen to the beautiful singing in 4 part harmony of the negroes in their own quarters away at the back of the orange grove. It was quite entrancing and this Jazz rot that has come from New York to Europe is a *horrible travesty* by New York Jews.

We often play the records of your works which Mr Gaisberg sent us. The Nursery Suite I did not know. It is charming: the Aubade is a gem. Introduction and Allegro I knew well and love it.

We both send you our New Year's greetings and the best of wishes!

Ever your aff^{te} friend
Frederick Delius

Letter in the hand of Jelka Delius, dated, written on headed notepaper.

The original is in the Hereford and Worcester County Record Office.

(597)
Frederick Delius to Edvard Munch

[Grez] 5.1.1934

Dear friend, We both send you our heartiest New Year greetings and hope all
is well with you. Won't you come to visit us in the spring?

Your faithful friend
Frederick Delius

Picture postcard: *Grez-sur-Loing (S.-et-M.) – Vue du Loing et les lavoirs*, in the hand of
Jelka Delius, dated, written in Norwegian. Addressed: Herr/Edvard Munch/Store
Kunstmaler./Skoyen/pr. Oslo/Norvège. Postmark: GREZ [date illegible].

The original is in the Munch Museum.

(598)
Edvard Munch to Frederick Delius

Dear Delius,

It was an enormous pleasure for me to receive your card and new year greetings
– And I am delighted that you are getting on well –
I have often thought of writing to you. I met Sinding recently – He was
looking well –
Jappe our old friend is dead – Helge Rode is certainly alright   He recently
wrote in Politikken about a book by Gauguin about me[1]
In it he talks about you and that summer we were together in Aasgaard-
strand –
I hear you have become a member of the music academy in London   Hearty
congratulations
The drawing is of my cottage in Aasgaardstrand. I am often there painting
I live completely like a hermit – Should I come to Paris at all I shall paint
you – We talked about it last time
Hearty greetings and wishes for a good year to you both.
Your devoted friend

Edvard Munch

Sköien pr Oslo 10/1 34

Autograph draft letter, signed and dated, written in Norwegian on notepaper headed
by a printed drawing of Munch's cottage at Aasgaardstrand.

The original, which was not sent, is in the Munch Museum.

1   *Politiken*, the Danish daily newspaper, had recently published an article by Rode on *Edvard Munch* (Oslo, Aschehoug, 1933), a biography by Paul Gauguin's son, Pola.

(599)
Jelka Delius to Eric Fenby

25.2.1934
GREZ-SUR-LOING (S & M)

My dear Eric, Well, we heard the lovely Songs of Farewell once more, but conditions were pretty bad. What came thro' best was the beginning, also N° 2. and Joy, Shipmate, Joy. That was truly heavenly and certainly Coates is so much more flexible and juicy than M.S. If one only could have heard properly! Fred was in bed and had the loud-speaker upstairs and to get the best results I stayed downstairs most of the time; but that is agony too, as one cannot hear properly. So I was always running up and down again. (I counted 27 ascensions!!)   A Journalist had come after lunch and told the sad news of Elgar's death[1] Then other phone calls etc kept us busy and Fred had to write a 100 word telegram for the United Press.

Why they all wanted Fred's opinion I cannot see. He was furious, of course. For poor Elgar it was best that it ended. He must have suffered terribly and was quite drugged in the end. We have a lot of records of his now. Falstaff is splendid. The new Gramophone is fine.

Keith Douglas asked Fred to write personally to Columbia about the recording. I wrote an extremely intense letter and also asked them for new sets of the old recordings. Ours are quite worn out. I wonder whether you are going to Manchester for the Hallé Concert on thursday?[2] Oh, I wish *I* could be there!

I heard old Goodson play the Concerto in Liverpool but could not get Fred to listen in, he is so dead tired of it. Fred was agreably surprised about the performance of Brigg Fair in Leeds. Barbirolli did it well and the orchestra, Fred thought were taking pains to do their best. In Huddersfield again the orchestra was too much subdued.

We have had a most trying long winter and it has frozen heavily all the time (6 to 10 degrees at night). It is only this last night that it rained *a little* – the Earth is so terribly dry. There are no little spring flowers out yet. We have never been so late – only a few Snowdrops.

26.2. Here I was interrupted. To-day Fred received a telegram from a man Lorenz (friend of Phil's he signs) to say that the performance of Paris was most stirring and exquisite (Beecham Sunday concert)   It gave us great pleasure.

God knows when I shall finish this. In a minute Wilhelm will come in and take Fred down, and then he (W.) is driving to Fontainebleau with André.[3] I thought of this just to give Wilhelm a little outing. I wish *you* were here to go with him as André is so stupid too; But –

Here I was told that I have to hand in my declaration of taxes at once – so farewell for now, and all the kind messages to Soldanella.[4]

In haste ever affly
Jelka

28th

Yesterday to add to all my tribulations the Radio-man came and tested our set for hours and I got a terrific headache, so I did not post this letter. In the late evening we heard the Dance Rhapsody 1 from Francfort. It was a very poetic and beautiful conception of the work quite unlike Wood and also much more wistful and imaginative and understood than any I heard before.

Jelka D.

Autograph letter, signed and dated, written on headed notepaper. Envelope addressed: Eric Fenby Esq/12 Mayville Avenue/Scarborough/Yorks/Angleterre. Postmark: GREZ [?] -2 34.

The original is in the Delius Trust Archive.

1   Elgar died on 23 February.

2   Beecham was to give an all-Delius (broadcast) concert with the Hallé on 1 March.

3   André Baron, the Deliuses' chauffeur.

4   Soldanella Oyler often visited her father Philip at Grez. He was separated from his Swedish wife who lived at Woodgreen, near Fordingbridge, Hampshire. Eric Fenby writes: 'A friendship with Philip eventually extended to his daughter, and after Delius's death I was invited to accompany mother and daughter for several weeks to stay with Mrs Oyler's brother, who was a professor at Upsala University. We were never engaged, as the family in Sweden objected to my being RC. They were all strict Swedenborgians.'

(600)

Universal Edition to Frederick Delius

Vienna, 1st March 1934.

Herrn
Frederick Delius,
Grez-sur-Loing
Seine et Marne

Dear Maestro Delius,

Mentor Film A.G., Zürich, propose to make a sound film of the short Keller novel "Romeo und Julia auf dem Dorfe" and would use the music from your opera if we "ask a very modest price for it", provided you think the music suitable for a sound film. We have not mentioned a price for the time being, but have asked the firm to let us know what price they would pay in this case. However, we would ask you kindly to confirm that we may conclude an agreement at the best possible price, and if agreement is reached, that we should receive a 25% share of the price for the permission to use the music for the sound film, while the price for the material that will have to be supplied for the purpose of the sound film will be calculated in the usual way.

Your immediate confirmation would be greatly appreciated.[1]

We remain
Yours very truly

Typed letter, signature illegible, dated, written in German.

From a carbon copy in the Universal Edition Archives.

1   The proposal appears to have got no further, Delius being worried that a mediocre film would do his work no good at all. When the Swiss film classic was finally made, in 1941, incidental music was commissioned from Jack Trommer.

(601)

Jelka Delius to Eric Fenby

GREZ-SUR-LOING (S & M)

3.3.34

My dear Eric,

We received a lot of cuttings to-day and among them this one from Huddersfield.[1] It is perhaps stupid of me, but I can't help feeling annoyed that all these people in the North shd think that poor Fred is left prostrate and quite alone, and that he hasn't even a soul to write his letters for him, since you have left. I almost wish you would write a few words to this Mr Ramsden and tell him that you are no longer constantly at Grez, but that for all matters that do not need musical notes annotation Delius has his wife and constant helpmate who attends to all that. You see, many people know that you have been in England for nearly a year; and it is dreadful that they think he is left quite alone and given up to misery.

However if you think this is nonsense just leave it.

I know that you have merited much more gratefulness from us and the world than the ordinary people will ever understand; but you have not been a nurse and factotum here.

Did you hear Beecham's concert? We heard it remarkably well. I had even called on all the people who have motors that afternoon and got them so interested and willing, that the baker baked his whole bread without electricity, that the Bourlots and Collarts pumped by hand to feed all their animals and the butcher lady also turned off her motor. It showed plainly that most of these disturbances come from these wretched motors. Eventyr, Fred thought was quite amazing, wonderful; he had never heard it like that. Songs of Sunset was lovely too, especially Olga Haley – Dennis Noble less good, a little stilted. But the suavity of the whole and the exquisiteness of the orchestra. The "Walk" was glorious too, rather more strong and passionate than our record. Appalachia came thro' less well, there was a lot of fading. And (between ourselves) the Hallé Chorus was rough, and did not understand the music one bit. Their "Heigh o" came so loud and sudden that I jumped up from my chair. That "Exceeding Sorrow" was really moving. Oh I enjoyed it immensely and it was so lovely to see Fred nodding so elatedly his head to the music. We heard it all downstairs and even Wilhelm was impressed.

I enclose you a cutting by that A. K. Holland[2] about a Liverpool performance of the Idyll; it will give you pleasure. Cohen[3] and the Singers must all have done it awfully well.

To-day is the first spring day and I do hope the beastly cold will not come back again. It must have been terrible up there in Yorks. too! How are you dear and how is your work going? Did you send in the Overture?[4]

I must rush this to the post, so goodbye dear

Love to you all!

Ever yrs
Jelka Delius

Autograph letter, signed and dated, written on headed notepaper. Envelope addressed: Eric Fenby Esq/12 Mayville Avenue/Scarborough/Yorks/Angleterre. Postmark illegible.

The original is in the Delius Trust Archive.

1   A note in the *Huddersfield Daily Examiner* of 26 February 1934 refers to a letter from Delius received by the president of the Huddersfield Choral Society, J. L. Ramsden.

2   Arthur Keith Holland, music critic of the *Liverpool Daily Post*, was later to write sensitively and in some detail on Delius's songs in a booklet published in 1951. His review of *Idyll* appeared in the *Post* on 27 February 1934. (Cf. Norman Cameron: 'Obituary: A. K. Holland, 1892–1980', *The Delius Society Journal*, 68 (July 1980), pp. 11–13.)

3   Louis Cohen was a Liverpool-born conductor and violinist. Eric Fenby, who was a friend of his, writes: 'A fine violinist, he conducted the orchestral concerts during the summer at Harrogate, and once when I visited Liverpool he conducted a splendid production of "Hassan".'

4   The overture referred to was Fenby's consummate musical pastiche, *Rossini on Ilkla Moor*, only recently completed.

(602)
Jelka Delius to Eric Fenby

GREZ-SUR-LOING (S & M)
12.3.34

Dear Eric,

After I wrote you last we got the terrible news about Norman O'Neill.[1] We had heard nothing about the accident. If it was in the paper I must have over-looked it   So it was really a dreadful shock and I have never seen Fred so deeply affected. The news was broadcast on sunday evening and we had had a letter from a relative in the morning to say he was *very ill*, that was all. I suppose you saw it all in the papers? Yesterday we had a letter from his brother: His accident was really quite like mine, and without your help it might have ended the same way. Norman was knocked down unconscious in Oxford Str., but he soon came to and was taken to the police station, where after a lot of delay they took him to a hospital. There they would not treat him, as it was not a "bed" case and sent him to another hospital, where they did nothing either but finally telefoned for his wife who took him home. The cuts were quite slight on the head. Next day he felt quite well and insisted on conducting his music at the Theatre. After that he collapsed and blood poisoning from the wounds set in. He was then delirious for 18 days and everything was tried to save him but it was too late. His brother says: if only someone had got a little iodine at the nearest Chemist *at once* and dabbed it on, he would have had no septic poisoning. It is heart rending. They left him too long and evidently also never did the anti tetanic injection. Well, my dear Eric, if I am here now, I owe it to you. The way you dragged me home in that car and got the owner to send the doctor!

Poor Norman was cremated on Wednesday: There were about 200 friends from music and theatre and bowers of flowers They cast the ashes on the rosebeds in Golders Green. It appears as he was always unconscious he did not know he was dying; that is a blessing.

I was quite amazed that they had not written a nice article about him on the Music-page in Saturdays Daily Telegraph and now there is nothing either in the Sunday Times. Already for his arduous and ungrateful work as Treasurer of the Philh. Society, he merited a warm tribute.

I wonder whether you are at Scarborough and whether perhaps Soldanella is there on a visit. Please give her my love and let me hear about it all.

Fred is alright. We read more than ever and there are so many letters to write, I never get done.

To-day we are to eat a big roast pork, with the fat and crisp skin left on. I brought it from Fontainebleau and Fred is quite exited about it   There have been negotiations about it for 3 weeks. Fred takes great interest in his food now, and I think that is a good sign, altho his forethought and imagination are always much bigger than his actual appetite.

My love to your dear mother and yourself

Jelka Delius

Tonight we are to hear Julian Clifford do the Summer Garden. I see that your organ arrangement of the Summer Garden[2] is out. I wish we could hear it!

Autograph letter, signed and dated, written on headed notepaper. Envelope addressed: Mons. Eric Fenby / 12 Mayville Avenue / Scarborough / Yorks / Angleterre. Postmark: GREZ 12 -3 34.

The original is in the Delius Trust Archive.

1   O'Neill's accident happened on 12 February in Holles Street, just off Oxford Street. He died on 3 March, at the age of fifty-eight.

2   In fact, *On hearing the first Cuckoo in Spring*.

(603)
Keith Douglas to Frederick Delius

President:
Sir Thomas Beecham.

Vice-Presidents:
Sir Granville Bantock,
Sir Henry J. Wood.

Chairman of Committee:
J. Michaud.[1]

Hon. Secretary:
Keith Douglas.

Hon. Treasurer:
Norman Peterkin.

Hon. Press Representative:
Norman Cameron.

Telephone: Museum 1888

The DELIUS SOCIETY

Founded by Delius lovers with the generous co-operation of musicians all over the world to do honour to a great Composer. To provide for the present and for posterity a fitting monument to Delius by means of gramophone records of his longer and previously un-recorded works.

40 *Langham Street*
LONDON W.1

March 21st, 1934.

Dear Mr. Delius,

I am off to Santa Margherita next Saturday for a fortnight, but before I go I must tell you that your letter to Columbia has worked wonders. Columbia had a long discussion, and then approached us and offered to sponser the Society, making use of their own dealers, etc, all over the world, and offering to start monthly announcements in their bulletins. They are also ready to start recording as soon as Sir Thomas and ourselves are ready. In other words, they are now prepared to do what we asked them to do months ago.

We cannot afford "Appalachia" for the first album, but we have sent to Sir Thomas to-day, suggesting six records, to contain "Paris", the third Violin Sonata, and four sides of Songs. This will, I think, bring in a large number of new members, and we shall hope to give "Appalachia" in the second album. Columbia anticipate a great sale in Japan, as well as in the U.S.A. There is no reason, if this is all approved of, why we should not make a start with the recording next week.

I am enormously relieved at the turn that things have taken, and I now feel that we shall go ahead. Will you, for the time being, regard this news as confidential? I shall write to you more openly as soon as things are settled.

My best wishes to you and to Mrs. Delius,

Sincerely yours,
Keith Douglas
Hon. Secretary.

Typed letter, signed and dated, written on headed notepaper.

The original is in the Delius Trust Archive. It is the only letter from Keith Douglas to Delius that has been found.

Keith Douglas: see Letter 529, note 1.

1   Jean Michaud was proprietor of the London music publishers Universal Music Agencies. He was London agent for Universal Edition, Leuckart, Josef Weinberger, and Eulenberg, and in 1929 played a part in the founding of the (first) Delius Society, of which he became Chairman.

(604)
Frederick Delius to Thomas Beecham

GREZ-SUR-LOING (S & M)
Delius dictates: 23.3.1934

Dear Thomas,

I am overjoyed to hear that the recording for the Delius Society is now going to begin and I am delighted that you are doing "Paris".[1] I wired you today asking you to play either "Cynara" or the Second Dance Rhapsody instead of Hassan. I might have added "A Song of Summer"

I have never been quite pleased with Hassan arranged without the voices. Or is it that this music belongs so entirely to the theatre?

With love
Frederick Delius.

Letter in the hand of Jelka Delius, dated, written on headed notepaper.

The original is in the Delius Trust Archive.

1   Beecham was to give *Paris* at Queen's Hall on 8 April with the London Philharmonic Orchestra. Recording sessions for the first (of three volumes) of the Delius Society records were to follow on 9 and 21 (or 22) April.

(605)
Jelka Delius to Eric Fenby

Grez 8.4.34

My dear Eric,

No, Fred is not seriously ill at present, but his urine contains a little Albumine and we must be most careful. The worst is that he is troubled with

the most dreadful shooting pains, that return every day at the same hour 5
p.m and persist thro' the whole night if he does not take a calming medicine,
which he generally does. But, of course, all that makes him feel weak and
fatigued in the morning.

This is what happened: A Mr Legge[1] (of whom we knew nothing) announced his visit for last saturday morning. Fred was already storming (and
said he would not see him)[2] because I said *I* would see him, if he could not.
Well imagine my *terrible heart-sinking* when at 10.30 he came accompanied by
Bax and Har. Cohen.[3] They had all met in Paris and decided to come along
here with Legge. They had come by the Auto car and Bax looked so puffed and
red, that his appearance quite frightened me. It had been so stuffy. I then at
last heard that Legge had come from Beecham-Columbia to announce all the
latest news about the recording for the Delius Society, all burningly interesting. But there was H.C. prattling away, Bax very huffy not to see Fred. Fred
coughing angrily upstairs, and sending for me every ten minutes. No conversation was possible and I shepherded them into the Garden and then into the
music room. Fred had said I must get rid of them *at once*. Of course I had to say
that Fred was very unwell. I think they wanted to lunch here with me, leaving
Fred upstairs. I nearly died and had at last to tell them that I must send them
away as Fred was in pain and needed me. So then we got the Grez carriage,
which took *untold ages* to come and take them to Fontainebleau. Now Fred was
downstairs and this H.C. had left gloves and umbrellas, and hairpins down
there and it was all I could do to prevent her from going in there. I'm sure I
must have looked tormented and dead tired: 2 hours of them! This is how the
rumour arose, and I could not help it.

I must say, dear Eric, we often long for you and if you were in earnest when
you said you would later pay us a visit – we should love you to come if you
could stay about a month. I am sure it would take Fred out of his groove to
talk music once more. I asked him and he said at once spontaneously: Oh I
always love having Eric.

9.4. I could not finish this yesterday. Of course, Eric, there is no actual
necessity for you to come, but it would be delightful and an unspeakable help
to me. So you must just tell us frankly how you feel about it and how it would
influence your work or possibly harm it. Please write about all this! You will
have seen in the papers that the Delius Soc. 1st Album is being recorded now.
"Paris" is the principal thing. Fred took Aspirine last night and had a good
rest and great perspiration. Maybe it will do him good. He sends you his love

Ever aff[ly] yrs
Jelka Delius

About "Koanga" Fred wants me first to ask Beecham what he thinks of the
plan. I think he will favour it.[4]

Autograph letter, signed and dated. Envelope addressed: Eric Fenby Esq/12 Mayville Avenue/Scarborough/Yorks/Angleterre.

The original is in the Delius Trust Archive.

1 Walter Legge (1906–79): recording manager with The Gramophone Company (HMV) and later with Columbia. He often worked with Beecham on recordings about this time. He was to become a noted musical administrator and impresario, founding the Philharmonia Orchestra in 1945. He married the soprano Elisabeth Schwarzkopf.

2 Added below the line.

3 Harriet Cohen (1895–1967): English pianist. She was an intimate of Bax, who dedicated two of his works to her. Shortly afterwards Bax mentioned his visit to Grez in a letter to Mary Gleaves: '. . . the old man was too ill to see me, I don't suppose I shall see [him] again.' (Foreman: *Bax*, p. 291.)

4 The Closing Scene from *Koanga* was to be included in Volume 1 of the Delius Society recordings published in November 1934.

(606)
Jelka Delius to Eric Fenby

16.5.1934

Dearest Eric

I am afraid I am very ill – I have gone on till I could not any more. They are going to fetch me this evening and operate me in a clinique in Fontainebleau.[1]

Please, Eric, be an angel and come over here as quick as you can and stay with Fred and keep him company. I send you a cheque for 15£ for the journey. I hope when they allow it you will come to see me, but Fred is the principal thing. I can not write any more, but please, dear, do not fail us

Yrs ever affly
Jelka Delius

If the money is not enough I will immediately send you more.

Autograph letter, signed and dated. Envelope addressed: Eric Fenby Esq/12 Mayville Avenue/Scarborough/Yorks/Angleterre. Postmark: GREZ 16 -5 34.

The original is in the Delius Trust Archive.

1 Jelka was to be operated on for cancer. The following day, she sent a telegram to Fenby: 'When are you coming? Am operated tomorrow Clinique St Joseph Fontainebleau.' Fenby came on 19 May.

(607)
Frederick Delius to H. Balfour Gardiner

[Grez, 19 May 1934]

Dear Balfour,

Eric will have already written to you to tell you of the calamity that has over-taken us and J's serious operation. Will you be the executor of my will? You are the only one of my friends whom I can entirely rely upon. I want you to have the entire furniture in this house as it stands, and to avoid any compli-cations with the French government, I want to give it to you now. Have a deed of gift made out, and I will sign it here before witnesses.

Ever your affectionate
Frederick Delius

dictated

59ᵃ Cornmarket St.
Oxford.

Pencilled draft letter in the hand of Eric Fenby, undated.

The original is in the Delius Trust Archive.

Delius revised his will – in draft form – on the same day in case he should outlive Jelka, as now seemed distinctly possible. A major point was that Fenby was to be entrusted with books, printed scores and manuscripts. 'The residue of my estate and future royalties I wish to be used to give a concert every year with the Philharmonic Orchestra; the programme must include one of my works, and the works of young British composers whose compositions merit a public performance.' The concert arrangements were largely to be entrusted to Sir Thomas Beecham.

(608)
Walter Legge to Frederick Delius

COLUMBIA GRAPHOPHONE COMPANY, LTD.

COLUMBIA HOUSE
98 TO 108, CLERKENWELL ROAD,
LONDON, E.C. 1.
21st. May, 1934.

Frederick Delius, Esq.,
Grez sur Loing,
Seine et Marne,
France.

Dear Mr. Delius,

Here are the records of "Paris". I think, and hope, you will be very pleased with them. Will you be so good as to let me know how you like them, and of course you will let me have your comments and suggestions. If you feel as enthusiastic about them as Sir Thomas and I do perhaps you will also be so kind as to write me a letter expressing your pleasure and approval of them, couched in terms that we can use for advertising purposes.

In a fortnight's time Sir Thomas is making more records, this time of the Interludes from "Fennimore and Gerda" and the final chorus of "Hassan"; the songs will be recorded at the end of June.

I hope you are feeling better than when I was in Paris at Easter. Arnold Bax, Cecil Gray and a host of other friends send their best wishes.

With kindest regards to yourself and Mrs. Delius.

Yours very sincerely,
Walter Legge.
DELIUS SOCIETY.

Typed letter, signed and dated, written on headed notepaper.

The original is in the Delius Trust Archive. It is the only letter from Walter Legge to Delius that has been found.

Walter Legge: see Letter 605, note 1. The records did not arrive in time for Delius to hear them.

(609)

H. Balfour Gardiner to Frederick Delius

FONTMELL HILL
IWERNE MINSTER
BLANDFORD
DORSET
May 26th 1934

My dear Fred,

Eric's letter of the 19th & yours of the 20th only reached me this morning, having been held up in Oxford. I am deeply concerned about Jelka and am telegraphing to you at once asking for news. Also of course I will act as your executor should it be needful; but as I have heard nothing further I very much hope that Jelka is now out of danger & that you will be able to continue the previous arrang[e]ments, whatever they were.

This is a terrible time – Norman's death, Gustav's death,[1] and now this serious news about Jelka. I am so glad that you have that kind and capable Eric with you. I await with anxiety your reply to my telegram.

Yours ever
H Balfour Gardiner

Autograph letter, signed and dated, written on headed notepaper. Envelope addressed: Frederic Delius Esq/Grez-sur-Loing/Seine et Marne/France. Postmark: BLANDFORD 26 May 34.

The original is in the Delius Trust Archive.

1 Following an operation in London on 23 May, Gardiner's great friend Holst died on 25 May.

(610)

H. Balfour Gardiner to Frederick Delius

FONTMELL HILL
IWERNE MINSTER
BLANDFORD
DORSET
May 26th 1934

My dear Fred,

Fenby's telegram was the greatest relief to me, and I am delighted Jelka is making good progress.

I see that your letter was dictated so long ago as last Sunday, and you were probably in a state of acute anxiety owing to the possibility that Jelka might not recover. But now that Jelka is out of danger, as I assume from the reassuring tone of Eric's telegram, would it not be better to wait a little time before I take over the executorship of your will? I do not know what the present arrangements are, but I think it would be wise to let them stand as they are for a little time – at least until we have had time to discuss the matter. This is best done verbally, but I am so busy at present that I cannot get away: in July I shall be able to, that is, in only about six weeks from now.

It is so kind of you to wish to leave me all the furniture and I shall accept it most gratefully. We can talk about this and all other details when I come to see you in July.

Yours affectionately
H Balfour Gardiner

Autograph letter, signed and dated, written on headed notepaper. Enclosed in envelope addressed: France/Monsieur Eric Fenby/chez Monsieur Delius/Grez-sur-Loing/Seine et Marne. Postmark: BLANDFORD 27 May 34.

The original is in the Delius Trust Archive.

A third letter dated 26 May was to Fenby: 'I am so glad you have been in Grez during this crisis, and grateful for all you have done.' Fenby replied to Gardiner on 28 May, telling him that Jelka was completely out of danger. And from Fontainebleau Jelka herself wrote to Fenby's mother on 30 May: 'It is so lonely and slow here; but of course that is inevitable and it seems I am doing well. My greatest treat is when Eric comes to see me. In fact if he had not come to Fred I do not know what I could have done . . . I have had such hard months behind me and shall have to count as an invalid for a long time.' Gardiner came to Grez on 7 June and stayed until the 9th. He returned on the 12th for Delius's interment.

Frederick Delius died on Sunday 10 June 1934.

Epilogue

Jelka Delius to Marie Clews

GREZ-SUR-LOING (S & M)
22.6.34

My dearest Marie,

I want to answer your friendly letter at once.

At present I am yet far from well, tho' I am getting on. But I could not envisage travelling for a long time after the life and death operation and the terrible parting from Fred. I want just to stay here, where he was and think of him. I have been surrounded by the kindest friends and they have helped me with all the necessary arrangements. It was all done with greatest care and exactly according to Fred's wishes, who wanted to be taken to a sunny little country churchyard in the South of England. As this could not be done at once for many reasons, I had a fine vault made here for him to lie in till the day of transfer. His coffin is of solid thick oak hermetically plumbed before witnesses, so that there will be no distressing scenes when he is exhumed. Of the provisoire funeral those silly journalists gave you a quite rotten idea. It was – as all told me the most impressive thing to see this coffin taken by a horse drawn herse emerge from our flower garden and all hidden under a wealth of roses and coloured wreaths and drive slowly and silently thro' the village street to its resting place, where about 6 dear friends and the civil authorities were waiting to witness it. I cannot tell you the difficulty we had in restraining the Pompiers, the Fanfare from Nemours and other Pseudo-musical Societies from following and bellowing their false notes into the beautiful peace and harmony of his drive to his resting place; as well as the curious and chattering public.

And please tell dear Mancha that everything was done to make a harmonious conclusion to dear Fred's life. He died in his sleep, surrounded by us all (I in a wheeled chair) without feeling the end, just as he would have wished.

He was then arranged remarkably well by *my* nurse and laid on the Divan in his music room. When the bandages were taken off he looked so natural and so beautiful and calm, after all this pain and unrest and sleeplessness that one could only feel thankful. He was in his white flannels, just as he used to lie on his couch in the garden and masses of roses all round. We had him photographed, and successfully, and we also had a mask in plaster taken, also of his beautiful hand. I have not seen the mask yet. There was no rush and I had myself wheeled into that peaceful room many a time and I was also able to make all the arrangements myself, always with the aid of Eric Fenby, Gardiner, Brooks, etc.

It was of course the most dreadful tragedy that Fred's progressing illness coïncided with my having to be operated of a large tumour. I had so hoped to be with Fred to the end first and *then* look after myself. So I waited till the very last moment and had to be taken away so hurriedly. I wired to Fenby and he came at once, but the shock of my desperate state was too much for Fred. But how could I have prepared him? He never would believe that anything could be the matter with me. When Fred got worse and worse I was in agony alone in the clinique and our house doctor saw that Fred *must* have me back and that I would never get better over there alone and heroically pulled me out of my bed with the wound not healed and brought me home. I owe it to him to have had a few days with Fred and to have seen his happiness about it. Fenby has been angelic in all that time watching over Fred day and night and now he is staying with me.

I had a piano brought down and he plays to me Fred's music and helps me in every way. But you know how it is in all these affairs; all these people without knowledge of the languages and of the french customs can do but little and I have now to struggle with the lawyers, testament, etc. and more or less defend myself against their unpractical help.

I am getting better, but shall never be my old self again – But what does it matter now?

Do, please come and see me when next you go to Paris and let me hear from you again. It was the greatest pity you both could not come last summer. We so often talked of you and Fred would have loved your visit

Yrs ever affly
Jelka

Autograph letter, signed and dated, written on headed notepaper.

The original is in the Delius Trust Archive.

Jelka Delius to Catherine Barjansky

[Grez, mid-May 1935]

My dear Katia,

I waited for you the whole time and I was all alone, as I am also now, because Fenby has gone to England to arrange the funeral. I have not been at all well for quite awhile. I have decided to take Madame Grespier to England with me, leaving here Wednesday afternoon.

I will spend the night in Paris in the Hôtel de Bourgogne, which is behind the Chambre des Députés and will then proceed Thursday to London, via Folk[e]stone, arriving at five-twenty in the afternoon. I will live there with Mrs. O'Neill. I will spend two days with her to have a rest.

The funeral will be in Limpsfield, Sunday afternoon at four. Then I shall go again to Mrs. O'Neill for a few days – will stay in London as short a time as possible, because I so need silence and rest. Fenby has been terribly busy with all the preparations. He will come back to Grez Saturday evening and then on the 25th will bring the coffin by automobile to Boulogne and proceed directly to Limpsfield, Surrey. Afterwards he will remain in London, where he will study conducting.

I should like to have a nurse-companion, because I can't bear this staying alone and being so sick. Oh, it is always so terribly cold! No spring at all. The whole of life seems so cold to me now. I am so delighted that your husband is to have a concert in London. He must come to see me at Mrs. O'Neill's.

In my devoted friendship,

Your
Jelka

From Catherine Barjansky: *Portraits with Backgrounds*, p. 112.

The funeral service was to be held at 4 p.m. on Sunday 26 May. Jelka wrote to Marie Clews on the 12th: 'I am going over to England on the 22^d and Eric Fenby, Fred's faithful amanuensis is going to travel with the Coffin in a motor car. He has been staying with me since Xmas. But of course it can not go on and I *must* advise him to follow his musical career in England ... I shall only stay about 10 days in London.'

The Funeral

David Howarth, later to become a writer of distinction, was in 1935 a youthful member of the recording department of the BBC. When the news department called for Delius's funeral service at Limpsfield to be recorded, so that extracts from it could be broadcast later that night, the assignment was given to Howarth. Much later he wrote down his memories of the event in the context of an article on Delius published in November 1961 – shortly before the centenary of the composer's birth – and entitled 'The Last Summer'. Two extracts from that article are here republished, with acknowledgements to *Harper's Magazine*.

There is much to be said for having a sort of funeral a year after a man is dead, instead of having it too soon. Some Africans bury their dead with very little ceremony, and then have a much bigger funeral on the anniversary of the death. If we did it like that, the sharp edge of grief would have worn away, and the man's friends could meet to do him honour without creating a public ordeal for the people who loved him best and miss him most. The funeral at Limpsfield was solemn, but it was far from gloomy: in fact, as it turned out, it was a perfect expression of the spirit of the dead man's music. Spring was just turning into summer, and it was one of those days when England, with all its blemishes, it still almost painfully beautiful. Sir Thomas Beecham had brought down a section of the London Philharmonic Orchestra, and they played the summery music in the church. I suppose nobody but a composer could have quite the same privilege of communicating with his own friends at his own funeral; it was a kind of victory over mortality. Afterwards, by the grave, Sir Thomas gave a funeral oration; and it was then that the blackbird sang. I do not remember what Sir Thomas said, but I am sure it was appropriate. He was a veteran conductor then, and an old friend of Delius', and he had done more than anyone else to bring Delius to the notice of the public; he remained a veteran conductor for another quarter of a century. While he was talking, I turned my microphone a little toward the yew trees. Whatever was said, it was certainly appropriate that a blackbird should sing at that funeral.

But although so many of Delius' friends were there that morning, his wife was not. She had come over from France for the occasion, but on the journey she had caught pneumonia . . .

I do not think I had ever heard of Jelka Delius until somebody, as we left the churchyard, said it was a pity she had been too ill to come. I took my records back to London, and broadcast parts of them in the news, and that was that. But the next day, or the next but one, the telephone on the desk in my office rang three times. Three rings had a special significance in Broadcasting House in that era; they meant that Sir John Reith, the Director General himself, was on the line. The effect on junior members of the staff was as if the Last Trump had sounded: I suppose he meant it to be. He asked me if I had recorded the funeral, and told me to take the records, and something to play them on, to a nursing home in Kensington, because somebody had suggested that Mrs Delius might like to hear them.

That regal command made no allowance for technical difficulties. Sound recording was a primitive business then, long before tape was invented. We used to record on soft cellulose discs, and the only portable apparatus we had for playing them was a clockwork gramophone which quickly wore them out. Moreover, the recording I had made of the music in the church was far below concert standard; the acoustics of the church had been difficult. So before I set off, I went to the gramophone library and borrowed the commercial records of my own favourite pieces of Delius: 'In a Summer Garden', the 'First Cuckoo', 'Summer Night on the River', and the 'Song before Sunrise'.

To excuse what I did that day, I must say again that I was young. I was not much over twenty, and young for my age, and I had very little experience of life and none of death; and so I just thought that if Mrs Delius was ill it might cheer her up to hear some of her husband's music, and I did not think in time that I might be meddling with more profound emotions.

The room in the nursing home was darkened. A woman took me in, and stayed while I was there. I thought she was a friend or a relation of Jelka Delius', not a nurse. I put my gramophone on a table near the bed; and I hardly dared look at the spare, drawn, motionless face on the pillow, because I had understood by then – though I do not think anyone had told me – that she was dying. I played one of the pieces I had recorded in the church, and the words of the service, and then Sir Thomas Beecham's funeral oration. The blackbird could be heard. At the end of his oration, she turned her head toward me where I stood in the half-darkness beside the bed, and she smiled and said: 'Dear Tommy.' That was the only time she spoke while I was there.

When I had finished, I whispered to the woman who was waiting: 'Do you think she would like to hear some music?'

'Yes, I think she would,' the woman said; and I put on one of the records I had brought. It was 'In a Summer Garden'.

Again, I do not know the technical words to describe that piece of music. But there again are all the images I have tried to put into words: love, youth, tranquillity, content; and superimposed on them, the gaiety of bright flowers, birdsong, and sunlight reflected on ripples of running water. The work ends in a shimmering series of chords so soft and so remote that the music seems almost not to move and not to end, but only to dissolve as trees and flowers dissolve in dusk when night falls on a garden. When the last of those chords was ended, the woman said: 'I do not think she can hear any more'; and I looked again at Jelka Delius. Her eyes were closed and she was perfectly still, and I could not read any expression on her face.

I read in the papers that she was dead; but it was not until many years later that I learned a little more about the music I had played her, and understood how reckless my choice had been. That was after the second war, when orchestral concerts began again in London, and I heard 'In a Summer Garden' again at the Albert Hall. Somebody lent me the score, and I saw for the first time the inscription that Delius had written on it. Even now I do not know what emotion I brought to that elderly lady in the last few conscious moments of her life: a happy recollection, or a regret for love and youth long past which is almost unbearable to imagine. 'In a Summer Garden' was written soon after Delius married her, before the misery of the war and the agony of his paralysis, and the garden it was written to evoke was their garden at Grez-sur-Loing. At the top of the score, he had written: 'To my wife Jelka': and he had added two lines which are quoted from Rossetti:

> All are my blooms, and all sweet blooms of love
> To thee I gave while spring and summer sang.

Jelka Delius died on Tuesday 28 May 1935.

Addenda/Corrigenda to Volume I

The recent accession to the Delius Trust Archive of a considerable quantity of musical MS material from the Beecham Library entails minor revision of a number of the references to Delius's works.

p. 5, line 2.   1 March, not 2 March.

p. 6, line 21.   For 'Zwei bräune Augen', read 'Zwei braune Augen'.

p. 8, line 8.   One of these part-songs, 'Durch den Wald' (RT IV/1), may have been composed in Danville, Virginia.

p. 12   [list of works]. Possibly dating from Delius's very early days in Paris are some rediscovered MS drafts entitled *Nuit en Florida* or *Rhapsody Floridienne* (DT reference TB/10/1). They have no material in common with 'La Quadroone' of 1889 (RT VI/6(a)).

p. 13   [footnote to Letter 3]. One further letter has recently been rediscovered. It was written in Copenhagen in 1935 by Nina Grieg to Jelka Delius.

p. 35   [list of works]. i. For *'Suite d'Orchestre'*, read *'Petite Suite d'Orchestre* (RT VI/6). May 1889.'
ii. Add to list: *'Suite de 3 Morceaux Caractéristiques pour orchestre* (RT VI/6(a)). Begun. (First movement, "La Quadroone (Une Rhapsodie Floridienne)" is dated 1889.)'

p. 46   [list of works]. i. For *'A l'Amore'*, read *'A l'Aurore* (RT VI/8).'
ii. For *'Petite Suite d'Orchestre'*, read *'Suite de 3 Morceaux Caractéristiques pour orchestre* (RT VI/6 (a)). Completed. (Second and third movements, "Skerzo" and "Marche Caprice", are dated 1890.)'
iii. Add to list: *'Marche Française* for orchestra (RT VI/6 (b)). Incomplete.'

iv. Add to list: '"Badinage" for piano (RT IX/4). Composed early to mid-nineties.'

p. 56 [list of works]. 'Lyse Naetter' (RT V/13). A sketch for a symphonic poem of this title dates from around the same period as the song. The musical material of the two is not connected.

p. 77 [footnote 1]. Delete 1889. The only fully-dated letter from Boutet de Monvel apparently reads '6 Juin 1895', and what is probably the earliest of these four letters can now be dated from internal evidence to August 1893.

p. 87, line 7. For 'Rover James', read 'Rorer James'.

p. 94 [list of works]. *Deux Mélodies* (RT V/16). Interestingly, an autograph of No. 1 is dedicated to André Messager.

p. 97 [list of works]. *Appalachia*, American Rhapsody for Orchestra (RT VI/12). Some sketch sheets for this work have recently been rediscovered. One bears the title *Nigger Rhapsody*, another *A Southern Night*.

p. 100 [footnote to Letter 61]. For 'Helene', read 'Helena'.

p. 112, line 18. For 'Lemanoff', read 'Lemmanoff'. Although it has been accepted by some commentators that the Princesse de Cystria was Delius's travelling companion in 1897, it must be admitted that the evidence would appear to be circumstantial.

p. 135 Letter 84 and footnote 3. For 'Equsquiza', read 'Egusquiza'.

p. 143 [list of works]. After '*Paris* ... (RT VI/14)', add: 'Begun October.'

p. 166 [list of works]. i. Add to list: '*Paris*, Nocturne (The Song of a great City) (RT VI/14). Completed February.'
ii. Add to list: '*Rhapsody for Piano and Orchestra* (RT VII/4(a)). Unfinished draft. Early 1900s?'

p. 177 8 lines from bottom. Delete bracketed question-mark after 'Averdieck'.

p. 260 [list of works]. The second entry should now read:
'*Songs of Sunset* [originally: *Songs of Twilight and Sadness*], for soprano and baritone solo, mixed chorus and orchestra (Ernest Dowson) (RT II/5). Begun September.'

p. 278 [list of works]. *Songs of Sunset* was completed in January.

p. 370   [Letter 292, paragraph 1, line 4]. For 'harmony', read 'wind
                [instruments].'

p. 373   [footnote to Letter 295]. Add: 'There are copies of just four-
                teen of Delius's letters to Harmonie Verlag in the Delius Trust
                Archive. Most are in carbon copy form and in Jelka's hand.
                Thirteen date from between 8 March 1908 and 9 July 1909. A
                final postcard is dated 4 January 1912.'

p. 389,   For 'run', read 'row'.
line 22.

p. 389,   For 'returned', read 'rowed'.
line 26.

Index: The entry for 'DELIUS, FRITZ' lacks references to plates 27 and 44.
———— The entry for 'Gerhardi, Ida' lacks references to *Fritz Delius, 1897*,
         plate 32; and *Frederick Delius, 1903*, plate 44.
———— The entry for 'Munch, Edvard' lacks a reference to *Fritz Delius: an
         early sketch*, plate 10.

Bibliography

Ackere, Jules van. 'Frederick Delius of de wellust van de klank'. *Academiae Analecta* (Brussels), 44, No. 3 (1983), pp. 59–122.

Allman, Anne Williams. *The Songs of Frederick Delius: an interpretive and stylistic analysis and performance of representative compositions*. Dissertation, Columbia University, 1983.

Anon. *Le Château de La Napoule*. La Napoule Art Foundation, Henry Clews Memorial, n.d.

Arnold, Cecily. 'A Singer's Memories of Delius'. *Music Teacher*, 29 (1950), p. 165–. Reprinted in *A Delius Companion*.

Backhouse, J. M. 'Delius Letters'. *The British Museum Quarterly*, 30, No. 1–2 (Autumn 1965), pp. 30–35.

Banfield, Stephen. *Sensibility and English Song: Critical studies of the early 20th century*. Cambridge: Cambridge University Press, 1985. 2 vols.

Barjansky, Catherine. *Portraits with Backgrounds*. New York: Macmillan, 1947; London: Geoffrey Bles, 1948.

Bartók Béla. ['Delius's First Performance in Vienna'.] *Zeneközlöny* (Budapest), 14 (1911), pp. 340–42.

———. *Béla Bartók Letters*. Collected, selected, edited and annotated by János Demény [transl. various]. London: Faber and Faber, 1971.

———. *Essays*. Ed. Benjamin Suchoff. London: Faber, 1976.

Beddington-Behrens, Edward. 'Violet and Sydney [Schiff]'. Chapter 5 of his *Look Back Look Forward*. London: Macmillan, 1963.

The Sir Thomas Beecham Society Newsletter. Ed. Denham V. Ford. Westcliff-on-Sea, Essex, 1966–1987.

Bennett, Joseph. Programme book (34 pp.), *Delius Orchestral Concert*, St James' Hall, London, 30 May 1899. The Concorde Concert Control, 1899.

Bergsagel, John. 'J. P. Jacobsen and Music'. Chapter 12 of *J. P. Jacobsen's Spor i ord, billeder og toner* [Essays by various authors, ed. F. J. Billeskov Jansen]. Copenhagen: C. A. Reitzels Forlag, 1985, pp. 283–313.

Boyle, Andrew J. 'Delius and Grieg: Aspects of Apprenticeship'. *The Delius Society Journal*, 79 (April 1983), pp. 7–12.

Brennan, Joseph Gerard. 'Delius and Whitman'. *Walt Whitman Review* (Wayne State University Press, Detroit), 18, No. 3 (September 1972), pp. 90–96.

Brian, Havergal. *Havergal Brian on Music. Selections from his Journalism. Volume One: British Music*, (Part Four: 'Delius, pp. 99–145.) Ed. Malcolm MacDonald. London: Toccata Press, 1986.

Brook, Donald. *Composers' Gallery: biographical sketches of contemporary composers.* London: Rockliff, 1946.

————. *International Gallery of Conductors*. London: Rockliff, 1951.

Cahill, Mary. *Delius in Danville*. Danville (Virginia): Danville Historical Society, 1986.

Carley, Lionel. 'Frederick Delius: 29 January 1862–10 June 1934: A Short Biography'. In *Delius: 1862–1934*, commemorative brochure published by The Delius Trust, London, 1984.

————. 'Genial Fastness: Clews and his Castle'. *The Delius Society Journal*, 90 (Summer 1986), pp. 5–9.

————. 'The Swedish Artists' Colony at Grez-sur-Loing in the 1880s'. *Adam* 1986 (text rev. Miron Grindea; first published in *The Delius Society Journal* (1974).)

Chisholm, Alastair. *Bernard van Dieren: an introduction*. London: Thames Publishing, 1984.

Clews, Henry, Junior. *Mumbo Jumbo*. London: Grant Richards, 1923.

Clews, Marie. Unpublished memoirs, in the collection of Mrs Katheryn Colton, Sarasota, Florida.

Colbeck, Maurice. 'Frederick Delius, 1862–1934'. In his *Yorkshire History Makers*. Wakefield: E. P. Publishing, 1976, pp. 32–40.

Cooke, Deryck. 'Delius: A Centenary Evaluation'. *The Listener*, 25 January 1962, pp. 195–6. Latest reprint in D. Cooke, *Vindications: Essays on Romantic Music*. London: Faber and Faber, 1982, pp. 116–22.

Copley, I. A. 'Warlock and Delius: A Catalogue'. *Music and Letters*, 49, No. 3 (July 1968), pp. 213–18.

Cox, Derek, 'Correspondances'. *The Delius Society Journal*, 47 (April 1975), pp. 6–9.

Cumberland, Gerald. 'Pen Portraits of Musicians: Frederick Delius'. *Musical Opinion*, July 1909. Reprinted in *A Delius Companion*.

Dean, Basil. 'Memories of "Hassan"'. *Radio Times*, 31 October 1952.

———. *Seven Ages: An Autobiography 1888–1927*. London: Hutchinson, 1970.

Delius, Frederick. 'At the Cross-Roads'. *The Sackbut* (London), 1, No. 5 (September 1902), pp. 205–8. Reprinted as 'The Present Cult: Charlatanism and Humbug in Music'. *The British Musician and Musical News*, November 1929, pp. 304–7; and elsewhere, including *A Delius Companion*.

———. [Libretto] *Irmelin*. Opera in Three Acts. Libretto from a text by the composer. London: Boosey & Hawkes, 1953.

———. [Libretto] *The Magic Fountain*. Lyric Drama in 3 Acts. Words and Music by Frederick Delius. Published by the Delius Society for The Delius Trust, London, 1977.

———. 'Musik in England im Kriege'. *Musikblätter des Anbruch* (Vienna), 1, No. 1 (November 1919), pp. 18–19. Reprinted, in translation by L. Carley, as 'Music in England during the War'. *Delius Society Newsletter*, 32 (Autumn 1971), p. 6.

Delius in Danville: An International Centennial Celebration 1886–1986. Programme book. Danville (Virginia), 1986.

Delius 1862–1934. [Brochure.] Compiled by The Delius Trust to mark the 50th anniversary of his death. London: The Delius Trust, 1984. [Contents include a Select Discography and List of Works, by Stephen Lloyd; and a Select Bibliography and Short Biography, by Lionel Carley.]

Demuth, Norman. *Musical Trends in the 20th Century*. London: Rockliff, 1952.

Dieren, Bernard van. 'Frederick Delius: January 29, 1863 – June 10, 1934'. *The Musical Times*, 75, No. 1097 (July 1934), pp. 598–604.

Douglas, Keith. 'Frederick Delius': A Paper read to the Incorporated Society of Musicians (Bradford). 15 February 1930.

———. 'Frederick Delius: An Appreciation'. *The Heaton Review*, 3 (1929), pp. 52–4.

Dowson, Ernest. *The Poetical Works of Ernest Christopher Dowson*. Edited, with an Introduction, by Desmond Flower. London: Cassell and the Bodley Head, 1934.

Elgar, Edward. 'My Visit to Delius'. *The Daily Telegraph*, 1 July 1933. Reprinted in *A Delius Companion*.

Elkin, Robert. *The Annals of the Royal Philharmonic Society*. London: Rider and Company, n.d.

Fenby, Eric. 'Before and After Grez: An interview with Dr Eric Fenby' [ed. Stephen Lloyd], *The Delius Society Journal*, 89 (Spring 1986), pp. 14–23.

————. 'Jelka Delius: A recollection by Dr Eric Fenby'. *The Delius Society Journal*, 79 (April 1983), pp. 7–12.

Fielding, Daphne. *Emerald and Nancy: Lady Cunard and her daughter*. London: Eyre & Spottiswoode, 1968.

Findon, B. W., ed. 'Hassan'. *The Play Pictorial* (London), 43, No. 261 (1923). [A description of the 1923 London production, with many photographs.]

Flecker, James Elroy. *Hassan: The Story of Hassan of Bagdad and how he came to make the Golden Journey to Samarkand*. A Play in Five Acts. London: William Heinemann, 1922.

Foreman, Lewis. *From Parry to Britten: British Music in Letters 1900–1945*. London: Batsford, 1987.

————. 'Oskar Fried: Delius and the Late Romantic School'. *The Delius Society Journal*, 86 (April 1985), pp. 4–22.

Foss, Hubert. 'Introduction', 'Additions, Annotations and Comments' and 'Postscript'. In Heseltine, *Frederick Delius*, 2nd ed., q.v., pp. 9–26, 137–90 and 191–5.

Foulds, John. *Music To-day: Its Heritage from the Past, and Legacy to the Future*. London: Ivor Nicholson and Watson, 1934.

Frederick Delius 1862–1934: An exhibition to mark the fiftieth anniversary of the composer's death. Exhibition catalogue. London Borough of Camden, March-April 1984.

Gerhardi, Evelin. 'My Reminiscences of Frederick and Jelka Delius at Grez-sur-Loing'. *The Delius Society Journal*, 52 (July 1976), pp. 4–9.

Grainger, Percy. *The Farthest North of Humanness: Letters of Percy Grainger 1901–14*. Ed. Kay Dreyfus. London and Melbourne: Macmillan, 1985.

Gray, Cecil. *A Survey of Contemporary Music*. London: Oxford University Press, 1924.

———. *Musical Chairs, or Between Two Stools: Being the Life and Memoirs of . . .* London: Home & Van Thal, 1948.

———. *Peter Warlock: A Memoir of Philip Heseltine*. With Contributions by Sir Richard Terry and Robert Nichols. Foreword by Augustus John. London: Jonathan Cape, 1934.

Greer, David, ed. *Hamilton Harty: His Life and Music*. Belfast: Blackstaff Press, n.d. [1978?]

Grew, Sydney. *Our Favourite Musicians, from Stanford to Holbrooke*. Edinburgh and London: T. N. Foulis, 1922.

Hadley, Patrick. 'Frederick Delius'. In *Dictionary of National Biography 1931–1940*. London: Oxford University Press, 1949, pp. 218–20.

Halliday, Francis, and Russell, John. *Matthew Smith*. London: George Allen and Unwin, 1962.

Harrison, Beatrice. *The Cello and the Nightingales: the autobiography of Beatrice Harrison*. Ed. Patricia Cleveland-Peck. London: John Murray, 1985.

Harrison, May. 'Delius'. *The Royal College of Music Magazine*, 33, No. 2 (1937), pp. 47–52. Reprinted in *A Delius Companion*.

'The Harrison Sisters Issue'. *The Delius Society Journal*, 87 (Autumn 1985), pp. 3–41. Includes articles by Frederick Arnold, Katrina Fountain, Beatrice Harrison, Margaret Harrison and May Harrison.

Hayes, J. I. *A History of Averett College*. Danville (Virginia): Averett College Press, 1984.

Hoare, Geoffrey G. 'Once I stayed in a Populous City: A Bradford Idyll'. *The Delius Society Journal*, 58 (December 1977), pp. 12–17.

Hove, Richard. 'Frederick Delius, 1862–1962, Et hundredeårsminde'. *Nordisk Tidskrift*, 1964, pp. 93–104.

Howarth, David. 'The Last Summer'. *Harper's Magazine*, 223, No. 1338 (November 1961), pp. 89–93.

Hunt, Norman T. *Frederick Delius: A Concert-Goer's Introduction to the Life and Music of a Great Composer*. Brighton: The Southern Publishing Co., n.d. [1945?]

Jacobsen, Jens Peter. *Niels Lyhne*. Translated from the Danish by Hanna Astrup Larsen. Introduction by Börge Gedsö Madsen. New York:

Twayne Publishers Inc. and The American-Scandinavian Foundation, 1967.

Jefferson, Alan. *Sir Thomas Beecham*. London: World Records, in association with Macdonald and Jane's, 1979.

Jenkins, Lyndon. 'When Delius came to Birmingham'. *Warwickshire and Worcestershire Life*, February 1982, pp. 44–5.

Jones, D. Marblacy. 'Look Back in Envy'. A series of reprints of early concert reviews published in four parts in the *Delius Society Newsletter*, [21] (November 1968), p. 5; 22 (February 1969), pp. 2–5; 26 (Winter [1969/] 1970), pp. 8–13; 27 (Spring 1970), pp. 8–14.

Jungheinrich, Hans-Klaus. 'Fremde Klange aus der Heimat: Zem 50. Todestage von Frederick Delius'. *Boosey & Hawkes Verlagsnachrichten* (Bonn), 48 (March 1984). Sequels in Nos 49 (June 1984), 50 (October 1984) and 51 (March 1985).

Keary, C.F. [Libretto] *Koanga*. Opera in Three Acts. Complete Libretto (text by C. F. Keary, revised by Sir Thomas Beecham, Bart. and Edward Agate). London: Winthrop Rogers Edition (Boosey & Hawkes), n.d.

———. [Libretto] *Koanga*. Oper in drei Akten . . . (Szenen aus dem Negerleben) von Frederick Delius. Text von C. F. Keary [transl. Jelka Delius?]. Elberfeld: J. H. Born [1904].

Keller, Gottfried. *A Village Romeo and Juliet*. Translated from the original German by Peter Tegel. London and Glasgow: Blackie, 1967.

Kennedy, Michael. *Barbirolli, Conductor Laureate*. The authorised biography. London: MacGibbon & Kee, 1971.

———. *The history of the Royal Manchester College of Music 1893–1972*. Manchester: Manchester University Press, 1971.

Klenau, Paul. 'The Approach to Delius'. *The Music Teacher*, January 1927, pp. 19–21. Reprinted in *A Delius Companion*.

Krohg, Christian. 'Fritz Delius', *Verdens Gang* (Oslo), 23 October 1897. (Transl. L. Carley in Lowe, Rachel: *Frederick Delius 1862–1934: A Catalogue of the Music Archive of the Delius Trust, London*, qv., pp. 172–4.)

Le Grand Baton. Journal of the Sir Thomas Beecham Society. Cleveland, Ohio, 1965–. [Delius/Harty number, 15, No. 4 (December 1978).]

Lloyd, Stephen. 'A Partnership of Genius' [Beecham]. *The Delius Society Journal*, 63 (April 1979), pp. 5–15.

————. 'Beecham: The Delius Repertoire'. *The Delius Society Journal*, Part 1, 71 (April 1981), pp. 9–19. Part 2, 75 (April 1982), pp. 12–22. Part 3, 79 (April 1983), pp. 13–20. Addenda and Corrigenda, 82 (April 1984), pp. 17–18.

————. 'Delius at the Proms'. *The Delius Society Journal*, 50 (January 1976), pp. [15–21].

————. 'Music from the Heart' [Hamilton Harty]. *The Delius Society Journal*, 65 (October 1979), pp. 3–7.

————. 'The Rumble of a Distant Drum ... Granville Bantock 1868–1946'. *The Delius Society Journal*, 80 (October 1983), pp. 4–28. [This Bantock issue also contains an essay on Bantock's music by Lewis Foreman, and interviews with Angus, Raymond and Myrrha Bantock.]

Lowe, Rachel [Rachel Lowe Dugmore]. *A Catalogue of the Music Archive of the Delius Trust*. Reprinted 1986, with minor corrections. The Delius Trust / Boosey & Hawkes.

————. 'Delius and Elgar: A Postscript'. *Studies in Music* (Perth: University of Western Australia), 8 (1974), pp. 92–100.

————. 'Documenting Delius'. *Studies in Music* (Perth: University of Western Australia). Part 1, 'The Years 1913–1915', 12 (1978), pp. 114–29. Part 2, '1916–1919', 13 (1979), pp. 44–62. 'Addendum', 14 (1980), p. 127.

————. 'Documenting Delius'. *The Delius Society Journal*, 65 (October 1979), pp. 7–14; 69 (October 1980), pp. 15–20.

————. 'Frederick Delius and Norway'. Reprinted in *A Delius Companion*.

Mead, William R. 'A Winter's Tale: Reflections on the Delius Festival (1946)'. *The Norseman* (Oslo), 1947, pp. 78–81.

Meyer, Michael. *Strindberg: A Biography*. London: Secker & Warburg, 1985.

Midgley, Samuel. *My 70 Years' Musical Memories (1860–1930)*. London: Novello, n.d.

Moore, Gerald. *Am I Too Loud? Memoirs of an accompanist*. London: Hamish Hamilton, 1962.

Moore, Jerrold Northrop. *Edward Elgar: a creative life*. Oxford: Oxford University Press, 1984.

————, ed. *Music and Friends: Seven decades of letters to Adrian Boult*. London: Hamish Hamilton, 1979.

Newman, Ernest. *From the World of Music*. Essays from 'The Sunday Times'. Selected by Felix Aprahamian. London: John Calder, 1956.

Nichols, Robert. 'Delius as I Knew Him'. In *Music Magazine*. Ed. Anna Instone and Julian Herbage. London: Rockliff, 1953, pp. 5–9. Reprinted in *A Delius Companion*.

Nietzsche, Friedrich. *Thus Spoke Zarathustra: A Book for Everyone and No One*. Translated with an introduction by R. J. Hollingdale. Harmondsworth: Penguin Books, 1961.

Orr, C. W. 'Frederick Delius: Some personal recollections'. *Musical Opinion*, August 1934. Reprinted in *A Delius Companion*.

Oyler, Philip. 'Frederick Delius in his garden'. *The Music Student*, 14, No. 7 (July 1934), pp. 121–3. Reprinted in *A Delius Companion*.

Palmer, Christopher. 'Eric Fenby – A Biographical Sketch'. In Fenby: *Delius as I Knew Him*. New and revised edition. London: G. Bell & Sons, 1981, pp. xv–xix.

———. 'Delius and Percy Grainger'. *Music and Letters*, 52, No. 4 (October 1971), pp. 418–25.

Parker, Maurice. *Sir Thomas Beecham, Bart, C. H. (1879–1961): A Calendar of his Concert and Theatrical performances*. [London: The Sir Thomas Beecham Society, 1985.] (Subsequent issues of *The Sir Thomas Beecham Society Newsletter* contain additions and amendments.)

Payne, Anthony. 'Frederick Delius'. In *Twentieth-century English Masters* (The New Grove Composer Biography Series). London: Macmillan, 1986, pp. 67–94.

Pirie, Peter J. 'Epitaph on a Centenary (Frederick Delius, 1862–1962)'. *The Music Review*, 23 (1962), pp. 221–37.

Proske, Beatrice Gilman. *Henry Clews, Jr., Sculptor*. Brookgreen (South Carolina), 1953. Cf. *Henry Clews, Jr. Sculpteur/Sculptor*. La Napoule: La Fondation d'Art de La Napoule, 1958.

Redlich, Hans F. 'Delius'. In *Die Musik in Geschichte und Gegenwart*, 3, cols 133–40. Kassel und Basel: Bärenreiter-Verlag, 1954.

Redwood, Christopher. 'Delius, his Sister and his Songs' and 'Some other Delius Descendants'. *The Delius Society Journal*, 68 (July 1980), pp. 6–10.

————. 'Grez-sur-Loing, 1932'. *The Delius Society Journal*, 52 (July 1976), pp. 4–9.

Redwood, Dawn. *Flecker and Delius – the making of 'Hassan'*. London: Thames Publishing, 1978.

————. 'Flecker, Dean and Delius: The History of "Hassan" Part I'. *The Delius Society Journal*, 50 (January 1976), pp. [6–15]. Part II, 51 (April 1976), pp. [4–10].

Runciman, John F. 'Fritz Delius, Composer'. *The Musical Courier*, 18 March 1903, pp. 16–17. Reprinted in *A Delius Companion*.

Seeley, Paul. 'Fritz Delius – the Bradford Years'. *The Delius Society Journal*, 58 (December 1977), pp. 5–11.

Simon, Heinrich. 'Frederick Delius' [obituary]. *Frankfurter Zeitung*, 29 June 1934.

————. 'Jelka Delius'. *The Monthly Musical Record*, December 1935, pp. 219–20. Reprinted in *A Delius Companion*.

Smyth, Ethel. *Beecham and Pharaoh*. London: Chapman & Hall, 1935.

Stevenson, Ronald. 'Delius's Sources'. *Tempo*, 151 (December 1984), pp. 24–7.

Tall, David. '"Five Little Pieces" by Delius orchestrated by Fenby'. *The Delius Society Journal*, 56 (July 1977), pp. 6–10 and 15–17.

————. 'The Fenby Legacy'. *The Delius Society Journal*, 61 (October 1978), pp. 5–10 and 15–20.

Tertis, Lionel. *Cinderella No More*. London: Peter Nevill, 1953.

————. *My Viola and I: A Complete Autobiography*. London: Paul Elek, 1974.

Threlfall, Robert. 'Delius as they saw him: A further attempt at an iconography'. *The Delius Society Journal*, 83 (July 1984), pp. 5–18.

————. *Frederick Delius: A Supplementary Catalogue*. London: The Delius Trust/Boosey & Hawkes, 1986.
[This volume updates the 1977 *Catalogue of the Compositions of Frederick Delius* by the same author; it also describes in full detail the many further music accessions received by the Trust since the original publication in 1974 of Rachel Lowe's *Catalogue of the Music Archive*.]

Tomlinson, Fred. *A Peter Warlock Handbook*. Vol. 1. London: Triad Press, 1974. Vol. 2. Rickmansworth: Triad Press, 1977.

————. *Warlock and Delius*. London: Thames Publishing, 1976.

————. *Warlock and van Dieren, with a van Dieren catalogue*. London: Thames Publishing, 1978.

Walker, Malcolm. 'Delius and Barbirolli'. *Delius Society Newsletter*, 34 (Easter 1972), pp. 8–16.
White, Eric Walter. *Stravinsky: The Composer and his Works*. London: Faber & Faber, 1966.
Whitman, Walt. *Leaves of Grass*. Revised edition. Philadelphia: David McKay, 1900.

Young, Percy M. *Elgar O.M.: a Study of a Musician*. London: Collins, 1955.

Index of Correspondents
(*by letter number*)

INDEX

Variant spellings found in the correspondence are given in parentheses
following the main entry in this index, which covers pp. 1–461. Numbers
in bold type indicate the principal reference, where the reader may be
referred to Volume I.

DATE DUE

HIGHSMITH 45-220